fifth edition

Writing Arguments
A Rhetoric with Readings

John D. Ramage
Arizona State University

John C. Bean
Seattle University

June Johnson
Seattle University

Allyn and Bacon
Boston ▪ London ▪ Toronto ▪ Sydney ▪ Tokyo ▪ Singapore

Vice President: Eben W. Ludlow
Editorial Assistant: Grace Trudow
Executive Marketing Manager: Lisa Kimball
Editorial Production Administrator: Susan Brown
Editorial-Production Service: Matrix Productions
Text Designer: Denise Hoffman
Composition Buyer: Linda Cox
Manufacturing Buyer: Suzanne Lareau
Compositor: Omegatype Typography, Inc.
Cover Administrator: Linda Knowles
Cover Designer: Susan Paradise

Copyright © 2001, 1998, 1995, 1992, and 1989 by Allyn & Bacon
A Pearson Education Company
160 Gould St.
Needham Heights, Mass. 02494
Internet: abacon.com

Library of Congress Cataloging-in-Publication Data

Ramage, John D.
    Writing arguments : a rhetoric with readings / John D. Ramage,
John C. Bean, June Johnson. — 5th ed.
        p.   cm.
    Includes index.
    ISBN 0-205-31745-6
    1. English language—Rhetoric.   2. Persuasion (Rhetoric)
3. College readers.   4. Report writing.   I. Bean, John C.
II. Johnson, June.   III. Title.
PE1431.R33   2000
808'.0427—dc21   00–021662
                                                                      CIP

Printed in the United States of America

10 9 8 7 6 5 4 3 2   RRDV   04 03 02 01

brief contents

contents

PART TWO
PRINCIPLES OF ARGUMENT   73

CHAPTER 4   The Core of an Argument:
A Claim with Reasons   75

CHAPTER 7   Moving Your Audience: Audience-Based Reasons, *Ethos,* and *Pathos*   132

CHAPTER 8   Accommodating Your Audience: Treating Differing Views   152

PART THREE
ARGUMENTS IN DEPTH:
SIX TYPES OF CLAIMS   181

CHAPTER 9   An Introduction to Types of Claims   183

CHAPTER 10   Categorical and Definitional Arguments: X Is (Is Not) a Y   192

CHAPTER 11   Causal Arguments: X Causes (Does Not Cause) Y   228

Student writer Daeho Ko responds to the Columbine High School shooting incident in Littleton, Colorado, and the flurry of conjectures about causes. Sympathizing with Dylan Klebold and Eric Harris, Ko faults public schools for their unqualified support of jocks and the sports team culture. In promoting these popular cliques, public schools damage and dangerously alienate students who aren't jocks and aren't popular.

Judith Kleinfeld, professor of psychology at the University of Alaska, argues that establishing more special programs for girls in mathematics and the sciences is a waste of money and a form of "social engineering." She claims that such sex-segregated programs will not advance women in science because even given choice and aptitude, females will continue to opt for other professions.

Student writer Holly Miller explores the multiple causes of the increase in teen sex. Although the media, peer pressure, and the failure of schools to emphasize love and morality and to equip girls to be less vulnerable to sexual pressure are all contributing causes, Miller asserts that parental involvement is the most important influence on teens' sexual behavior.

CHAPTER 13   Evaluation Arguments: X Is (Is Not) a Good Y   280

 Student writer Sam Isaacson, addressing a gay audience, evaluates the potential impact of gay marriage on the gay community.

 Weak as musicians and actresses, the Spice Girls have succeeded splendidly at making money through their understanding of girl fashion, their fun-seeking image, their appeal to individualism, and their curious blend of sexually objectified and liberated womanhood. Granting them their marketing success, student writer Pat Inglenook nevertheless faults them for being poor role models for young girls through their emphasis of voyeuristic sex.

CHAPTER 14   Proposal Arguments: We Should (Should Not) Do X   307

CHAPTER 15   Ethical Arguments   346

PART FOUR
WRITING FROM SOURCES: THE ARGUMENT
AS A FORMAL RESEARCH PAPER   359

APPENDIXES   431

PART FIVE
AN ANTHOLOGY OF ARGUMENTS   463

Social Causes of Teen Violence   467

The Social Impact of Popular Culture   488

Distribution of Wealth: What Responsibility Do the Rich Have for the Poor?   531

Civil Disobedience   557

Censorship on the Internet   578

Instead of censoring the Internet, we should combat negative information such as extremist hate propaganda by expanding Internet access to all minority listeners and voices, thereby broadening the base of accurate information and counteracting "cyberhate."

Dr. Alvin Schrader advises teachers against using Internet filtering devices on the grounds that they are technically and philosophically flawed. Further, reducing access to sites means limiting diverse ideas and intellectual freedom. Instead, adults should teach children to think critically about what they view on the Internet.

Although the Supreme Court has awarded the Internet the same free speech protection as printed materials, many industry leaders promise to regulate the flow of information on the Internet. Such regulation, however, is unconstitutional and may create a homogenized information superhighway. Instead, the American Civil Liberties Union supports actions to provide consumers with more information about how to navigate the Internet.

Internet consultant John Carr argues that some amount of Internet censorship is necessary to protect consumers, especially children, from unwanted images and information. Strong anticensorship advocates are needlessly concerned, he says, as long as censors strive to develop rating systems to suit both liberal and conservative interests.

Sexual Harassment: When Is Offensiveness a Civil Offense?   607

Psychology professor Riger analyzes reasons for the paucity of sexual harassment complaints. She concludes that gender bias is built into the way sexual harassment policies are written.

Munson questions present definitions of sexual harassment and confusion between harassing remarks and innuendo. The writer blames "feminist rage" for much of the failure to distinguish between harassment and normal insensitivity in the workplace.

Forbes writer Morgenson argues that "the alleged increase in sexual harassment [is] more a product of propaganda from self-interested parties" than from substantive cases.

Attorney Susan Crawford offers a pragmatic defense of sexual harassment laws based on lost employee work time, inefficient use of the workday, and costly lawsuits growing out of sexual harassment issues.

Egg Donors and Reproductive Technology   675

Corporate Responsibility and World Markets   715

abusing workers and by trying to hide the abuses to create a favorable public image, the Nike Corporation—the lawsuit claims—is guilty of unfair business practices.

Journalist David Lamb, touring a Nike factory in Bien Hoa, Vietnam, asks whether Nike is helping workers escape poverty or exploiting them through abusive sweatshop practices. Showing how Nike has improved conditions in its factories, Lamb contrasts the apparent job satisfaction of the Vietnamese workers with the complaints against Nike by sweatshop critics.

Stung by criticism of labor abuses in its overseas factories and pressured by shamed employees in the United States, the Nike Corporation is striving for a kinder, gentler image, claims journalist Stephanie Salter. Led by the company's new vice president for corporate and social responsibility, Maria Eitel, Nike offers to reveal the location of its overseas factories and to allow critics to examine working conditions.

In their effort to eliminate sweatshops, college students are calling for reform that ultimately will harm workers in developing countries. So claims *Business Week* staff writer Aaron Bernstein, who argues that a better approach would be to persuade the apparel industry to join the Fair Labor Association (FLA) despite its current weak regulations.

preface

Overview

Through its first four editions, *Writing Arguments* has earned its place as the leading college textbook in argumentation. It has been especially praised for teaching the critical thinking that helps students *write* arguments: how to analyze the occasion for an argument; how to ground an argument in the values and beliefs of the targeted audience; how to develop and elaborate an argument; and how to respond sensitively to objections and alternative views. By treating argument as a means of discovery as well as persuasion, the text shows students how arguing involves productive dialog in search of the best solutions to problems rather than pro-con debate with winners and losers. Adopters of *Writing Arguments* testify that students using this text write better arguments—arguments that are more critically thoughtful, more fully developed and elaborated, and more in tune with the demands of their audience. Available in three versions—a regular edition, which includes an anthology of readings; a brief edition, which offers the complete rhetoric without the anthology; and a concise edition with fewer readings and examples—*Writing Arguments* has been used successfully at every level, from first-year composition to advanced argumentation courses.

For the fifth edition, we have made judicious changes that reflect our own evolving understanding of the theory and practice of argumentation and our awareness of what concepts and skills students need to write thoughtful and effective arguments. We also have increased the book's interest level for students by using examples and readings that connect more directly to their own lives. As in previous editions, our aim is to integrate a comprehensive study of argument with a process approach to writing and critical thinking. In both its treatment of argumentation and its approach to teaching writing, the text is rooted in current research and theory. Our emphasis throughout is on providing a teaching tool that really works in the classroom.

The fifth edition of *Writing Arguments* is particularly strengthened by the presence of a new coauthor, June Johnson, a colleague of John Bean's at Seattle University. Her background in contemporary literary and rhetorical theory and her research interests in popular culture and civic argument—along with extensive classroom experience and training in pedagogy—have made June an invaluable writing partner.

What's New in the Fifth Edition?

The fifth edition retains all the features that have made earlier editions successful. In addition, the fifth edition contains the following improvements:

- Substantial revision of Chapter 2, "Reading Arguments," aimed at shortening the chapter and increasing student interest. We have replaced the Charles Murray article on welfare reform with two arguments on gender pay equity. Besides teaching summary writing and critical analysis, the chapter shows students how to seek out alternative views, pose questions about facts and values, and use disagreement productively to prompt further investigation. Throughout, we treat the process of reading arguments as a step toward writing arguments.

- Increased focus on audience, on real-world occasions for argument, and on analyzing rhetorical context. Throughout the text, we have infused a philosophical view of argument that emphasizes audience and rhetorical context at every stage of the construction of an argument. Our revisions of Chapter 3, "Writing Arguments," particularly reflect this focus.

- Reconceptualization of Chapter 9, "An Introduction to the Types of Claims," to reflect our evolving understanding of stasis theory. Using lasik eye surgery as an extended example, we show how knowledge of the claim types—combined with an analysis of audience—can help writers focus an argument and generate ideas. Also, in this edition we have added a sixth claim type, called "simple categorical arguments."

- A revision of Chapter 10, now titled "Categorical and Definitional Arguments." This chapter now explains both simple categorical arguments and definitional arguments. The revised chapter makes it easy for students to appreciate the universality of these two claim types, to understand the argumentative moves they entail, and to produce their own categorical or definitional arguments. Additionally, Chapter 11, on causal arguments, is significantly streamlined and clarified

- Six new student essays selected for the quality of their arguments and the appeal of their subject matter. Drawn from popular culture issues and other contemporary concerns, these readings connect effectively to the interests of today's students. For example, one student essay persuades readers to change their misconception of skateboarders ("'Half-Criminals' or Urban Athletes? A Plea for Fair Treatment of Skateboarders," pp. 129–31); another evaluates the marketing wizardry of the Spice Girls ("The Spice Girls: Good at Marketing but Not Good for Their Market," pp. 296–99); still another identifies high school cliques as a possible cause for the Columbine massacre ("The Monster That Is High School," pp. 247–49).

- Ten new professional essays in the rhetoric portion of the text, chosen for the appeal of their subject matter and for the range of genres represented. Among the new professional essays are John Leo's analysis of racial stereotypes in the film *The Phantom Menace* ("Stereotypes No Phantom in New *Star Wars* Movie," pp. 218–19); law professor Vicki Schultz's definitional argument on sexual harassment ("Sex Is the Least of It: Let's Focus Harassment Law on Work, Not Sex," pp. 223–27); and physician Ezekiel Emanuel's evaluation argument on fertility drugs ("Eight Is Too Many: The Case against Octuplets," pp. 303–06). In addition to new professional essays, the rhetoric portion also includes screen captures from several Web sites (on gender pay equity, on sweatshops) and several examples of visual arguments (photographs on Kosovo and on Makah whaling; tables and graphs related to wealth and income distribution).

- In the rhetoric portion, the addition of discussion questions following each reading, both student and professional. These questions prompt students to analyze writers' persuasive strategies, including how writers frame their arguments and situate them in larger social conflicts. Also we now introduce each reading with a brief headnote describing the reading's rhetorical context.

- Attention to visual arguments, with a special section devoted to visual arguments in Chapter 7, "Moving Your Audience: Audience-Based Reasons, *Ethos*, and *Pathos*."

- A new section on using humor to appeal to resistant audiences in Chapter 8, "Accommodating Your Audience: Treating Differing Views."

- Expanded treatment of electronic sources including explanations of how to evaluate Web sites and how to understand the logic of electronic searching—for example, the differences between licensed databases and the World Wide Web.

- More concise explanations throughout the text with the goal of making the style crisper and more engaging.

- A greatly improved anthology section with new readings on issues selected for their appeal to students and for their wide range of genres and argument types. We have replaced the units on immigration policy, mercy killing, legalization of drugs, recycling, and welfare reform with new units on causes of teenage violence, the social impact of popular culture, egg donors and reproductive technology, environmentalism versus culturalism, and corporate responsibility and world markets. Additionally, the unit on Internet censorship has completely new readings. The provocative arguments that compose each unit often respond to each other. They also show how different points of view lead to different ways of framing an issue and conceiving an audience.

- The anthology now contains 57 professional readings in 11 units; 39 of the readings are new while 18 are retained from the 4th edition. Genres range widely from op-ed pieces (Chuck Shelton's "When White Boys Kill, White Dads Fail") to legal briefs ("Kaske versus Nike"); from scholarly articles ("Women and Weight: Gendered Messages on Magazine Covers") to philosophical pieces aimed at popular audiences (James Garbarino's "Children in a Violent World: A Metaphysical Perspective"); from film reviews ("*South Park* Movie Revels in Its Really Bad Behavior") to organizational white papers (the ACLU's "Fahrenheit 451.2: Is Cyberspace Burning?"); from Web site advocacy pieces ("Where Is the Whales' Manifesto? Sea Shepherd's Response to the Makah Manifesto") to advocacy pieces in serious public affairs magazines (Andrew Sullivan's *New Republic* piece "Here Comes the Groom: A (Conservative) Case for Gay Marriage").

What Hasn't Changed? The Distinguishing Features of *Writing Arguments*

Building on earlier success, we have preserved all the features of earlier editions praised by students, instructors, and reviewers. The fifth edition provides the same teachable material but in a more streamlined and lively style. Specifically, the fifth edition retains the following successful features from the fourth edition:

- Focus throughout on writing arguments. Grounded in composition theory, this text combines explanations of argument with class-tested discussion tasks, exploratory writing tasks, and sequenced writing assignments aimed at developing skills of writing and critical thinking.

- Extensive treatment of invention including use of the Toulmin system of analyzing arguments combined with use of the enthymeme as a discovery and shaping tool.

- Detailed explanations of *logos*, *pathos*, and *ethos* as persuasive appeals.

- Comprehensive treatment of stasis theory identified for students as "types of claims."

- Focus on both the reading and the writing of arguments with emphasis on argument as inquiry and discovery as well as persuasion.

- Focus on the critical thinking that underlies effective arguments, particularly the skills of critical reading, of believing and doubting, of empathic listening, of active questioning, and of negotiating ambiguity and seeking synthesis.

- Focus on strategies for analyzing rhetorical context, for rooting arguments in the values and beliefs of the intended audience, and for basing decisions about content, structure, and style on analysis of audience and context.

- Copious treatment of the research paper, including two student examples—one using the MLA system and one using the APA system.

- Numerous "For Class Discussion" exercises and sequenced writing assignments designed to teach critical thinking and build argumentative skills. All "For Class Discussion" exercises can be used either for whole class discussions or for collaborative group tasks.

- Numerous student and professional arguments used to illustrate argumentative strategies and stimulate discussion, analysis, and debate. The rhetoric portion contains thirteen student essays of varied length and complexity as well as fourteen professional essays. Additionally, the fifth edition contains four letters to the editor from citizens, several screen captures from Web sites, and several examples of visual arguments.

Our Approaches to Argumentation

Our interest in argumentation grows out of our interest in the relationship between writing and thinking. When writing arguments, writers are forced to lay bare their thinking processes in an unparalleled way, grappling with the complex interplay between inquiry and persuasion, between issue and audience. In an effort to engage students in the kinds of critical thinking that argument demands, we draw on four major approaches to argumentation:

- *The enthymeme as a rhetorical and logical structure.* This concept, especially useful for beginning writers, helps students "nutshell" an argument as a claim with one or more supporting *because* clauses. It also helps them see how real-world arguments are rooted in assumptions granted by the audience rather than in universal and unchanging principles.
- *The three classical types of appeal*—**logos, ethos,** *and* **pathos.** These concepts help students place their arguments in a rhetorical context focusing on audience-based appeals; they also help students create an effective voice and style.
- *Toulmin's system of analyzing arguments.* Toulmin's system helps students see the complete, implicit structure that underlies an enthymeme and develop appropriate grounds and backing to support the claim. It also highlights the rhetorical, social, and dialectical nature of argument.
- *Stasis or claim-type theory.* This approach stresses the heuristic value of learning different patterns of support for different types of claims and often leads students to make surprisingly rich and full arguments.

Throughout the text these approaches are integrated and synthesized into generative tools for both producing and analyzing arguments.

Structure of the Text

The text has five main parts plus two appendixes. Part One gives an overview of argumentation. The first three chapters present our philosophy of argument, showing how argument helps writers clarify their own thinking and connect with the values and beliefs of a questioning audience. Throughout we link the process of arguing—articulating issue questions, formulating propositions, examining alternative points of view, and creating structures of supporting reasons and evidence—with the processes of reading and writing.

Part Two examines the principles of argument. Chapters 4 through 6 show that the core of an argument is a claim with reasons. These reasons are often stated as enthymemes, the unstated premise of which must sometimes be brought to the surface and supported. Discussion of Toulmin logic shows students how to discover the stated and unstated premises of their arguments and to provide structures of reasons and evidence to support them. Chapters 7 and 8 focus on the rhetorical context of arguments. These chapters discuss the writer's relationship with an audience, particularly with finding audience-based rea-sons, with using *pathos* and *ethos* effectively and responsibly, and with accommodating arguments to different kinds of audiences from sympathetic to neutral to resistant.

Part Three discusses six different types of argument: simple categorical arguments, definitional arguments, causal arguments, resemblance arguments, evaluation arguments, and proposal arguments. These chapters introduce students to two recurring strategies of argument that cut across the different category types: criteria-match arguing, in which the writer establishes criteria for making a judgment and argues whether a specific case does or does not meet those criteria, and causal arguing, in which the writer shows that one event or phenomenon can be linked to others in a causal chain. The last chapter of Part Three deals with the special complexities of moral arguments.

Part Four shows students how to incorporate research into their arguments. It explains how writers use sources, with a special focus on the skills of summary, paraphrase, and judicious quotation. Unlike standard treatments of the research paper, our discussion explains to students how the writer's meaning and purpose control the selection and shaping of source materials. Part Four explains both the MLA and the APA documentation systems, which are illustrated by two student examples of researched arguments. Throughout Chapters 16 and 17, we incorporate discussions of electronic searching and the challenges of detecting what is useful on the World Wide Web.

The appendixes provide important supplemental information useful for courses in argument. Appendix One gives an overview of informal fallacies. Appendix Two shows students how to get the most out of collaborative groups in an argument class. Appendix Two also provides a sequence of collaborative tasks that will help students learn to peer-critique their classmates' arguments-in-progress. The numerous "For Class Discussion" exercises within the text provide additional tasks for group collaboration.

Finally Part Five, the anthology, provides a rich selection of professional arguments arranged under eleven high-interest topic areas ranging from sweatshop controversies to the ethics of reproductive technology. The anthology selections are grouped by topic rather than by issue question to encourage students to see that any conversation of alternative views gives rise to numerous embedded and intertwined issues. Formulating the issue question, targeting an audience, framing the issue as a claim, and determining the depth and complexity of the argument are all part of the writer's task. Many of the issues raised in the anthology are first raised in the rhetoric (Parts One through Four). For example, Chapter 10 has a reading on sexual harassment; Chapters 11 and 12 on causes of teenage violence; Chapter 13 on the social impact of popular culture, on reproductive technology, and on same-sex marriage; Chapter 14 on the mentally ill homeless; and Chapter 16 on sweatshops.

Writing Assignments

The text provides a variety of sequenced writing assignments, including exploratory tasks for discovering and generating arguments, "microthemes" for practicing basic argumentative moves (for example, supporting a reason with statistical evidence), cases, and numerous other assignments calling for complete arguments. Thus the text provides instructors with a wealth of options for writing assignments on which to build a coherent course.

An Expanded and Improved Instructor's Manual

The Instructor's Manual has been revised and expanded to make it more useful for teachers and writing program administrators. Written by co-author June Johnson, the new Instructor's Manual has the following features:

- Discussion of planning decisions an instructor must make in designing an argument course: for example, how to use readings; how much to emphasize or de-emphasize Toulmin or claim-type theory; how much time to build into the course for invention, peer review of drafts, and other writing instruction; and how to select and sequence assignments.

- Three detailed sample syllabi showing how *Writing Arguments* can support a variety of course structures and emphases:

  Syllabus #1: This course emphasizes argumentative skills and strategies, uses readings for rhetorical analysis, and asks students to write on issues drawn from their own experience.

  Syllabus #2: This more rigorous course works intensely with the logical structure of argument, the classical appeals, the Toulmin schema, and claim-type theory. It uses readings for rhetorical analysis and for an introduction to the argumentative controversies that students will address in their papers.

  Syllabus #3: This course asks students to experiment with genres of argument (for example, op-ed pieces, white papers, visual arguments, and researched freelance or scholarly arguments) and focuses on students' choice of topics and claim types.

- For instructors who include Toulmin, an independent, highly teachable introductory lesson on the Toulmin schema.

- For new teachers, a helpful discussion of how to sequence writing assignments and how to use a variety of collaborative tasks in the classroom to promote active learning and critical thinking.

- Chapter-by-chapter responses to the For Class Discussion exercises.

- Numerous teaching tips and suggestions placed strategically throughout the chapter material.

- Helpful suggestions for using the exercises on critiquing readings in Part Three, "Arguments in Depth: Six Types of Claims." By focusing on rhetorical context as well as the strengths and weaknesses of these arguments, our suggestions will help students connect their reading of arguments to their writing of arguments.

- At the end of each claim-type chapter in Part Three, a list of anthology readings that employ the same claim type, either as a major claim or as a substantial portion of the argument.

- A substantially revised approach to our analysis of anthology readings that better connects the anthology to the rhetoric portion of the text. Using a bulleted, quick-reference format, each analysis briefly discusses (1) the core of the argument, (2) the major or dominant claims of the argument, (3) the argument's use of evidence and argumentative strategies, (4) the appeals to *ethos* and *pathos* in the argument, and (5) the argument's genre. This easy-to-scan format helps instructors select readings and provides good starting points for class discussion. Our analyses also point out striking connections among readings, suggesting how the readings participate in larger societal argumentative conversations.

Companion Web Site

The *Writing Arguments* Companion Web Site, http://www.abacon.com/ramage, enables instructors to access online writing activities and Web links keyed to specific chapters, post and make changes to their syllabi, hold chat sessions with individual students or groups of students, and receive e-mail and essay assignments directly from students.

Acknowledgments

We are happy for this opportunity to give public thanks to the scholars, teachers, and students who have influenced our approach to composition and argument. We would especially like to thank Darlene Panvini of Vanderbilt University for her advice on our treatment of the wetlands controversy in Chapter 10. Additional thanks go to Seattle University librarian Sandra Brandt for her help with our explanations of library and Internet databases and retrieval and to Daniel Anderson of the University of North Carolina, Chapel Hill, for his material on electronic communication. Thanks also to Susan Meyer, Stephen Bean, and Sarah Bean for their research assistance in preparing the fifth edition.

Particular thanks go to the following reviewers, who gave us helpful and cogent advice at various stages of the revision process: Jonathan Ayres, the University of Texas at Austin; Linda Bensel-Meyers, University of Tennessee–Knoxville; Deborah Core, Eastern Kentucky University; Richard Fulkerson, Texas A&M University–Commerce; Carol A. Lowe, McLennan Community College; David Mair, University of Oklahoma; Tim McGee, the College of New Jersey; Thomas A. Wallis, North Carolina State University; and Irene Ward, Kansas State University, for their reviews of *Writing Arguments,* Fourth Edition, and draft chapters of this fifth edition.

We also would like to thank our editor of more than fifteen years, Eben Ludlow, who well deserves his reputation as a premier editor in college publishing. In fact, it has been a joy for us to work with the whole Allyn & Bacon English team: Lisa Kimball, English marketing manager; Susan Brown, editorial production administrator; and Doug Day, English sales specialist. Additional thanks go to Merrill Peterson of Matrix Productions, who professionally managed many key aspects of production.

Finally, we would like to thank our families. John Bean: Thanks to my wife, Kit, whose own work as an ESL instructor has produced wonderful discussions of argument and pedagogy in a multicultural setting, and to my children Matthew, Andrew, Stephen, and Sarah for their love and support. June Johnson: Thanks to my husband, Kenneth Bube, and my daughter, Jane Ellen, for their keen insights, loving encouragement, and inspirational humor.

Overview of Argument

1 Argument

An Introduction

At the outset of a book on argument, we ought to explain what an argument is. Instead, we're going to explain why no simple definition is possible. Philosophers and rhetoricians have disagreed over the centuries about the meaning of the term and about the goals that arguers should set for themselves. This opening chapter introduces you to some of these controversies. Our goal is to introduce you to various ways of thinking about argument as a way of helping you become a more powerful arguer yourself.

We begin by asking what we mean by argument and then proceed to three defining features: *Argument* requires justification of its claims, it is both a product and a process, and it combines elements of truth seeking and persuasion. We then explore more deeply the relationship between truth seeking and persuasion by asking questions about the nature of "truth" that arguments seek. Finally, we give you an example of a successful arguing process.

WHAT DO WE MEAN BY ARGUMENT?

Let's begin by examining the inadequacies of two popular images of argument—fight and debate.

Argument Is Not a Fight or a Quarrel

To many, the word *argument* connotes anger and hostility, as when we say, "I just got in a huge argument with my roommate," or "My mother and I argue all the time." What we picture here is heated disagreement, rising pulse rates, and an urge to slam doors. Argument imagined as fight conjures images of shouting talk-show guests, name-calling letter writers, or fist-banging speakers.

But to our way of thinking, argument doesn't imply anger. In fact, arguing is often pleasurable. It is a creative and productive activity that engages us at high levels of inquiry and critical thinking, often in conversation with persons we like and respect. For your primary image of argument, we invite you to think not of a fist-banging speaker but of a small group of reasonable persons seeking the best solution to a problem. We will return to this image throughout the chapter.

Argument Is Not Pro-Con Debate

Another popular image of argument is debate—a presidential debate, per-haps, or a high school or college debate tournament. According to one popular dic-tionary, *debate* is "a formal contest of argumentation in which two opposing teams defend and attack a given proposition." While formal debate can develop critical thinking, its weakness is that it can turn argument into a game of winners and losers rather than a process of cooperative inquiry.

For an illustration of this weakness, consider one of our former students, a champion high school debater who spent his senior year debating the issue of prison reform. Throughout the year he argued for and against propositions such as "The United States should build more prisons" and "Innovative alternatives to prison should replace prison sentences for most crimes." We asked him, "What do you personally think is the best way to reform prisons?" He replied, "I don't know. I haven't thought about what I would actually choose."

Here was a bright, articulate student who had studied prisons extensively for a year. Yet nothing in the atmosphere of pro-con debate had engaged him in truth-seeking inquiry. He could argue for and against a proposition, but he hadn't ex-perienced the wrenching process of clarifying his own values and taking a personal stand. As we explain throughout this text, argument entails a desire for truth; it aims to find the best solutions to complex problems. We don't mean that arguers don't passionately support their own points of view or expose weaknesses in views they find faulty. Instead, we mean that their goal isn't to win a game but to find and promote the best belief or course of action.

Arguments Can Be Explicit or Implicit

Before proceeding to some defining features of argument, we should note also that arguments can be either explicit or implicit. An *explicit* argument states di-rectly a controversial claim and supports it with reasons and evidence. An *implicit* argument, in contrast, doesn't look like an argument. It may be a poem or short story, a photograph or cartoon, a personal essay or an autobiographical narrative. But like an explicit argument, it persuades its audience toward a certain point of view. John Steinbeck's *Grapes of Wrath* is an implicit argument for the unionization of farm workers, just as the following poem is an implicit argument against the premise that it is sweet and fitting to die for one's country.

Dulce et Decorum Est

Bent double, like old beggars under sacks,
Knock-kneed, coughing like hags, we cursed through sludge
Till on the haunting flares we turned our backs,
And towards our distant rest began to trudge.
Men marched asleep. Many had lost their boots,
But limped on, blood-shod. All went lame, all blind;
Drunk with fatigue; deaf even to the hoots
Of gas-shells dropping softly behind.

Gas! Gas! Quick, boys—An ecstasy of fumbling,
Fitting the clumsy helmets just in time,
But someone still was yelling out and stumbling
And flound'ring like a man in fire or lime.
Dim through the misty panes and thick green light,
As under a green sea, I saw him drowning.

In all my dreams before my helpless sight
He plunges at me, guttering, choking, drowning.

If in some smothering dreams, you too could pace
Behind the wagon that we flung him in,
And watch the white eyes writhing in his face,
His hanging face, like a devil's sick of sin,
If you could hear, at every jolt, the blood
Come gargling from the froth-corrupted lungs
Bitter as the cud
Of vile, incurable sores on innocent tongues,—
My friend, you would not tell with such high zest
To children ardent for some desperate glory,
The old lie: *Dulce et decorum est*
*Pro patria mori.**

                                        —Wilfred Owen

Here Wilfred Owen makes a powerful case against the "old lie"—that war is honorable, that dying for one's country is sweet and fitting. But the argument is implicit: It is carried in the horrible image of a soldier drowning in his own fluids from a mustard gas attack rather than through an ordered structure of thesis, rea-

---

*"How sweet and fitting it is to die for one's country." Wilfred Owen (1893–1918) was killed in World War I and wrote many of his poems while in the trenches.

sons, and evidence. Visual images can also make implicit arguments, often by evoking powerful emotions in audiences. The perspective photos take, the stories they tell, or the vivid details of place and time they display compel viewers literally to see the issue from a particular angle. Take, for instance, the photo (Figure 1.1) of Albanian refugees during the Kosovo War. The photographer conveys the nightmare of this war by foregrounding the old woman, probably a grandmother, perched precariously atop a heavily loaded wheelbarrow, her canes or crutches sticking out from the pile, and the five other persons in the scene hastening down a stark road against an ominous gray background. Here *showing* the urgency of the Albanians' flight for their lives and the helplessness of the two who can't walk is an effective strategy to arouse sympathy for the Albanians. Photographs of this kind regularly appeared in American newspapers during the war, serving to heighten U.S. support of NATO bombing. Meanwhile, Serbs complained that no American newspapers showed photographs of KLA (Kosovo Liberation Army) atrocities against Serbs.

FIGURE 1.1   Albanian refugees during the Kosovo War
Newsweek, April 12, 1999, p. 33.

FOR CLASS DISCUSSION

1. In your own words, how do explicit and implicit arguments differ?

2. Imagine that you wanted to take a photograph that creates an implicit argument persuading (1) teenagers against smoking; (2) teenagers against becoming sexually active; (3) the general public toward banning handguns; (4) the general public against banning handguns; (5) the general public toward saving endangered species; (6) the general public toward supporting timber companies' desire to harvest old-growth forests. Working individually or in small groups, describe a photograph you might take that would create an appropriate implicit argument.

   EXAMPLE: To create an implicit argument against legalizing hard drugs, you might photograph a blank-eyed, cadaverous teenager plunging a needle into her arm.

Although implicit arguments can be powerful, the predominant focus of this text is on explicit argument. We don't leave implicit arguments entirely, however, because their strategies—especially the persuasive power of stories and narratives—can often be incorporated into explicit arguments, as we discuss more fully in Chapter 7.

THE DEFINING FEATURES OF ARGUMENT

We turn now to examine argument in more detail. (From here on, when we say "argument," we mean "explicit argument.") This section examines three defining features.

Argument Requires Justification of Its Claims

To begin defining argument, let's turn to a humble but universal site of disagreement: the conflict between a parent and a teenager over rules. In what way and in what circumstances do such conflicts constitute arguments?

Consider the following dialogue:

YOUNG PERSON (*racing for the front door while putting coat on*): Bye. See you later.

PARENT: Whoa! What time are you planning on coming home?

YOUNG PERSON (*coolly, hand still on doorknob*): I'm sure we discussed this earlier. I'll be home around 2 A.M. (*The second sentence, spoken very rapidly, is barely audible.*)

PARENT (*mouth tightening*):   We did *not* discuss this earlier and you're *not* staying out till two in the morning. You'll be home at twelve.

At this point in the exchange, we have a quarrel, not an argument. Quarrelers exchange antagonistic assertions without any attempt to support them rationally. If the dialogue never gets past the "Yes-you-will/No-I-won't" stage, it either remains a quarrel or degenerates into a fight.

Let us say, however, that the dialogue takes the following turn:

YOUNG PERSON (*tragically*):   But I'm *sixteen years old*!

Now we're moving toward argument. Not, to be sure, a particularly well-developed or cogent one, but an argument all the same. It's now an argument because one of the quarrelers has offered a reason for her assertion. Her choice of curfew is satisfactory, she says, *because* she is sixteen years old, an argument that depends on the unstated assumption that sixteen-year-olds are old enough to make decisions about such matters.

The parent can now respond in one of several ways that will either advance the argument or turn it back into a quarrel. The parent can simply invoke parental authority ("I don't care—you're still coming home at twelve"), in which case argument ceases. Or the parent can provide a reason for his or her view ("You will be home at twelve because your dad and I pay the bills around here!"), in which case the argument takes a new turn.

So far we've established two necessary conditions that must be met before we're willing to call something an argument: (1) a set of two or more conflicting assertions and (2) the attempt to resolve the conflict through an appeal to reason.

But good argument demands more than meeting these two formal requirements. For the argument to be effective, an arguer is obligated to clarify and support the reasons presented. For example, "But I'm sixteen years old!" is not yet a clear support for the assertion "I should be allowed to set my own curfew." On the surface, Young Person's argument seems absurd. Her parent, of all people, knows precisely how old she is. What makes it an argument is that behind her claim lies an unstated assumption—all sixteen-year-olds are old enough to set their own curfews. What Young Person needs to do now is to support that assumption.* In doing so, she must anticipate the sorts of questions the assumption will raise in the minds of her parent: What is the legal status of sixteen-year-olds? How psychologically mature, as opposed to chronologically mature, is Young Person? What is the actual track record of Young Person in being responsible? and so forth. Each of these questions will force Young Person to reexamine and clarify her assumptions about the proper degree of autonomy for sixteen-year-olds. And her response to those questions should in turn force the parents to reexamine their

---

*Later in this text we will call the assumption underlying a line of reasoning its *warrant* (see Chapter 5).

assumptions about the dependence of sixteen-year-olds on parental guidance and wisdom. (Likewise, the parents will need to show why "paying the bills around here" automatically gives them the right to set Young Person's curfew.)

As the argument continues, Young Person and Parent may shift to a different line of reasoning. For example, Young Person might say: "I should be allowed to stay out until 2 A.M. because all my friends get to stay out that late." (Here the unstated assumption is that the rules in this family ought to be based on the rules in other families.) The parent might in turn respond, "But I certainly never stayed out that late when I was your age"—an argument assuming that the rules in this family should follow the rules of an earlier generation.

As Young Person and Parent listen to each other's points of view (and begin realizing why their initial arguments have not persuaded their intended audience), both parties find themselves in the uncomfortable position of having to examine their own beliefs and to justify assumptions that they have taken for granted. Here we encounter one of the earliest senses of the term *to argue*, which is "to clarify." As an arguer begins to clarify her own position on an issue, she also begins to clarify her audience's position. Such clarification helps the arguer see how she might accommodate her audience's views, perhaps by adjusting her own position or by developing reasons that appeal to her audience's values. Thus Young Person might suggest an argument like this:

> I should be allowed to stay out until 2 on a trial basis because I need enough space to demonstrate my maturity and show you I won't get into trouble.

The assumption underlying this argument is that it is good to give teenagers freedom to demonstrate their maturity. Because this reason is likely to appeal to her parent's own values (the parent wants to see his or her daughter grow in maturity) and because it is tempered by the qualifier "on a trial basis" (which reduces some of the threat of Young Person's initial demands), it may prompt productive discussion.

Whether or not Young Person and Parent can work out a best solution, the preceding scenario illustrates how argument leads persons to clarify their reasons and provide justifications that can be examined rationally. The scenario also illustrates two specific aspects of argument that we will explore in detail in the next sections: (1) Argument is both a process and a product. (2) Argument combines truth seeking and persuasion.

Argument Is Both a Process and a Product

As the preceding scenario revealed, argument can be viewed as a *process* in which two or more parties seek the best solution to a question or problem. Argument can also be viewed as a *product*, each product being any person's contribution to the conversation at a given moment. In an informal discussion, the products are usually short, whatever time a person uses during his or her turns in the conversation. Under more formal settings, an orally delivered product might be a short impromptu speech (say, during an open-mike discussion of a campus issue) or a longer, carefully prepared formal speech (as in an oral brief before a judge, a presentation to a legislative subcommittee, or an argument at a public hearing for or against a proposed city project).

Similar conversations occur in writing. Roughly analogous to a small-group discussion is an e-mail discussion of the kind that occurs regularly through informal chat groups or professional listservs. In an online discussion, participants have more thinking time to shape their messages than they do in a real-time oral discussion. Nevertheless, messages are usually short and informal, making it possible over the course of several days to see participants' ideas shift and evolve as conversants modify their initial views in response to others' views.

Roughly equivalent to a formal speech would be a formal written argument composed through multiple drafts over the course of days or weeks and submitted as a college essay assignment, a grant proposal, a guest column for the op-ed* section of a newspaper, a letter to a congressional representative, a legal brief for a judge, or an article for an organizational newsletter, popular magazine, or professional journal. In each of these instances, the written argument (a product) enters a conversation (a process)—in this case, a conversation of readers, many of whom will carry on the conversation by writing their own responses or by discussing the writer's views with others. The goal of the community of writers and readers is to find the best solution to the problem or issue under discussion.

Argument Combines Truth Seeking and Persuasion

In thinking about argument as a product, the writer will find herself continually moving back and forth between truth seeking and persuasion—that is, between questions about the subject matter (What is the best solution to this problem?) and about audience (What do my readers already believe or value? What reasons and evidence will most persuade them?). Back and forth she'll weave, alternately absorbed in the subject of her argument and in the audience for that argument.

Neither of the two focuses is ever completely out of mind, but their relative importance shifts during different phases of the development of a paper. Moreover, different rhetorical situations place different emphases on truth seeking versus persuasion. We could thus place arguments on a kind of continuum that

---

*Op-ed stands for "opposite-editorial." It is the generic name in journalism for a signed argument that voices the writer's opinion on an issue, as opposed to a news story that is supposed to report events objectively, uncolored by the writer's personal views. Op-ed pieces appear in the editorial-opinion section of newspapers, which generally feature editorials by the resident staff, opinion pieces by syndicated columnists, and letters to the editor from readers. The term op-ed is often extended to syndicated columns appearing in news magazines.

measures the degree of attention a writer gives to subject matter versus audience. At the far truth-seeking end of the continuum might be an exploratory piece that lays out several alternative approaches to a problem and weighs the strengths and weaknesses of each with no concern for persuasion. At the other end of the continuum would be outright propaganda, such as a political campaign advertisement that reduces a complex issue to sound bites and distorts an opponent's position through out-of-context quotations or misleading use of data. (At its most blatant, propaganda obliterates truth seeking; it will do anything, including the knowing use of bogus evidence, distorted assertions, and outright lies, to win over an audience.) In the middle ranges of the continuum, writers shift their focuses back and forth between truth seeking and persuasion but with varying degrees of emphasis.

As an example of a writer focusing primarily on truth seeking, consider the case of Kathleen, who, in her college argument course, addressed the definitional question "Is American Sign Language (ASL) a 'foreign language' for purposes of meeting the university's foreign language requirement?" Kathleen had taken two years of ASL at a community college. When she transferred to a four-year college, the chair of the foreign languages department at her new college would not allow her ASL proficiency to count for the foreign language requirement. ASL isn't a "language," the chair said summarily. "It's not equivalent to learning French, German, or Japanese."

Kathleen disagreed, so she immersed herself in developing her argument. While doing research, she focused almost entirely on subject matter, searching for what linguists, brain neurologists, cognitive psychologists, and sociologists had said about the language of deaf people. Immersed in her subject matter, she was only tacitly concerned with her audience, whom she thought of primarily as her classmates and the professor of her argument class—persons who were friendly to her views and interested in her experiences with the deaf community. She wrote a well-documented paper, citing several scholarly articles, that made a good case to her classmates (and the professor) that ASL was indeed a distinct language.

Proud of the big red A the professor had placed on her paper, Kathleen returned to the chair of the foreign languages department with a new request to count ASL for her language requirement. The chair read her paper, congratulated her on her good writing, but said her argument was not persuasive. He disagreed with several of the linguists she cited and with the general definition of *language* that her paper assumed. He then gave her some additional (and to her fuzzy) reasons why the college would not accept ASL as a foreign language.

Spurred by what she considered the chair's too-easy dismissal of her argument, Kathleen decided, for a subsequent assignment in her argument class, to write a second paper on ASL—but this time aiming it directly at the chair of foreign languages. Now her writing task falls closer to the persuasive end of our continuum. Kathleen once again immersed herself in research, but this time it focused not on subject matter (whether ASL is a distinct language) but on audience. She researched the history of the foreign language requirement at her college and discovered some of the politics behind it (an old foreign language requirement had been dropped in the 1970s and reinstituted in the 1990s, partly—a math professor told her—to boost enrollments in foreign language courses). She also interviewed foreign language teachers to find out what they knew and didn't know about ASL. She discovered that many teachers thought ASL was "easy to learn," so that accepting ASL would allow students a Mickey Mouse way to avoid the rigors of a "real" foreign language class. Additionally, she learned that foreign language teachers valued immersing students in a foreign culture; in fact, the foreign language requirement was part of her college's effort to create a multicultural curriculum.

This new understanding of her target audience helped Kathleen totally reconceptualize her argument. She condensed and abridged her original paper down to one line of reasoning in her new argument. She added sections showing the difficulty of learning ASL (to counter her audience's belief that learning ASL was easy), showing how the deaf community formed a distinct culture with its own customs and literature (to show how ASL met the goals of multiculturalism), and showing that the number of transfer students with ASL credits would be negligibly small (to allay fears that accepting ASL would threaten enrollments in language classes). She ended her argument with an appeal to her college's public emphasis (declared boldly in its mission statement) on eradicating social injustice and reaching out to the oppressed. She described the isolation of deaf people in a world where almost no hearing people learn ASL, and she argued that the deaf community on her campus could be integrated more fully into campus life if more students could "talk" with them. Thus the ideas included in her new argument—the reasons selected, the evidence used, the arrangement and tone—all were determined by her primary focus on persuasion.

Our point, then, is that all along the continuum writers are concerned both to seek truth and to persuade, but not necessarily with equal balance. Kathleen could not have written her second paper, aimed specifically at persuading the chair of foreign languages, if she hadn't first immersed herself in truth-seeking research that convinced her that ASL was indeed a distinct language. Nor are we saying that her second argument was better than her first. Both fulfilled their purposes and met the needs of their intended audiences. Both involved truth seeking and persuasion, but the first focused primarily on subject matter whereas the second focused primarily on audience.

ARGUMENT AND THE PROBLEM OF TRUTH

The tension that we have just examined between truth seeking and persuasion raises one of the oldest issues in the field of argument: Is the arguer's first obligation to truth or to winning the argument? And just what is the nature of the truth to which arguers are supposed to be obligated? To this second question we now turn.

When Does Argument Become Propaganda?
The Debate between Socrates and Callicles

One of the first great debates on the issue of truth versus victory occurs in Plato's dialogue the *Gorgias,* in which the philosopher Socrates takes on the rhetorician Callicles.

Socrates was a great philosopher known to us today primarily through his student Plato, whose "dialogues" depict Socrates debating various friends and antagonists. Socrates' stated goal in these debates was to "rid the world of error." In dialogue after dialogue, Socrates vanquishes error by skillfully leading people through a series of questions that force them to recognize the inconsistency and implausibility of their beliefs. He was a sort of intellectual judo master who takes opponents' arguments the way they want to go until they suddenly fall over.

Callicles, in contrast, is a shadowy figure in history. We know him only through his exchange with Socrates—hence only through Plato's eyes. But Callicles is easily recognizable to philosophers as a representative of the Sophists, a group of teachers who schooled ancient Greeks in the fine art of winning arguments. The Sophists were a favorite, if elusive, target of both Socrates and Plato. Indeed, opposition to the Sophists' approach to life lies at the core of Platonic philosophy. Having said all that, let's turn to the dialogue.

Early in the debate, Socrates is clearly in control. He easily—too easily, as it turns out—wins a couple of preliminary rounds against some less-determined Sophists before confronting Callicles. But in the long and arduous debate that follows, it's not at all clear that Socrates wins. In fact, one of the points being made in the *Gorgias* seems to be that philosophers committed to "clarifying" and discovering truth may occasionally have to sacrifice winning the debate in the name of their higher ends. Although Plato makes an eloquent case for enlightenment as the goal of argument, he may well contribute to the demise of this noble principle if he should happen to lose. Unfortunately, it appears that Socrates can't win the argument without sinning against the very principle he's defending.

The effectiveness of Callicles as a debater lies in his refusal to allow Socrates *any* assumptions. In response to Socrates' concern for virtue and justice, Callicles responds dismissively that such concepts are mere conventions, invented by the weak to protect themselves from the strong. In Callicles' world, "might makes right." The function of argument in such a world is to extend the freedom and power of the arguer, not to arrive at some vision of "truth." Indeed, the power to decide what's "true" belongs to the winner of the debate. For Callicles, a truth that never wins is no truth at all because it will soon disappear. In sum, Callicles sees the ends (winning the argument) as justifying the means (refusing to grant any assumptions, using ambiguous language, and so forth). Socrates, in contrast, believes that no good end can come from questionable means.

Based on what we've said up to this point about our belief in argument as truth seeking, you might guess that our sympathies are with Socrates. To a great extent they are. But Socrates lived in a much simpler world than we do, if by "simple" we mean a world where the True and the Good were, if not universally agreed-upon notions, at least ones around which a clear consensus formed. For Socrates, there was one True Answer to any important question. Truth resided in the ideal world of forms, and through philosophic rigor humans could transcend the changing, shadowlike world of everyday reality to perceive the world of universals where Truth, Beauty, and Goodness resided.

Callicles, however, rejects the notion that there is only one possible truth at which all arguments will necessarily arrive. For Callicles, there are different degrees of truth and different kinds of truths for different situations or cultures. In raising the whole nettlesome question—How "true" is a "truth" that you can't get anyone to agree to?—Callicles is probably closer to the modern world than is Plato. Let's expand on Callicles' view of truth by examining some contemporary illustrations.

What Is Truth? The Place of Argument in Contemporary Life

Although the debate between Socrates and Callicles appears to end inconclusively, many readers over the centuries conceded the victory to Socrates almost by default. Callicles was seen as cheating. The term *sophistry* came to be synonymous with trickery in argument. The Sophists' relativistic beliefs were so repugnant to most people that they refused to grant any merit to the Sophists' position. In our century, however, the Sophists have found a more sympathetic readership, one that takes some of the questions they raised quite seriously.

One way of tracing this shift in attitude toward truth is by looking at a significant shift in the definition of the verb *to argue* over the centuries. On the one hand, as we have seen, one of the earliest meanings of *to argue* was "to clarify," a definition focusing on truth seeking. Another early meaning was "to prove"—a definition that focuses simultaneously on truth seeking and on persuasion in that it implies that truth can be both known (truth seeking) and "proved" (persuasion). Argument in this sense was closely associated with mathematical demonstrations in which you move from axioms to proofs through formulae. An argument of this sort is nearly irrefutable—unless we play Callicles and reject the axioms.

Today, on the other hand, *to argue* is usually taken to mean something like "to provide grounds for inferring." The better the argument, the better the reasons and evidence one provides, the more likely is the audience to infer what the arguer has inferred. Instead of "proving" one's claim, the best an arguer can hope for is to make an audience *more likely to agree with* the arguer's claim. One contemporary philosopher says that argument can hope only to "increase adherence" to ideas, not absolutely convince an audience of the necessary truth of ideas.

In the twentieth century, absolute, demonstrable truth is seen by many thinkers, from physicists to philosophers, as an illusion. Some would argue that truth is merely a product of human beings' talking and arguing with each other.

These thinkers say that when considering questions of interpretation, meaning, or value one can never tell for certain whether an assertion is true—not by examining the physical universe more closely or by reasoning one's way toward some Platonic form or by receiving a mystical revelation. The closest one can come to truth is through the confirmation of one's views from others in a community of peers. "Truth" in any field of knowledge, say these thinkers, is simply an agreement of knowledgeable people in that field.

To illustrate the relevance of Callicles to contemporary society, suppose for the moment that we wanted to ask whether sexual fidelity is a virtue. A Socratic approach would assume a single, real Truth about the value of sexual fidelity, one that could be discovered through a gradual peeling away of wrong answers. Callicles, meanwhile, would assume that sexual morality is culturally relative; hence, he might point out all the societies in which monogamous fidelity for one or both sexes is not the norm. Clearly, our world is more like Callicles'. We are all exposed to multiple cultural perspectives directly and indirectly. Through television, newspapers, travel, and education we experience ways of thinking and valuing that are different from our own. It is difficult to ignore the fact that our personal values are not universally shared or even respected. Thus, we're all faced with the need to justify our views in such a diverse society.

It should be clear, then, that when we speak of the truth-seeking aim of argument, we mean not the discovery of an absolute "right answer," but the willingness to think through the complexity of an issue and to consider respectfully a wide range of views. The process of argument allows social groups, through the thoughtful exchange of ideas, to seek the best solution to a problem. The value of argument is its ability to help social groups make decisions in a rational and humane way without resorting to violence or to other assertions of raw power.

FOR CLASS DISCUSSION

On any given day, newspapers provide evidence of the complexity of living in a pluralistic culture. Issues that could be readily decided in a completely homogeneous culture raise many questions for us in a society that has few shared assumptions.

What follows are two brief news stories from the Associated Press wires. Choose one story or the other and conduct a "simulation game" in which various class members role play the points of view of the characters involved in the controversy. If you choose the first case, for example, one class member should role-play the attorney of the woman refusing the Caesarean section, another the "court-appointed representative of the woman's fetus," and another the doctor. If you wish, conduct a court hearing in which other members role-play a judge, cross-examining attorneys, and a jury. No matter which case you choose, your class's goal should be to represent each point of view as fully and sympathetically as possible to help you realize the complexity of the values in conflict.

Illinois Court Won't Hear Case of Mom Who Refuses Surgery

1   CHICAGO—A complex legal battle over a Chicago woman's refusal to undergo a Caesarean section, even though it could save the life of her unborn child, essentially was settled yesterday when the state's highest court refused to hear the case.

2   The court declined to review a lower court's ruling that the woman should not be forced to submit to surgery in a case that pitted the rights of the woman, referred to in court as "Mother Doe," against those of her fetus.

3   The 22-year-old Chicago woman, now in the 37th week of her pregnancy, refused her doctors' advice to have the surgery because she believes God intended her to deliver the child naturally.

4   The woman's attorneys argued that the operation would violate her constitutional rights to privacy and the free exercise of her religious beliefs.

5   Cook County Public Guardian Patrick Murphy, the court-appointed representative of the woman's fetus, said he would file a petition with the U.S. Supreme Court asking it to hear the case. He has 90 days to file the petition, but he acknowledged future action would probably come too late.

6   Doctors say the fetus is not receiving enough oxygen from the placenta and will either die or be retarded unless it is delivered by Caesarean section. Despite that diagnosis, the mother has stressed her faith in God's healing powers and refused doctors' advice to submit to the operation.

Homeless Hit the Streets to Protest Proposed Ban

1   SEATTLE—The homeless stood up for themselves by sitting down in a peaceful but vocal protest yesterday in Seattle's University District.

2   About 50 people met at noon to criticize a proposed set of city ordinances that would ban panhandlers from sitting on sidewalks, put them in jail for repeatedly urinating in public, and crack down on "intimidating" street behavior.

3   "Sitting is not a crime," read poster boards that feature mug shots of Seattle City Attorney Mark Sidran, who is pushing for the new laws. [. . .] "This is city property; the police want to tell us we can't sit here," yelled one man named R.C. as he sat cross-legged outside a pizza establishment.

4   Marsha Shaiman stood outside the University Book Store holding a poster and waving it at passing cars. She is not homeless, but was one of many activists in the crowd. "I qualify as a privileged white yuppie," she said. "I'm offended that the privileged people in this country are pointing at the poor, and people of color, and say they're causing problems. They're being used as scapegoats."

Many local merchants support the ban saying that panhandlers hurt business by in-   5
timidating shoppers and fouling the area with the odor of urine, vomited wine, and sometimes even feces.

A SUCCESSFUL PROCESS
OF ARGUMENTATION:
THE WELL-FUNCTIONING COMMITTEE

We have said that neither the fist-banging speaker nor the college debate team
represents our ideal image of argument. The best image for us, as we have implied,
is a well-functioning small group seeking a solution to a problem. In professional
life such small groups usually take the form of committees.

We must acknowledge that many people find committee deliberations hopelessly muddled and directionless—the very antithesis of good argumentation. Our
collective suspicion of committees is manifest in the many jokes we make about
them. (For example, do you know the definition of the word *committee*? It's a place
where people keep minutes and waste hours. Or: What is a zebra? A horse designed by a committee.)

Our society relies on committees, however, for the same reason that Winston
Churchill preferred democracy: However imperfect it may be, the alternatives are
worse. A single individual making decisions may be quirky, idiosyncratic, and insensitive to the effects of a decision on different groups of people; worse yet, he or
she may pursue self-interests to the detriment of an entire group. But too large a
group makes argumentative discussion impossible. Hence, people have generally
found it useful to delegate many decision- and policy-making tasks to a smaller,
representative group—a committee.

We use the word *committee* in its broadest sense to indicate all sorts of important work that grows out of group conversation and debate. The Declaration of
Independence is essentially a committee document with Thomas Jefferson as the
chair. Similarly, the U.S. Supreme Court is in effect a committee of nine judges who
rely heavily, as numerous books and articles have demonstrated, on small-group
decision-making processes to reach their judgments and formulate their legal
briefs.

To illustrate our committee model for argument, let's briefly consider the
workings of a university committee on which coauthor John Ramage once served,
the University Standards Committee. The Arizona State University (ASU) Standards Committee plays a role in university life analogous to that of the Supreme
Court in civic life. It's the final court of appeal for ASU students seeking exceptions to various rules that govern their academic lives (such as registering under
a different catalog, waiving a required course, or being allowed to retake a course
for the third time).

The Standards Committee is a large committee, comprising nearly two dozen members who represent the whole spectrum of departments and offices across campus. Every two weeks, the committee meets for two or more hours to consider between twenty and forty appeals. Several days before each meeting, committee members receive a hefty packet of materials relevant to the cases (such as, originals of the students' appeals, including the responses of those who've heard the appeal earlier, complete transcripts of each student's grades, and any supporting material or new information the student might wish to provide). Students may, if they choose, appear before the committee personally to make their cases.

The issues that regularly come before the committee draw forth all the argumentative strategies discussed in detail throughout this text. For example, all of the argument types discussed in Part Three regularly surface during committee deliberations. The committee deals with definition issues ("Is math anxiety a 'learning disability' for purposes of exempting a student from a math requirement? If so, what criteria can we establish for math anxiety?"); cause/consequence issues ("What were the causes of this student's sudden poor performance during spring semester?" "What will be the consequences of approving or denying her appeal?"); resemblance issues ("How is this case similar to an earlier case that we considered?"); evaluation issues ("Which criteria should take precedence in assessing this sort of appeal?"); and proposal issues ("Should we make it a policy to allow course X to substitute for course Y in the General Studies requirements?").

On any given day, the committee's deliberations showed how dialogue can lead to clarification of thinking. On many occasions, committee members' initial views shifted as they listened to opposing arguments. In one case, for example, a student petitioned to change the catalog under which she was supposed to graduate because the difference in requirements would let her graduate a half-year sooner. Initially, most committee members opposed the petition. They reminded the committee that in several earlier cases it had denied petitions to change catalogs if the petitioner's intent was to evade the more rigorous graduation requirements imposed by a new General Studies curriculum. Moreover, the committee was reminded that letting one student change catalogs was unfair to other students who had to meet the more rigorous graduation standards.

However, after emphatic negative arguments had been presented, a few committee members began to voice support for the student's case. While acknowledging the truth of what other committee members had said, they pointed out reasons to support the petition. The young woman in question had taken most of the required General Studies courses; it was mostly changes in the requirements for her major that delayed her graduation. Moreover, she had performed quite well in what everyone acknowledged to be a demanding course of study. Although the committee had indeed turned down previous petitions of this nature, in none of those cases had the consequences of denial been so dire for the student.

After extended negotiations between the two sides on this issue, the student was allowed to change catalogs. Although the committee was reluctant to set a bad precedent (those who resisted the petition foresaw a deluge of similar petitions from less worthy candidates), it recognized unique circumstances that legitimately made this petitioner's case different. Moreover, the rigor of the student's curriculum, the primary concern of those who opposed the change, was shown to be greater than the rigor of many who graduated under the newer catalog.

As the previous illustration suggests, what allowed the committee to function as well as it did was the fundamental civility of its members and their collective concern that their decisions be just. Unlike some committees, this committee made many decisions, the consequences of which were not trivial for the people involved. Because of the significance of these outcomes, committee members were more willing than they otherwise might have been to concede a point to another member in the name of reaching a better decision and to view their deliberations as an ongoing process of negotiation rather than a series of win-lose debates.

To give you firsthand experience at using argument as a process of clarification, we conclude this chapter with an actual case that came before the University Standards Committee. We invite you to read the following letter, pretending that you are a member of the University Standards Committee, and then proceed to the exercises that follow.

Petition to Waive the University Mathematics Requirement

Standards Committee Members,

I am a 43-year-old member of the Pawnee Tribe of Oklahoma and a very nontraditional   1
student currently pursuing Justice Studies at the Arizona State University (ASU) College of Public Programs. I entered college as the first step toward completion of my goal—becoming legal counsel for my tribe, and statesman.

I come before this committee in good faith to request that ASU suspend, in my special   2
case, its mathematics requirement for undergraduate degree completion so I may enter the ASU college of Law during Fall 1993. The point I wish to make to this committee is this: I do not need algebraic skills; I will never use algebra in my intended profession; and, if forced to comply with ASU's algebra requirement, I will be needlessly prevented from graduating in time to enter law school next fall and face an idle academic year before my next opportunity in 1994. I will address each of these points in turn, but a few words concerning my academic credentials are in order first.

Two years ago, I made a vow of moral commitment to seek out and confront injustice.   3
In September of 1990, I enrolled in college. Although I had only the benefit of a ninth grade education, I took the General Equivalency Diploma (GED) examination and placed in the top ten percent of those, nationwide, who took the test. On the basis of this score I was accepted into Scottsdale Community College (SCC). This step made me the first in my entire family, and practically in my tribe, to enter college. During my first year at SCC I maintained a 4.0 GPA, I was placed on the President's list twice, was active in the Honors Program,

received the Honors Award of Merit in English Humanities, and was conferred an Honors Scholarship (see attached) for the Academic year of 1991–1992 which I declined, opting to enroll in ASU instead.

4   At the beginning of the 1991 summer semester, I transferred to ASU. I chose to graduate from ASU because of the courses offered in American Indian studies, an important field ignored by most other Universities but necessary to my commitment. At ASU I currently maintain a 3.6 GPA, although my cumulative GPA is closer to 3.9, I am a member of the Honors and Justice Colleges, was appointed to the Dean's List, and awarded ASU's prestigious Maroon and Gold Scholarship twice. My academic standing is impeccable. I will enter the ASU College of Law to study Indian and criminal law during the Fall of 1993—if this petition is approved. Upon successful completion of my juris doctorate I will return to Oklahoma to become active in the administration of Pawnee tribal affairs as tribal attorney and advisor, and vigorously prosecute our right to sovereignty before the Congress of the United States.

5   When I began my "college experience," I set a rigid time schedule for the completion of my goal. By the terms of that self-imposed schedule, founded in my belief that I have already wasted many productive years, I allowed myself thirty-five months in which to achieve my Bachelor of Science degree in Justice Studies, for indeed justice is my concern, and another thirty-six months in which to earn my juris doctorate—summa cum laude. Consistent with my approach to all endeavors, I fell upon this task with zeal. I have willingly assumed the burden of carrying substantial academic loads during fall, spring and summer semesters. My problem now lies in the fact that in order to satisfy the University's math requirement to graduate I must still take MAT-106 and MAT-117. I submit that these mathematics courses are irrelevant to my goals, and present a barrier to my fall matriculation into law school.

6   Upon consideration of my dilemma, the questions emerged: Why do I need college algebra (MAT-117)? Is college algebra necessary for studying American Indian law? Will I use college algebra in my chosen field? What will the University gain or lose, from my taking college algebra—or not? I decided I should resolve these questions.

7   I began my inquiry with the question: "Why do I need college algebra (MAT-117)?" I consulted Mr. Jim _____ of the Justice College and presented this question to him. He referred to the current ASU catalog and delineated the following answer: I need college algebra (1) for a minimum level of math competency in my chosen field, and (2) to satisfy the university math requirement in order to graduate. My reply to the first answer is this: I already possess ample math skills, both practical and academic; and, I have no need for algebra in my chosen field. How do I know this? During the spring 1992 semester at ASU I successfully completed introductory algebra (MAT-077), scoring the highest class grade on one test (see attached transcript and test). More noteworthy is the fact that I was a machine and welding contractor for fifteen years. I used geometry and algebra commonly in the design of many welded structures. I am proficient in the use of Computer Assisted Design (CAD) programs, designing and drawing all my own blueprints for jobs. My blueprints and designs are always approved by city planning departments. For example, my most recent job consisted of the manufacture, transportation and installation of one linear mile of anodized, aluminum handrailing at a luxury resort condo on Maui, Hawaii. I applied extensive use of

math to calculate the amount of raw materials to order, the logistics of mass production and transportation for both men and materials from Mesa to Maui, the job site installation itself, and cash flow. I have successfully completed many jobs of this nature—all without a mathematical hitch. As to the application of math competency in my chosen field, I can guarantee this committee that there will not be a time in my practice of Indian law that I will need algebra. If an occasion ever occurs that I need algebra, I will hire a mathematician, just as I would an engineer if I need engineering, or a surgeon if I need an operation.

I then contacted Dr. _____ of the ASU Mathematics Department and presented him 8 with the same question: "Why do I need college algebra?" He replied: (1) for a well rounded education; (2) to develop creative thinking; and (3) to satisfy the university math requirement in order to graduate. Responding to the first answer, I have a "well rounded education." My need is for a specific education in justice and American Indian law. In fact, I do not really need the degree to practice Indian law as representative of my tribe, just the knowledge. Regarding the second, I do not need to develop my creative thinking. It has been honed to a keen edge for many years. For example, as a steel contractor, I commonly create huge, beautiful and intricate structures from raw materials. Contracting is not my only experience in creative thinking. For twenty-five years I have also enjoyed the status of being one of this country's foremost designers and builders of racebikes. Machines I have designed and brought into existence from my imagination have topped some of Japan and Europe's best engineering efforts. To illustrate this point, in 1984 I rode a bike of my own design to an international victory over Honda, Suzuki, Laverda, BMW and Yamaha. I have excelled at creative thinking my entire life—I called it survival.

Expanding on the question of why I need college algebra, I contacted a few friends who 9 are practicing attorneys. All responded to my question in similar manner. One, Mr. Billy _____, Esq., whose law firm is in Tempe, answered my two questions as follows: "When you attended law school, were there any courses you took which required algebra?" His response was "no." "Have you ever needed algebra during the many years of your practice?" Again, his response was "no." All agreed there was not a single occasion when they had need for algebra in their professional careers.

Just to make sure of my position, I contacted the ASU College of Law, and among 10 others, spoke to Ms. Sierra _____. I submitted the question "What law school courses will I encounter in which I will need algebra?" The unanimous reply was, they knew of none.

I am not proposing that the number of credit hours I need for graduation be lowered. 11 In fact, I am more than willing to substitute another course or two in its place. I am not trying to get out of anything hard or distasteful, for that is certainly not my style. I am seeking only to dispose of an unnecessary item in my studies, one which will prevent me from entering law school this fall—breaking my stride. So little holds up so much.

I agree that a young adult directly out of high school may not know that he needs 12 algebraic skills. Understandably, he does not know what his future holds—but I am not that young adult. I claim the advantage. I know precisely what my future holds and that future holds no possibility of my needing college algebra.

Physically confronting injustice is my end. On reservations where government apathy 13 allows rapacious pedophiles to pose as teachers; in a country where a million and a half American Indians are held hostage as second rate human beings whose despair results in a suicide, alcohol and drug abuse rate second to no other people; in prisons where helpless inmates are beaten like dogs by sadistic guards who should be the inmates—this is the realm of my chosen field—the disenfranchised. In this netherworld, algebra and justice exist independently of one another.

14   In summary, I am convinced that I do not need college algebra for a minimum level of math competency in my chosen field. I do not need college algebra for a well rounded education, nor to develop my creative thinking. I do not need algebra to take the LSAT. I do not need algebra for any courses in law school, nor will I for any purpose in the practice of American Indian law. It remains only that I need college algebra in order to graduate.

15   I promise this committee that ASU's integrity will not be compromised in any way by approving this waiver. Moreover, I assure this committee that despite not having a formal accreditation in algebra, I will prove to be nothing less than an asset to this University and its Indian community, both to which I belong, and I will continue to set a standard for integrity, excellence and perseverance for all who follow. Therefore, I ask this committee, for all the reasons described above, to approve and initiate the waiver of my University mathematics requirement.

[Signed: Gordon Adams]

FOR CLASS DISCUSSION

1. Before class discussion, decide how you would vote on this issue. Should this student be exempted from the math requirement? Write out the reasons for your decision.

2. Working in small groups or as a whole class, pretend that you are the University Standards Committee, and arrive at a group decision on whether to exempt this student from the math requirement.

3. After the discussion, write for five to ten minutes in a journal or notebook describing how your thinking evolved during the discussion. Did any of your classmates' views cause you to rethink your own? Class members should share with each other their descriptions of how the process of argument led to clarification of their own thinking.

We designed this exercise to help you experience argument as a clarifying process. But we had another purpose. We also designed the exercise to stimulate thinking about a problem we introduced at the beginning of this chapter: the difference between argument as clarification and argument as persuasion. Is a good argument necessarily a persuasive argument? In our opinion, this student's letter to the committee is a *good* argument. The student writes well, takes a clear stand, offers good reasons for his position, and supports his reasons with effective evidence. To what extent, however, is the letter a *persuasive* argument? Did it win its case? You know how you and your classmates stand on this issue. But what do you think the University Standards Committee at ASU actually decided during its deliberations?

We will return to this case again in Chapter 7.

CONCLUSION

In this chapter we have explored some of the complexities of argument, showing you why we believe that argument is a matter not of fist banging or of win-lose debate but of finding, through a process of rational inquiry, the best solution to a problem or issue. What is our advice for you at the close of this introductory chapter? Briefly, to see the purpose of argument as truth seeking as well as persuasion. We suggest that throughout the process of argument you seek out a wide range of views, that you especially welcome views different from your own, that you treat these views respectfully, and that you see them as intelligent and rationally defensible. (Hence you must look carefully at the reasons and evidence on which they are based).

Our goal in this text is to help you learn skills of argument. If you choose, you can use these skills, like Callicles, to argue any side of any issue. Yet we hope you won't. We hope that, like Socrates, you will use argument for truth seeking and that you will consequently find yourselves, on at least some occasions, changing your position on an issue while writing a rough draft (a sure sign that the process of arguing has complicated your views). We believe that the skills of reason and inquiry developed through the writing of arguments can help you get a clearer sense of who you are. If our culture sets you adrift in pluralism, argument can help you take a stand, to say, "These things I believe." In this text we will not pretend to tell you what position to take on any given issue. But as responsible beings, you will often need to take a stand, to define yourself, to say, "Here are the reasons that choice A is better than choice B, not just for me but for you also." If this text helps you base your commitments and actions on reasonable grounds, then it will have been successful.

2 Reading Arguments

WHY READING ARGUMENTS IS IMPORTANT FOR WRITERS

In the previous chapter we explained how reading and writing arguments is a social phenomenon growing out of people's search for the best answers to questions. In this chapter we'll focus on the first half of that social dynamic—the thoughtful reading of arguments.

Much of the advice we offer about reading applies equally to listening. In fact, it is often helpful to think of reading as a conversation. We like to tell students that a college library is not so much a repository of information as a discussion frozen in time until you as reader bring it to life. Those books and articles, stacked neatly on library shelves or stored in Web sites or databases, are arguing with each other, carrying on a great extended conversation. As you read, you bring those conversations to life. And when you write in response to your reading, you enter those conversations.

SUGGESTIONS FOR IMPROVING YOUR READING PROCESS

Before we offer specific strategies for reading arguments, let's examine some general reading strategies applicable to most complex texts.

1. *Slow down.* Ads for speed-reading courses misleadingly suggest that expert readers read rapidly. In fact, experts read difficult texts slowly, often reread-

ing them two or three times, treating their first readings like first drafts. They hold confusing passages in mental suspension, hoping that later parts of the essay will clarify earlier parts. They "nutshell" or summarize passages in the margins. They interact with the text by asking questions, expressing disagreements, linking the text with other readings or with personal experience.

2. *Get the dictionary habit.* When you can't tell a word's meaning from context, get in the habit of looking it up. One strategy is to make small check marks next to words you're unsure of; then look them up after you're done so as not to break your concentration.

3. *Lose your highlighter/find your pen.* Relying on yellow highlighters makes you too passive. Next time you get the urge to highlight a passage, write in the margin why you think it's important. Is it a major new point in the argument? A significant piece of support? A summary of the opposition? A particularly strong or particularly weak point? Use the margins to summarize the text, protest vehemently, ask questions, give assent—don't just color the pages.

4. *Reconstruct the rhetorical context.* Train yourself to ask questions such as these: Who is this author? What audience is he or she writing for? What occasion prompted this writing? What is the author's purpose? Any piece of writing makes more sense if you think of its author as a real person writing for some real purpose out of real historical context.

5. *Continue the conversation after your reading.* After you've read a text, try completing the following statements in a journal: "The most significant question this essay raises is. . . ." "The most important thing I learned from this essay is. . . ." "I agree with the author about. . . ." "However, I have doubts about. . . ." These questions help you remember the reading and urge you to respond actively to it.

6. *Try "translating" difficult passages.* When you stumble over a difficult passage, try "translating" it into your own words. Converting the passage into your own language forces you to focus on the precise meanings of words. Although your translation may not be exactly what the author intended, you see more clearly where the sources of confusion lie and what the likely range of meanings might be.

STRATEGIES FOR READING ARGUMENTS: AN OVERVIEW

Whereas the preceding suggestions can be applied to all sorts of reading tasks, the rest of this chapter focuses on reading strategies specific to arguments. Because argument begins in disagreements within a social community, we recommend that you examine any argument as if it were only one voice in a larger conversation. We therefore recommend the following strategies in sequence:

1. Read as a believer.
2. Read as a doubter.
3. Consider alternative views and analyze sources of disagreement.
4. Use disagreement productively to prompt further investigation.

Let's now explore each of these strategies in turn.

STRATEGY 1: READING AS A BELIEVER

When you read as a believer, you practice what psychologist Carl Rogers calls *empathic listening*. Empathic listening requires you to see the world through the author's eyes, to adopt temporarily the author's beliefs and values, and to suspend your skepticism and biases long enough to hear what the author is saying.

Because empathic listening is such a vital skill, we will invite you shortly to try it on a controversial op-ed piece from conservative columnist George Will on the subject of equal pay for men and women. First, though, here is some background.

Each year, the federal government, using data collected by the Census Bureau and other sources, publishes wage data showing earnings broken down by state, region, profession, ethnicity, gender, and other categories. One of the most controversial statistics is the wage gap between the average earnings of men and women. The figure widely published in 1999, based on 1996 census data, was that women, on average, earn 74 cents to a man's dollar. When President Bill Clinton, in his 1999 State of the Union address, vowed to enforce equal-pay laws, he received hearty bipartisan applause. However, the issue is being hotly debated in both state legislatures and the United States Congress.

FOR CLASS DISCUSSION

Working individually or in groups, respond to the following questions:

1. Do you think the pay gap between women and men is a small, moderate, or major social and economic problem?

2. Has this problem affected you or your family? How might this problem affect you in the future? (Think ahead to your career and possible plans for a family.)

Now individually or in groups, examine Figure 2.1, which reproduces a Web page from the site of the nation's largest labor organization, the AFL-CIO (American Federation of Labor and Congress of Industrial Organizations). This advocacy Web site presents one of the main perspectives on the issue of pay equity. It aims to persuade workers to join the cause of pay equity for women. After looking at this site's examples of the wage gap in different occupational categories, respond to the following questions:

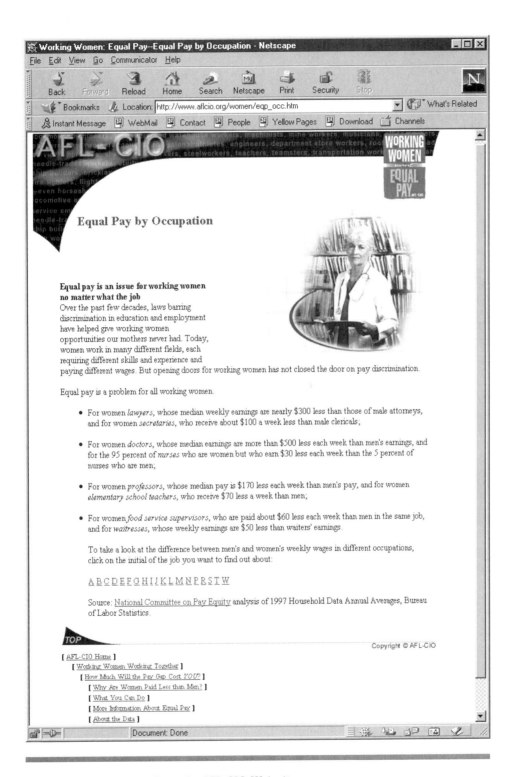

FIGURE 2.1   Web page from the AFL-CIO Web site

1. What do you think are the causes of pay gaps between men and women?

2. Supporters of pay equity legislation generally have two areas of concern: First, they desire "equal pay for equal work." This idea means that female mechanics should receive the same pay as male mechanics or female college professors the same pay as male college professors. Second, they desire "equal pay for comparable work." This idea means that jobs held mostly by women, such as social workers, should pay the same wages as comparable jobs held mostly by men, such as parole officers. Supporters propose to measure comparable worth by using criteria such as education and training required for entry into the field, the levels of stress and responsibility demanded by the work, and the social value of the work. Based on these criteria, do you think an elementary teacher with an M.A. degree should earn more or less than an accountant with a B.A. degree? Do you think a secretary with an A.A. degree should earn more or less than an auto mechanic with an A.A. degree?

3. Who, if anyone, should be responsible for establishing fair pay? Businesses and employers alone? The government?

Now that you have some background on the pay equity issue, you are ready to read George Will's argument.

Lies, Damned Lies, and . . .

George F. Will

1   With the Dow Average nearing a fifth digit, Americans are cheerful. However, soon the women's division of the Great American Grievance Industry will weigh in, saying women remain trapped beneath the "glass ceiling" and in the "pink ghetto." Brace yourself for a blizzard of statistics purporting to prove that women are suffering a "wage gap" primarily caused by discrimination that requires government actions like affirmative action, quotas and set-asides.

2   But a counterblizzard has blown in from Diana Furchtgott-Roth and Christine Stolba, authors of "Women's Figures: An Illustrated Guide to the Economic Progress of Women in America." Furchtgott-Roth is a fellow at The American Enterprise Institute and Stolba is a historian living in Washington, and both had better mind their manners. Feminists are not famous for their sense of humor and may frown at the authors' dedication of their book to their husbands "who have always appreciated our figures."

3   The National Committee On Pay Equity and other participants in the theatrics of Equal Pay Day will not appreciate the figures Furchtgott-Roth and Stolba marshal. The premise of Equal Pay Day is that women work from Jan. 1 until early April essentially for no pay because women earn only 74 cents for every dollar men earn. That uninformative number is the basis for the allegation that the average woman loses approximately $420,000 in wages

and benefits during her working life. The 74 cents factoid is prima facie proof of "the demeaning practice of wage discrimination," according to President Clinton, who opposes everything demeaning to women.

Furchtgott-Roth and Stolba argue that the 74 cents statistic is the product of faulty   4
methodology that serves the political agenda of portraying women as victims needing yet more government intervention in the workplace. The authors demonstrate that income disparities between men and women have been closing rapidly and that sex discrimination, which has been illegal for 30 years, is a negligible cause of those that remain, which are largely the result of rational personal choices by women.

Between 1960 and 1994 women's wages grew 10 times faster than men's, and today,   5
among people 27 to 33, women who have never had a child earn about 98 cents for every dollar men earn. Children change the earnings equations. They are the main reason that meaningful earnings contrasts must compare men and women who have similar experiences and life situations. Earnings differentials often reflect different professional paths that are cheerfully chosen because of different preferences, motivations, and expectations.

The "adjusted wage gap," adjusted for age, occupation, experience, education and time   6
in the work force, is primarily the product of personal choices women make outside the work environment. Eighty percent of women bear children and 25 percent of working women work part-time, often to accommodate child rearing. Many women who expect to have children choose occupations where job flexibility compensates for somewhat lower pay, and occupations (e.g., teaching) in which job skills deteriorate slower than in others (e.g., engineering). And it is not sex discrimination that accounts for largely male employment in some relatively high-paying occupations (e.g., construction, oil drilling and many others) which place a premium on physical strength. (Workers in some such occupations pay a price: the 54 percent of all workers who are male account for 92 percent of all job-related deaths.)

Still, between 1974 and 1993 women's wages have been rising relative to men's in all   7
age groups, and most dramatically among the youngest workers. The rise would be more dramatic if many women did not make understandable decisions to favor family over higher pay and more rapid job advancement purchased by 60-hour weeks on the fast track.

Some victimization theorists say the fast track is pointless for women because they are   8
held down by the "glass ceiling" that limits their rise in business hierarchies. In 1995 the government's Glass Ceiling Commission (the propagandistic title prejudged the subject) saw proof of sex discrimination in the fact that women are only 5 percent of senior managers at Fortune 1000 industrial and Fortune 500 service companies. But Furchtgott-Roth and Stolba note that typical qualifications for such positions include an M.B.A. and 25 years' work experience. The pool of women with those qualifications is small, not because of current discrimination but because of women's expectations in the 1950s and 1960s. In 1970 women received only 4 percent of all M.B.A. degrees, 5 percent of law degrees.

Which lends support to the optimistic "pipeline" theory: women are rising in economic   9
life as fast as they pour from the educational pipeline—which is faster than men. Since 1984 women have outnumbered men in undergraduate and graduate schools. Women are receiving a majority of two-year postsecondary degrees, bachelor's and master's degrees, almost 40 percent of M.B.A degrees, 40 percent of doctorates, more than 40 percent of law and medical degrees. Education improves economic opportunities—and opportunities

encourage education, which has higher rewards for women than for men because men without college degrees or even high-school diplomas can get those high-paying, physically demanding—and dangerous—jobs.

10   The supposed "pink ghetto" is where women are, in the Glass Ceiling Commission's words, "locked into" low-wage, low-prestige, dead-end jobs. Such overheated rhetoric ignores many women's rational sacrifices of pay and prestige for job flexibility in occupations in which skills survive years taken off for raising children. Women already predominate in the two economic sectors expected to grow fastest in the near future, service/trade/retail and finance/insurance/real estate.

11   The 74 cents statistic and related propaganda masquerading as social science are arrows in the quivers of those waging the American left's unending struggle to change the American premise, which stresses equality of opportunity, not equality of outcomes. Furchtgott-Roth and Stolba have better figures.

Summary Writing as a Way of Reading to Believe

Now that you have finished the article, ask yourself how well you "listened" to it. If you listened well, you should be able to write a summary of Will's argument in your own words. A *summary* (also called an *abstract*, a *précis*, or a *synopsis*) presents only a text's major points and eliminates supporting details. Writers often incorporate summaries of other writers' views into their own arguments, either to support their own claims or to represent alternative views that they intend to address. Summaries can be any length, depending on the writer's purposes, but usually they range from several sentences to one or two paragraphs.

Practicing the following steps should help you be a better summary writer:

Step 1: Read the argument first for general meaning. Don't judge it; put your objections aside; just follow the writer's meaning, trying to see the issue from the writer's perspective. Try to adopt the writer's values and belief system. Walk in the writer's shoes.

Step 2: Read the argument slowly a second and a third time, writing in the margins brief *does* and *says* statements for each paragraph (or group of closely connected paragraphs). A *does* statement identifies a paragraph's function, such as "summarizes an opposing view," "introduces a supporting reason," "gives an example," or "uses statistics to support the previous point." A *says* statement summarizes a paragraph's content. Figure 2.2 shows a page from a passage from Will's article with *does* and *says* statements intermixed in the margins. What follows are our *does* and *says* statements for the first six paragraphs of Will's article.

DOES/SAYS ANALYSIS OF WILL'S ARTICLE

Paragraph 1: *Does:* Introduces issue by summarizing the wage gap argument that Will opposes. *Says:* Although most Americans are cheerful about the

Furchtgott-Roth and Stolba argue that the 74 cents statistic is the product of faulty methodology that serves the political agenda of portraying women as victims needing yet more government intervention in the workplace. The authors demonstrate that income disparities between men and women have been closing rapidly and that sex discrimination, which has been illegal for 30 years, is a negligible cause of those that remain, which are largely the result of rational personal choices by women.   [4]

> 74¢ statistic is faulty. Sex discrimination is negligible. Gap caused by personal choices.

Between 1960 and 1994 women's wages grew 10 times faster than men's, and today, among people 27 to 33, women who have never had a child earn about 98 cents for every dollar men earn. Children change the earnings equations. They are the main reason that meaningful earnings contrasts must compare men and women who have similar experiences and life situations. Earnings differentials often reflect different professional paths that are cheerfully chosen because of different preferences, motivations, and expectations.   [5]

> Women's wages in general rising faster than men's.
> Main cause of women's lower pay is children.

The "adjusted wage gap," adjusted for age, occupation, experience, education and time in the work force, is primarily the product of personal choices women make outside the work environment. Eighty percent of women bear children and 25 percent of working women work part-time, often to accommodate child rearing. Many women who expect to have children choose occupations where job flexibility compensates for somewhat lower pay, and occupations (e.g., teaching) in which job skills deteriorate slower than in others (e.g., engineering). And it is not sex discrimination that accounts for largely male employment in some relatively high-paying occupations (e.g., construction, oil drilling and many others) which place a premium on physical strength. (Workers in some such occupations pay a price: the 54 percent of all workers who are male account for 92 percent of all job-related deaths.)   [6]

> Women choose careers that accommodate child-rearing.
> Some lower paying female jobs result of work flexibility   Many higher paying male jobs result of danger

Still, between 1974 and 1993 women's wages have been rising relative to men's in all age groups, and most dramatically among the youngest workers. The rise would be more dramatic if many women did not make understandable decisions to favor family over higher pay and more rapid job advancement purchased by 60-hour weeks on the fast track.   [7]

> Dramatic rise in women's wages would be higher if women didn't favor family.

Some victimization theorists say the fast track is pointless for women because they are held down by the "glass ceiling" that limits their rise in business hierarchies. In 1995 the government's Glass Ceiling Commission (the propagandistic title prejudged the subject) saw proof of sex discrimination in the fact that women are only 5 percent of senior managers at Fortune 1000 industrial and Fortune 500 service companies. But Furchtgott-Roth and Stolba note that typical qualifications for such positions include an M.B.A. and 25 years' work experience. The pool of women with those qualifications is small, not because of current discrimination but because of women's expectations in the 1950s and 1960s. In 1970 women received only 4 percent of all M.B.A. degrees, 5 percent of law degrees.   [8]

> Refutes glass ceiling argument. Women haven't been in professional jobs long enough to reach highest levels.

FIGURE 2.2   Reading-to-believe notes for Will argument

boom economy, the "American Grievance Industry" will soon complain that women suffer a wage gap that will require government intervention.

Paragraph 2:   *Does:*   Introduces two authors whose research debunks the wage gap argument. *Says:*   Diana Furchtgott-Roth and Christine Stolba provide a very different interpretation of the data on men's and women's wages.

Paragraph 3:   *Does:*   Summarizes the wage gap argument of the National Committee on Pay Equity. *Says:*   According to the National Committee on Pay Equity, women earn only 74 cents for every dollar that men earn, so the average woman loses $420,000 in wages over a career, thus proving wage discrimination.

Paragraph 4:   *Does:*   Summarizes the counterargument of Diana Furchtgott-Roth and Christine Stolba. *Says:*   The 74-cent "factoid" is not proof of wage discrimination; the pay gap has been closing rapidly, and whatever pay gap remains can be explained by women's personal career choices.

Paragraph 5:   *Does:*   Further develops this argument by focusing on the impact on children. *Says:*   Women's pay has risen ten times faster than men's since 1960, and childless women ages 27 to 33 earn 98 percent of men's wages; having children makes the difference, causing women to choose different career paths.

Paragraph 6:   *Does:*   Further develops the child-raising explanation. *Says:* The lower wages of women are the result of women's choosing jobs with flexibility in occupations from which they can take time off.

FOR CLASS DISCUSSION

Working individually or in groups, make *does* and *says* statements for the remaining paragraphs in Will's article.

Step 3:   Examine your *does* and *says* statements to determine the major sections of the argument, and create a list of major points and subpoints. If you are visually oriented, you may prefer to make a flowchart or diagram of the article. (See Figure 2.3 for our flowchart of Will's article.)

Step 4:   Turn your list, outline, flowchart, or diagram into a prose summary. Typically, writers do this in one of two ways. Some start by joining all their *says* statements into a lengthy paragraph-by-paragraph summary and then prune it. Others start with a one-sentence summary of the argument's thesis and major supporting reasons and then gradually flesh it out with more supporting ideas.

Step 5:   Revise your summary until it is the desired length and is sufficiently clear, concise, and complete. When you incorporate a summary of someone else's argument into your own essay, you must distinguish that author's

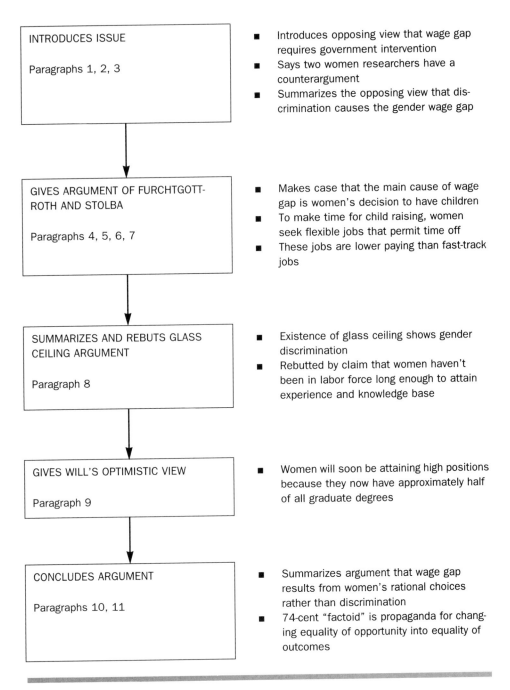

FIGURE 2.3 Flowchart for Will argument

words and ideas from your own by using *attributive tags* (expressions like "Will says," "according to Will," or "Will further explains"), by putting any directly borrowed language in quotation marks, and by citing the original author using appropriate conventions for documenting sources.[*]

As illustrations, we will show you our summaries of Will's article—a one-paragraph version and a single-sentence version. In the one-paragraph version we illustrate the MLA documentation system in which page numbers for direct quotations are placed in parentheses after the quotation and complete bibliographic information is placed in a Works Cited list at the end of the paper. See Chapter 17 for a complete explanation of the MLA and APA documentation systems.

ONE-PARAGRAPH SUMMARY OF WILL'S ARGUMENT

Identification of author and source

Insertion of a short quotation; MLA documentation style shows page number in parentheses

attributive tag

main claim of the article

attributive tag

attributive tag

attributive tag with transition

another short quotation

attributive tag

attributive tag

In a recent *Newsweek* editorial entitled "Lies, Damned Lies and . . .," conservative columnist George Will questions the claim that women, in earning 74 cents to a man's dollar, are victims of gender-based wage discrimination that "requires government actions like affirmative action, quotas, and set-asides" (28). Citing a recent book by Diana Furchtgott-Roth and Christine Stolba, Will argues that the 74-cents statistic is a "factoid" (29) that indicates personal career choices, not wage discrimination. Arguing that the wage gap is rapidly closing and has virtually disappeared for childless women between ages 27 and 33, Will claims that the remaining wage gap results from women's sacrificing pay and prestige for flexible jobs that allow time off for child raising. Women's dramatic increases in pay, Will asserts, would be even more dramatic if women desiring children didn't drop out of the fast track. Will then examines the objection made by "victimization theorists" (29) that the absence of high-level women executives in Fortune 1000 companies reveals a glass ceiling. He rebuts this argument by claiming that women haven't occupied professional jobs long enough to gain the experience and qualifications to attain upper-level positions, a situation that will soon end now that half of advanced degrees are earned by women. Will concludes that the 74-cent statistic is mere propaganda aimed at changing the traditional American value of equal opportunity into the leftist value of equal outcomes. (236 words)

---

[*]The most frequently used documentation systems in academic writing are those of the Modern Language Association (MLA) and the American Psychological Association (APA). Both systems are explained in detail in Chapter 17.

Will article cited completely in MLA documentation format; in a formal paper the Works Cited list begins a new page

Work Cited

Will, George F. "Lies, Damned Lies and . . ." *Newsweek* 29 Mar. 1999: 84. Rpt. in *Writing Arguments: A Rhetoric with Readings.* John D. Ramage, John C. Bean, and June Johnson. 5th ed. Needham: Allyn, 2001. 28–30.

ONE-SENTENCE SUMMARY OF WILL'S ARGUMENT

In a recent *Newsweek* editorial, conservative columnist George Will argues that the supposed wage gap between men and women is the result not of wage discrimination but of women's rational choices to sacrifice the pay and prestige of fast-track careers for flexible jobs that allow time off for child raising. (51 words)

Whether you write a very short summary or a more detailed one, your goal should be to come as close as possible to a fair, accurate, and balanced condensation of the author's argument and to represent the relationships among the parts fairly and accurately. We don't want to pretend that summary writing is easy; often it's not, especially if the argument is complex and if the author doesn't explicitly highlight his or her thesis and main supporting reasons. Nonetheless, being able to summarize the arguments of others in your own words is an important skill for arguers.

Suspending Doubt: Willing Your Own Belief in the Writer's Views

Summarizing an argument is only the first step in your effort to believe it. You must also suspend doubt and will yourself to adopt the writer's view. Suspending doubt is easy if you already agree with the author. But if an author's views affront your own values, then "believing" can be a hard but valuable exercise. By struggling to believe strange, threatening, or unfamiliar views, we can grow as learners and thinkers.

To believe an author, search your mind for personal experiences, values, and beliefs that affirm his or her argument. Here is how one female student wrote a journal entry trying to believe Will's argument.

JOURNAL ENTRY SHOWING STUDENT'S ATTEMPT TO BELIEVE WILL

When I first read the Web page from the AFL-CIO, I was outraged at the low pay women got. I thought that this was outright discrimination against women. I thought of all the money that women lost during their careers because men automatically got more pay than women just because people don't think women's work is worth as much. But then when I read George Will I saw that maybe there was another explanation. It is really true that many women worry how they are going to balance a career with having children, and I can see how women might seek out jobs that don't demand 80-hour workweeks and that give them some flexibility in hours so that they can spend more time with their children. Although I think dads ought to make the same sacrifices, I can see how women are more likely to focus on family issues. So if enough women are opting for less prestigious jobs, then the average wages of all women would be lower. It's a shame that women rather than men have to sacrifice their careers for children, but I can see Will's point that their lower earnings are a result of personal choices rather than discrimination.

STRATEGY 2: READING AS A DOUBTER

Reading as a believer is only half of being a powerful reader. You must also read as a doubter by raising objections, asking questions, expressing skepticism, and withholding assent. In the margins of the text, as a doubter, you add a new layer of notes demanding more proof, doubting evidence, challenging the author's assumptions and values, and so forth. Figure 2.4 shows one reader's marginal notes doubting Will's argument. (For purposes of illustration, this reader's believing notes—efforts to map and summarize the argument—aren't shown. Marginal notes usually intermingle believing and doubting commentary.)

FOR CLASS DISCUSSION

Return now to Will's article, reading it skeptically. Raise questions, offer objections, and express doubts. Then, working as a class or in small groups, list all doubts you have about Will's argument.

Now that you've doubted Will's article, compare your doubts to some of those raised by our students.

- Are all Americans happy about the healthy stock market, as Will suggests? Does this mean economic prosperity for everyone? What about all those people who don't own stocks?
- Will implies that mainly feminists believe that a gender wage gap exists. Who exactly is protesting the gender wage gap?
- What is the background of the two authors—Diana Furchtgott-Roth and Christine Stolba?
- What is the source of Will's claim that in the last thirty years women's wages have been rising ten times faster than men's? The AFL-CIO Web page doesn't agree at all with this claim. We wonder what jobs and careers he is describing.
- Will automatically assumes that if a job is flexible it ought to pay less. What's wrong with good-paying jobs being flexible? Also, can you really

Furchtgott-Roth and Stolba argue that the 74 cents statistic is the product of faulty methodology that serves the political agenda of portraying women as victims needing yet more government intervention in the workplace. The authors demonstrate that income disparities between men and women have been closing rapidly and that sex discrimination, which has been illegal for 30 years, is a negligible cause of those that remain, which are largely the result of rational personal choices by women.   [4]

Between 1960 and 1994 women's wages grew 10 times faster than men's, and today, among people 27 to 33, women who have never had a child earn about 98 cents for every dollar men earn. Children change the earnings equations. They are the main reason that meaningful earnings contrasts must compare men and women who have similar experiences and life situations. Earnings differentials often reflect different professional paths that are (cheerfully) chosen because of different preferences, motivations, and expectations.   [5]

Why do these figures not jibe with AFL/CIO data from Web site?

Are these choices really "cheerful"??!

The "adjusted wage gap," adjusted for age, occupation, experience, education and time in the work force, is primarily the product of personal choices women make outside the work environment. Eighty percent of women bear children and 25 percent of working women work part-time, often to accommodate child rearing. Many women who expect to have children choose occupations where job flexibility compensates for somewhat lower pay, and occupations (e.g., teaching) in which job skills deteriorate slower than in others (e.g., engineering). And it is not sex discrimination that accounts for largely male employment in some relatively high-paying occupations (e.g., construction, oil drilling and many others) which place a premium on physical strength. (Workers in some such occupations pay a price: the 54 percent of all workers who are male account for 92 percent of all job-related deaths.)   [6]

Why should job flexibility have to mean lower pay?

Seems to justify low pay of teachers because job skills don't deteriorate rapidly. Doesn't seem right.

Still, between 1974 and 1993 women's wages have been rising relative to men's in all age groups, and most dramatically among the youngest workers. The rise would be more dramatic if many women did not make understandable decisions to favor family over higher pay and more rapid job advancement purchased by 60-hour weeks on the fast track.   [7]

What percentage of men actually work 60 hours per week?

Some victimization theorists say the fast track is pointless for women because they are held down by the "glass ceiling" that limits their rise in business hierarchies. In 1995 the government's Glass Ceiling Commission (the propagandistic title prejudged the subject) saw proof of sex discrimination in the fact that women are only 5 percent of senior managers at Fortune 1000 industrial and Fortune 500 service companies. But Furchtgott-Roth and Stolba note that typical qualifications for such positions include an M.B.A. and 25 years' work experience. The pool of women with those qualifications is small, not because of current discrimination but because of women's expectations in the 1950s and 1960s. In 1970 women received only 4 percent of all M.B.A. degrees, 5 percent of law degrees.   [8]

Interesting explanation. But what about all the examples we hear about outright discrimination against women? Old boys club?

FIGURE 2.3   Reading-to-doubt notes for Will argument

justify paying teachers less because teaching skills don't deteriorate rapidly if you take time off?

- Will assumes that if a job is dangerous (he mentions construction and others) it ought to pay more. What about jobs in athletic-shoe sweatshops in Asia and Mexico where women workers are exposed to dangerous chemicals? By Will's argument, they ought to be making a mint.

- Will assumes a two-parent family where the father has the main career. He completely ignores mothers who must work and single mothers who can't afford to take time off from work and who must pay for child care.

- He also ignores working-class women. His optimistic picture involves college-educated women who are willing to forgo having children.

These are only some of the objections that might be raised against Will's argument. Perhaps you and your classmates have other objections that are equally important. Our point is that you should practice "doubting" an argument as well as "believing" it. Both skills are essential. *Believing* helps you expand your view of the world or modify your arguments and beliefs in response to others. *Doubting* helps protect you from becoming overpowered by others' arguments and teaches you to stand back, consider, and weigh points carefully.

STRATEGY 3: SEEKING OUT ALTERNATIVE VIEWS AND ANALYZING SOURCES OF DISAGREEMENT

When you analyze an argument, you shouldn't isolate it from the general conversation of differing views that form its context. If you were an arbitrator, you wouldn't think of settling a dispute between A and B on the basis of A's testimony only. You would also insist on hearing B's side of the story. In analyzing an argument, therefore, you should try to seek out the views of those who disagree with the author to appreciate the full context of the issue.

As you listen to differing views, try to identify sources of disagreement, which often fall into two categories: (1) disagreement about the facts or reality of the case and (2) disagreement about underlying beliefs, values, or assumptions, including assumptions about definitions or appropriate analogies. Let's look at each in turn.

Disagreement about Facts or Reality

Theoretically, a fact is a piece of empirical data on which everyone agrees. Often, however, what one person takes as fact another takes as a misconception or an opinionated misinterpretation. Thus in the 1996 presidential elections, Bob Dole claimed that President Clinton had pushed through "the largest tax increase in U.S. history," whereas Clinton claimed in turn that an earlier tax increase passed during President Bush's administration (and voted for by Senator Dole) was in "adjusted dollars" much higher. Here Dole and Clinton disagree about "facts"— in this case, the truth represented by raw numbers that can be selected and arranged in a variety of ways. Other examples of disagreements about facts or reality include the following:

- In arguing whether silver-mercury amalgam tooth fillings should be banned, dental researchers disagree on the amount of mercury vapor released by older fillings; they also disagree on how much mercury vapor has to be present before it is harmful.

- In arguing about the legalization of drugs, writers disagree about the degree to which Prohibition reduced alcohol consumption; they also disagree on whether crack cocaine is "crimogenic" (has chemical properties that induce violent behavior).

Disagreement about Values, Beliefs, or Assumptions

A second source of disagreement concerns differences in values, beliefs, or assumptions. Here are some examples:

- Persons A and B might agree that a huge tax on gasoline would cut down on the consumption of petroleum. They might agree further that the world's supply of petroleum will eventually run out. Thus Persons A and B agree at the level of facts. But they might disagree about whether the United States should enact a huge gas tax. Person A might support the law in order to conserve oil. Person B might oppose it, perhaps because B believes that scientists will find alternative energy sources before the petroleum runs out or because B believes the short-term harm of such a tax outweighs distant benefits.

- Person A and Person B might agree that capital punishment deters potential murderers (an agreement on facts). Person A supports capital punishment for this reason, but Person B opposes it, believing that the taking of a human life is always wrong in principle even if the state does it legally (a disagreement about basic beliefs).

Sometimes differing beliefs or values present themselves as disagreements about definitions or appropriate analogies.

- Social Theorist A and Social Theorist B disagree about whether the covers of some women's magazines like *Cosmopolitan* are pornographic. This disagreement turns on the definition of *pornography*, with different definitions reflecting different underlying values and beliefs.

- In supporting a Texas law forbidding flag burning, Chief Justice William Rehnquist argued that desecration of a flag in the name of free speech is similar to desecrating the Washington Monument. He thus makes this analogy: Just as we would forbid desecration of a national monument, so should we forbid desecration of the flag. Opposing justices did not think the analogy was valid.

■ Person A and Person B disagree on whether it is ethically acceptable to have Down's syndrome children undergo plastic surgery to correct some of the facial abnormalities associated with this genetic condition. Person A supports the surgery, arguing that it is analogous to any other cosmetic surgeries done to improve appearance. Person B argues against such surgery, saying it is analogous to the racial self-hatred of some minority persons who have tried to change their ethnic appearance and become lily white. (The latter analogy argues that Down's syndrome is nothing to be ashamed of and that persons should take pride in their difference.)

FOR CLASS DISCUSSION

As discussed in Chapter 1, we live in a pluralistic world wherein many differing systems of values and beliefs compete for our allegiance. It is not surprising, therefore, that people disagree on the issue of pay equity. What follows is a syndicated column by journalist Ellen Goodman, written about the same time as George Will's *Newsweek* piece. Read Goodman's column carefully. Then, working as a whole class or in small groups, answer the following questions:

1. To what extent do Will and Goodman disagree about the basic facts concerning men's and women's wages?

2. In what ways are the disagreements between Will and Goodman related to their differing values, beliefs, and underlying assumptions?

A New Campaign for Pay Equity

Ellen Goodman

1   Somewhere in the recesses of my desk drawer there is a battered old pink pin bearing the message: 59 cents. This was not the price of the pin. It was the price of being a working woman circa 1969.

2   When these pins first began to appear at political conferences and conventions, women were earning 59 cents for every male dollar. Today, after 30 years of change, guess what? Women are earning 74 cents for every male dollar.

3   We have, in short, made economic progress at roughly half a cent a year. And before you choke over this breakneck pace, consider that three-fifths of the "progress" in closing the gender gap has come from men's falling wages, not women's rising wages.

Somehow or other the unsexy issue of the paycheck—equal pay for the same or equiv-   4
alent work— dropped off the economic agenda. But it never left the minds of women. In
surveys, women workers went on rating pay equity as "very important," and a third said
they didn't have it. These are the same women who worry about balancing work and family, but many said, if we get a fair paycheck, we'll work it out.

Now, without a whole lot of fanfare, the issue of pay equity is back.   5

Remember that moment in the State of the Union address when the president told Con-   6
gress to "make sure women and men get equal pay by strengthening enforcement of the
equal pay laws"? To everyone's surprise he got a bipartisan Standing O. Since then the president proposed a $14 million equal pay initiative with most of the money going to better
enforcement of the existing laws.

Now, as spring rolls in, new legislation for pay equity is being planted in 24 state-   7
houses. This campaign has a two-part strategy. Part One: Get the old laws enforced. Part
Two: Expand the notion of equal pay to include work of equal value.

As for Part One, if you have any doubts that the old laws aren't enforced enough,   8
click onto the depressing union Web page, www.aflcio.org/women/. There's a lot of bad
news.

The gender gap between male and female accountants is $201 a week. The gap be-   9
tween bartenders is $48. And, to pick another occupation out of a hat, the gap between
male and female reporters and editors—ahem—is $163. The Web site will also help you
figure out your own lifetime net loss.

As for Part Two, if you have any doubts that the old laws are too narrow, even if women   10
were paid equally for the same job, most don't hold the same jobs. The jobs held primarily
by women are "worth less" than the ones held primarily by men. That's true even if they
involve roughly the same skills, effort, responsibility and working conditions.

For this reason, a 911 dispatcher is paid less in many places than an emergency opera-   11
tor at the Fire Department. A social worker is paid less than a probation officer. And in some
states we have the tale of two nursery workers, one working with plants, the other with
children. Guess who gets paid more?

Underlying the new campaign for pay equity are attitudes that are changing faster than   12
wages. When the 59-cent button first appeared, it was assumed that any woman who
wanted to get paid "like a man" had to do a "man's job."

At the Center for Policy Alternatives, Linda Tarr-Whelan says, "In this economy we
have a diminished sense that the work women do with people is worth the same amount   13
as the work men do with machines and dollars." Many are finally asking why "women's
jobs" should be "worth less"?

For a long time, the glib excuse for the gender values gap has been market values: "the   14
marketplace." Now it's being reframed as a matter of fairness and discrimination.

Not surprisingly, the legislative campaign will begin at the state level—where the per-   15
centage of women legislators is twice as high as in Congress—and build momentum before
it goes to Washington.

In the meantime, there is a figure from the new survey to keep in mind: $200 billion.   16
That's the amount families of working women lose every year to the gender gap. At that
rate, half a cent a year just won't hack it.

Writing an Analysis of a Disagreement

A common writing assignment in argument courses asks students to analyze the sources of disagreement between two or more writers who take different positions on an issue. In writing such an analysis, you need to determine whether the writers disagree primarily about facts/reality or values (or both). Specifically, you should pose the following questions:

1. Where do the writers disagree about facts and/or the interpretation of facts?
2. Where do the writers disagree about underlying beliefs, values, or assumptions?
3. Where do the writers disagree about key definitions or about appropriate analogies? How do these differences imply differences in values, beliefs, or assumptions?

To illustrate how these three questions can help you write an analysis, we've constructed the following model: our own brief analysis of the sources of disagreement between Will and Goodman written as a short, formal essay.

An Analysis of the Sources of Disagreement between Will and Goodman

1   The op-ed pieces of George Will and Ellen Goodman on the gender pay gap show disagreements of both fact and value. Will and Goodman agree that there is a gender wage gap reflected in the statistic that women earn only 74 cents to a man's dollar. However, they disagree about the causes of this pay gap. Goodman attributes the gap to gender discrimination in the workplace, whereas Will attributes it to women's personal choices in opting for flexible jobs that permit time off for child raising. Will therefore calls the 74-cent statistic a meaningless "factoid" rather than a meaningful fact.

2   This basic disagreement about cause explains each author's choice of data for framing the issue. Goodman accepts the statistics disseminated on the AFL-CIO web site. She believes that women have made little progress in closing the wage gap in the last thirty years and argues that "three-fifths of the 'progress' in closing the gender gap has come from men's falling wages, not women's rising wages" (40). Goodman sees discrimination operating at two levels—in the disparate wages paid to men and women in the same jobs and in the lower worth placed on women's jobs.

3   In contrast, Will's selection of data paints an optimistic picture of women's progress. Drawing statistics from Furchtgott-Roth and Stolba, Will asserts that the 74-cents figure is not accurate for all women, citing instead the data that women's wages grew ten times faster than men's in the last thirty years and that "today, among people 27 to 33, women

who have never had a child earn about 98 cents for every dollar men earn" (29). Thus Goodman and Will disagree on which "facts" are significant. Their selection of data creates different views of reality.

Will's and Goodman's different views of the facts reflect deep differences in values. 4 Will, a political conservative, upholds the free market and opposes "government actions like affirmative action, quotas and set-asides" (28). Will claims that the American left is trying to "change the American premise, which stresses equality of opportunity, not equality of outcomes" (30). Underneath Will's belief that women "cheerfully" opt for lower-paying jobs in order to raise children is a belief in the two-parent, nuclear family and in traditional gender roles that make child rearing primarily the mother's responsibility. In contrast, Goodman, a political liberal, sees the gender wage gap as an unfair, discriminatory situation that should be corrected by government. Moreover, she sees it as a problem for men and for families as well as for women.

Typical of many op-ed pieces, both Will and Goodman adopt a breezy, joking style, but 5 the different ways they joke also reflect and convey their values. Will adopts a flippant, trivializing "guess who is complaining now?" tone. His frequent use of the phrase "women's figures" and his statement that women are just making up the problem ("victimization theorists") and that feminists like to complain ("the Great American Grievance Industry") suggest an anger directed at feminists rather than a concern for the social consequences of low-paying jobs for women. Although less filled with loaded words, Goodman's piece is also a little sarcastic. Her "guess what—the problem isn't going away" tone conveys her impatience with free-market proponents and with people who don't acknowledge the discrimination that seems so clear to her: "We have, in short, made economic progress at roughly half a cent a year. And before you choke over this breakneck pace [. . .]" (40). Both writers risk alienating readers, but both appear to decide that their tone fits with their aims and perceptions of their audiences. At least, both writers whip up the enthusiasm of readers who already share their values.

Not surprisingly, both Will's and Goodman's different interpretations of facts and their 6 different values lead to different proposals for action. Believing that women are making progress through higher education and more professional experience, Will asserts that the gender wage gap is correcting itself. In contrast, Goodman calls for immediate political action and change. She is concerned with working-class jobs as well as professional, white-collar careers and supports enactment of new laws to "expand the notion of equal pay to include work of equal value" (41).

In sum, Will and Goodman disagree about both facts and values. 7

Works Cited

Goodman, Ellen. "A New Campaign for Pay Equity." *Buffalo News* 16 Mar. 1999: 3B. Rpt. in *Writing Arguments: A Rhetoric with Readings.* John D. Ramage, John C. Bean, and June Johnson. 5th ed. Needham: Allyn, 2001. 40–41.

Will, George F. "Lies, Damned Lies and . . ." *Newsweek* 29 Mar. 1999: 84. Rpt. in *Writing Arguments: A Rhetoric with Readings.* John D. Ramage, John C. Bean, and June Johnson. 5th ed. Needham: Allyn, 2001. 28–30.

STRATEGY 4: USING DISAGREEMENT PRODUCTIVELY TO PROMPT FURTHER INVESTIGATION

Our fourth strategy—using disagreement productively to prompt further investigation—is both a powerful strategy for reading arguments and a bridge toward constructing your own arguments. Our goal is to suggest ways to help you proceed when the experts disagree. Encountering divergent points of view, such as the disagreement between Will and Goodman, can create intense intellectual pressure. Inexperienced arguers sometimes opt for easy escape routes. Either they throw up their hands, claim that "everyone has a right to his own opinion," and leave the argumentative arena, or they latch on to one of the competing claims, defend it against all comers, and shut off opportunity for growth and change. What our fourth strategy invites you to do is stay in the argumentative arena. It urges you to become an active questioner and thinker—to seek answers where possible to disputed questions of fact and value and to articulate and justify your own beliefs and assumptions, which will ultimately inform the positions you take on issues.

As you sort through conflicting viewpoints, your goal is not to identify one of them as "correct" but to ask what is the best solution to the problem being debated here. You may eventually decide that one of the current viewpoints is indeed the best solution. Or you may develop a synthesis that combines strengths from several divergent viewpoints. In either case, you will emerge from the process with an enlarged, informed understanding. You will have developed the ability to remain intellectually flexible while listening to alternative viewpoints. Most important, you will have learned how to avoid falling into a valueless relativism. Responding productively to disagreement thus becomes part of your preparation for writing ethically responsible arguments.

To try to illustrate the process of responding to disagreements, we now show you how we responded to the disagreement between Will and Goodman over pay equity.

Accepting Ambiguity and Uncertainty as a Prompt for Further Investigation

When confronted with conflicting positions, you must learn to cope with ambiguity. If there were no disagreements, of course, there would be no need for argument. It is important to realize that experts can look at the same data, can analyze the same arguments, can listen to the same authorities, and still reach different conclusions. Seldom will one expert's argument triumph over another's in a field of dissenting claims. More often, one expert's argument will modify another's and in turn will be modified by yet another. Accepting ambiguity is a way of suspending judgment as you enter the complexity of an issue. A willingness to live with ambiguity enables you to delve deeply into an issue and to resist easy answers.

Seeking Out Sources of Facts and More Complete Versions of Alternative Views

After analyzing the sources of disagreement between Will and Goodman (see our sample essay on pp. 42–43), we next attempted to use these disagreements productively by striving for a more complete understanding of alternative views. We began by pursuing the sources cited by Will and Goodman. We needed to determine whether the book by Furchtgott-Roth and Stolba cited by Will or the data compiled by the AFL-CIO cited by Goodman seemed more reliable and persuasive. We also hoped to determine if there is a majority position among commentators.

Our searching for sources helped us see a pattern in the views of experts. We discovered that Will's perspective is endorsed by the American Enterprise Institute (a conservative think tank of which Furchtgott-Roth is a fellow) and by the Senate Republican Committee. Because conservatives tend to favor free markets, these endorsements seemed understandable. Numerous other organizations, however, believe that the gender pay gap is a serious problem: the Bureau of Labor Statistics, the Institute for Women's Policy Research, Catalyst (a women's research group), and the National Committee on Pay Equity. Furthermore, the results of the AFL-CIO's 1997 "Ask A Working Woman" survey, which strongly argues that a gender pay gap exists, are presented very clearly in their Web site (www.aflcio.org). Because these organizations are aligned with labor or with women's advocacy groups, they understandably favor proactive policies to boost wages of low-pay workers.

However, these pro-labor groups did provide strong evidence to confirm the reality of a gender pay gap. These sources gave extensive national and state data, based on what seemed to us factual information about wages, to show that a wage gap exists, that it varies by state, and that the gap is bigger for women of color.

Our search for fuller understanding inspired us to seek out information on the Fair Pay Act and the Paycheck Fairness Act currently before Congress to see how the legislators propose to deal with this problem. We discovered that pro-business commentators think that new laws could lead to costly litigation as women sue for back pay and could lead to government micro-management of corporations. These concerns are valid, but we also found that one main goal of the legislation is to encourage corporations and institutions to self-audit for internal equity in hiring and in establishing equitable policies for evaluations for salaries, promotions, and benefits.

We were also drawn to arguments that framed the gender pay gap as an issue affecting women, men, children, and families. The families of working women, and particularly of single mothers, are suffering the most from the inequity in wages of wives and mothers. These sources persuasively widened their concerns to show that equal pay for women affects children's security, health care, the poverty rate, domestic violence, Social Security, pensions, and family stability. The issue thus has enormous social repercussions.

Determining What Values Are at Stake for You in the Issue and Articulating Your Own Values

In responding to disagreement, you need to articulate your own values and to try to justify them by explaining the reasons you hold them. The authors of this text, for example, tend to support the need for greater pay equity and question Will's emphasis on women's choices as a complete explanation for lower pay for women. We know that for many women and families, working isn't a choice; it is a necessity. We have seen that women often sacrifice salaries and advancements when they have to take time off for children and that these choices are not always "cheerfully" made, as Will claims, but involve agonizing conflicts between job and family. Thinking about the fairness of pay reminds us that the United States has the highest poverty rate, the highest rate of children in poverty, and the biggest disparity of income distribution among industrialized nations. Therefore, we tend to favor government policies that boost the earnings of people at the bottom of the economic ladder.

Considering Ways to Synthesize Alternative Views

As a final step in your evaluation of conflicting sources, you should consider what you have gained from the different perspectives. How do the alternative views modify each other or otherwise "speak to each other"? If conflicting views don't lead to a synthesis, how do the different perspectives at least lead to an informed, enlarged vision of the issue?

What valuable points could we take from the opposing stands on this topic if we were to write our own argument on pay equity? What perspective could we synthesize from the free-market optimism of Will and the need for reform voiced by Goodman? Will claims that more women are earning college and graduate degrees and that these qualifications will equip them for better jobs; basically, he argues, the situation for women is improving and any inequalities will fix themselves. Yet Goodman believes that rigorous enforcement of pay equity laws *and* the enactment of new ones are needed. Could an argument on pay equity acknowledge the progress that Will cites and the urgency of the problems that Goodman discusses? We concluded that an informed position would need to recognize the economic progress of college-educated, professional women willing to forego childbearing, while at the same time pointing out the injustice of persistently low wages for women in working class jobs. Our goal would be to find ways to connect the pay equity problem to issues of family and poverty.

When you try to synthesize points from conflicting positions, as we did here, you tap into the dialectical nature of argument, questioning and modifying positions in response to new perspectives. We cannot claim that the position we are tentatively formulating on the pay equity issue is the right one. We can claim only that it is a reasonable and responsible one in light of the available facts and our own values. We have tried to show how the process of responding to disagreement—coping with ambiguity, pursuing researched answers to questions about fact and value, articulating your own values, and seeking possible syntheses—launches you on the path to becoming a responsible writer of arguments.

CONCLUSION

This chapter has explained why reading arguments is crucially important to writers of argument and has offered suggestions for improving your own reading process. We have suggested four main strategies for deep reading: (1) Read as a believer. (2) Read as a doubter. (3) Consider alternative views and analyze sources of disagreement. (4) Use disagreement productively to prompt further investigation. This chapter has also shown you how to summarize an article and incorporate summaries into your own writing through the use of attributive tags.

In the next chapter we turn from the reading of arguments to the writing of arguments, suggesting ways that you can generate ideas for arguments, structure your arguments, and improve your own writing processes.

3 Writing Arguments

As the opening chapters suggest, when you write an argument, you try to achieve two goals: (1) to persuade your audience toward your stance on an issue and (2) to see the issue complexly enough so that your stance reflects an ethical consideration of conflicting views. Because managing these tasks takes time, the quality of any argument depends on the quality of the thinking and writing processes that produced it. In this chapter, we suggest ways that you can improve these processes. We begin by looking at the social contexts that produce arguments, asking who writes arguments and why. We then present some writing tips based on the composing practices of experienced writers. Finally, we describe nuts-and-bolts strategies for generating ideas and organizing an argument for an intended audience, concluding with two sets of exploratory exercises that can be adapted to any kind of argumentative task.

WHO WRITES ARGUMENTS AND WHY?

To help you see how writers operate in a social context—how they are spurred to write by a motivating occasion and by a desire to change the views of particular audiences—we begin by asking you to consider more fully why someone would produce an argument.

In the classical period of ancient Greece and Rome, when the discipline of rhetoric was born, arguers usually made speeches before deliberative bodies. Arguers today, however, can present their views in a wide range of media and genres: speeches at public hearings, at committee meetings, or on talk radio; letters to legislators, bosses, or newspaper editors; professional proposals, marketing plans, or workplace memos; posters and pamphlets advocating a cause; e-mail letters or posts to chat rooms or personal Web sites; paid advertisements—even T-shirts and bumper stickers. Experienced writers and media specialists have even more options: freelance articles, books, syndicated columns, TV documentaries, and so forth.

To illustrate these multiple contexts for persuasion, let's return to the issue of gender pay equity that we used in Chapter 2. Who in our culture actually writes arguments on pay equity? To whom are they writing and why? Here is a partial list of these writers and their contexts:

- *Lobbyists and advocacy groups.*   Advocacy groups commit themselves to a cause, often with passion, and produce avidly partisan arguments aimed at persuading voters, legislators, or other targeted decision makers. Well-financed groups such as the American Civil Liberties Union or the National Rifle Association hire professional researchers, writers, media specialists, and lobbyists. Smaller advocacy groups might create their own Web sites, produce low-budget documents such as pamphlets and newsletters, and orchestrate letter-writing campaigns to legislators and newspapers. Numerous advocacy groups have coalesced around the pay equity issue. The organizations mentioned in Chapter 2 are all advocacy groups arguing for or against pay equity legislation.

- *Legislators.*   Whenever new laws are proposed in legislatures, staffers do research for elected representatives and write "white papers" recommending positions for their bosses to take on an issue. Because pay equity is a hot issue, numerous staff researchers have produced white papers on the subject in both state legislatures and Congress.

- *Business professionals.*   Businesses and corporations produce numerous internal documents aimed at researching data and recommending policy. Whenever pay equity issues arise in a business or corporation, managers and executives (accountants, comptrollers, planners, labor/management negotiators) analyze pay equity data, debate courses of action, and produce position papers.

- *Employment and corporate lawyers and judges.*   Employment lawyers, representing clients with pay equity grievances, write briefs supporting their client's case. Meanwhile, corporate lawyers defend the corporation's interests against pay equity lawsuits. When the decisions of lower courts are appealed to higher judicial courts, arguments become increasingly philosophical. Often other lawyers, particularly law professors, file "friends of the court" briefs aimed at influencing the decision of judges. Finally, judges write court opinions explaining their decisions on a case.

- *Media commentators.* Whenever pay equity issues get in the news, media commentators (journalists, editorial writers, syndicated columnists) write on the issue, filtering it through the perspective of their own political views. The Will and Goodman editorials analyzed in Chapter 2 fall into this category.

- *Professional freelance or staff writers.* Some of the most thoughtful analyses of public issues are composed by freelance or staff writers for public forum magazines such as *Atlantic Monthly,* the *Nation, Ms.,* the *National Review,* and *Utne Reader.* Arguments on pay equity surface whenever the topic seems timely to magazine editors.

- *Scholars and academics.* A key public role played by college professors comes from their scholarly research. Almost all public debates on social policy derive at least some data and analysis from the scholarship of college professors. Although no research can be purely objective—unshaped by the biases of the researcher—scholarly research differs substantially from advocacy argument in its systematic attempt to arrive at the best answers to questions based on the full examination of all relevant data. Much scholarship has been devoted to the pay equity issue—primarily by economists and sociologists. Scholarly research is usually published in refereed academic journals rather than popular magazines. (Of course, scholars can also take personal positions on social issues and use their research for advocacy arguments.)

- *Citizens.* Average citizens influence social policy through letters, contributions to advocacy Web sites, guest editorials for newspapers, or pieces in professional newsletters or other media. The pay equity issue reaches national consciousness when enough individuals make their views heard.

Where do student writers fit on this list? As a student you are already a member of both the "citizen" group and the "scholars and academics" group. Moreover, you may often be given opportunities to role-play membership in other groups as well. As a professional-in-training, you can practice both advocacy arguments and inquiry-based research pieces. Some students taking argument courses in college publish their work as letters to the editor or guest editorials (in the case of advocacy pieces) or present their work at undergraduate research conferences (in the case of scholarly pieces). Others try to influence public opinion by writing persuasive letters to legislators, submitting proposals to decision makers in the workplace, or posting their arguments on Web sites.

What all these writers have in common is a deep engagement with their issues. They share a strong belief that an issue matters, that decisions have consequences, and that the stakes are often high. You can engage an issue either by having a strong position to advocate or by seeking to clarify your stand on a complex problem. What is important to note is how fluid a writer's position can be along this continuum from advocate to inquirer (analogous to the continuum between "persuasion" and "truth seeking" discussed in Chapter 1, pp. 10–12). An advocate, while writing an argument, might discover an issue's complexity and be drawn into inquiry. Likewise, an inquirer, in the course of studying an issue, might clarify her thinking, establish a strong claim, and become an advocate. It is also possible to write arguments from any position on the continuum: You can be a tentative advocate as well as an avidly committed one, or you can be a cautious skeptic. You can even remain an inquirer by arguing that no proposed solution to a problem is yet adequate.

So how do you become engaged? We suggest that you immerse yourself in the arguments of the communities to which you belong—your classroom community, your dorm or apartment community, your work community, your civic community—and look for points of entry into these conversations: either places where you can take a stand or places where you are puzzled and uncertain. By opening yourself to the conversations of your culture, and by initiating these conversations when you encounter situations you would like to change, you will be ready to write arguments.

LEARNING FROM EXPERTS: TIPS FOR IMPROVING YOUR WRITING PROCESS

Once you are motivated to write, you can improve your arguing ability if you know something about the writing processes of experienced writers. Too often inexperienced writers cut this process short, producing undeveloped arguments that don't speak effectively to the needs of the intended audience. Although no two writers follow the same process, we can describe the evolution of an argument in a loose way and offer tips for making your writing processes more effective. You should regard the writing process we are about to describe as *recursive*, meaning that writers often loop back to earlier phases by changing their minds on an issue, by throwing out a draft and starting over, or by going back to do more research late in the process.

Starting point: Most writers of arguments start with an issue about which they are undecided or a claim they want to assert. At the outset, they may pose questions such as these: Who are the interested parties in this conversation? What are the causes of disagreement? What is the best way to solve the problem being debated? Who is the audience that must be persuaded? What is the best means of persuading members of that audience? What are the subtleties and complexities of this issue? Often a specific occasion spurs them to write. They feel hooked.

Tips for Starting the Process

- In many cases arguers are motivated to write because they find situations in their lives that they want to change. You can often focus on argument by asking yourself who has the power to make the changes you desire. How can you craft an argument that connects your desired changes to this audience's beliefs and values? What obstacles in your audience's environment might constrain individuals in that audience from action? How can these obstacles be overcome? This rhetorical focus—identifying the decision makers who have the power to change a situation and looking at the constraints that keep them from action—can give you a concrete sense of audience and clarify how your argument might proceed.

- In a college context you sometimes may have only a secondary occasion for writing—an assignment due date rather than an issue that hooks you. In such cases you can use some of the exploratory exercises described later in this chapter. These exercises help you inventory issues within the communities to which you belong, find points of engagement, and articulate the values and consequences that are at stake for you. Knowing why an issue matters to you can help you make it matter to others.

- Discuss issues with friends and classmates. Talking about ideas in small groups may help you discover claims that you want to make or issues that you find significant yet perplexing. By questioning claims and presenting multiple points of view, groups can help you understand points of disagreement on an issue.

Exploration, research, and rehearsal: To discover, refine, and support their claims, writers typically research their issues carefully, trying to understand arguments on all sides, to resolve disagreements about facts or reality, to clarify their own values, and to identify the beliefs and values of their audience. While researching their issues, writers often discover that their own views evolve. During research, writers often do exploratory writing in online chat rooms, e-mail exchanges, or a writer's journal, sometimes drafting whole pieces of an argument.

Tips for Exploring, Researching, and Rehearsing

- When you research an issue, focus on your rhetorical context. You need to research the issue itself, but also the values and beliefs of your targeted audience, and obstacles in your audience's social environment that might prevent individuals from acting on your claim or adopting your beliefs. The exploratory writing strategies and idea-generating procedures described later in this chapter will help you establish and maintain this focus.

- As you explore divergent views on your issue through library or Internet research or through interviews and field research, pay particular attention to why your views may be threatening to others. Later chapters in this text explain strategies for overcoming audience resistance.

- As you take notes on your research and imagine ways of shaping an argument for an intended audience, try some of the visual techniques suggested later in this chapter. Many writers find that idea maps and tree diagrams help them brainstorm for ideas and visualize structure.

■ Stay in conversation with others. Active discussion of your issue—especially with persons who don't agree with you—is a powerful way to explore an argument and find the best means of persuasion. As you talk through your argument, note where listeners look confused or skeptical and where they question your points. Skeptics may find holes in your reasoning, argue from different values, surprise you by conceding points you thought had to be developed at length, and challenge you by demanding more justification of your claim.

Writing a first draft: At some point in the process, a writer's attention begins to shift away from gathering data and probing an issue to composing a first draft. The act of writing a draft forces deep and focused thinking, which may then send the writer back to do more research and exploration. Effective first drafts are likely to be jumbled, messy, and full of gaps. Ideas appear at the point the writer thought of them rather than where readers need them. The writer's tone and style may be inappropriate, needed evidence may be entirely missing, the audience's beliefs and values may not be adequately addressed, and the whole draft may be confusing to an outside reader. Moreover, writers may discover that their own views are still shifting and unstable. Nevertheless, such drafts are a crucial first step. They get your ideas onto paper and give you material to work with.

Tips for Writing a First Draft

■ Try lowering your expectations. Writers can quickly create writer's block if they aim for perfection on the first draft. If you get blocked, keep writing. Don't worry about grammar, correctness, or polish. Just get ideas on paper.

■ Rehearse your ideas orally. Working in pairs with another student, talk through your argument orally before you write it down. Make a scratch outline first to prompt you as you talk. Then let your partner question you to help you flesh out your argument with more details.

■ For a first draft, try following the template for a "classical argument" described on pages 63–65. This strategy will help you consider and respond to opposing views as well as clarify the reasons and evidence that support your own claim.

■ Do the exploration tasks entitled "Set 2: Exploration and Rehearsal" (pp. 70–71) prior to writing a first draft. These exercises will help you brainstorm most of the ideas you'll need for an initial draft.

Revising through multiple drafts: After completing a first draft, you have materials out on the table to work with. Most writers need multiple drafts to convert an early draft into a persuasive finished product. Sometimes writers revise their claims significantly during revision, having discovered hidden complexities in the issue while composing the first draft.

Tips for Revising

- Don't manicure your drafts; rebuild them. Cross out whole paragraphs and rewrite them from scratch. Move blocks of text to new locations. Make a mess. Inexperienced writers often think of revision as polishing and correcting rather than as making substantial changes (what writing teachers call "global revision"). Revising means to rethink your whole argument. Some writers even throw away the first draft and start fresh.

- Improve your mechanical procedures. We recommend that you revise off double-spaced hard copy rather than off the computer screen. Leave lots of space between lines and in the margins on your drafts so that you have room to draw arrows and make pencil or pen deletions and inserts. When your draft becomes too messy, keyboard your changes back into the computer. If you manage all your drafts on computer, you may find that copying to a new file for each new draft gives you more freedom to experiment with changes (since you can always recover an earlier draft).

- As you revise, think of your audience. Many first drafts show why the writer believes the claim but not why the intended audience should believe it or act on it. As we explain later in this text (especially Chapters 7 and 8), first drafts often contain "writer-based reasons" rather than "audience-based reasons." How can you hook into your audience's beliefs and values? Look also at the obstacles or constraints that keep your audience from adopting your beliefs or acting on your claim. How can you address those constraints in your revision?

- As you revise, also consider the image of yourself conveyed in your tone and style. Do you want to come across as angry? As sarcastic? As conciliatory and sympathetic? Also, to what extent do you want to appeal to readers' emotions and imagination as well as to their logical intellects? These concerns are discussed in Chapter 7 under the headings *ethos* and *pathos.*

- Exchange drafts with classmates. Ask classmates where your argument is not persuasive, where your tone is offensive, where they have doubts, where your writing is unclear or undeveloped. Ask your classmates to role-play your intended audience. Explain the values and beliefs of this audience and the constraints members face. Let them give you their reactions and advice. Classmates can also help you meet your readers' needs for effective organization, development, and style.

- Loop back to do more exploration and research. Writing is a recursive process during which writers frequently loop back to earlier stages. Revising your first draft may involve considerably more research and exploration.

Editing for style, impact, and correctness: Writers now polish their drafts, rephrasing sentences, finding the precise word, and establishing links between sentences. At this point, you should turn to surface features such as spelling, punctuation, and grammar as well as to the appearance and form of the final manuscript.

Tips for Editing

- Read your draft out loud. Your ear can often pick up problems missed by the eye.
- Use your computer's spell check program. Remember, however, that spell checkers won't pick up mistakes with homonyms like *to/two/too, here/hear,* or *affect/effect.* Be skeptical of computerized grammar checkers, which cannot "read" with human intelligence but can only mechanically count, sort, and match. Your instructor can guide you on what grammar checkers can and cannot do.
- Use a good handbook for up-to-date advice on usage, punctuation, style, and manuscript form.
- Ask a classmate or friend to proofread your paper.
- Be prepared to loop back again to earlier stages. Sometimes thinking of a better way to word a sentence uncovers larger problems of clarity and meaning requiring you to rewrite a whole section of your argument.

USING EXPLORATORY WRITING TO DISCOVER IDEAS AND DEEPEN THINKING

What follows is a compendium of strategies to help you discover and explore ideas. None of these strategies works for every writer. But all of them are worth trying. Each requires practice, so don't give up on the strategy if it doesn't work at first. We recommend that you keep your exploratory writing in a journal or in easily identified files in your word processor so you can review it later and test the "staying power" of ideas produced by the different strategies.

Freewriting or Blind Writing

Freewriting is useful at any stage of the writing process. When you freewrite, you put pen to paper and write rapidly *nonstop,* usually ten to fifteen minutes at a stretch. The object is to think of as many ideas as possible without stopping to edit your work. On a computer, freewriters often turn off the monitor so that they can't see the text being produced. Such "blind writing" frees the writer from the urge to edit or correct the text and simply to let ideas roll forth. Some freewriters or blind writers achieve a stream-of-consciousness style, recording their ideas at the very moment they bubble into consciousness, stutters and stammers and all. Others produce more focused chunks, though without clear connections among them. You will probably find your initial reservoir of ideas running out in three to five minutes. If so, force yourself to keep writing or typing. If you can't think of anything to say, write "relax" or "I'm stuck" over and over until new ideas emerge.

Here is an example of a freewrite from a student named Stephen, exploring his thoughts on the question "What can be done about the homeless?" (Stephen eventually wrote the proposal argument found on pages 334–42.)

> Let's take a minute and talk about the homeless. Homeless homeless. Today on my way to work I passed a homeless guy who smiled at me and I smiled back though he smelled bad. What are the reasons he was out on the street? Perhaps an extraordinary string of bad luck. Perhaps he was pushed out onto the street. Not a background of work ethic, no place to go, no way to get someplace to live that could be afforded, alcoholism. To what extent do government assistance, social spending, etc, keep people off the street? What benefits could a person get that stops "the cycle"? How does welfare affect homelessness, drug abuse programs, family planning? To what extent does the individual have control over homelessness? This question of course goes to the depth of the question of how community affects the individual. Relax, relax. What about the signs that I see on the way to work posted on the windows of businesses that read, "please don't give to panhandlers it only promotes drug abuse etc" a cheap way of getting homeless out of the way of business? Are homeless the natural end of unrestricted capitalism? What about the homeless people who are mentally ill? How can you maintain a living when haunted by paranoia? How do you decide if someone is mentally ill or just laughs at society? If one can't function obviously. How many mentally ill are out on the street? If you are mentally ill and have lost the connections to others who might take care of you I can see how you might end up on the street. What would it take to get treatment? To what extent can mentally ill be treated? When I see a homeless person I want to ask, How do you feel about the rest of society? When you see "us" walk by how do you think of us? Do you possibly care how we avoid you.

▼ FOR CLASS DISCUSSION

Individual task: Choose one of the following controversial claims (or another chosen by your instructor) and freewrite your response to it for five or ten minutes. **Group task:** Working in pairs, in small groups, or as a whole class, share your freewrite with classmates. Don't feel embarrassed if your freewrite is fragmentary or disjointed. Freewrites are not supposed to be finished products; their sole purpose is to generate a flow of thought. The more you practice the technique, the better you will become.

1. A student should report a fellow student who is cheating on an exam or plagiarizing an essay.

2. States should legalize marriages between homosexuals.

3. Companies should not be allowed to enforce English-only policies in the workplace.

4. Spanking children should be considered child abuse.

5. State and federal governments should legalize hard drugs.

6. For grades 1 through 12, the school year should be extended to eleven months.

7. Taxpayer money should not be used to fund professional sports stadiums.

8. Violent video games such as Mortal Kombat should be made illegal.

9. Rich people are morally obligated to give part of their wealth to the poor.

10. Women should be assigned to combat duty equally with men.

Idea Mapping

Another good technique for exploring ideas is *idea mapping*. When you make an idea map, draw a circle in the center of the page and write some trigger idea (a broad topic, a question, or working thesis statement) in the center of the circle. Then record your ideas on branches and subbranches extending from the center circle. As long as you pursue one train of thought, keep recording your ideas on the branch. But when that line of thinking gives out, start a new branch. Often your thoughts jump back and forth between branches. That's a major advantage of "picturing" your thoughts; you can see them as part of an emerging design rather than as strings of unrelated ideas.

Idea maps usually generate more ideas, though less well-developed ones, than freewrites. Writers who practice both techniques report that each strategy causes them to think about their ideas very differently. When Stephen, the free-writer on homelessness, created an idea map (see Figure 3.1), he was well into an argument disagreeing with a proposal by columnist Charles Krauthammer advocating the confinement of the homeless mentally ill in state mental hospitals. Stephen's idea map helped him find some order in his evolving thoughts on homelessness and his reasons for disagreeing with Krauthammer.

FOR CLASS DISCUSSION

Choose a controversial issue—national, local, or campus—that's interesting to the class. The instructor will lead a class discussion on the issue, recording ideas on an idea map as they emerge. Your goal is to appreciate the fluidity of idea maps as a visual form of idea generation halfway between an outline and a list.

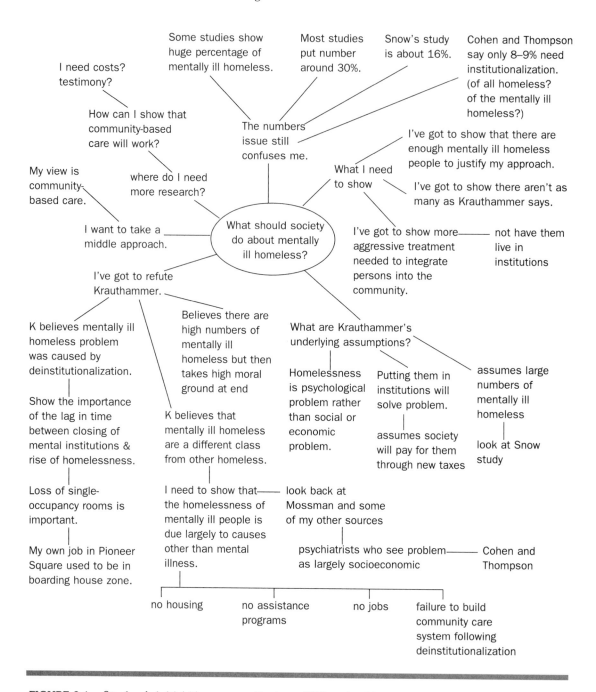

FIGURE 3.1   Stephen's initial idea map on the issue "What should society do about the mentally ill homeless?"

Playing the Believing and Doubting Game

The believing/doubting game* is an excellent way to imagine views different from your own and to anticipate responses to those views.

As a believer, your role is to be wholly sympathetic to an idea, to listen carefully to it, and to suspend all disbelief. You must identify all the ways in which the idea might appeal to different audiences and all the reasons for believing the idea. The believing game is easy so long as you already accept an idea. But in dealing with ideas that strike you as shaky, false, or threatening, you will find that the believing game can be difficult, even frightening.

The doubting game is the opposite of the believing game. As a doubter, your role is to be judgmental and critical, to find faults with an idea. You do your best to find counterexamples and inconsistencies that undermine it. Again, it is easy to play the doubting game with ideas you reject, but doubting those you've invested in can be threatening.

When you play the believing and doubting game with an assertion, simply write two different chunks, one chunk arguing for the assertion (the believing game) and one chunk opposing it (the doubting game). Freewrite both chunks, letting your ideas flow without censoring. Or, alternatively, make an idea map with believing and doubting branches.

Here is how one student played the believing and doubting game as part of a class discussion about the following classified ad seeking young college women to be egg donors for an infertile couple.

Infertile professional couple seeks egg-donor for artificial insemination. Donor should be slim, athletic, blue-eyed with 1400 SAT's or better. $50,000 and all medical expenses. Must be discrete and willing to sign documents giving up all legal rights to a baby that might be produced.

This student is responding to the assertion "Recent advances in reproductive technology, including the use of egg donors, are good for society."

BELIEVING EXAMPLE

The latest advances in reproductive technology are good for society. Up until now, infertile couples had only adoption to turn to if they wanted a child. Using egg donation enables the parents to feel like real parents because the mother does carry the child. The parents can be a bit more selective about the child they get because egg donors are carefully screened. I think egg donors are more stable and safe than women who carelessly or accidentally get pregnant and give up their babies for adoption. Egg donors can be smart, healthy young women, such as college

---

*A term coined by Peter Elbow, *Writing without Teachers* (New York: Oxford UP, 1973), 147–90.

students. These young women also get an opportunity to make some money. Another point is that women can preserve some of their own eggs from their youth and actually have a child much later in life when they are ready for such a commitment. I can see how egg donation can help infertile couples, young women, and older women.

DOUBTING EXAMPLE

While egg donation sounds promising, I think the supporters of it often leave out the dark side and the moral implications. The process is changing having babies from a natural experience to a completely commercial one. Eggs are bought and judged like any other product. The high prices reaching even tens of thousands of dollars mean that only rich couples will be able to afford the process. The fact that the preferred egg donors have common traits (are Ivy League students, are tall, blonde, and blue eyed) only serves to increase a certain elitism. The donor part has pitfalls too. I can understand the attraction of the large sums of money, but the medical process is not easy. The young women must take fertility drugs and injections to boost their egg production. These drugs may have side effects and long-term complications. I wouldn't want my girlfriend to undergo this process.

Although this writer condemns these medical advances in reproductive technology, he does a good job of trying to sympathize with women who are involved in them. Playing the believing and doubting game has helped him see the issue more complexly.

FOR CLASS DISCUSSION

Return to the ten controversial claims in the For Class Discussion on pages 56–57. **Individual task:** Choose one of the claims and play the believing and doubting game with it by freewriting for five minutes trying to believe the claim and then for five minutes trying to doubt the claim. Or, if you prefer, make an idea map by creating a believing spoke and a doubting spoke off the main hub. Instead of freewriting, enter ideas onto your idea map, moving back and forth between believing and doubting. **Group task:** Share what you produced with members of your group or with the class as a whole.

Repeat the exercise with another claim.

Brainstorming for Pro and Con
Because Clauses

This activity is similar to the believing and doubting game in that it asks you to brainstorm ideas for and against a controversial assertion. In the believing and doubting game, however, you simply freewrite or make an idea map on both sides of the issue. In this activity, you try to state your reasons for and against the proposition as *because* clauses. The value of doing so is discussed in depth in Chapter 4, which shows how a claim with *because* clauses can form the core of an argument.

Here is an example of how you might create *because* clauses for and against the claim "The recent advances in reproductive technology, including the use of egg donors, are good for society."

PRO

The recent advances in reproductive technology, including the use of egg donors, are good for society.

- because children born using this technology are really wanted and will be given loving homes
- because infertility is a medical disorder that can destroy marriages
- because curing this disorder will support marriages and create loving families
- because this technology restores to parents some measure of control over their reproductive capabilities

CON

The recent advances in reproductive technology, including the use of egg donors, are dangerous to society.

- because this technology could lead to situations in which persons have no idea to whom they are genetically related
- because the technology might harm persons such as the egg donors who do not know what the long-term consequences of tampering with their reproductive systems through the use of fertility drugs might be
- because using donor eggs is equivalent to "special ordering" children who may not live up to the parents' expectations (to be smart, tall)
- because the expense of reproductive technology (especially when it results in multiple births) is too large for individuals, insurance companies, or the state to bear

FOR CLASS DISCUSSION

Generating *because* clauses like these is an especially productive discussion activity for groups. Once again return to the ten controversial claims in the For Class Discussion exercise on pages 56–57. Select one or more of these claims (or others provided by your instructor) and, working in small groups, generate pro and con *because* clauses supporting and attacking the claim. Share your group's *because* clauses with those of other groups.

Brainstorming a Network of Related Issues

The previous exercise helps you see how certain issues can provoke strong pro-con stances. Occasionally in civic life, an issue is presented to the public in such a pro-con form, as when voters are asked to approve or disapprove a referendum or when a jury must decide the guilt or innocence of a defendant.

But in most contexts, the argumentative situation is more open-ended and fluid. You can easily oversimplify an issue by reducing it to two opposing sides. Because most issues are embedded in a network of subissues, side issues, and larger issues, seeing an issue in pro-con terms can often blind you to other ways to join a conversation. For example, a writer might propose a middle ground between adversarial positions, examine a subissue in more depth, connect an issue to a related side issue, or redefine an issue to place it in a new context.

Consider, for example, the assertion about reproductive technology. Rather than arguing for or against this claim, a writer might focus on reproductive technology in a variety of other ways:

- Who should determine the ethics of reproductive technology? Families? Doctors? Government?
- How can risky physical outcomes such as multiple births (mothers carrying seven and eight babies) be avoided?
- What effect will the new reproductive technologies have on our concepts of motherhood and family?
- In case of divorce, who has legal rights to frozen embryos and other genetic material?
- Will reproductive technology lead to control over the sex and genetic makeup of children? Should it?
- What is the difference between paying someone to donate a kidney (which is illegal) and paying a woman to donate her eggs (which is currently legal)?
- Currently many adopted children want to seek out their birth mothers. Would children born from donated eggs want to seek out their genetic mothers?
- Who should pay for reproductive technology?

FOR CLASS DISCUSSION

Working as a whole class or in small groups, choose one or more of the controversial assertions on pages 56–57. Instead of arguing for or against them, brainstorm a number of related issues (subissues, side issues, or larger issues) on the same general subject. For example, brainstorm a number of issues related to the general topics of cheating, gay marriage, women in combat, and so forth.

SHAPING YOUR ARGUMENT
FOR YOUR INTENDED AUDIENCE

We turn now from discovery strategies to organizing strategies. As you begin drafting, you need some sort of plan. How elaborate that plan is varies considerably from writer to writer. Some writers plan extensively before writing; others write extensively before planning. But somewhere along the way, all writers must decide on a structure. This section offers two basic organizing strategies: (1) using the conventional structure of "classical argument" as an initial guide and (2) using a tree diagram instead of a traditional outline.

Classical Argument as an Initial Guide

In drafting, writers of argument often rely on knowledge of typical argument structures to guide their thinking. One of the oldest models is the *classical argument*—so called because it follows a pattern recommended by ancient rhetoricians. In traditional Latin terminology, classical argument has the following parts: the *exordium* (which gets the audience's attention); the *narratio* (which provides needed background); the *propositio* (which introduces the speaker's proposition or thesis); the *partitio* (which forecasts the main parts of the speech); the *confirmatio* (which presents arguments supporting the proposition); the *confutatio* (which refutes opposing views); and the *peroratio* (which sums up the argument, calls for action, and leaves a strong last impression). Classical arguments are often best suited for undecided or neutral audiences (see Chapter 8).

In slightly homelier terms (see Figure 3.2), writers of classical argument typically begin with a dramatic story or a startling statistic that commands attention. Then they focus the issue, often by stating it directly as a question and perhaps by briefly summarizing opposing views. Next, they contextualize the issue by providing needed background, explaining the immediate context, or defining key terms. They conclude the introduction by presenting the thesis and forecasting the argument's structure.

Next, in usually the longest part of the classical argument, writers present the major reasons and evidence supporting their thesis, typically trying to develop reasons that appeal to their audience's values and beliefs. Often, each reason is developed in its own section. Each section opens with a statement of the reason, which is then supported with evidence or chains of other reasons. Along the way, writers guide their readers with appropriate transitions.

Subsequently, alternative views are summarized and critiqued. (Some writers put this section *before* the presentation of their own argument.) If opposing arguments consist of several parts, writers may either (1) summarize all opposing arguments before responding or (2) summarize and respond one part at a time. Writers may respond to opposing views either by refuting them or by conceding their strengths but shifting to a different field of values where these strengths are less decisive.

Finally, in their conclusion, writers will sum up their argument, often calling for some kind of action, thereby creating a sense of closure and leaving a strong final impression.

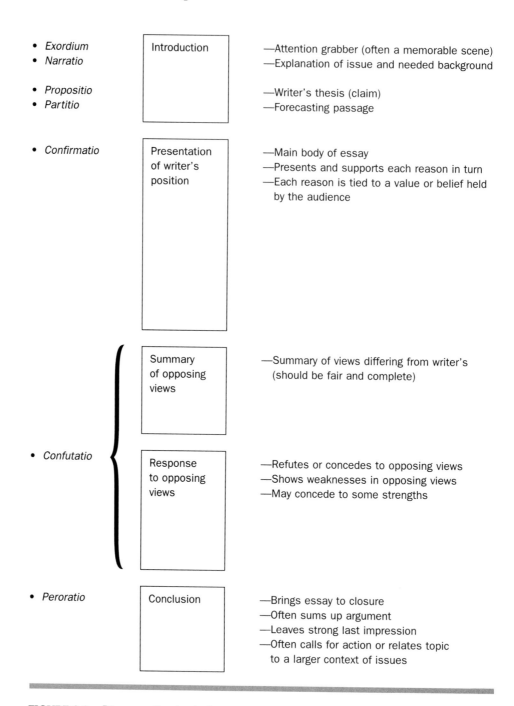

FIGURE 3.2   Diagram of a classical argument

For all its strengths, the classical argument may not always be your best model. In some cases, for example, delaying your thesis or ignoring alternative views may be justified (see Chapter 8). Even in these cases, however, the classical argument is a useful planning tool. Its call for a thesis statement and a forecasting statement in the introduction helps you see the whole of your argument in miniature. And by requiring you to summarize and consider opposing views, classical argument alerts you to the limits of your position and to the need for further reasons and evidence. Moreover, the classical argument is a particularly persuasive mode of argument when you address a neutral or undecided audience.

The Power of Tree Diagrams

The classical argument offers a general guide for shaping arguments, but it doesn't help you wrestle with particular ideas. It is one thing to know that you need one or more reasons to support your thesis, but quite another to figure out what those reasons are, to articulate them clearly, and to decide what evidence supports them. Traditionally, writers have used outlines to help them flesh out a structure. For some writers, however, a visual strategy called *tree diagramming* may be more effective.

A *tree diagram* differs from an outline in that headings and subheadings are indicated by spatial relationships rather than by a system of letters and numerals. Figure 3.3 reveals the plan for a classical argument opposing a campus ban on hate speech. The writer envisions the argument as a guest editorial in the campus newspaper aimed at persuading campus opinion away from a proposed ban. The inverted triangle at the top of the tree represents the writer's introduction. The main reasons appear on branches beneath the claim, and the supporting evidence and arguments for each reason are displayed beneath each reason.

The same argument displayed in outline form would look like this:

THESIS: Colleges should not try to ban hate speech.

   I. A ban on hate speech violates the First Amendment.

  II. A ban on hate speech doesn't solve the problem of hate.
     A. It doesn't allow people to understand and hear each other's anger.
     B. It disguises hatred instead of bringing it out in the open where it can be dealt with.
     C. The ability to see both sides of an issue would be compromised.

 III. Of course, there are good arguments in support of a ban on hate speech.
     A. Banning hate speech creates a safer environment for minorities.
     B. It helps eliminate occasions for violence.
     C. It teaches good manners and people skills.
     D. It shows that ignorant hate speech is not the same as intelligent discussion.

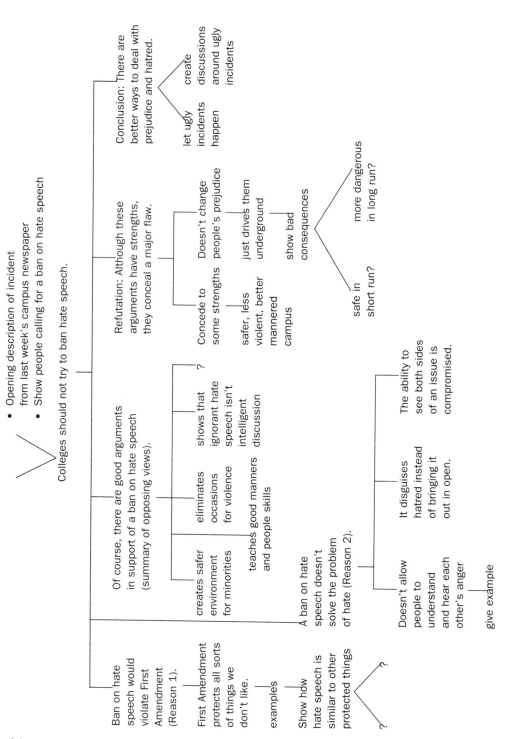

FIGURE 3.3   Tree diagram of an argument opposing a ban on hate speech

66

IV. Although these arguments have strengths, they conceal a major flaw.
   A. I concede that a hate speech ban might make a safer, less violent campus and might help teach good manners.
   B. But in the long run, it doesn't change people's prejudices; it just drives them underground.
V. CONCLUSION: There are better ways to deal with prejudice and hatred.
   A. Instead of repressing hate, let ugly incidents happen.
   B. Create discussions around the ugly incidents.

In our experience, tree diagrams often lead to fuller, more detailed, and more logical arguments than do traditional outlines. Their strength results from their several advantages. First, they are visual. The main points are laid out horizontally and support is displayed vertically. Writers can literally "see" where they need more support and can move freely between dimensions as they construct their argument.

Second, they are flexible. While traditional outlines require a division of each whole into two or more parts (every A must have a B—based on the principle that no whole can logically have just one part), tree diagrams can represent additional relationships. For example, a tree diagram can logically show a single line descending vertically from a higher-level point to represent, say, a generalization illustrated by a single example. Additionally, the descending lines on a tree diagram function as an informal flowchart, letting you plan out a chain of reasons. (This flexibility explains why the tree diagram in Figure 3.3 contains so much more information than the outline for the same argument.)

Finally, tree diagrams are powerful aids to invention because they invite you to insert question marks as placeholders for information you know you need but haven't yet found. For instance, if you know you need more data to support a point, you can write out your point on the tree diagram and place one or more question marks on descending lines below the point. (See the writer's use of question marks in Figure 3.3.)

DISCOVERING IDEAS:
TWO SETS OF EXPLORATORY
WRITING TASKS

The following tasks use exploratory writing to help you generate ideas. The first set of tasks helps you gather ideas early in a writing project either by helping you think of issues to write about or by deepening and complicating your response to readings. The second set of tasks helps you think about your ideas systematically before you compose a first draft.

Set 1: Starting Points

Task 1: Make an Inventory of the Communities to Which You Belong. What Issues Arise in Those Communities?

All of us belong to a variety of communities. For example, you have a class-room community for each course you are taking. Each club or organization has its own community, as does the community where you live (dorm, apartment, your family). Beyond these small communities, you have your campus community and beyond that your city, state, region, nation, and world communities. You may also belong to a work or job community, to a church/mosque/synagogue community, or to communities related to your hobbies or avocations.

The occasion for argument grows out of your life in these communities—your desire to make a difference on some issue that divides or troubles the community. As an arguer, you might tackle a big issue in your world community (What is the best way to prevent destruction of rain forests?) or a small issue in your dorm (Should quiet hours be enforced?). In your classroom community, you might tackle a practical problem (What should the instructor do about persons coming in late?) or intellectual issues in the discipline itself (Is Frankenstein's monster good or evil? Is gender socially constructed?).

For this task make a list of the communities to which you belong. Then brain-storm controversies in these communities—issues that are being debated or that you would like to see debated. You might find one or more of the following "trig-ger questions" helpful:

- Persons in my dorm (at work, in the state legislature, at the United Nations) disagree about . . . .

- Our campus (this dorm, my hometown, my worksite, our state, our country) would be a better place if . . . .

- Something that really makes me mad about this campus (my apartment life, city government, our society) is . . . .

- In the career I hope to pursue, X is a serious problem that needs to be addressed.

- Person X believes . . . ; however, I believe . . . .

Task 2: Make an Inventory of Issues That Interest You

The previous task can overwhelm students with the sheer number of issues that surround them. Once you broaden out to the large communities of city, state, nation, and world, the numbers of issues multiply rapidly. Moreover, each large issue has numerous subissues. For this task make an inventory of ten to fifteen possible issues that you would like to explore more deeply and possibly write about. Share your list with classmates, adding their ideas to yours.

Task 3: Choose Several Areas of Controversy for Exploration

For this task choose two or three possible controversies from the list above and explore them through freewriting or idea mapping. Try responding to the following questions: (a) What is my position on this issue and why? (b) What are opposing or alternative positions on this issue? (c) Why do people disagree about this issue? (Do they disagree about the facts of the case? About underlying values, assumptions, and beliefs?) (d) To argue a position on this issue, what evidence do I need to find and what further research will be required?

Task 4: Choose a Local Issue and Explore Its Rhetorical Context

For this task choose a local issue (some situation that you would like to see changed on your campus, in your place of work, or in your town or city) and explore its rhetorical context: (a) What is the situation you would like to change? (b) Who has the power to change that situation? (c) What are the values and beliefs of these decision makers? (d) What obstacles or constraints may prevent these decision makers from acting on your desires? (e) What reasons and evidence would exert the most pressure on these decision makers? (How can you make acting on your proposal a good thing for them?)

Task 5: Identify and Explore Issues That Are Problematic for You

A major assignment often given in argument courses is to write a research-based argument on an issue or problem initially puzzling to you. Perhaps you don't know enough about the issue (for example, establishing international controls on pesticides), or perhaps the issue draws you into an uncomfortable conflict of values (for example, assisted suicide, legalization of drugs, noncriminal incarceration of sexual predators). Your goal for this task is to identify several issues about which you are undecided, to choose one, and to explore your current uncertainty. Why can't you make up your mind on this issue?

Task 6: Deepen Your Response to Readings

This task requires you to read a collection of arguments on an issue and to explore them thoughtfully. As you read the arguments assigned by your instructor, annotate the margins with believing and doubting notes as explained in Chapter 2. Then respond to one or more of the following prompts, using freewriting or idea mapping:

- Why do the writers disagree? Are there disagreements about facts? About underlying values, beliefs, and assumptions?

- Identify "hot spots" in the readings—passages that evoke strong agreement or disagreement, anger, confusion, or any other memorable response—and explore your reaction to these passages.

- Explore the evolution of your thinking as you read and later review the essays. What new questions have they raised? How did your thinking change? Where do you stand now and why?

- If you were to meet one of the authors on a plane or at a ball game, what would you say to him or her?

Set 2: Exploration and Rehearsal

The following tasks are designed to help you once you have chosen a topic and begun to clarify your thesis. While these tasks may take two or more hours to complete, the effort pays off by helping you produce a full set of ideas for your rough draft. We recommend using these tasks each time you write an argument for this course.

Task 1

What issue do you plan to address in this argument? Try wording the issue as a one-sentence question. Reword your question in several different ways because each version will frame the issue somewhat differently. Then put a box around your best version of the question.

Task 2

Now write out your tentative answer to the question. This will be your beginning thesis statement or claim. Put a box around this answer. Next write out one or more different answers to your question. These will be alternative claims that a neutral audience might consider.

Task 3

Why is this a controversial issue? Is there insufficient evidence to resolve the issue, or is the evidence ambiguous or contradictory? Are definitions in dispute? Do the parties disagree about basic values, assumptions, or beliefs?

Task 4

What personal interest do you have in this issue? What are the consequences for you if your argument succeeds or doesn't succeed? How does the issue affect you? Why do you care about it? (Knowing why you care about it might help you get your audience to care about it.)

Task 5

Who is the audience that you need to persuade? If your argument calls for an action, who has the power to act on your claim? Can you address these persons of power directly? Or do you need to sway others (such as voters) to exert pressure on persons in power? With regard to your issue, what are the values and beliefs of the audience you are trying to sway?

Task 6

What obstacles or constraints in the social or physical environment prevent your audience from acting on your claim or accepting your beliefs? What are some ways these obstacles can be overcome? If these obstacles cannot be overcome, should you change your claim?

Task 7

In this task you will rehearse the main body of your paper. Using freewriting or idea mapping, think of the main reasons and evidence you could use to sway your intended audience. Brainstorm everything that comes to mind that might help you support your case. Because this section will eventually provide the bulk of your argument, proceed rapidly without worrying whether your argument makes sense. Just get ideas on paper. As you generate reasons and evidence, you are likely to discover gaps in your knowledge. Where could your argument be bolstered by additional data such as statistics, examples, and expert testimony? Where and how will you do the research to fill these gaps?

Task 8

Now reread what you wrote for Tasks 5 and 6, in which you examined your audience's perspective. Role-playing that audience, imagine all the counterarguments members might make. Where does your claim threaten them or oppose their values? What obstacles or constraints in their environment are individuals likely to point to? ("I'd love to act on your claim, but we just don't have the money" or "If we grant your request, it will set a bad precedent.") Brainstorm all the objections your audience might raise to your argument.

Task 9

How can you respond to those objections? Take them one by one and brainstorm possible responses.

Task 10

Finally, explore again why this issue is important. What are its broader implications and consequences? What other issues does it relate to? Thinking of possible answers to these questions may prove useful when you write your introduction or conclusion.

WRITING ASSIGNMENTS
FOR CHAPTERS 1–3

OPTION 1: *An Argument Summary*   Write a 250-word summary of an argument selected by your instructor. Then write a one-sentence summary of the same argument. Use as models the summaries of George Will's argument on pay equity in Chapter 2.

OPTION 2: *An Analysis of Sources of Disagreement in a Controversy*   Using as a model the analysis of the controversy between Will and Goodman on pay equity in Chapter 2, write an analysis of the sources of disagreement in any two arguments that take differing views on the same issue.

OPTION 3: *Evaluating Your Use of Exploratory Writing*   For this option your instructor will assign one or more of the exploratory exercises in Chapter 3 for you to do as homework. Do the tasks as well as you can, submitting your exploratory writing as an exhibit for evidence. Then write a reflective evaluation of how well the assignment worked for you. In your evaluation address questions such as these:

    a. Did the exercise help you develop ideas? (Why or why not?)

    b. What are examples of some of the ideas you developed?

    c. What did the exercise teach you about the demands of good arguments?

    d. What did the exercise teach you about your own writing and thinking process?

OPTION 4: *Propose a Problem for a Major Course Project*   An excellent major project for an argument course is to research an issue about which you are initially undecided. Your final essay for the course could be an argument in which you take a stand on this issue. Choose one of the issues you listed in "Set 1: Starting Points," Task 5—"I am unable to take a stand on the issue of . . ."—and make this issue a major research project for the course. During the term keep a log of your research activities and be ready, in class discussion or in writing, to explain what kinds of arguments or evidence turned out to be most persuasive in helping you take a stand.

    For this assignment, write a short letter to your instructor identifying the issue you have chosen, and explain why you are interested in it and why you can't make up your mind at this time.

Principles of Argument

4

The Core of an Argument

A Claim with Reasons

THE RHETORICAL TRIANGLE

Before we examine the structure of arguments, we should explain briefly their social context, which can be visualized as a triangle with interrelated points labeled *message, writer/speaker,* and *audience* (see Figure 4.1). Effective arguments consider all three points on this *rhetorical triangle.* As we will see in later chapters, when you alter one point of the triangle (for example, when you change the audience for whom you are writing), you often need to alter the other points (by restructuring the message itself and perhaps by changing the tone or image you project as writer/speaker). We have created a series of questions based on the "rhetorical triangle" to help you plan, draft, and revise your argument.

Each point on the triangle in turn corresponds to one of the three kinds of persuasive appeals that ancient rhetoricians named *logos, ethos,* and *pathos. Logos* (Greek for "word") refers primarily to the internal consistency and clarity of the message and to the logic of its reasons and support. The impact of *logos* on an audience is referred to as its *logical appeal.*

Ethos (Greek for "character") refers to the credibility of the writer/speaker. *Ethos* is often conveyed through the tone and style of the message, through the care with which the writer considers alternative views, and through the writer's investment in his or her claim. In some cases, it's also a function of the writer's reputation for honesty and expertise independent of the message. The impact of *ethos* on an audience is referred to as its *ethical appeal* or *appeal from credibility.*

Our third term, *pathos* (Greek for "suffering" or "experience"), is often associated with emotional appeal. But *pathos* appeals more specifically to an audience's imaginative sympathies—their capacity to feel and see what the writer feels and

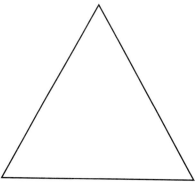

Message
(LOGOS: *How can I make the argument
internally consistent and logical?
How can I find the best reasons and
support them with the best evidence?*)

Audience
(PATHOS: *How can I make the reader
open to my message? How can I best
appeal to my reader's values and
interests? How can I engage my
reader emotionally and imaginatively?*)

Writer or Speaker
(ETHOS: *How can I present myself
effectively? How can I enhance my
credibility and trustworthiness?*)

FIGURE 4.1   The rhetorical triangle

sees. Thus, when we turn the abstractions of logical discourse into a palpable and immediate story, we are making a pathetic appeal. While appeals to *logos* and *ethos* can further an audience's intellectual assent to our claim, appeals to *pathos* engage the imagination and feelings, moving the audience to deeper appreciation of the argument's significance.

In Part Two, we treat all three elements of the rhetorical triangle in detail. Although all three terms overlap, Chapters 4–6 focus primarily on *logos*, and Chapters 7 and 8 focus primarily on *ethos* and *pathos*.

Given this background on the rhetorical triangle, let's turn now to *logos*—the logic and structure of arguments.

ISSUE QUESTIONS AS THE ORIGINS OF ARGUMENT

At the heart of any argument is an issue, which we can define as a controversial topic area such as "criminal rights" or "the minimum wage," that gives rise to differing points of view and conflicting claims. A writer can usually focus an issue by asking an issue question that invites at least two alternative answers. Within any complex issue—for example, the issue of abortion—there are usually a number of separate issue questions: Should abortions be legal? Should the federal government authorize Medicaid payments for abortions? When does a fetus become a human being (at conception? at three months? at quickening? at birth?)? What are the effects of legalizing abortion? (One person might stress that legalized abortion leads to greater freedom for women. Another person might respond that it lessens a society's respect for human life.)

Difference between an Issue Question and an Information Question

Of course, not all questions are issue questions that can be answered reasonably in two or more differing ways; thus not all questions can lead to effective argument essays. Rhetoricians have traditionally distinguished between *explication*, which is writing that sets out to inform or explain, and *argumentation,* which sets out to change a reader's mind. On the surface, at least, this seems like a useful distinction. If a reader is interested in a writer's question mainly to gain new knowledge about a subject, then the writer's essay could be considered explication rather than argument. According to this view, the following questions about abortion might be called information questions rather than issue questions:

How does the abortion rate in the United States compare with the rate in Sweden?

If the rates are different, why?

Although both questions seem to call for information rather than for argument, we believe the latter one would be an issue question if reasonable people disagreed on the answer. Thus, two writers might agree that abortion rates in the United States and Sweden differ significantly, but they might disagree in their explanations of why. One might say that Sweden has a higher abortion rate because of the absence of a large Catholic or conservative Protestant population in the country. The other might attribute the higher rate to Sweden's generous national health coverage or to differences in sex education in the schools. Thus, underneath the surface of what looks like a simple explication of the "truth" is really a controversy.

You can generally tell whether a question is an issue question or an information question by examining your purpose in relationship to your audience. If your relationship to your audience is that of teacher to learner, so that your audience hopes to gain new information, knowledge, or understanding that you possess, then your question is probably an information question. But if your relationship to your audience is that of advocate to decision maker or jury, so that your audience needs to make up its mind on something and is weighing different points of view, then the question you address is an issue question.

Often the same question can be an information question in one context and an issue question in another. Let's look at the following examples:

- How does a diesel engine work? (This is probably an information question since reasonable people who know about diesel engines will probably agree on how they work. This question would be posed by an audience of new learners.)

- Why is a diesel engine more fuel-efficient than a gasoline engine? (This also seems to be an information question since all experts will probably agree on the answer. Once again, the audience seems to be new learners, perhaps students in an automotive class.)

- What is the most cost-effective way to produce diesel fuel from crude oil? (This could be an information question if experts agree and you are addressing new learners. But if you are addressing engineers and one engineer says process X is the most cost-effective and another argues for process Y, then the question is an issue question.)

- Should the present highway tax on diesel fuel be increased? (This is certainly an issue question. One person says yes; another says no; another offers a compromise.)

FOR CLASS DISCUSSION

Working as a class or in small groups, try to decide which of the following questions are information questions and which are issue questions. Many of them could be either, depending on the rhetorical context. For such questions, create hypothetical contexts to show your reasoning.

1. What percentage of single-parent families receive welfare support?

2. What is the cause of the large number of out-of-wedlock births in the United States?

3. Should the United States eliminate welfare support for unwed mothers?

4. What percentage of TV shows during prime-time hours depict violence?

5. What is the effect of violent TV shows on children?

6. Are chiropractors legitimate health professionals?

7. How does chiropractic treatment of illness differ from a medical doctor's treatment?

8. Are caffeinated sodas harmful to children?

9. Should a woman with a newly detected breast cancer opt for a radical mastectomy (complete removal of the breast and surrounding lymph tissue) or a lumpectomy (removal of the malignant lump without removal of the whole breast)?

10. Is Simone de Beauvoir correct in calling marriage an outdated, oppressive, capitalist institution?

DIFFERENCE BETWEEN A GENUINE ARGUMENT AND A PSEUDO-ARGUMENT

While every argument features an issue question with alternative answers, not every dispute over answers is a rational argument. Rational arguments require two additional factors: (1) reasonable participants who operate within the conventions of reasonable behavior and (2) potentially sharable assumptions that can serve as a starting place or foundation for the argument. Lacking one or both of these conditions, disagreements remain stalled at the level of pseudo-arguments.

Pseudo-Arguments: Fanatical Believers and Fanatical Skeptics

A reasonable argument assumes the possibility of growth and change; disputants may modify their views as they acknowledge strengths in an alternative view or weaknesses in their own. Such growth becomes impossible—and argument degenerates to pseudo-argument—when disputants are fanatically committed to their positions. Consider the case of the fanatical believer or the fanatical skeptic.

Fanatical believers believe their claims are true because they say so, period. They may cite some authoritative text—the Bible, the *Communist Manifesto*, or *The Road Less Traveled*—but in the end it's their narrow and quirky reading of the text or their faith in the author (which others might not share) that underlies their argument. Disagreeing with a fanatical believer is like ordering the surf to quiet down. The only response is another crashing wave.

The fanatical skeptic, in contrast, dismisses the possibility of proving anything. So what if the sun has risen every day of recorded history? That's no proof that it will rise tomorrow. Short of absolute proof, which never exists, fanatical skeptics accept nothing. In a world where the most we can hope for is increased audience adherence to our ideas, the fanatical skeptic demands an ironclad logical demonstration of our claim's rightness. In the presence of fanatical believers or skeptics, then, genuine argument is impossible.

Another Source of Pseudo-Arguments:
Lack of Shared Assumptions

A reasonable argument is difficult to conduct unless the participants share common assumptions on which the argument can be grounded. Like axioms in geometry, these shared assumptions serve as the starting point for the argument. Consider the following conversation, in which Randall refuses to accept Rhonda's assumptions:

RHONDA: Smoking should be banned because it causes cancer.

RANDALL: So it causes cancer. What's so bad about that?

RHONDA: Don't be perverse, Randy. Cancer causes suffering and death.

RANDALL: Rhonda, my dear girl, don't be such a twinkie. Suffering and death are just part of the human condition.

RHONDA: But that doesn't make them desirable, especially when they can be avoided.

RANDALL: Perhaps in particular cases they're avoidable for a while, but in the long run, we all suffer and we all die, so who cares if smoking causes what's inevitable anyway?

This, we would suggest, is a doomed argument. Without any shared assumptions (for example, that cancer is bad, that suffering should be minimized and death delayed), there's no "bottom" to this argument, just an endless regress of reasons based on more reasons. While calling assumptions into question is a legitimate way to deepen and complicate our understanding of an issue, the unwillingness to accept any assumption makes argument impossible.

Our smoking example may be a bit heavy handed, but less obvious variants of this debate happen all the time. Whenever we argue about purely personal opinions—opera is boring, soccer is better than baseball, pizza is tastier than nachos—we're condemned to a bottomless dispute. Because there are no common criteria for "boring" or "better" or "tastier," we can't put our claims to any common test. We can only reassert them.

Of course, reasonable arguments about these disputes become possible once common assumptions are established. For example, a nutritionist could argue that pizza is better than nachos because it provides a better balance of nutrients per calorie. Such an argument can succeed if the disputants accept the nutritionist's assumption that "a better balance of nutrients per calorie" is a criterion for "better." But if one of the disputants responds, "Nah, nachos are better than pizza because nachos taste better," then he makes a different assumption—"My sense of taste is better than your sense of taste." This is a wholly personal standard, an assumption that others are unable to share.

FOR CLASS DISCUSSION

The following questions can all be answered in alternative ways. However, not all of them will lead to reasonable arguments. Try to decide which questions will lead to reasonable arguments and which will lead only to pseudo-arguments.

1. Is Spike Lee a good film director?

2. Is postmodern architecture beautiful?

3. Should cities subsidize professional sports venues?

4. Is this abstract oil painting by a monkey smearing paint on a canvas a true work of art?

5. Are nose rings and tongue studs attractive?

FRAME OF AN ARGUMENT: A CLAIM SUPPORTED BY REASONS

We have said earlier that an argument originates in an *issue question*, which by definition is any question that provokes disagreement about the best answer. When you write an argument, your task is to take a position on the issue and to support it with reasons and evidence. The *claim* of your essay is the position you want your audience to accept. To put it another way, your claim is your essay's thesis statement, a one-sentence summary answer to your issue question. Your task, then, is to make a claim and support it with reasons.

What Is a Reason?

A *reason* (also called a *premise*) is a claim used to support another claim. In speaking or writing, a reason is usually linked to the claim with connecting words such as *because, since, for, so, thus, consequently,* and *therefore,* indicating that the claim follows logically from the reason.

Let's take an example. In one of our recent classes a woman naval ROTC student surprised her classmates by remarking that women should not be allowed to serve on submarines. A heated discussion quickly followed, expanding into the more general issue of whether women should be allowed to join military combat units. Here are frameworks the class developed for two alternative positions on that issue:

One View

CLAIM: Women should be barred from joining military combat units.

REASON 1:   Women for the most part don't have the strength or endurance for combat roles.

REASON 2:   Serving in combat isn't necessary for women's career advancement in the military.

REASON 3:   Women in close-knit combat units would hurt unit morale by introducing sexual jealousies.

REASON 4:   Pregnancy or need to care for infants and small children would make women less reliable to a unit.

REASON 5:   Women haven't been socialized into fighters and wouldn't have the "Kill them with a bayonet!" spirit that men can get.

Alternative View

CLAIM: Women should be allowed to join combat units in the military.

REASON 1:   Millions of women are stronger and more physically fit than most men; women selected for combat duty would have the strength and endurance to do the job.

REASON 2:   The image of women as combat soldiers would help society overcome harmful gender stereotyping.

REASON 3:   Serving in combat units would open up many more opportunities for women's career advancement in the military.

REASON 4:   The justice of equal rights for women demands that women be allowed to serve in combat units.

Formulating a list of reasons in this way breaks your argumentative task into a series of subtasks. It gives you a frame for building your argument in parts. In the previous example, the frame for the argument opposing women in combat suggests five different lines of reasoning a writer might pursue. A writer might use all five reasons or select only two or three, depending on which reasons would most persuade the intended audience. Each line of reasoning would be developed in its own separate section of the argument.

For example, one section of an argument opposing women in combat might open with the following sentence: "Women shouldn't be allowed to join combat units because they don't have the strength or endurance for combat roles." In this section, the writer would describe the levels of strength and endurance currently required for combat service and provide evidence that these requirements would have to be lowered if women were to join combat units. In this section the writer might also need to support the unstated assumption that underlies this reason—that a high level of physical strength and endurance is a necessary criterion for combat effectiveness. (How one articulates and supports the underlying assumptions of an argument will be developed in Chapter 5 in our discussion of warrants and backing.)

The writer would proceed the same way for each separate section of the argument. Each section would open with a clear statement of the reason to be developed. The writer would then support each reason with evidence or chains of other reasons. In addition, if needed for the intended audience, the writer would support any underlying assumptions on which the reason depends.

To summarize our point in this section, the frame of an argument consists of a claim (the thesis statement of the essay), which is supported by one or more reasons, which are in turn supported by evidence or sequences of further reasons.

Advantages of Expressing Reasons in *Because* Clauses

Chances are that when you were a child the word *because* contained magical explanatory powers:

DOROTHY: I want to go home now.

TOMMY: Why?

DOROTHY: Because.

TOMMY: Because why?

DOROTHY: Just because.

Somehow *because* seemed decisive. It persuaded people to accept your view of the world; it changed people's minds. Later, as you got older, you discovered that *because* only introduced your arguments and that it was the reasons following *because* that made the difference. Still, *because* introduced you to the powers potentially residing in the adult world of logic.

Of course, there are many other ways to express the logical connection between a reason and a claim. Our language is rich in ways of stating *because* relationships:

- Women shouldn't be allowed to join combat units because they don't have the strength or endurance for combat roles.
- Women don't have the strength or endurance for combat roles. Therefore women should not be allowed to join combat units.
- Women don't have the strength or endurance for combat roles, so they should not be allowed to join combat units.
- One reason why women should not be allowed to join combat units is that they don't have the strength or endurance for combat roles.
- My argument that women should not be allowed to join combat units is based mainly on evidence that women don't have the strength or endurance for combat roles.

Even though logical relationships can be stated in various ways, writing out one or more *because* clauses seems to be the most succinct and manageable way to clarify an argument for oneself. We therefore suggest that sometime in the writing process you create a *working thesis statement* that summarizes your main reasons as *because* clauses attached to your claim.* Just when you compose your own working thesis statement depends largely on your writing process. Some writers like to plan out their whole argument from the start and often compose their working thesis statements with *because* clauses before they write their rough drafts. Others discover their arguments as they write. And sometimes it is a combination of both. For these writers, an extended working thesis statement is something they might write halfway through the composing process as a way of ordering their argument when various branches seem to be growing out of control. Or they might compose a working thesis statement at the very end as a way of checking the unity of the final product.

Whenever you write your extended thesis statement, the act of doing so can be simultaneously frustrating and thought provoking. Composing *because* clauses can be a powerful discovery tool, causing you to think of many different kinds of arguments to support your claim. But it is often difficult to wrestle your ideas into the *because* clause shape, which sometimes seems to be overly tidy for the complex network of ideas you are trying to work with. Nevertheless, trying to summarize your argument as a single claim with reasons should help you see more clearly what you have to do.

FOR CLASS DISCUSSION

Try this group exercise to help you see how writing *because* clauses can be a discovery procedure. Divide into small groups. Each group member should contribute an issue that he or she might like to explore. Discussing one person's issue at a time, help each member develop a claim supported by several reasons. Express each reason as a *because* clause. Then write out the working thesis statement for each person's argument by attaching the *because* clauses to the claim. Finally, try to create *because* clauses in support of an alternative claim for each issue. Recorders should select two or three working thesis statements from the group to present to the class as a whole.

---

*A working thesis statement for an argument opposing women in combat units might look like this: *Women should not be allowed to join combat units because they lack the strength, endurance, and "fighting spirit" needed in combat; because being pregnant or having small children would make them unreliable for combat at a moment's notice; and because women's presence would hurt morale of tight-knit combat units.* (A working thesis statement for an argument supporting women in combat is found on page 86.)

You might not put a bulky thesis statement like this into your essay itself; rather, a working thesis statement is a behind-the-scenes way of summarizing your argument for yourself so that you can see it whole and clear.

APPLICATION OF THIS CHAPTER'S PRINCIPLES TO YOUR OWN WRITING

In Chapter 2 we discussed the difficulties of summarizing various types of arguments. Generally, an argument is easiest to summarize when the writer places her thesis in the introduction and uses explicit transitions to highlight the argument's reasons and structural frame. Such arguments are said to have a *self-announcing structure* because they announce their thesis (and sometimes supporting reasons) and forecast their shape at the outset. Such self-announcing arguments typically follow the conventional format of classical argument discussed in Chapter 3. The invention strategies set forth in this chapter—generating parallel *because* clauses and nutshelling them in a working thesis statement—lead naturally to a classical argument with a self-announcing structure. Each *because* clause, together with its supporting evidence, becomes a separate section of the argument.

An argument with an *unfolding structure*, in contrast, is considerably harder to summarize. In an unfolding structure, the thesis is delayed until the end or is unstated and left to be inferred by the reader from a narrative that may be both complex and subtle. As we explain in Chapter 8, unfolding structures can be especially effective for dealing with hostile audiences or with troubling or tangled issues. In contrast, classical arguments are often best for neutral or undecided audiences weighing alternative views on a clearcut issue.*

In our own classes, we ask students initially to write arguments with self-announcing structures, thereby forcing them to articulate their arguments clearly to themselves and helping them to master the art of organizing complex ideas. Later on in the course, we invite students to experiment with structures that unfold their meanings in subtler, more flexible ways.

In writing classical arguments, students often ask how much of the argument to summarize in the introduction. Consider the following options. You might announce only your claim:

Women should be allowed to join combat units.

Or you could also forecast a series of parallel reasons:

Women should be allowed to join combat units for several reasons.

Or you could forecast the actual number of reasons:

Women should be allowed to join combat units for four reasons.

---

*Instead of the terms *self-announcing* and *unfolding*, rhetoricians sometimes use the terms *closed form* and *open form*. *Closed-form* structures tell the reader in advance where the argument is headed. In choosing to use a closed form, which forecasts the structure in the introduction, the writer also chooses to follow through with that structure in a straightforward, undeviating way. In contrast, *open-form* structures are like stories or narratives, keeping the reader in suspense about the argument's final destination.

Or you could forecast the whole argument:

> Women should be allowed to join combat units because they are physically capable of doing the job; because the presence of women in combat units would weaken gender stereotypes; because opening combat units to women would expand their military career opportunities; and because it would advance the cause of civil rights.

Those, of course, are not your only options. If you choose to delay your thesis until the end (a typical kind of unfolding argument), you might place the issue question in the introduction without giving away your own position:

> Is the nation well served by allowing women to join combat units?

No formula can tell you how much of your argument to forecast in the introduction. In Chapters 7 and 8 we discuss how forecasting or withholding your thesis affects your *ethos*. We also show how a delayed thesis argument may be a better option for hostile audiences. It is clear at this point, though, that the more you forecast, the clearer your argument is to your reader, whereas the less you forecast, the more surprising your argument will be. The only general rule is this: Readers sometimes feel insulted by too much forecasting. In writing a self-announcing argument, forecast only what is needed for clarity. In short arguments readers often need only your claim. In longer arguments, however, or in especially complex ones, readers appreciate your forecasting the complete structure of the argument (claim with reasons).

APPLICATION OF THIS CHAPTER'S PRINCIPLES TO THE READING OF ARGUMENTS

When you read a complex argument that lacks explicit forecasting, it is often hard to discern its structural core, to identify its claim, and to sort out its reasons and evidence. The more "unfolding" its structure, the harder it is to see exactly how the writer makes his or her case. Moreover, extended arguments often contain digressions and subarguments. Thus there may be dozens of small interlinked arguments going on inside a slowly unfolding main argument.

When you feel yourself getting lost in an unfolding structure, try converting it to a self-announcing structure. (It might help to imagine that the argument's author must state the argument as a claim with *because* clauses. What working thesis statement might the writer construct?) Begin by identifying the writer's claim. Then ask yourself: What are the one, two, three, or four main lines of argument this writer puts forward to support that claim? State those arguments as *because* clauses attached to the claim. Then compare your *because* clauses with your classmates'. You can expect disagreement—indeed, disagreement can enrich your understanding of a text—because the writer has left it to you to infer her intent. You should, however, find considerable overlap in your responses.

Once you have converted the support for the claim to *because* clauses and reached consensus on them, you will find it much easier to analyze the writer's reasoning, underlying assumptions, and use of evidence.

CONCLUSION

This chapter has introduced you to the rhetorical triangle with its key concepts of *logos, ethos,* and *pathos.* It has also shown how arguments originate in issue questions, how issue questions differ from information questions, and how arguments differ from pseudo-arguments. At the heart of this chapter we explained that the frame of an argument is a claim supported by reasons. As you generate reasons to support your own arguments, it is often helpful to articulate them as *because* clauses attached to the claim. Finally, we explained how you can apply the principles of this chapter to your own writing and reading of arguments.

In the next chapter we will see how to support a reason by examining its logical structure, uncovering its unstated assumptions, and planning a strategy of development.

5 The Logical Structure of Arguments

In Chapter 4 you learned that the core of an argument is a claim supported by reasons and that these reasons can often be stated as *because* clauses attached to a claim. In the present chapter we examine the logical structure of arguments in more depth.

AN OVERVIEW OF *LOGOS:* WHAT DO WE MEAN BY THE "LOGICAL STRUCTURE" OF AN ARGUMENT?

As you will recall from our discussion of the rhetorical triangle, *logos* refers to the strength of an argument's support and its internal consistency. *Logos* is the argument's logical structure. But what do we mean by "logical structure"?

First of all, what we *don't* mean by logical structure is the kind of precise certainty you get in a philosophy class in formal logic. Logic classes deal with symbolic assertions that are universal and unchanging, such as "If all *p*s are *q*s and if *r* is a *p*, then *r* is a *q*." This statement is logically certain so long as *p*, *q*, and *r* are pure abstractions. But in the real world, *p*, *q*, and *r* turn into actual things, and the relationships among them suddenly become fuzzy. For example, *p* might be a class of actions called "Sexual Harassment," while *q* could be the class called "Actions That Justify Dismissal from a Job." If *r* is the class "Telling Off-Color Stories," then the logic of our *p–q–r* statement suggests that telling off-color stories (*r*) is an instance of sexual harassment (*p*), which in turn is an action justifying dismissal from one's job (*q*).

Now, most of us would agree that sexual harassment is a serious offense that might well justify dismissal from a job. In turn, we might agree that telling off-color stories, if the jokes are sufficiently raunchy and are inflicted on an unwilling audience, constitutes sexual harassment. But few of us would want to say categorically that all people who tell off-color stories are harassing their listeners and ought to be fired. Most of us would want to know the particulars of the case before making a final judgment.

In the real world, then, it is difficult to say that *rs* are always *ps* or that every instance of a *p* results in *q*. That is why we discourage students from using the word *prove* in claims they write for arguments (as in "This paper will prove that euthanasia is wrong"). Real-world arguments seldom *prove* anything. They can only make a good case for something, a case that is more or less strong, more or less probable. Often the best you can hope for is to strengthen the resolve of those who agree with you or weaken the resistance of those who oppose you. If your audience believes *x* and you are arguing for *y*, you cannot expect your audience suddenly, as the result of your argument, to start believing *y*. If your argument causes an audience to experience a flicker of doubt or an instant of open-mindedness, if you win some small measure of agreement, you've done well. So proofs and dramatic shifts in position are not what real-world arguments are about.

A key difference, then, between formal logic and real-world argument is that real-world arguments are not grounded in abstract, universal statements. Rather, as we shall see, they must be grounded in beliefs, assumptions, or values granted by the audience. A second important difference is that in real-world arguments these beliefs, assumptions, or values are often unstated. So long as writer and audience share the same assumptions, it's fine to leave them unstated. But if these underlying assumptions aren't shared, the writer has a problem.

To illustrate the nature of this problem, consider one of the arguments we introduced in the last chapter.

> Women should be allowed to join combat units because the image of women in combat would help eliminate gender stereotypes.

On the face of it, this is a plausible argument. But the argument is persuasive only if the audience agrees with the writer's assumption that it is a good thing to eliminate gender stereotyping. The writer assumes that gender stereotyping (for example, seeing men as the fighters who are protecting the women and children back home) is harmful and that society would be better off without such fixed gender roles. But what if you believed that some gender roles are biologically based, divinely intended, or otherwise culturally essential and that society should strive to maintain these gender roles rather than dismiss them as "stereotypes"? If such were the case, you might believe as a consequence that our culture should socialize women to be nurturers, not fighters, and that some essential trait of "womanhood" would be at risk if women served in combat. If these were your beliefs, the argument wouldn't work for you because you would reject its underlying assumption. To persuade you with this line of reasoning, the writer would have to show not only how women in combat would help eliminate gender stereotypes but also why these stereotypes are harmful and why society would be better off without them.

The previous core argument ("Women should be allowed to join combat units because the image of women in combat would help eliminate gender stereotypes") is what the Greek philosopher Aristotle would call an enthymeme. An *enthymeme* is an incomplete logical structure that depends, for its completeness, on one or more unstated assumptions (values, beliefs, principles) that serve as the starting point of the argument. The successful arguer, said Aristotle, is the person who knows how to formulate and develop enthymemes so that the argument is rooted in the audience's values and beliefs.

To clarify the concept of "enthymeme," let's go over this same territory again more slowly, examining what we mean by "incomplete logical structure." The sentence "Women should be allowed to join combat units because the image of women in combat would help eliminate gender stereotypes" is an enthymeme. It combines a claim (women should be allowed to join combat units) with a reason expressed as a *because* clause (because the image of women in combat would help eliminate gender stereotypes). To render this enthymeme logically complete, you must supply an unstated assumption—that gender stereotypes are harmful and should be eliminated. If your audience accepts this assumption, then you have a starting place on which to build an effective argument. If your audience doesn't accept this assumption, then you must supply another argument to support it, and so on until you find common ground with your audience.

To sum up:

1. Claims are supported with reasons. You can usually state a reason as a *because* clause attached to a claim (see Chapter 4).

2. A *because* clause attached to a claim is an incomplete logical structure called an enthymeme. To create a complete logical structure from an enthymeme, the unstated assumption (or assumptions) must be articulated.

3. To serve as an effective starting point for the argument, this unstated assumption should be a belief, value, or principle that the audience grants.

Let's illustrate this structure by putting the previous example—plus a new one— into schematic form.

INITIAL ENTHYMEME:	Women should be allowed to join combat units because the image of women in combat would help eliminate gender stereotypes.
CLAIM:	Women should be allowed to join combat units.
STATED REASON:	because the image of women in combat would help eliminate gender stereotypes

UNSTATED ASSUMPTION:	Gender stereotypes are harmful and should be eliminated.
INITIAL ENTHYMEME:	Cocaine and heroin should be legalized because legalization would eliminate the black market in drugs.
CLAIM:	Cocaine and heroin should be legalized.
STATED REASON:	because legalization would eliminate the black market in drugs
UNSTATED ASSUMPTION:	An action that eliminates the black market in drugs is good. (Or, to state the assumption more fully, the benefits to society of eliminating the black market in drugs outweigh the negative effects to society of legalizing drugs.)

FOR CLASS DISCUSSION

Working individually or in small groups, identify the claim, stated reason, and unstated assumption that completes each of the following enthymemic arguments.

EXAMPLE:
Rabbits make good pets because they are gentle.

CLAIM:	Rabbits make good pets.
STATED REASON:	because they are gentle
UNSTATED ASSUMPTION:	Gentle animals make good pets.

1. We shouldn't elect Joe as committee chair because he is too bossy.

2. Buy this stereo system because it has a powerful amplifier.

3. Drugs should not be legalized because legalization would greatly increase the number of drug addicts.

4. Practicing the piano is good for kids because it teaches discipline.

5. Welfare benefits for unwed mothers should be eliminated because doing so will greatly reduce the nation's illegitimacy rate.

6. Welfare benefits for unwed mothers should not be eliminated because these benefits are needed to prevent unbearable poverty among our nation's most helpless citizens.

7. We should strengthen the Endangered Species Act because doing so will preserve genetic diversity on the planet.

8. The Endangered Species Act is too stringent because it severely damages the economy.

9. The doctor should not perform an abortion in this case because the mother's life is not in danger.

10. Abortion should be legal because a woman has the right to control her own body. (This enthymeme has several unstated assumptions behind it; see if you can recreate all the missing premises.)

ADOPTING A LANGUAGE FOR DESCRIBING ARGUMENTS: THE TOULMIN SYSTEM

Understanding a new field usually requires us to learn a new vocabulary. For example, if you were taking biology for the first time, you'd spend days memorizing dozens and dozens of new terms. Luckily, the field of argument requires us to learn a mere handful of new terms. A particularly useful set of argument terms, one we'll be using occasionally throughout the rest of this text, comes from philosopher Stephen Toulmin. In the 1950s, Toulmin rejected the prevailing models of argument based on formal logic in favor of a very audience-based courtroom model.

Toulmin's courtroom model differs from formal logic in that it assumes that (1) all assertions and assumptions are contestable by "opposing counsel" and that (2) all final "verdicts" about the persuasiveness of the opposing arguments will be rendered by a neutral third party, a judge or jury. Keeping in mind the "opposing counsel" forces us to anticipate counterarguments and to question our assumptions. Keeping in mind the judge and jury reminds us to answer opposing arguments fully, without rancor, and to present positive reasons for supporting our case as well as negative reasons for disbelieving the opposing case. Above all else, Toulmin's model reminds us not to construct an argument that appeals only to those who already agree with us. In short, it helps arguers tailor arguments to their audiences.

The system we use for analyzing arguments combines Toulmin's system with Aristotle's concept of the enthymeme. The purpose of this system is to provide writers with an economical language for articulating the structure of argument and, in the process, to help them anticipate their audience's needs. More particularly, it helps writers see enthymemes—in the form of a claim with because clauses—as the core of their argument and the other structural elements from Toulmin as strategies for elaborating and supporting that core.

This system builds on the one you have already been practicing. We simply need to add a few more key terms from Toulmin. The first key term is Toulmin's *warrant*, the name we will now use for the unstated assumption that turns an enthymeme into a complete logical structure. For example:

INITIAL ENTHYMEME:	Women should be allowed to join combat units because the image of women in combat would help eliminate gender stereotypes.
CLAIM:	Women should be allowed to join combat units.
STATED REASON:	because the image of women in combat would help eliminate gender stereotypes
WARRANT:	Gender stereotypes are harmful and should be eliminated.
INITIAL ENTHYMEME:	Cocaine and heroin should be legalized because legalization would eliminate the black market in drugs.
CLAIM:	Cocaine and heroin should be legalized.
STATED REASON:	because legalization would eliminate the black market in drugs
WARRANT:	An action that eliminates the black market in drugs is good.

Toulmin derives his term *warrant* from the concept of "warranty" or "guarantee." The warrant is the value, belief, or principle that the audience has to hold if the soundness of the argument is to be guaranteed or warranted. We sometimes make similar use of this word in ordinary language when we say, "That is an unwarranted conclusion," meaning one has leapt from information about a situation to a conclusion about that situation without any sort of general principle to justify or "warrant" that move. Thus if we claim that cocaine and heroin ought to be legalized because legalization would end the black market, we must be able to cite a general principle or belief that links our prediction that legalization would end the black market to our claim that legalization ought to occur. In this case the warrant is the statement "An action that eliminates the black market for drugs is good." It is this underlying belief that warrants or guarantees the argument. Just as automobile manufacturers must provide warranties for their cars if they want skeptical customers to buy them, we must provide warrants linking our reasons to our claims if we expect skeptical audiences to "buy" our arguments.

But arguments need more than claims, reasons, and warrants. These are simply one-sentence statements—the frame of an argument, not a developed argument. To flesh out our arguments and make them convincing, we need what Toulmin calls *grounds* and *backing*. Grounds are the supporting evidence—facts, data, statistics, testimony, or examples—that cause you to make a claim in the first place or that you produce to justify a claim in response to audience skepticism. Toulmin suggests that grounds are "what you have to go on" in an argument. In short, they are collectively all the evidence you use to support a reason. It sometimes helps to think of grounds as the answer to a "How do you know that . . . ?" question preceding a reason. (How do you know that letting women into combat units would help eliminate gender stereotypes? How do you know that legalizing drugs will end the black market?) Here is how grounds fit into our emerging argument schema.

CLAIM:	Women should be allowed to join combat units.
STATED REASON:	because the image of women in combat would help eliminate gender stereotypes
GROUNDS:	data and evidence showing that a chief stereotype of women is that they are soft and nurturing whereas men are tough and aggressive. The image of women in combat gear packing a rifle, driving a tank, firing a machine gun from a foxhole, or radioing for artillery support would shock people into seeing women not as "soft and nurturing" but as equal to men.

CLAIM:	Cocaine and heroin should be legalized.
STATED REASON:	because legalization would eliminate the black market in drugs
GROUNDS:	data and evidence showing how legalizing cocaine and heroin would eliminate the black market (statistics, data, and examples describing the size and effect of current black market, followed by arguments showing how selling cocaine and heroin legally in state-controlled stores would lower the price and eliminate the need to buy them from drug dealers)

In many cases, successful arguments require just these three components: a claim, a reason, and grounds. If the audience already accepts the unstated assumption behind the reason (the warrant), then the warrant can safely remain in the background unstated and unexamined. But if there is a chance that the audience will question or doubt the warrant, then the writer needs to back it up by providing an argument in its support. *Backing* is the argument that supports the warrant. Backing answers the question "How do you know that . . . ?" or "Why do you believe that . . . ?" prefixed to the warrant. (Why do you believe that gender stereotyping is harmful? Why do you believe that the benefits of ending the black market outweigh the costs of legalizing cocaine and heroin?) Here is how *backing* is added to our schema:

> WARRANT: Gender stereotypes are harmful and should be eliminated.
>
> BACKING: arguments showing how the existing stereotype of soft and nurturing women and tough and aggressive men is harmful to both men and women (examples of how the stereotype keeps men from developing their nurturing sides and women from developing autonomy and power; examples of other benefits that come from eliminating gender stereotypes include more egalitarian society, no limits on what persons can pursue, deeper respect for both sexes)

> WARRANT: An action that eliminates the black market in drugs is good.
>
> BACKING: an argument supporting the warrant by showing why eliminating the black market in drugs is good (statistics and examples about the ill effects of the black market, data on crime and profiteering, evidence that huge profits make drug dealing more attractive than ordinary jobs, the high cost of crime created by the black market, the cost to taxpayers of waging the war against drugs, the high cost of prisons to house incarcerated drug dealers.)

Finally, Toulmin's system asks us to imagine how a resistant audience would try to refute our argument. Specifically, the adversarial audience might challenge our reason and grounds by showing how letting women become combat soldiers wouldn't do much to end gender stereotyping or how legalizing drugs would *not* end the black market. Or the adversary might attack our warrant and backing by showing how some gender stereotypes are worth keeping, or how the negative consequences of legalizing drugs might outweigh the benefit of ending the black market.

In the case of the argument supporting women in combat, an adversary might offer one or more of the following rebuttals:

CONDITIONS OF REBUTTAL

Rebutting the reasons and grounds: Evidence that letting women join combat units wouldn't overcome gender stereotyping (very few women would want to join combat units; those that did would be considered freaks; most girls would still identify with Barbie doll models, not with female infantry)

Rebutting the warrant and backing: Arguments showing that it is important to maintain gender role differences because they are biologically based, divinely inspired, or otherwise important culturally; women should be nurturers and mothers, not fighters; essential nature of "womanhood" sullied by putting women in combat

As this example shows, adversaries can question an argument's reasons and grounds or its warrant and backing or sometimes both. Conditions of rebuttal remind writers to look at their arguments from the perspective of skeptical readers. To help writers imagine how skeptics might see weaknesses in an argument, conditions of rebuttal are often stated as conditionals using the word *unless*, as in, "It is good to overcome gender stereotyping *unless* those stereotypes are biologically based or otherwise essential for society." Conditions of rebuttal name the exceptions to the rule, the circumstances under which your reason or warrant might not hold. Stated in this manner, the conditions of rebuttal for the legalization-of-drugs argument might look like this:

CONDITIONS OF REBUTTAL

Rebutting the reason and grounds: Legalizing cocaine and heroin would eliminate the black market in drugs unless taxes on legal drugs kept the price high enough that a black market would still exist; unless new kinds of illegal designer drugs were developed and sold on the black market.

Rebutting the warrant and backing: Ending the black market is good unless the increased numbers of drug users and addicts were unacceptably high; unless harmful changes in social structure due to acceptance of drugs were too severe; unless the health and economic consequences of increased number of drug users were catastrophic; unless social costs to families and communities associated with addiction or erratic behavior during drug-induced "highs" were too great.

Toulmin's final term, used to limit the force of a claim and indicate the degree of its probable truth, is *qualifier.* The qualifier reminds us that real-world arguments almost never prove a claim. We may say things like "very likely," "probably," or "maybe" to indicate the strength of the claim we are willing to draw from our grounds and warrant. Thus if there are exceptions to your warrant or if your grounds are not very strong, you will have to qualify your claim. For example, you might say, "Except in rare cases, women should not be allowed in combat units," or "With full awareness of the potential dangers, I suggest we consider the option of legalizing drugs as a way of ending the ill effects of the black market."

Although the system just described might at first seem complicated, it is actually fairly easy to use after you've had some opportunity to practice. The following chart will help you review the terms:

ORIGINAL ENTHYMEME: your claim with *because* clause

CLAIM: the point or position you are trying to get your audience to accept

STATED REASON: your *because* clause*; your reasons are the subordinate claims you make in support of your main claim

GROUNDS: the evidence (data, facts, testimony, statistics, examples) supporting your stated reason

WARRANT: the unstated assumption behind your enthymeme, the statement of belief, value, principle, and so on, that, when accepted by an audience, warrants or underwrites your argument

BACKING: evidence or other argumentation supporting the warrant (if the audience already accepts the warrant, then backing is usually not needed, but if the audience doubts the warrant, then backing is essential)

CONDITIONS OF REBUTTAL: your acknowledgment of the limits of your claim—those conditions under which it does not hold true, in anticipation of an adversary's counterargument against your reason and grounds or against your warrant and backing

QUALIFIER: words or phrases limiting the force of your claim

To help you practice using these terms, on pages 98–99 are two more examples, displayed this time so that the conditions of rebuttal are set in an opposing column next to the reason/grounds and the warrant/backing.

---

*Most arguments have more than one *because* clause or reason in support of a claim. Each enthymeme thus develops only one line of reasoning, one piece of your whole argument.

INITIAL ENTHYMEME: Women should be barred from combat duty because the presence of women would harm unit morale.

CLAIM: Women should be barred from combat duty.

STATED REASON: because the presence of women would harm unit morale

GROUNDS: evidence and examples of how presence of women would lead to romantic or sexual relationships and create sexual competition and jealousy; evidence that male bonding is difficult when women are present; fear that a woman wouldn't be strong enough to carry a wounded buddy off a battlefield, etc.; fear that men couldn't endure watching a woman with her legs blown off in a minefield

WARRANT: Combat units need high morale to function effectively.

BACKING: arguments supporting the warrant by showing that combat soldiers have to have an utmost faith in buddies to do their job; anything that disrupts male bonding will make the unit less likely to stick together in extreme danger or endure being prisoners of war; examples of how unit cohesion is what makes a fighting unit able to withstand battle

CONDITIONS OF REBUTTAL:
Rebutting the reason and grounds: arguments that letting women join combat units would *not* harm unit morale (times are changing rapidly; men are used to working professionally with women; examples of successful mixed-gender sports teams and mountain-climbing teams; example of women astronauts working in close quarters with men; arguments that sexual and romantic liaisons would be forbidden and sexual activity punished; after a period of initial discomfort, men and women would overcome modesty about personal hygiene, etc.)

Rebutting the warrant and backing: arguments that unit morale is not as important for combat efficiency as are training and discipline; unit morale is not as important as promoting women's rights; men will have to learn to deal with the presence of women and treat them as fellow soldiers; men can learn to act professionally even if their morale is lower

QUALIFIER: In many cases the presence of women would hurt morale.

ORIGINAL ENTHYMEME: The exclusionary rule is a bad law because it allows drug dealers to escape prosecution.*

CLAIM: The exclusionary rule is a bad law.

STATED REASON: because it allows drug dealers to escape prosecution

GROUNDS: numerous cases wherein the exclusionary rule prevented police from presenting evidence in court; examples of nitpicking rules and regulations that allowed drug dealers to go free; testimony from prosecutors and police about how the exclusionary rule hampers their effectiveness

WARRANT: It is beneficial to our country to prosecute drug dealers.

BACKING: arguments showing the extent and danger of the drug problem; arguments showing that prosecuting and imprisoning drug dealers will reduce the drug problem

CONDITIONS OF REBUTTAL:
Rebuttal of reason and grounds:
evidence that the exclusionary rule does not allow many drug dealers to escape prosecution (counter-evidence showing numerous times when police and prosecutors followed the exclusionary rule and still obtained convictions; statistical analysis showing that the percentage of cases in which exclusionary rule threw evidence out of court is very low)

Rebuttal of warrant and backing:
arguments that reversing the exclusionary rule would have serious costs that outweigh benefits; arguments that softening the exclusionary rule would have serious costs (arguments showing that the value of protecting individual liberties outweighs the value of prosecuting drug dealers)

QUALIFIER: perhaps, tentatively

---

*The exclusionary rule is a court-mandated set of regulations specifying when evidence can and cannot be introduced into a trial. It excludes all evidence that police obtain through irregular means. In actual practice, it demands that police follow strict procedures. Opponents of the exclusionary rule claim that its "narrow technicalities" handcuff police.

FOR CLASS DISCUSSION

Working individually or in small groups, imagine that you have to write arguments developing the ten enthymemes listed in the For Class Discussion exercise on pages 91–92. Use the Toulmin schema to help you determine what you need to consider when developing each enthymeme. As an example, we have applied the Toulmin schema to the first enthymeme.

ORIGINAL ENTHYMEME: We shouldn't elect Joe as committee chair because he is too bossy.

CLAIM: We shouldn't elect Joe as committee chair.

STATED REASON: because he is too bossy

GROUNDS: various examples of Joe's bossiness; testimony about his bossiness from people who have worked with him

WARRANT: Bossy people make bad committee chairs.

BACKING: arguments showing that other things being equal, bossy people tend to bring out the worst rather than the best in those around them; bossy people tend not to ask advice, make bad decisions; etc.

CONDITIONS OF REBUTTAL: *Rebuttal of reason and grounds:* perhaps Joe isn't really bossy (counterevidence of Joe's cooperativeness and kindness; testimony that Joe is easy to work with; etc.)

Rebuttal of the warrant and backing: perhaps bossy people sometimes make good chairpersons (arguments showing that at times a group needs a bossy person who can make decisions and get things done); perhaps Joe has other traits of good leadership that outweigh his bossiness (evidence that, despite his bossiness, Joe has many other good leadership traits such as high energy, intelligence, charisma, etc.)

QUALIFIER: In most circumstances, bossy people make bad committee chairs.

USING TOULMIN'S SCHEMA TO DETERMINE A STRATEGY OF SUPPORT

Having introduced you to Toulmin's terminology for describing the logical structure of arguments, we can turn directly to a discussion of how to use these concepts for developing your own arguments. As we have seen, the claim, supporting reasons, and warrant form the frame for a line of reasoning. The majority of words in an argument, however, are devoted to grounds and backing—the supporting sections that develop the argument frame. Generally these supporting sections take one of two forms: either (1) *evidence* such as facts, examples, case studies, statistics, and testimony from experts or (2) a *sequence of reasons*—that is, further conceptual argument. The Toulmin schema can help you determine what kind of support your argument needs. Let's look at each kind of support separately.

Evidence as Support

It's often easier for writers to use evidence rather than chains of reasons for support because using evidence entails moving from generalizations to specific details—a basic organizational strategy that most writers practice regularly. Consider the following hypothetical case. A student, Ramona, wants to write a complaint letter to the head of the philosophy department about a philosophy professor, Dr. Choplogic, whom Ramona considers incompetent. Ramona plans to develop two different lines of reasoning: (1) Choplogic's courses are disorganized. (2) Choplogic is unconcerned about students. Let's look briefly at how she can develop her first main line of reasoning, which is based on the following enthymeme:

Dr. Choplogic is an ineffective teacher because his courses are disorganized.

The grounds for this argument will be all the evidence Ramona can muster showing that Choplogic's courses are disorganized. Figure 5.1 shows her initial brainstorming notes based on the Toulmin schema. The information Ramona lists under "grounds" is what she sees as the facts of the case—the hard data she will use as evidence to support her reason. Here is how this argument might look when placed into written form:

FIRST PART OF RAMONA'S ARGUMENT

Claim and reason	One reason that Dr. Choplogic is ineffective is that his courses are poorly organized. I have had him for two courses—Introduction to Philosophy and Ethics—and both were disorganized. He never gave us a syllabus or explained his grading system. At the beginning of the course he wouldn't tell us how many papers he would require, and he never seemed to know how much of the textbook material he planned to cover. For Intro he told us to read the whole text, but he covered only half of it in class. A week before the final I asked him how much of the text would be on the exam and he said he hadn't decided. The Ethics class was even more disorganized. Dr. Choplogic told us to read the text, which provided one set of terms for ethical arguments, and then he told us he didn't like the text and presented us in lecture with a wholly different set of terms. The result was a whole class of confused, angry students.
Grounds (evidence in support of reason)	

Claim: Dr. Choplogic is an ineffective teacher.
Stated reason: because his courses are disorganized
Grounds: What evidence is there that his courses are disorganized?
    —no syllabus in either Intro or Ethics
    —never announced how many papers we would have
    —didn't know what would be on tests
    —didn't like the textbook he had chosen; gave us different terms
    —didn't follow any logical sequence in his lectures

FIGURE 5.1   Ramona's initial planning notes

As you can see, Ramona has plenty of evidence to support her contention that Choplogic is disorganized. But how effective is this argument as it stands? Is this all she needs? The Toulmin schema also encourages Ramona to examine the warrant, backing, and conditions of rebuttal for this argument. Figure 5.2 shows how her planning notes continue.

This section of her planning notes helps her see her argument more fully from the audience's perspective. She believes that no one can challenge her reason and grounds—Choplogic is indeed a disorganized teacher. But she recognizes that some people might challenge her warrant ("Disorganized teachers are ineffective"). A supporter of Dr. Choplogic might say that some teachers, even though they are hopelessly disorganized, might nevertheless do an excellent job of stimulating thought and discussion. Moreover, such teachers might possess other valuable traits that outweigh their disorganization. Ramona therefore decides to address these concerns by adding another section to this portion of her argument.

CONTINUATION OF RAMONA'S ARGUMENT

Backing for warrant (shows why disorganization is bad)

Dr. Choplogic's lack of organization makes it difficult for students to take notes, to know what to study, or to relate one part of the course to another. Moreover, students lose confidence in the teacher because he doesn't seem to care enough to prepare for class.

Response to conditions of rebuttal

In Dr. Choplogic's defense, it might be thought that his primary concern is involving students in class discussions or other activities to teach us thinking skills or get us involved in philosophical discussions. But this isn't the case. Students rarely get a chance to speak in class. We just sit there listening to rambling, disorganized lectures.

Claim: Dr. Choplogic is an ineffective
   teacher.
Stated reason: because his
   courses are disorganized
Grounds: What evidence is there
   that his courses are disorganized?
   —no syllabus in either Intro or
      Ethics
   —never announced how many
      papers we would have
   —didn't know what would be on
      tests
   —didn't like the textbook he had
      chosen; gave us different terms
   —didn't follow any logical
      sequence in his lectures
Warrant: Disorganized teachers
   are ineffective.
Backing:
   —organization helps you learn
   —gets material organized in a
      logical way
   —helps you know what to study
   —helps you take notes and relate
      one part of course to another
   —when teacher is disorganized,
      you think he hasn't prepared for
      class; makes you lose confidence

Conditions of rebuttal: Would
   anybody doubt my reasons and
   grounds?
   —No. Every student I have ever
      talked to agrees that these
      are the facts about Choplogic's
      courses. Everyone agrees that
      he is disorganized. Of course,
      the department chair might
      not know this, so I will have
      to provide evidence.
Would anybody doubt my warrant
   and backing? Maybe they would.
   —Is it possible that in some cases
      disorganized teachers are good
      teachers? Have I ever had a
      disorganized teacher who was
      good? My freshman sociology
      teacher was disorganized, but
      she really made you think. You
      never knew where the course was
      going but we had some great
      discussions. Choplogic isn't like
      that. He isn't using classtime to
      get us involved in philosophical
      thinking or discussions.
   —Is it possible that Choplogic
      has other good traits that
      outweigh his disorganization?
      I don't think he does, but I will
      have to make a case for this.

FIGURE 5.2   Ramona's planning notes, continued

   As the marginal notations show, this section of her argument backs the warrant that disorganized teachers are ineffective and anticipates some of the conditions for rebuttal that an audience might raise to defend Dr. Choplogic. Throughout her draft, Ramona has supported her argument with effective use of evidence. The Toulmin schema has shown her that she needed evidence primarily to support her stated reason ("Choplogic is disorganized"). But she also needed some evidence to support her warrant ("Disorganization is bad") and to respond to possible conditions of rebuttal ("Perhaps Choplogic is teaching thinking skills").

In general, the evidence you use for support can come either from your own personal experiences and observations or from reading and research. Although many arguments depend on your skill at research, many can be supported wholly or in part from your own personal experiences, so don't neglect the wealth of evidence from your own life when searching for data. Chapter 6 is devoted to a more detailed discussion of evidence in arguments.

Sequence of Reasons as Support

So far we have been discussing how reasons can be supported with evidence. Often, however, reasons require for their support further conceptual arguing rather than empirical data. Reasons of this kind must be supported with a sequence of other reasons. Consider, for example, a writer proposing a mandatory death penalty for convicted serial killers. Let's assume that this writer, living in a state where the death penalty is legal but seldom used, is angry that a recently convicted serial killer was sentenced to life imprisonment. His claim, along with his main supporting reason, is as follows:

CLAIM:	The law should mandate capital punishment for serial killers.
STATED REASON:	Serial killings belong in a class of their own, that of exceptionally heinous crimes.
WARRANT:	Crimes that are exceptionally heinous deserve a more severe punishment than other crimes.

To make this argument, the writer can use empirical evidence to show that serial killing is heinous (data about the grisliness of the crimes). But the main thrust of the argument requires something more. The writer must show that serial killing is *exceptionally* heinous, an argument requiring a sequence of further reasons. So why should the law single out serial killers for a mandatory death sentence but not other murderers? Since all murders are heinous, what is unique about those committed by serial killers that justifies executing them while letting other murderers get by with lesser sentences? To support his stated reason and gain acceptance for his warrant that a different order of crime deserves a different order of punishment, the writer must establish the peculiarity of serial killings. To distinguish serial killings from other murders, the writer develops the following list of potential reasons:

- Serial killers have murdered more than one person, usually many; the crime is multiple.

- Serial murders are calculated crimes, often requiring extensive planning that goes far beyond the mere "intent" required in first-degree murder cases.

- Serial murders typically involve torture of at least some of the victims in order to satisfy the serial killer's deep need not just to kill but to dominate his victims.

- The repetitious nature of the crime indicates that serial killers cannot be rehabilitated.

- The repetitious nature of the crime also means that the chances of mistakenly executing a defendant, which are minuscule to begin with, are virtually nonexistent with serial killers.

Having developed a list of reasons for singling out serial killers, the writer is ready to draft this part of his argument. Here is a portion of the argument, picking up after the writer has used evidence (in the form of gruesome narratives) to demonstrate the heinous nature of serial murders.

A LINE OF ARGUMENT DEVELOPED WITH A SEQUENCE OF REASONS

These stories show the heinous nature of serial murders. "But aren't all murders heinous?" someone might ask. What makes serial murders exceptionally heinous? Why single these criminals out for a mandatory death sentence while leaving the fate of other murderers to the discretion of judges and juries?

Serial murders represent a different order of crime from other murders and belong in a class of exceptionally heinous crimes. First, serial murderers have killed more than one person, sometimes as many as twenty or thirty. Moreover, these killings are ruthless and brutal. Typically they involve torture of at least some of the victims to satisfy the serial killer's deep need not just to kill but also to humiliate and dominate his victims. Whereas most killers kill for a motive such as greed, jealousy, or momentary rage, the serial killer derives pleasure from killing. Serial killers are particularly frightening because they use their rational intelligence to plot their attack on their next victim. Their crimes are calculated, often involving extensive planning that goes beyond the mere "intent" required for other first-degree murder convictions. The very repetition of this crime indicates that serial killers cannot be rehabilitated. Lastly, when the serial killer is finally caught, he has left behind so many signature marks that it is virtually impossible to execute the wrong person. This frequent objection to capital punishment—that an innocent person may be executed—isn't an issue with serial killers, who differ substantially from other criminals.

As you can tell, this section is considerably more complex than one that simply cites data as evidence in support of a reason. Here the writer must use a sequence of reasons to make his point, showing all the ways that serial killers' crimes belong in a class of their own and thus should be punished differently. Certainly, this argument is not definitive and rests on the cumulative persuasiveness of the reasons themselves, but such an argument is considerably more compelling than simply asserting a claim without elaboration. Although developing a line of argument with a sequence of reasons is harder than using empirical evidence, many arguments will require this kind of support.

CONCLUSION

Chapters 4 and 5 have provided an anatomy of argument. They have shown that the core of an argument is a claim with reasons that usually can be summarized in one or more *because* clauses attached to the claim. Often, it is as important to support the unstated premises in your argument as it is to support the stated ones. In order to plan out an argument strategy, arguers can use the Toulmin schema, which helps writers discover grounds, warrants, and backings for their arguments and to test them through conditions for rebuttal. Finally, we saw how stated reasons and warrants are supported through the use of evidence or through sequences of other reasons. In the next chapter we will look more closely at the uses of evidence in argumentation.

FOR CLASS DISCUSSION

1. Working individually or in small groups, consider ways you could use evidence from personal experience to support the stated reason in each of the following partial arguments:
   a. Another reason to oppose a state sales tax is that it is so annoying.
   b. Professor X should be rated down on his (her) teaching because he (she) doesn't design homework effectively to promote real learning.
   c. Professor X is an outstanding teacher because he (she) generously spends so much time outside of class counseling students with personal problems.

2. Now try to create a sequence-of-reasons argument to support the warrants in each of the partial arguments in exercise 1. The warrants for each of the arguments are stated below.
   a. Support this warrant: We should oppose taxes that are annoying.
   b. Support this warrant: The effective design of homework to promote real learning is an important criterion for rating teachers.
   c. Support this warrant: Time spent counseling students with personal problems is an important criterion for rating teachers.

3. Using Toulmin's conditions of rebuttal, work out a strategy for refuting either the stated reasons or the warrants or both in each of the arguments above.

6 Evidence in Arguments

In the previous chapter, we examined two basic ways to support arguments: through reasons supported by evidence and through reasons supported by a sequence of other reasons. In this chapter we return to a discussion of evidence— how to find, use, and evaluate it. We focus on four categories of evidence: (1) data from personal experience—either from memory or from observation; (2) data from interviews, surveys, and questionnaires; (3) data from reading, especially library research; and (4) numerical or statistical data. At the end of the chapter, we discuss how to evaluate evidence in order to use it fairly, responsibly, and persuasively.

USING EVIDENCE FROM PERSONAL EXPERIENCE

Your own life can be the source of supporting evidence in many arguments. You can draw examples from your own experience or tell your experiences as narratives to illustrate important points. Personal examples and narratives can build bridges to readers who often find personal experience more engaging and immediate than dry lists of facts or statistics. Moreover, when readers sense a writer's personal connection to and investment in an issue, they are more likely to find the writer's position creditable.

Using Personal Experience Data Collected from Memory

Many arguments can be supported extensively, sometimes even exclusively, by information gathered from personal experience or recalled from memory. Here, for example, is how a student used personal experience to help support her argument that foreign language instruction in the United States should be started in elementary school. In the following passage she supports one of her reasons: Young children can learn foreign languages faster than adults.

> We need to start foreign language training early because young children can pick up a language much faster than adults. This truth is exemplified by the experience of several of my family members. In 1993, my uncle was transferred to Switzerland by his employer. A small village named Ruthi in northeastern Switzerland became the new home of my uncle, his wife, and their two young boys, ages six and nine. To add to the difficulty of the move, no one in the family spoke German. Their experience with language acquisition ended up being a textbook case. The youngest child was able to learn German the fastest; the older child also picked it up, but not as quickly. By contrast, my uncle and aunt, who were in their early forties, could not learn the language at all. This same pattern was repeated several years later when they were transferred again, this time to Japan.

The personal examples in this paragraph support the writer's point that foreign language instruction should begin as early as possible in a child's schooling.

Using Personal Experience Data
Collected from Observations

For other arguments you can gather evidence through personal observations, as in the following example:

> The intersection at 5th and Montgomery is particularly dangerous. Traffic volume on Montgomery is so heavy that pedestrians almost never find a comfortable break in the flow of cars. On April 29, I watched fifty-seven pedestrians cross this intersection. Not once did cars stop in both directions before the pedestrian stepped off the sidewalk onto the street. Typically, the pedestrian had to move into the street, start tentatively to cross, and wait until a car finally stopped. On fifteen occasions, pedestrians had to stop halfway across the street, with cars speeding by in both directions, waiting for cars in the far lanes to stop before they could complete their crossing.

USING EVIDENCE FROM INTERVIEWS, SURVEYS, AND QUESTIONNAIRES

In addition to direct observations, you can gather evidence by conducting interviews, taking surveys, or passing out questionnaires.

Conducting Interviews

Interviewing people is a useful way not only to gather expert testimony and important data but also to learn about alternative views. To conduct an effective interview, you must first have a clear sense of purpose: Why are you interviewing the person, and what information is he or she uniquely able to provide? In turn, you need to be professional and courteous.

It's crucial that you write out all questions you intend to ask beforehand, making sure that every question is related to the purpose of your interview. (Of course, be ready to move in unexpected directions if the interview opens up new territory.) Find out as much as possible about the interviewee before the interview. Your knowledge of his or her background will help establish your credibility and build a bridge between you and your source. Be punctual and respectful of your interviewee's time.

In most cases, it is best to present yourself as a listener seeking clarity on an issue rather than as an advocate of a particular position. Except in rare cases, it is a mistake to enter into argument with your interviewee, or to indicate through body language or tone of voice an antagonism toward his or her position. During the interview, play the believing role. Save the doubting role for later, when you are looking over your notes. While conducting the interview, plan either to tape it (in which case you must ask the interviewee's permission) or to take good notes. Immediately after the interview, while your memory is fresh, rewrite your notes more fully and completely.

When you use interview data in your own writing, put quotation marks around any direct quotations. Except when unusual circumstances might require anonymity, identify your source by name and indicate his or her title or credentials—whatever will convince the reader that this person's remarks are to be taken seriously. Here is how one student used interview data to support an argument against carpeting dorm rooms:

> Finally, university-provided carpets will be too expensive. According to Robert Bothell, Assistant Director of Housing Services, the cost will be $300 per room for the carpet and installation. The university would also have to purchase more vacuum cleaners for the students to use. Altogether, Bothell estimated the cost of carpets to be close to $100,000 for the whole campus.

Using Surveys or Questionnaires

Still another form of field research data can come from surveys or questionnaires. Sometimes an informal poll of your classmates can supply evidence persuasive to a reader. One of our students, in an argument supporting public transportation, asked every rider on her bus one morning the following two questions:

> Do you enjoy riding the bus more than commuting by car? If so, why?

She was able to use her data in the following paragraph:

Last week I polled forty-eight people riding the bus between Bellevue and Seattle. Eighty percent said they enjoyed riding the bus more than commuting by car, while 20 percent preferred the car. Those who enjoyed the bus cited the following reasons in this order of preference: It saved them the hassle of driving in traffic; it gave them time to relax and unwind; it was cheaper than paying for gas and parking; it saved them time.

More formal research can be done through developing and distributing questionnaires. Developing a good questionnaire is a task of sufficient complexity that some academic disciplines devote whole courses to the topic. In general, problems with questionnaires arise when the questions are confusing or when response categories don't allow the respondent enough flexibility of choices. If you are writing an argument that depends on an elaborate questionnaire, consider checking out a book from your library on questionnaire design. A simple questionnaire, however, can be designed without formal training. Type it neatly so that it looks clean, uncluttered, and easy to complete. At the head of the questionnaire you should explain its purpose. Your tone should be courteous and, if possible, you should offer the reader some motivation to complete the questionnaire.

INEFFECTIVE EXPLANATION FOR QUESTIONNAIRE

The following questionnaire is very important for my research. I need it back by Tuesday, January 19, so please fill it out as soon as you get it. Thanks. [doesn't explain purpose; reasons for questionnaire are stated in terms of writer's needs, not audience's need]

MORE EFFECTIVE EXPLANATION

This questionnaire is aimed at improving the quality of Dickenson Library for students and staff. It should take no more than three or four minutes of your time and gives you an opportunity to say what you presently like and don't like about the library. Of course, your responses will be kept anonymous. To enable a timely report to the library staff, please return the questionnaire by Tuesday, January 19. Thank you very much. [purpose is clear; respondents see how filling out questionnaire may benefit them]

When you pass out questionnaires, you should seek a random distribution so that any person in your target population has an equal chance of being selected. Surveys lose their persuasiveness if the respondents are unrepresentative of the total population you intended to survey. For example, if your library questionnaire went only to dorm residents, then you wouldn't know how commuting students feel about the library.

USING EVIDENCE FROM READING

Although you can base some arguments on evidence from personal experience or from questionnaires and interviews, most arguments require research evidence gleaned from reading: books, magazines, journals, newspapers, government documents, computerized data banks, Internet sources, chat groups, specialized encyclopedias and almanacs, corporate bulletins, and so forth. How to find such data; how to incorporate it into your own writing through summary, paraphrase, and quotation; and how to cite it and document it are treated in detail in Part Four of this text (Chapters 16 and 17).

When you use research data from reading, it often takes one or more of the following forms: facts and examples, summaries of research studies, and testimony.

Facts and Examples

A common way to incorporate evidence from reading is to cite facts and examples. Here is how one student writer argues that plastic food packaging and Styrofoam cups aren't necessarily damaging to the environment.

> It's politically correct today to scorn plastic food wrapping and Styrofoam cups. But in the long run these containers may actually help the environment. According to environmentalist writer John Tierney, a typical household in countries that don't use plastic food wrapping produces one-third more garbage from food spoilage than do U.S. households. Those plastic wrappers on foods allow us to buy foods in small quantities and keep them sterile until use. Tierney also claims that plastic packaging requires far less energy to produce than does paper or cardboard and is lighter to transport (27). Similarly, he claims that the energy costs of producing a ceramic coffee mug and of washing it after each use make it less environmentally friendly than throwaway Styrofoam cups (44).*

Knowing that experts can disagree about what is a "fact," this writer attributes her evidence to Tierney ("Tierney claims . . . ") rather than stating Tierney's claims baldly as facts and simply citing him in parentheses.

Summaries of Research

An argument can often be supported by summarizing or quoting summary statements from research studies. Here is how a student writer used a summary statement to support his opposition to mandatory helmet laws for motorcycle riders:

---

*Here the writer is using the MLA (Modern Language Association) system for citing sources. The reader would look under "Tierney" in the Works Cited list at the end of the paper for complete bibliographic information. The numbers in parentheses are page numbers in the Tierney article. See Chapter 17.

However, a helmet won't protect against head injury when one is traveling at normal traffic speeds. According to a U.S. Department of Transportation study, "There is no evidence that any helmet thus far, regardless of cost or design, is capable of rejecting impact stress above 13 mph" ("Head Injuries" 8).*

Testimony

Research data can also take the form of *testimony,* an expert's opinion that you cite to help bolster your case. Testimony, which we might call secondhand evidence, is often blended with other kinds of data. Using testimony is particularly common wherever laypersons cannot be expected to be experts. Thus you might cite an authority on the technical feasibility of cold fusion, the effects of alcohol on fetal tissue development, or the causes of a recent airplane crash. Here is how a student writer used testimony to bolster an argument on global warming:

We can't afford to wait any longer before taking action against global warming. At a recent Senate hearing of the Subcommittee on Environmental Pollution, Senator Chafee warned: "There is a very real possibility that man—through ignorance or indifference or both—is irreversibly altering the ability of our atmosphere to [support] life" (qtd. in Begley 64). At this same hearing, Robert Watson of the National Aeronautics and Space Administration (which monitors the upper atmosphere) claimed: "Global warming is inevitable—it's only a question of magnitude and time" (qtd. in Begley 66).**

Here the writer uses no factual or statistical data that indicate that global warming is occurring; rather, she cites the testimony of experts.

USING NUMERICAL DATA AND STATISTICS

Among the most pervasive kinds of evidence in modern arguments are numerical data and statistics. Many of us, however, are understandably mistrustful of numerical data. "There are three kinds of lies," we have all heard: "lies, damned lies, and statistics."

Those who gather, use, and analyze numerical data have their own language for degrees of data manipulation. *Teasing* and *tweaking* data are usually legitimate attempts to portray data in a better light; *massaging* data may involve a bit of subterfuge but is still within acceptable limits. When the line is crossed and ma-

---

*Here the writer cites a government document listed under "Head Injuries" in the Works Cited list. The quotation is from page 8.

**In this passage the quotations come from an article listed under "Begley" in the Works Cited list. The pages, respectively, are 64 and 66. Again the citation system being used is MLA.

nipulation turns into outright, conscious misrepresentation, however, we say the data have been *cooked*—an unsavory fate for data and people alike. If we are to use data responsibly and protect ourselves from others' abuses of them, it's important for us to understand how to analyze them.

In this section, we explain basic forms of graphic representations—tables, line graphs, bar graphs, and pie charts—and then examine ways to use numerical data both responsibly and persuasively.

Representing Numbers in Tables, Graphs, and Charts

One of the simplest means for presenting numerical data to your audience is in a table. Halfway between a picture and a list, a *table* presents numerical data in columns (vertical groupings) and rows (horizontal groupings), thereby allowing us to see relationships relatively quickly.

The table presented as Figure 6.1 is intended to help people perceive how much progress a large southwestern university has made toward diversifying its faculty during a given decade. It offers snapshots of the faculty's ethnic composition in 1984 and again in 1994, followed by a summary of the changes that took place in between.

You read tables in two directions: from the top down and from left to right. The title of the table is usually at the top. In this case, the title "Southwest State University: A historical review of minority students, faculty, and staff" tells us the most general content of the table—the change over time in the ethnic makeup of the university community. Directly below, we encounter the subtitle "Full-Time faculty by tenure status, fall 1984 and fall 1994." This subtitle tells us which of the three components of the university community identified in the title—SSU faculty—is the subject of the table and the principle means—tenure status and time—used to organize the table's contents.

Continuing down the table, in the first row of categories beneath the labels we find a breakdown of the major ethnic groups ("Native American," "Asian American," etc.) composing SSU's faculty. We then move to the top of the far left column, where we find "Tenure Status." There are three variations of tenure status: "Tenured," "On track" ("on track" faculty typically are eligible to become tenured after six years of successful teaching and scholarship at the institution), and "Not on track"—a category that includes adjunct faculty who were hired with no expectation of a long-term contractual commitment from the university.

Immediately below "Tenure Status" we find the data broken down into "1984 Total," "1994 Total," and "10-Year % Change." Reading across each row, we see a series of numbers telling us the number of people in each category and the percentage of the whole that number represents. In this case, the whole is the number in the "Total" column on the right. Thus, in 1984 there were six tenured Native American faculty, representing 0.6 percent of the 937 tenured faculty in the university.

Southwest State University: A historical review of minority students, faculty, and staff

Full-Time faculty by tenure status, fall 1984 and fall 1994

Tenure status	Native American		Asian American		African American		Hispanic		White		Total		Minority	
	No.	%	No.	%	No.	%	No.	%	No.	%	No.	%	No.	%
1984 Total	9	0.6	64	4.2	21	1.4	44	2.9	1,371	90.9	1,509	100.0	138	9.1
Tenured	6	0.6	30	3.2	10	1.1	24	2.6	867	92.5	937	100.0	70	7.5
On track	2	0.7	15	5.5	5	1.8	13	4.7	240	87.3	275	100.0	35	12.7
Not on track	1	0.3	19	6.4	6	2.0	7	2.4	264	88.9	297	100.0	33	11.1
1994 Total	15	0.8	137	7.5	37	2.0	102	5.6	1,533	84.0	1,824	100.0	291	16.0
Tenured	6	0.5	54	4.9	15	1.4	49	4.5	973	88.7	1,097	100.0	124	11.3
On track	8	2.5	32	9.9	11	3.4	39	12.1	232	72.0	322	100.0	90	28.0
Not on track	1	0.2	51	12.6	11	2.7	14	3.5	328	81.0	405	100.0	77	19.0
10-Year % Change	6	66.7	73	114.1	16	76.2	58	131.8	162	11.8	315	20.9	153	110.9
Tenured	0	0.0	24	80.0	5	50.0	25	104.2	106	12.2	160	17.1	54	77.1
On track	6	300.0	17	113.3	6	120.0	26	200.0	−8	−3.3	47	17.1	55	157.1
Not on track	0	0.0	32	168.4	5	83.3	7	100.0	64	24.2	108	36.4	44	133.3

Source: SSU Office of Institutional Analysis.

FIGURE 6.1   A table showing relationships among numerical data

When you read a table, avoid the temptation simply to plunge into all the numbers. After you've read the title and headings to make basic sense of what the table is telling you, try randomly selecting several numbers in the table and saying aloud what those numbers "mean" to be sure you understand what the table is really about.

Line Graphs

At first glance, line graphs seem significantly simpler to read than tables. Sometimes we literally see the significance of a line graph at a glance. A *line graph* achieves this simplicity by converting numerical data into a series of points on an imaginary grid created by horizontal and vertical axes, and then by connecting those points. The resulting line gives us a picture of the relationship between whatever is represented on the horizontal x-axis and whatever is represented on the vertical y-axis. Although they are extremely economical, graphs can't convey the same richness of information that tables can. They are most useful when your focus is on a single relationship.

To illustrate how graphs work, consider Figure 6.2, which contains a graphic representation of a learning curve for assembly-line workers. To determine what this graph is telling you, you must first clarify what's represented on the two axes. In this case, the x-axis represents "Units produced," and the y-axis represents

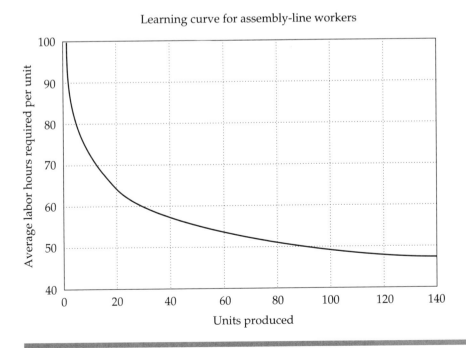

FIGURE 6.2 A line graph depicting a dynamic relationship between two variables

"Average labor hours required." The first point on the *x*-axis indicates that the number of hours a worker requires to produce the first unit is 100. By the time a worker gets to the 20th unit, however, the number of hours required is down to 63. By the 140th unit, production time is down to only 48 hours.

So what does this graph tell us? How would we generally characterize the nature of the relationship between the variables on the *x*-axis and the *y*-axis? Generally, we could say that they are "inversely related": As the number of units produced gets larger, the average number of hours required per unit gets smaller. That general description will hold for all line graphs that look like this one, sloping downward from left to right.

In simple English, we might translate this relationship to something like the following: "As you produce more units of anything, you learn how to produce those units more efficiently and thus spend less time producing each one." But note that the line's slope (its angle of ascent or descent) flattens out as it moves to the right, suggesting that over time the *rate* at which efficiency improves slows down. In the language of data analysis, the flattened slope indicates that changes in the *y*-axis variable are less and less "sensitive" to changes in the *x*-axis variable. At some point, presumably, you would see no further increases in efficiency, and the learning curve would be perfectly parallel to the *x*-axis, meaning that the *y*-variable is no longer sensitive to the *x*-variable.

Bar Graphs

Bar graphs use bars of varying length and width, extending either horizontally or vertically, to contrast two or more quantities. As with any graphic presentation, you should read from the top down, being especially careful to note the graph's title. Most bar graphs also have *legends,* or explanations of how to read the graph. Bars are typically shaded in various hues, crosshatched, left clear, or filled in with slanting lines, to differentiate among the quantities or items being compared. The legend identifies what quantity or item each bar represents.

The bar graph in Figure 6.3 is from the national newspaper, *USA Today,* well known for its extensive use of graphics as a means of simplifying complex concepts for a broad audience. The title tells us that the purpose of the graph is to illustrate "How Congress could solve the deficit problem in seven years by holding spending to the projected 3% inflation rate" instead of spending at the rate projected by the Congressional Budget Office (CBO). The legend, in turn, shows us which quantity each of the bars in the graph represents: The lightest bar represents revenues, the darkest bar represents the CBO's projected spending, and the medium-colored bar represents spending at the 3 percent inflation rate.

Reading across the *x*-axis, we find the *independent variable,* time—in this case a year-by-year comparison of the three quantities from 1995 to 2002. On the *y*-axis, we find the *dependent variable,* dollars received and expended. As we move from left to right, the revenue bar and the 3 percent growth bar gradually inch closer together, until by 2002 they are exactly equal, meaning that revenue and spending would be balanced. The black middle bar, the CBO's estimated spending, inches

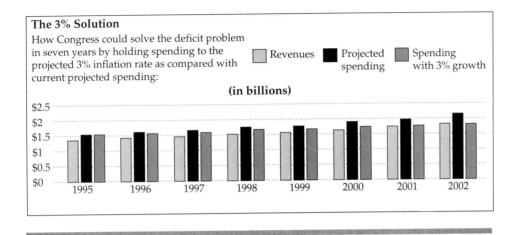

FIGURE 6.3   A bar graph that simplifies a complex concept

Source: Congressional Budget Office.

past the other two bars until finally it represents a significant imbalance between revenue and spending.

The power of this visual is that it takes a particularly dodgy set of figures and gives them the certitude of an accomplished fact. National revenue and spending figures are notoriously difficult to project. Both can be markedly affected by a number of economic factors over which we have very limited control. And the further out we make those projections, the more problematic they become. Seven years, in the world of macroeconomics, is an extraordinarily long time to project into the future. But cast into a series of bars, each one only slightly different from the previous one, the change seems not only plausible but almost inevitable. Hey, that 3 percent solution is a great idea!

Pie Charts

Pie charts, as the name suggests, depict different percentages of a total (the pie) in the form of slices. At tax time, pie charts are a favorite way of depicting all the different places that your tax dollars go. If your main point is to demonstrate that a particular portion of a whole is disproportionately large—perhaps you're arguing that too many of our tax dollars are spent on Medicaid or defense—the pie chart can demonstrate that at a glance. (Conversely, of course, it can also demonstrate that some other part of the whole is undersized relative to other shares.) The effectiveness of pie charts diminishes as we add too many slices. In most cases, you'll begin to confuse readers if you include more than five or six.

Figure 6.4 shows a pie chart from *USA Today* that, in combination with a line graph, effectively illustrates the size of three parts relative to one another. Note how the editors of *USA Today* chose to use a line graph to plot the growth in

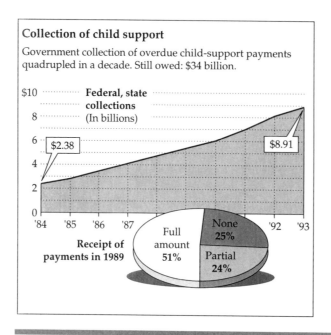

Collection of child support

Government collection of overdue child-support payments quadrupled in a decade. Still owed: $34 billion.

FIGURE 6.4   Pie chart showing relative sizes of three parts

Source: Office of Child Support Enforcement; Census Bureau. By Cliff Vancura, *USA Today.*

collections of child-support payments from 1984 to 1993. The impressive upward slope of the line nicely underscores the editors' point that child-support collections nearly quadrupled during that time period. They use a line graph to do what line graphs do best—illustrate change over time for a given dependent variable. But when they wanted to depict a static relationship, the editors naturally chose a pie chart to show that a great deal of support is still owed: In 1989, only 51 percent of children granted child support in a divorce settlement received their full amount, while 25 percent received nothing. (In place of a legend, the editors simply identify what each slice of the pie represents within the graph itself.)

Using Graphics for Effect

Any time we present numerical data pictorially, the potential for enhancing the rhetorical presence of our argument, or of manipulating our audience outright, increases substantially. By *presence*, we mean the immediacy and impact of our material. For example, raw numbers and statistics, in large doses, are likely to dull people's minds and perplex an audience. But numbers turned into pictures are very immediate. Graphs, charts, and tables help an audience see at a glance what long strings of statistics can only hint at.

We can have markedly different effects on our audience according to how we design and construct a graphic. For example, by coloring one variable prominently and enlarging it slightly, a graphic artist can greatly distort the importance of that variable. Although such depictions may carry warnings that they are "not to scale," the visual impact is often more memorable than the warning.

One of the subtlest ways of controlling an audience's perception of a numerical relationship is the way you assign values to the horizontal *x*-axis and vertical *y*-axis of a line graph. Consider, for example, the graph in Figure 6.5 depicting the monthly net profits of an ice-cream sandwich retailer. When you look at this graph, you may think that Bite O' Heaven's net profits are shooting heavenward. But if you were considering investing in an ice-cream sandwich franchise, you would want to consider how the graph was constructed. One can easily distort or overstate a rate of change on a graph.

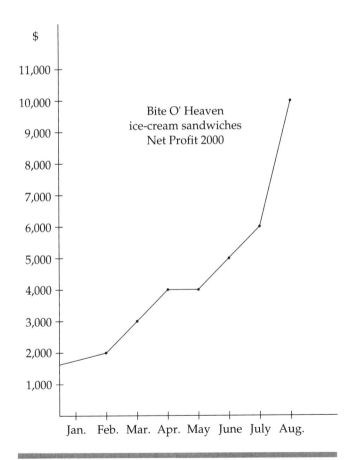

FIGURE 6.5   A line graph that distorts the data

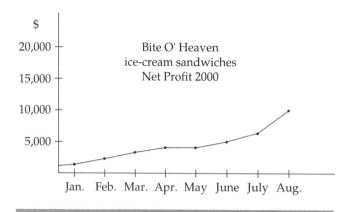

FIGURE 6.6   A line graph that more accurately depicts data

Although Figure 6.5 does represent the correct quantities, the designer's choice of increments on the *x*-axis leads to a wildly exaggerated depiction of success. If the Bite O' Heaven folks had chosen a larger increment—say, $5,000 instead of $1,000—the company's rise in profitability would look like the graph in Figure 6.6.

Another way to create a rhetorical effect with a line graph is to vary the scope of time it covers. Note that Figures 6.5 and 6.6 cover net sales from January through August. What do you think the sales figures for this company might typically be from September through December?

FOR CLASS DISCUSSION

In small groups, create a line graph for Bite O' Heaven's net profits for a whole year based on your best estimates of when people are most likely to buy ice-cream sandwiches. Then draw graphs showing net profits, quarter by quarter, over a three-year period to represent the following conditions:

1. Bite O' Heaven maintains a stable market share with no increase or decrease in the rate of profits over the three years.

2. Bite O' Heaven increases its market share, and each year is more profitable than the preceding one.

3. Bite O' Heaven loses market share, and each year is leaner than the previous one.

Using Numbers Strategically

As we have suggested, your choice and design of a graphic can markedly affect your audience's perception of your subject. But you can also influence your audience through the kinds of numbers you use: raw numbers versus percentages; or raw numbers versus "adjusted" numbers (for example, wages "adjusted for inflation"); or a statistical presentation versus a narrative one. The choice always depends on the audience you're addressing and the purpose you want to achieve.

One of the most common choices writers have to make is between citing raw numbers or citing percentages or rates. In some cases, a raw number will be more persuasive than a percentage. If you were to say that the cost of attending a state college will increase at a rate 15 percent greater than the Consumer Price Index over the next decade, most audiences would be lost—few would know how to translate that number into terms they could understand. But if you were to say that in the year 2007 the cost of attending a state college for one year will be about $21,000, you would surely grab your audience's attention. So, if you were a financial planner trying to talk a young couple into saving money for their children's college education, you would be inclined to use the raw number rather than the percentage increase. But if you were a college administrator trying to play down the increasing costs of college to a hostile legislator, you might well use the percentage increase rather than the raw number.

In turn, how you state raw numbers can markedly increase or decrease their impact on an audience. For example, to say that newspapers consume huge amounts of wood pulp is mildly interesting. To say that publication of the *New York Times* requires 248 million tons of pulp each year is even more impressive. To say that publication of just one Sunday edition of the *New York Times* requires the cutting of 75,000 trees is mind-boggling. Again, translate the number into what is most meaningful to your audience and the impact you wish to have on that audience.

Finally, in using numbers you often have a choice of presenting *indexed* or *adjusted* numbers as opposed to simple raw numbers. In the case of economic data, this difference can be particularly important. For example, in the 1996 presidential debates, Republican supporters suggested that President Clinton had signed the "largest tax increase in history" into law. Clinton supporters retorted that if adjustments were made for inflation, the tax increase was in fact smaller than one signed into law by Republican President Bush. Because of the extremely high rates of inflation during the 1980s, any economic data from that decade or prior to it should be adjusted for inflation in making comparisons to present-day dollar values.

FOR CLASS DISCUSSION

A proposal to build a new ballpark in Seattle, Washington, yielded a wide range of statistical arguments. All of the following statements are reasonably faithful to the same facts:

- The ballpark would be paid for by raising the sales tax from 8.2 percent to 8.3 percent over a twenty-year period.

- The sales tax increase is one-tenth of 1 percent.

- This increase represents an average of $7.50 per person per year—about the price of a movie ticket.

- This increase represents $750 per five-person family over the twenty-year period of the tax.

- For a family building a new home in the Seattle area, this tax will increase building costs by $200.

- This is a $250 million tax increase for the residents of the Seattle area.

How would you describe the costs of the proposed ballpark if you opposed the proposal? How would you describe the costs if you supported the proposal?

WRITING YOUR OWN ARGUMENT: USING EVIDENCE PERSUASIVELY

Once you have arrived at a position on an issue, often after having written a draft that enables you to explore and clarify your own views, you need to select the best evidence possible and to use it persuasively. Whether your evidence comes from research or from personal experience, the following guidelines may be helpful.

When Possible, Select Your Data from Sources Your Reader Trusts

Other things being equal, choose data from sources you think your reader will trust. After immersing yourself in an issue, you will get a sense of who the participants in a conversation are and what their reputations tend to be. One needs to know the political biases of sources and the extent to which a source has a financial or personal investment in the outcome of a controversy. When the global-warming controversy first struck the national consciousness, two prolific writers on the subject were Carl Sagan and Dixie Lee Ray. Both writers held Ph.D. degrees in science, and both had national reputations for speaking out in the popular press on technical and scientific issues. Carl Sagan, however, was an environmentalist, and Dixie Lee Ray tended to support business and industry. To some audiences, neither of these writers was as persuasive as more cautious and less visible scientists who publish primarily in scientific journals. Similarly, citing a conservative magazine such as *Reader's Digest* is likely to be ineffective to liberal audiences, just as citing a Sierra Club publication would be ineffective to conservatives.

Increase Persuasiveness of Factual Data by Ensuring Recency, Representativeness, and Sufficiency

Other things being equal, choose data that are recent, representative, and sufficient. The more your data meet these criteria, the more persuasive they are.

Recency: Although some timeless issues don't depend on recent evidence, most issues, especially those related to science and technology or to current political and economic issues, depend on up-to-date information. Make sure your supporting evidence is the most recent you can find.

Representativeness: Supporting examples are more persuasive when the audience believes they are typical examples instead of extreme cases or rare occurrences. Ensuring representativeness is an especially important concern of statisticians, who seek random samples to avoid bias toward one point of view. Seeking representative examples helps you guard against selective use of data—starting with a claim and then choosing only those data that support it, instead of letting the claim grow out of a careful consideration of all the data.

Sufficiency: One of the most common reasoning fallacies, called *hasty generalization* (see pp. 441–42), occurs when a person leaps to a sweeping generalization based on only one or two instances. The criterion of sufficiency (which means having enough examples to justify your point) helps you guard against hasty generalization.

In Citing Evidence, Distinguish Fact from Inference or Opinion

In citing research data, you should be careful to distinguish facts from inferences or opinions. A *fact* is a noncontroversial piece of data that is verifiable through observation or through appeal to communally accepted authorities. Although the distinction between a fact and an inference is a fuzzy one philosophically, at a pragmatic level all of the following can loosely be classified as facts:

The Declaration of Independence was signed in 1776.

An earthquake took place in San Francisco on the opening day of the World Series in 1989.

The amount of carbon dioxide in the atmosphere has increased by 7 percent since 1955.

An *inference,* in contrast, is an interpretation or explanation of the facts that may be reasonably doubted. This distinction is important because, when reading as a doubter, you often call into question a writer's inferences. If you treat these inferences as facts, you are likely to cite them as facts in your own arguments, thereby opening yourself up to easy rebuttal. For the most part, inferences should be handled as testimony rather than as fact.

> **WEAK:**   Flohn informs us that the warming of the atmosphere will lead to damaging droughts by the year 2035. [treats Flohn's inference as a fact about global warming]
>
> **BETTER:**   Flohn interprets the data pessimistically. He believes that the warming of the atmosphere will lead to damaging droughts by the year 2035. [makes it clear that Flohn's view is an inference, not a fact]

FOR CLASS DISCUSSION

Suppose that you developed a questionnaire to ascertain students' satisfaction with your college library as a place to study. Suppose further that you got the following responses to one of your questions (numbers in parentheses indicate percentage of total respondents who checked each response):

The library provides a quiet place to study.

Strongly agree (10%)

Agree (40%)

Undecided (5%)

Disagree (35%)

Strongly disagree (10%)

Without distorting any facts, you can report these data so that they place the current library atmosphere in either favorable or unfavorable light. Working individually or in small groups, use the data provided to complete the following sentences:

There seemed to be considerable satisfaction with the library as a quiet place to study. In response to our questionnaire . . . [complete this sentence by selecting data from the above responses].

Students seem dissatisfied with the noise level of the library. In response to our questionnaire . . . [complete this sentence by selecting data from the above responses].

CONCLUSION

Good arguers use evidence effectively. As we have seen, evidence includes facts, examples, statistics, testimony, and other forms of data, and it can come from personal experience as well as from reading and research. It is important to select data from sources that your reader will trust, to ensure the recency, representativeness, and sufficiency of your evidence, and to distinguish between facts and inferences.

WRITING ASSIGNMENTS
FOR CHAPTERS 4–6

OPTION 1: *A Microtheme That Supports a Reason with Personal Experience Data* Write a one- or two-paragraph argument in which you support one of the following enthymemes, using evidence from personal experience. Most of your microtheme should support the stated reason with personal experience data. However, also include a brief passage supporting the implied warrant. The opening sentence of your microtheme should be the enthymeme itself, which serves as the thesis statement for your argument.

1. Reading fashion magazines can be detrimental to teenage girls because such magazines can lower a girl's self-esteem.

2. Learning to surf the Web might harm your studying because it causes you to waste time.

3. Getting a part-time job in college might improve your grades because the job will teach you time management.

4. X (a teacher/professor of your choosing) is an outstanding teacher because she (he) generously spends time counseling students with personal problems.

5. Any enthymeme (a claim with *because* clause) of your choice that can be supported through personal experience. Clear your enthymeme with your instructor.

OPTION 2: *A Microtheme That Uses Evidence from Research*   The purpose of this microtheme is to help you learn how to support reasons with evidence gathered from research. The following presentation of data attempts to simulate the kinds of research evidence one might typically gather on note cards during a research project. (See Chapters 16 and 17 for further advice on incorporating research data into your own writing. For this assignment, assume you are writing for a popular magazine so that you do not need to use academic citations.)
   The situation: By means of startling "before and after" photographs of formerly obese people, the commercial diet industry heavily advertises rapid weight loss diets that use liquids and powders or special low-calorie frozen dinners. **Your**

task: Drawing on the following data, write a short argument warning people of the hazards of these diets.

Source: Representative Ron Wyden (D–Oregon), chairman of a congressional sub-committee investigating the diet industry.

- Wyden fears that diet programs now include many shoddy companies that use misleading advertisements and provide inadequate medical supervision of their clients.
- "This industry has been built almost overnight on a very shaky foundation."
- "All the evidence says that losing large amounts of weight very fast does more harm than good."
- Wyden believes that the diet industry may need to be federally regulated.

Source: Theodore B. VanItallie, M.D., a founder of the Obesity Research Center at St. Luke's Roosevelt Hospital Center in New York.

- Rapid weight loss systems (such as liquid diets) were originally designed for morbidly obese individuals.
- For people who are only slightly overweight, rapid weight loss can be hazardous.
- When weight loss is too rapid, the body begins using lean muscle mass for fuel instead of excess fat. The result is a serious protein deficiency that can bring on heart irregularities.
- "If more than 25 percent of lost weight is lean body mass, the stage is set not only for early regain of lost weight but for a higher incidence of fatigue, hair loss, skin changes, depression and other undesirable side effects."

Source: Bonnie Blodgett, freelance writer on medical/health issues.

- Rapid weight loss may accelerate formation of gallstones. 179 people are currently suing a major diet company because of gallstone complications while pursuing the company's diet. The company denies responsibility.
- For every five people who start a commercial weight-loss program, only one stays with it long enough to lose a significant amount of weight.
- Up to 90 percent of dieters who lose more than 25 pounds gain it all back within two years.
- Only one in fifty maintains the weight loss for seven years.
- The best way to lose weight is through increased exercise, moderate reduction of calories, and a lifelong change in eating habits.

- Unless one is grossly obese and dieting under a physician's supervision, one should strive to lose no more than 1 or 2 pounds per week.

Source: Philip Kern, M.D., in a study appearing in *The New England Journal of Medicine.*

- Rapid weight loss programs result in the "yo-yo" syndrome—a pattern of compulsive fasting followed by compulsive bingeing.
- This pattern may upset the body's metabolism by producing an enzyme called lipoprotein lipase.
- This protein helps restore fat cells shrunken by dieting.
- It apparently causes formerly fat people to crave fatty foods, thereby promoting regain of lost weight.*

OPTION 3: *A Microtheme That Uses Statistical Data to Support a Point*   Defend one of the following theses:

Thesis A—"Women (blacks) made only negligible progress toward job equality between 1972 and 1981."

Thesis B—"Women (blacks) made significant progress toward job equality between 1972 and 1981."

Support your thesis with evidence drawn from the table on page 128. You can write your microtheme about the job progress of either women or blacks.

OPTION 4: *A Classical Argument*   Write a classical argument that uses at least two reasons to support your claim. Classical argument is explained in detail in Chapter 3. As we explain further in Chapter 8, classical argument is particularly effective when you are addressing neutral or undecided audiences. It has a self-announcing or closed-form structure in which you state your claim at the end of the introduction, begin body paragraphs with clearly stated reasons, and use effective transitions throughout to keep your reader on track. In developing your own argument, place your most important reason last, where it will have the greatest impact on your readers. Typically, a classical argument also summarizes anticipated objections to the writer's argument and responds to them briefly. You can place this section either before or after you develop your main argument. (Chapter 8, pages 156–65, gives a detailed explanation of how to respond to objections and alternative views.) See page 64 for a diagram of a classical argument.

The student essay on pages 129–31 illustrates a classical argument.

---

*Source of these data is Bonnie Blodgett, "The Diet Biz," *Glamour* Jan. 1991: 136ff.

TABLE FOR OPTION 3   Employed persons, by sex, race, and occupation, 1972 and 1981

Occupation	1972 Total Employed (1,000)	Percentage Female	Percentage Black and Other	1981 Total Employed (1,000)	Percentage Female	Percentage Black and Other
Professional, Technical	11,538	39.3	7.2	16,420	44.6	9.9
Accountants	720	21.7	4.3	1,126	38.5	9.9
Dentists	108	1.9	5.6	130	4.6	6.2
Engineers	1,111	0.8	3.4	1,537	4.4	7.3
Lawyers	322	3.8	1.9	581	14.1	4.6
Librarians	158	81.6	7.0	192	82.8	5.7
Physicians	332	10.1	8.2	454	13.7	14.5
Registered nurses	807	97.6	8.2	1,654	96.8	12.3
College teachers	464	28.0	9.2	585	35.2	9.2
Administrators	8,081	17.6	4.0	11,540	27.5	5.8
Bank officers	430	19.0	2.6	696	37.5	5.5
Office managers	317	41.9	1.0	504	70.6	4.0
Sales managers	574	15.7	1.6	720	26.5	4.6
Clerical Workers	14,329	75.6	8.7	18,564	80.5	11.6
Bank tellers	290	87.5	4.9	569	93.5	7.6
File clerks	274	84.9	18.0	315	83.8	22.9
Secretaries	2,964	99.1	5.2	3,917	99.1	7.2
Skilled Crafts	10,867	3.6	6.9	12,662	6.3	8.5
Carpenters	1,052	0.5	5.9	1,122	1.9	5.8
Construction	2,261	0.6	9.0	2,593	1.9	10.2
Mechanics	1,040	0.5	8.5	1,249	0.6	8.7
Transportation	3,233	4.2	14.8	3,476	8.9	15.5
Bus drivers	253	34.1	17.1	360	47.2	21.1
Truck drivers	1,449	0.6	14.4	1,878	2.7	13.9
Unskilled Labor	4,242	6.0	20.2	4,583	11.5	16.5
Service Workers	9,584	57.0	18.5	12,391	59.2	18.4
Food service	3,286	69.8	13.9	4,682	66.2	14.0
Nurses' aides	1,513	87.0	24.6	1,995	89.2	24.3
Domestic cleaners	715	97.2	64.2	468	95.1	51.5

"Half-Criminals" or Urban Athletes?
A Plea for Fair Treatment of Skateboarders
David Langley (Student)

For skateboarders, the campus of the University of California at San Diego is a wide-open, huge, geometric, obstacle-filled, stair-scattered cement paradise. The signs posted all over campus read, "No skateboarding, biking, or rollerblading on campus except on Saturday, Sunday, and Holidays." I have always respected these signs at my local skateboarding spot. On the first day of 1999, I was skateboarding here with my hometown skate buddies and had just landed a trick when a police officer rushed out from behind a pillar, grabbed me, and yanked me off my board. Because I didn't have my I.D. (I had emptied my pockets so I wouldn't bruise my legs if I fell—a little trick of the trade), the officer started treating me like a criminal. She told me to spread my legs and put my hands on my head. She frisked me and then called in my name to police headquarters. 1

"What's the deal?" I asked. "The sign said skateboarding was legal on holidays." 2

"The sign means that you can only *roll* on campus," she said. 3

But that's *not* what the sign said. The police officer gave one friend and me a warning. Our third friend received a fifty-dollar ticket because it was his second citation in the last twelve months. 4

Like other skateboarders throughout cities, we have been bombarded with unfair treatment. We have been forced out of known skate spots in the city by storeowners and police, kicked out of every parking garage in downtown, compelled to skate at strange times of day and night, and herded into crowded skateboard parks. However, after I was searched by the police and detained for over twenty minutes in my own skating sanctuary, the unreasonableness of the treatment of skateboarders struck me. Where are skateboarders supposed to go? Cities need to change their unfair treatment of skateboarders because skateboarders are not antisocial misfits as popularly believed, because the laws regulating skateboarding are ambiguous, and because skateboarders are not given enough legitimate space to practice their sport. 5

Possibly because to the average eye most skateboarders look like misfits or delinquents, adults think of us as criminal types and associate our skateboards with antisocial behavior. But this view is unfair. City dwellers should recognize that skateboards are a natural reaction to the urban environment. If people are surrounded by cement, they are going to figure out a way to ride it. People's different environments have always produced transportation and sports to suit the conditions: bikes, cars, skis, ice skates, boats, canoes, surfboards. If we live on snow, we are going to develop skis or snowshoes to move around. If we live in an environment that has flat panels of cement for ground with lots of curbs and stairs, we are going to invent an ingeniously designed flat board with wheels. Skateboards are as natural to cement as surfboards are to water or skis to snow. Moreover, the resulting sport is as healthful, graceful, and athletic. A fair assessment of skateboarders should respect our elegant, nonpolluting means of transportation and sport, and not consider us hoodlums. 6

7   A second way that skateboarders are treated unfairly is that the laws that regulate skateboarding in public places are highly restrictive, ambiguous, and open to abusive application by police officers. My being frisked on the UCSD campus is just one example. When I moved to Seattle to go to college, I found the laws in Washington to be equally unclear. When a sign says "No Skateboarding," that generally means you will get ticketed if you are caught skateboarding in the area. But most areas aren't posted. The general rule then is that you can skateboard so long as you do so safely without being reckless. But the definition of "reckless" is up to the whim of the police officer. I visited the front desk of the Seattle East Precinct and asked them exactly what the laws against reckless skateboarding meant. They said that skaters are allowed on the sidewalk as long as they travel at reasonable speed and the sidewalks aren't crowded. One of the officers explained that if he saw a skater sliding down a handrail with people all around, he would definitely arrest the skater. What if there were no people around, I asked? The officer admitted that he might arrest the lone skater anyway and not be questioned by his superiors. No wonder skateboarders feel unfairly treated.

8   One way that cities have tried to treat skateboarders fairly is to build skateboard parks. Unfortunately, for the most part these parks are no solution at all. Most parks were designed by nonskaters who don't understand the momentum or gravity pull associated with the movement of skateboards. For example, City Skate, a park below the Space Needle in Seattle, is very appealing to the eye, but once you start to ride it you realize that the transitions and the verticals are all off, making it unpleasant and even dangerous to skate there. The Skate Park in Issaquah, Washington, hosts about thirty to fifty skaters at a time. Collisions are frequent and close calls, many. There are simply too many people in a small area. The people who built the park in Redmond, Washington, decided to make a huge wall in it for graffiti artists "to tag on" legally. They apparently thought they ought to throw all us teenage "half criminals" in together. At this park, young teens are nervous about skating near a gangster "throwing up his piece," and skaters become dizzy as they take deep breaths from their workouts right next to four or five cans of spray paint expelling toxins in the air.

9   Of course, many adults probably don't think skateboarders deserve to be treated fairly. I have heard the arguments against skateboarders for years from parents, storeowners, friends, police officers, and security guards. For one thing, skateboarding tears up public and private property, people say. I can't deny that skating leaves marks on handrails and benches, and it does chip cement and granite. But in general skateboarders help the environment more than they hurt it. Skateboarding places are not littered or tagged up by skaters. Because skaters need smooth surfaces and because any small object of litter can lead to painful accidents, skaters actually keep the environment cleaner than the average citizen does. As for the population as a whole, skateboarders are keeping the air a lot cleaner than many other commuters and athletes such as boat drivers, car drivers, and skiers on ski lifts. In the bigger picture, infrequent repair of curbs and benches is cheaper than attempts to heal the ozone.

10   We skateboarders aren't going away, so cities are going to have to make room for us somewhere. Here is how cities can treat us fairly. We should be allowed to skate when others are present as long as we skate safely on the sidewalks. The rules and laws should be clearer so that skaters don't get put into vulnerable positions that make them easy targets

for tickets. I do support the opening of skate parks, but cities need to build more of them, need to situate them closer to where skateboarders live, and need to make them relatively wholesome environments. They should also be designed by skateboarders so that they are skater-friendly and safe to ride. Instead of being treated as "half criminals," skaters should be accepted as urban citizens and admired as athletes; we are a clean population, and we are executing a challenging and graceful sport. As human beings grow, we go from crawling to walking; some of us grow from strollers to skateboards.

7 Moving Your Audience

Audience-Based Reasons, *Ethos,* and *Pathos*

In Chapters 5 and 6 we discussed *logos*—the logical structure of reasons and evidence in an argument. When writers focus on *logos,* they are often trying to clarify their own thinking as much as to persuade. In this chapter and the next, we shift our attention increasingly toward persuasion, in which our goal is to move our audience as much as possible toward our own position on an issue. In this chapter we examine strategies for connecting our argument to our audience's values and beliefs (audience-based reasons), for ensuring that we are credible and trustworthy in their eyes (*ethos*), and for ensuring that our presentation affects their sympathies (*pathos*). In Chapter 8 we explain strategies for varying the tone and structure of an argument to accommodate different kinds of audiences.

Although all these strategies could be misused—that is, they could be exploited to manipulate or mislead an audience—our discussion of them presupposes a responsible arguer whose position is based on a reasoned investigation of evidence and a sincere commitment to consistent values and beliefs that can be articulated. When these strategies are employed responsibly, they can help you create arguments that are not only rationally sound but also effective for a given audience.

STARTING FROM YOUR READERS' BELIEFS: THE POWER OF AUDIENCE-BASED REASONS

Whenever you ask whether a given piece of writing is persuasive, the immediate rejoinder should always be, "Persuasive to whom?" What seems a good reason to you may not be a good reason to others. The force of a logical argument, as Aristotle showed in his explanation of enthymemes, depends on the audience's acceptance of underlying assumptions, values, or beliefs (see pp. 90–92). Finding audience-based reasons means discovering enthymemes that are effectively rooted in your audience's values.

Difference between Writer- and Audience-Based Reasons

To illustrate the difference between writer- and audience-based reasons, consider the following hypothetical case. Suppose you believed that the government should build a dam on the nearby Rapid River—a project bitterly opposed by several environmental groups. Which of the following two arguments might you use to address environmentalists?

1. The government should build a dam on the Rapid River because the only alternative power sources are coal-fired or nuclear plants, both of which pose greater risk to the environment than a hydroelectric dam.
2. The government should build a hydroelectric dam on the Rapid River because this area needs cheap power to attract heavy industry.

Clearly, the warrant of Argument 1 ("Choose the source of power that poses least risk to the environment") is rooted in the values and beliefs of environmentalists, whereas the warrant of Argument 2 ("Growth of industry is good") is likely to make them wince. To environmentalists, new industry means more congestion, more smokestacks, and more pollution. However, Argument 2 may appeal to out-of-work laborers or to the business community, to whom new industry means more jobs and a booming economy.

From the perspective of *logos* alone, Arguments 1 and 2 are both sound. They are internally consistent and proceed from reasonable premises. But they will affect different audiences very differently. Neither argument proves that the government should build the dam; both are open to objection. Passionate environmentalists, for example, might counter Argument 1 by asking why the government needs to build any power plant at all. They could argue that energy conservation would obviate the need for a new power plant. Or they might argue that building a dam hurts the environment in ways unforeseen by dam supporters. Our point, then, isn't that Argument 1 will persuade environmentalists. Rather, our point is that Argument 1 will be more persuasive than Argument 2 because it is rooted in beliefs and values that the intended audience shares.

Let's consider a second example by returning to Chapter 1 and student Gordon Adams's petition to waive his math requirement. Gordon's central argument, as you will recall, was that as a lawyer he would have no need for algebra. In Toulmin's terms, Gordon's argument looks like this:

CLAIM: I should be exempted from the algebra requirement.

STATED REASON: because in my chosen field of law I will have no need for algebra

GROUNDS: testimony from lawyers and others that lawyers never use algebra

WARRANT: (largely implicit in Gordon's argument) General education requirements should be based on career utility (that is, if a course isn't needed for a particular student's career, it shouldn't be required).

BACKING: (not provided) arguments that career utility should be the chief criterion for requiring general education courses

In our discussions of this case with students and faculty, students generally vote to support Gordon's request, whereas faculty generally vote against it. And in fact, the University Standards Committee rejected Gordon's petition, thus delaying his entry into law school.

Why do faculty and students differ on this issue? Mainly they differ because faculty reject Gordon's warrant that general education requirements should serve students' individual career interests. Most faculty believe that general education courses, including math, provide a base of common learning that links us to the past and teaches us modes of understanding useful throughout life.

Gordon's argument thus challenges one of college professors' most cherished beliefs—that the liberal arts are innately valuable. Further, it threatens his immediate audience, the committee, with a possible flood of student requests to waive other general education requirements on the grounds of their irrelevance to a particular career choice.

How might Gordon have created a more persuasive argument? In our view, Gordon might have prevailed had he accepted the faculty's belief in the value of the math requirement and argued that he had fulfilled the "spirit" of that requirement through alternative means. He could have based his argument on an enthymeme like this:

> I should be exempted from the algebra requirement because my experience as a contractor and inventor has already provided me with equivalent mathematical knowledge.

Following this audience-based approach, he would drop all references to algebra's uselessness for lawyers and expand his discussion of the mathematical savvy he acquired on the job. This argument would honor faculty values and reduce the faculty's fear of setting a bad precedent. Few students are likely to have Gordon's background, and those who do could apply for a similar exemption without threatening the system. Again, this argument might not have won, but it would have gotten a more sympathetic hearing.

Arguments like Gordon's that call fundamental assumptions into doubt may have a long-range effect even though they lose in the short range. Although he probably would have greatly improved his chances of getting a waiver by appealing to his audience's values and beliefs, his challenge of those beliefs might in the long run contribute to the systemic change he desires. By arguing that he's a special case, Gordon would have left the rule unchallenged. By challenging the rule itself, he followed a high-risk/high-gain strategy that, even if unsuccessful, might force reexamination of the faculty's basic beliefs. If successful, meanwhile, it could affect thousands of students.

FOR CLASS DISCUSSION

Working in groups, decide which of the two reasons offered in each instance would be more persuasive to the specified audience. Be prepared to explain your reasoning to the class. Write out the implied warrant for each *because* clause and decide whether the specific audience would likely grant it.

1. Audience: a beleaguered parent
   a. I should be allowed to stay out until 2 A.M. because all my friends do.
   b. I should be allowed to stay out until 2 A.M. because only if I'm free to make my own decisions will I mature.

2. Audience: a prospective employer
   a. I would be a good candidate for a summer job at the Happy Trails Dude Ranch because I have always wanted to spend a summer in the mountains and because I like to ride horses.
   b. I would be a good candidate for a summer job at the Happy Trails Dude Ranch because I am a hard worker, because I have had considerable experience serving others in my volunteer work, and because I know how to make guests feel welcome and relaxed.

3. Audience: people who oppose the present grading system on the grounds that it is too competitive
   a. We should keep the present grading system because it prepares people for the dog-eat-dog pressures of the business world.
   b. We should keep the present grading system because it tells students that certain standards of excellence must be met if individuals are to reach their full potential.

4. Audience: young people ages fifteen to twenty-five
   a. You should become a vegetarian because an all-vegetable diet is better for your heart than a meaty diet.
   b. You should become a vegetarian because that will help eliminate the suffering of animals raised in factory farms.

5. Audience: conservative proponents of "family values"
   a. Same-sex marriages should be legalized because doing so will promote public acceptance of homosexuality.
   b. Same-sex marriages should be legalized because doing so will make it easier for gay people to establish and sustain long-term stable relationships.

Finding Audience-Based Reasons: Asking Questions about Your Audience

As the preceding exercise makes clear, reasons are most persuasive when linked to your audience's values. This principle seems simple enough, yet it is easy to forget. For example, employers frequently complain about job interviewees whose first concern is what the company will do for them, not what they might do for the company. Conversely, job search experts agree that most successful job candidates do extensive background research on a prospective company so that in an interview they can relate their own skills to the company's problems and needs. Successful arguments typically grow out of similar attention to audience needs.

To find out all you can about an audience, we recommend that you explore the following questions:

1. *Who is your audience?* Your audience might be a single, identifiable person. For example, you might write a letter to your student body president arguing for a change in intramural policies or to a vice president for research proposing a new research and development project for your company. Or your audience might be a decision-making body such as the University Standards Committee or a philanthropic organization to which you're writing a grant proposal. At other times your audience might be the general readership of a newspaper, church bulletin, magazine, or journal, or you might produce a flier to be handed out on street corners.

2. *How much does your audience know or care about your issue?* Are members of this audience currently part of the conversation on this issue, or do they need considerable background information? If you are writing to specific decision makers (for example, the administration at your college about restructuring the student orientation program), are they currently aware of the problem or issue you are addressing, and do they care about it? If not, how can you get their attention? Your answers to these questions will especially affect your introduction and conclusion.

3. *What is your audience's current attitude toward your issue?* Are members of this audience supportive of your position on the issue? Neutral or undecided? Skeptical? Strongly opposed? What other points of view besides your own will your audience be weighing? In Chapter 8, we will explain how your answers to these questions can help you decide the structure and tone of your argument.

4. *What will be your audience's likely objections to your argument?* What weaknesses will audience members find? What aspects of your position will be most threatening to them and why? How are your basic assumptions, values, or beliefs different from your audience's? Your answers here will help determine the content of your argument and will alert you to extra research you may need to do to bolster your response to audience objections.

5. *Finally, what values, beliefs, or assumptions about the world do you and your audience share?* Despite differences of view on this issue, where can you find common links with your audience? How might you use these links to build bridges to your audience?

Suppose, for example, that you support universal mandatory testing for the HIV virus. It's important from the start that you understand and acknowledge the interests of those opposed to your position. Who are they, and what are their concerns? Gays and others in high-risk categories may fear finding out whether they are infected; certainly they will fear discrimination from being publicly identified as HIV carriers. Moreover, gays may see mandatory AIDS testing as part of an ongoing attempt by homophobes to stigmatize the gay community. Liberals, meanwhile, will question the necessity of invading people's privacy and compromising their civil liberties in the name of public health.

What shared values might you use to build bridges to those opposed to mandatory testing? At a minimum, you share a desire to find a cure for AIDS and a fear of the horrors of an epidemic. Moreover, you also share a respect for the dignity and humanity of those afflicted with AIDS and do not see yourself as part of a backlash against gays.

Given all that, you begin to develop a strategy to reduce your audience's fears and to link your reasons to their values. Your thinking might go something like this:

PROBLEM:	How can I create an argument rooted in shared values?
POSSIBLE SOLUTIONS:	I can try to reduce the audience's fear that mandatory AIDS testing implies a criticism of gays. I must assure that my plan ensures confidentiality. I must make clear that my first priority is stopping the spread of the disease and that this concern is shared by the gay community.
PROBLEM:	How can I reduce fear that mandatory HIV-testing will violate civil liberties?
POSSIBLE SOLUTIONS:	I must show that the enemy here is the HIV virus, not victims of the disease. Also, I might cite precedents for how we fight other infectious diseases. For example, many states require marriage license applicants to take a test for sexually transmitted diseases,

and many communities have imposed quarantines to halt the spread of epidemics. I could also argue that the right of everyone to be free from this disease outweighs the right to privacy, especially when confidentiality is assured.

The preceding example shows how a writer's focus on audience can shape the actual invention of the argument.

FOR CLASS DISCUSSION

Working individually or in small groups, plan an audience-based argumentative strategy for one or more of the following cases. Follow the thinking process used by the writer of the mandatory HIV-testing argument: (1) State several problems that the writer must solve to reach the audience, and (2) develop possible solutions to those problems.

1. An argument for the right of software companies to continue making and selling violent video games: Aim the argument at parents who oppose their children's playing these games.

2. An argument to reverse grade inflation by limiting the number of A's and B's a professor can give in a course. Aim the argument at students who fear the results of getting lower grades.

3. An argument supporting a $1-per-gallon increase in gasoline taxes as an energy conservation measure: Aim your argument at business leaders who oppose the tax for fear it will raise the cost of consumer goods.

4. An argument supporting the legalization of cocaine: Aim your argument at readers of *Reader's Digest,* a conservative magazine that supports the current war on drugs.

ETHOS AND *PATHOS* AS PERSUASIVE APPEALS: AN OVERVIEW

The previous section focused on audience-based reasons as a means of moving an audience. In terms of the rhetorical triangle introduced in Chapter 4 (see Figure 4.1), searching for audience-based reasons can be seen primarily as a function of *logos*—finding the best structure of reasons and evidence to sway an audience—although, as we shall see, it also affects the other points of the triangle. In what follows, we turn to the power of *ethos* (the appeal to credibility) and *pathos* (the appeal to an audience's sympathies) as further means of making your arguments more effective.

It's tempting to think of these three kinds of appeals as "ingredients" in an essay, like spices you add to a casserole. Succumbing to this metaphor, you might say to yourself something like this: "Just enough *logos* to give the dish body; but for more piquancy it needs a pinch of *pathos*. And for the back of the palate, a tad more *ethos*."

But this metaphor is misleading because *logos*, *ethos*, and *pathos* are not substances; they are ways of seeing rather than objects of sight. A better metaphor might be that of different lamps and filters used on theater spotlights to vary lighting effects on a stage. Thus, if you switch on a *pathos* lamp (possibly through using more concrete language or vivid examples), the resulting image will engage the audience's sympathy and emotions more deeply. If you overlay an *ethos* filter (perhaps by adopting a different tone toward your audience), the projected image of the writer as a person will be subtly altered. If you switch on a *logos* lamp (by adding, say, more data for evidence), you will draw the reader's attention to the logical appeal of the argument. Depending on how you modulate the lamps and filters, you shape and color your readers' perception of the issue.

Our metaphor is imperfect, of course, but our point is that *logos*, *ethos*, and *pathos* work together to create an impact on the reader. Consider, for example, the different impacts of the following arguments, all having roughly the same logical appeal:

1. People should adopt a vegetarian diet because only through vegetarianism can we prevent the cruelty to animals that results from factory farming.

2. I hope you enjoyed your fried chicken this evening. You know, of course, how much that chicken suffered just so you could have a tender and juicy meal. Commercial growers cram the chickens so tightly together into cages that their beaks must be cut off to keep them from pecking each other's eyes out. The only way to end the torture is to adopt a vegetarian diet.

3. People who eat meat are no better than sadists who torture other sentient creatures to enhance their own pleasure. Unless you enjoy sadistic tyranny over others, you have only one choice: Become a vegetarian.

4. People committed to justice might consider the extent to which our love of eating meat requires the agony of animals. A visit to a modern chicken factory—where chickens live their entire lives in tiny darkened coops without room to spread their wings—might raise doubts about our right to inflict such suffering on sentient creatures. Indeed, such a visit might persuade us that vegetarianism is a more just alternative.

Each argument has roughly the same logical core:

CLAIM:	People should adopt a vegetarian diet.
STATED REASON:	because only vegetarianism will end the suffering of animals subjected to factory farming
GROUNDS:	the evidence of suffering in commercial chicken farms, where chickens are crammed together, and lash out at

WARRANT: If we have an alternative to making animals suffer, we should adopt it.

But the impact of each argument varies. The difference between Arguments 1 and 2, most of our students report, is the greater emotional power of Argument 2. Whereas Argument 1 refers only to the abstraction "cruelty to animals," Argument 2 paints a vivid picture of chickens with their beaks cut off to prevent their pecking each other blind. Argument 2 makes a stronger appeal to *pathos* (not necessarily a stronger argument), stirring feelings by appealing simultaneously to the heart and to the head.

The difference between Arguments 1 and 3 concerns both *ethos* and *pathos*. Argument 3 appeals to the emotions through highly charged words like *torture, sadist,* and *tyranny*. But Argument 3 also draws attention to its writer, and most of our students report not liking that writer very much. His stance is self-righteous and insulting. In contrast, Argument 4's author establishes a more positive *ethos*. He establishes rapport by assuming his audience is committed to justice and by qualifying his argument with conditional terms such as *might* and *perhaps*. He also invites sympathy for his problem—an appeal to *pathos*—by offering a specific description of chickens crammed into tiny coops.

Which of these arguments is best? They all have appropriate uses. Arguments 1 and 4 seem aimed at receptive audiences reasonably open to exploration of the issue, whereas Arguments 2 and 3 seem designed to shock complacent audiences or to rally a group of True Believers. Even Argument 3, which is too abusive to be effective in most instances, might work as a rallying speech at a convention of animal liberation activists.

Our point thus far is that *logos, ethos,* and *pathos* are different aspects of the same whole, different lenses for intensifying or softening the light beam you project onto the screen. Every choice you make as a writer affects in some way each of the three appeals. The rest of this chapter examines these choices in more detail.

HOW TO CREATE AN EFFECTIVE *ETHOS:* THE APPEAL TO CREDIBILITY

The ancient Greek and Roman rhetoricians recognized that an argument would be more persuasive if the audience trusted the speaker. Aristotle argued that such trust resides within the speech itself, not in the prior reputation of the speaker. In the speaker's manner and delivery, in the speaker's tone, word choice, and arrangement of reasons, in the sympathy with which he or she treats alternative views, the speaker creates a trustworthy persona. Aristotle called the impact of the speaker's credibility the appeal from *ethos*. How does a writer create credibility? We will suggest three ways.

Be Knowledgeable about Your Issue

The first way to gain credibility is to *be* credible—that is, to argue from a strong base of knowledge, to have at hand the examples, personal experiences, statistics, and other empirical data needed to make a sound case. If you have done your homework, you will command the attention of most audiences.

Be Fair

Besides being knowledgeable about your issue, you need to demonstrate fairness and courtesy to alternative views. Because true argument can occur only where persons may reasonably disagree with one another, your *ethos* will be strengthened if you demonstrate that you understand and empathize with other points of view. There are times, of course, when you may appropriately scorn an opposing view. But these times are rare, and they mostly occur when you address audiences predisposed to your view. Demonstrating empathy to alternative views is generally the best strategy.

Build a Bridge to Your Audience

A third means of establishing credibility—building a bridge to your audience—has been treated at length in our earlier discussion of audience-based reasons. By grounding your argument in shared values and assumptions, you demonstrate your goodwill and enhance your image as a trustworthy person respectful of your audience's views. We mention audience-based reasons here to show how this aspect of *logos*—finding the reasons that are most rooted in the audience's values—also affects your *ethos* as a person respectful of your readers' views.

HOW TO CREATE *PATHOS:* THE APPEAL TO BELIEFS AND EMOTIONS

At the height of the Vietnam protest movement, a group of demonstrators "napalmed" a puppy by dousing it with gasoline and setting it on fire, thereby outraging people all across the country. Many sent indignant letters to their local newspapers, provoking the following response from the demonstrators: "Why are you outraged by the napalming of a single puppy when you are not outraged by the daily napalming of human babies in Vietnam?"

From the demonstrators' view, napalming the puppy constituted an appeal from *pathos*. *Logos*-centered arguments, the protesters felt, numbed the mind to human suffering; in napalming the puppy, they intended to reawaken in their audience a capacity for gut-level revulsion that had been dulled by too many statistics, too many abstract moral appeals, and too much superficial TV coverage of the war.

Of course, the napalmed puppy was a real-life event, a street theater protest, not a written argument. But writers often use a similar strategy. Anti-abortion proponents use it whenever they graphically describe the dismemberment of a fetus during abortion; euthanasia proponents use it when they describe the prolonged suffering of a terminally ill patient hooked hopelessly to machines. And a student uses it when he argues that a professor ought to raise his grade from a C to a B, lest he lose his scholarship and leave college, shattering the dreams of his dear old grandmother.

Are such appeals legitimate? Our answer is yes, if they intensify our response to an issue rather than divert our attention from it. Because understanding is a matter of feeling as well as perceiving, *pathos* can give access to nonlogical, but not necessarily nonrational, ways of knowing. Used effectively, pathetic appeals reveal the fullest human meaning of an issue, helping us walk in the writer's shoes. That is why arguments are often improved through the use of sensory details that allow us to see the reality of a problem or through stories that make specific cases and instances come alive.

Appeals to *pathos* become illegitimate, we believe, when they confuse an issue rather than clarify it. To the extent that students' grades should be based on performance or effort, the student's image of the dear old grandmother is an illegitimate appeal to *pathos* because it diverts the reader from rational to irrational criteria. The weeping grandmother may provide a legitimate motive for the student to study harder but not for the professor to change a grade.

Although it is difficult to classify all the ways that writers can create appeals from *pathos,* we will focus on four strategies: concrete language; specific examples and illustrations; narratives; and connotations of words, metaphors, and analogies. Each of these strategies lends "presence" to an argument by creating immediacy and emotional impact.

Use Concrete Language

Concrete language—one of the chief ways that writers achieve voice—can increase the liveliness, interest level, and personality of a writer's prose. When used in argument, concrete language typically heightens *pathos.* For example, consider the differences between the first and second drafts of the following student argument:

First draft: People who prefer driving a car to taking a bus think that taking the bus will increase the stress of the daily commute. Just the opposite is true. Not being able to find a parking spot when in a hurry to work or school can cause a person stress. Taking the bus gives a person time to read or sleep, etc. It could be used as a mental break.

Second draft: Taking the bus can be more relaxing than driving a car. Having someone else behind the wheel gives people time to chat with friends or cram for an exam. They can balance their checkbooks, do homework, doze off, read the daily newspaper, or get lost in a novel rather than foaming at the mouth looking for a parking space.

In this revision, specific details enliven the prose by creating images that trigger positive feelings. Who wouldn't want some free time to doze off or to get lost in a novel?

Use Specific Examples and Illustrations

Specific examples and illustrations serve two purposes in an argument: They provide evidence that supports your reasons; simultaneously, they give your argument presence and emotional resonance. Note the flatness of the following draft arguing for the value of multicultural studies in a university core curriculum:

> *Early draft:* Another advantage of a multicultural education is that it will help us see our own culture in a broader perspective. If all we know is our own heritage, we might not be inclined to see anything bad about this heritage because we won't know anything else. But if we study other heritages, we can see the costs and benefits of our own heritage.

Now note the increase in "presence" when the writer adds a specific example:

> *Revised draft:* Another advantage of multicultural education is that it raises questions about traditional Western values. For example, owning private property (such as buying your own home) is part of the American dream and is a basic right guaranteed in our Constitution. However, in studying the beliefs of American Indians, students are confronted with a very different view of private property. When the U.S. government sought to buy land in the Pacific Northwest from Chief Sealth, he replied:
>> The president in Washington sends words that he wishes to buy our land. But how can you buy or sell the sky? The land? The idea is strange to us. If we do not own the freshness of the air and the sparkle of the water, how can you buy them? [. . .] We are part of the earth and it is part of us. [. . .] This we know: The earth does not belong to man, man belongs to the earth.
>
> Our class was shocked by the contrast between traditional Western views of property and Chief Sealth's views. One of our best class discussions was initiated by this quotation from Chief Sealth. Had we not been exposed to a view from another culture, we would have never been led to question the "rightness" of Western values.

The writer begins his revision by evoking a traditional Western view of private property, which he then questions by shifting to Chief Sealth's vision of land as open, endless, and unobtainable as the sky. Through the use of a specific example, the writer brings to life his previously abstract point about the benefit of multicultural education.

Use Narratives

A particularly powerful way to evoke *pathos* is to tell a story that either leads into your claim or embodies it implicitly and that appeals to your readers' feelings and imagination. Brief narratives—whether true or hypothetical—are particularly effective as opening attention grabbers for an argument. To illustrate how an introductory narrative (either a story or a brief scene) can create pathetic appeals, consider the following first paragraph to an argument opposing jet skis:

> I dove off the dock into the lake, and as I approached the surface I could see the sun shining through the water. As my head popped out, I located my cousin a few feet away in a rowboat waiting to escort me as I, a twelve-year-old girl, attempted to swim across the mile-wide, pristine lake and back to our dock. I made it, and that glorious summer day is one of my most precious memories. Today, however, no one would dare attempt that swim. Jet skis have taken over this small lake where I spent many summers with my grandparents. Dozens of whining jet skis crisscross the lake, ruining it for swimming, fishing, canoeing, row-boating, and even water-skiing. More stringent state laws are needed to control jet-skiing because it interferes with other uses of lakes and is currently very dangerous.

This narrative makes a case for a particular point of view toward jet skis by winning our identification with the writer's experience. She invites us to relive that experience with her while she also taps into our own treasured memories of summer experiences that have been destroyed by change.

Opening narratives to evoke *pathos* can be powerfully effective, but they are also risky. If they are too private, too self-indulgent, too sentimental, or even too dramatic and forceful, they can backfire on you. If you have doubts about an opening narrative, read it to a sample audience before using it in your final draft.

FOR CLASS DISCUSSION

Suppose that you want to write arguments on the following issues. Working individually or in groups, think of an introductory scene or brief story that would create a pathetic appeal favorable to your argument.

1. a. an argument supporting the use of animals for biomedical research
   b. an argument opposing the use of animals for biomedical research
   (Note that the purpose of the first narrative is to create sympathy for the use of animals in medical research; perhaps you could describe the happy homecoming of a child cured by a medical procedure developed through testing on animals. The second narrative, aimed at evoking sympathy for abolishing animal research, might describe a lab rabbit's suffering.)

2. a. an argument for a program to restore a national park to its natural condition

b. an argument for creating more camping places and overnight sites for recreational vehicles in national parks

3. a. an argument favoring legalization of drugs
   b. an argument opposing legalization of drugs

In addition to their use as opening scenes or as examples and illustrations, narratives can sometimes inform a whole argument. If the argument is conveyed entirely through narrative, then it is an *implicit* rather than *explicit* argument (see Chapter 1, pp. 4–9). But explicit arguments can sometimes contain an extensive narrative component. One source of the powerful appeal of Gordon Adams's petition to waive his math requirement (Chapter 1, pp. 19–22) is that the argument embodies aspects of his personal story.

In his appeal to the Standards Committee, Gordon Adams uses numerous standard argument devices (for example, testimony from legal practitioners that knowledge of algebra is not required in the study or practice of law). But he also makes a strong pathetic appeal by narrating the story of how he assembled his case. By foregrounding his encounters with all the people from whom he seeks information, he makes himself an actor in a story that might be called "Gordon's Quest for Truth."

The story of Gordon's construction of his argument, meanwhile, is situated inside a larger story that lends weight to the points he makes in the smaller story. The larger story, the story of Gordon's "awakening" to injustice and his fierce commitment to overcoming injustice for his people, links Gordon's desire to waive his algebra requirement to a larger, more significant story about overcoming oppression. And beyond Gordon's story lies an even larger, richer story, the history of Native American peoples in the United States over the past century, which lends an even greater resonance and clarity to his personal story. By telling his story, Gordon makes himself more human and familiar, more understandable and less threatening. This is why whenever we want to break down difference, overcome estrangement, grow closer to people we don't know well, we tell them our stories. Telling his story allowed Gordon to negotiate some considerable differences between himself and his audience of mostly white, middle-class faculty members. Even though he lost his case, he made a powerful argument that was taken seriously.

Choose Words, Metaphors, and Analogies with Appropriate Connotations

Another way of appealing to *pathos* is to select words, metaphors, or analogies with connotations that match your aim. A rapidly made decision by a city council might be called "haughty and autocratic" or "bold and decisive," depending on whether you oppose or support the council. Similarly, writers can use favorable or unfavorable metaphors and analogies to evoke different imaginative or emotional responses. A tax bill might be viewed as a "potentially fatal poison pill" or as "unpleasant but necessary economic medicine."

The writer's control over word selection raises the problem of slant or bias. Some contemporary philosophers argue that bias-free, perfectly transparent language is impossible because all language is a lens. Thus, when we choose word A rather than word B, when we put this sentence in the passive voice rather than the active, when we select this detail and omit that detail, we create bias.

Let's illustrate. When you see an unshaven man sitting on a city sidewalk with his back up against a doorway, wearing old, slovenly clothes, and drinking from a bottle hidden in a sack, what is the objective, "true" word for this person?

a person on welfare?	a welfare leech?	a beggar?
a panhandler?	a bum?	a hobo?
a wino?	a drunk?	an alcoholic?
a crazy guy?	a homeless person?	a transient?

None of these words can be called "true" or perfectly objective because each creates its own slant. Each word causes us to view the person through that word's lens. If we call the person a beggar, for example, we evoke connotations of helpless poverty and of the biblical call to give alms to the poor. *Beggar,* then, is slightly more favorable than *panhandler,* which conjures up the image of someone pestering you for money. Calling the person *homeless* shifts the focus away from the person's behavior and onto a faulty economic system that fails to provide sufficient housing. The word *wino* identifies a different cause for the person's condition—alcoholism rather than economics.

Our point, then, is that purely objective language may be impossible. But the absence of pure objectivity doesn't mean that all language is equally slanted or that truth can never be discerned. Readers can recognize degrees of bias in someone's language and distinguish between a reasonably trustworthy passage and a highly distortive one. By being on the lookout for slanted language—without claiming that any language can be totally objective—we can defend ourselves from distortive appeals to *pathos* while recognizing that responsible use of connotation can give powerful presence to an argument.

FOR CLASS DISCUSSION

Outside class rewrite the introduction to one of your previous papers (or a current draft) to include more appeals to *pathos.* Use any of the strategies for giving your argument presence: concrete language, specific examples, narratives, metaphors, analogies, and connotative words. Bring both your original and your rewritten introductions to class. In pairs or in groups, discuss the comparative effectiveness of these introductions in trying to reach your intended audience.

USING VISUAL ARGUMENTS FOR EMOTIONAL APPEAL

One of the most powerful ways to engage an audience emotionally is to use photos or other visual images. If you think of any news event that has captured wide media attention, you will probably recall memorable photos. Think of the famous photograph of three-year-old John F. Kennedy Jr. saluting his father's coffin. Or think of the image most frequently used to accompany stories of the U.S. women's soccer team winning the world championship in 1999—not the great goal-keeping photo of African American Briana Scurry blocking the last penalty kick, but the photo of Brandi Chastain removing her jersey to reveal a black sports bra. Sometimes we are only partially aware of how the specific subject matter selected for a photo, its angle and cropping, the arrangement and posing of figures, and other details can encode an argument. Many analysts, for example, observed that the famous Brandi Chastain photograph linked women's sports with stereotypical views of women as sex objects rather than with athletic prowess.

Because of the power of visual images, professional writers often try to use photographs or drawings to enhance their arguments. Visual images accompanying an argument can be particularly effective at grabbing viewers' attention, conveying the seriousness of an issue, and evoking strong emotions ranging from compassion to revulsion.

One especially charged kind of visual argument is the political cartoon. Political cartoons are often mininarratives that can portray an issue dramatically, compactly, and humorously. They may illustrate the cartoonist's perspective on an issue by exaggerating and exposing the absurdity of those who take the other side or by humorously illustrating the consequences of pursuing a course of action. Political cartoons have a long history. For example, consider a cartoon on one of the most controversial issues of mid-nineteenth-century America: women's rights. The cartoon shown in Figure 7.1, from an 1868 issue of *Harper's Weekly*, depicts the cartoonist's vision of a society gone awry. It shows gender roles confused and reversed—men knitting, sewing, and struggling with babies in a crowded room while the women lounge and smoke in a saloon. The disagreeable "unnaturalness" of this gender reversal supports the cartoonist's argument that women's attempts to gain more rights threaten to undo the social order. The cartoon appealed to its nineteenth-century audience by arousing anxiety while inspiring a mocking rejection of the women's rights cause.

Although many written arguments do not lend themselves to visual illustrations, we suggest that when you construct arguments you consider the potential of visual support. Imagine that your argument is to appear in a newspaper or

HOW IT WOULD BE, IF SOME LADIES HAD THEIR OWN WAY.

FIGURE 7.1   Mid-nineteenth-century political cartoon

magazine where space will be provided for one or two visuals. What photographs or drawings might help persuade your audience toward your perspective? When visual images work well, they are analogous to the verbal strategies of concrete language, specific illustrations, narratives, and connotative words. The challenge in using visuals is to find material that is straightforward enough not to require elaborate explanations, that is timely and relevant, and that clearly adds impact to a specific part of your argument.

FOR CLASS DISCUSSION

In the following exercise, we ask you to consider the effect of visual images on a recent event that pitted cultural values against the interests of environmentalists and animal rights activists, as well as raising numerous issues related to world trade and international fisheries. This conflict centered on the Makah people's desire to resume their traditional practice of hunting gray whales—a right guaranteed them by treaty. When a U.S. federal court granted the tribe permission to resume whaling (the tribe was allotted four whales), an extended conflict broke out between the tribe and antiwhaling protesters. Both sides hired public relations firms to help sway the general public toward their views and interests. On the day that the Makah killed their first whale, the media filmed the event, creating photographs that were a public relations disaster for the tribe.

For this exercise, we ask you to read the following excerpt from an op-ed newspaper article and then answer the questions that follow. The purpose of the whole article is to give a balanced description of the killing from the viewpoints of both the Makah themselves and the antiwhaling protesters. This excerpt focuses on the power of visual images.

From "Tradition vs. a Full-Blown PR Problem: Now Come Reactions to a Very Public Death"

Eric Sorensen

You are a big public-relations firm and your client, the Makah Tribe, has just killed a whale.   1

Live. On television. And the hunt is now being replayed on screens across the nation.   2

The harpoon going in. The whale taking off. The speedboat pulling alongside and firing several shots that explode in the sea. The whale rolling. The towline going slack.   3

In Neah Bay, this is cause for celebration, a triumphant embrace of tradition and heritage, a culture's central symbol giving itself up for the kill.   4

But in living rooms across the country, unaccustomed to hunting or the ways of an obscure Northwest tribe, it's a tough moment.   5

If you're doing PR for the tribe, you're in a tough spot.   6

"The pictures are brutal," said David Margulies, president of a Dallas-based public-relations firm specializing in crisis communications. "As one of the reporters said, 'It's a brutal killing.' The average person is going to say, 'I don't see the point of doing that.'"   7

ABC anchor Peter Jennings called it "a bad chapter" in the battle over protecting whales and protecting tradition. NBC's Tom Brokaw called it "a day of ritual, death and protest." CBS referred to the "death of a beautiful titan of the sea."   8

All three showed ample footage of the whale being killed.   9

And the Makahs saw their long-simmering public-relations difficulties grow into what some experts call a full-blown PR problem.   10

Where before they juggled interview requests and stressed that whale hunting helps preserve their heritage, they now must deal with the more visceral reaction that comes from watching a big animal die a nine-minute public death.   11

Video is that powerful. It's why the U.S. military has clamped down on media access since television turned public opinion against the Vietnam War.   12

"The picture is always the most powerful element of the story," said Margulies, who advises clients on how to deal with hard-hitting programs such as *60 Minutes.*   13

"One of the first things you want to do in public relations is control the picture. Whichever side has the better picture very often controls the argument," Margulies said.   14

Moreover, he said, the picture of a dying whale now stands to be replayed over the coming months and years, whenever a television producer needs images to go with an update of the Makahs whaling controversy.   15

Jim McCarthy, a Washington, D.C.–based public-relations consultant who has advised the Makahs, suggested last year they hunt in the early morning darkness to avoid being photographed. The tribe refused.   16

17   "The bottom line is they have nothing to hide," said McCarthy, a frequent adviser of tribal groups. "They're proud of what they're doing."

18   The task for the tribe now is to appeal to the public's intellect, asking it to apply to non-Indian culture the same standard it might be asking of the Makahs, he said.

19   "There's a kind of schizophrenia going on here," McCarthy said. "More than 50,000 animals are killed for the mainstream public every day. That is often done in a more graphic way than what the Makahs are doing."

20   The killing underscores the cultural gap between tribal customs that condone killing a whale and nontribal values that cherish the imagery of *Free Willy.*

Working in small groups or as a whole class, respond to the following questions:

1. Figures 7.2 and 7.3 show two photographs taken during the day of the whale killing. Freewrite your response to these photos. How would you describe their emotional impact on the viewer? Then share your freewrites with classmates.

FIGURE 7.2   Media photograph of a scene from a whale killing

FIGURE 7.3   Another photograph of a scene from a whale killing

2. In the preceding extract, the author quotes a public relations officer who says, "One of the first things you want to do in public relations is control the picture. Whichever side has the better picture very often controls the argument." If you were a public relations consultant for the Makah, which of the two photos would you select to support the tribe's view of whale hunting as noble action—an ancient tribal custom in harmony with the tribe's traditional values? Why?

3. Which picture would best support the protesters' anti-whaling views? Why?

4. Find several different photos of a historical event or a recent news event and explain how these photos have been used to present different perspectives on the event. What emotions do the photos appeal to?

CONCLUSION

In this chapter, we have explored ways that writers can strengthen the persuasiveness of their arguments by using audience-based reasons and by creating appeals to *ethos* and *pathos*. Arguments are more persuasive if they are rooted in underlying assumptions, beliefs, and values of the intended audience. Similarly, arguments are more persuasive if readers trust the credibility of the writer and if the argument appeals to readers' hearts and imaginations as well as their intellects. Sometimes visual images may reinforce the argument by evoking strong emotional responses, thus enhancing *pathos*.

8

Accommodating Your Audience

Treating Differing Views

In the previous chapter we discussed ways of moving an audience. In this chapter we discuss a writer's options for accommodating differing views on an issue—whether to omit them, refute them, concede to them, or incorporate them through compromise and conciliation. In particular, we show you how your choices about structure, content, and tone may differ depending on whether your audience is sympathetic, neutral, or strongly resistant to your views. The strategies explained in this chapter will increase your flexibility as an arguer and enhance your chance of persuading a wide variety of audiences.

ONE-SIDED VERSUS MULTISIDED ARGUMENTS

Arguments are sometimes said to be one-sided or multisided. A *one-sided* argument presents only the writer's position on the issue without summarizing and responding to alternative viewpoints. A *multisided* argument presents the writer's position but also summarizes and responds to possible objections that an audience might raise. Which kind of argument is more persuasive to an audience?

According to some researchers, if people already agree with a writer's thesis, they usually find one-sided arguments more persuasive. A multisided argument appears wishy-washy, making the writer seem less decisive. But if people initially disagree with a writer's thesis, a multisided argument often seems more persuasive because it shows that the writer has listened to other views and thus seems more open-minded and fair. An especially interesting effect has been documented for neutral audiences. In the short run, one-sided arguments seem more persuasive to neutral audiences, but in the long run multisided arguments seem to have more staying power. Neutral audiences who've heard only one side of an issue tend to change their minds when they hear alternative arguments. By anticipating and in some cases refuting opposing views, the multisided argument diminishes the surprise and force of subsequent counterarguments and also exposes their weaknesses.

In the rest of this chapter we will show you how your choice of writing one-sided or multisided arguments is a function of how you perceive your audience's resistance to your views.

DETERMINING YOUR AUDIENCE'S RESISTANCE TO YOUR VIEWS

When you write an argument, you must always consider your audience's point of view. One way to imagine your relationship to your audience is to place it on a scale of resistance ranging from strong support of your position to strong opposition (see Figure 8.1). At the "Accord" end of this scale are like-minded people who basically agree with your position on the issue. At the "Resistance" end are those who strongly disagree with you, perhaps unconditionally, because their values, beliefs, or assumptions sharply differ from your own. Between "Accord" and "Resistance" lies a range of opinions. Close to your position will be those leaning in your direction but with less conviction than you have. Close to the resistance position will be those basically opposed to your view but willing to listen to your argument and perhaps willing to acknowledge some of its strengths. In the middle are those undecided people who are still sorting out their feelings, seeking additional information, and weighing the strengths and weaknesses of alternative views.

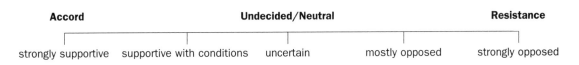

FIGURE 8.1   Scale of resistance

Seldom, however, will you encounter an issue in which the range of disagreement follows a simple line from accord to resistance. Often resistant views fall into different categories so that no single line of argument appeals to all those whose views are different from your own. You have to identify not only your audience's resistance to your ideas but also the causes of that resistance.

Consider, for example, an issue that divided the state of Washington when the Seattle Mariners baseball team demanded a new stadium. A ballot initiative asked citizens to raise taxes to build a new retractable-roof stadium for the Mariners.

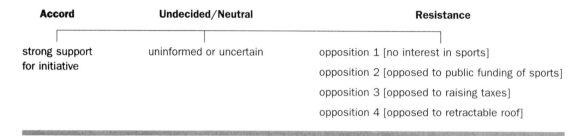

FIGURE 8.2   Scale of resistance, baseball stadium issue

Supporters of the initiative faced a complex array of resisting views (see Figure 8.2). Opponents of the initiative could be placed into four categories. Some simply had no interest in sports, cared nothing about baseball, and saw no benefit in building a huge sports facility in downtown Seattle. Another group loved baseball, perhaps followed the Mariners passionately, but was philosophically opposed to subsidizing rich players and owners with taxpayer money. This group argued that the whole sports industry needed to be restructured so that stadiums were paid for out of sports revenues. Still another group was opposed to tax hikes in general. It focused on the principle of reducing the size of government and of using tax revenues only for essential services. Finally, another powerful group supported baseball and supported the notion of public funding of a new stadium but opposed the kind of retractable-roof stadium specified in the initiative. This group wanted an old-fashioned, open-air stadium like Baltimore's Camden Yards or Cleveland's Jacobs Field.

Writers supporting the initiative found it impossible to address all these resisting audiences at once. If a supporter of the initiative wanted to aim an argument at sports haters, he or she could stress the spinoff benefits of a new ballpark (for example, the new ballpark would attract tourist revenue, renovate the deteriorating Pioneer Square neighborhood, create jobs, make sports lovers more likely to vote for public subsidies of the arts, and so forth). But these arguments were irrelevant to those who wanted an open-air stadium, who opposed tax hikes categorically, or who objected to public subsidy of millionaires.

Another kind of complexity occurs when a writer is positioned between two kinds of resisting views. Consider the position of student writer Sam, a gay man who wished to argue that gay and lesbian people should actively support legislation to legalize same-sex marriage (see Figure 8.3). Most arguments that support same-sex marriage are aimed at conservative heterosexual audiences who tend to disapprove of homosexuality and stress traditional family values. But Sam imagined writing for a gay magazine such as the *Harvard Gay and Lesbian Review* or *The Advocate,* and he wished to aim his argument at liberal gay and lesbian activists who opposed traditional marriage on different grounds. These thinkers, critiquing traditional marriage for the way it stereotypes gender roles and limits the freedom

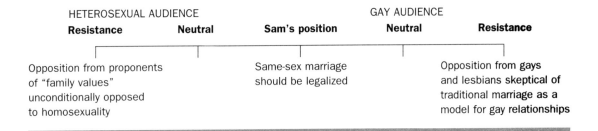

FIGURE 8.3 Scale of resistance for same-sex marriage issue

of partners, argued that heterosexual marriage wasn't a good model for relationships in the gay community. These persons constituted an audience 180 degrees removed from the conservative proponents of family values who oppose same-sex marriage on moral and religious grounds.

In writing his early drafts, Sam was stymied by his attempt to address both audiences at once. Only after he blocked out the conservative "family values" audience and imagined an audience of what he called "liberationist" gays and lesbians was he able to develop a consistent argument. (You can read Sam's essay on pages 294–96.)

The Mariners example and the same-sex marriage example illustrate the difficulty of adapting your argument to your audience's position on the scale of resistance. Yet doing so is important because you need a stable vision of your audience before you can determine an effective content, structure, and tone for your argument. As we showed in Chapter 7, an effective content derives from your choosing audience-based reasons that appeal to your audience's values, assumptions, and beliefs. As we show in the rest of this chapter, an effective structure and tone are often a function of where your audience falls on the scale of resistance. The next sections show how you can adjust your arguing strategy depending on whether your audience is supportive, neutral, or hostile.

APPEALING TO A SUPPORTIVE AUDIENCE: ONE-SIDED ARGUMENT

Although arguing to a supportive audience might seem like preaching to the choir, such arguments are common. Usually, the arguer's goal is to convert belief into action—to inspire a party member to contribute to a senator's campaign or a bored office worker to sign up for a change-your-life weekend seminar.

Typically, appeals to a supportive audience are structured as one-sided arguments that either ignore opposing views or reduce them to "enemy" stereotypes. Filled with motivational language, these arguments list the benefits that will ensue from your donations to the cause and the horrors just around the corner if the other side wins. One of the authors of this text recently received a fundraising letter from an environmental lobbying group declaring, "It's crunch time for the polluters and their pals on Capitol Hill." The "corporate polluters" and "anti-environment politicians," the letter continues, have "stepped up efforts to roll back our environmental protections—relying on large campaign contributions, slick PR firms and well-heeled lobbyists to get the job done before November's election." This letter makes the reader feel part of an in-group of good guys fighting the big business "polluters." Nothing in the letter examines environmental issues from business's perspective or attempts to examine alternative views fairly. Since the intended audience already believes in the cause, nothing in the letter invites readers to consider the issues more complexly. Rather, the goal is to solidify support, increase the fervor of belief, and inspire action. Most appeal arguments make it easy to act, ending with an 800 phone number to call, a tear-out postcard to send in, or a congressperson's address to write to.

APPEALING TO A NEUTRAL OR UNDECIDED AUDIENCE: CLASSICAL ARGUMENT

The in-group appeals that motivate an already supportive audience can repel a neutral or undecided audience. Because undecided audiences are like jurors weighing all sides of an issue, they distrust one-sided arguments that caricature other views. Generally the best strategy for appealing to undecided audiences is the classical argument described in Chapter 3 (pp. 63–65).

What characterizes the classical argument is the writer's willingness to summarize opposing views fairly and to respond to them openly—either by trying to refute them or by conceding to their strengths and then shifting to a different field of values. Let's look at these strategies in more depth.

Summarizing Opposing Views

The first step toward responding to opposing views in a classical argument is to summarize them fairly. Follow the *principle of charity,* which obliges you to avoid loaded, biased, or "straw man" summaries that oversimplify or distort opposing arguments, making them easy to knock over.

Consider the differences between an unfair and a fair summary of George Will's "Lies, Damned Lies, and . . ." (pp. 28–30), which we examined in Chapter 2.

UNFAIR SUMMARY

In a recent *Newsweek* editorial, right-wing columnist George Will parrots the capitalist party line about the virtues and successes of the free enterprise system. He mocks women who complain about the gender pay gap, labeling them whiny feminists. Citing biased statistics gathered by two ultra-conservative, antifeminist women authors, Will claims that women are not discriminated against in the workplace even though they make only 74 cents to a man's dollar and even though only a tiny percentage of top executives in Fortune 500 companies are women. He insults women by claiming that women's unequal pay is the result of their "cheerful" acceptance of their natural roles as mothers that lead them to desire flexible jobs rather than well-paying ones. He blindly dismisses the need for government action. Normal women, he claims, should be able to see that women have the best of all possible worlds because our wonderful economy lets them combine family with jobs.

This summary both distorts and oversimplifies Will's position. By adopting a sarcastic tone ("our wonderful economy") and by using loaded phrases ("right-wing," "parrots the capitalist party line," and so forth), the writer reveals a bias against Will that neutral readers will distrust. In failing to summarize Will's statistical explanations for both the current pay gap and the absence of women in top executive positions, the writer oversimplifies Will's argument, preventing the reader from understanding Will's reasoning. The writer thus sets up a straw man that is easier to knock over than is Will's original argument.

For an example of fair summaries of Will, see the versions we have written in Chapter 2 (pp. 34–35). In those examples we follow the principle of charity by summarizing Will's views as justly and accurately as possible.

FOR CLASS DISCUSSION

Suppose that you believe that ROTC courses ought to receive academic credit and thus you oppose the views of the student writer of "ROTC Courses Should Not Get College Credit" on pp. 458–60. Working individually or in groups, prepare two different summaries of this writer's views, as follows:

1. Unfair summary using loaded language or straw man oversimplification or distortion

2. Fair summary following the principle of charity

When you are finished, be prepared to read your summaries aloud to the class as a whole.

Refuting Opposing Views

Once you have summarized opposing views, you can either refute them or concede to their strengths. In refuting an opposing view, you attempt to convince readers that its argument is logically flawed, inadequately supported, or based on erroneous assumptions. In refuting an argument, you can rebut (1) the writer's stated reason and grounds, (2) the writer's warrant and backing, or (3) both. Put in less specialized language, you can rebut a writer's reasons and evidence or the writer's underlying assumptions. Let's begin with a simple example. Suppose you wanted to refute this argument:

We shouldn't elect Joe as committee chair because he is too bossy.

Displayed in Toulmin's terms, the argument looks like this:

CLAIM:	We shouldn't elect Joe as committee chair.
STATED REASON:	because he is too bossy
GROUNDS:	evidence that Joe is bossy
WARRANT:	Bossy people make bad committee chairs.

One way to refute this argument is to rebut the stated reason and grounds:

REBUTTAL OF REASON AND GROUNDS

I disagree with you that Joe is bossy. In fact, Joe is very unbossy. He's a good listener who's willing to compromise, and he involves others in decisions. The example you cite for his being bossy wasn't typical. It was a one-time circumstance that doesn't represent his normal behavior. [The writer could then provide examples of Joe's cooperative nature.]

Or you could concede that Joe is bossy but rebut the argument's warrant that bossiness is a bad trait:

REBUTTAL OF WARRANT

I agree that Joe is bossy, but in this circumstance bossiness is just the trait we need. This committee hasn't gotten anything done for six months and time is running out. We need a decisive person who can come in, get the committee organized, assign tasks, and get the job done.

Let's now illustrate these strategies in a more complex situation. For an example, we'll look at the issue of whether recycling is an effective strategy for saving the environment. A controversial subissue of recycling is whether the United States is running out of space for sanitary landfills. Here is how one environmental writer argues that there are no places left to dump our garbage:

Because the United States is running out of landfill space, Americans will simply not be able to put the 180 million tons of solid waste they generate each year into landfills, where 70 percent of it now goes. Since 1979, the United States has exhausted more than two-thirds of its landfills; projections indicate that another one-fifth will close over the next five years. Between 1983 and 1987, for example, New York closed 200 of its 500 landfills; this year Connecticut will exhaust its landfill capacity. If the problem seemed abstract to Americans, it became odiously real in the summer of 1989 as most of the nation watched the notorious garbage barge from Islip, New York, wander 6,000 miles, searching for a place to dump its rancid 3,100-ton load.*

This passage tries to persuade us that the United States is running out of landfill space. Now watch how writer John Tierney attempts to refute this argument in an influential 1996 *New York Times Magazine* article entitled "Recycling Is Garbage:"

REBUTTAL OF ARGUMENT THAT AMERICA IS RUNNING OUT OF LANDFILL SPACE

[Proponents of recycling believe that] our garbage will bury us. The *Mobro's*[†] saga was presented as a grim harbinger of future landfill scarcity, but it actually represented a short-lived scare caused by new environmental regulations. As old municipal dumps were forced to close in the 1980's, towns had to send their garbage elsewhere and pay higher prices for scarce landfill space. But the higher prices predictably encouraged companies to open huge new landfills, in some regions creating a glut that set off price-cutting wars. Over the past few years, landfills in the South and Middle West have been vying for garbage from the New York area, and it has become cheaper to ship garbage there than to bury it locally.

America has a good deal more landfill space available than it did 10 years ago. [...] A. Clark Wiseman, an economist at Gonzaga University in Spokane, Wash., has calculated that if Americans keep generating garbage at current rates for 1,000 years, and if all their garbage is put in a landfill 100 yards deep, by the year 3000 this national garbage heap will fill a square piece of land 35 miles on each side.

This doesn't seem a huge imposition in a country the size of America. The garbage would occupy only 5 percent of the area needed for the national array of solar panels proposed by environmentalists. The millennial landfill would fit on one-tenth of 1 percent of the range land now available for grazing in the continental United States.[‡]

In this case, Tierney uses counterevidence to rebut the reason and grounds of the original enthymeme: "Recycling is needed because the United States is running out of landfill space." Tierney attacks this argument by disagreeing with the stated reason that the United States is running out of landfill space.

Writers are also likely to question the underlying assumptions (warrants) of an opposing view. For an example, consider another recycling controversy: From

*George C. Lodge and Jeffrey F. Rayport, "Knee-Deep and Rising: America's Recycling Crisis," *Harvard Business Review* Sept–Oct. 1991, 132.

[†]*Mobro* is the name of the notorious garbage barge from Islip, New York, referred to at the end of the previous quotation.

[‡]John Tierney, "Recycling Is Garbage," *New York Times Magazine* 30 June 1996, 28.

an economic perspective, is recycling cost-effective? In criticizing recycling, Tierney argues that recycling wastes money; he provides evidence that "every time a sanitation department crew picks up a load of bottles and cans from the curb, New York City loses money." In Toulmin's terms, Tierney's line of reasoning is structured as follows:

TIERNEY'S ENTHYMEME:	Promoting recycling is bad policy because it costs more to recycle material than to bury the same material in a landfill.
CLAIM:	Promoting recycling is bad policy.
STATED REASON:	because it costs more to recycle material than to bury the same material in a landfill
GROUNDS:	evidence of the high cost of recycling [Tierney cites evidence that it costs New York City $200 more per ton to collect and dispose of recyclables than to bury them]
WARRANT:	We should dispose of garbage in the least expensive way.

In rebutting Tierney's argument, proponents of recycling typically accepted Tierney's figures on recycling costs in New York City (that is, they agreed that in New York City recycling was more expensive than burying garbage). But in various ways they attacked his warrant. Typically, proponents of recycling said that even if the costs of recycling were higher than burying wastes in a landfill, recycling still benefited the environment by reducing the amount of virgin materials taken from nature. This argument says, in effect, that saving virgin resources takes precedence over economic costs.

These examples show how a refutation can focus either on the stated reasons and grounds of an argument or on the warrants and backing.

FOR CLASS DISCUSSION

Imagine how each of the following arguments might be fleshed out with grounds and backing. Then attempt to refute each argument by suggesting ways to rebut the reason and grounds, or the warrant and backing, or both.

1. Writing courses should be pass/fail because the pass/fail system would encourage more creativity.

2. The government should make cigarettes illegal because cigarettes cause cancer and heart disease.

3. Majoring in engineering is better than majoring in music because engineers make more money than musicians.

4. People should not eat meat because doing so causes needless pain and suffering to animals.

5. The endangered species law is too stringent because it seriously hampers the economy.

Strategies for Rebutting Evidence

Whether you are rebutting an argument's reasons and grounds or its warrant and backing, you will frequently need to question a writer's use of evidence. Here are some strategies that you can use.

Deny the Truth of the Data

What one writer considers a fact another may consider a case of wrong information. If you have reason to doubt a writer's facts, then call them into question.

Cite Counterexamples or Countertestimony

One of the most effective ways to counter an argument based on examples is to cite a counterexample. The effect of counterexamples is to deny the conclusiveness of the original data. Similarly, citing an authority whose testimony counters other expert testimony is a good way to begin refuting an argument based on testimony.

Cast Doubt on the Representativeness or Sufficiency of Examples

Examples are powerful only if the audience feels them to be representative and sufficient. Many environmentalists complained that John Tierney's attack on recycling was based too largely on data from New York City and that it didn't accurately take into account the more positive experiences of other cities and states. When data from outside New York City were examined, the cost-effectiveness and positive environmental impact of recycling seemed more apparent.

Cast Doubt on the Relevance or Recency of the Examples, Statistics, or Testimony

The best evidence is up-to-date. In a rapidly changing universe, data that are even a few years out-of-date are often ineffective. For example, as the demand for recycled goods increases, the cost of recycling will be reduced. Out-of-date statistics will skew any argument about the cost of recycling. Another problem with data is their occasional lack of relevance. For example, in arguing that an adequate ozone layer is necessary for preventing skin cancers, it is not relevant to cite statistics on the alarming rise of lung cancers.

Call into Question the Credibility of an Authority

If an opposing argument is based on testimony, you can undermine its persuasiveness if you show that a person being cited lacks up-to-date or relevant expertise in the field. (This procedure is different from the *ad hominem* fallacy discussed in Appendix 1 because it doesn't attack the personal character of the authority but only the authority's expertise on a specific matter.)

Question the Accuracy or Context of Quotations

Evidence based on testimony is frequently distorted by being either misquoted or taken out of context. Often scientists qualify their findings heavily, but these qualifications are omitted by the popular media. You can thus attack the use of a quotation by putting it in its original context or by restoring the qualifications accompanying the quotation in its original source.

Question the Way Statistical Data Were Produced or Interpreted

Chapter 6 provides fuller treatment of how to question statistics. In general, you can rebut statistical evidence by calling into account how the data were gathered, treated mathematically, or interpreted. It can make a big difference, for example, whether you cite raw numbers or percentages or whether you choose large or small increments for the axes of graphs.

Example of a Student Essay Using Refutation Strategy

The following extract from a student essay is the refutation section of a classical argument appealing to a neutral or undecided audience. In this essay, student writer Marybeth Hamilton argues the claim that First Place, an alternative public school for homeless children that also provides support services for their families, should continue to be publicly funded because it provides the emotional and educational support homeless children need to become mainstreamed. In the beginning of her essay, Marybeth explains that First Place provides not only a nurturing, supportive educational environment for its homeless students but also services such as counseling and therapy for the students' families. At least 80 percent of the children at First Place have witnessed domestic violence or have experienced physical, sexual, or emotional abuse. Lacking permanent housing, many of these children have moved from school to school. Because running First Place is costly and can accommodate only 4 percent of her city's homeless children who need help, Marybeth recognizes that her audience may object to First Place. Consequently, to reach the neutral and resistant members of her audience, she devotes the following portion of her argument to summarizing and refuting opposing views.

From "First Place: A Healing School for Homeless Children"

Marybeth Hamilton (Student)

... As stated earlier, the goal of First Place is to prepare students for returning to main-   1
stream public schools. Although there are many reasons to continue operating an agency
like First Place, there are some who would argue against it. One argument is that the school
is too expensive, costing many more taxpayer dollars per child than a mainstream school.
I can understand this objection to cost, but one way to look at First Place is as a preventative action by the city to reduce the future costs of crime and welfare. Because all the students at First Place are at-risk for educational failure, drug and alcohol abuse, or numerous
other long-term problems, a program like First Place attempts to stop the problems before
they start. In the long run, the city could be saving money in areas such as drug rehabilitation, welfare payments, or jail costs.

Others might criticize First Place for spending some of its funding on social services   2
for the students and their families instead of spending it all on educational needs. When
the city is already making welfare payments and providing a shelter for the families, why
do they deserve anything more? Basically, the job of any school is to help a child become
educated and have social skills. At First Place, students' needs run deep, and their entire
families are in crisis. What good is it to help just the child when the rest of the family is
still suffering? The education of only the child will not help the family out of poverty. Therefore, First Place helps parents look for jobs by providing job search help including assistance
with résumés. They even supply clothes to wear to an interview. First Place also provides
a parent support group for expressing anxieties and learning coping skills. This therapy
helps parents deal with their struggles in a productive way, reducing the chance that they
will take out their frustration on their child. All these "extras" are an attempt to help the
family get back on its feet and become self-supporting.

Another objection to an agency like First Place is that the short-term stay at First Place   3
does no long-term good for the student. However, in talking with Michael Siptroth, a
teacher at First Place, I learned that the individual attention the students receive helps
many of them catch up in school quite quickly. He reported that some students actually
made a three-grade-level improvement in one year. This improvement definitely contributes
to the long-term good of the student, especially in the area of self-esteem. Also, the students
at First Place are in desperate situations. For most, any help is better than no help. Thus
First Place provides extended day care for the children so they won't have to be unsuper-
vised at home while their parents are working or looking for work. For example, some
homeless children live in motels on Aurora Avenue, a major highway that is overrun with
fast cars, prostitutes, and drugs. Aurora Avenue is not a safe place for children to play, so
the extended day care is important for many of First Place's students.

Finally, opponents might question the value of removing students from mainstream   4
classrooms. Some might argue that separating children from regular classrooms is not good
because it further highlights their differences from the mainstream children. Also, the separation period might cause additional alienation when the First Place child does return to

a mainstream school. In reality, though, the effects are quite different. Children at First Place are sympathetic to each other. Perhaps for the first time in their lives, they do not have to be on the defensive because no one is going to make fun of them for being homeless; they are all homeless. The time spent at First Place is usually a time for catching up to the students in mainstream schools. When students catch up, they have one fewer reason to be seen as different from mainstream students. If the students stayed in the mainstream school and continued to fall behind, they would only get teased more.

5   First Place is a program that merits the community's ongoing moral and financial support. With more funding, First Place could help many more homeless children and their families along the path toward self-sufficiency. While this school is not the ultimate answer to the problem of homelessness, it is a beginning. These children deserve a chance to build their own lives, free from the stigma of homelessness, and I, as a responsible citizen, feel a civic and moral duty to do all I can to help them.

FOR CLASS DISCUSSION

Having worked as a teacher's aide at First Place school, Marybeth Hamilton is familiar with the public criticism that the school receives. Individually or in groups, analyze the refutation strategies she employs in her argument.

1. Summarize each of the opposing reasons that Marybeth anticipates from her audience.

2. How does she attempt to refute each line of reasoning in the opposing argument? In each case does she refute her audience's reason and grounds, the warrant, or both?

3. Which of her counterexamples and counter-reasons do you think is her strongest? After reading her argument, would you as a city resident vote for the allotment of more public money for this school? Why or why not?

Conceding to Opposing Views

In writing a classical argument, a writer must sometimes concede to an opposing argument rather than refute it. Sometimes you encounter portions of an argument that you simply can't refute. For example, suppose you support the legalization of hard drugs such as cocaine and heroin. Adversaries argue that legalizing hard drugs will increase the number of drug users and addicts. You might dispute the size of their numbers, but you reluctantly agree that they are right. Your strategy in this case is not to refute the opposing argument but to concede to it by admitting that legalization of hard drugs will promote heroin and cocaine addiction. Having made that concession, your task is then to show that the benefits of drug legalization still outweigh the costs you've just conceded.

As this example shows, the strategy of a concession argument is to switch from the field of values employed by the writer you disagree with to a different field of values more favorable to your position. You don't try to refute the writer's stated reason and grounds (by arguing that legalization will *not* lead to increased drug usage and addiction) or the writer's warrant (by arguing that increased drug use and addiction is not a problem). Rather, you shift the argument to a new field of values by introducing a new warrant, one that you think your audience can share (that the benefits of legalization—eliminating the black market and ending the crime and violence associated with procurement of drugs—outweigh the costs of increased addiction). To the extent that opponents of legalization share your desire to stop drug-related crime, shifting to this new field of values is a good strategy. Although it may seem that you weaken your own position by conceding to an opposing argument, you may actually strengthen it by increasing your credibility and gaining your audience's goodwill. Moreover, conceding to one part of an opposing argument doesn't mean that you won't refute other parts of that argument.

APPEALING TO A RESISTANT AUDIENCE: DELAYED THESIS OR ROGERIAN ARGUMENT

Whereas classical argument is effective for neutral or undecided audiences, it is often less effective for audiences strongly opposed to the writer's position. Because resisting audiences often hold values, assumptions, or beliefs widely different from the writer's, they are unswayed by classical argument, which attacks their worldview too directly. On many values-laden issues such as abortion, gun control, gay rights, and welfare reform, the distance between a writer and a resisting audience can be so great that dialogue hardly seems possible.

Because of these wide differences in basic beliefs and values, a writer's goal is seldom to convert resistant readers to the writer's position. The best that the writer can hope for is to reduce somewhat the level of resistance, perhaps by opening a channel of conversation, increasing the reader's willingness to listen, and preparing the way for future dialogue. If you can get a resistant audience to say, "Well, I still don't agree with you, but I now understand you better and respect your views more," you will have been highly successful.

Delayed-Thesis Argument

In many cases you can reach a resistant audience by using a *delayed-thesis* structure in which you wait until the end of your argument to reveal your thesis. Classical argument asks you to state your thesis in the introduction, support it with reasons and evidence, and then summarize and refute opposing views. Rhetorically, however, it is not always advantageous to tell your readers where you stand at the start of your argument or to separate yourself so definitively from alternative views. For resistant audiences, it may be better to keep the issue open, delaying the revelation of your own position until the end of the essay.

To illustrate the different effects of classical versus delayed-thesis arguments, we invite you to read a delayed-thesis argument by nationally syndicated columnist Ellen Goodman. The article appeared shortly after the nation was shocked by a brutal gang rape in New Bedford, Massachusetts, in which a woman was raped on a pool table by patrons of a local bar.*

Minneapolis Pornography Ordinance

Ellen Goodman

1   Just a couple of months before the pool-table gang rape in New Bedford, Mass., *Hustler* magazine printed a photo feature that reads like a blueprint for the actual crime. There were just two differences between *Hustler* and real life. In *Hustler,* the woman enjoyed it. In real life, the woman charged rape.

2   There is no evidence that the four men charged with this crime had actually read the magazine. Nor is there evidence that the spectators who yelled encouragement for two hours had held previous ringside seats at pornographic events. But there is a growing sense that the violent pornography being peddled in this country helps to create an atmosphere in which such events occur.

3   As recently as last month, a study done by two University of Wisconsin researchers suggested that even "normal" men, prescreened college students, were changed by their exposure to violent pornography. After just ten hours of viewing, reported researcher Edward Donnerstein, "the men were less likely to convict in a rape trial, less likely to see injury to a victim, more likely to see the victim as responsible." Pornography may not cause rape directly, he said, "but it maintains a lot of very callous attitudes. It justifies aggression. It even says you are doing a favor to the victim."

4   If we can prove that pornography is harmful, then shouldn't the victims have legal rights? This, in any case, is the theory behind a city ordinance that recently passed the Minneapolis City Council. Vetoed by the mayor last week, it is likely to be back before the Council for an overriding vote, likely to appear in other cities, other towns. What is unique about the Minneapolis approach is that for the first time it attacks pornography, not because of nudity or sexual explicitness, but because it degrades and harms women. It opposes pornography on the basis of sex discrimination.

5   University of Minnesota Law Professor Catherine MacKinnon, who co-authored the ordinance with feminist writer Andrea Dworkin, says that they chose this tactic because they believe that pornography is central to "creating and maintaining the inequality of the sexes. . . . Just being a woman means you are injured by pornography."

*The rape occurred in 1985 and was later made the subject of an Academy Award–winning movie, *The Accused,* starring Jodie Foster.

They defined pornography carefully as, "the sexually explicit subordination of women,   6
graphically depicted, whether in pictures or in words." To fit their legal definition it must
also include one of nine conditions that show this subordination, like presenting women
who "experience sexual pleasure in being raped or . . . mutilated. . . ." Under this law, it
would be possible for a pool-table rape victim to sue *Hustler.* It would be possible for a
woman to sue if she were forced to act in a pornographic movie. Indeed, since the law describes pornography as oppressive to all women, it would be possible for any woman to sue
those who traffic in the stuff for violating her civil rights.

In many ways, the Minneapolis ordinance is an appealing attack on an appalling prob-   7
lem. The authors have tried to resolve a long and bubbling conflict among those who have
both a deep aversion to pornography and a deep loyalty to the value of free speech. "To
date," says Professor MacKinnon, "people have identified the pornographer's freedom with
everybody's freedom. But we're saying that the freedom of the pornographer is the subordination of women. It means one has to take a side."

But the sides are not quite as clear as Professor MacKinnon describes them. Nor is the   8
ordinance.

Even if we accept the argument that pornography is harmful to women—and I do—   9
then we must also recognize that anti-Semitic literature is harmful to Jews and racist literature is harmful to blacks. For that matter, Marxist literature may be harmful to government
policy. It isn't just women versus pornographers. If women win the right to sue publishers
and producers, then so could Jews, blacks, and a long list of people who may be able to
prove they have been harmed by books, movies, speeches or even records. The Manson
murders, you may recall, were reportedly inspired by the Beatles.

We might prefer a library or book store or lecture hall without *Mein Kampf* or the   10
Grand Whoever of the Ku Klux Klan. But a growing list of harmful expressions would inevitably strangle freedom of speech.

This ordinance was carefully written to avoid problems of banning and prior restraint,   11
but the right of any woman to claim damages from pornography is just too broad. It seems
destined to lead to censorship.

What the Minneapolis City Council has before it is a very attractive theory. What   12
MacKinnon and Dworkin have written is a very persuasive and useful definition of pornography. But they haven't yet resolved the conflict between the harm of pornography and the
value of free speech. In its present form, this is still a shaky piece of law.

Consider now how this argument's rhetorical effect would be different if Ellen
Goodman had revealed her thesis in the introduction using the classical argument
form. Here is how this introduction might have looked:

GOODMAN'S INTRODUCTION REWRITTEN IN CLASSICAL FORM

Just a couple of months before the pool-table gang rape in New Bedford,
Mass., *Hustler* magazine printed a photo feature that reads like a blueprint for the
actual crime. There were just two differences between *Hustler* and real life. In *Hustler,* the woman enjoyed it. In real life, the woman charged rape. Of course, there
is no evidence that the four men charged with this crime had actually read the

magazine. Nor is there evidence that the spectators who yelled encouragement for two hours had held previous ringside seats at pornographic events.

But there is a growing sense that the violent pornography being peddled in this country helps to create an atmosphere in which such events occur. One city is taking a unique approach to attack this problem. An ordinance recently passed by the Minneapolis City Council outlaws pornography not because it contains nudity or sexually explicit acts, but because it degrades and harms women. Unfortunately, despite the proponents' good intentions, the Minneapolis ordinance is a bad law because it has potentially dangerous consequences.

Even though Goodman's position can be grasped more quickly in this classical form, our students generally find the original-delayed thesis version more effective. Why is this?

Most people point to the greater sense of complexity and surprise in the delayed-thesis version, a sense that comes largely from the delayed discovery of the writer's position. Whereas the classical version immediately labels the ordinance a "bad law," the original version withholds judgment, inviting the reader to examine the law more sympathetically and to identify with the position of those who drafted it. Rather than distancing herself from those who see pornography as a violation of women's rights, Goodman shares with her readers her own struggles to think through these issues, thereby persuading us of her genuine sympathy for the ordinance and for its feminist proponents. In the end, her delayed thesis renders her final rejection of the ordinance not only more surprising but more convincing.

Clearly, then, a writer's decision about when to reveal her thesis is critical. Revealing the thesis early makes the writer seem more hardnosed, more sure of her position, more confident about how to divide the ground into friendly and hostile camps, more in control. Delaying the thesis, in contrast, complicates the issues, increases reader sympathy for more than one view, and heightens interest in the tension among alternative views and in the writer's struggle for clarity.

Rogerian Argument

An even more powerful strategy for addressing resistant audiences is a conciliatory strategy often called *Rogerian argument,* named after psychologist Carl Rogers, who used this strategy to help people resolve differences.* Rogerian argument emphasizes "empathic listening," which Rogers defined as the ability to see an issue sympathetically from another person's perspective. He trained people to withhold judgment of another person's ideas until after they listened attentively to the other person, understood that person's reasoning, appreciated that

---

*See Carl Rogers's essay "Communication: Its Blocking and Its Facilitation" in his book *On Becoming a Person* (Boston: Houghton Mifflin, 1961), 329–37. For a fuller discussion of Rogerian argument, see Richard Young, Alton Becker, and Kenneth Pike, *Rhetoric: Discovery and Change* (New York: Harcourt Brace, 1972).

person's values, respected that person's humanity—in short, walked in that person's shoes. Before disagreeing with another person, Rogers would tell his clients, you must be able to summarize that person's argument so accurately that he or she will say, "Yes, you understand my position."

What Carl Rogers understood is that traditional methods of argumentation are threatening. When you try to persuade people to change their minds on an issue, Rogers claimed, you are actually demanding a change in their worldview—to get other people, in a sense, to quit being their kind of person and start being your kind of person. Research psychologists have shown that persons are often not swayed by a logical argument if it somehow threatens their own view of the world. Carl Rogers was therefore interested in finding ways to make arguments less threatening. In Rogerian argument the writer typically waits until the end of the essay to present his position, and that position is often a compromise between the writer's original views and those of the resisting audience. Because Rogerian argument stresses the psychological as well as logical dimensions of argument, and because it emphasizes reducing threat and building bridges rather than winning an argument, it is particularly effective when dealing with emotionally laden issues.

Under Rogerian strategy, the writer reduces the sense of threat in her argument by showing that *both writer and resistant audience share many basic values.* Instead of attacking the audience as wrongheaded, the Rogerian writer respects the audience's intelligence and humanity and demonstrates an understanding of the audience's position before presenting her own position. Finally, the Rogerian writer never asks the audience to capitulate entirely to the writer's side—just to shift somewhat toward the writer's views. By acknowledging that she has already shifted toward the audience's views, the writer makes it easier for the audience to accept compromise. All of this negotiation ideally leads to a compromise between—or better, a synthesis of—the opposing positions.

The key to successful Rogerian argument, besides the art of listening, is the ability to point out areas of agreement between the writer's and reader's positions. For example, if you support a woman's right to choose abortion and you are arguing with someone completely opposed to abortion, you're unlikely to convert your reader, but you might reduce the level of resistance. You begin this process by summarizing your reader's position sympathetically, stressing your shared values. You might say, for example, that you also value babies; that you also are appalled by people who treat abortion as a form of birth control; that you also worry that the easy acceptance of abortion diminishes the value society places on human life; and that you also agree that accepting abortion lightly can lead to lack of sexual responsibility. Building bridges like these between you and your readers makes it more likely that they will listen to you when you present your own position.

In its emphasis on establishing common ground, Rogerian argument has much in common with recent feminist theories of argument. Many feminists criticize classical argument as rooted in a male value system and tainted by metaphors of war and combat. Thus, classical arguments, with their emphasis on assertion and refutation, are typically praised for being "powerful" or "forceful." The writer "defends" his position and "attacks" his "opponent's" position using facts and data as "ammunition" and reasons as "big guns" to "blow away" his opponent's claim. According to some theorists, viewing argument as war can lead to inauthenticity, posturing, and game playing. The traditional pro-con debate—defined in one of our desk dictionaries as "a formal contest of argumentation in which two opposing teams defend and attack a given proposition"—treats argument as verbal jousting, more concerned to determine a winner than to clarify an issue.

One of our female students, who excelled as a debater in high school and received straight A's in argument classes, recently explained in an essay her growing alienation from male rhetoric: "Although women students are just as likely to excel in 'male' writing [. . .] we are less likely to feel as if we were saying something authentic and true." Later the student elaborated on her distrust of "persuasion":

> What many writing teachers have told me is that "the most important writing/ speaking you will ever do will be to persuade someone." My experience as a person who has great difficulty naming and expressing emotions is that the most important communication in my life is far more likely to be simply telling someone how I feel. To say "I love you," or "I'm angry with you," will be far more valuable in most relationship contexts than to say "These are the three reasons why you shouldn't have done what you did [. . .] ."*

Writers who share this woman's distrust of classical argumentation often find Rogerian argument appealing because it stresses self-examination, clarification, and accommodation rather than refutation. Rogerian argument is more in tune with win-win negotiation than with win-lose debate.

To illustrate a conciliatory or Rogerian approach to an issue, here is how one student wrote a letter to her boss recommending a change in the kind of merchandise stocked in a small-town music store.

Letter to Beth Downey

Ms. Beth Downey, Owner/Manager
Downey's Music
Grayfish

Dear Ms. Downey:

1   I would just like to comment on the success of "Downey's Music" in Grayfish and say that, as owner and manager, you have done a wonderful job. I'm sure that you have the most ex-

---

*Our thanks to Catherine Brown for this paragraph from an unpublished paper written at Seattle University.

tensive classical music, music teaching books, piano and acoustic guitar inventory of any store in a 100-square-mile area. After working for you for three years, I have encountered music teachers and classical music lovers coming as far as 70 miles to buy their music from Downey's. All have had nothing but compliments for you and for the store. However, I would once again like to bring up the subject of introducing an inventory of electronic music equipment to the store. Since Grayfish is mainly a tourist town, many times a week I have people from touring bands, visiting Canadians, and also locals coming into the store looking for such things as electronic keyboards, electric guitars, and amplifiers. I know that you have qualms about this idea, but I believe that I have a suggestion that we could both agree on.

First, let me restate your reasons for objecting to such a move. You have already stated   2 that if a change will benefit the store, the initial investment is well worth the expense in the long run (e.g., when pianos were added to the inventory). Therefore, I assume that cost is not a factor at this time. However, you feel that the "kind of people" that electronics may draw could possibly offend our present clientele. You feel, as well as others, that the people who are drawn by electronics are often long-haired, dirty, and give a bad impression. This would in effect change the store's image. Also, you are afraid that the noise caused by these instruments could turn classical music lovers away from the store. The sounds of electronic instruments are not always pleasing, and since most of our clientele are older, more refined persons, you feel that these sounds will force some to go to other stores. Mainly, however, you are worried about the result that the change in the store's image could have upon a community the size of Grayfish. Many people in this area, I realize, feel that electronic music means heavy rock music, while this in turn means alcohol and drugs.

Basically, I agree with you that Grayfish needs a "classical" music store and that the   3 culture that your store brings to Grayfish greatly enhances the area. I also love classical music and want to see it growing and alive. I also have some of the same fears about adding electronic music to the inventory. I enjoy the atmosphere of Downey's, and I have always enjoyed working there, so I don't want to see anything adverse happen to it, either. On the other hand, I feel that if a large electronic music section were added to the store with soundproof rooms, a "sit and try it" atmosphere, and a catalog inventory large enough to special-order anything that a customer might want that is not in the store, it would help immensely in the success of the store. With the way that Downey's is built, on two levels, it would be very easy to accommodate the needs of both departments. Even now we are only using about half the floor space available, while the rest is empty storage area. By building soundproof rooms on the lower level, we could easily double the in-use floor area, increase our tourist clientele, have the music business in *all* areas cornered for approximately 60 square miles, and also add practice rooms for our present customers to use when they are choosing music.

I know that you are wrestling with this idea of such a drastic changeover, so I would   4 like to propose a nonthreatening, easy-to-reverse first step. My solution is to start slowly, on a trial basis, and see how it works. I suggest that we start with a few small electronic keyboards, a few electric guitars, and one or two amps. In this way, we could begin to collect the information and literature on other electronic equipment that may be added later on, see how the community responds to such a move, find out how our present clientele reacts, get a feel for the demand in this field, and yet still be a small hometown music store without a great investment in this electronic area. I still feel that a large addition would be more successful, but I also believe that this little test may help prove to you, or disprove to me, that electronic music instruments in this area are in high demand. I honestly feel that electronics could produce fantastic profits for the people who get into the business first. I would love it if these "people" could be the owners and workers at Downey's Music.

Sincerely,

Mary Doe

FOR CLASS DISCUSSION

1. In this letter, what shared values between writer and audience does the writer stress?

2. Imagine the letter rewritten as a classical argument. How would it be different?

APPEALING TO A RESISTANT AUDIENCE: USING HUMOR

Another strategy that can sometimes appeal to a resistant audience is humor. Anyone who has experienced moments of hilarity with others—friends, a lover, family members, coworkers—knows how powerful laughing together can be in building relationships. Humor can also relieve stress and open up fresh perspectives, even momentarily turn the world upside down to show us what we couldn't see before. In arguments, humor can strengthen the bonds among people who already agree by solidifying their common ground. It can also be used in arguments to win over resistant audiences, often by neutralizing their objections through entertaining amusement. Humor, especially when it evokes laughter, is disarming; it melts opposition, sometimes winning our assent to ideas we might reject if they were presented seriously. Humor can also be a way for you, the arguer, to express your concern, exasperation, or anger about an issue more productively than through direct or serious confrontation with your audience. When and how you use humor in your arguments has to be your call, based on context. Despite our fondness for humorous writing, we have to offer this caveat: Using humor in arguments is risky business that may backfire on you, especially if a resistant audience feels ridiculed. But humor may be powerfully persuasive.

Although we can't give you simple rules to determine when to use humor in your arguments, we can briefly explain some of the tools you can employ to construct an argument using humor. Some of the humorist's main tools are these imaginative uses of language: hyperbole (or exaggeration), understatement, repetition, and witty, memorable lines. *Hyperbole* refers to a writer's exaggeration of an idea. Often, inflating or blowing up an idea to enormous proportions compels an audience to see that idea as ridiculous and to laugh with you about it. *Understatement* works in an opposite manner: A writer leaves unsaid, but strongly implies, an idea, drawing the audience into a "shared" joke by asking the audience to see beyond the words. When you use understatement, you express an idea so far below the intensity it deserves that you push readers to supply the unsaid meaning in their own minds. *Repetition* of an idea builds up momentum (that "on a roll now" feeling) and collaborates with exaggeration by piling up details or ideas to ridiculous levels, conveying an idea through the sheer weight and rhythm of the language. *Witty, memorable lines* are funny flashes of insight expressed in well-placed colorful images or surprisingly suitable words; they can be those zingers or punch lines that drive home a point and leave the audience amazed and amused.

To show you how these tools of humor can operate in argument, we present below excerpts from the transcript of a public hearing in New York City on the possible relocation of Richard Serra's *Tilted Arc,* a sculpture placed in the plaza of the Jacob Javits Federal Building in lower Manhattan.* Some members of the community found this gigantic piece of metal offensive. In this hearing, the artist and his sympathizers argued that art should resist easy comprehension and challenge, even disturb, our perceptions. Other people at the hearing condemned and rejected this notion of art.

In the following passage, Phil La Basi, a federal employee who worked in a building on the plaza, protests the artist's definition of art and uses hyperbole, repetition, and witty lines to try to make the audience see his vision of this sculpture.

USING HYPERBOLE, WIT, AND REPETITION TO ARGUE A POSITION

Hyperbole

What I see there is something that looks like a tank trap to prevent an armed attack from Chinatown in case of a Soviet invasion. In my mind it probably wouldn't even do that well, because one good Russian tank could probably take it out.

Witty lines playing on "tilted arc"

To be very serious, I wouldn't call it *Tilted Arc.* To me it looks like crooked metal or bent metal. I think we can call anything art if we call that art. I think any one of those people here could come along with an old broken bicycle that perhaps got run over by a car, or some other piece of material, and put it up and call it art and name it something. I think that is what was done here. [. . .]

Hyperbole

Repetition

---

*A more complete version of the transcripts of the public hearing in New York City on *Tilted Arc* is printed in Margaret P. Battin, John Fisher, Ronald Moore, and Anita Silvers, *Puzzles about Art* (New York: St. Martin's Press, 1989). Phil La Basi's remarks appear on pages 186–87; Peter Hirsh's testimony is on pages 183–84.

Another speaker at the hearing, Peter Hirsh, the research director and legal counsel for the Association of Immigration Attorneys, used understatement to denounce the sculpture. Notice the low-key way in which Hirsh basically says he thinks the sculpture is garbage.

USING UNDERSTATEMENT TO MAKE A POINT

Understatement leaving unsaid the writer's full dislike and disgust

My membership has authorized me to say that we are entirely opposed to *Tilted Arc*. My own personal view is that a good place to put *Tilted Arc* would be in the Hudson River. [. . .] I am told that they are going to have to put artificial things in the river to provide shelter for the striped bass. I think *Tilted Arc* would make a very fine shelter.

Humorous arguments can often take the form of satire or parody. In *satire*, a writer adopts an ironic point of view and appears to praise the very thing he or she is holding up for criticism. Often by exaggerating the weaknesses, foolishness, wrongness, or evils of some issue while seeming to support the issue (saying the opposite of what is really thought or meant), the writer can expose those weaknesses to ridicule. In this indirect and disruptive way, satire seeks to win the audience's acceptance of the writer's perspective. On a continuum ranging from "playfully critical and funny" to "harshly condemning and biting," satire often leans toward the latter.

Humorous argument can also be written as parody. A *parody* imitates a serious piece of work or even an event but seeks to ridicule it. It takes the familiar but changes it into something new that reminds readers of the original, plays off it, and in some way criticizes the original.

As a reaction to the recent volatile discussions of government regulation of guns in the House of Representatives, an article entitled "The Gun Commandments" appeared in the magazine *The Economist*.* In the passages from this article that follow, you can see that the piece employs both satire and parody. The article satirizes the House's ineffective approach to gun control by appearing to side with the anti–gun control position and by exaggerating that position to absurd proportions. It also parodies the House's stance toward gun control and its decision to post the Ten Commandments in schools by rewriting the Ten Commandments as Gun Commandments.

USING SATIRE AND PARODY TO ARGUE A POSITION

Satire

It is in the spirit of Mr. DeLay that the House decided, rather than controlling guns, to allow the Ten Commandments to be posted on the walls of every public school in America. That will teach them.

---

*"The Gun Commandments," *Economist* 26 June 1999, 22. The article is anonymous.

Satire

It is, of course, possible that the Supreme Court (a Godless institution) will decide that this offends against the separation of church and state. If this happens, Congress has an alternative set of commandments ready. They will do just as well.

Parody
{

1. Honour the National Rifle Association, and remember that it doth contribute $4m to congressional campaigns. [. . .]
3. Honour the Sabbath day and keep it holy. Six days shalt thou labour and do all thy work, and on the seventh thou shalt do target practice. [. . .]
5. Thou shalt not kill, except when provoked. But if thou dost, remember that thy *gun* had nothing to do with it. [. . .]

In this example of satire and parody, the writer manages to express harsh criticism of and anger at Congress and the anti–gun control faction but does so in a clever, surprising way that makes even a resistant audience listen before turning off. The piece lures readers into its perspective, couching its real view of gun control in irony. If nothing else, the writer makes the audience think of the gun control issue in a wacky, distorted way that exposes the flaws in the anti–gun control position and the weaknesses in Congress's response.

As you contemplate both your investment in your claim and the level of resistance of your intended audience, determine whether humor as a main approach or as a way to make a point here and there might be an effective means to diminish your audience's resistance and perhaps even warm the audience up to your argument.

◤ FOR CLASS DISCUSSION

George F. Will's article "The Perils of Brushing" appeared in the May 10, 1999, issue of *Newsweek* as a "The Last Word" column. After reading this piece, work individually or in groups to answer the questions that follow.

The Perils of Brushing
George F. Will

All of us have seen lots of them, those words of warning or instruction that appear on products we buy. "Do not eat this sled." "For best results do not apply this floor wax to your teeth." "This antifreeze is not intended for pouring on breakfast cereal." We hardly notice them, let alone consider what they say about the times in which we live. The sled,   1 wax and antifreeze warnings are apocryphal. But you could not know that. After all, *The American Enterprise* magazine offers these from real life:

2   On a bag of Fritos: "You could be a winner! No purchase necessary. Details inside." On a bread pudding: "Product will be hot after heating." On a bar of Dial soap: "Use like regular soap." On a hotel shower cap: "Fits one head." On a package of Nytol sleeping aid: "May cause drowsiness." On a string of Christmas lights: "For indoor or outdoor use only." On the packaging of a Rowenta iron. "Do not iron clothes on body."

3   The warning about a product's being hot after heating may be a response to the famous case wherein a woman successfully sued McDonald's because she was burned when she spilled—she was a passenger in a stationary car at the time, with the cup between her legs—the hot McDonald's coffee she had just bought. (If the coffee had been cool, a complaint about that could have been packaged as a lawsuit.) But try to picture in your mind the event involving two or more heads that the manufacturer of the shower cap was worried about.

4   Give up? Well, then, answer this: If there are people who press their pants while in their pants, are they the sort of people whose behavior will be changed by a warning on the packaging the iron comes in? If there are people who have done that once, are there any who have done it twice? If not, does that demonstrate that even the dimmest among us has a learning curve that actually curves?

5   Such questions are stirred by the great toothbrush litigation just getting underway in Chicago. What Charles Dickens did with *Jarndyce v. Jarndyce* in *Bleak House* as an index of cultural conditions, perhaps some modern novelist will do with *Trimarco v. Colgate Palmolive et al.*

6   The et al.'s include some other manufacturers of toothbrushes, and the American Dental Association. All are to be hauled before the bar of justice by Mark Trimarco, speaking for himself and—this is a class-action suit—"all others similarly situated." The others are suffering from what Trimarco's complaint calls "a disease known as 'toothbrush abrasion'." Abrasion a disease? The plaintiff's materials also call it "an injury." And "a distinct clinical entity caused by toothbrushes of the following bristle types: firm, medium and soft, both natural and synthetic."

7   The complaint says people suffering from this self-inflicted injury are consumers who were not "informed or warned about the danger of toothbrush abrasion." And: "It was the duty of the defendant manufacturers to furnish a product, i.e., toothbrush, which was in reasonably safe condition when put to a use in a manner that was reasonably foreseeable considering the nature and intended function of the product."

8   But the toothbrushes "were unsafe and unreasonably dangerous for their intended use in that the packaging contained no warning as to the risks of toothbrush abrasion or instructions on how to brush to avoid toothbrush abrasion." The American Dental Association is a defendant because it gave its seal of approval to the toothbrushes.

9   The complaint charges negligence because the manufacturers knew or should have known about the disease/injury/clinical entity since "at least 1949" but continued to manufacture toothbrushes that were "likely" to cause abrasion. *Likely?* If the result is "likely," you would think that the class of plaintiffs would be a majority of all who brush their teeth.

10   If toothbrushes are, as charged, "unreasonably dangerous" because of the absence of warnings and instructions, try to imagine the words which, if printed on toothbrush packages, would immunize manufacturers against such a complaint. "Warning: In brushing, too

much is too much." "Instructions: Hold brush in hand. Insert the end with the bristles into your mouth. Move brush up and down. Stop before you wear out your teeth." Or perhaps: "Look, this toothbrush is not normally a dangerous implement, but neither is it intended for ninnies who can't figure out how to brush their teeth without doing them irreparable harm."

This suit is just part of a great American growth industry—litigation that expresses the   11
belief that everyone has an entitlement to compensation for any unpleasantness; litigation that displaces responsibility from individuals to corporations with money. This industry was, of course, up and running before the tobacco litigation, but that taught lawyers just how lucrative it could be to blame individuals' foolishness on, say, Joe Camel.

Now many cities are suing gun manufacturers for the "costs"—the numbers are   12
guesses—of shootings. In a new wrinkle in tort law—a move that would make a trial lawyer blush, if that were possible—individuals who have been shot are suing groups of manufacturers without claiming to have been injured by a product made by any of the targeted manufacturers.

If you—your teeth *are* suddenly feeling a bit abraded, are they not?—want to climb   13
aboard the latest gravy train pulling out of the station, log on to www.toothbrushlawsuit. com. You will be greeted warmly: "Welcome to the Toothbrush Lawsuit Web Site." Illinois residents can dial 1-877-SORE GUMS. From the Web site you will learn that the disease is "progressive." That means not that Al Gore likes it, but that it gets worse if you keep making it worse. You also will learn that toothbrush abrasion "is most prevalent in those with good oral hygiene, i.e., people who brush their teeth." And "there are studies that show that people who do not brush their teeth, never develop" symptoms of toothbrush abrasion. Consider yourself warned.

1. What examples of hyperbole, understatement, repetition, and witty lines can you find in this article?

2. Do you see elements of satire and parody in this article? If so, where?

3. What is Will's main claim in this argument? In other words, what is the position he is arguing?

4. As you think about rhetorical context—Will's purpose, audience, genre, and style—speculate why humor is an effective approach to convey this argument. What audiences does Will reach that might not have listened to him had he written a more serious, straightforward argument? Do you agree or disagree with Will's argument? Has his humor moved you or changed your perspective in any way?

CONCLUSION

This chapter has shown you the difference between one-sided and multisided arguments and explained why multisided arguments are likely to be more persuasive to neutral or resisting audiences. A multisided argument generally includes a fair summary of differing views, followed by either refutation, concession, or

Rogerian synthesis. The strategies you use for treating resistant views depend on the audience you are trying to reach and your purpose. We explained how audiences can be placed on a scale of resistance ranging from "strongly supportive" to "strongly resistant." In addressing supportive audiences, writers typically compose one-sided arguments with strong motivational appeals to action. Neutral or undecided audiences generally respond most favorably to classical arguments that set out strong reasons in support of the writer's position yet openly address alternative views, which are first summarized and then either rebutted or conceded to. When the audience is strongly resistant, a delayed thesis or Rogerian strategy is most effective at reducing resistance and helping move the audience slightly toward the writer's views. Sometimes humor is also effective at winning consideration from a resistant audience.

WRITING ASSIGNMENT
FOR CHAPTERS 7 AND 8

The assignment for Chapters 7 and 8 has two parts. Part One is an actual argument you will write. Part Two is your own self-reflective analysis on how you chose to appeal to and accommodate your audience.

PART ONE: For this assignment, argue against a popular cultural practice or belief that you think is wrong, or argue for an action or belief that you think is right even though it will be highly unpopular. Your claim, in other words, must be controversial—going against the grain of popular actions, values, and beliefs—so that you can anticipate considerable resistance to your views. This essay invites you to stand up for something you believe in even though your view will be highly contested. Your goal is to persuade your audience toward your position.

In writing and revising your argument, draw upon appropriate strategies from Chapters 7 and 8. From Chapter 7 consider the concept of audience-based reasons and strategies for increasing your appeals to *ethos* and *pathos*. From Chapter 8 consider strategies for appealing to audiences according to their level of resistance. Choose the most resistant audience that you think you can sway to your point of view. Whether you use a refutation strategy, a delayed-thesis strategy, a Rogerian strategy, a humorous strategy, or some combination of these approaches is up to you.

PART TWO: Attach to your argument a self-reflective letter to your instructor and classmates explaining and justifying the choices you made for appealing to your audience and accommodating their views. In your letter address questions such as the following:

1. At the most resistant end of the spectrum, why are people opposed to your claim? How does your claim challenge their views and perhaps threaten their own value system?

2. Whom did you picture as the audience you were trying to sway? Where on the spectrum from "accord" to "resistance" did you address your argument? Why?

3. What strategies did you use for appealing to that audience?

4. What choices did you make in trying to accommodate differing views?

5. What challenges did this assignment present for you? How successful do you think you were in meeting those challenges?

part three

Arguments in Depth

Six Types of Claims

9

An Introduction to the Types of Claims

In Part One of this text, we discussed the reading and writing of arguments, linking argument to both persuasion and inquiry. In Part Two we examined the internal structure of arguments and showed how persuasive writers link their arguments to the beliefs and values of their audience. We also showed how writers can vary their content, structure, and style to reach audiences with varying degrees of resistance to the writer's views.

Now in Part Three we examine arguments in depth by explaining six types of claims and by showing how each type has its own characteristic patterns of development and support. Because almost all arguments use one or more of these types of claims as basic argumentative "moves" or building blocks, knowing how to develop each claim type will advance your skills in argument. The types of claims to be examined in Part Three are related to an ancient rhetorical concept called *stasis* from a Greek term meaning "stand" as in "to take a *stand* on something." There are many competing theories of stasis, so no two rhetoricians discuss stasis in exactly the same way. But all the theories have valuable components in common.

In Part Three we present our own version of stasis theory, or, to use more ordinary language, our own approach to argument based on the types of claims. The payoff for you will be twofold. First, understanding the types of claims will help you focus an argument and generate ideas for it. Second, a study of claim types teaches you characteristic patterns of support for each type, thereby helping you organize and develop your arguments.

AN OVERVIEW OF THE TYPES OF CLAIMS

To appreciate what a study of claim types can do, imagine one of those heated but frustrating arguments—let's suppose it's about gun control—where the question at issue keeps shifting. Everyone talks at cross-purposes, each speaker's point unconnected to the previous speaker's. The disputants start gesticulating at each other, faces contorted, voice levels rising. Sometimes you can get such a discussion back on track if one person says, "Hold it for a moment. What are we actually disagreeing about here? Are we debating whether the government should enact gun control? Whether gun ownership prevents crime? Whether getting a gun license is like getting a car license? Let's figure out what we agree on and where we disagree because we can't debate all these questions at once." Whether she recognizes it or not, this person is applying the concept of claim types to get the argument focused.

To understand how claim types work, let's return to the concept of stasis. A *stasis* is an issue or question that focuses a point of disagreement. You and your audience might agree on the answer to Question A and so have nothing to argue about. Likewise you might agree on the answer to Question B. But on Question C you disagree. Question C constitutes a *stasis* where you and your audience diverge. It is the place where disagreement begins, where as an arguer you take a *stand* against another view. Thus you and your audience might agree that handgun ownership is legal. You might agree further that widespread ownership of handguns reduces crime. But if you ask the question "Is widespread handgun ownership a good thing?" you and your audience might disagree. This last question constitutes a *stasis*, the point where you and your audience part company.

Rhetoricians have discovered that the kinds of questions that divide people have classifiable patterns. In this text we identify six broad types of claims—each type originating in a different kind of question. To emphasize the structural pattern of each type, we will first use an X and a Y to represent slots so that you can focus on the structure rather than the content of the claim type. Then we'll move quickly to actual examples. Here is a brief overview of the six claim types.

Type 1: Simple Categorical Arguments (Is X a Y? [Where You and Your Audience Agree on the Meaning of Y])

A *categorical argument* occurs when persons disagree about the category (Y) that a given thing (X) belongs to. A categorical question is said to be simple if there is no dispute about the meaning of the Y term. Examples of questions leading to simple categorical arguments are the following:

Was Richard Nixon a workaholic?

Is surfing the Internet a new kind of addiction?

Was Senator Weasel's vote for increased military spending politically motivated?

In these examples, we assume that writer and audience agree on the meaning of "workaholic," "addiction," and "politically motivated." At issue is whether Nixon, surfing the Internet, and Senator Weasel belong to these categories.

The strategy for conducting a simple categorical argument is to provide examples or other evidence to show that X does or does not belong to category Y. Yes, Nixon was a workaholic (provide examples). Yes, surfing the Internet is a new kind of addiction (provide examples, testimony from psychologists). No, Senator Weasel's support for new weapons funding was not politically motivated (provide evidence that Weasel has a long record of pro-military spending). Simple categorical arguments are discussed in the first part of Chapter 10.

Type 2: Definitional Arguments (Is X a Y? [Where the Definition of Y Is Contested])

A categorical argument becomes more complex if you and your audience disagree about the meaning of the Y term. In this second type of claim, you have to define the Y term and defend your definition against objections and alternative definitions. Suppose, for example, you want to argue that using animals for medical research constitutes cruelty to animals. Here you would have to define what you mean by "cruelty to animals" and show how using animals for medical research fits your definition. Almost all legal disputes require definitional arguing because courts must determine whether an action meets or does not meet the criteria for a crime or civil tort as defined by a law, statute, or series of previous court rulings. Examples of questions leading to definitional arguments are the following:

Is occasional telling of off-color jokes in the workplace an instance of sexual harassment?

Is flag burning constitutionally protected free speech?

Is Pluto a planet or an asteroid?

The general strategy for conducting a definitional argument is to define the second term and then argue whether the first term meets or does not meet the definition. We call this strategy *criteria-match arguing* because to define the second term you must specify the criteria that something must meet to fit the category. Then you must argue that your first term does or does not match these criteria. Definitional arguments are treated in depth in Chapter 10.

Type 3: Cause/Consequence Arguments (Does X Cause Y? Is Y a Consequence of X?)

Another major argument type entails cause and effect reasoning. Often such arguments arise from disagreements about the cause of an event or a trend: "What caused the crash of American Airlines Flight 800?" or "What causes teenage males to become violent?" Just as frequently, causal arguments arise from speculations about the possible consequences of an action: "What will be the consequences of changing from a progressive to a flat income tax?" "Will gun control legislation reduce violence in the schools?"

The general strategy for conducting causal arguments is to describe the chain of events that lead from X to Y. If a causal chain cannot be directly established, you can argue indirectly, using inductive methods, statistical analyses, or analogies. Causal arguments are treated in detail in Chapter 11.

Type 4: Resemblance Arguments (Is X like Y?)

A fourth argument type involves disputes about appropriate analogies or precedents. Suppose you disapproved of investing in the stock market and wanted to argue that stock market investing is like gambling. In showing the similarities between investing and gambling, you would be making a resemblance argument. Examples of questions that lead to resemblance arguing are the following:

Was Slobodan Milosovic's policy of "ethnic cleansing" in Kosovo like Hitler's "final solution" against the Jews?

Is killing starlings in your attic like killing rats in your attic? (Are starlings like rats?)

Does pornography disparage women the way neo-Nazi propaganda disparages people of color? (Is pornography like racist propaganda?)

The general strategy for resemblance arguments is to compare the first term to the second, pointing out similarities between them (if your goal is to make X like Y) or differences between them (if your goal is to make X unlike Y). Resemblance arguments are covered in Chapter 12.

Type 5: Evaluation Arguments (Is X Good or Bad? Is X a Good or Bad Y?)

Categorical, causal, and resemblance arguments (types 1–4) are often called reality or truth arguments. In such arguments, people question the way things are, were, or will be; they are disagreeing about the nature of reality. In contrast, evaluation and proposal arguments (types 5 and 6) deal with values, what people consider important, good, or worth doing. Although a person's values often begin as feelings founded on personal experience, they can nevertheless form the basis of reasonable argument in the public sphere if they are articulated and justified. When you articulate your values, explain their source (if necessary), and apply them consistently to specific cases, you make your values transpersonal and shareable and can use them to build coherent and reasonable arguments.

Evaluation arguments (type 5) ask questions about whether X is good or bad. Examples of evaluation questions are the following:

Is a European-style, single-payer health insurance system a good policy for the United States to enact?

Is acquiring job experience between college and graduate school a good career plan?

Is a sports utility vehicle a good urban vehicle?

The general strategy for evaluation arguments uses criteria-match arguing similar to that used for definitional arguments: You first establish your criteria for "good" in the specific case and then show how your first term does or does not meet the criteria. Evaluation arguments are covered in Chapter 13. A special category of evaluation arguments—dealing with ethical or moral issues (for example, "Is it morally justifiable to spank children?" or "Are cloning experiments ethical?")—is treated in Chapter 15.

Type 6: Proposal Arguments (Should We Do X?)

Whereas argument types 1–5 all involve changing your audience's beliefs about something—whether about reality (types 1–4) or about the value of something (type 5)—proposal arguments call for action. Proposals ask your audience to *do* something, to act in some way. Typically, proposals use words like *should, ought,* or *must* followed by an action of some kind. The following questions all lead to proposal arguments:

Should the United States shift from a progressive to a flat income tax?

Should teens who commit crimes receive the same sentences as adult criminals?

Should gay marriages be legalized?

The most typical strategy for making proposal arguments is to follow a problem-solution-justification structure whereby the opening section convinces the audience that a problem exists, the second section proposes a solution to solve the problem, and the last section justifies the solution by demonstrating that the benefits of acting on the proposal outweigh the costs or that the inherent "rightness" of the solution (on moral grounds) compels action. Proposal arguments are covered in Chapter 14.

FOR CLASS DISCUSSION

Working as a whole class or in small groups, decide which claim type is represented by each of the following questions. Sometimes the argument categories overlap or blend together. For example, the question "Is airline travel safe?" might be considered either a simple categorical question or an evaluation question.

1. Should violent video games be made illegal?

2. How effective is aspirin in reducing the risk for heart attacks and stroke?

3. Why is anorexia nervosa primarily a white, middle-class female disease?

4. Is depression in the elderly common in Asian cultures?

5. Will military intervention in Country X be like U.S. intervention in Vietnam or like U.S. intervention in Iraq?

6. Should professional baseball impose a salary cap on its superstar players?

7. Is this Web site racist?

8. Is tobacco a drug?

9. Are Nike's Asian shoe factories sweatshops?

10. What causes American girls to lose self-esteem when they reach puberty?

WHAT IS THE VALUE OF STUDYING CLAIM TYPES?

Having provided an overview of the types of claims, we conclude this chapter by showing you two substantial benefits you will derive from knowing about each type: help in focusing and generating ideas for an argument and help in organizing and developing an argument.

Help in Focusing an Argument and Generating Ideas

Knowing the different types of claims can help you focus an argument and generate ideas for it. Understanding claim types helps you focus by asking you to determine what's at stake between you and your audience. Where do you and your audience agree and disagree? What are the questions at issue? It helps you generate ideas by guiding you to pose questions that suggest lines of development.

To illustrate, let's take a hypothetical case—one Isaac Charles Little (affectionately known as I. C. Little), who desires to chuck his contact lenses and undergo the new lasik procedure to cure his near-sightedness. ("Lasik" is the common name for laser in-situ keratomileusis, a recent advance in surgical treatments for myopia. Sometimes known as "flap and zap" surgery, it involves using a laser to cut a layer of the corneal tissue thinner than a human hair and then flattening the cornea. It's usually not covered by insurance and is quite expensive.) I. C. has two different arguments he'd like to make: (1) He'd like to talk his parents into helping him pay for the procedure, and (2) he'd like to convince insurance companies that the lasik procedure should be covered under standard medical insurance policies. In the discussions that follow, note how the six types of claims can help I. C. identify points of disagreement for each audience and simultaneously suggest lines of argument for persuading each one. Note, too, how the questions at issue vary for each audience.

First imagine what might be at stake in I. C.'s discussions with his parents.

Claim Type Analysis: Parents as Audience

- *Simple categorical argument:* I. C.'s parents will be concerned about the safety and effectiveness of this procedure. Is lasik safe? Is it effective? (These are the first questions at issue. I. C.'s mom has heard a horror story about an earlier surgical procedure for myopia, so I. C. knows he will have to persuade her that lasik is safe and effective.)

- *Definitional argument:* With parents as audience, I. C. will have to define what lasik surgery is so they won't have misconceptions about what is involved. However, he can't think of any arguments that would ensue over this definition, so he proceeds to the next claim type.

- *Causal argument:* Both parents will question I. C.'s underlying motivation for seeking this surgery. "What causes you to want this lasik procedure?" they will ask. (I. C.'s dad, who has worn eyeglasses all his adult life, will not be swayed by cosmetic desires. "If you don't like contacts," he will say, "just wear glasses.") Here I. C. needs to argue that permanently correcting his near sightedness will improve his quality of life. I. C. decides to emphasize his desire for an active, outdoor life, and especially his passion for water sports including swimming and scuba diving, where his need for contacts or glasses is a serious handicap. Also, I. C. says that if he doesn't have to wear contacts he can get a summer job as a lifeguard.

- *Resemblance argument:* I. C. can't think of any resemblance questions at issue.

- *Evaluation argument:* When the pluses and minuses are weighed, is lasik a good thing? Would the results of the surgery be beneficial enough to justify the cost and the risks? In terms of costs, I. C. might argue that even though the procedure is initially expensive (from $1,000 to $4,000), over the years he will save money by not needing contacts or glasses. The pleasure of seeing well in the water and not being bothered by contacts or glasses while hiking and camping constitutes a major psychological benefit. (The cosmetic benefits—I. C. thinks he'll look cooler without glasses—he decides to leave out, since his dad thinks wearing glasses is fine.)

- *Proposal:* Should I. C. (or a person in general) get this operation for treatment of myopia? (All the previous points of disagreement are subissues related to this overarching proposal issue.)

What this example should help you see is that the values arguments in the last two claim types (evaluation and proposal) depend on the writer's resolving related reality/truth questions in one or more of the first four types (simple categorical, definition, cause, resemblance). In this particular case, before convincing his parents that they should help him pay for the lasik procedure (I. C.'s proposal claim), I. C. would need to convince them that the procedure is safe and effective (simple categorical arguments), that there are significant recreational and professional reasons for this surgery (causal argument), and that the benefits outweigh the costs (evaluation argument). Almost all arguments combine subarguments in this way so that lower-order claims provide supporting materials for addressing higher-order claims.

The previous illustration focused on parents as audience. If we now switch audiences, we can use our theory of claim types to identify different questions at issue. Let's suppose I. C. wants to persuade insurance companies to cover the lasik procedure. He imagines insurance company decision makers as his primary audience, along with the general public and state legislators who may be able to influence them.

Claim Type Analysis: Insurance Decision Makers as Audience

- *Simple categorical argument:* No disagreements come immediately to mind (This audience shares I. C.'s belief that lasik is safe and effective.)

- *Definitional argument:* Should lasik be considered "cosmetic surgery" (as insurance companies contend) or as "medically justifiable surgery" (as I. C. contends)? This definitional question constitutes a major stasis. I. C. wants to convince his audience that lasik belongs in the category of "medically justifiable surgery" rather than "cosmetic surgery." He will need to define "medically justifiable surgery" in such a way that lasik can be included.

- *Causal argument:* What will be the consequences to insurance companies and to the general public of making insurance companies pay for lasik? For this audience, consequence issues are crucial. Will insurance companies be overloaded with claims? What will happen to insurance rates? Will optometrists and eyeglass manufacturers go out of business?

- *Resemblance argument:* Does lasik more resemble a facelift (not covered by insurance) or plastic surgery to repair a cleft palate (covered by insurance)?

- *Evaluation argument:* Would it be good for society as a whole if insurance companies had to pay for lasik?

- *Proposal argument:* Should insurance companies be required to cover lasik?

As this analysis shows, the questions at issue change when you consider a different audience. Now the chief question at issue is definition: Is lasik cosmetic surgery or medically justifiable surgery? I. C. needs to spend no time arguing that the surgery is safe and effective (major concerns for his parents); instead he must establish criteria for "medically justifiable surgery" and then argue that lasik meets these criteria. Again note how the higher-order issues of value depend on resolving one or more lower-order issues of truth/reality.

So what can a study of claim types teach you about focusing an argument and generating ideas? First, it teaches you to analyze what's at stake between you and your audience by determining major points of disagreement. Second, it shows that you can make any of the claim types your argument's major focus. Rather than tackle a values issue, you might tackle only a reality/truth issue. You could, for example, focus an entire argument on the simple categorical question "Is lasik safe?" (an argument requiring you to research the medical literature). Likewise you could write a causal argument focusing on what might happen to optometrists and eyeglass manufacturers if the insurance industry decided to cover lasik. Often arguers jump too quickly to issues of value without first resolving issues of reality/truth. Finally, a study of claim types helps you pose questions that generate ideas and suggest lines of reasoning. Later in Part Three, we will show you a particularly powerful way of using lower-order questions about reality/truth to generate supporting ideas for a proposal argument (see Chapter 14, pp. 313–17).

FOR CLASS DISCUSSION

Select an issue familiar to most members of the class—perhaps a current campus issue, an issue prominent in the local or national news, or an issue that the class has recently discussed—and analyze it using our sequence of claim types. Consider how a writer or speaker might address two different audiences on this issue. Hypothesizing the writer/speaker's perspective and claim, make a list of points of agreement and disagreement for both audiences, using as a pattern our claim types analyses for lasik.

Help in Organizing and Developing an Argument

The second main benefit of studying claim types will become clearer as you read the chapters in Part Three. Because each type of claim has its own characteristic pattern of development, learning these patterns will help you organize and develop your arguments. Studying claim types shows you how different arguments are typically structured, teaching you generic moves needed in many different kinds of argumentative situations. If, for example, you make a proposal claim, a study of claim types will show you the generic moves typically needed in proposal arguments. If one of your supporting reasons is a definition claim or an evaluation claim, study of claim types will show you how to do the criteria-match arguing typical of such claims. Likewise such a study shows you how to develop each of the other claim types to help you construct arguments that tap into your audience's values and that include strong support to overcome your audience's resistance.

In the following chapters in Part Three, we discuss each of the claim types in depth.

10

Categorical and Definitional Arguments

X Is (Is Not) a Y

CASE 1

The impeachment trial of President Bill Clinton, following his affair with Monica Lewinsky, involved a number of definitional issues: Did Clinton's behavior with Lewinsky and his evasions of the truth while testifying to a grand jury in the Paula Jones lawsuit constitute "Treason, Bribery, or other high Crimes and Misdemeanors"—the constitutional phrase that describes an impeachable offense? More narrowly, did Clinton's testimony in the Paula Jones lawsuit, when he denied having sexual relations with Monica Lewinsky, constitute "perjury"? More narrowly still, did Clinton's behavior with Monica Lewinsky meet the legal definition of "sexual relations"? At each of these levels of debate, lawyers and pundits put forth competing definitions of these disputed terms and argued that Clinton's actions did or did not meet the definitions.

CASE 2

Recent developments in reproductive technology are spurring mind-numbing ethical and legal questions. For example, suppose an infertile couple conceives several embryos in a test tube and then freezes the fertilized embryos for future use. What happens when the couple divorces and disagrees about the disposition of the frozen embryos? (In one actual case, the woman wanted to use the frozen embryos to try to get pregnant, and the man wanted to destroy the embryos.) What should be done with the embryos and who decides? Should frozen embryos be treated as "persons," thus becoming analogous to children in custody arguments? Or should they be divided up as "property" with the man getting one half of the frozen embryos and the woman getting the other half? Or should a new legal category be created for them that regards them as more than property but less than actual persons? In one court case, the judge decided that frozen embryos "are not, strictly speaking, either 'persons' or 'property,' but occupy an interim category that entitles them to special respect because of their potential for human life."*

AN OVERVIEW OF CATEGORICAL ARGUMENTS

Categorical arguments are among the most common argument types you will encounter. They can occur whenever you claim that any given X belongs in category Y. Did NATO bombing of Serbia during the Kosovo crisis belong in the category "a just war"? Does skateboarding belong in the category "a true sport"? Does my swerving across the center lane while trying to slap a bee on my windshield belong in the category "reckless driving"?

We place items in categories all the time, and the categories we choose can have subtle but powerful rhetorical effects, creating implicit mini-arguments. Consider, for example, how a review of the film *American Pie* categorizes first-time sex for teens: "In what must be the raunchiest coming-of-age film ever, 'American Pie' tackles the most hallowed rite of teenage passage: losing one's virginity."† Here loss of virginity is placed in the category "hallowed rite of teenage passage." By placing teenage sexuality in this category, the reviewer urges readers to view first-time sex for teens as a humorous coming-of-age moment like getting a driver's license or chugging your first beer. Later in the review, those who might object to the movie's depersonalized, comic, amoral depiction of sexuality are categorized as "Victorians." The review implicitly divides readers into two categories: prudish Victorians and normal people who enjoy raunchy movies and see teenage sex as a rite of passage. But there are other categories into which teenage sex can be placed. Some commentators see teenage sex as a national disaster leading to out-of-wedlock pregnancy, a frightening rise in STDs, and the decline of the stable, two-parent family. Often, the categories we create rhetorically have real-life consequences: They can shape legislation, influence court decisions, even determine our personal values and behavior.

Similar examples of implicit categorical claims can be found in almost any kind of text. Consider the competing categories proposed for whales in an international whaling controversy accelerated in the late 1990s by the Makahs' pursuit of their U.S. treaty rights to hunt whales. What category does a whale belong to? Some arguers placed whales in the category "sacred animals" that should never be killed because of their intelligence, beauty, grace, and power. Others categorized

---

*See Vincent F. Stempel, "Procreative Rights in Assisted Reproductive Technology: Why the Angst?" *Albany Law Review 62* (1999), 1187.

†*Review* (1999). Sharon Pian Chan, " 'American Pie' Sweet but Raunchy," rev. of *American Pie, Seattle Times* 9 July 1999, F1, F3.

whales as a "renewable food resource" like tuna, crabs, cattle, and chickens. Others worried whether the specific kinds of whales being hunted were an "endangered species"—a concept that argues for the preservation of whale stocks but not necessarily for a ban on controlled hunting of individual whales once population numbers rise sufficiently. Each of these whaling arguments places whales within a different category that implicitly urges the reader to adopt that category's perspective on whaling.

Categorical claims shift from implicit to explicit arguments whenever the arguer supplies reasons and evidence to persuade us that X does (or does not) belong in category Y. In the rest of this chapter we discuss two kinds of categorical arguments: (1) simple categorical arguments in which the writer and an audience agree on the meaning of the Y term and (2) definitional arguments in which the meaning of the Y term is itself controversial.

SIMPLE CATEGORICAL ARGUMENTS

A categorical argument can be said to be "simple" if there is no disagreement about the meaning of the Y term. For example, suppose you are discussing with fellow committee members whom to select as committee chairperson. You want to make the case that "David won't make a good committee chair because he is too bossy." Your supporting reason ("David is too bossy") is a simple categorical claim. You assume that everyone agrees what *bossy* means; the point of contention is whether David is or is not bossy. To support your claim, you would supply examples of David's bossiness. To refute it, someone else might supply counterexamples of David's cooperative and kind nature. As this example suggests, the basic procedural rule for developing a simple categorical claim is to supply examples and other data that show how X is (or is not) a member of category Y.

Difference between Facts and Simple Categorical Claims

Simple categorical claims are interpretive statements about reality. They claim that something does (or does not) exist or that something does (or does not) possess the qualities of a certain category. Often simple categorical claims look like facts, so it is important to distinguish between a fact and a simple categorical claim.

A *fact* is a statement that can be verified in some way, either by empirical observation or by reference to a reliable source (say, an encyclopedia) trusted by you and your audience. Here are some facts: Water freezes at 32 degrees. Boise is in Idaho, not Montana. The bald eagle is no longer on the EPA's endangered species list. These are all facts because they can be verified; no supporting arguments are needed or called for.

In contrast, a *simple categorical claim* is a contestable interpretation of facts. Consider the difference between these two sentences:

Fact: The bald eagle is no longer on the EPA's endangered species list.

Simple categorical claim: The bald eagle is no longer an endangered species.

The factual statement can be verified by looking at the list of endangered species published by the Environmental Protection Agency. We can see the date the bald eagle was placed on the list and the date it was removed. The second statement is a claim. Imagine all the debates and arguments the EPA must have had as it poured over statistical data about eagle population numbers and over field reports from observers of eagles before deciding to remove the bald eagle from the list.

Often, it is difficult to draw the line between a fact and a claim. The acceptance or skepticism of a given audience can determine what passes as a fact or what becomes a claim that the arguer needs to support. Consider the statement "John F. Kennedy was killed by Lee Harvey Oswald." Most people call this statement a fact; to them, the report of the Warren Commission appointed to investigate the assassination is a reliable document that settles the issue. But conspiracy theorists, many of whom regard the Warren report as an unreliable rush to judgment, consider the statement above a highly contestable claim.

FOR CLASS DISCUSSION

Working individually or in small groups, determine which of the following statements are facts and which are categorical claims. If you think a statement could be a "fact" for some audiences and a "claim" for others, explain your reasoning.

1. State sales taxes are not deductible on your federal income tax form.

2. State sales taxes are annoying to both buyers and sellers.

3. State sales taxes are a hardship on low-income families.

4. *The Phantom Menace* is a George Lucas film.

5. *The Phantom Menace* was not well received by movie critics.

6. *The Phantom Menace* is a racist movie.

7. Eleanor Roosevelt was a very unconventional woman.

8. Eleanor Roosevelt was the most influential first lady ever to inhabit the White House.

9. Eleanor Roosevelt sometimes seemed anti-Semitic.

10. Eleanor Roosevelt was one of the drafters of the United Nations' Universal Declaration of Human Rights.

Variations in the Wording
of Simple Categorical Claims

Simple categorical claims typically take the grammatical structure "X is a Y." Grammarians describe this structure as a subject followed by a linking verb (such as *to be* or *to seem*) followed by a predicate noun or adjective:

> David is bossy.
>
> State sales taxes are annoying.
>
> Eleanor Roosevelt sometimes seemed anti-Semitic.

But other grammatical constructions can be used to make the same categorical claims:

> David frequently bosses people around. (He belongs to the category "people who are bossy.")
>
> Sales taxes really annoy people. (Sales taxes belong to the category "things that are annoying.")
>
> On occasion, Eleanor Roosevelt made anti-Semitic remarks. (Eleanor Roosevelt belongs to the category "people who occasionally seem anti-Semitic.")

Almost any kind of interpretive statement about reality (other than causal statements, which are covered in Chapter 11) is a categorical claim of some kind. Here are a couple more examples of different kinds of categorical claims that can be translated into an "X is Y" format:

> The Kosovo Liberation Army waged terrorism against the Serbs. (The Kosovo Liberation Army was in part an anti-Serb terrorist organization.)
>
> Corporations often exaggerate the money they give to charities. (Corporate claims about their charitable giving are often exaggerated.)

Our point is to demonstrate that categorical claims are very common. Whether they are worded directly as "X is Y" statements or disguised in different grammatical structures, they assert that item X belongs in category Y or possesses the features of category Y.

Supporting Simple Categorical Claims:
Supply Examples

The basic strategy for supporting a simple categorical claim is to give examples or other data showing how X belongs in category Y. If you want to argue that Sam is a party animal, provide examples of his partying behavior. If you want to argue that Eleanor Roosevelt sometimes seemed anti-Semitic, quote excerpts of anti-Semitic statements from her personal correspondence.* Because simple categorical arguments are common building blocks for longer, more complex arguments, they often take no more than one or two paragraphs inside a longer piece.

For an example of a simple categorical argument, consider the following paragraph from an article supporting regulated hunting of whales. In this article, the writer explains that many countries oppose whaling because they are no longer dependent on whale oil, having found synthetic substitutes. Whaling was never a deep part of the culture of these industrialized countries. As part of his argument, the writer wants to contrast these countries with traditional whaling countries. He makes the categorical claim that in Norway and Japan whaling was an "ancient occupation" worthy of respect. The following paragraph supports that categorical claim:

> Things were different in other nations, especially Norway and Japan, where whaling is an ancient occupation worthy of the respect and support that Americans award to, say, the running of a farm. Norwegians view whaling as part of the hard, honorable life of a fisherman—a reliable slow-season activity that helps fishing communities to make it through the year. The Japanese who come from a long line of whalers have deeply held moral beliefs about maintaining their family tradition. To be prevented from honoring their ancestors in this manner is a source of shame. After the 1982 moratorium [on whaling] some Norwegian fishers went bankrupt. The same thing happened in Iceland. Given the abundance of the whale stocks, these nations ask, why can't such people be free to practice their traditional livelihood? Anthropologists have long observed the primary role played by traditional foods in the social structure and moral norms of a community—a role that is captured in the widely repeated aphorism "you are what you eat." Asking people to give up their customary diet is in many ways like asking them to give up part of their identity.[†]

Of course, a simple categorical claim can also be the thesis for a whole argument. We provide such an example on pages 218–19, where columnist John Leo cites numerous examples from the Star Wars movie *Episode I: The Phantom Menace* to argue that this film "is packed with awful stereotypes."

---

*Roosevelt's biographer Blanche Wiesen Cook deals sensitively with this complex issue, largely exonerating Roosevelt from the charge of anti-Semitism. See *Eleanor Roosevelt*, vol. 2, *1933–38* (New York: Viking, 1999).

[†]William Aron, William Burke, and Milton Freeman. "Flouting the Convention." *Atlantic*, May, 1999, p. 26.

Refuting Simple Categorical Claims

If you wish to challenge or question someone else's simple categorical claim, you have three common strategies at your disposal:

- *Deny the accuracy or truth of the examples and data.* "You say that David is bossy. But you are remembering incorrectly. That wasn't David who did those bossy things; that was Paul."

- *Provide counterexamples that place X in a different category.* "Well, maybe David acted bossy on a few occasions. But more often he is kind and highly cooperative. For example . . ."

- *Raise definitional questions about the Y term.* "Well, that depends on what you mean by 'bossy.' What you call bossiness, I call decisiveness."

The last of these strategies shows how easily a simple categorical claim can slip into a definitional dispute. In the rest of this chapter we turn our attention to definitional arguments.

▼ FOR CLASS DISCUSSION

Working as a whole class or in small groups, prepare brief arguments in support of each of the following categorical claims. Then discuss ways that you might call these claims into question.

1. Americans today are obsessed with their appearance.

2. Professional athletes are overpaid.

3. The video games most enjoyed by children are extremely violent.

AN OVERVIEW OF DEFINITIONAL ARGUMENTS

As we turn now to definitional arguments, it is important to distinguish between cases where definitions are needed and cases where definitions are *disputed.* Many arguments require a definition of key terms. If you are arguing, for example, that after-school jobs are harmful to teenagers because they promote materialism, you will probably need to define *materialism* somewhere in your argument. Writers regularly define key words for their readers by providing synonyms, by citing a dictionary definition, by stipulating a definition, or by some other means. In the rest of this chapter, we focus on arguments in which the meaning of a key term is disputed. Consider, for example, the environmental controversy over the definition of *wetlands.* Section 404 of the federal Clean Water Act provides for federal protection of wetlands, but it leaves the task of defining wetlands to administrative agencies and the courts. Currently about 5 percent of the land surface of the contiguous forty-eight states is potentially affected by the wetlands provision, and 75 percent of this land is privately owned. Efforts to define wetlands have created a battleground between pro-environment and pro-development (or pro–private property rights) groups. Farmers, homeowners, and developers often want a narrow definition of wetlands so that more property is available for commercial or private use. Environmentalists favor a broad definition in order to protect different habitat types and maintain the environmental safeguards that wetlands provide (control of water pollution, spawning grounds for aquatic species, floodwater containment, and so forth). The problem is that defining wetlands is tricky. For example, one federal regulation defines a wetland as any area that has a saturated ground surface for twenty-one consecutive days during the year. But how would you apply this law to a pine flatwood ecosystem that was wet for ten days this year but thirty days last year? And how should the courts react to lawsuits claiming that the regulation itself is either too broad or too narrow? One can see why the wetlands controversy provides hefty incomes for lawyers and congressional lobbyists.

THE CRITERIA-MATCH STRUCTURE OF DEFINITIONAL ARGUMENTS

As the wetlands example suggests, definitional arguments usually have a two-part structure—a definition part that tries to establish the meaning of the Y term (What do we mean by *wetland?*) and a match part that argues whether a given X meets that definition (Does this 30-acre parcel of land near Swan Lake meet the criteria for a wetland?) We use the term *criteria-match* to describe this structure, which occurs regularly not only in definitional arguments but also, as we shall see in Chapter 13, in evaluation arguments of the type "X is (is not) a good Y." The *criteria* part of the structure defines the Y term by setting forth the criteria that must be met for something to be considered a Y. The *match* part examines whether the X term meets these criteria. Here are some examples:

- *Definitional issue:* In a divorce proceeding, is a frozen embryo a "person" rather than "property"?

  Criteria part: What legal criteria must be met for something to be a "person"?

  Match part: Does a frozen embryo meet these criteria?

- *Definitional issue:* For purposes of my feeling good about buying my next pair of running shoes, is the Hercules Shoe Company a socially responsible company?

  Criteria part: What criteria must be met for a company to be deemed "socially responsible"?

  Match part: Does the Hercules Shoe Company meet these criteria?

To show how a definitional issue can be developed into a claim with supporting reasons, let's look more closely at this second example. Let's suppose you work for a consumer information group that wishes to encourage patronage of socially responsible companies while boycotting irresponsible ones. Your group's first task is to define *socially responsible company*. After much discussion and research, your group establishes three criteria that a company must meet to be considered socially responsible:

> *Your definition:* A company is socially responsible if it (1) avoids polluting the environment, (2) sells goods or services that contribute to the well-being of the community, and (3) treats its workers justly.

The criteria section of your argument would explain and illustrate these criteria.

The match part of the argument would then try to persuade readers that a specific company does or does not meet the criteria. A typical thesis statement might be as follows:

> *Your thesis statement:* Although the Hercules Shoe Company is nonpolluting and provides a socially useful product, it is *not* a socially responsible company because it treats workers unjustly.

Here is how the core of the argument could be displayed in Toulmin terms (note how the criteria established in your definition serve as warrants for your argument):

INITIAL ENTHYMEME:	The Hercules Shoe Company is not a socially responsible company because it treats workers unjustly.
CLAIM:	The Hercules Shoe Company is *not* a socially responsible company.
STATED REASON:	because it treats workers unjustly
GROUNDS:	evidence that the company manufactures its shoes in East Asian sweatshops; evidence of the inhumane conditions in these shops; evidence of hardships imposed on displaced American workers
WARRANT:	Socially responsible companies treat workers justly.
BACKING:	arguments showing that just treatment of workers is right in principle and also benefits society; arguments that capitalism helps society as a whole only if workers achieve a reasonable standard of living, have time for leisure, and are not exploited
POSSIBLE CONDITIONS OF REBUTTAL	Opponents of this thesis might argue that justice needs to be considered from an emerging nation's

standpoint: The wages paid workers are low by
American standards but are above average by
East Asian standards. Displacement of American
workers is part of the necessary adjustment of
adapting to a global economy and does not mean
that a company is unjust.

As this Toulmin frame illustrates, the writer's argument needs to contain a criteria section (warrant and backing) showing that just treatment of workers is a criterion for social responsibility and a match section (stated reason and grounds)
showing that the Hercules Shoe Company does not treat its workers justly. Your
audience's initial beliefs determine how much emphasis you need to place on justifying each criterion and supporting each match. The conditions of rebuttal help
the writer imagine alternative views and see places where opposing views need
to be acknowledged and rebutted.

FOR CLASS DISCUSSION

Consider the following definitional claims. Working as individuals or in small
groups, identify the criteria issue and the match issue for each of the following
claims.

EXAMPLE: A Honda assembled in Ohio is (is not) an American-made car.

CRITERIA PART: What criteria have to be met before a car can be called "American made"?

MATCH PART: Does a Honda assembled in Ohio meet these criteria?

1. Computer programming is (is not) a creative profession.

2. Writing graffiti on subways is (is not) vandalism.

3. American Sign Language is (is not) a "foreign language" for purposes of a college graduation requirement.

4. Beauty contests are (are not) sexist events.

5. Bungee jumping from a crane is (is not) a "carnival amusement ride" subject
to state safety inspections.

CONCEPTUAL PROBLEMS OF DEFINITION

Before moving on to discuss ways of defining the Y term in a definitional
argument, we should explore briefly some of the conceptual difficulties of definition. Language, for all its wonderful powers, is an arbitrary system that requires

agreement among its users before it can work. And it's not always easy to get that agreement. In fact, the task of defining something can be devilishly complex.

Why Can't We Just Look in the Dictionary?

What's so hard about defining? you might ask. Why not just look in a dictionary? To get a sense of the complexity of defining something, consider again the word *wetland*. A dictionary can tell us the ordinary meaning of a word (the way it is commonly used), but it can't resolve a debate between competing definitions when different parties have interests in defining the word in different ways. For example, the *Webster's Seventh New Collegiate Dictionary* defines *wetland* as "land containing much soil moisture"—a definition that is hardly helpful in determining whether the federal government can prevent the development of a beach resort on some landowner's private property. Moreover, dictionary definitions rarely tell us such things as *to what degree* a given condition must be met before it qualifies for class membership. How wet does a wetland have to be before it is *legally* a wetland? How long does this wetness have to last? When is a wetland a mere swamp that ought to be drained rather than protected?

Definitions and the Rule of Justice: At What Point Does X Quit Being a Y?

For some people, all this concern about definition may seem misplaced. How often, after all, have you heard people accuse each other of getting bogged down in "mere semantics"? But how we define a given word can have significant implications for people who must either use the word or have the word used on them. Take, for example, what some philosophers refer to as the *rule of justice*. According to this rule, "Beings in the same essential category should be treated in the same way." Should an insurance company, for example, treat anorexia nervosa as a physical illness like diabetes (in which case treatment is paid for by the insurance company) or as a mental illness like paranoia (in which case insurance payments are minimal)? Or, to take another example, if a company gives "new baby" leave to a mother, should it also give "new baby" leave to a father? In other words, is this kind of leave "new mother" leave, or is it "new parent" leave? And what if a couple adopts an infant? Should "new mother" or "new parent" leave be available to adoptive parents also? These questions are all definitional issues involving arguments about what class of beings an individual belongs to and about what actions to take to comply with the rule of justice, which demands that all members of that class be treated equally.

The rule of justice becomes even harder to apply when we consider Xs that grow, evolve, or otherwise change through time. When Young Person back in Chapter 1 argued that she could set her own curfew because she was mature, she raised the question "What are the attributes or criteria of a 'mature' person?" In this case, a categorical distinction between two separate kinds of things ("mature" versus "not mature") evolves into a distinction of degree ("mature enough"). So perhaps we should ask not whether Young Person is mature but whether she is "mature enough." At what point does a child become an adult? (When does a fetus become a human person? When does a social drinker become an alcoholic?)

Although we may be able arbitrarily to choose a particular point and declare, through stipulation, that "mature" means eighteen years old or that "human person" includes a fetus at conception, or at three months, or at birth, in the everyday world the distinction between child and adult, between egg and person, between social drinking and alcoholism seems an evolution, not a sudden and definitive step. Nevertheless, our language requires an abrupt shift between classes. In short, applying the rule of justice often requires us to adopt a digital approach to reality (switches are either on or off, either a fetus is a human person or it is not), whereas our sense of life is more analogical (there are numerous gradations between on and off, there are countless shades of gray between black and white).

As we can see by the preceding examples, the promise of language to fix what psychologist William James called "the buzz and confusion of the world" into an orderly set of categories turns out to be elusive. In most definitional debates, an argument, not a quick trip to the dictionary, is required to settle the matter.

FOR CLASS DISCUSSION

Suppose your landlord decides to institute a "no pets" rule. The rule of justice requires that all pets have to go—not just your neighbor's barking dog, but also Mrs. Brown's cat, the kids' hamster downstairs, and your own pet tarantula. That is, all these animals have to go unless you can argue that some of them are not "pets" for purposes of a landlord's "no pets" rule.

1. Working in small groups or as a whole class, define *pets* by establishing the criteria an animal would have to meet to be included in the category "pets." Consider your landlord's "no pets" rule as the rhetorical context for your definition.

2. Based on your criteria, which of the following animals is definitely a pet that would have to be removed from the apartment? Based on your criteria, which animals could you exclude from the "no pets" rule? How would you make your argument to your landlord?
   - a German shepherd dog
   - a small housecat
   - a tiny, well-trained lapdog
   - a gerbil in a cage
   - a canary
   - a tank of tropical fish
   - a tarantula

KINDS OF DEFINITIONS

In this section we discuss two methods of definition commonly used in definitional arguments: Aristotelian and operational.

Aristotelian Definition

Aristotelian definitions, regularly used in dictionaries, define a term by placing it within the next larger class or category and then showing the specific attributes that distinguish the term from other terms within the same category. For example, a *pencil* is a "writing implement" (next larger category) that differs from other writing implements in that it makes marks with lead or graphite rather than ink. You could elaborate this definition by saying, "Usually the lead or graphite is a long, thin column embedded in a slightly thicker column of wood with an eraser on one end and a sharpened point, exposing the graphite, on the other." You could even distinguish a wooden pencil from a mechanical pencil, thereby indicating again that the crucial identifying attribute is the graphite, not the wooden column.

As you can see, an Aristotelian definition of a term identifies specific attributes or criteria that enable you to distinguish it from other members of the next larger class. We created an Aristotelian definition in our example about socially responsible companies. A socially responsible company, we said, is any company (next larger class) that meets three criteria: (1) It doesn't pollute the environment; (2) it creates goods or services that promote the well-being of the community; and (3) it treats its workers justly.

In constructing Aristotelian definitions, you may find it useful to employ the concepts of accidental, necessary, and sufficient criteria. An *accidental criterion* is a usual but not essential feature of a concept. For example, "made out of wood" is an accidental feature of a pencil. Most pencils are made out of wood, but something can still be a pencil even if it isn't made out of wood (a mechanical pencil). In our example about socially responsible companies, "makes regular contributions to charities" might be an accidental criterion; most socially responsible companies contribute to charities, but some do not. And many socially irresponsible companies also contribute to charities—often as a public relations ploy.

A *necessary criterion* is an attribute that *must* be present for something to belong to the category being defined. For example, the property of "being a writing implement" is a necessary criterion for an object to be a pencil. The property of "marking with graphite or lead" is also a necessary criterion. However, neither of these criteria is a sufficient criterion for an object to be a pencil because many writing implements are not pencils (for example, pens), and many things that mark with graphite or lead aren't pencils (for example, a lead paperweight can make lead marks). Because an object that possesses both of these criteria together must be a pencil, we say that these two qualities together form a *sufficient criterion* for an object to be a pencil.

To show you how these concepts can help you carry on a definitional argument with more precision, let's apply them to a few examples. Suppose Felix

Ungar and Oscar Madison are arguing whether an original Dodge Stealth is a true sports car. At issue are the criteria for "true sports car." Felix might argue that a Stealth is not a true sports car because it has rear seats. (To Felix, having seating for only two people is thus a necessary criterion for a true sports car.) Oscar Madison might argue, however, that having two seats is only an accidental feature of sports cars and that a Stealth is indeed a true sports car because it has a racy appearance and is designed to handle superbly on narrow curving roads. (For Oscar, racy appearance and superb handling are together sufficient criteria for a true sports car.)

As another example, consider again our defining criteria for a "socially responsible" company: (1) The company must avoid polluting the environment; (2) the company must create goods or services that contribute to the well-being of the community; and (3) the company must treat its workers justly. In this definition, each criterion is necessary, but none of the criteria alone is sufficient. In other words, to be defined as socially responsible, a company must meet all three criteria at once. It is not enough for a company to be nonpolluting (a necessary but not sufficient criterion); if that company makes a shoddy product or treats its workers unjustly, it fails to meet the other necessary criteria and can't be deemed socially responsible. Because no one criterion by itself is sufficient, all three criteria together must be met before a company can be deemed socially responsible.

In contrast, consider the following definition of *sexual harassment* as established by the U.S. Equal Employment Opportunity Commission in its 1980 guidelines:

> Unwelcome sexual advances, requests for sexual favors, and other verbal or physical conduct of a sexual nature constitute sexual harassment when (1) submission to such conduct is made either explicitly or implicitly a term or condition of an individual's employment, (2) submission to or rejection of such conduct by an individual is used as the basis for employment decisions affecting such individual, or (3) such conduct has the purpose or effect of unreasonably interfering with an individual's work performance or creating an intimidating, hostile, or offensive working environment.*

Here each of these criteria is sufficient but none is necessary. In other words, an act constitutes sexual harassment if any one of the three criteria is satisfied.

FOR CLASS DISCUSSION

Working individually or in small groups, try to determine whether each of the following is a necessary criterion, a sufficient criterion, an accidental criterion, or

---

*Quoted by Stephanie Riger, "Gender Dilemmas in Sexual Harassment Policies and Procedures," *American Psychologist* 46 (May 1991), 497–505.

no criterion for defining the indicated concept. Be prepared to explain your reasoning and to account for differences in points of view.

CRITERION	CONCEPT TO BE DEFINED
presence of gills	fish
profane and obscene language	R-rated movie
birthplace inside the United States	American citizen
age of 65 or older	senior citizen
line endings that form a rhyming pattern	poem
spanking a child for discipline	child abuse
diet that excludes meat	vegetarian
killing another human being	murder
good sex life	happy marriage

Effect of Rhetorical Context on Aristotelian Definitions

It is important to appreciate how the context of a given argument can affect your definition of a term. The question "Is a tarantula kept in the house a pet?" may actually have opposing answers, depending on the rhetorical situation. You may argue that your tarantula is or is not a pet, depending on whether you are trying to exclude it from your landlord's "no pet" rule or include it in your local talk show's "weird pet contest." Within one context you will want to argue that what your landlord really means by *pet* is an animal (next larger class) capable of disturbing neighbors or harming the landlord's property (criteria that distinguish it from other members of the class). Thus you could argue that your tarantula isn't a pet in your landlord's sense because it is incapable of harming property or disturbing the peace (assuming you don't let it loose!). In the other context you would argue that a pet is "any living thing" (note that in this context the "next larger class" is much larger) with which a human being forms a caring attachment and which shares its owner's domicile. In this case you might say, "Tommy Tarantula here is one of my dearest friends and if you don't think Tommy is weird enough, wait 'til I show you Vanessa, my pet Venus's-flytrap."

To apply the same principle to a different field of debate, consider whether obscene language in a student newspaper should be protected by the First Amendment. The purpose of school officials' suspending editors responsible for such language is to maintain order and decency in the school. The school officials thus hope to narrow the category of acts that are protected under the free-speech amendment in order to meet their purposes. In contrast, the American Civil Liberties Union (which has long defended student newspaper editors) is intent on avoiding any precedent that will restrict freedom of speech any more than is absolutely necessary. The different definitions of *free speech* that are likely to emerge thus reflect the different purposes of the disputants.

The problem of purpose shows why it is so hard to define a word out of context. Some people try to escape this dilemma by returning to the "original intent" of the authors of precedent-setting documents such as the Constitution. But if we try to determine the original intent of the writers of the Constitution on such matters as "free speech," "cruel and unusual punishment," or the "right to bear arms," we must still ask what their original purposes were in framing the constitutional language. If we can show that those original purposes are no longer relevant to present concerns, we have begun to undermine what would otherwise appear to be a static and universal definition to which we could turn.

Operational Definitions

In some rhetorical situations, particularly those arising in the physical and social sciences, writers need precise definitions that can be measured empirically and are not subject to problems of context and disputed criteria. Consider, for example, an argument involving the concept "aggression": "Do violent television programs increase the incidence of aggression in children?" To do research on this issue, a scientist needs a precise, measurable definition of *aggression.* Typically, a scientist might measure "aggression" by counting the number of blows or kicks a child gives to an inflatable bozo doll over a fifteen-minute period when other play options are available. The scientist might then define *aggressive behavior* as six or more blows to the bozo doll. In our wetlands example, a federal authority created an operational definition of *wetland:* A wetland is a parcel of land that has a saturated ground surface for twenty-one consecutive days during the year. Such definitions are useful because they are precisely measurable, but they are also limited because they omit criteria that may be unmeasurable but important. Many scientists, for example, object to definitions of *wetland* based on consecutive days of wetness. What is more relevant, they argue, is not the duration of wetness in any parcel of land but the kind of plants and animals that depend on the wetland as a habitat. As another example, we might ask whether it is adequate to define a *superior student* as someone with a 3.5 GPA or higher or a *successful sex education program* as one that results in a 25 percent reduction in teenage pregnancies. What important aspects of a superior student or a successful sex education program are not considered in these operational definitions?

STRATEGIES FOR DEFINING THE CONTESTED TERM IN A DEFINITIONAL ARGUMENT

In constructing criteria to define your contested term, you can take two basic approaches—what rhetoricians call reportive and stipulative definitions. A *reportive definition* cites how others have used the term. A *stipulative definition* cites how you define the term. To put it another way, you can take a reportive approach by turning to standard or specialized dictionaries, judicial opinions, or expert testimony to establish a definition based on the authority of others. A lawyer defining a wetland based on twenty-one consecutive days of saturated ground surface would be using a reportive definition with a federal regulation as her source. The other approach is to use your own critical thinking to stipulate a definition, thereby defining the contested term yourself. Our definition of a socially responsible company, specifying three criteria, is an example of a stipulative definition. This section explains these approaches in more detail.

Reportive Approach: Research How Others Have Used the Term

When you take a reportive approach, you research how others have used the term, searching for authoritative definitions acceptable to your audience yet favorable to your case. Student writer Kathy Sullivan uses this approach in her argument that photographs displayed at the Oncore Bar are not obscene (see pp. 220–22). To define *obscenity*, she turns to *Black's Law Dictionary* and Pember's *Mass Media Laws*. (Specialized dictionaries are a standard part of the reference section of any library. See your reference librarian for assistance.) Other sources of specialized definitions are state and federal appellate court decisions, legislative and administrative statutes, and scholarly articles examining a given definitional conflict. Lawyers use this research strategy exhaustively in preparing court briefs. They begin by looking at the actual text of laws as passed by legislatures or written by administrative authorities. Then they look at all the court cases in which the laws have been tested and examine the ways courts have refined legal definitions and applied them to specific cases. Using these refined and elaborated definitions, lawyers then apply them to their own case at hand.

When research fails to uncover a definition favorable to the arguer's case, the arguer can sometimes adopt an *original intentions strategy*. For example, if a scientist is dissatisfied with definitions of *wetland* based on consecutive days of saturated ground surface, she might proceed as follows: "The original intention of the Congress in passing the Clean Water Act was to preserve the environment." What Congress intended, she could then claim, was to prevent development of those wetland areas that provide crucial habitat for wildlife or that inhibit water pollution. She could then propose an alternative definition (either a stipulative one that she develops herself or a reportive one that she uncovers in research) based on criteria other than consecutive days of ground saturation. (Of course, original intentions arguments can often be refuted by a "times have changed" strategy or by a "we can't know what they originally intended; we can only know what they wrote" strategy.)

Another way to make a reportive definition is to employ a strategy based on etymology, or *earlier meaning strategy*. Using an etymological dictionary or the *Oxford English Dictionary* (which traces the historical evolution of a word's meaning), an arguer can often unveil insights favorable to the writer's case. For example, if you wanted to argue that portrayal of violence in films is *obscene,* you could point to the etymology of the word, which literally means "offstage." The word derives from the practice of classical Greek tragedy, where violent acts occurred offstage and were only reported by a messenger. This strategy allows you to show how the word originally applied to violence rather than to sexual explicitness.

Stipulative Approach: Create Your Own Definition Based on Positive, Contrastive, and Borderline Cases*

Often, however, you need to create your own definition of the contested term. An effective strategy for developing your own definition is to brainstorm examples of positive, contrastive, and borderline cases. Suppose, for example, you wanted to argue the claim that "Computer programming is (is not) a creative activity." Your first goal is to establish criteria for creativity. You could begin by thinking of examples of obvious creative behaviors, then of contrastive behaviors that seem similar to the previous behaviors but yet are clearly not creative, and then finally of borderline behaviors that may or may not be creative. Your list might look like this:

EXAMPLES OF CREATIVE BEHAVIORS

Beethoven composes a violin concerto.

An architect designs a house.

Edison invents the lightbulb.

An engineer designs a machine that will make widgets in a new way.

A poet writes a poem. (Later revised to "A poet writes a poem that poetry experts say is beautiful"—see following discussion.)

CONTRASTIVE EXAMPLES OF NONCREATIVE BEHAVIORS

A conductor transposes Beethoven's concerto into a different key.

A carpenter builds a house from the architect's plan.

I change a lightbulb in my house.

A factory worker uses the new machine to stamp out widgets.

A graduate student writes sentimental "lovey/dovey" verses for greeting cards.

---

*The defining strategies and collaborative exercises in this section are based on the work of George Hillocks and his research associates at the University of Chicago. See George Hillocks Jr., Elizabeth A. Kahn, and Larry R. Johannessen, "Teaching Defining Strategies as a Mode of Inquiry: Some Effects on Student Writing," *Research in the Teaching of English 17* (October 1983), 275–84. See also Larry R. Johannessen, Elizabeth A. Kahn, and Carolyn Calhoun Walter, *Designing and Sequencing Prewriting Activities* (Urbana, IL: NCTE, 1982).

EXAMPLES OF BORDERLINE CASES

A woman gives birth to a child.

An accountant figures out your income tax.

A musician arranges a rock song for a marching band.

A monkey paints an oil painting by smearing paint on canvas; a group of art critics, not knowing a monkey was the artist, call the painting beautiful.

Next you can begin developing your criteria by determining what features the "clearly creative" examples have in common and what features the "clearly non-creative" examples lack. Then refine your criteria by deciding on what grounds you might include or eliminate your borderline cases from the category "creative." For example, you might begin with the following criterion:

DEFINITION: FIRST TRY

For an act to be creative, it must result in an end product that is significantly different from other products.

But then, by looking at some of the examples in your creative and noncreative columns, you decide that just producing a different end product isn't enough. A bad poem might be different from other poems, but you don't want to call a bad poet creative. So you refine your criteria:

DEFINITION: SECOND TRY

For an act to be creative, it must result in an end product that is significantly different from other products and is useful or beautiful.

This definition would allow you to include all the acts in your creative column but eliminate the acts in the noncreative column.

Your next step is to refine your criteria by deciding whether to include or reject items in your borderline list. You decide to reject the childbirth case by arguing that creativity must be a mental or intellectual activity, not a natural process. You reject the monkey as painter example on similar grounds, arguing that although the end product may be both original and beautiful, it is not creative because it is not a product of the monkey's intellect. However, when you consider the example of the musician who arranges a rock song for a marching band, you encounter disagreement. One member of your group says that arranging music is not creative. This person says that the musician, like a carpenter who makes a few alterations in the blueprint of a house, isn't designing a new product but rather is adapting an already existing one.

A musician in the group reacts angrily, arguing that musicians—in their arrangements of music and in their renditions of musical pieces—"interpret" music. She contends that different renditions of music are actually significantly different pieces that are experienced differently by audiences, and therefore both arranging music and playing a piece in a different musical style are creative acts. The group hesitantly acknowledges that arranging a rock song in marching-band style is different from the example of a carpenter who adds a door between the kitchen and the dining room in a new house. The group concedes to the music major and includes the example of arranging a musical piece in a different musical style.

Your group's final definition, then, looks like this:

DEFINITION: THIRD TRY

> For an act to be creative, it must be produced by intellectual design, and it must result in an end project that is significantly different from the other products and is useful or beautiful.

Having established these criteria, you are ready to apply them to your controversial case of computer programming. Based on your criteria, you decide to argue that computer programming exists on a continuum ranging from "noncreative activity" to "highly creative activity." At the "noncreative" end of the continuum, computer programmers churn out lines of code following algorithmic procedures requiring intelligence, knowledge, problem-solving skills, and a high level of craftsmanship, but not creative thought. Such programmers apply established procedures to new situations; although the applications are new, the programs themselves are not significantly different or innovative. At the other end of the continuum, computer programmers are highly creative. The original Macintosh computer, with its icon-based operating system (later imitated by Microsoft in its Windows© programs), has been heralded as one of the twentieth century's most creative inventions. Programmers who develop ideas for new products, who solve old problems in new ways, or who do research in artificial intelligence, computer simulation, or other interdisciplinary fields requiring synthetic thought are all meeting the criteria of significant newness, usefulness (or beauty), and intellectual design required by our stipulated definition of *creativity.*

This strategy using positive examples, contrastive examples, and borderline cases produces a systematic procedure for developing a definitional argument. Moreover, it provides the examples you will need to explain and illustrate your criteria.

FOR CLASS DISCUSSION

1. Suppose you wanted to define the concept "courage." Working in groups, try to decide whether each of the following cases is an example of courage:
   a. A neighbor rushes into a burning house to rescue a child from certain death and emerges, coughing and choking, with the child in his arms. Is the neighbor courageous?

b. A firefighter rushes into a burning house to rescue a child from certain death and emerges with the child in her arms. The firefighter is wearing protective clothing and a gas mask. When a newspaper reporter calls her courageous, she says, "Hey, this is my job." Is the firefighter courageous?

c. A teenager rushes into a burning house to recover a memento given to him by his girlfriend, the first love of his life. Is the teenager courageous?

d. A parent rushes into a burning house to save a trapped child. The fire marshal tells the parent to wait because there is no chance that the child can be reached from the first floor. The fire marshal wants to try cutting a hole in the roof to reach the child. The parent rushes into the house anyway and is burned to death. Was the parent courageous?

2. As you make your decisions on each of these cases, create and refine the criteria you use.

3. Make up your own series of controversial cases, like those above for "courage," for one or more of the following concepts:
   a. cruelty to animals
   b. child abuse
   c. true athlete
   d. sexual harassment
   e. free speech protected by the First Amendment

Then, using the strategy of positive, contrastive, and borderline cases, construct a definition of your chosen concept.

CONDUCTING THE MATCH PART OF A DEFINITIONAL ARGUMENT

In conducting a match argument, you need to supply examples and other evidence showing that your contested case does (does not) meet the criteria you established in your definition. In essence, you support the match part of your argument in much the same way you would support a simple categorical claim.

For example, if you were developing the argument that the Hercules Shoe Company is not socially responsible because it treats its workers unjustly, your match section would provide evidence of this injustice. You might supply data about the percentage of shoes produced in East Asia, about the low wages paid these workers, and about the working conditions in these factories. You might also describe the suffering of displaced American workers when Hercules closed its American factories and moved operations to Asia, where the labor was non-union and cheap. The match section should also summarize and respond to opposing views.

WRITING A DEFINITIONAL ARGUMENT

WRITING ASSIGNMENT FOR CHAPTER 10

Write an argument that develops a definitional claim of the form "X is (is not) a Y," where Y is a controversial term with a disputed definition. Typically your argument will have a criteria section in which you develop an extended definition of your Y term and a match section in which you argue that your X does (does not) meet the criteria for Y.

Exploring Ideas

Ideally, in writing this argument you will join an ongoing conversation about a definitional issue that interests you. What cultural and social issues that concern you involve disputed definitions? In the public area, you are likely to find numerous examples simply by looking through a newspaper—the strategy used by student writer Kathy Sullivan, who became interested in the controversy over allegedly obscene photographs in a gay bar (see pp. 220–22). Others of our students have addressed definitional issues such as these: Is Dr. Kevorkian a murderer (because he administered a lethal dosage to a paralyzed patient on national TV)? Are skateboarders punks or athletes? Is spanking a form of child abuse? Is flag burning protected free speech? Are today's maximum security prisons "cruel and unusual punishment"? Is tobacco a drug for purposes of federal regulation? Are chiropractors "real doctors"?

If you have trouble discovering a local or national issue that interests you, you can create fascinating definitional controversies among your classmates by asking whether certain borderline cases are "true" examples of some category: Are highly skilled video game players (race car drivers, synchronized swimmers, marbles players) true athletes? Is a gourmet chef a true artist? Is rap music truly misogynist? Is the novel (or film) *Sophie's Choice* a true tragedy? Working as a whole class or in small groups inside or out of class, create an argumentative discussion on one or more of these issues. Listen to the various voices in the controversy, and then write out your own argument.

You can also stimulate definitional controversies by brainstorming borderline cases for such terms as *courage* (Is mountain climbing an act of courage?), *cruelty to animals* (Are rodeos [zoos, catch-and-release trout fishing, use of animals for medical research] cruelty to animals?), or *police brutality* (Is use of a stun gun an example of police brutality?).

As you explore your definitional issue, try to determine how others have defined your Y term (a reportive procedure). If no stable definition emerges from your search, stipulate your own definition by deciding what criteria must be met for any X to be deemed a Y. Try using the strategy of positive examples, negative examples, and borderline cases that we discussed on pages 209–12 with reference to creativity. Once you have determined your criteria for your Y term, freewrite for five or ten minutes, exploring whether your X term meets each of the criteria. Before writing your first draft, you might also explore your ideas further by doing the ten freewriting tasks on pages 70–71 in Chapter 3.

Organizing a Definitional Argument

As you compose a first draft of your essay, you may find it helpful to know a prototypical structure for definitional arguments. Here are several possible plans.

Plan 1 (Criteria and Match in Separate Sections)

- Introduce the issue by showing disagreements about the definition of a key term or about its application to a problematic case.
- State your claim.
- Present your definition of the key term.

  State and develop criterion 1.

  State and develop criterion 2.

  Continue with rest of criteria.

- Summarize and respond to possible objections to your definition.
- Restate your claim about the contested case (it does [does not] meet your definition).

  Apply criterion 1 to your case.

  Apply criterion 2 to your case.

  Continue the match argument.

- Summarize and respond to possible objections to your match argument.
- Conclude your argument.

Plan 2 (Criteria and Match Interwoven)

- Introduce the issue by showing disagreements about the definition of a key term or about its application to a problematic case.
- Present your claim.

  State criterion 1 and argue that contested case meets (does not meet) criterion.

State criterion 2 and argue that contested case meets (does not meet) criterion.

Continue with criteria-match sections for additional criteria.

■ Summarize opposing views.

■ Refute or concede to opposing views.

■ Conclude your argument.

Revising Your Draft

Once you have written a discovery draft, your goal should be to make your argument more clear and persuasive to your audience. Where might your audience call your claim, reasons, or evidence into question? Reengage with your audience to better appreciate the complexity of your issue. One way to strengthen your appeal to your readers is to use a Toulmin analysis to determine where your reasoning needs to be bolstered for your particular audience. In a definitional argument, the criteria established in your definition of the Y term are the warrants for your match argument. You might find it helpful at this time to summarize your argument as a claim with *because* clauses and to test it with Toulmin's schema. Here is how student writer Kathy Sullivan used Toulmin to analyze a draft of her essay examining the possible obscenity of photographs displayed in a gay bar in Seattle. The final version of this essay is printed on pages 220–22.

ENTHYMEME:	The photographs displayed in the Oncore bar are not obscene because they do not violate the community standards of the patrons of the bar, because they do not appeal to prurient interest, because children are not likely to be exposed to them, and because they promote an important social value, safe sex, in order to prevent AIDS.
CLAIM:	The photographs are not obscene.
STATED REASONS:	(1) They don't violate community standards. (2) They do not appeal to prurient interests. (3) Children are not exposed to them. (4) They promote an important social purpose of preventing AIDS through safe sex.
GROUNDS:	(1) evidence that most Oncore patrons are homosexual and that these photographs don't offend them (no complaints, etc.); (2) purpose of photographs is not prurient sexuality, they don't depict explicit sexual acts, the only thing complained about by the

	liquor board is visible body parts; (3) because this is a bar, children aren't allowed; (4) evidence that the purpose of these photographs is to promote safe sex, thus they have a redeeming social value
WARRANT:	Things that don't violate community standards, do not appeal to prurient interests, don't come in view of children, and promote an important purpose are not obscene.
BACKING:	These criteria come from the definition of *obscenity* in *Black's Law Dictionary,* which in turn is based on recent court cases. This is a very credible source. In addition, arguments showing why the community standard here should be that of the homosexual community rather than the community at large; arguments showing that the social importance of safe sex overrides other considerations.
CONDITIONS OF REBUTTAL:	An opponent might say that the community standards should be those of the Seattle community at large, not those of the gay community. An opponent might say that photographs of male genitalia in a gay bar appeal to prurient interest.
QUALIFIER:	Those photographs would be obscene if displayed anywhere but in a gay bar.

As a result of this analysis, Kathy revised her final draft considerably. By imagining where her arguments were weak ("conditions of rebuttal"), she realized that she needed to include more backing by arguing that the community standards to be applied in this case should be those of the homosexual community rather than the community at large. She also added a section arguing that visible genitalia in the photographs didn't make the photos obscene. By imagining how your readers might rebut your argument, you will see ways to strengthen your draft. Consequently, we close out this chapter by looking more carefully at the ways a definitional argument can be rebutted.

QUESTIONING AND CRITIQUING A DEFINITIONAL ARGUMENT

Another powerful way to stimulate revision of a draft is to role-play a skeptical audience. The following means of questioning a definitional argument can be applied to your own draft to help you strengthen it or to someone else's definitional argument as a means of critiquing it closely. In critiquing a definitional argument, you need to appreciate its criteria-match structure. Your critique can question the argument's criteria, the match, or both.

Questioning the Criteria

Might a skeptic claim that your criteria are not the right ones? This is the most common way to attack a definitional argument. Skeptics might say that one or more of your argument's criteria are only accidental criteria, not necessary or sufficient ones. Or they might argue for different criteria or point out crucial missing criteria.

Might a skeptic point out possible bad consequences of accepting your argument's criteria? Here a skeptic could raise doubts about your definition by showing how it would lead to unintended bad consequences.

Might a skeptic cite extraordinary circumstances that weaken your argument's criteria? Skeptics might argue that your criteria are perfectly acceptable in ordinary circumstances but are rendered unacceptable by extraordinary circumstances.

Might a skeptic point out a bias or slant in your definition? Writers create definitions favorable to their case. By making this slant visible, a skeptic may be able to weaken the persuasiveness of your definition.

Questioning the Match

A match argument usually uses examples and other evidence to show that the contested case meets (does not meet) the criteria in the definition. The standard methods of refuting evidence apply (see pp. 161–62). Thus skeptics might ask one or more of the following questions:

Are your examples out-of-date or too narrow and unrepresentative?

Are your examples inaccurate?

Are your examples too extreme?

Are there existing counterexamples that alter the case?

By using these questions to test your own argument, you can reshape and develop your argument to make it thought provoking and persuasive for your audience.

READINGS

Our first reading makes a simple categorical claim about the *Star Wars* movie *Episode I: The Phantom Menace.* The movie's appearance in May 1999 was a media event generating much discussion in the newspapers. In this op-ed piece, syndicated columnist John Leo argues that this film recirculates and perpetuates old racist stereotypes.

Stereotypes No Phantom
in New Star Wars Movie

John Leo

1   Everyone's a victim these days, so America's touchiness industry is dedicated to seeing group slights everywhere. But sometimes even touchy people are right. Complaints about the new *Star Wars* movie, for instance, are correct. *Episode I: The Phantom Menace* is packed with awful stereotypes.

2   Consider the evil Neimodians. They are stock Oriental villains out of black-and-white B movies of the 1930s and 1940s, complete with Hollywood Asian accents, sinister speech patterns, and a space-age version of stock Fu Manchu clothing.

3   Watto, the fat, greedy junk dealer with wings, is a conventional, crooked Middle Eastern merchant. This is a generic and anti-Semitic image, Jewish if you want him to be, or Arab if you don't.

4   Law Professor Patricia Williams says Watto looks strikingly like an anti-Jewish caricature published in Vienna at the turn of the century—round-bellied, big-nosed, with spindly arms, wings sprouting from his shoulders, and a scroll that says "anything for money."

5   Perhaps Watto isn't supposed to be Jewish. Some people thought he sounded Italian. But by presenting the character as an unprincipled, hook-nosed merchant (and a slave-owner, to boot), the movie is at least playing around with traditional anti-Semitic imagery. It shouldn't.

6   The loudest criticism has been directed at Jar Jar Binks, the annoying, computer-generated amphibian who looks like a cross between a frog and a camel and acts, as one critic put it, like a cross between Butterfly McQueen and Stepin Fetchit. His voice, the work of a black actor, is a sort of slurred, pidgin Caribbean English, much of it impossible to understand.

7   "Me berry, berry scay-yud," says Jar Jar, in one of his modestly successful attempts at English. For some reason, he keeps saying "yousa" and "meesa," instead of "you" and "me." He is the first character in the four *Star Wars* movies to mess up Galactic Basic (the English language) on a regular basis.

8   Trouble with English in one of the key traits of a racist caricature, from all the 19th-century characters named Snowball down to the sophisticated wit of Amos 'n' Andy. Whether endearing or pathetic, this trouble with language is supposed to demonstrate the intellectual inferiority of blacks.

9   Childlike confusion is another familiar way of stereotyping blacks, and Jar Jar shows that trait too. He steps in alien-creature doo-doo, gets his tongue caught in a racing engine and panics during the big battle scene. He is, in fact, a standard-issue black caricature.

10   A stereotype on this level is more than insult. It is a teaching instrument and a powerful, non-verbal argument saying that racial equality is a hopeless cause. If blacks talk and act like this movie says they do, how can they possibly expect equal treatment?

11   What is going on in this movie? George Lucas, director of the *Star Wars* movies, says media talk about stereotypes is creating "a controversy out of nothing."

But many visual cues support the charge that stereotypes are indeed built into the film. Jar Jar has head flaps drawn to look like dreadlocks. The ruler of his tribe, Boss Nass, wears what looks to be an African robe and African headdress. (Nass, fat and slobbering, seems to come right out of an old movie about the Zulu.)   12

A Neimodian senator named Lott (Trent Lott?), representing the evil viceroy Nute Gunray (Newt Gingrich?), wears a version of a Catholic bishop's miter and a Catholic priest's stole over a dark robe. This can't be an accident. It duplicates, almost exactly, the appearance of a real bishop. It's a small reference, but an unmistakable one. So Catholics, along with Asians and Republicans, are at least vaguely associated with Neimodian treachery.   13

Lucas is a visually sophisticated and careful moviemaker. In a TV interview, he said that he researched imagery of Satan in every known culture before deciding on how evil warrior Darth Maul should look in the film (tattooed, with horns). A *Star Wars* book that came out with the movie, *The Visual Dictionary,* describes in detail almost every image used in the film. So it's hard to believe that all the stereotyped imagery just happened.   14

One of the keys to Lucas' success is that his movies are made up of brilliantly reimagined themes and scenes from earlier films (World War II aerial dogfights, cowboys and Indians, swashbuckling sword fights, a *Ben Hur* chariot race, etc.). After three very inventive *Star Wars* movies, the not-so-inventive fourth seems to have fallen back on some tired Hollywood ethnic themes and characters he mostly avoided in the first three.   15

So *The Phantom Menace* offers us revived versions of some famous stereotypes. Jar Jar Binks as the dithery Butterfly McQueen; Watto, a devious, child-owning wheeler-dealer, as the new Fagin; the two reptilian Neimodian leaders as the inscrutably evil Fu Manchu and Dr. No. What's next—an interplanetary version of the Frito Bandito?   16

The *Star Wars* films deserve better than this. Let's put all these characters to sleep and start over in the next movie.   17

Critiquing "Stereotypes No Phantom in New 'Star Wars' Movie"

1. Simple categorical arguments are typically developed by the use of examples to support the claim. What examples does Leo use to demonstrate that stereotypes are common in *The Phantom Menace?*

2. Leo assumes his audience is familiar with Butterfly McQueen (who played the maid Prissy in *Gone with the Wind*), Fagin (the hook-nosed Jewish stereotype in Charles Dickens's *Oliver Twist*), Stepin Fetchit (the stereotype of the black sidekick/servant), Fu Manchu (the stereotype of the threatening, inscrutable Asian), Dr. No (the ethnically "other" villain), and the Frito Bandito (a Mexican stereotype used in Frito advertisements)—famous stereotypes from an earlier era. Share any knowledge you have of these stereotypes. Does *The Phantom Menace* deserve to be classified with earlier films that are now justly castigated for perpetuating racial and ethnic stereotypes?

3. Leo's article is a simple categorical argument rather than a definitional argument because there is no controversy over the meaning of the Y term "stereotype."

However, Lucas claims that critics' complaints about stereotyping in the film are "a controversy over nothing." How does Leo argue that the stereotypes are both intentional and damaging? What is the larger conversation about the influence of art on society that Leo's article is joining? Do you agree with Leo's implicit claim in this larger conversation—namely, that films have a powerful influence on society?

The second reading, by student Kathy Sullivan, was written for the definition assignment on page 213. The definitional issue that she addresses—"Are the Menasee photographs obscene?"—became a local controversy in the state of Washington when the state liquor control board threatened to revoke the liquor license of a Seattle gay bar, the Oncore, unless it removed a series of photographs that the board deemed obscene.

Oncore, Obscenity, and the Liquor Control Board

Kathy Sullivan (student)

1   In early May, Geoff Menasee, a Seattle artist, exhibited a series of photographs with the theme of "safe sex" on the walls of an inner city, predominantly homosexual restaurant and lounge called the Oncore. Before hanging the photographs, Menasee had to consult with the Washington State Liquor Control Board because, under the current state law, art work containing material that may be considered indecent has to be approved by the board before it can be exhibited. Of the almost thirty photographs, six were rejected by the board because they partially exposed "private parts" of the male anatomy. Menasee went ahead and displayed the entire series of photographs, placing Band-Aids over the "indecent" areas, but the customers continually removed the Band-Aids.

2   The liquor control board's ruling on this issue has caused controversy in the Seattle community. The *Seattle Times* has provided news coverage, and a "Town Meeting" segment was filmed at the restaurant. The central question is this: Should an establishment that caters to a predominantly homosexual clientele be enjoined from displaying pictures promoting "safe sex" on the grounds that the photographs are obscene?

3   Before I can answer this question, I must first determine whether the art work should truly be classified as obscene. To make that determination, I will use the definition of obscenity in *Black's Law Dictionary:*

Material is "obscene" if to the average person, applying contemporary community standards, the dominant theme of material taken as a whole appeals to prurient interest, if it is utterly without redeeming social importance, if it goes substantially beyond customary limits of candor in description or representation, if it is characterized by patent offensiveness, and if it is hard core pornography.

An additional criterion is provided by Pember's *Mass Media Laws:* "A work is obscene if it has a tendency to deprave and corrupt those whose minds are open to such immoral influences (children for example) and into whose hands it might happen to fall" (394). The art work in question should not be prohibited from display at predominantly homosexual establishments like the Oncore because it does not meet the above criteria for obscenity.

First of all, to the average person applying contemporary community standards, the predominant theme of Menasee's photographs is not an appeal to prurient interests. The first element in this criterion is "average person." According to Rocky Breckner, manager of the Oncore, 90 percent of the clientele at the Oncore is made up of young white homosexual males. This group therefore constitutes the "average person" viewing the exhibit. "Contemporary community standards" would ordinarily be the standards of the Seattle community. However, this art work is aimed at a particular group of people—the homosexual community. Therefore, the "community standards" involved here are those of the gay community rather than the city at large. Since the Oncore is not an art museum or gallery, which attracts a broad spectrum of people, it is appropriate to restrict the scope of "community standards" to that group who voluntarily patronize the Oncore.   4

Second, the predominant theme of the photographs is not "prurient interest" nor do the photographs go "substantially beyond public limits of candor." There are no explicit sexual acts found in the photographs; instead, their theme is the prevention of AIDS through the practice of safe sex. Homosexual displays of affection could be viewed as "prurient interest" by the larger community, but same-sex relationships are the norm for the group at whom the exhibit is aimed. If the exhibit were displayed at McDonald's or even the Red Robin it might go "substantially beyond customary limits of candor," but it is unlikely that the clientele of the Oncore would find the art work offensive. The manager stated that he received very few complaints about the exhibit and its contents.   5

Nor is the material pornographic. The liquor control board prohibited the six photographs based on their visible display of body parts such as pubic hair and naked buttocks, not on the basis of sexual acts or homosexual orientation. The board admitted that the photographs depicted no explicit sexual acts. Hence, it can be concluded that they did not consider the suggestion of same-sex affection to be hard-core pornography. Their sole objection was that body parts were visible. But visible genitalia in art work are not necessarily pornographic. Since other art work, such as Michelangelo's sculptures, explicitly depict both male and female genitalia, it is arguable that pubic hair and buttocks are not patently offensive.   6

It must be conceded that the art work has the potential of being viewed by children, which would violate Pember's criterion. But once again the incidence of minors frequenting this establishment is very small.   7

But the most important reason for saying these photographs are not obscene is that they serve an important social purpose. One of Black's criteria is that obscene material is "utterly without redeeming social importance." But these photographs have the explicit purpose of promoting safe sex as a defense against AIDS. Recent statistics reported in the *Seattle Times* show that AIDS is now the leading cause of death of men under forty in the Seattle area. Any methods that can promote the message of safe sex in today's society have strong redeeming social significance.   8

9   Those who believe that all art containing "indecent" material should be banned or covered from public view would most likely believe that Menasee's work is obscene. They would disagree that the environment and the clientele should be the major determining factor when using criteria to evaluate art. However, in the case of this exhibit I feel that the audience and the environment of the display are factors of overriding importance. Therefore, the exhibit should have been allowed to be displayed because it is not obscene.

Critiquing "Oncore, Obscenity, and the Liquor Control Board"

1. Kathy Sullivan here uses a reportive approach for defining her Y term "obscenity." Based on the definitions of *obscenity* in *Black's Law Dictionary* and Pember's *Mass Media Laws,* what criteria for obscenity does Kathy use?

2. How does she argue that the Menasee photographs do *not* meet the criteria?

3. Working as a whole class or in small groups, share your responses to the following questions: (a) If you find Kathy's argument persuasive, which parts were particularly influential or effective? (b) If you are not persuaded, which parts of her argument do you find weak or ineffective? (c) How does Kathy shape her argument to meet the concerns and objections of her audience? (d) How might a lawyer for the liquor control board rebut Kathy's argument?

Our last reading concerns sexual harassment, which continues to be a hotly debated legal, economic, and social issue. Vicki Schultz, a Yale law professor, first wrote a version of the article "Sex Is the Least of It: Let's Focus Harassment Law on Work, Not Sex," for the *Yale Law Journal.* She then rewrote this article for a more general audience, and this is the version we are printing here. It appeared in the May 25, 1998, issue of the *Nation,* a moderately liberal magazine devoted to politics and public issues. Here she addresses the complex issue of how sexual harassment should be defined. She looks at current definitions, shows the bad social consequences of following these definitions, and poses a new definition based on new criteria.

As background for reading this article, you should understand some of the context that it addresses. In the controversy over sexual harassment, most parties agree on the *quid pro quo* criterion (Latin for "something for something"—something given for something received), which covers those direct incidents of sexual harassment where a superior demands sexual favors in exchange for job benefits (or threatens demotion or firing if the favors are not granted). But the standard definition of *sexual harassment* (see the definition from the Equal Employment Opportunity Commission that we reprinted on p. 205) also includes a "hostile workplace" criterion, which has led to extensive confusion and debate. It is worded as follows in the EEOC guidelines: Sexual harassment occurs if someone's "conduct has the purpose or effect of unreasonably interfering with an individual's work performance or creating an intimidating, hostile, or offensive working environment." In this article, Schultz argues that limiting the defining features of a hostile environment to sexual conditions (such as telling off-color jokes) has unfortunate consequences.

Sex Is the Least of It: Let's Focus Harassment Law on Work, Not Sex

Vicki Schultz

The Clarence Thomas hearings, the Tailhook incident, the Gene McKinney trial, the Clinton scandals—if these events spring to mind when you hear the words "sexual harassment," you are not alone. That such images of powerful men making sexual come-ons toward female subordinates should be the defining ones simply proves the power of the popular perception that harassment is first and foremost about sex. It's easy to see why: The media, the courts and some feminists have emphasized this to the exclusion of all else. But the real issue isn't sex, it's sexism on the job. The fact is, most harassment isn't about satisfying sexual desires. It's about protecting work—especially the most favored lines of work—as preserves of male competence and authority.

This term the Supreme Court heard three cases involving sex harassment in the workplace. Along with media coverage of current events, the Court's decisions will shape our understanding of this issue into the next century, for all these controversies raise the same fundamental question: Does sex harassment require a special body of law having to do with sexual relations, or should it be treated just like any other form of workplace discrimination?

If the Court decides that harassment is primarily a problem of sexual relations, it will be following the same misguided path some courts have taken since they first accepted that such behavior falls under the prohibitions of Title VII of the Civil Rights Act, the major federal statute forbidding sex discrimination in employment. Early decisions outlawed what is known as quid pro quo harassment—typically, a situation where a supervisor penalizes a subordinate who refuses to grant sexual favors. It was crucial for the courts to acknowledge that sexual advances and other interactions *can* be used in the service of discrimination. Yet their reasoning spelled trouble. The courts said harassment was sex bias because the advances were rooted in a sexual attraction that the harasser felt for a woman but would not have felt for another man. By locating the problem in the sexual character of the advances rather than in the workplace dynamics of which they were a part—for instance, the paternalistic prerogative of a male boss to punish an employee on the job for daring to step out of her "place" as a woman—the decisions threatened to equate sex harassment with sexual pursuits. From there it was a short step to the proposition that sex in the workplace, or at least sexual interactions between men and women in unequal jobs, is inherently suspect.

Yet the problem we should be addressing isn't sex, it's the sexist failure to take women seriously as workers. Sex harassment is a means for men to claim work as masculine turf.

By driving women away or branding them inferior, men can insure the sex segregation of the work force. We know that women who work in jobs traditionally held by men are more likely than other women to experience hostility and harassment at work. Much of the harassment they experience isn't "sexual" in content or design. Even where sexually explicit harassment occurs, it is typically part of a broader pattern of conduct intended to reinforce gender difference and to claim work as a domain of masculine mastery. As one experienced electrician put it in Molly Martin's *Hard-Hatted Women,* "[We] . . . face another pervasive and sinister kind of harassment which is gender-based, but may have nothing to do with sex. It is harassment aimed at us simply because we are women in a 'man's' job, and its function is to discourage us from staying in our trades."

5   This harassment can take a variety of forms, most of which involve undermining a woman on the job. In one case, male electricians stopped working rather than submit to the authority of a female subforeman. In another, Philadelphia policemen welcomed their new female colleagues by stealing their case files and lacing their uniforms with lime that burned their skin. Even more commonly, men withhold the training and assignments women need to learn to do the job well, or relegate them to menial duties that signal they are incompetent to perform the simplest tasks. Work sabotage is all too common.

6   Nor is this a purely blue-collar phenomenon. About one-third of female physicians recently surveyed said they had experienced sexual harassment, but almost half said they'd been subjected to harassment that had no sexual or physical component but was related simply to their being female in a traditionally male field. In one 1988 court case, a group of male surgical residents went so far as to falsify a patient's medical records to make it appear as though their female colleague had made an error.

7   Men do, of course, resort to sexualized forms of harassment Sexual overtures may intimidate a woman or label her incompetent in settings where female sexuality is considered incompatible with professionalism. In one 1993 Supreme Court case, a company president suggested that a female manager must have had sex with a client to land an important account. Whether or not the harassment assumes a sexual form, however, what unites all these actions is that they create occupational environments that define womanhood as the opposite of what it takes to be a good worker.

8   From this starting point, it becomes clear that the popular view of harassment is both too narrow and too broad. Too narrow, because that focus on rooting out unwanted sexual activity has allowed us to feel good about protecting women from sexual abuse while leading us to overlook equally pernicious forms of gender-based mistreatment. Too broad because the emphasis on sexual conduct has encouraged some companies to ban all forms of sexual interaction, even when these do not threaten women's equality on the job.

9   How has the law become too narrow? The picture of harassment-as-sex that developed out of the quid pro quo cases has overwhelmed the conception of the hostile work environment, leading most courts to exonerate seriously sexist misconduct if it does not resemble a sexual come-on. In *Turley v. Union Carbide Corp.,* a court dismissed the harassment claim of a woman whose foreman "pick[ed] on [her] all the time" and treated her worse than the men. Citing Catharine MacKinnon's definition of sexual harassment as "the unwanted imposition of sexual requirements in the context of a relationship of unequal power," the court concluded that the case did not involve actionable harassment

because "the foreman did not demand sexual relations, he did not touch her or make sexual jokes."

By the same reasoning, in *Reynolds v. Atlantic City Convention Center,* the court ruled against a female electrical subforeman, Reynolds, whose men refused to work for her, made obscene gestures and stood around laughing while she unloaded heavy boxes. Not long before, the union's business agent had proclaimed, "[Now] is not the time, the place or the year, [nor] will it ever be the year for a woman foreman." When the Miss America pageant came to town, an exhibitor asked that Reynolds be removed from the floor—apparently, the incongruity between the beauty contestants and the tradeswoman was too much to take—and Reynolds's boss replaced and eventually fired her. Yet the court concluded that none of this amounted to a hostile work environment: The obscene gestures that the court considered "sexual" were too trivial, and the rest of the conduct wasn't sufficiently sexual to characterize as gender-based.

These are not isolated occurrences. I recently surveyed hundreds of Title VII hostile work environment cases and found that the courts' disregard of nonsexual forms of harassment is an overwhelming trend. This definitely works against women in male-dominated job settings, but it has also hurt women in traditionally female jobs, who share the experience of harassment that denigrates their competence or intelligence as workers. They are often subjected to sexist forms of authority, humiliation and abuse—objectified not only as sexual commodities but as creatures too stupid or worthless to deserve respect, fit only to be controlled by others ("stupid women who have kids," "too fat to clean rooms," "dumb females who [can't] read or write").

Just as our obsession with sexual misconduct obscures many debilitating forms of harassment facing women, it also leads us to overlook some pernicious harassment confronting men on the job. If the legal cases provide any indication, the most common form of harassment men experience is not, as the film *Disclosure* suggests, a proposition from a female boss. It is, instead, hostility from male co-workers seeking to denigrate or drive away men who threaten the work's masculine image. If a job is to confer manliness, it must be held by those who project the desired sense of manhood. It isn't only women who can detract from that image. In some work settings, men are threatened by the presence of any man perceived to be gay—for homosexuality is often seen as gender deviance—or any other man perceived to lack the manly competence considered suitable for those who hold the job. The case logs are filled with harassment against men who are not married, men who are not attractive to women, men who are seen as weak or slow, men who are openly supportive of women, men who wear earrings and even young men or boys. Some men have taunted and tormented, battered and beaten other men in the name of purging the brotherhood of wimps and fags—not suitable to stand alongside them as workers.

We have been slow to name this problem sex-based harassment because it doesn't fit our top-down, male-female, sexual come-on image of harassment. In *Goluszek v. Smith,* the court ruled against an electronic maintenance mechanic who was disparaged and driven out by his fellow workers. They mocked him for not having a wife, saying a man had to be married to be a machinist. They used gender-based images to assault his competence, saying that if he couldn't fix a machine they'd send in his "daddy"—the supervisor—to do it. They drove jeeps at him and threatened to knock him off his ladder, and when he filed a grievance, his supervisor wrote him up for carelessness and eventually fired him. Not only did the court dismiss Goluszek's claim, the judge simply couldn't conceive that what happened to him was sexual harassment. "The 'sexual harassment' that is actionable under Title VII 'is the exploitation of a powerful position to impose sexual demands or pressures on an unwilling but less powerful person,' " the judge wrote. Perhaps lower courts will adopt a broader view now that the Supreme Court has ruled, in the recent *Oncale v. Sundowner Offshore Services* decision, that male-on-male harassment may be actionable even when it is not sexual in design.

14   Meanwhile, the traditional overemphasis on sex can lead to a repressive impulse to eliminate all hints of sexual expression from the workplace, however benign. Instead of envisioning harassment law as a tool to promote women's equality as workers, the popular understanding of harassment encourages courts and companies to "protect" women's sexual sensibilities. In *Fair v. Guiding Eyes for the Blind,* a heterosexual woman who was the associate director of a nonprofit organization claimed her gay male supervisor had created an offensive environment by making gossipy conversation and political remarks involving homosexuality. It is disturbing that current law inspired such a claim, even though the court correctly ruled that the supervisor's conduct was not sexual harassment.

15   Other men haven't fared so well. In *Pierce v. Commonwealth Life Insurance Co.,* a manager was disciplined for participating in an exchange of sexually explicit cards with a female office administrator. One of the cards Pierce had sent read, "Sex is a misdemeanor. De more I miss, de meanor I get." After thirty years with the company, he was summarily demoted and transferred to another office, with his pay slashed and his personal belongings dumped at a roadside Hardee's. True, Pierce was a manager and he was responsible for enforcing the company's harassment policy. Still, the reasoning that led to his ouster is unsound—and dangerous. According to his superiors, he might as well have been a "murderer, rapist or child molester; that wouldn't be any worse [than what he had done]." This sort of thing gives feminism a bad name. If companies want to fire men like Pierce, let them do it without the pretense of protecting women from sexual abuse.

16   Equally alarming are reports that, in the name of preventing sexual harassment, some companies are adopting policies that prohibit a man and woman from traveling or staying at the same hotel together on business, or prevent a male supervisor from giving a performance evaluation to a female underling behind closed doors without a lawyer present. One firm has declared that its construction workers can't even look at a woman for more than five seconds. With such work rules, who will want to hire women? How will women obtain the training they need if their male bosses and colleagues can't interact with them as equals?

17   It's a mistake to try to outlaw sexual interaction in the workplace. The old Taylorist project of purging organizations of all sexual and other emotional dynamics was deeply flawed. Sexuality is part of the human experience, and so long as organizations still employ people rather than robots, it will continue to flourish in one form or another. And sexuality is not simply a tool of gender domination; it is also a potential source of empowerment and even pleasure for women on the job. Indeed, some research suggests that where men and women work as equals in integrated settings, sex harassment isn't a problem. Sexual talk and joking continues, but it isn't experienced as harassment. It's not impossible to imag-

ine sexual banter as a form of playfulness, even solidarity, in a work world that is increasingly competitive and stressful.

Once we realize that the problem isn't sex but sexism, we can re-establish our concept   18
of harassment on firmer ground. Title VII was never meant to police sexuality. It was meant to provide people the chance to pursue their life's work on equal terms—free of pressure to conform to prescribed notions of how women and men are supposed to behave in their work roles. Properly conceived, quid pro quo harassment is a form of discrimination because it involves men exercising the power to punish women, as workers, who have the temerity to say no, as women. Firing women who won't have sex on the job is no different from firing black women who refuse to perform cleaning work, or female technicians who refuse to do clerical work, that isn't part of their job descriptions.

So, too, hostile-work-environment harassment isn't about sexual relations; it's about   19
how work relations engender inequality. The legal concept was created in the context of early race discrimination cases, when judges recognized that Jim Crow systems could be kept alive not just through company acts (such as hiring and firing) but also through company atmospheres that made African-American workers feel different and inferior. That discriminatory environments are sometimes created by "sexual" conduct is not the point. Sex should be treated just like anything else in the workplace: Where it furthers sex discrimination, it should go. Where it doesn't, it's not the business of our civil rights laws.

It's too easy to allow corporate America to get away with banning sexual interaction   20
without forcing it to attend to the larger structures of workplace gender discrimination in which both sexual and not-so-sexual forms of harassment flourish. Let's revitalize our understanding of harassment to demand a world in which all women and even the least powerful men can work together as equals in whatever endeavors their hearts and minds desire.

Critiquing "Sex Is the Least of It: Let's Focus Harassment Law on Work, Not Sex"

1. Try to restate Schultz's main argument in your own words. What does she mean when she says, "Yet the problem we should be addressing isn't sex, it's the sexist failure to take women seriously as workers. Sex harassment is a means for men to claim work as masculine turf"? What definition of *sexual harassment* is she advocating?

2. Give a typical example of what the courts currently mean by a "hostile workplace" based on prevailing sexual criteria. Then give a typical example of a "hostile workplace" as Schultz would define it. How do the two examples differ?

3. What does Schultz mean when she says that the "popular view of harassment is both too narrow and too broad"?

4. What contribution does Schultz make to the conflicted conversation about sexual harassment in the workplace? What would be the consequences of adopting her enlarged definition of *sexual harassment?* Are there any drawbacks to her definition?

11

Causal Arguments

X Causes (Does Not Cause) Y

CASE 1

In the Spring of 1999 two male students of Columbine High School in Littleton, Colorado, opened fire on their classmates. Twelve students and a teacher were killed, and the two boys killed themselves; twenty-three were wounded. For months following the killings, social scientists and media commentators analyzed the massacre, trying to determine what caused it and what solutions might be enacted to reduce teen violence. Among the causes proposed were the following: violent movies, violent video games, violent TV, the music of Marilyn Manson, easy access to guns, breakdown of the traditional family, absence of parental involvement in teen lives, erosion of school discipline, inadequate school counseling, Internet neo-Nazi chat rooms, Internet lessons on how to make bombs, and the irresponsible prescribing of antidepressants to teenagers (one of the assailants was taking Prozac). For each proposed cause, the arguer suggested a different approach for reducing teen violence.

CASE 2

Four years ago, the Fiji Islands got satellite television, and Fijians began watching such American television shows as *Beverly Hills 90210* and *Melrose Place*. In the next four years, the number of teens at risk for eating disorders doubled. According to columnist Ellen Goodman, "74 percent of the Fiji teens in a study said they felt 'too big or fat' at least some of the time and 62 percent said they had dieted in the past month." Emphasizing eating as pleasure and a rite of hospitality, Fiji culture has traditionally valued ample flesh and a robust shape for women, an image very opposite from that of thin American television stars. A Harvard anthropologist and psychiatrist has been studying this connection between television and eating disorders. Although "a direct causal link" may not be easy to support, there does seem to be a connection between projected television images of women and illness. Goodman poses the question of what harm television images can cause to women.*

AN OVERVIEW OF CAUSAL ARGUMENTS

We encounter causal issues all the time. What caused the Columbine High School massacre? What caused young women in Fiji to start feeling fat? What would be the consequences of legalizing drugs? What are the causes of illegal immigration into the United States and of the federal government's failure to stem it? (One proposed answer to the last question: Many powerful U.S. businesses want illegal immigration to continue because they rely on illegal immigrants as a source of cheap labor.)

Sometimes an argument can be devoted entirely to a causal issue. Just as frequently, causal arguments support proposal arguments in which the writer argues that we should (should not) do X *because doing X will lead to good (bad) consequences.* Convincing readers how X will lead to these consequences—a causal argument—thus bears on the success of many proposal arguments.

Because causal arguments require close analysis of phenomena, effective causal arguing is closely linked to critical thinking. Studies of critical thinking show that good problem solvers systematically explore the causes of a problem before proposing a solution. Equally important, before making a decision, good problem solvers predict and weigh the consequences of alternative solutions to a problem, trying to determine a solution that produces the greatest benefits with the least cost. Adding to the complexity of causal arguing is the way a given event can have multiple causes and multiple consequences. In an effort to save salmon, for example, environmentalists have proposed the elimination of several dams on the Snake River above Lewiston, Idaho. Will the removal of these dams save the salmon? Nobody knows for sure, but three universally agreed-upon consequences of removing the dams will be the loss of several thousand jobs in the Lewiston area, loss of some hydroelectric power, and the shift in wheat transportation from river barges to overland trucks and trains. So the initial focus on consequences to salmon soon widens to include consequences to jobs, to power generation, and to agricultural transportation.

THE NATURE OF CAUSAL ARGUING

Typically, causal arguments try to show how one event brings about another. On the surface, causal arguments may seem a fairly straightforward matter—more

---

*Ellen Goodman, "The Skinny on Fiji's Loss of a Robust Cultural Identity," *Seattle Times* 28 June 1999, B3.

concrete, to be sure, than the larger moral issues in which they are often embed-ded. But consider for a moment the classic illustration of causality—one billiard ball striking another on a pool table. Surely we are safe in saying that the move-ment of the second ball was "caused" by a transfer of energy from the first ball at the moment of contact. Well, yes and no. British philosopher David Hume (among others) argued long ago that we don't really perceive "causality"; what we per-ceive is one ball moving and then another ball moving. We infer the notion of causality, which is a human construct, not a property of billiard balls.

When humans become the focus of a causal argument, the very definition of causality is immediately vexed. When we say that a given factor X "caused" a person to do Y, what do we mean? On the one hand, we might mean that X "forced her to do Y," thereby negating her free will (for example, the presence of a brain tumor caused my erratic behavior, which caused me to lose my job). On the other hand, we might simply mean that factor X "motivated" her to do Y, in such a way that doing Y is still an expression of freedom (for example, my love of the ocean caused me to give up my job as a Wal-Mart greeter and become a California surf bum).

When we argue about causality in human beings, we must guard against con-fusing these two senses of "cause" or assuming that human behavior can be pre-dicted or controlled in the same way that nonhuman behavior can. A rock dropped from a roof will always fall to the ground at 32 feet per second squared, and a rat zapped for making left turns in a maze will always quit making left turns. But if we raise interest rates, will consumers save more? If so, how much? This is the sort of question we debate endlessly.

Fortunately, most causal arguments can avoid the worst of these scientific and philosophical quagmires. As human beings, we share a number of assumptions about what causes events in the observable world, and we can depend on the goodwill of our audiences to grant us most of these assumptions. Most of us, for example, would be satisfied with the following explanation for why a car went into a skid: "In a panic the driver locked the brakes of his car, causing the car to go into a skid."

panic → slamming brake pedal → locking brakes → skid

We probably do not need to defend this simple causal chain because the audience will grant the causal connections between events A, B, C, and D. The sequence seems reasonable according to our shared assumptions about psychological causality (panic leads to slamming brake pedal) and physical causality (locked brakes lead to skid).

But if you are an attorney defending a client whose skidding car caused con-siderable damage to an upscale boutique, you might see all sorts of additional causal factors. ("Because the stop sign at that corner was obscured by an untrimmed willow tree, my client innocently entered what he assumed was an open intersection only to find a speeding beer truck bearing down on him. When my client took immediate decelerating corrective action, the improperly maintained, oil-slicked roadway sent his car into its near-fatal skid and into the boutique's bow windows—windows that extrude into the walkway 11 full inches beyond the limit allowed by city code.") Okay, now what's the cause of the crash, and who's at fault?

As the previous example shows, explaining causality entails creating a plausible chain of events linking a cause to its effect. Let's take another example—this time a real rather than hypothetical one. Consider an argument put forward by syndicated columnist John Leo as an explanation for the Columbine High School massacre.* Leo attributes part of the cause to the desensitizing effects of violent video games. After suggesting that the Littleton killings were partly choreographed on video game models, Leo suggests the following causal chain:

> Many youngsters are left alone for long periods of time → they play violent video games obsessively → their feelings of resentment and powerlessness "pour into the killing games" → the video games break down a natural aversion to killing, analogous to psychological techniques employed by the military → realistic touches in modern video games blur the "boundary between fantasy and reality" → youngsters begin identifying not with conventional heroes but with sociopaths who get their kicks from blowing away ordinary people ("pedestrians, marching bands, an elderly woman with a walker") → having enjoyed random violence in the video games, vulnerable youngsters act out the same adrenaline rush in real life.

DESCRIBING A CAUSAL ARGUMENT IN TOULMIN TERMS

Because causal arguments can involve lengthy or complex causal chains, they are often harder to summarize in *because* clauses than are other kinds of arguments. Likewise, they are not as likely to yield quick analysis through the Toulmin schema. Nevertheless, a causal argument can usually be stated as a claim with *because* clauses. Typically, a *because* clause for a causal argument pinpoints one or two key elements in the causal chain rather than trying to summarize every link. Leo's argument could be summarized in the following claim with *because* clause:

> Violent video games may have been a contributing cause to the Littleton massacre because playing these games can make random, sociopathic violence seem pleasurable.

---

*John Leo, "Kill-for-Kicks Video Games Desensitizing Our Children," *Seattle Times* 27 Apr. 1999, B4.

Once stated as an enthymeme, the argument can be analyzed using Toulmin's schema. (It is easiest to apply Toulmin's schema to causal arguments if you think of the grounds as the observable phenomena at any point in the causal chain and the warrants as the shareable assumptions about causality that join links together.)

CLAIM:	Violent video games may have been a contributing cause to the Littleton massacre
STATED REASON:	because playing these games can make random, sociopathic violence seem pleasurable
GROUNDS:	evidence that the killers, like many young people, played violent video games; evidence that the games are violent; evidence that the games involve random, sociopathic violence (not heroic cops against aliens or gangsters, but a killer blowing away ordinary people— marching bands, little old ladies, and so forth); evidence that young people derive pleasure from these games
WARRANT:	If youngsters derive pleasure from random, sociopathic killing in video games, then they can transfer this pleasure to real life, thus leading to the Littleton massacre.
BACKING:	testimony from psychologists; evidence that violent video games desensitize persons to violence; analogy to military training where video game strategies are used to "make killing a reflex action"; evidence that the distinction between fantasy and reality becomes especially blurred for unstable children.
CONDITIONS OF REBUTTAL:	*Questioning the reason and grounds:* Perhaps the killers didn't play video games; perhaps the video games are no more violent than traditional kids' games (such as cops and robbers); perhaps the video games do not feature sociopathic killing.
	Questioning the warrant and backing: Perhaps kids are fully capable of distinguishing fantasy from reality; perhaps the games are just fun with no transference to real life; perhaps these video games are substantially different from military training strategies.

QUALIFIER: (Claim is already qualified by *may* and *contributing cause*)

FOR CLASS DISCUSSION

1. Working individually or in small groups, create a causal chain to show how the item mentioned in the first column could help lead to the item mentioned in the second.

   a. invention of the automobile   redesign of cities

   b. invention of the automobile   changes in sexual mores

   c. invention of the telephone   loss of sense of community in neighborhoods

   e. development of the "pill"   rise in the divorce rate

   f. development of way to prevent rejections in transplant operations   liberalization of euthanasia laws

2. For each of your causal chains, compose a claim with an attached *because* clause summarizing one or two key links in the causal chain. For example, "The invention of the automobile helped cause the redesign of cities because automobiles made it possible for people to live farther away from their places of work."

THREE METHODS FOR ARGUING THAT ONE EVENT CAUSES ANOTHER

One of the first things you need to do when preparing a causal argument is to note exactly what sort of causal relationship you're dealing with. Are you concerned with the causes of a specific event or phenomenon such as NATO's decision to bomb Serbia or the crash of John F. Kennedy Jr.'s private airplane? Or are you planning to write about the cause of some recurring phenomenon such as eating disorders or the economic forces behind global warming? Or are you writing about a puzzling trend such as the decline of salmon runs on the Columbia River or the rising popularity of extreme sports?

With recurring phenomena or with trends, you have the luxury of being able to study multiple cases over long periods of time and establishing correlations between suspected causal factors and effects. In some cases you can even intervene in the process and test for yourself whether diminishing a suspected causal factor results in a lessening of the effect or whether increasing the causal factor results in a corresponding increase in the effect. Additionally, you can spend a good deal of time exploring just how the mechanics of causation might work.

But with a one-time occurrence your focus is on the details of the event and specific causal chains that may have contributed to the event. Sometimes evidence has disappeared or changed its nature. You often end up in the position more of a detective than of a scientific researcher, and your conclusion will have to be more tentative as a result.

Having briefly stated these words of caution, let's turn now to the various ways you can argue that one event causes another.

First Method: Explain the Causal Mechanism Directly

The most convincing kind of causal argument identifies every link in the causal chain, showing how X causes A, which causes B, which in turn causes C, which finally causes Y. In some cases, all you have to do is fill in the missing links. In other cases—when your assumptions about causality may seem questionable to your audience—you have to argue for the causal connection with more vigor.

A careful spelling out of each step in the causal chain is the technique used by science writer Robert S. Devine in the following passage from his article "The Trouble with Dams."* Although the benefits of dams are widely understood (cheap, pollution-free electricity; flood control; irrigation; barge transportation), the negative effects are less commonly known and understood. In this article, Devine tries to persuade readers that dams have serious negative consequences. In the following passage, he explains how dams reduce salmon flows by slowing the migration of smolts (newly hatched young salmon) to the sea.

CAUSAL ARGUMENT DESCRIBING A CAUSAL CHAIN

Such transformations lie at the heart of the ongoing environmental harm done by dams. Rivers are rivers because they flow, and the nature of their flows defines much of their character. When dams alter flows, they alter the essence of rivers.

Consider the erstwhile river behind Lower Granite [a dam on Idaho's Snake River]. Although I was there in the springtime, when I looked at the water it was moving too slowly to merit the word "flow"—and Lower Granite Lake isn't even one of the region's enormous storage reservoirs, which bring currents to a virtual halt. In the past, spring snowmelt sent powerful currents down the Snake during April and May. Nowadays hydropower operators of the Columbia and Snake systems store the runoff behind the dams and release it during the winter, when demand—and the price—for electricity rises. Over the ages, however, many populations of salmon have adapted to the spring surge. The smolts used the strong flows to migrate, drifting downstream with the current. During the journey smolts' bodies undergo physiological changes that require them to reach salt

*Robert S. Devine, "The Trouble with Dams," *Atlantic* Aug. 1995, 64–75. The example quotation is from page 70.

water quickly. Before dams backed up the Snake, smolts coming down from Idaho got to the sea in six to twenty days; now it takes from sixty to ninety days, and few of the young salmon reach salt water in time. The emasculated current is the single largest reason that the number of wild adult salmon migrating up the Snake each year has crashed from predevelopment runs of 100,000–200,000 to what was projected to be 150–75 this year.

This tightly constructed passage connects various causal chains to explain the decline of salmon runs:

Smolts use river flow to reach the sea $\rightarrow$ dams restrict flow of river $\rightarrow$ a trip that before development took 6–20 days now takes 60–90 days $\rightarrow$ migrating smolts undergo physiological changes that demand quick access to salt water $\rightarrow$ delayed migration time kills the smolts.

Describing each link in the causal chain—and making each link seem as plausible as possible—is the most persuasive means of convincing readers that X causes Y.

Second Method: Use Various Inductive Methods to Establish a High Probability of a Causal Link

If we can't explain a causal link directly, we often employ a reasoning strategy called *induction.* Through induction we infer a general conclusion based on a limited number of specific cases. For example, if on several occasions you got a headache after drinking red wine but not after drinking white wine, you would be likely to conclude inductively that red wine causes you to get headaches. However, because there are almost always numerous variables involved, because there are exceptions to most principles arrived at inductively, and because we can't be certain that the future will always be like the past, inductive reasoning gives only probable truths, not certain ones.

When your brain thinks inductively, it sorts through data looking for patterns of similarity and difference. But the inductive process does not explain the causal mechanism itself. Thus, through induction you know that red wine gives you a headache, but you don't know how the wine actually works on your nervous system—the causal chain itself.

In this section we explain three kinds of inductive reasoning: informal induction, scientific experimentation, and correlation.

Informal Induction

Informal induction is our term for the habitual kind of inductive reasoning we do all the time. Toddlers think inductively when they learn the connection between flipping a wall switch and watching the ceiling light come on. They hold all variables constant except the position of the switch and infer inductively a causal connection between the switch and the light. Typical ways that the mind infers causality described by the nineteeth-century philosopher John Stuart Mill include looking for a common element that can explain a repeated circumstance. For example, psychologists attempting to understand the causes of anorexia have discovered that many anorexics (but not all) come from perfectionist, highly work-oriented homes that emphasize duty and responsibility. This common element is thus a suspected causal factor leading to anorexia. Another of Mill's methods is to look for a single difference. When infant death rates in the state of Washington shot up in July and August 1986, one event stood out making these two months different: increased radioactive fallout from the Chernobyl nuclear meltdown in the Ukraine. This single difference led some researchers to suspect radiation as a possible cause of infant deaths. Informal induction typically proceeds from this kind of "common element" or "single difference" reasoning.

Largely because of its power, informal induction can often lead you to wrong conclusions. You should be aware of two common fallacies of inductive reasoning that can tempt you into erroneous assumptions about causality. (Both fallacies are treated more fully in Appendix 1.)

The *post hoc, ergo propter hoc* fallacy ("after this, therefore because of this") mistakes precedence for cause. Just because event A regularly precedes event B doesn't mean that event A causes event B. The same reasoning that tells us that flipping a switch causes the light to go on can make us believe that low levels of radioactive fallout from the Chernobyl nuclear disaster caused a sudden rise in infant death rates in the state of Washington. The nuclear disaster clearly preceded the rise in death rates. But did it clearly *cause* it? Our point is that precedence alone is no proof of causality and that we are guilty of this fallacy whenever we are swayed to believe that X causes Y primarily because X precedes Y. We can guard against this fallacy by seeking plausible link-by-link connections showing how X causes Y.

The *hasty generalization* fallacy occurs when you make a generalization based on too few cases or too little consideration of alternative explanations: You flip the switch, but the lightbulb doesn't go on. You conclude—too hastily—that the power has gone off. (Perhaps the lightbulb has burned out or the switch is broken.) How many trials does it take before you can make a justified generalization rather than a hasty generalization? It is difficult to say for sure. Both the *post hoc* fallacy and the hasty generalization fallacy remind us that induction requires a leap from individual cases to a general principle and that it is always possible to leap too soon.

Scientific Experimentation

One way to avoid inductive fallacies is to examine our causal hypotheses as carefully as possible. When we deal with a recurring phenomenon such as cancer, we can create scientific experiments that give us inductive evidence of causality with a fairly high degree of certainty. If, for example, we were concerned that a particular food source such as spinach might contain cancer-causing chemicals, we could test our hypothesis experimentally. We could take two groups of rats and control their environment carefully so that the only difference between them (in theory, anyway) was that one group ate large quantities of spinach and the other group ate none. Spinach eating, then, would be the one variable between the two groups that we are testing. After a specified period of time, we would check to see what percentage of rats in each group developed cancer. If twice as many spinach-eating rats contracted cancer, we could probably conclude that our hypothesis held up.

Correlation

Still another method of induction is *correlation*, which expresses a statistical relationship between X and Y. A correlation between X and Y means that when X occurs, Y is likely to occur also, and vice versa. To put it another way, correlation establishes a possibility that an observed link between an X and a Y is a causal one rather than a mere coincidence. The existence of a correlation, however, does not tell us whether X causes Y, whether Y causes X, or whether both are caused by some third phenomenon. For example, there is a fairly strong correlation between near-sightedness and intelligence. (That is, in a given sample of nearsighted people and people with normal eyesight, a higher percentage of the nearsighted people will be highly intelligent. Similarly, in a sample of high-intelligence people and people with normal intelligence, a higher percentage of the high-intelligence group will be nearsighted.) But the direction of causality isn't clear. It could be that high intelligence causes people to read more, thus ruining their eyes (high intelligence causes nearsightedness). Or it could be that near-sightedness causes people to read more, thus raising their intelligence (near-sightedness causes high intelligence). Or it could be that some unknown phenomenon inside the brain causes both near-sightedness and high intelligence.

In recent years, correlation studies have been made stunningly sophisticated through the power of computerized analyses. For example, we could attempt to do the spinach-cancer study without resorting to a scientific experiment. If we identified a given group that ate lots of spinach (for example, vegetarians) and another group that ate little if any spinach (Inuits) and then checked to see if their rates of cancer correlated to their rates of spinach consumption, we would have the beginnings of a correlation study. But it would have no scientific validity until we factored out all the other variables between vegetarians and Inuits that might skew the findings—variables such as lifestyle, climate, genetic inheritance, and differences in diet other than spinach. Factoring out such variables is one of the complex feats that modern statistical analyses attempt to accomplish. But the fact remains that the most sophisticated correlation studies still cannot tell us the direction of causality or even for certain that there is causality.

Conclusion about Inductive Methods

Induction, then, can tell us within varying degrees of certainty whether X causes Y. It does not, however, explain the causal mechanism itself. Typically, the *because* clause structure of an inductive argument would take one of the following three shapes: (1) "Although we cannot explain the causal mechanism directly, we believe that X and Y are very probably causally linked because we have repeatedly observed their conjunction"; (2) " . . . because we have demonstrated the linkage through controlled scientific experiments"; or (3) " . . . because we have shown that they are statistically correlated and have provided a plausible hypothesis concerning the causal direction."

▼ FOR CLASS DISCUSSION

Working individually or in small groups, develop plausible causal chains that might explain the correlations between the following pairs of phenomena:

a. A person who registers a low stress level on an electrochemical stress meter — Does daily meditation

b. A person who regularly consumes frozen dinners — Is likely to vote for improved rapid transit

c. A person who is a high achiever — Is a first-born child

d. A person who is a member of the National Rifle Association — Favors tough treatment of criminals

Third Method: Argue by Analogy or Precedent

Another common method of causal arguing is through analogy or precedent. (See also Chapter 12, which deals in more depth with the strengths and weaknesses of this kind of arguing.) When you argue through resemblance, you try to find a case that is similar to the one you are arguing about but is better known and less controversial to the reader. If the reader agrees with your view of causality in the similar case, you then try to transfer this understanding to the case at issue. In the following example, the writer tries to explain the link between environmental and biological factors in the creation of teen violence. In this analogy, the biological predisposition for violent behavior is compared to some children's biological predisposition for asthma. Cultural and media violence is then compared to air pollution.

CAUSAL ARGUMENT BY ANALOGY

To deny the role of these influences [bad parenting, easy access to guns, violence in the media] is like denying that air pollution triggers childhood asthma. Yes, to develop asthma a child needs a specific, biological vulnerability. But as long as some children have this respiratory vulnerability—and some always will—then allowing pollution to fill our air will make some children wheeze, and cough, and die. And as long as some children have a neurological vulnerability [to violent behavior]—and some always will—then turning a blind eye to bad parenting, bullying, and the gun culture will make other children seethe, and withdraw, and kill.*

Causal arguments by analogy and precedent are logically weaker than arguments based on causal chains or scientific induction. Although they can be powerfully persuasive, you should be aware of their limits. If any two things are alike in some ways (analogous), they are different in others (disanalogous), and these differences shouldn't be ignored. Consider the following example:

> A huckster markets a book called *30 Days to a More Powerful Brain*. The book contains logical puzzles and other brain-teasing exercises that he calls "weight training for the mind."

This argument depends on the warrant that the brain is like a muscle. Because the audience accepts the causal belief that weight training strengthens muscles, the marketers hope to transfer that same belief to the field of mental activity (mind exercises strengthen the brain). However, cognitive psychologists have shown that the brain does *not* work like a muscle, so the analogy is false. Although the argument seems powerful, you should realize that the warrant that says X is like Y is almost always vulnerable.

All resemblance arguments, therefore, are in some sense "false analogies." But some analogies are so misleading that logicians have labeled them "fallacious"—the fallacy of *false analogy*. The false analogy fallacy covers those truly blatant cases where the differences between X and Y are too great for the analogy to hold. An example might be the following: "Putting red marks all over students' papers causes great emotional distress just as putting knife marks over their palms would cause great physical distress." It is impossible to draw a precise line, however, between an analogy that has true clarifying and persuasive power and one that is fallacious. Whether the analogy works in any situation depends on the audience's shared assumptions with the arguer.

GLOSSARY OF TERMS ENCOUNTERED IN CAUSAL ARGUMENTS

Because causal arguments are often easier to conduct if writer and reader share a few specialized terms, we offer the following glossary for your convenience.

Fallacy of Oversimplified Cause: One of the greatest temptations when establishing causal relationships is to fall into the habit of looking for *the* cause

---

*Sharon Begley, "Why the Young Kill," *Newsweek* 3 May 1999, 35.

of something. Most phenomena, especially the ones we argue about, have multiple causes. For example, scientists know that a number of different causes must work together to create a complex disease such as cancer. But though we know all this, we still long to make the world less complex by looking for *the* cause of cancer, thus attributing a single cause to puzzling effects.

Universal/Existential Quantifiers: Closely related to the fallacy of the single clause is the tendency to confuse what logicians call the universal quantifier *(all)* with the existential quantifier *(some)*. The mixing up of universal and existential quantifiers can falsify an argument. For example, to argue that *all* the blame for recent school shootings comes from the shooters' playing violent video games is to claim that playing violent video games is the sole cause—a universal statement. An argument will be stronger and more accurate if the arguer makes an existential statement: *Some* of the blame for this violent behavior can be attributed to playing violent video games. Arguers sometimes deliberately mix up these quantifiers to misrepresent and dismiss opposing views. For example, someone might argue that because the violent video games are not totally and exclusively responsible for the students' violent behavior, they are not an influential factor at all. In this instance, arguers are attempting to dismiss potential causes by framing them as universal statements that can be rejected because they are too extreme and indefensible. Because something is not a sole or total cause does not mean that it could not be a partial cause.

Immediate/Remote Causes: Every causal chain links backward indefinitely into the past. An immediate cause is the closest in time to the event being examined. When John F. Kennedy Jr.'s plane crashed into the Atlantic Ocean south of Martha's Vineyard in July 1999, experts speculated that the *immediate cause* was Kennedy's becoming disoriented in the night haze, losing visual control of the plane, and sending the plane into a fatal dive. A slightly less immediate cause was his decision to make an over-water flight at night without being licensed for instrument flying. The cause of that decision was the need to get to Hyannis Port quickly to attend a wedding. Farther back in time were all the factors that made Kennedy the kind of risk taker who took chances with his own life. For example, several months earlier he had broken an ankle in a hang-gliding accident. Many commentators said that the numerous tragedies that befell the Kennedy family helped shape his risk-taking personality. Such causes going back into the past are considered *remote causes.* It is sometimes difficult to determine the relative significance of remote causes. Immediate causes are obviously linked to an event, but remote causes often have to be dug out or inferred. It's difficult to know, for example, just how seriously to take Hillary Clinton's explanation for her husband's extramarital affairs with Monica Lewinsky and other women. Clinton's womanizing tendencies, she claimed, were caused by "a terrible conflict between his mother and grandmother" when Clinton was four years old. During this period, she said, he "was scarred by abuse."*

Precipitating/Contributing Causes: These terms are similar to *immediate* and *remote* causes but don't designate a temporal linking going into the past. Rather, they refer to a main cause emerging out of a background of subsidiary causes. The *contributing causes* are a set of conditions that give rise to the *precipitating cause,* which triggers the effect. If, for example, a husband and wife decide to separate, the precipitating cause may be a stormy fight over money, which itself is a symptom of their inability to communicate with each other any longer. All the factors that contribute to that inability to communicate— preoccupation with their respective careers, anxieties about money, in-law problems—may be considered contributing causes. Note that the contributing causes and precipitating cause all coexist simultaneously in time—none is temporally more remote than another. But the marriage might have continued had the contributing causes not finally resulted in frequent angry fighting, which doomed the marriage.

Constraints: Sometimes an effect occurs not because X happened but because another factor—a *constraint*—was removed. At other times a possible effect will not occur because a given constraint prevents it from happening. A constraint is a kind of negative cause that limits choices and possibilities. As soon as the constraint is removed, a given effect may occur. For example, in the marriage we have been discussing, the presence of children in the home might have been a constraint against divorce; as soon as the children graduate from high school and leave home, the marriage may well dissolve.

Necessary/Sufficient Causes: A *necessary cause* is one that has to be present for a given effect to occur. For example, fertility drugs are necessary to cause the conception of septuplets. Every couple who has septuplets must have used fertility drugs. In contrast, a *sufficient cause* is one that always produces or guarantees a given effect. Smoking more than a pack of cigarettes per day is sufficient to raise the cost of one's life insurance policy. This statement means that if you are a smoker life insurance companies will always place you in a higher risk bracket and charge you more for life insurance. In some cases, a single cause can be both necessary and sufficient. For example, lack of ascorbic acid is both a necessary and a sufficient cause of scurvy. (Think of all those old sailors who didn't eat fruit for months.) It is a necessary cause because you can't get scurvy any other way except through absence of ascorbic acid; it is a sufficient cause because the absence of ascorbic acid always causes scurvy.

---

*"First Lady's Remarks Take White House by Surprise," *Seattle Times* 2 Aug. 1999, A1.

FOR CLASS DISCUSSION

The terms in the preceding glossary can be effective brainstorming tools for thinking of possible causes of an event. For the following events, try to think of as many causes as possible by brainstorming possible *immediate causes, remote causes, precipitating causes, contributing causes,* and *constraints*:

1. Working individually, make a list of different kinds of causes/constraints for one of the following:
    a. your decision to attend your present college
    b. an important event in your life or your family (a job change, a major move, etc.)
    c. a personal opinion you hold that is not widely shared

2. Working as a group, make a list of different kinds of causes/constraints for one of the following:
    a. why women's fashion and beauty magazines are the most frequently purchased magazines in college bookstores
    b. why the majority of teenagers don't listen to classical music
    c. why the number of babies born out of wedlock has increased dramatically in the last thirty years

WRITING YOUR CAUSAL ARGUMENT

WRITING ASSIGNMENT
FOR CHAPTER 11

Choose an issue about the causes or consequences of a trend, event, or other phenomenon. Write an argument that persuades an audience to accept your explanation of the causes or consequences of your chosen phenomenon. Within your essay you should examine alternative hypotheses or opposing views and explain your reasons for rejecting them. You can imagine your issue either as a puzzle or as a disagreement. If a puzzle, your task will be to create a convincing case for an audience that doesn't have an answer to your causal question already in mind. If a disagreement, your task will be more overtly persuasive since your goal will be to change your audience's views.

Exploring Ideas

Arguments about causes and consequences abound in public, professional, or personal life, so you shouldn't have difficulty finding a causal issue worth investigating and arguing. Angered by media explanations for the Columbine High School massacre, student writer Daeha Ko contributed his own argument to the conversation by blaming popular cliques and the school establishment that supports them (see pp. 247–49). Others of our students have focused on causal issues such as these: What causes promiscuous teen sex? What effect does TV violence have on children? What would be the consequences of breaching dams on the Snake River? What causes anorexia? What will be the consequences of allowing the Makah to hunt whales? What are the chief causes of the destruction of tropical rain forests? Why does it take so long to approve experimental drugs in the United States? What would be the consequences of raising the retirement age as a means of saving Social Security? What are the causes of different sexual orientations?

If you find yourself uninterested in major public issues involving cause or consequence, you can often create provocative controversies among your classmates through the following strategies:

- *Make a list of unusual likes and dislikes.*   Think about unusual things that people like or dislike. We find it really strange, for example, that so many people like professional wrestling or dislike bats. You could summarize the conventional explanations that persons give for an unusual pleasure or aversion and then argue for a surprising or unexpected cause. Why do people like playing the lottery? What attracts people to extreme sports? What causes math phobia? How do you explain the popularity of the new VW Beetle?

- *Make a list of puzzling events or trends.*   Another strategy is to make a list of puzzling phenomena and try to explain their causes. Start with one-time events (the sudden appearance of deformed frogs in Minnesota lakes; the Senate acquittal of Bill Clinton in his impeachment trial). Then list puzzling repeatable events (infant sudden death syndrome; failure of many children to become good readers). Finally, list some recent trends (growth of naturopathic medicine; teen interest in the gothic; hatred of women in much gangsta rap). Engage classmates in discussions of one or more of the items on your list. Look for places of disagreement as entry points into the conversation.

- *Brainstorm consequences of a recent or proposed action.*   Arguments about consequences are among the most interesting and important of causal disputes. If you can argue for an unanticipated consequence of a real, hypothetical, or proposed action—for example, a bad consequence of an apparently positive event or a good consequence of an apparently negative event—you can make an important contribution to the conversation. What might be the consequences, for example, of some of the following: a cure for cancer; total prevention of illegal immigration; the legalization of same-sex marriage; a heavy tax on families having more than two children; replacement of federal income tax with a federal sales tax; ending "social promotion" in the schools; depletion of the world's oil supply; any similar recent, hypothetical, or proposed event or action?

Organizing a Causal Argument

At the outset, it is useful to know some of the standard ways that a causal argument can be organized. Later, you may decide on a different organizational pattern, but these standard ways will help you get started.

Plan 1

When your purpose is to describe and explain all the links in a causal chain:

- Introduce phenomenon to be explained and show why it is problematical.
- Present your thesis in summary form.
- Describe and explain each link in the causal chain.

Plan 2

When your purpose is to explore the relative contribution of a number of causes to a phenomenon or to explore multiple consequences of a phenomenon:

- Introduce the phenomenon to be explained and suggest how or why it is controversial.
- Devote one section to each possible cause/consequence and decide whether it is necessary, sufficient, contributory, remote, and so forth. (Arrange sections so that those causes most familiar to the audience come first and the most surprising ones come last.)

Plan 3

When your purpose is to argue for a cause or consequence that is surprising or unexpected to your audience:

- Introduce a phenomenon to be explained and show why it is controversial.
- One by one, examine and reject the causes or consequences your audience would normally assume or expect.
- Introduce your unexpected or surprising cause or consequence and argue for it.

Plans 2 and 3 are similar in that they examine numerous possible causes or consequences. Plan 2, however, tries to establish the relative importance of each cause or consequence, whereas plan 3 aims at rejecting the causes or consequences normally assumed by the audience and argues for an unexpected surprising cause or consequence.

Plan 4

When your purpose is to change your audience's mind about a cause or consequence:

- Introduce the issue and show why it is controversial.
- Summarize your opponent's causal argument and then refute it.
- Present your own causal argument.

Plan 4 is a standard structure for all kinds of arguments. This is the structure you would use if you were the attorney for the person whose car skidded into the boutique (pp. 230–31). The opposing attorney would blame your client's reckless driving. You would lay blame on a poorly signed intersection, a speeding beer truck, and violation of building codes.

QUESTIONING AND CRITIQUING A CAUSAL ARGUMENT

Because of the strenuous conditions that must be met before causality can be proven, causal arguments are vulnerable at many points. The following strategies will generally be helpful.

If you described every link in a causal chain, would skeptics point out weaknesses in any of the links? Describing a causal chain can be a complex business. A skeptic can raise doubts about an entire argument simply by questioning one of the links. Your best defense is to make a diagram of the linkages and role-play a skeptic trying to refute each link in turn. Whenever you find possible arguments against your position, see how you can strengthen your own argument at that point.

If your argument is based on a scientific experiment, could skeptics question the validity of the experiment? The scientific method attempts to demonstrate causality experimentally. If the experiment isn't well designed, however, the demonstration is less likely to be acceptable to skeptical audiences. Here are ways to question and critique a scientific argument:

- *Question the findings.* Skeptics may have reason to believe that the data collected were not accurate or representative. They might provide alternative data or simply point out flaws in the way the data were collected.

- *Question the interpretation of the data.*   Many research studies are divided into "findings" and "discussion" sections. In the discussion section the researcher analyzes and interprets the data. A skeptic might provide an alternative interpretation of the data or otherwise argue that the data don't support what the original writer claims.

- *Question the design of the experiment.*   A detailed explanation of research design is beyond the scope of this text, but we can give a brief example of how a typical experiment did go wrong. When home computers were first developed in the 1980s, a group of graduate students conducted an experiment to test the effect of word processors on students' writing in junior high school. They reported that students who used the word processors for revising all their essays did significantly better on a final essay than a control group of students who didn't use word processors. It turned out, however, that there were at least two major design flaws in the experiment. First, the researchers allowed students to volunteer for the experimental group. Perhaps these students were already better writers than the control group from the start. (Can you think of a causal explanation of why the better students might volunteer to use the computers?) Second, when the teachers graded essays from both the computer group and the control group, the essays were not retyped uniformly. Thus the computer group's essays were typed with "computer perfection," whereas the control group's essays were handwritten or typed on ordinary typewriters. Perhaps the readers were affected by the pleasing appearance of the computer-typed essays. More significantly, perhaps the graders were biased in favor of the computer project and unconsciously scored the computer-typed papers higher.

If you have used correlation data, could skeptics argue that the correlation is much weaker than you claim or that you haven't sufficiently demonstrated causality?   As we discussed earlier, correlation data tell us only that two or more phenomena are likely to occur together. They don't tell us that one phenomenon caused the other. Thus correlation arguments are usually accompanied by hypotheses about causal connections between the phenomena. Correlation arguments can often be refuted as follows:

- Find problems in the statistical methods used to determine the correlation.
- Weaken the correlation by pointing out exceptions.
- Provide an alternative hypothesis about causality.

If you have used an analogy argument, could skeptics point out disanalogies?   Although among the most persuasive of argumentative strategies, analogy arguments are also among the easiest to refute. The standard procedure is to counter your argument that X is like Y by pointing out all the ways that X is *not* like Y. Once again, by role-playing an opposing view, you may be able to strengthen your own analogy argument.

Could a skeptic cast doubt on your argument by reordering your priority of causes? Up to this point we've focused on refuting the claim that X causes Y. However, another approach is to concede that X helps cause Y but that X is only one of several contributing causes and not the most significant one at that.

READINGS

The following essay, by student writer Daeha Ko, appeared as an op-ed piece in the *University of Washington Daily* on 9 May 1999, several weeks after the Columbine High School massacre in Littleton, Colorado. Daeha's motivation for writing is his anger at media attempts to explain the massacre—none of which focuses on the cliquish social structure of high school itself.

The Monster That Is High School
Daeha Ko (student)

In the past weeks, intensive media coverage has surrounded the shooting incident   1 in Littleton, Colorado, where 12 students and a teacher died, along with 23 wounded. Yet people forget the real victims of the Littleton massacre are Dylan Klebold and Eric Harris.

What they did was against the law, but let's face it—the incident was waiting to happen.   2 And there's nothing surprising about it.

The social priorities of high school are to blame. In truth, high school is a place where   3 jocks, cheerleaders and anyone associated with them can do whatever they want and get away with it. Their exploits are celebrated in pep rallies, printed in school papers and shown off in trophy cases. The popular cliques have the most clout, and are—in a sense— local celebrities. If they ever run into disciplinary problems with the school or police, they get let off the hook under the guise that they are just kids.

Public schools claim to support all students, but in reality choose to invest their prior-   4 ities in activities associated with popular cliques. Schools are willing to go to any means necessary to support the sports teams, for example. They care less about students who don't belong to popular cliques, leaving them almost nothing. School becomes less about getting a good education, instead priding itself on the celebration of elite cliques.

The popular cliques are nice to their own but spit out extremely cruel insults to those   5 who don't fit in. As noted in *Time,* jocks admitted they like to pick on unpopular kids "because it's just fun to do." Their insulting words create deep emotional wounds, while school authorities ignore the cruelty of the corrupt high-school social system.

6   Schools refuse to accept any accountability and point to parents instead. While it is the job of parents to condition their kids, it is impossible for them to supervise their kids 24 hours a day.

7   As an outcast, I was harrassed on an everyday basis by jocks, and received no help from school authorities. It got so bad that I attempted suicide.

8   Yes, I did (and still do) wear all black, play Doom and listen to raucous heavy metal, punk and Goth music. I was into the occult and had extensive knowledge on guns and how to build bombs.

9   I got into several fights, including one where I kicked the shit out of a basketball player. The only reason why I didn't shoot him and his jock cronies is because I lacked access to guns. I would've blown every single one of them away and not cared.

10   To defend myself, I carried around a 7-inch blade. If anyone continued to mess with me, I sent them anonymous notes with a big swastika drawn on them. I responded to harassment with "Yeah, heil Hitler," while saluting.

11   They got the hint. Eventually, I found some friends who were also outcasts. We banded together and didn't judge each other by the way we looked or what we liked. But I still held contempt for jocks whom I believed should be shot and fed to the sharks.

12   Even in their deaths, Klebold and Harris are still treated like outcasts. How dare *Time* call them "The Monsters Next Door." News analysis poured over the "abnormal" world of "Goth" culture, Marilyn Manson, violent computer games and gun control. It also targeted other outcast students as trenchcoat-goth, submerged, socially challenged kids who fail to fit the "correct" image of American teens.

13   The popular cliques have their likeness reinforced through the images of trashy teen media as seen on MTV, *90210,* and *Dawson's Creek.* It's heard in the bubble-gum pop of Britney Spears and Backstreet Boys, along with their imitators. Magazines like *YM* and *Seventeen* feature pretty-looking girls, offering advice on the latest trends in dress, makeup and dating.

14   Media coverage was saturated with memorials and funeral services of the deceased. Friends and family remembered them as "good kids." Not all those killed knew or made fun of Klebold or Harris. Obviously there were members of the popular cliques who made fun of them and escaped harm. But innocent people had to die in order to bring injustices to light that exist in our society.

15   It's tragic, but perhaps that's the price that had to be paid. Perhaps they are shocked by the fact that some "nerds" have actually defeated them for once because teasing isn't fun and games anymore.

16   With the last of the coffins being laid to rest, people are looking for retribution, someone to prosecute. Why? The two kids are dead—there is no sense in pursuing this problem any further. But lawyers are trying to go after those who they believe influenced Harris and

Klebold: namely their parents, gun dealers, and the Trenchcoat Mafia. Police heavily questioned Harris' girlfriend about the guns she gave them and arrested one person.

The families of the deceased, lawyers and the police need to get a clue and leave the   17
two kids' families and friends alone. They are dealing with just as much grief and do not
need to be punished for someone else's choices. Filing lawsuits will drag on for years, burdening everyone and achieving little.

It's not like you can bring your loved ones back to life after you've won your case.   18

What we need is bigger emphasis on academic discipline and more financing toward   19
academic programs. Counselors and psychiatrists need to be hired to attend to student
needs. People need practical skills, not the pep-rally fluff of popular cliques.

The people of Littleton need to be at peace with the fate of their town and heal wounds   20
instead of prying them open with lawsuits.

Critiquing "The Monster That Is High School"

1. Summarize Daeha Ko's argument by creating a plausible causal chain leading from popular high school cliques to the Littleton massacre. How persuasive is Daeha's argument?

2. Daeha is angered at *Time* magazine for characterizing Klebold and Harris as "the monsters next door." How would you characterize Daeha's *ethos* in this piece? Do you see him as "monstrous" himself? Or does his *ethos* help create sympathy for social outcasts in high school culture?

3. Daeha presents his causal argument as a contribution to the frantic, contentious social conflict that raged among social scientists, columnists, and other media commentators after the shootings at Columbine High School in Littleton, Colorado (see a summary of this discussion in Case 1, p. 228). Which alternative explanations for the shooting does Daeha address? What strategy does he use to rebut alternative causal arguments? Do you regard Daeha's argument as a valuable contribution to the controversy? Why or why not?

Our second reading, by a professor of psychology at the University of Alaska, appeared in the journal *Academic Questions,* a publication of the National Association of Scholars. This philosophically conservative organization tries to preserve traditional humanistic values, believes the academic curriculum has been debased by educational fads, and actively opposes postmodernism and the "political correctness" movement associated with liberal politics. In this article, Judith Kleinfeld attacks the Morella Bill, a federal funding program aimed at attracting women into scientific and technical fields. Her article explores the puzzling causal question "Why do so few women go into science?" and provides an answer contrary to the causal explanations espoused by most liberals.

The Morella Bill, My Daughter Rachel, and the Advancement of Women in Science
Judith Kleinfeld

1   The advancement of women in science and mathematics has become something of a cottage industry fueled by federal dollars. The Morella Bill, passed in the fall of 1998 by the 105th Congress, is the latest effort. This bill established yet another commission to figure out why women are underrepresented in scientific and technical fields. The commission, in turn, is apt to recommend more of the same science programs for young women that we already have. Many of these special programs, as a practical matter, are closed to boys. Leaving aside the questions of the ethics and the legality of such sex-segregated federal programs, let us ask if these kinds of programs are even in the interests of women themselves? My own experience in trying to get my daughter Rachel interested in mathematics and science suggests the risks of such social engineering.

2   The Program for Women and Girls in the National Science Foundation's Directorate for Human Resources and Education is a good example of what is likely to emerge from the Morella Bill. The NSF Program for Women and Girls spends close to $10 million a year on a potpourri of educational initiatives. Many are designed to get young girls, especially those from low-income families, interested in science, mathematics, and technology. The program "Creating After School Science" is a typical example:

> *Creating After School Science Opportunities for Girls in NYC Settlement Houses: A Model Project.* Supports the piloting of a hands-on science/gender equity model for girls 6 to 11 in after school programs at four New York City settlement houses. Builds on the Educational Equity Concept's "Playtime is Science" program. Start date August 1, 1996, NSF Award #9633332241, $119,053 (Estimated).[1]

3   The NSF Program for Women and Girls also funds a multitude of programs designed to make sure that teachers are up to date on the cooperative, rather than competitive, methods of teaching that are supposedly more congruent with the fragile female psyche. While most of these programs are funded in the $100,000 range, Arizona State University managed to pick up this plum:

> *Guiding Math/Science Talented Girls and Women.* Supports one-week summer and winter seminars where counselors, administrators, and science educators will be taught the knowledge and skills for guiding career development of math/science talented girls and especially at-risk girls. Start Date May 1, 1997, NSF Award #9619121, $730,382 (Estimated).

Such summer camps and after-school programs should be interesting and enjoyable, with their emphasis on field trips, cooperative projects, and hands-on science activities. But boys do not get to participate in these stimulating activities. The "Frequently Asked Questions and Answers" page of the NSF Program for Women and Girls website indeed gives potential grantees this counsel:

Question #2. Do you have any information about Title IX? Can a federally funded education program exclude boys?

> NSF programs for girls may not exclude boys. However, projects can be proposed and conducted by organizations which serve girls primarily, can actively recruit girls, and can study girls as their focus. They do not have to make an effort to include boys; they just can't categorically keep them out.

After clarifying the law, the potential grantee is shown, as a practical matter, how to flout it:

> It is rare that, for example, boys want to come to an after-school Girls Club event, or "Girls in Science Day" or such. (There is a natural disinterest, for example—boys wanting to be Girl Scouts.)

The author of these questions and answers evidently believes there can be a "natural disinterest" on the part of boys, although suggesting any natural disinterest on the part of girls would not be acceptable.

Do such programs succeed in increasing the number of women in mathematics, the physical sciences, engineering, and computer science? When I posed this question to an NSF administrator, she responded with admirable candor.[2] These programs provide interesting activities for girls, especially low-income girls, who might otherwise not have another way to go to summer camp, she told me. But she doubted they did much to advance women in science.

4

The Morella Bill—The Wisdom of WISETECH

Effective or not, more such programs are on their way. On 9 November 1997, Representative Connie Morella (R–Maryland) with sixteen cosponsors introduced H.R. 3007, "a bill to establish the Commission on the Advancement of Women and Minorities in Science, Engineering, and Technology Development" (dubbed WISETECH). The commission is charged with such tasks as reviewing the research on the number of women in science, engineering, and technology and identifying barriers to their advancement. It is required to report its findings and recommendations in one year.

5

As the Congressional Budget Office points out, in estimating the cost of WISETECH at $1 million, such a short time span means that the commission would have to "rely heavily on available information."[3] A great deal of information indeed is available. To take just one example, the National Research Council established in 1991 a Committee on Women in Science and Engineering, which compiled a list of organizations working to increase the participation of women in science and engineering. They located 290 organizations.

6

The White House indeed opposed the Morella Bill on the grounds of expensive duplication.[4] The actual basis for White House opposition was probably political—Congresswoman Morella is a Republican who stood for reelection in 1998.[5] Needed or not, WISETECH made it through the legislative process. The bill sailed through committee hearings with barely an objection.

7

Women and the Physical Sciences—The Puzzle

8   Since the 1960s, women have vastly increased their numbers in the professions and the biological sciences.[6] In 1994, women attained more than 40 percent of all professional degrees, up from less than 3 percent in 1961. In such professional fields as veterinary medicine, women now receive the majority of professional degrees (65 percent). The gender gap in the biological sciences is also closing. Indeed, American women in 1994 received 43 percent of the doctorates in biology and 63 percent of the doctorates in health.[7] Still, only 24 percent of the doctorates in mathematics, 22 percent of the doctorates in the physical sciences, 18 percent of the doctorates in computer sciences, and 15 percent of the doctorates in engineering went to American women.

9   In noting this gender gap, it is also important to note that the careers and prospects of very few women are affected. An important point, constantly forgotten, is how few people, men or women, choose scientific and technical careers. The number of doctorates awarded to American men in the physical sciences, mathematics, engineering, and the computer sciences in 1994 totaled only 5,532; the number awarded to American women totaled 1,291. But almost 17,000 women got law degrees that year.

10   Still, success in science is an important cultural symbol. Men like Albert Einstein, Richard Feynman, and Stephen Hawking create our popular images of spectacular intellectual achievement. Most undergraduates, in my experience, can name no famous female scientist other than Marie Curie.

Cultural and Biological Explanations for the Gender Gap

11   So what is a program to do? Can the Morella Bill, the Program for Women and Girls at the National Science Foundation, the Committee on Women in Science and Engineering of the National Research Council, or any of the other 290 organizations fighting on the ramparts make a difference?

12   Attempts to explain the gender gap in science and mathematics are not wanting. In a paper reviewing the literature on what causes gender differences, for example, Gita Wilder cites so many studies that her references take up eighteen pages.[8] Virtually every serious effort to understand the gender gap, as Wilder points out, acknowledges the importance of both biological and cultural influences.

13   **Cultural Influences—The Negative Stereotype Effect.**   Cultural stereotypes are one prominent explanation for the gender gap in science and mathematics. Some of the most convincing research on the effect of negative cultural stereotypes has been done by Claude Steele, a psychologist at Stanford University.[9] Steele and his colleagues recruited male and female college students with talent in mathematics, who saw themselves as strong math students. He gave them a difficult mathematics test taken from the Graduate Record Examinations. In one condition, the students were told that the test typically showed gender differences in favor of males. In the other condition, students were told this test showed no gender differences.

When threatened with the negative stereotype about female abilities in mathematics, women indeed performed significantly worse than men. When told that the test showed no gender differences, men and women got approximately equal scores. Steele sees this result as evidence of the negative influence of female stereotypes, and he is right. What he does not point out is that the scores became equal not only because women's mathematics scores went up but also because men's scores went down. Steele also neglects to point out that the women in this study never achieved mathematics scores as high as men reached, even when the threat of cultural stereotypes was removed.

Biological Explanations—The Testosterone Effect.   While Steele's studies and similar research do demonstrate the negative effects of cultural stereotypes on women, this research does not succeed in dismissing biological explanations. Strong spatial-rotational abilities, for example, are important to advanced mathematical reasoning and to scientific achievement in physics. Reviewing the research literature, psychologist Diane Halpern emphasizes that testosterone is clearly linked to such skills:

> The spatial-skills performance of normal males fluctuates in concert with daily variations in testosterone and seasonal variations. . . . When normal, aging men were given testosterone to enhance sexual functioning, they also showed improved performance on visual-spatial tests.
>
> Additionally, when female-to-male transsexuals were given high doses of testosterone in preparation for sex change therapy, their visual spatial skills improved dramatically and their verbal fluency skills declined dramatically within three months. The results of these studies and others provide a strong causal link between levels of adult hormones and sex-typical patterns of performance.[10]

Cultural influences reinforce and amplify these biological patterns. Women tend to excel in verbal skills while men tend to excel in spatial reasoning.[11] This is the distribution of abilities that such policy initiatives as the Morella Bill are fighting.

What My Daughter Rachel and (Many) Women Want

Still, some women have strong spatial abilities and talent in mathematics and science. Would these women be helped by the kinds of programs apt to come out of the Morella Bill?

The voluminous research literature on gender offers surprisingly few case studies that would give us some insight into why women with talent in science and mathematics do not choose these fields. For this reason, I offer here, in the spirit of a case study, my experience with my own daughter, Rachel. She is just the kind of young woman who would be the target of the program efforts likely to emerge from the Morella Bill. Indeed, she was the target of my own extensive efforts to interest her in science and mathematics, efforts far more determined than any likely to come from a federal program. But Rachel, like so many other young women, insisted that she was "not interested" in science and wanted "to work with people." Why?

19   I first realized Rachel was gifted in mathematics when she entered junior high school. She had scored high on a mathematics test that her school gave to choose students for "MathCounts," a national mathematics competition. MathCounts winners are overwhelmingly male.[12] Rachel was hardly a victim of cultural stereotypes about women. She was the only one of our three children (the other two are boys) who learned to use tools. For her birthdays, she asked for building sets. On her sixth birthday, I found her packing up the new Barbie doll her grandmother had sent her. "If grandma likes dolls so much," she said with disgust, "she can have all of mine."

20   The more I thought about Rachel's interests and skills, the more it all fell into place. I had a mathematically and technically inclined daughter whose talents I should develop. Rachel was already getting tutored in advanced mathematics twice a week to prepare her for the statewide MathCounts meet. Her school had arranged private tutoring for her and another high-scoring student, a boy. But there was more I could do! I got her to enroll in a science course sponsored by the Center for Talented Youth. She had qualified for both the writing and science courses but had always chosen the writing courses.

21   To give her practical experience in a scientific career and let her meet female role models, I arranged for her to work after school with a doctoral student (female, of course) at the University of Alaska's Institute for Arctic Biology. Rachel got to look at samples of Bering Sea water using an electron microscope. I was thrilled. Rachel was not. She told me to lay off.

22   "I am not part of your agenda for the advancement of women in science," she informed me in a tone that left no room for further discussion. "I want to work with people. I want to help people."

23   These are the standard reasons women give when they explain why they are not interested in scientific careers. As I thought more about Rachel's experience, I realized that there was a lot more to her decision than her preference for working with people. This reason masked other reasons, good reasons, for not choosing science as a career.

24   Let us take a closer look at Rachel's actual skills from the viewpoint of where she has the greatest "comparative advantage." Yes, Rachel did score about as high as the male student in the local MathCounts competition. But the tutoring sessions revealed great differences in their mathematical gifts. The young boy could solve problems in a flash while she had to struggle. I asked him how he did it, but he wasn't very verbal. "I don't know," he said. "The solutions just come to me." The solutions did not "just come" to Rachel. In the pressure of the statewide MathCounts competition, the boy did much better. Rachel's reaction was again typical of what girls say—she did not like the "competitiveness" of the math contest. But the issue was not male versus female competitiveness. Rachel was an avid competitor when her chances of winning were high.

25   The science course also gave Rachel valuable information about her areas of comparative advantage. In her writing courses with the Center for Talented Youth, she had always been at the top. In the CTY science course, she found herself stuck in the middle. Her reaction—she was "not interested" in science.

26   Like most of us, Rachel finds most interesting the areas she is best at. But Rachel was able to discover her relative strengths and weaknesses only because she was in mathematics and science settings where both males and females were present. Had she been in sex-segregated programs, like the ones likely to come out of the Morella Bill, she would have

been deprived of valuable information about her abilities. In an all-girls program, she would most likely have been a star.

Lop-Sided Males and Balanced Females

Many females with talent in science and mathematics, in my experience, resemble my daughter Rachel. They are "balanced," apt to be bright in both verbal skills and mathematics skills. These young women have a wide range of choices—to go into a scientific field or to go into another field where their verbal skills are valuable.   27

Many males with talent in science and mathematics, in my experience, resemble the young boy who was also competing in MathCounts. These males are "lop-sided," strong in mathematical skills but far weaker in verbal skills. These young men, playing to their strengths, are apt to choose scientific and technical fields. Of course, some young men will have strength in both the verbal and mathematical areas. But I suspect a larger number of young men, compared to young women, will have this "lop-sided" pattern. I am currently testing this theory through an analysis of SAT scores, in order to see what proportions of females and males who have high scores on the mathematics section of the SAT also have high scores on the verbal section of the test. My bet is that women who have high mathematical skills will also tend to have high verbal skills, while men who have high mathematical skills are more apt to be "lop-sided."   28

In a free society, where people can make their own career choices, it should not be surprising that males and females choose somewhat different careers.[13] A 1996 survey of college freshmen, for example, shows that 20 percent of females but less than 10 percent of males are choosing professional careers. Women are indeed seeking high-status and high-paying careers but they prefer the professions. This survey also showed that over 20 percent of male college freshmen compared to 6 percent of females are choosing careers in physical sciences, engineering, and the computer sciences. Despite all the efforts of federal agencies, females and males seek out work they enjoy and work at which they excel.   29

Is there anything really wrong with this picture? I think not. The danger of the Morella Bill and the sex-segregated programs this legislation is likely to spawn is that young women will be pressured, or seduced by scholarships, into scientific and technical careers which do not fit them well and which they will not find satisfying. Science may need women in order to meet current demands for political correctness, but women have many other satisfying career choices.   30

Notes

1. These examples are drawn from the web page of the Program for Women and Girls at the National Science Foundation. On the web, go to http://www.nsf.gov/verity/srchawd.htm and type 1544 in the dialog window.
2. I deliberately leave the identity of this NSF administrator vague because I do not wish to embarrass her. We were speaking on the record, but she may have been too open.
3. This Congressional Budget Office Cost Estimate was prepared on 21 May 1998 and can be found on this web site: http://www.thomas.loc.gov by following the queries.

4. Letter from Kerri-Ann Jones, Acting Director, Office of Science and Technology Policy, Executive Office of the President, sent to The Honorable William F. Goodling, Chairman of the Committee on Education and the Workforce, 11 May 1998.

5. These points come from a source in the Committee on Education and the Workforce.

6. Precise documentation for these statistics and others in this essay may be found in *The Myth That Schools Shortchange Girls* (Washington, DC: Women's Freedom Network, 1998).

7. These statistics track the proportion of American women who receive doctorates in the sciences, compared to American men. Reports on gender equity often underestimate the progress of American women, because they ignore the preponderance of foreign students who are receiving doctorates from American universities. These foreign students are overwhelmingly (in a ratio of 3 to 1) male.

8. See Gita Wilder, "Antecedents of Gender Differences," in *Supplement to Gender and Fair Assessment* (Princeton, NJ: Educational Testing Service, 1997).

9. See Claude M. Steele, "A Threat in the Air: How Stereotypes Shape Intellectual Identity and Performance," *American Psychologist* 52, 6 (1997): 613–629.

10. See Diane Halpern, "Sex Differences in Intelligence: Implications for Education," *American Psychologist* 52, 20, 1091–1102.

11. For a review of the specific evidence, using both grades and standardized test scores, see W. W. Willingham and N. S. Cole, *Gender and Fair Assessment* (Mahwah, NJ: Lawrence Erlbaum, 1997).

12. For a discussion of MathCounts, see C. A. Dwyer and L. M. Johnson, "Grades, Accomplishments, and Correlates," in Willingham and Cole, *Gender and Fair Assessment,* 127–156.

13. See the survey conducted by Alexander Austin, reported in Y. Bae and T. M. Smith, "Women in Mathematics and Science," in National Center for Educational Statistics, *The Condition of Education 1997* (Washington, DC: U.S. Department of Education, 1997), 13–21.

Critiquing "The Morella Bill, My Daughter Rachel, and the Advancement of Women in Science"

1. The central puzzle Kleinfeld addresses is why a significantly smaller percentage of women than men pursue careers in mathematics, science, and engineering. What are the usual causes cited for this phenomenon? What is Kleinfeld's explanation?

2. In wrestling with the question of scientific careers for women, Kleinfeld joins a larger social controversy about girls and education. For example, education professors Myra and David Sadker in their book *Failing at Fairness: How American Schools Cheat Girls* (1994) and groups such as the American Association of University Women argue that girls are still being short-changed intellectually and that many gaps in girls' education still persist. What contribution does Kleinfeld make to this larger conversation?

3. It is unusual (and often dangerous) to base a causal argument on a single case study. How persuasive do you find Kleinfeld's use of her daughter Rachel?

What rhetorical strategies does Kleinfeld use to increase the persuasiveness of the material based on Rachel?

4. Role-play a debate on the Senate floor preceding a vote on the Morella Bill. Have one group of students represent Kleinfeld's view in the debate. Have another group support the Morella Bill.

Our final causal argument, by student writer Holly Miller, examines the causes of teen sexual behavior. It uses the documentation form of the American Psychological Association (APA).

The Causes of Teen Sexual Behavior

Holly M. Miller (Student)

Teen sex, leading all too frequently to casual promiscuity, abortion, single motherhood, or STDs including AIDS, is a widely discussed problem in our culture. According to a recent survey conducted by the Kaiser Family Foundation, whereas only 35 percent of girls and 55 percent of boys had had sex by their eighteenth birthdays in the early 1970s, 56 percent of teenage girls and 73 percent of boys had had sex by age eighteen in 1996. The same study revealed that only "one in five teenagers do not have intercourse during their teenage years." Fifty-five percent of the teens cite readiness as the reason they have sex. Simply, "they think they are ready" (Survey, 1996).

However, there should be little doubt that most teens are not ready for sexual activity. High rates of pregnancy and STDs indicate that teens do not properly protect themselves, and high numbers of abortions suggest that they are not ready for parenthood. Moreover, much sexual behavior seems attributable to emotional immaturity, which may contribute to the particularly disturbing statistic that many girls are pressured to have sex or do so involuntarily. Seventy percent of the girls who had sex before age fourteen, and 60 percent of the girls who had sex prior to their fifteenth birthday claimed that the sexual intercourse was involuntary. Additionally, "six out of ten teenage girls say another reason why teen girls may have sex is because a boyfriend is pressuring them" (Survey, 1996).

There can be no question that teen sexual behavior is a growing problem, but the explanation for this increase in sexual activity is controversial. This paper's focus is on the causes of teen sexual behavior. Why are teens having sex? Who or what is the greatest influence on teen sexual behavior? How can we slow the rate of teen sexual activity?

Although many causes work together to influence teen sex, one of the most significant contributing causes is the media. Victor C. Strasburger (1997), an expert on adolescence, notes, "Teenagers watch an average of three hours of TV per day" (p. 18). A study cited by the Kaiser Foundation examined TV shows most popular with teenagers in 1992–1993. This study "found that one in four interactions among characters per episode conveyed a sexual message. . . . Only two of the ten shows included messages about sexual responsibility" (Entertainment, 1996). Popular shows in 1992–1993, such as *90210* and *Melrose*

Place, were just the trailblazers for the prime-time dramas now aimed at teens, such as *Dawson's Creek, Party of Five,* and *Felicity.* Beyond the sexually explicit story lines of programs, commercials use sex appeal to sell everything from cars to potato chips, and teens see twenty thousand commercials per year (Strasburger, 1997, p. 18). Another multimedia influence on teens is pornography. While statistics are hard to find because selling pornography to children is illegal, it is obvious that teens have access to pornography. One fifteen-year-old boy interviewed by *Life* magazine claimed, "No one tells you how to [have sex]. You learn it from watching pornos" (Adato, 1999, p. 38).

5   The effect of the media on teenage sexuality is probably subtle rather than direct. The media don't encourage teenagers to have sex, at least explicitly. But the influence is still there. Hollywood has long been blamed for desensitizing our culture to violence; it is entirely plausible that they have also desensitized our culture, and youth, to sex. According to Drew Altman, president of the Kaiser Family Foundation, "With the problems facing adolescents today, how sex is shown on TV is just as important as how much sex is shown on TV" (Entertainment, 1996). The frequent and graphic depictions of sex normalize the behavior for teenagers. Watching stars play characters their own age—characters with whom they can identify, characters who, just like them, have part-time jobs, too much homework, and problems with their parents—encourages teens to emulate the sexual behaviors of Bailey, Sara, Dawson, or Joey.

6   Teenagers themselves, however, will usually deny that they emulate TV characters, so we need to look also at other factors. Another contributing cause of teen sexual activity is peer pressure. The problem comes from teens' willingness to say and do things to impress others. The tendency to brag about sexual exploits was egregiously illustrated by the Spur Posse scandal of 1993. A group of popular high school "jocks" from a suburban California community formed a clique with the purpose of sleeping with girls. In fact, they competed with each other to see who could sleep with the most girls, going so far as to pressure girls as young as ten to have sex. Once exposed, several members were charged with lewd conduct, felony intercourse, and rape. The Posse members themselves say they learned about sex "the old-fashioned way": from older brothers and friends (Gelman, 1993, p. 29). Few, if any, of the guys would probably have gone to such extremes to sleep with girls had their friends not been competing in the same contest.

7   Another contributing cause is schools. According to many critics, sex education programs in the schools do little to promote safe sexual behavior, and they are often criticized by conservatives as promoting the message that it is good and normal to be sexually active (so long as you use a condom). Why are sex education programs so ineffective? One critic notes that sex education classes focus on the mechanics of sex and avoid issues of emotions, love, and morality. "They talk about zygotes," according to one fourteen-year-old boy (Adato, 1999, p. 38). Another critic, NYU psychology professor Paul C. Vitz (1999), reviewed leading high school health textbooks and is troubled by their lack of focus on "the meaning and possibility of true love and its relationship to sexual union and marriage." Vitz claims that textbooks encourage students to evaluate behavior in terms of their own needs rather than the needs of their partners or of a relationship. He claims that "[o]ur growing

tolerance of the adult 'do your own thing' morality runs smack up against the need to socialize and protect the young" (p. 547). In short, Vitz desires a sex education program that emphasizes love and morality. Yet schools avoid creating such programs because while parents are generally comfortable with their kids learning about sex from school, they are not as complacent when it comes to schools teaching morality.

The schools are criticized from another direction by some feminist scholars who have blamed conventional schooling for the vulnerability of girls. Nancy J. Perry (1992), citing an American Association of University Women study showing that teachers pay less attention to girls than to boys, charges that "girls come out of school ill-prepared to get ahead in society" (p. 83). Though the AAUW did not address the sexual behavior of girls, their hypothesis that schools marginalize girls, making them vulnerable, may contribute to the fact that between 60 and 70 percent of teenage girls feel pressured into sex.

In explaining why adolescence is so difficult for girls, however, Perry puts primary responsibility not on the schools but on parents. Although she acknowledges that peer pressure and the media's portrayal of women as sex objects are contributing factors to sexual activity among teenage girls, she identifies parental involvement as the critical factor in the development of young girls.

In fact, differences in parenting styles might be the chief variable that influences teenage sexual behavior. Drs. Sharon D. White and Richard R. DeBlassie, writing in the journal *Adolescence,* point out that "parents are the earliest and most important influence on sexuality" (1992, p. 184). According to their research, different parenting styles have a measurable influence on teenagers' sexual behavior. The highest rates of sexual activity come from teenagers with permissive parents who set no rules. The next highest rates, ironically, come from teenagers whose parents are unduly strict and controlling, a parenting style that often fosters rebellion. The lowest rates of sexual activity come from teenagers whose parents set firm but reasonable and moderate rules. White and DeBlassie show that parents who insist on reasonable curfews, and who supervise their teens' dating by knowing whom they are with and where they are going, produce teens with the most responsible attitudes toward sex. They suggest also that parents' implicit values—for example, abstinence until marriage or at least sex linked to love and commitment—are most likely to be transmitted to teens when the teens feel connected to their parents in a safe environment with rules.

So what can be done to reduce the problems of teen sexuality? Research suggests that parents have the most direct and strongest influence over teens' sexual behavior, but by no means are they the only influences. Thus, television producers ought to provide role models of teens with less promiscuous views of sex. Teachers need to pay better attention to the needs of their students, whether the teens need to hear about emotional sides of sex or the advantages of waiting until marriage to have intercourse. Parents need to turn off the TV and open dialogue with their children. Parents need to set moderate and reasonable rules for their teens and carefully supervise their behavior. Only when parents take the lead in responsibly educating their children about sex, and in pressuring the media and the schools to create a holistic view of sex in the context of love and commitment, can we curb the trend of teen sex and its unhealthy consequences.

References

Adato, A. (1999, March 1). The secret lives of teens. *Life,* p. 38.

Entertainment media as "sex educators?" and other ways teens learn about sex, contraception, STDs, and AIDS. (1996). Kaiser Family Foundation. Retrieved May 16, 1999 from the World Wide Web: http://www.kff.org (Scroll "Reproductive and Sexual Health." Then choose "surveys.")

Gelman, D. (1993, April 12). Mixed messages. *Newsweek,* p. 29.

Perry, N. (1992, August 10). Why it's so tough to be a girl. *Fortune,* pp. 82–84.

Strasburger, V. (1997, May 19). Tuning in to teenagers. *Newsweek,* pp. 18–19.

Survey on teens and sex: What they say teens today need to know, and who they listen to. (1996). Kaiser Family Foundation. Retrieved May 16, 1999, from the World Wide Web: http://www.kff.org (Scroll "Reproductive and Sexual Health." Then choose "surveys.")

Vitz, P. (1999, March). Cupid's broken arrow. *Phi Delta Kappan,* p. 547.

White, S., & DeBlassie, R. (1992). Adolescent sexual behavior. *Adolescence, 27,* 183–191.

Critiquing "The Causes of Teen Sexual Behavior"

1. How does Holly Miller establish the issue of teen sexuality and suggest the controversy surrounding it?

2. What kind of causal links does Holly employ to explain why teenagers have sex? What data does she use to support those links? Are these data persuasive? What would make her interpretations more persuasive?

3. What features of causal argument contribute to the strength of her argument? What insights does this argument add to the ongoing social conflict and confusion over teen sexuality?

12 Resemblance Arguments

X Is (Is Not) like Y

CASE 1

When NATO began bombing Serbia during the Kosovo crisis, the Clinton administration, along with the U.S. media, likened Yugoslavian president Slobodan Milosovic to Adolf Hitler and compared the "ethnic cleansing" of Kosovo to the Nazis' "final solution" against the Jews. When justifying the bombing, Clinton frequently evoked the Holocaust and the lessons of World War II. "Never again," he said. Meanwhile, the Serbian community in the United States (and many Balkan scholars) criticized the Holocaust analogy. The Serbian community likened the Kosovo crisis not to the Nazi annihilation of the Jews but to a civil war in which Serbs were protecting their homeland against Albanian terrorists. They pointed to explanatory precedents when the Serbs themselves were victims, especially the "ethnic cleansing" of Serbs from Croatia in 1995.

CASE 2

When the voting age was reduced from twenty-one to eighteen, many people argued for the lower voting age by saying, "If you are old enough to fight for your country in a war, you are old enough to vote." But author Richard Weaver claimed that this analogy was true "only if you believe that fighting and voting are the same kind of thing which I, for one, do not. Fighting requires strength, muscular coordination and, in a modern army, instant and automatic response to orders. Voting requires knowledge of men, history, reasoning power; it is essentially a deliberative activity. Army mules and police dogs are used to fight; nobody is

261

interested in giving them the right to vote. This argument rests on a false analogy."* Someone else might argue that Weaver's counteranalogy is also weak.

AN OVERVIEW OF
RESEMBLANCE ARGUMENTS

Resemblance arguments support a claim by comparing one thing to another
with the intention of transferring the audience's understanding of (or feelings
about) the second thing back to the first. Sometimes an entire argument can be devoted to a resemblance claim. More commonly, brief resemblance arguments are
pieces of larger arguments devoted to a different stasis. Thus lawyer Charles Rem-
bard, in attacking the American Civil Liberties Union for its opposition to mandatory reporting of AIDS at the start of the AIDS crisis, compared the ACLU's desire
to protect the privacy of individuals to out-of-date war tactics:

> [The ACLU] clings to once useful concepts that are inappropriate to current prob-
> lems. Like the French military, which prepared for World War II by building the
> Maginot Line, which was nicely adapted to the trench warfare of World War I, the
> ACLU sometimes hauls up legal arguments effective to old libertarian battles but
> irrelevant to those at hand.†

The strategy of resemblance arguments is to take the audience's understanding
of the point made in the comparison (you shouldn't fight World War II with
out-of-date strategies from World War I) and transfer it to the issue being debated
(you shouldn't fight the battle against AIDS with an out-of-date libertarian
philosophy).

In some cases it may seem that a resemblance argument (X is like Y) is not very
different from a definitional argument (X is Y). For example, if you were to say that
Slobodan Milosovic is "like" Adolf Hitler, you might simply be making a definitional argument, claiming that both men belong to the same class—say, the class
"fascist dictators" or "racial supremacists." Their similarities would be restricted
to the traits of whatever class they are put into. In effect, the *like* statement is a definitional claim in which both X and Y are said to belong to class Z.

But a resemblance argument doesn't work in quite this way. For one thing, in
a resemblance argument the overarching class Z is usually not mentioned but left
to the audience's imagination; the focus stays on Y—that is, on the specific case to
which X is being compared. Often, in fact, there is no single overarching category
Z that effectively sums up all the points of comparison between X and Y. (What
common category do the ACLU's position on AIDS testing and France's building
of the Maginot Line belong to?) This definitional blurring moves resemblance

---

*Richard M. Weaver, "A Responsible Rhetoric," *The Intercollegiate Review,* Winter 1976–77: 86–87.

†Charles Rembar, *New York Times,* 15 May 1987: I, 31:2.

arguments away from strict logic and toward a kind of metaphoric or imaginative persuasiveness.

The persuasive power of resemblance arguments comes from their ability to clarify an audience's conception of contested issues while conveying powerful emotions. Resemblance arguments typically take the form X is (is not) like Y. Resemblance arguments work best when the audience has a clear (and sometimes emotionally charged) understanding of the Y term. The writer then hopes to transfer this understanding, along with accompanying emotions, to the X term. The danger of resemblance arguments, as we shall see, is that the differences between the X and Y terms are often so significant that the resemblance argument collapses under close examination.

Like most other argument types, resemblance arguments can be analyzed using the Toulmin schema. Suppose, for example, that you wanted to write an argument favoring a balanced federal budget. In one section of your argument you might develop the following claim of resemblance: "Just as a family will go bankrupt if it continually spends more than it makes, so the federal government will go bankrupt if its expenses exceed its revenues." This claim depends on the resemblance between the fiscal problems of the federal government and the fiscal problems of a private family. The argument can be displayed in Toulmin terms as follows:

ENTHYMEME:	If the federal government doesn't balance its budget, it will go bankrupt because the federal government is like a family that goes bankrupt when it fails to balance its budget.
CLAIM:	If the federal government doesn't balance its debt, it will go bankrupt.
STATED REASON:	because the federal government is like a family that goes bankrupt when it fails to balance its budget
GROUNDS:	evidence showing that families that overspend their budgets go bankrupt
WARRANT:	The economic laws that apply to families apply also to governments.
BACKING:	evidence that when governments and families behave in economically similar ways, they suffer similar consequences
CONDITIONS OF REBUTTAL:	all cases in which governments and families behaved in similar ways and did not suffer similar consequences; all the ways that families and governments differ
QUALIFIER:	The claim is supported by the analogy only to the extent that family and government economics resemble each other.

For many audiences, this comparison of the government to a family might be persuasive: It uses an area of experience familiar to almost everyone (the problem of balancing the family budget) to help make sense of a more complex area of experience (the problem of balancing the federal budget). At its root is the warrant that what works for the family will work for the federal government.

But this example also illustrates the dangers of resemblance arguments, which often ignore important differences or *disanalogies* between the terms of comparison. One can think, for instance, of many differences between the economics of a family and that of the federal government. For example, unlike a private family, the federal government prints its own money and does most of its borrowing from its own members. Perhaps these differences negate the claim that family debt and federal debt are similar in their effects. Thus an argument based on resemblance is usually open to refutation if a skeptic points out important disanalogies.

We turn now to the two types of resemblance arguments: analogy and precedent.

ARGUMENTS BY ANALOGY

The use of *analogies* can constitute the most imaginative form of argument. If you don't like your new boss, you can say that she's like a marine drill sergeant, the cowardly captain of a sinking ship, or a mother hen. Each of these analogies suggests a different management style, clarifying the nature of your dislike while conveying an emotional charge. The ubiquity of analogies undoubtedly stems from their power to clarify the writer's understanding of an issue through comparisons that grip the audience.

Of course, this power to make things clear comes at a price. Analogies often clarify one aspect of a relationship at the expense of other aspects. Thus, for example, in nineteenth-century America many commentators were fond of justifying certain negative effects of capitalism (for example, the squalor of the poor) by comparing social and economic processes to Darwinian evolution—the survival of the fittest. In particular, they fastened on one aspect of evolution, competition, and spoke darkly of life as a cutthroat struggle for survival. Clearly the analogy clarified one aspect of human interaction: People and institutions do indeed compete for limited resources, markets, and territory. Moreover, the consequences of failure are often dire (the weak get eaten by the strong).

But competition is only one aspect of evolution—albeit a particularly dramatic one. The ability to dominate an environment is less important to long-term survival of a species than the ability to adapt to that environment. Thus the mighty dinosaur disappeared, but the lowly cockroach continues to flourish because of the latter's uncanny ability to adjust to circumstance.

The use of the evolutionary analogies to stress the competitive nature of human existence fit the worldview (and served the interests) of those who were most fond of invoking them, in particular the so-called robber barons and conservative Social Darwinists. But in overlooking other dimensions of evolution, especially the importance of adaptation and cooperation to survival, the analogy created a great deal of mischief.

So analogies have the power to get an audience's attention like virtually no other persuasive strategy. But seldom are they sufficient in themselves to provide full understanding. At some point with every analogy you need to ask yourself, "How far can I legitimately go with this? At what point are the similarities between the two things I am comparing going to be overwhelmed by their dissimilarities?" They are useful attention-getting devices; used carefully and cautiously, they can be extended to shape an audience's understanding of a complex situation. But they can conceal and distort as well as clarify.

With this caveat, let's look at the uses of both undeveloped and extended analogies.

Using Undeveloped Analogies

Typically, writers will use short, *undeveloped analogies* to drive home a point (and evoke an accompanying emotion) and then quickly abandon the analogy before the reader's awareness of disanalogies begins to set in. Thus conservative columnist James Kilpatrick, in arguing that it is not unconstitutional to require drug testing of federal employees, compares giving a urine specimen when applying for a federal job to going through an airport metal detector when flying:

> The Constitution does not prohibit all searches and seizures. It makes the people secure in their persons only from "unreasonable" searches and seizures. [. . .] A parallel situation may be observed at every airport in the land. Individuals may have a right to fly, but they have no right to fly without having their persons and baggage inspected for weapons. By the same token, the federal worker who refuses a urine specimen [has no right to a federal job].*

Kilpatrick wants to transfer his audience's general approval of weapons searches as a condition for airplane travel to drug testing as a condition for federal employment. But he doesn't want his audience to linger too long on the analogy. (Is a urine specimen for employment really analogous to a weapons search before an airplane trip?)

Using Extended Analogies

Sometimes writers elaborate an analogy so that it takes on a major role in the argument. As an example of a claim based on an *extended analogy,* consider the following excerpt from a professor's argument opposing a proposal to require a writing proficiency exam for graduation. In the following portion of his argument,

---

*From "A Conservative View" by James J. Kilpatrick. ©Universal Press Syndicate. Reprinted with permission. All rights reserved.

the professor compares development of writing skills to the development of physical fitness.

> A writing proficiency exam gives the wrong symbolic messages about writing. It suggests that writing is simply a skill, rather than an active way of thinking and learning. It suggests that once a student demonstrates proficiency then he or she doesn't need to do any more writing.
>
> Imagine two universities concerned with the physical fitness of their students. One university requires a junior-level physical fitness exam in which students must run a mile in less than 10 minutes, a fitness level it considers minimally competent. Students at this university see the physical fitness exam as a one-time hurdle. As many as 70 percent of them can pass the exam with no practice; another 10–20 percent need a few months' training; and a few hopeless couch potatoes must go through exhaustive remediation. After passing the exam, any student can settle back into a routine of TV and potato chips having been certified as "physically fit."
>
> The second university, however, believing in true physical fitness for its students, is not interested in minimal competency. Consequently, it creates programs in which its students exercise 30 minutes every day for the entire four years of the undergraduate curriculum. There is little doubt which university will have the most physically fit students. At the second university, fitness becomes a way of life with everyone developing his or her full potential. Similarly, if we want to improve our students' writing abilities, we should require writing in every course throughout the curriculum.

If you choose to write an extended analogy such as this, you will focus on the points of comparison that serve your purposes. The writer's purpose in the preceding case is to support the achievement of mastery rather than minimalist standards as the goal of the university's writing program. Whatever other disanalogous elements are involved (for example, writing requires the use of intellect, which may or may not be strengthened by repetition), the comparison reveals vividly that a commitment to mastery involves more than a minimalist test. The analogy serves primarily to underscore this one crucial point. In reviewing the different groups of students as they "prepare" for the fitness exam, the author makes clear just how irrelevant such an exam is to the whole question of mastery. Typically, then, in developing your analogy, you are not developing all possible points of comparison so much as you are bringing out those similarities consistent with the point you are trying to make.

FOR CLASS DISCUSSION

The following is a two-part exercise to help you clarify for yourself how analogies function in the context of arguments. Part 1 is to be done outside class; part 2 is to be done in class.

PART 1   Think of an analogy that accurately expresses your feeling toward each of the following topics. Then write your analogy in the following one-sentence format:

X is like Y: A, B, C . . . (where X is the main topic being discussed; Y is the analogy; and A, B, and C are the points of comparison).

EXAMPLES:

Cramming for an exam to get better grades is like pumping iron for 10 hours straight to prepare for a weightlifting contest: exhausting and counterproductive.

A right-to-lifer bombing an abortion clinic is like a vegetarian bombing a cattle barn: futile and contradictory.

a. Spanking a child to teach obedience is like . . .

b. Building low-cost housing for poor people is like . . .

c. The use of steroids by college athletes is like . . .

d. Mandatory AIDS testing for all U.S. residents is like . . .

e. A legislative proposal to eliminate all federally subsidized student loans is like . . .

f. The effect of American fast food on our health is like . . .

g. The personal gain realized by people who have committed questionable or even illegal acts and then made money by selling book and movie rights is like . . .

In each case, begin by asking yourself how you feel about the subject. If you have negative feelings about a topic, then begin by calling up negative pictures that express those feelings (or if you have positive feelings, call up positive comparisons). As they emerge, test each one to see if it will work as an analogy. An effective analogy will convey both the feeling you have toward your topic and your understanding of the topic. For instance, the writer in the "cramming for an exam" example obviously believes that pumping iron for 10 hours before a weightlifting match is stupid. This feeling of stupidity is then transferred to the original topic—cramming for an exam. But the analogy also clarifies understanding. The writer imagines the mind as a muscle (which gets exhausted after too much exercise and which is better developed through some exercise every day rather than a lot all at once) rather than as a large container (into which lots of stuff can be "crammed").

PART 2   Bring your analogies to class and compare them to those of your classmates. Select the best analogies for each of the topics and be ready to say why you think they are good.

ARGUMENTS BY PRECEDENT

Precedent arguments are like analogy arguments in that they make comparisons between an X and a Y. In precedent arguments, however, the Y term is usually a past event where some sort of decision was reached, often a moral, legal, or political decision. An argument by precedent tries to show that a similar decision should be (should not be) reached for the present issue X because the situation of X is (is not) like the situation of Y. For example, if you wanted to argue that your college or university could increase retention by offering seminars for first-year students, you could point to the good results at other colleges that have instituted first-year seminars. If you wanted to argue that antidrug laws will never eradicate drug use, you could point to the failure of alcohol prohibition in the United States in the 1920s.

A good example of a precedent argument is the following excerpt from a speech by President Lyndon Johnson in the early years of the Vietnam War:

> Nor would surrender in Vietnam bring peace because we learned from Hitler at Munich that success only feeds the appetite of aggression. The battle would be renewed in one country and then another country, bringing with it perhaps even larger and crueler conflict, as we have learned from the lessons of history.*

Here the audience knows what happened at Munich: France and Britain tried to appease Hitler by yielding to his demand for a large part of Czechoslovakia, but Hitler's armies continued their aggression anyway, using Czechoslovakia as a staging area to invade Poland. By arguing that surrender in Vietnam would lead to the same consequences, Johnson brings to his argument about Vietnam the whole weight of his audience's unhappy knowledge of World War II. Administration white papers developed Johnson's precedent argument by pointing toward the similarity of Hitler's promises with those of the Viet Cong: You give us this and we will ask for no more. But Hitler didn't keep his promise. Why should the Viet Cong?

Johnson's Munich precedent persuaded many Americans during the early years of the war and helps explain U.S. involvement in Southeast Asia. Yet many scholars attacked Johnson's reasoning. Let's analyze the Munich argument, using Toulmin's schema:

ENTHYMEME:　　　　The United States should not withdraw its troops from Vietnam because conceding to the Viet Cong will have the same disastrous consequences as did conceding to Hitler in Munich.

*From *Public Papers of the Presidents of the United States*, vol. 2, *Lyndon B. Johnson* (Washington, DC: GPO, 1965), 794.

CLAIM:	The United States should not withdraw its troops from Vietnam.
STATED REASON:	because conceding to the Viet Cong will have the same disastrous consequences as did conceding to Hitler in Munich
GROUNDS:	evidence of the disastrous consequences of conceding to Hitler at Munich: Hitler's continued aggression; his using of Czechoslovakia as a staging area to invade Poland
WARRANT:	What happened in Europe will happen in Southeast Asia.
BACKING:	evidence of similarities between 1939 Europe and 1965 Southeast Asia (for example, similarities in political philosophy, goals, and military strength of the enemy; similarities in the nature of the conflict between the disputants)
CONDITIONS OF REBUTTAL:	acknowledged differences between 1939 Europe and 1965 Southeast Asia that might make the outcomes different

Laid out like this, we see that the persuasiveness of the comparison depends on the audience's acceptance of the warrant, which posits close similarity between 1939 Europe and 1965 Southeast Asia. But many critics of the Vietnam War attacked this warrant.

During the Vietnam era, historian Howard Zinn attacked Johnson's argument by claiming three crucial differences between Europe in 1939 and Southeast Asia in 1965: First, Zinn argued, the Czechs were being attacked from outside by an external aggressor (Germany), whereas Vietnam was being attacked from within by rebels as part of a civil war. Second, Czechoslovakia was a prosperous, effective democracy, whereas the official Vietnam government was corrupt and unpopular. Third, Hitler wanted Czechoslovakia as a base for attacking Poland, whereas the Viet Cong and North Vietnamese aimed at reunification of their country as an end in itself.*

The Munich example shows again how arguments of resemblance depend on emphasizing the similarities between X and Y and playing down the dissimilarities. One could try to refute the counterargument made by Zinn by arguing first that the Saigon government was more stable than Zinn thinks and second that the Viet Cong and North Vietnamese were driven by goals larger than reunification of

---

*Based on the summary of Zinn's argument in J. Michael Sproule, *Argument: Language and Its Influence* (New York: McGraw-Hill, 1980), 149–50.

Vietnam, namely, communist domination of Asia. Such an argument would once again highlight the similarities between Vietnam and prewar Europe.

FOR CLASS DISCUSSION

1. Consider the following claims of precedent, and evaluate how effective you think each precedent might be in establishing the claim. How would you develop the argument? How would you cast doubt on it?
   a. Don't vote for Governor Frick for president because governors have not proven to be effective presidents.
   b. Gays should be allowed to serve openly in the U.S. military because they are allowed to serve openly in the militaries of most other Western countries.
   c. Gun control will reduce violent crime in the United States because many countries that have strong gun control laws (such as Japan and England) have low rates of violent crime.

2. Advocates for "right to die" legislation legalizing active euthanasia under certain conditions often point to the Netherlands as a country where acceptance of euthanasia works effectively. Assume for the moment that your state has a ballot initiative legalizing euthanasia. Assume further that you are being hired as a lobbyist for (against) the measure and have been assigned to do research on euthanasia in the Netherlands. Working in small groups, make a list of research questions you would want to ask. Your long-range rhetorical goal is to use your research to support (attack) the ballot initiative by making a precedence argument focusing on the Netherlands.

WRITING A RESEMBLANCE ARGUMENT

WRITING ASSIGNMENT FOR CHAPTER 12

Write a letter to the editor of your campus or local newspaper or a slightly longer guest editorial in which you try to influence public opinion on some issue through the use of a persuasive analogy or precedent. T. D. Hylton's argument against using sirens in radio commercials is a student piece written for this assignment (see p. 273).

Exploring Ideas

Because letters to the editor and guest editorials are typically short, writers often lack space to develop full arguments. Because of their clarifying and emotional power, arguments from analogy or precedent are often effective in these situations.

Newspaper editors usually print letters or guest editorials only on current issues or on some current problem to which you can draw attention. For this assignment look through the most recent back issues of your campus or local newspaper, paying particular attention to issues being debated on the op-ed pages. Join one of the ongoing conversations about an existing issue, or draw attention to a current problem or situation that annoys you. In your letter or guest editorial, air your views. As part of your argument, include a persuasive analogy or precedent.

Organizing a Resemblance Argument

The most typical way to develop a resemblance argument is as follows:

- Introduce the issue and state your claim.
- Develop your analogy or precedent.
- Draw the explicit parallels you want to highlight between your claim and the analogy or precedent.
- Anticipate and respond to objections (optional depending on space and context).

Of course, this structure can be varied in many ways, depending on your issue and rhetorical context. Sometimes writers open an argument with the analogy, which serves as an attention grabber.

QUESTIONING AND CRITIQUING A RESEMBLANCE ARGUMENT

Once you have written a draft of your letter or guest editorial, you can test its effectiveness by role-playing a skeptical audience. What follows are some typical questions audiences will raise about arguments of resemblance.

Will a skeptic say I am trying to prove too much with my analogy or precedent? The most common mistake people make with resemblance arguments is to ask them to prove more than they're capable of proving. Too often, an analogy is treated as if it were a syllogism or algebraic ratio wherein necessary truths are deduced (*a* is to *b* as *c* is to *d*) rather than as a useful but basically playful figure that suggests uncertain but significant insight. The best way to guard against this charge is to qualify your argument and to find other means of persuasion to supplement an analogy or precedent argument.

For a good example of an analogy that tries to do too much, consider President Ronald Reagan's attempt to prevent the United States from imposing economic sanctions on South Africa. Ronald Reagan wanted to argue that harming South Africa's economy would do as much damage to blacks as to whites. In making this argument, he compared South Africa to a zebra and concluded that one couldn't hurt the white portions of the zebra without also hurting the black.

The zebra analogy might work quite well to point up the interrelatedness of whites and blacks in South Africa. But it has no force whatsoever in supporting Reagan's assertion that economic sanctions would hurt blacks as well as whites. To refute this analogy, one need only point out the disanalogies between the zebra stripes and racial groups. (There are, for example, no differences in income, education, and employment between black and white stripes on a zebra.)

Will a skeptic point out disanalogies in my resemblance argument?   Although it is easy to show that a country is not like a zebra, finding disanalogies is sometimes quite tricky. As one example, we have already shown you how Howard Zinn identified disanalogies between Europe in 1939 and Southeast Asia in 1965. To take another similar example, during the Kosovo conflict critics of NATO policy questioned the NATO claim that Milosovic's "ethnic cleansing" of ethnic Albanians in Kosovo was analogous to Hitler's extermination of the Jews (see Case 1, p. 261). Although acknowledging the horror of Serbian atrocities, critics pointed out several disanalogies between the Serbs and the Nazis: (1) Jews in Germany and Poland were not engaged in a land dispute with the Germans, unlike ethnic Albanians, who wanted political control over Kosovo. (2) There was no Jewish equivalent of the Kosovo Liberation Army, which was committing terrorist acts against Serbs in Kosovo. (3) Although Germany was traumatized by its defeat in World War I, the Germans themselves were not recent victims of "ethnic cleansing," as were the Serbs in Croatia. (4) The Serbs were not motivated by a centralized philosophy of racial superiority supposedly grounded in evolutionary theory. (5) The Serbs' goal was to drive ethnic Albanians out of Kosovo, not to systematically exterminate an "inferior" race. Critics were not denying the evil of the Serbs' actions. But they held the Holocaust as a darker and "purer" form of evil, something of unique malignance not to be lumped in the same category as the ethnic wars in the Balkans or even the horrors of Pol Pot's killing fields in Cambodia or Stalin's massacre of the Russian peasants.*

---

*NATO's comparison of Kosovo to the Holocaust came during a decade when many scholars were reexamining the historical significance of the Holocaust. For an overview of these debates, see Karen Winkler, "German Scholars Sharply Divided over Place of Holocaust in History," *Chronicle of Higher Education* 27 May 1987, 4–5.

READINGS

Our first reading is a student argument written in response to the assignment on page 270. Notice how this student uses an analogy to analyze and protest an experience that has troubled her.

Don't Fake Sirens!

T. D. Hylton (Student)

As I drove down I-5 slightly over the 65-mph speed limit, I heard the scream of a siren. 1
Naturally my adrenaline started to flow as I transferred attention from the road ahead to searching for the source of the howling siren. Then I realized my mistake: I had not heard a real emergency vehicle; I had heard a radio commercial. Distracted by the sound of the siren, I had put my fellow drivers at risk. The use of sirens in commercials has potentially dangerous consequences. We should not wait for a fatal car accident to ban such commercials.

Compare this type of commercial to a prank call. Pretend that your sister called you 2
up, told you that a loved one had just died unexpectedly, and said that she would get back to you about details as soon as she heard. You would be upset, right? Your attention would no longer be focused on what you had been doing before the phone call. Then, after getting all worked up, pretend that your sister called you back and said it was all a joke. During the time you were distracted, something bad might have happened: You might have left the stove on high or failed to meet an important deadline at work.

While this case is more extreme than a radio commercial siren, hearing a siren while 3
driving does release in us a flood of fears and anxieties. I suspect my reaction is typical: I start to think I did something wrong. Am I speeding? I instinctively look at my speedometer and begin braking. Then I start scanning the road, searching my rear-view mirror for flashing lights, and even pulling into the right lane. Flustered and distracted, I become momentarily a less safe driver. Then I realize that the commercial has played a joke on me.

Just as we would get mad at our sisters for a stupid prank, we should get mad at the 4
commercial writers for fooling us with a siren. It is currently a crime to impersonate a police officer; it ought to be a crime to fake an emergency vehicle. Let's ban these distracting commercials.

Critiquing "Don't Fake Sirens"

1. What is the analogy in this piece?

2. How effective is this analogy? How does T. D. Hylton attempt to draw readers into her perspective?

The second and third readings were published respectively as a guest editorial and a letter to the editor in the *Seattle Times*. They are responses to proposals for stronger gun control laws following the Columbine High School massacre in Littleton, Colorado.

Creeping Loopholism Threatens Our Rights
Michael D. Lubrecht

1   Imagine for a moment that ethanol is recognized as a primary root of crime and social dysfunction in America. Not alcoholism, not drunken driving, not teen drinking, but ethanol, grain alcohol, booze.

2   To address the serious issues arising from the presence of ethanol in society, Congress passes "reasonable" legislation to ban malt liquor, reduce six-packs of beer to four-packs, and prohibit the import of fine French Bordeaux. When these "reasonable" efforts don't stop the problems, the search expands to find "loopholes" in the previous legislation and plug them. We limit the alcohol content in microbrews, require labeling changes on wine coolers, and ban the particularly evil double-malt Scotches. That doesn't work either.

3   The process goes on until there is no legal way left to purchase alcohol. The end result is functionally equivalent to Prohibition, and guess what—it didn't work. Alcohol abuse was rampant, crime soared and a new black market was created.

4   At least the misguided congressmen who engineered the original Prohibition had the courage to stand up and lay their principles on the line. Our current crop of gun-control proponents know that guns in the hands of law-abiding citizens do not increase criminal activity; in many demonstrated ways, they actually reduce crime. The current examples of gun prohibition in countries like Australia show astounding increases in violent crime when guns are removed from the citizenry.

5   But still, these proponents keep chipping away incrementally at, not criminal behavior, but the guns themselves—guns with bayonet lugs, guns that are inexpensive, guns that are painted black, guns that hold too many bullets, guns from other countries, guns that look too evil.

6   Before the Youth Violence Bill—with its "loophole filling" background checks, gunsmith licensing, and other misdirected contents—was even voted Yea or Nay, Rep. Rod Blagojevich (D–Ill.) introduced a new bill to restrict access to rifles in .50 caliber. These rifles, of course, are designed only for killing people.

7   Now, I could write a treatise advancing a plausible hunting sporting or self-defense justification for individual ownership of each and every weapon on the gun-banners' list, despite the fact that we "know" they are all really just death-dealing instruments of destruction. But I won't, for the simple fact is that the gun-control lobby's ultimate goal is the total prohibition of firearms. No matter what "reasonable" law is compromised on, there is another waiting in the wings, to add to the stack of restrictions.

8   It is time to stop defending the functionality, "sporting use" or other arbitrarily selected evil qualities of particular classes of firearms, stand fast, and say, "No More!"

Congress? If guns are the root of all evil, then let's see the House resolution to ban 'em 9
all, right here, right now. If you really think restricting law-abiding citizens' access to particular types of guns will reduce crime in America, then banning them all should halt crime
entirely. If you believe that restricting firearms possession by citizens who are too young
or too poor will make the streets safer, then getting rid of all the guns will restore our
streets to perfect safety. If restricting magazine capacity to 10 rounds will reduce homicides
by some arbitrary number, then reducing their capacity to zero should result in a null homicide rate.

History will not agree with you, but let's try your social experiment. Summon up some 10
backbone and ban them already. Show the character to reveal your agenda in one courageous piece of legislation and be done with it.

Or, come to your senses, address the real issues, leave guns and gun owners alone and 11
stop this endless, senseless, pointless trend of creeping loopholism.

Violence Is a Symptom
(Letter to the Editor)
Rev. Marilyn Redmond

Editor, The Times:

Letters to the Editor and television shows discussing the shootings such as in Littleton, 1
Colo., miss the point. *Guns don't kill people, people kill people.*

Violence is a symptom, like alcoholism is a symptom, of something deeper. We need 2
to grow out of the denial and see the reality of pain and misery. These people have a medical condition called addiction. It needs medical treatment and therapy.

I speak from my 50 years of a violent childhood and marriage. Unless appropriate help 3
is available from therapists and counselors who understand the imbalance—physically, mentally, emotionally and spiritually—recovery is not possible.

All the talk, laws and programs in the world will not heal an illness. A genetic, heredi- 4
tary condition aggravated by generational conditioning needs analysis for the root causes,
not superficial bandages of laws and blame from feeling powerless.

Without appropriate solutions, the epidemic will still erupt with other destructive sub- 5
stitutions, because the illness—a chronic and progressive condition—is not healed. Proactive responsible decisions create resolution and health.

Critiquing "Creeping Loopholism Threatens
Our Rights" and "Violence Is a Symptom"

1. What analogy does each writer use in these pieces?

2. These pieces join the social controversy over gun control reinvigorated by
the Columbine school shootings. What beliefs, assumptions, and values would an

audience have to hold to accept the analogies of each writer? Do these arguments consider alternative views and speak to them? Do any disanalogies come to mind? How effective are these arguments for you?

Our last reading is from feminist writer Susan Brownmiller's *Against Our Will: Men, Women, and Rape.* First published in 1975, Brownmiller's book was chosen by the *New York Times Book Review* as one of the outstanding books of the year. In the following excerpt, Brownmiller makes an argument from resemblance, claiming that pornography is "anti-female propaganda."

From Against Our Will
Men, Women, and Rape
Susan Brownmiller

1   Pornography has been so thickly glossed over with the patina of chic these days in the name of verbal freedom and sophistication that important distinctions between freedom of political expression (a democratic necessity), honest sex education for children (a societal good) and ugly smut (the deliberate devaluation of the role of women through obscene, distorted depictions) have been hopelessly confused. Part of the problem is that those who traditionally have been the most vigorous opponents of porn are often those same people who shudder at the explicit mention of any sexual subject. Under their watchful, vigilante eyes, frank and free dissemination of educational materials relating to abortion, contraception, the act of birth, the female biology in general is also dangerous, subversive and dirty. (I am not unmindful that frank and free discussion of rape, "the unspeakable crime," might well give these righteous vigilantes further cause to shudder.) Because the battle lines were falsely drawn a long time ago, before there was a vocal women's movement, the anti-pornography forces appear to be, for the most part, religious, Southern, conservative and right-wing, while the pro-porn forces are identified as Eastern, atheistic and liberal.

2   But a woman's perspective demands a totally new alignment, or at least a fresh appraisal. The majority report of the President's Commission on Obscenity and Pornography (1970), a report that argued strongly for the removal of all legal restrictions on pornography, soft and hard, made plain that 90 percent of all pornographic material is geared to the male heterosexual market (the other 10 percent is geared to the male homosexual taste), that buyers of porn are "predominantly white, middle-class, middle-aged married males" and that the graphic depictions, the meat and potatoes of porn, are of the naked female body and of the multiplicity of acts done to that body.

3   Discussing the content of stag films, "a familiar and firmly established part of the American scene," the commission report dutifully, if foggily, explained, "Because pornography historically has been thought to be primarily a masculine interest, the emphasis in stag films seems to represent the preferences of the middle-class American male. Thus male homosexuality and bestiality are relatively rare, while lesbianism is rather common."

The commissioners in this instance had merely verified what purveyors of porn have always known: hard-core pornography is not a celebration of sexual freedom; it is a cynical exploitation of female sexual activity through the device of making all such activity, and consequently all females, "dirty." Heterosexual male consumers of pornography are frankly turned on by watching lesbians in action (although never in the final scenes, but always as a curtain raiser); they are turned off with a sudden swiftness of a water faucet by watching naked men act upon each other. One study quoted in the commission report came to the unastounding conclusion that "seeing a stag film in the presence of male peers bolsters masculine esteem." Indeed. The men in groups who watch the films, it is important to note, are *not* naked. 4

When male response to pornography is compared to female response, a pronounced difference in attitude emerges. According to the commission, "Males report being more highly aroused by depictions of nude females, and show more interest in depictions of nude females than [do] females." Quoting the figures of Alfred Kinsey, the commission noted that a majority of males (77 percent) were "aroused" by visual depictions of explicit sex while a majority of females (68 percent) were not aroused. Further, "females more often than males reported 'disgust' and 'offense.'" 5

From whence comes this female disgust and offense? Are females sexually backward or more conservative by nature? The gut distaste that a majority of women feel when we look at pornography, a distaste that, incredibly, it is no longer fashionable to admit, comes, I think, from the gut knowledge that we and our bodies are being stripped, exposed and contorted for the purpose of ridicule to bolster that "masculine esteem" which gets its kick and sense of power from viewing females as anonymous, panting playthings, adult toys, dehumanized objects to be used, abused, broken and discarded. 6

This, of course, is also the philosophy of rape. It is no accident (for what else could be its purpose?) that females in the pornographic genre are depicted in two cleanly delineated roles: as virgins who are caught and "banged" or as nymphomaniacs who are never sated. The most popular and prevalent pornographic fantasy combines the two: an innocent, untutored female is raped and "subjected to unnatural practices" that turn her into a raving, slobbering nymphomaniac, a dependent sexual slave who can never get enough of the big, male cock. 7

There can be no "equality" in porn, no female equivalent, no turning of the tables in the name of bawdy fun. Pornography, like rape, is a male invention, designed to dehumanize women, to reduce the female to an object of sexual access, not to free sensuality from moralistic or parental inhibition. The staple of porn will always be the naked female body, breasts and genitals exposed, because as man devised it, her naked body is the female's "shame," her private parts the private property of man, while his are the ancient, holy, universal, patriarchal instrument of his power, his rule by force over *her*. 8

Pornography is the undiluted essence of anti-female propaganda. Yet the very same liberals who were so quick to understand the method and purpose behind the mighty propaganda machine of Hitler's Third Reich, the consciously spewed-out anti-Semitic caricatures and obscenities that gave an ideological base to the Holocaust and the Final Solution, the very same liberals who, enlightened by blacks, searched their own conscience and came to understand that their tolerance of "nigger" jokes and portrayals of shuffling, rolling-eyed 9 servants in movies perpetuated the degrading myths of black inferiority and gave an ideological base to the continuation of black oppression—these very same liberals now fervidly maintain that the hatred and contempt for women that find expression in four-letter words used as expletives and in what are quaintly called "adult" or "erotic" books and movies are a valid extension of freedom of speech that must be preserved as a Constitutional right.

10   To defend the right of a lone, crazed American Nazi to grind out propaganda calling for the extermination of all Jews, as the ACLU has done in the name of free speech, is, after all, a self-righteous and not particularly courageous stand, for American Jewry is not currently threatened by storm troopers, concentration camps and imminent extermination, but I wonder if the ACLU's position might change if, come tomorrow morning, the bookstores and movie theaters lining Forty-second Street in New York City were devoted not to the humiliation of women by rape and torture, as they currently are, but to a systematized commercially successful propaganda machine depicting the sadistic pleasures of gassing Jews or lynching blacks?

11   Is this analogy extreme? Not if you are a woman who is conscious of the ever-present threat of rape and the proliferation of a cultural ideology that makes it sound like "liberated" fun. The majority report of the President's Commission on Obscenity and Pornography tried to pooh-pooh the opinion of law enforcement agencies around the country that claimed their own concrete experience with offenders who were caught with the stuff led them to conclude that pornographic material is a causative factor in crimes of sexual violence. The commission maintained that it was not possible at this time to scientifically prove or disprove such a connection.

12   But does one need scientific methodology in order to conclude that the antifemale propaganda that permeates our nation's cultural output promotes a climate in which acts of sexual hostility directed against women are not only tolerated but ideologically encouraged? A similar debate has raged for many years over whether or not the extensive glorification of violence (the gangster as hero; the loving treatment accorded bloody shoot-'em-ups in movies, books and on TV) has a causal effect, a direct relationship to the rising rate of crime, particularly among youth. Interestingly enough, in this area—nonsexual and not specifically related to abuses against women—public opinion seems to be swinging to the position that explicit violence in the entertainment media does have a deleterious effect; it makes violence commonplace, numbingly routine and no longer morally shocking.

13   More to the point, those who call for a curtailment of scenes of violence in movies and on television in the name of sensitivity, good taste and what's best for our children are not accused of being pro-censorship or against freedom of speech. Similarly, minority group organizations, black, Hispanic, Japanese, Italian, Jewish, or American Indian, that campaign against ethnic slurs and demeaning portrayals in movies, on television shows and in commercials are perceived as waging a just political fight, for if a minority group claims to be offended by a specific portrayal, be it Little Black Sambo or the Frito Bandito, and relates it to a history of ridicule and oppression, few liberals would dare to trot out a Constitutional argument in theoretical opposition, not if they wish to maintain their liberal credentials. Yet when it comes to the treatment of women, the liberal consciousness remains fiercely obdurate, refusing to be budged, for the sin of appearing square or prissy in the age of the so-called sexual revolution has become the worst offense of all.

Critiquing the Passage from *Against Our Will: Men, Women, and Rape*

1. Summarize Brownmiller's argument in your own words.

2. Brownmiller states that pornography degrades and humiliates women the same way that anti-Semitic literature degrades and humiliates Jews or that myths of black inferiority degrade and humiliate blacks. According to Brownmiller, how does pornography degrade and humiliate women?

3. What disanalogies might a skeptic point out between pornography and anti-Semitic or other racist propaganda?

4. One reviewer of Brownmiller's book said, "Get into this book and hardly a single thought to do with sex will come out the way it was." How does this passage from Brownmiller contribute to a public conversation about sexuality? What is thought provoking about this passage? How does it cause you to view sex differently?

13 Evaluation Arguments

X Is (Is Not) a Good Y

CASE 1

A young engineer has advanced to the level of a design group leader. She is now being considered for promotion to a management position. Her present supervisor is asked to write a report evaluating her as a prospective manager. He is asked to pay particular attention to four criteria: technical competence, leadership, interpersonal skills, and communication skills.

CASE 2

The federal government has long contemplated reforming the federal tax system. Many competing models have been proposed, each with characteristic strengths and weaknesses. How can one evaluate a tax system? What criteria should be applied? Murray Weidenbaum, an economic analyst for the *Christian Science Monitor,* proposed six criteria. The tax system, he said, should (1) be fair to the average taxpayer, (2) be understandable to the average tax payer, (3) eliminate costly loopholes, (4) promote savings and investment, (5) make it easier to start a new business, and (6) foster a strong, sustainable economy. According to Weidenbaum, any tax system that meets these criteria would be vastly superior to our present system.*

---

*Murray Weidenbaum, "How to Reform the Federal Tax System: Just the Basics, Please," *Christian Science Monitor* 18 July 1996.

AN OVERVIEW OF
EVALUATION ARGUMENTS

In our roles as citizens and professionals we are continually expected to make difficult evaluations, to defend them, and even to persuade others to accept them. Often we will defend our judgments orally—in committees making hiring and promotion decisions, in management groups deciding which of several marketing plans to adopt, or at parent advisory meetings evaluating the success of school policies. Sometimes, too, we will be expected to put our arguments in writing.

Practice in thinking systematically about the process of evaluation, then, is valuable experience. In this chapter we focus on evaluation arguments of the type "X is (is not) a good Y" or "X is good (bad)" and on the strategy needed for conducting such arguments.* In Chapter 15, we will return to evaluation arguments to examine in more detail some special problems raised by ethical issues.

CRITERIA-MATCH STRUCTURE
OF EVALUATION ARGUMENTS

An "X is (is not) a good Y" argument follows the same criteria-match structure that we examined in definitional arguments (see Chapter 10). A typical claim for such an argument has the following form:

X is (is not) a good Y because it meets (fails to meet) criteria A, B, and C.

The main structural difference between an evaluation argument and a definition argument involves the Y term. In a definition argument, one argues whether a particular Y term is the correct class in which to place X. (Does this swampy area qualify as a *wetland*?) In an evaluation argument, we know the Y term—that is, what class to put X into (Dr. Choplogic is a *teacher*)—but we don't know whether X is a good or bad instance of that class. (Is Dr. Choplogic a *good* teacher?) As in definition arguments, warrants specify the criteria to be used for the evaluation, whereas the stated reasons and grounds assert that X meets these criteria.

Let's look at an example that, for the sake of illustration, asserts just one criterion for "good" or "bad." (Most arguments will, of course, develop several criteria.)

ENTHYMEME:	Computer-aided instruction (CAI) is an effective teaching method because it encourages self-paced learning. (The complete argument would develop other reasons also.)

---

*In addition to the contrasting words *good/bad*, a number of other evaluative terms involve the same kinds of thinking: *effective/ineffective, successful/unsuccessful, workable/unworkable,* and so forth. Throughout this chapter, terms such as these can be substituted for *good/bad*.

CLAIM:	Computer-aided instruction is an effective teaching method.
STATED REASON:	Computer-aided instruction encourages self-paced learning.
GROUNDS:	evidence that CAI encourages self-paced learning; examples of different learners working at different paces
WARRANT (CRITERION):	Self-paced learning is an effective teaching method.
BACKING:	explanations of why self-paced learning is effective; research studies or testimonials showing effectiveness of self-pacing
CONDITIONS OF REBUTTAL:	*Attacking stated reason and grounds:* Perhaps students don't really pace themselves in CAI.
	Attacking the warrant and backing: Perhaps self-paced learning isn't any more effective than other methods; perhaps the disadvantages of other features of CAI outweigh the value of self-pacing.

As this Toulmin schema shows, the writer needs to show that self-paced learning is an effective teaching method (the warrant or criterion) and that computer-aided instruction meets this criterion (the stated reason and grounds—the match argument).

GENERAL STRATEGY FOR EVALUATION ARGUMENTS

The general strategy for evaluation arguments is to establish criteria and then to argue that X meets or does not meet the criteria. In writing your argument, you have to decide whether your audience is likely to accept your criteria. If you want to argue, for example, that pit bulls do not make good pets because they are potentially vicious, you can assume that most readers will share your assumption that viciousness is bad. Likewise, if you want to praise the new tax bill because it cuts out tax cheating, you can probably assume readers agree that tax cheating is bad.

Often, however, selecting and defending your criteria are the most difficult parts of a criteria-match argument. For example, people who own pit bulls because they *want* a vicious dog for protection may not agree that viciousness is bad. In this case, you would need to argue that another kind of dog, such as a German shepherd or a Doberman pinscher would make a better choice than a pit bull or that the bad consequences of owning a vicious dog outweigh the benefits. Several kinds of difficulties in establishing criteria are worth discussing in more detail.

The Problem of Standards:
What's Commonplace or What's Ideal?

To get a sense of this problem, consider again Young Person's archetypal argument with Parent about her curfew (see Chapter 1). She originally argued that staying out until 2 A.M. is fair "because all the other kids' parents let their kids stay out late," to which Parent might respond: "Well, *ideally*, all the other parents should not let their kids stay out that late." Young Person based her criterion for fairness on what is *commonplace*; her standards arose from common practices of a social group. Parent, however, argued from what is *ideal*, basing her or his criteria on some external standard that transcends social groups.

We experience this dilemma in various forms throughout our lives. It is the conflict between absolutes and cultural relativism, between written law and customary practice. There is hardly an area of human experience that escapes the dilemma: Is it fair to get a ticket for going 70 mph on a 65-mph freeway when most of the drivers go 70 mph or higher? Is it better for high schools to pass out free contraceptives to students because the students are having sex anyway (what's *commonplace*), or is it better not to pass them out in order to support abstinence (what's *ideal*)? When you select criteria for an evaluation argument, you may well have to choose one side or the other of this dilemma, arguing for what is ideal or for what is commonplace. Neither position should be seen as necessarily better than the other; common practice may be corrupt just as surely as ideal behavior may be impossible.

The Problem of Mitigating Circumstances

When confronting the dilemma raised by the "commonplace" versus the "ideal," we sometimes have to take into account circumstances as well as behavior. In particular, we have the notion of *mitigating* circumstances, or circumstances that are extraordinary or unusual enough to cause us to change our standard measure of judgment. Ordinarily it is wrong to be late for work or to miss an exam. But what if your car had a flat tire?

When you argue for mitigating circumstances as a reason for modifying judgment in a particular case, you are arguing against the conditions of both common behavior and ideal behavior as the proper criterion for judgment. Thus, when you make such an argument, you will likely assume an especially heavy burden of proof. People assume the rightness of usual standards of judgment unless there are compelling arguments for abnormal circumstances.

The Problem of Choosing
between Two Goods or Two Bads

Not all arguments of value, of course, clearly deal with bad and good. Some deal with choosing between two bads or two goods. Often we are caught between a rock and a hard place. Should we cut pay or cut people? Put our parents in a nursing home or let them stay at home where they have become a danger to themselves? In such cases one has to weigh conflicting criteria, knowing that the choices are too much alike—either both bad or both good.

The Problem of Seductive Empirical Measures

The need to make distinctions among relative goods or relative bads has led many persons to seek quantifiable criteria that can be weighed mathematically. Thus we use grade point averages to select scholarship winners, MCAT scores to decide who gets into medical school, and student evaluation scores to decide which professor gets the University Teaching Award.

In some cases, such empirical measures can be quite acceptable. But they can be dangerous if they don't adequately measure the value of the people or things they purportedly evaluate. (Some people would argue that they *never* adequately measure anything significant.) To illustrate the problem further, consider the problems of relying on grade point average as a criterion for employment. Many employers rely heavily on grades when hiring college graduates. But according to every major study of the relationship between grades and **work** achievement, grades are about as reliable as palm reading when it comes to predicting life success. Why do employers continue to rely so heavily on grades? Clearly because it is so easy to classify job applicants according to a single empirical measure that appears to rank order everyone along the same scale.

The problem with empirical measures, then, is that they seduce us into believing that complex judgments can be made mathematically, thus rescuing us from the messiness of alternative points of view and conflicting criteria. Empirical measures seem extremely persuasive next to written arguments that try to qualify and hedge and raise questions. We suggest, however, that a fair evaluation of any X might require such hedging.

The Problem of Cost

A final problem that can crop up in evaluations is cost. In comparing an X to others of its kind, we may find that on all the criteria we can develop, X comes out on top. X is the best of all possible Ys. But if X costs too much, we have to rethink our evaluation.*

If we're looking to hire a new department head at Median State University, and the greatest scholar in the field, a magnificent teacher, a regular dynamo of diplomacy, says she'll come—for a hundred Gs a year—we'll probably have to withdraw our offer. Whether the costs are expressed in dollars or personal dis-

---

*We can avoid this problem somewhat by placing items into different classes on the basis of cost. For example, a Mercedes may come out far ahead of a Hyundai, but the more relevant evaluative question to ask is "How does a Mercedes compare to a Cadillac?"

comfort or moral repugnance or some other terms, our final evaluation of X must take cost into account, however elusive that cost might be.

HOW TO DETERMINE CRITERIA
FOR YOUR ARGUMENT

Now that we have explored some of the difficulties you may encounter in establishing and defending criteria for your evaluation of X, let's turn to the practical problem of trying to determine criteria themselves. How do you go about finding the criteria you'll need for distinguishing a good teacher from a poor teacher, a good movie from a bad movie, a successful manager from an unsuccessful manager, a healthy diet from an unhealthy diet, and so forth?

Step 1: Determine the Category in Which
the Object Being Evaluated Belongs

In determining the quality or value of any given X, you must first figure out what your standard of comparison is. If, for example, you asked one of your professors to write you a letter of recommendation for a summer job, what class of things should the professor put you into? Is he or she supposed to evaluate you as a student? a leader? a worker? a storyteller? a party animal? or what? This is an important question because the criteria for excellence in one class (student) may be very different from criteria for excellence in another class (party animal).

To write a useful letter, your professor should consider you first as a member of the general class "summer job holder" and base her evaluation of you on criteria relevant to that class. To write a truly effective letter, however, your professor needs to consider your qualifications in the context of the smallest applicable class of candidates: not "summer job holder," but "law office intern" or "highway department flagperson" or "golf course groundsperson." Clearly, each of these subclasses has very different criteria for excellence that your professor needs to address.

We thus recommend placing X into the smallest relevant class because of the apples-and-oranges law. That is, to avoid giving a mistaken rating to a perfectly good apple, you need to make sure you are judging an apple under the class "apple" and not under the next larger class "fruit" or a neighboring class "orange." And to be even more precise, you may wish to evaluate your apple in the class "eating apple" as opposed to "pie apple" because the latter class is supposed to be tarter and the former class juicier and sweeter.

Obviously, there are limits to this law. For example, the smallest possible class of apples would contain only one member—the one being evaluated. At that point, your apple is both the best and the worst member of its class, and evaluation of it is meaningless. Also, we sometimes can't avoid apples-and-oranges comparisons because they are thrust on us by circumstances, tradition, or some other factor. Thus the Academy Award judges selecting "best movie" aren't allowed to distinguish between "great big box office hits" and "serious little films that make socially significant points."

Step 2: Determine the Purpose
or Function of This Class

Once you have located X in its appropriate class, you should next determine what the purpose or function of this class is. Let's suppose that the summer job you are applying for is tour guide at the city zoo. The function of a tour guide is to make people feel welcome, to give them interesting information about the zoo, to make their visit pleasant, and so forth. Consequently, you wouldn't want your professor's evaluation to praise your term paper on Napoleon Bonaparte or your successful synthesis of some compound in your chemistry lab. Rather, the professor should highlight your dependability, your neat appearance, your good speaking skills, and your ability to work with groups. But if you were applying for graduate school, then your term paper on Bonaparte or your chem lab wizardry would be relevant. In other words, the professor has to evaluate you according to the class "tour guide," not "graduate student," and the criteria for each class derive from the purpose or function of the class.

Let's take another example. Suppose that you are the chair of a committee charged with evaluating the job performance of Lillian Jones, director of the admissions office at Clambake College. Ms. Jones has been a controversial manager because several members of her staff have filed complaints about her management style. In making your evaluation, your first step is to place Ms. Jones into an appropriate class, in this case, the general class "manager," and then the more specific class "manager of an admissions office at a small, private college." You then need to identify the purpose or function of these classes. You might say that the function of the general class "managers" is to "oversee actual operations of an organization so that the organization meets its goals as harmoniously and efficiently as possible," whereas the function of the specific class "manager of an admissions office at a small, private college" is "the successful recruitment of the best students possible."

Step 3: Determine Criteria Based
on the Purposes or Function
of the Class to Which X Belongs

Once you've worked out the purposes of the class, you are ready to work out the criteria by which you judge all members of the class. Criteria for judgment will be based on those features of Y that help it achieve the purposes of its class. For example, once you determine the purpose and function of the position filled by Lillian Jones, you can develop a list of criteria for managerial success:

1. Criteria related to "efficient operation"
   - articulates priorities and goals for the organization
   - is aggressive in achieving goals
   - motivates fellow employees
   - is well organized, efficient, and punctual
   - is articulate and communicates well

2. Criteria related to "harmonious operation"
   - creates job satisfaction for subordinates
   - is well groomed, sets good example of professionalism
   - is honest, diplomatic in dealing with subordinates
   - is flexible in responding to problems and special concerns of staff members

3. Criteria related to meeting specific goals of a college admissions office
   - creates a comprehensive recruiting program
   - demonstrates that recruiting program works

Step 4: Give Relative Weightings to the Criteria

Even though you have established criteria, you must still decide which of the criteria are most important. In the case of Lillian Jones, is it more important that she bring in lots of students to Clambake College or that she create a harmonious, happy office? These sorts of questions are at the heart of many evaluative controversies. Thus a justification for your weighting of criteria may well be an important part of your argument.

DETERMINING WHETHER X MEETS THE CRITERIA

Once you've established your criteria, you've got to figure out how well X meets them. You proceed by gathering evidence and examples. The success of the recruiting program at Clambake College can probably be measured empirically, so you gather statistics about applications to the college, SAT scores of applicants, number of acceptances, academic profiles of entering freshmen, and so forth. You might then compare those statistics to those compiled by Ms. Jones's predecessor or to her competitors at other, comparable institutions.

You can also look at what the recruiting program actually does—the number of recruiters, the number of high school visitations, the quality of admissions brochures and other publications. You can also look at Ms. Jones in action, searching for specific incidents or examples that illustrate her management style. For example, you can't measure a trait such as diplomacy empirically, but you can find specific instances where the presence or absence of this trait was demonstrated. You could turn to examples where Ms. Jones may or may not have prevented a potentially divisive situation from occurring or where she offered or failed to offer encouragement at psychologically the right moment to keep someone from getting demoralized. As with criteria-match arguments in definition, one must provide examples of how the X in question meets each of the criteria that have been set up.

Your final evaluation of Ms. Jones, then, might include an overview of her strengths and weaknesses along the various criteria you have established. You might say that Ms. Jones has done an excellent job with recruitment (an assertion you can support with data on student enrollments over the last five years) but was relatively poor at keeping the office staff happy (as evidenced by employee complaints, high turnover, and your own observations of her rather abrasive management style). Nevertheless, your final recommendation might be to retain Ms. Jones for another three-year contract because you believe that an excellent recruiting record is the most important criterion for her position at Clambake. You might justify this heavy weighting of recruiting on the grounds that the institution's survival depends on its ability to attract adequate numbers of good students.

FOR CLASS DISCUSSION

The following small-group exercise can be accomplished in one or two class hours. It gives you a good model of the process you will need to go through in order to write your own evaluation essay. Working in small groups, suppose that you are going to evaluate a controversial member of one of the following classes:

    a. a teacher
    b. a political figure
    c. an athlete
    d. a school newspaper or school policy
    e. a play or film or Web site
    f. a recent Supreme Court decision
    g. a rock singer or group or MTV video
    h. a dorm or living group
    i. a restaurant or college hangout
    j. an X of your choice

1. Choose a controversial member within one of these classes as the specific person, thing, or event you are going to evaluate (Professor Choplogic, the Wild Dog Bar, Eminem, and so forth).

2. Narrow the general class by determining the smallest relevant class to which your X belongs (from "athlete" to "basketball guard"; from "college hangout" to "college hangout for people who want to hold late-night bull sessions").

3. Make a list of the purposes or functions of that class, and then list the criteria that a good member of that class would have to have in order to accomplish the purposes.

4. If necessary, rank-order your criteria.

5. Evaluate your X by matching X to each of the criteria.

WRITING AN EVALUATION ARGUMENT

WRITING ASSIGNMENT FOR CHAPTER 13

Write an argument in which you try to change someone's mind about the value of X. The X you choose should be controversial or at least problematic. While you would be safe in arguing that a Mercedes is a good car or that smoking is bad for your health, your claim would be unlikely to surprise anyone. By *controversial* or *problematic*, we mean that people are likely to disagree with your evaluation or X, that they are surprised at your evaluation, or that you are somehow opposing the common or expected view of X. By choosing a controversial or problematic X, you will be able to focus on a clear issue. Somewhere in your essay you should summarize alternative views and either refute them or concede to them (see Chapter 8).

Note that this assignment asks you to do something different from a typical movie review, restaurant review, or product review in a consumer magazine. Many reviews are simply informational or analytical; the writer's purpose is to describe the object or event being reviewed and explain its strengths and weaknesses. In contrast, your purpose here is persuasive. You must change someone's mind about the evaluation of X.

Exploring Ideas

Evaluation issues are all around us, sometimes in subtle forms. The most frequent evaluation arguments occur when we place an X in its most common or expected class: Was Bill Clinton a good president? Is *Ally McBeal* a good TV drama? But more interesting and provocative evaluation issues can sometimes arise if we place X in a different class: Was Bill Clinton a good liberal? Is *Ally McBeal* a good feminist drama? Does *Ally McBeal* portray legal issues effectively? If you think again of the various communities to which you belong, chances are each community has disagreements over the evaluation of many Xs.

If no ideas come immediately to mind, try creating idea maps with spokes chosen from among the following categories: *people* (athletes, political leaders, musicians, clergypeople, entertainers, businesspeople); *science and technology* (weapons systems, word-processing programs, spreadsheets, automotive advancements, treatments for diseases); *media* (a newspaper, a magazine or journal, a TV program, a radio station, an advertisement); *government and world affairs* (an economic policy, a Supreme Court decision, a law or legal practice, a government custom or practice, a foreign policy); *the arts* (a movie, a book, a building, a painting, a piece of music); *your college or university* (a course, a teacher, a textbook, a curriculum, an administrative policy, the financial aid system); *world of work* (a job, a company operation, a dress policy, a merit pay system, a hiring policy, a supervisor); or any other categories of your choice.

Then brainstorm possibilities for controversial Xs that might fit into the categories on your map. As long as you can imagine disagreement about how to evaluate X, you have a potentially good topic for this assignment.

Once you have found an issue and have taken a tentative position on it, explore your ideas by freewriting your responses to the ten guided tasks in Chapter 3, (pp. 70–71).

Organizing an Evaluation Argument

As you write a draft, you might find useful the following prototypical structures for evaluation arguments. Of course, you can always alter these plans if another structure better fits your material.

Plan 1 (Criteria and Match in Separate Sections)

- Introduce the issue by showing disagreements about how to evaluate a problematic X (Is X a good Y?).
- State your claim.
- Present your criteria for evaluating members of class Y.
  State and develop criterion 1.
  State and develop criterion 2.
  Continue with the rest of your criteria.
- Summarize and respond to possible objections to your criteria.
- Restate your claim, asserting that X is (is not) a good member of class Y.
  Apply criterion 1 to your case.
  Apply criterion 2 to your case.
  Continue the match argument.

- Summarize and respond to possible objections to your match argument.
- Conclude your argument.

Plan 2 (Criteria and Match Interwoven)

- Introduce the issue by showing disagreements about how to evaluate a problematic X (Is X a good Y?).
- Present your claim.
  State criterion 1 and argue that your X meets (does not meet) this criterion.
  State criterion 2 and argue that your X meets (does not meet) this criterion.
  Continue with criteria-match sections for additional criteria.
- Summarize opposing views.
- Refute or concede to opposing views.
- Conclude your argument.

Revising Your Draft

Once you have written a rough draft, your goal is to make it clearer and more persuasive to your audience. Where might your audience question your claim, demand more evidence, or ask for further clarification and support of your criteria? One way to evaluate your draft's persuasiveness is to analyze it using the Toulmin schema.

Imagine that you are on a committee to determine whether to retain or fire Ms. Lillian Jones, the director of admissions at Clambake College (see details about Ms. Jones in our example on pages 286–88). You have been asked to submit a written argument to the committee. Here is how you might use Toulmin to suggest revision strategies for making your argument more persuasive (your thinking processes are indicated in italics):

ENTHYMEME:	Despite some weaknesses, Ms. Jones has been a good manager of the admissions office at Clambake College because her office's recruiting record is excellent.
CLAIM:	Ms. Jones has been a good manager of the admissions office at Clambake College.
STATED REASON:	Her office's recruitment record is excellent.
GROUNDS:	*My draft has statistical data showing the good results of Ms. Jones's recruiting efforts. Can I get more data? Do I need more data? Would other grounds be useful such as testimony from other college officials or comparison with other schools?*

WARRANT:	Successful recruitment is the most important criterion for rating job performance of the director of admissions.
BACKING:	*In my draft I don't have any backing. I am just assuming that everyone will agree that recruiting is the most important factor. But a lot of people are angry at Ms. Jones for personnel problems in her office. How can I argue that her recruitment record is the most important criterion? I could mention that maintaining a happy, harmonious staff serves no purpose if we have no students. I could remind people of how much tuition dollars drive our budget; if enrollments go down, we're in big trouble.*
CONDITIONS OF REBUTTAL:	*How could committee members who don't like Ms. Jones question my reason and grounds? Could they show that her recruitment record isn't that good? Might they argue that plenty of people in the office could do the same good job of recruitment—after all, Clambake sells itself— without stirring up any of the personnel problems that Ms. Jones has caused? Maybe I should add to the draft the specific things that Ms. Jones has done to improve recruiting.*
	Will anyone attack my warrant by arguing that staff problems in Ms. Jones's office are severe enough that we ought to search for a new director? How can I counter that argument?
QUALIFIER:	*I will need to qualify my general rating of an excellent record by acknowledging Ms. Jones's weaknesses in staff relations. But I want to be definite in saying that recruitment is the most important criterion and that she should definitely keep her job because she meets this criterion fully.*

QUESTIONING AND CRITIQUING AN EVALUATION ARGUMENT

To strengthen your draft of an evaluation argument, you can role-play a skeptic by asking the following questions:

Will a skeptic accept my criteria?   Many evaluative arguments are weak because the writers have simply assumed that readers will accept their criteria. Whenever your audience's acceptance of your criteria is in doubt, you will need to make your warrants clear and provide backing in their support.

Are my criteria based on the "smallest applicable class" for X?   For example, the film *The Blair Witch Project* will certainly be a failure if you evaluate it in the general class "movies," in which it would have to compete with *Citizen Kane* and other great classics. But if you evaluated it as a "horror film" or a "low-budget film," it would have a greater chance for success and hence of yielding an arguable evaluation.

Will a skeptic accept my general weighting of criteria?   Another vulnerable spot in an evaluation argument is the relative weight of the criteria. How much anyone weights a given criterion is usually a function of his or her own interests relative to the X in question. You should always ask whether some particular group affected by the quality of X might not have good reasons for weighting the criteria differently.

Will a skeptic question my standard of reference?   In questioning the criteria for judging X, we can also focus on the standard of reference used—what's commonplace versus what's ideal. If you have argued that X is bad because it doesn't live up to what's ideal, you can expect some readers to defend X on the basis of what's common. Similarly, if you argue that X is good because it is better than its competitors, you can expect some readers to point out how short it falls from what is ideal.

Will a skeptic criticize my use of empirical measures?   The tendency to mistake empirical measures for criteria is a common one that any critic of an argument should be aware of. As we have discussed earlier, what's most measurable isn't always significant when it comes to assessing the essential traits needed to fulfill whatever function X is supposed to fulfill. A 95-mph fastball is certainly an impressive empirical measure of a pitcher's ability—but if the pitcher doesn't get batters out, that measure is a misleading gauge of performance.

Will a skeptic accept my criteria but reject my match argument?   The other major way of testing an evaluation argument is to anticipate how readers might object to your stated reasons and grounds. Will readers challenge you by finding sampling errors in your data or otherwise find that you used evidence selectively? For example, if you think your opponents will emphasize Lillian Jones's abrasive management style much more heavily than you did, you may be able to undercut their arguments by finding counterexamples that show Ms. Jones acting diplomatically. Be prepared to counter objections to your grounds.

READINGS

Our first reading, by student writer Sam Isaacson, was written for the assignment on page 289.

Would Legalization of Gay Marriage Be Good for the Gay Community?

Sam Isaacson (student)

1 For those of us who have been out for a while, nothing seems shocking about a gay pride parade. Yet at this year's parade, I was struck by the contrast between two groups—the float for the Toys in Babeland store (with swooning drag queens and leather-clad, whip-wielding, topless dykes) and the Northwest chapters of Integrity and Dignity (Episcopal and Catholic organizations for lesbians and gays), whose marchers looked as conservative as the congregation of any American church.

2 These stark differences in dress are representative of larger philosophical differences in the gay community. At stake is whether or not we gays and lesbians should act "normal." Labeled as deviants by many in straight society, we're faced with various opposing methods of response. One option is to insist that we are normal and work to integrate gays into the cultural mainstream. Another response is to form an alternative gay culture with its own customs and values; this culture would honor deviancy in response to a society which seeks to label some as "normal" and some as "abnormal." For the purposes of this paper I will refer to those who favor the first response as "integrationists" and those who favor the second response as "liberationists." Politically, this ideological clash is most evident in the issue of whether legalization of same-sex marriage would be good for the gay community. Nearly all integrationists would say yes, but many liberationists would say no. My belief is that while we must take the objections of the liberationists seriously, legalization of same-sex marriage would benefit both gays and society in general.

3 Let us first look at what is so threatening about gay marriage to many liberationists. Many liberationists fear that legalizing gay marriage will reinforce current social pressures that say monogamous marriage is the normal and right way to live. In straight society, those who choose not to marry are often viewed as self-indulgent, likely promiscuous, and shallow—and it is no coincidence these are some of the same stereotypes gays struggle against. If gays begin to marry, married life will be all the more the norm and subject those outside of marriage to even greater marginalization. As homosexuals, liberationists argue, we should be particularly sensitive to the tyranny of the majority. Our sympathies should lie with the deviants—the transsexual, the fetishist, the drag queen, and the leather-dyke. By choosing marriage, gays take the easy route into "normal" society; we not only abandon the sexual minorities of our community, we strengthen society's narrow notions of what is "normal" and thereby further confine both straights and gays.

4 Additionally, liberationists worry that by winning the right to marry gays and lesbians will lose the distinctive and positive characteristics of gay culture. Many gay writers have commented on how as a marginalized group gays have been forced to create different forms of relationships that often allow for a greater and often more fulfilling range of life experiences. Writer Edmund White, for instance, has observed that there is a greater fluidity in the relationships of gays than straights. Gays, he says, are more likely than straights to stay friends with old lovers, are more likely to form close friendships outside the romantic relationship, and are generally less likely to become compartmentalized into isolated

couples. It has also been noted that gay relationships are often characterized by more equality and better communication than are straight relationships. Liberationists make the reasonable assumption that if gays win the right to marry they will be subject to the same social pressure to marry that straights are subject to. As more gays are pressured into traditional life patterns, liberationists fear the gay sensibility will be swallowed up by the established attitudes of the broader culture. All of society would be the poorer if this were to happen.

I must admit that I concur with many of the arguments of the liberationists that I have 5 outlined above. I do think if given the right, gays would feel social pressure to marry; I agree that gays should be especially sensitive to the most marginalized elements of society; and I also agree that the unique perspectives on human relationships that the gay community offers should not be sacrificed. However, despite these beliefs, I feel that legalizing gay marriage would bring valuable benefits to gays and society as a whole.

First of all, I think it is important to put the attacks the liberationists make on marriage 6 into perspective. The liberationist critique of marriage claims that marriage in itself is a harmful institution (for straights as well as gays) because it needlessly limits and normalizes personal freedom. But it seems clear to me that marriage in some form is necessary for the well-being of society. Children need a stable environment in which to be raised. Studies have shown that children whose parents divorce often suffer long-term effects from the trauma. Studies have also shown that people tend to be happier in stable long-term relationships. We need to have someone to look over us when we're old, when we become depressed, when we fall ill. All people, gay or straight, parents or nonparents, benefit from the stabilizing force of marriage.

Second, we in the gay community should not be too quick to overlook the real bene- 7 fits that legalizing gay marriage will bring. We are currently denied numerous legal rights of marriage that the straight community enjoys: tax benefits, insurance benefits, inheritance rights, and the right to have a voice in medical treatment or funeral arrangements for a dying partner.

Further, just as important as the legal impacts of being denied the right to marriage is 8 the socially symbolic weight this denial carries. We are sent the message that while gay sex in the privacy of one's home will be tolerated, gay love will not be respected. We are told that it is not important to society whether we form long-term relationships or not. We are told that we are not worthy of forming families of our own. By gaining the same recognitions by the state of our relationships and all the legal and social weight that recognition carries, the new message will be that gay love is just as meaningful as straight love.

Finally, let me address what I think is at the heart of the liberationist argument against 9 marriage—the fear of losing social diversity and our unique gay voice. The liberationists are wary of society's normalizing forces. They fear that if gays win the right to marry gay relationships will simply become imitations of straight relationships—the richness gained through the gay experience will be lost. I feel, however, this argument unintentionally plays into the hands of conservatives. Conservatives argue that marriage is, by definition, the union between man and woman. As a consequence, to the broad culture gay marriage can only be a mockery of marriage. As gays and lesbians we need to argue that conservatives are imposing arbitrary standards on what is normal and not normal in society. To fight the conservative agenda, we must suggest instead that marriage is, in essence, a contract of love and commitment between two people. The liberationists, I think, unwittingly feed into conservative identification and classification by pigeonholing gays as outsiders. Reacting against social norms is simply another way of being held hostage by them.

10   We need to understand that the gay experience and voice will not be lost by gaining the right to marry. Gays will always be the minority by simple biological fact and this will always color the identity of any gay person. But we can only make our voice heard if we are seen as full-fledged members of society. Otherwise we will remain an isolated and marginalized group. And only when we have the right to marry will we have any say in the nature and significance of marriage as an institution. This is not being apologetic to the straight culture, but is a demand that we not be excluded from the central institutions of Western culture. We can help merge the fluidity of gay relationships with the traditionally more compartmentalized married relationship. Further, liberationists should realize that the decision *not* to marry makes a statement only if one has the ability to choose marriage. What would be most radical, most transforming, is two women or two men joined together in the eyes of society.

Critiquing "Would Legalization of Gay Marriage Be Good for the Gay Community?"

1. Who is the audience that Sam Isaacson addresses in this argument?

2. Ordinarily when we think of persons opposing gay marriage, we imagine socially conservative heterosexuals. However, Sam spends little time addressing the anti-gay marriage arguments of straight society. Rather, he addresses the anti-marriage arguments made by "liberationist" gay people. What are these arguments? How well does Sam respond to them?

3. What are the criteria Sam uses to argue that legalizing gay marriage would be good for the gay community?

4. How persuasive do you think Sam's argument is to the various audiences he addresses?

Our second reading, another student essay also written for the assignment on page 289, evaluates the Spice Girl phenomenon of the late 1990s. At the time this essay was written, Ginger Spice had just left the band. Critics predicted a quick decline of Spice Girl popularity.

The Spice Girls: Good at Marketing but Not Good for Their Market

Pat Inglenook (student)

1   When my eight-year-old sister asked for a Baby Spice talking doll (It plays Baby Spice's voice saying "In my bed I've got two teddies, a rabbit, two dollies," and "Fantastic. I love it."), and my eleven-year-old sister and her friends seemed to be dancing to Spice Girl CDs

all the time, I started to wonder about this strange relationship between capitalism and culture in the late 1990s. What is it about the Spice Girls—Ginger Spice, Posh Spice, Baby Spice, Scary Spice, and Sporty Spice—that has attracted mobs of screaming, hysterical girls, aged 7–14, and created for the Spice Girls a multi-million-dollar industry almost overnight? Clearly, my two sisters and their friends with their three-inch Spice Girl figurines ($3.99 each) and their seven-inch Spice Girl dolls ($7.99 each) and their Spice Girl Hair Play set, Nail Salon set, and Tattoo Graphix set ($9.97 each), to say nothing of the CDs ($16.85 each), have helped to support this industry. But why? As I have watched my sisters I have wondered, What is the fascination here? The Spice Girls do wear hip, hot-looking outfits, but the group's music is bubblegum for the brain. One critic says that the Spice Girl music is an "ideal hollow-commodity for a world increasingly obsessed with 'low': low-fat, low-sodium, low-calorie, low-IQ" (Crumley). Neither do they fare well in the category "actresses," where they won the anti-Oscar "Golden Raspberry Award" as "Worst Actress" for 1998. According to the judge, "They have the talent of one bad actress between them" ("Shiteworld").

So if we place the Spice Girls in the categories "musician" or "actress," they fail miserably. But if we evaluate them in the category "marketers," they obviously excel. They are excellent marketers because, in targeting a specific audience of preteen girls, they have shrewdly created an image that appeals to that audience's interests and psychological desires. 2

Their first mark of excellence is that they understand girl psychology, which wants sexy fashion without sex. As any good marketer knows, the younger part of the Spice Girls' target audience values Barbie dolls, and so the Spice Girls created a Barbie image of décolletage and fashion without any Madonna-like interest in real sex. In their film *Spice World,* the girls look music-video sexy, but they aren't seeking sex. When one of the directors tries to put some buff male dancers on the stage, the girls do an "Ick, Boys" routine and mock them. No real boy friends intrude on this Barbie doll world. 3

Instead of sex, the Spice Girls value an endless slumber party where giggling girls share secrets. In *Spice World,* they bond together like fun-seeking little girls on vacation from the grown-up world of responsibility represented by their manager. In this intimate little girl world, they look out for each other like Care Bears. They are even willing to miss their concert date to stay with their friend who is having a baby. 4

Another example of their marketing shrewdness is the way that the Spice Girls appeal to individualism and the belief that any self has many sides. Just as it was a calculatingly clever marketing move for the Barbie people to create an astronaut Barbie, a teacher Barbie, and a doctor Barbie, so was it brilliant to give each Spice Girl a different personality type and a different style of hot, sexy clothes. On any given day, your typical ten-year-old girl can live out her baby side, her posh side, her sporty side, her scary side, and her fun-loving Ginger side. 5

But their shrewdest marketing move is to create an illusion that a girl can be both a sex object and a liberated woman. Popular culture today pummels young girls with two contradictory messages. First, it tells girls to make themselves objects of sexual desire by being consumers of beauty and glamour products and purchasers of fashion magazines. Conversely, it tells girls to be liberated women, fully equal to men, with men's freedom and power and array of career choices. The Spice Girls, with their "girl power" logos on midriff 6

T's worn over micro-skirts, send both messages simultaneously. Their girl power side is acted out in *Spice World* by their defiance of the male authority figures. For instance, they "steal" a boat and go for a frolicking excursion on a speedboat. Later in the movie, their "heroic" bus ride (a parody of James Bond pursuit scenes) shows the girls having another adventure and taking control of their lives. Even their rise from poverty to fame in a music culture dominated by men demonstrates girl power. Their object-of-sexual-desire side is portrayed constantly by their sexy clothes and dance routines. The effect is to urge young girls to become capitalist consumers of beauty products while believing they possess power as girls. Girls get the same illusion when they comb the hair of their astronaut Barbies.

7   Despite the overwhelming marketing success of the Spice Girls, I question whether monetary gain should be the main measure of this cultural product. Furthermore, although the Spice Girls sell themselves as models for young girls and appear to succeed, are they promoting models that can and should be imitated?

8   Some people would say that combining sexuality and girl power is good and beneficial. Critics of feminism often complain that hard-line feminists want women to give up beauty and sex appeal. These critics don't like that de-sexed view of women. They think a truly liberated woman should be able to use *all* her powers, and some of this power comes from her being a sex object. This view would say that beauty pageant contestants, topless dancers, and even prostitutes could be liberated women if they use their sexuality to get what they want and if they feel good about themselves. From this perspective, the Spice Girls use their sexuality in the name of liberation. This view perhaps led the United Nations to send Geri Halliwell (the former Ginger Spice) to be an ambassador of goodwill for the United Nations Population Fund to promote contraceptives in Third World countries ("Church Attacks" A18).

9   But to me this argument doesn't work. I think the Spice Girls are confusing, even bad, models for helping young girls integrate sexuality and liberation. The sex is voyeuristic only. The Spice Girls flaunt their sexuality but don't show any signs of establishing healthy adult relationships. The projected scene of married life in *Spice World* shows fat or pregnant housewives bored out of their skulls—no love, no husbands, no families. Equally strange is the childbirth scene where the Spice Girls seem to know nothing about female bodies. It is closer to a stork delivery than to the real thing: no messy water, blood, and umbilical cords. The cherubic, powdered baby pops out like toast from a toaster.

10   The Spice Girl image sends all kinds of mixed messages, urging preteens to become sex objects while remaining little girls. I'm surprised that parents aren't up in arms (but they are the ones, of course, who supply the money that drives the Spice enterprise). In a review of *Spice World* from *Screen It: Entertainment Reviews for Parents,* the reviewers rated the movie "mild" for sex/nudity (parents were concerned primarily about naked male butts in one scene), and under the criteria "topics to talk about" they found almost nothing in the movie that needs discussion with one's children. On the lookout for things like visible nipples, sex scenes, and violence, parents have failed to see the unhealthy, fragmented, and warped view of womanhood the Spice Girls project to their young audience. Their strange clashing mixture of sexuality and liberation promotes confusion, not health.

Near the end of *Spice World* the girls are stopped by a cop who aims to give them a   11
ticket for reckless driving. Undaunted, they turn to Baby Spice, who gives Daddy Policeman
her best I'm-a-sorry-little-girl smile, and his heart melts. Rather than face the consequences
of choice making in an adult world, Baby Spice knows just the right daddy-pleasing gesture
to make all their troubles go away. I grant that the Spice Girls are great at marketing themselves, but I don't think their product is good for their market. Maybe soon all the Spice
Girl dolls and CDs in my house will be given away like other outgrown, faddish toys. I hope
the next pop cultural sensation aimed at preteen girls has more wholesome substance than
this mixture of illusory independence, sexiness, and lollipops.

Works Cited

"Church Attacks Ex-Spice Girl's Sex-Education Tour." *Seattle Times* 15 June 1999: A18.

Crumley, Bruce. "Spice Invaders." *Culture* Kiosque 12 June 1997. Paris. 23 Aug. 1999 <http://www.culturekiosque.com/nouveau/comment/rhespice.htm>.

Rev. of *Spice World,* dir. Bob Spiers. *Screen It! Entertainment Reviews for Parents.* 12 Jan. 1998. 24 Aug. 1999 <http://www.screenit.com/movies/1998/spice_world.html>.

"Shiteworld: The Movies." *New Musical Express Online.* 23 Aug. 1999 <http://nme.com/newsdesk/19990222143334news.html>.

Critiquing "The Spice Girls: Good at Marketing but Not Good for Their Market"

1. Inglenook evaluates the Spice Girls in four different categories: musician, actress, marketer, and role model. Explain how each category requires different criteria for excellence.

2. What criteria does Inglenook use to argue that the Spice Girls are excellent marketers? What criteria does she use to argue that the Spice Girls are not good role models for preteen girls?

3. Why do you suppose that many parents have no objections to the Spice Girls and in fact encourage Spice Girl adoration by doling out the money for Spice Girls products? Similarly, why did the parents reviewing *Spice World* find it so mild and nonobjectionable? Do you think Inglenook does a good job of persuading her audience that the Spice Girls are a bad influence on preteen girls?

4. How effectively does Inglenook summarize and respond to alternative assessments of the Spice Girls?

Our third reading evaluates the B-2 stealth bomber, a highly controversial, in-credibly expensive Air Force plane that made its military debut in the air war against Yugoslavia during the Kosovo crisis. Carrying a crew of two persons, each plane costs $2.1 billion. With its radar-absorbing black paint and its flat sawtooth shape that deflects radar signals, the plane is nearly undetectable by enemy sur-veillance. In an introductory sidebar, the author, Paul Richter, writing for the *Los*

Angeles Times, states: "Once mocked as the Pentagon's ultimate boondoggle, the B-2 is suddenly looking like the answer to the kind of conflict the U.S. has faced in the Balkans and the Persian Gulf."

Stealth Bomber Proves Its Mettle

Paul Richter

1   KNOB KNOSTER, Mo.—Two years ago, an Air Force ground crew rolled a B-2 stealth bomber from a hanger here and hosed it down before a skeptical civilian audience to settle a question: Would an afternoon cloudburst melt the bomber's delicate skin and knock the plane out of the sky?

2   These days when the B-2 emerges from its shelter at Whitman Air Force Base, onlookers ponder a far different question: Is a plane once mocked by critics as the Pentagon's ultimate boondoggle about to become America's weapon of choice in the early 21st century?

3   The most expensive and controversial warplane ever built, the B-2 has undergone a stunning reversal of fortune with its combat debut in the air war against Yugoslavia. With its radar-evading capacity and huge payload, the bat-winged bomber is suddenly looking like the answer to the kind of military emergencies that the U.S. has encountered in the Balkans, the Persian Gulf and the terrorist training camps of Afghanistan.

4   With only 24 hours' notice and apparently minimal risk to its crew, the B-2 can accurately drop as many as 16 2,000-pound bombs on heavily guarded targets in any corner of the world. The B-1 bomber is faster, and the 37-year-old B-52 can carry more bombs, but the B-2's stealth qualities give the Air Force the ability to strike anywhere before the enemy knows an attack is underway.

Technological Success Story

5   Although some technical questions remain, the B-2 in many circumstances can strike with more speed and punch than the cruise missiles that have become the hallmark of the Clinton administration's approach to warfare.

6   Some military officers, including Air Force Lt. Gen. Michael Short, U.S. air commander in the Kosovo campaign, have called the B-2 and its all-weather, satellite-guided bombing system the greatest technology success story of Operation Allied Force. They are predicting that America's regional military commanders, who are cautious about using unproved systems and who delayed the B-2's debut for months, will now turn to it regularly.

7   Development of the B-2 began in 1981 in the early days of President Reagan's arms buildup. The Pentagon's objective was to acquire a heavy nuclear bomber that, barely visible to radar, could penetrate Soviet air defenses to destroy elusive mobile nuclear missiles.

8   The sleek plane, shaped like a boomerang, has a wingspan of 172 feet and a length of only 69 feet. Its tailless, horizontal design, radar-absorbing plastic composite skin and other features make it very hard to track with radar. It is also tough to find with sensors that pick up heat, sound or electromagnetic impulses.

The Toughest Targets

The B-2 was used from the first night of the airstrikes on Yugoslavia to smash well-protected and fixed targets, including air defenses that put other NATO planes at risk. 9

Flying in pairs on a 30-hour round-trip mission from Whitman Air Force Base 60 miles southeast of Kansas City, the B-2s smashed Yugoslav command bunkers, radar installations, communications sites, bridges, arms factories and other heavily defended targets. The B-2s were refueled in the air twice each way. 10

The B-2's mission was to "go in after the highest threat and the hardest targets," said Air Force Brig. Gen. Leroy Barnidge Jr., commander of the 509th Bomber Wing, which includes all the B-2s. 11

A major ingredient in the B-2's successful combat debut is a new technology that uses satellite guidance to direct bombs to their targets. Unlike laser munitions, which are disabled by clouds, these Joint Direct Attack Munitions can be dropped under any weather conditions. 12

As a result, the B-2s were sometimes the only bombers on the attack during frequent bouts of bad weather that hampered the air campaign through much of April. 13

Overall, the six B-2s used in the war flew about 50 missions, less than 1 percent of the total. But they dropped about 11 percent of the bombs used, nearly 700. 14

Stealth and Accuracy

Defense officials have declined to release a full list of the plane's targets. But they have disclosed that it was a B-2 that dropped three bombs on the Chinese Embassy in Belgrade, killing three people. 15

The blunder was not a mistake by the air crew but rather by NATO strike planners, who mistakenly thought they were striking a military supply center nearby. 16

The mission illustrates that the airplane was considered stealthy enough and accurate enough to be sent against sites in congested downtown Belgrade, where air defenses were formidable and the risk of unintended damage was high. 17

Andrew Krepinevitch, executive director of the Center for Strategic and Budgetary Assessments, a nonpartisan defense think tank, praises the B-2's performance in the Balkans but says the "jury is still out" on some key technological issues. 18

Also, some senior military officials say the Pentagon's regional commanders will be cautious in calling the B-2 into service because the cost of the plane is so high it is considered a "national asset." 19

"No one wants to be the first to lose a B-2," said one Pentagon planner. 20

The Bomber's Assets

Nevertheless, even some longtime critics acknowledge that the B-2's debut proved the plane has a combination of assets that will make it highly attractive to military leaders: 21

- It can be flown from the U.S. heartland, at a time when it is increasingly difficult to find forward bases for U.S. aircraft.

- With a turnaround time of 24 or more hours, it often can reach faraway targets faster than Tomahawk cruise missiles, which are carried on ships that sometimes take days to steam into position.

- And its radar-evading capacity, although not conclusively proved in the Kosovo air war, is doubted by few. Experts predict that the B-2's stealthiness will be valued more and more as politicians' tolerance for casualties declines.

22   The advent of the B-2, said William Arkin, an air-power expert, has now "really eclipsed the era of the cruise missile."

23   A key ingredient is the B-2's sophisticated radar targeting system, considered the best of its kind, that gives the pilots nearly photo-quality pictures of the targets they are about to hit. The pilots compare this information to spy-satellite images and correct the targeting data loaded into their bombs.

24   "The real capability is the fliers, and all the people who plan the mission," said Gen. Ronald Marcotte, the 8th Air Force commander who oversees all U.S. heavy bombers.

Pilots as Problem-Solvers

25   The 51 B-2 pilots are picked in a competitive selection process somewhat like the one used to choose astronauts. The Air Force does not want hot-dog fighter jocks piloting its B-2s; it is looking instead for sober fliers in their 30s.

26   Their most important skill is not what they can do with the joystick—there is little need to manually steer the highly automated B-2, even in combat, pilots said. Rather, the Air Force wants pilots with good judgment and analytical problem-solving skills.

27   During the airstrikes against Yugoslavia, the pilots often used their judgment to calibrate bomb fuses to destroy the intended targets without causing excessive collateral damage. Instead of setting the fuse to detonate the bomb several feet above ground, which would cause maximum destruction, pilots often delayed detonation for several milliseconds, to put off the explosion until the bomb's nose was buried in the ground.

28   The B-2's capabilities send a clear and powerful message to adversaries, said one B-2 pilot: "If the United States is angry enough, they can go anywhere in the world—you won't even know they're coming—to strike you."

Critiquing "Stealth Bomber Proves Its Mettle"

1. Critics of the military often attack the Pentagon's penchant for expensive weapons and runaway costs (jokes about thousand-dollar toilet seats and five-hundred-dollar hammers abound). The B-2 stealth bomber was bitterly opposed by critics because of its cost. Yet Richter argues that the plane may be worth it. What criteria does Richter use for his evaluation of the B-2? In your own words, summarize his argument.

2. How does Richter justify and defend these criteria? How do these criteria relate specifically to war in a post-Cold War era?

3. Theologians and philosophers raised questions about whether the war in Kosovo was a "just war." One of the questions raised was whether it was just that no NATO or U.S. soldiers were killed in the war. Two pilots, reasonably safe in a two-billion-dollar plane, could drop tons of explosives on the enemy. Such air-power meant that NATO could wage war without using ground troops, even though many critics of the war argued that early use of ground troops might have prevented much of the suffering of the Kosovo refugees. Why do you suppose that, in Richter's words, "politicians' tolerance for casualties" has declined? How might the presence of the B-2 bomber have contributed to the way the war was fought?

Our final reading, "Eight Is Too Many: The Case against the Octuplets," is by Dr. Ezekiel Emanuel, the chair of the department of clinical bioethics at the National Institute of Health. The public, he observes, is always fascinated by multiple births, praising the miracle of life and the heroism of the parents. Dr. Emanuel, writing for the *New Republic,* attempts to reverse that evaluation.

Eight Is Too Many: The Case against Octuplets

Dr. Ezekiel J. Emanuel

Just like the McCaughey septuplets of Iowa, whose first birthday recently made head- 1
lines in *People* magazine, the Chukwu octuplets of Texas have become a media spectacle. Daily bulletins detailing each child's respiratory status, ultrasound results, and other developments fill the papers—not just the tabloids, but respectable outlets like the *New York Times* and the *Washington Post,* as well. Inevitably, writers describe the eight live births in glowing terms—amazing, wonderful, even a miracle; they describe the mother as the brave survivor of adversity; they portray the hard-battling physicians as heroes and champions.

But what are we all celebrating? Modern reproductive technologies have brought the 2
miracle of children to many infertile couples, thereby producing enormous good. The McCaughey septuplets and Chukwu octuplets, however, represent too much of that good thing. They are the product of fertility technology misused—an error, not a wonder, and one that even the few public voices of skepticism seem not fully to appreciate.

First and most obvious, large multiple births lead to all sorts of medical problems, for 3
mothers and children alike. Nkem Chukwu had to stay in the hospital for months prior to delivery, on a bed that tilted her nearly upside down. It's too early to know how well her surviving children will fare (one died seven days after birth), but the odds do not favor them. Among children born prematurely and weighing just two pounds or less—the largest of the Chukwu infants weighed one pound, eleven ounces at birth—breathing difficulties, brain damage, and fluid imbalances are not rare.

The result is a comparatively high level of infant mortality and, in the survivors, long- 4
term complications. Studies of low-birth-weight children (not from multifetal pregnancies

but from premature births) have shown that approximately 20 percent have severe disabilities; among those weighing less than 750 grams (1.7 pounds) at birth, 50 percent have functional impairments. A recent study that followed these very small infants to school showed that up to 50 percent of them scored low on standardized intelligence tests, including 21 percent who were mentally retarded. In addition, nine percent had cerebral palsy, and 25 percent had severe vision problems. As a result, 45 percent ended up enrolling in special-education programs.

5   Equally important, but rarely articulated, are the emotional health risks children in multiple births face. Loving and raising children through the normal developmental milestones is enormously wonderful and rewarding. But it is also hard work. Raising children is not a sprint to a healthy birth but a marathon through variable terrain until the goal of independent adulthood. The real way to assess these miraculous pregnancies—indeed, any pregnancy—is whether they are ultimately good for children. Quite clearly, they are not.

6   Attending to the physical, emotional, intellectual, and social needs of children for 18 years is hard and demanding. For infants and toddlers there are the simple physical demands—feeding, changing diapers, bathing, chasing after them to prevent injuries. Then there are the emotional and intellectual demands—cuddling them, talking to them, responding meaningfully to their smiles and first words, reading books to them, playing with them and their toys, handling the tantrums, and so on. And, while the physical demands may lessen once children grow (although parents who often feel like chefs, maids, chauffeurs, and all-around gofers may disagree with that), the emotional and intellectual demands become more complex with time. Older children need help with homework, mediation of sibling rivalry, constructive discipline, support in the trials and tribulations of friendships, encouragement in their participation in sports and other activities, help in coping with losses and defeats, and guidance through the many pitfalls of adolescence.

7   It is challenging enough to balance the demands of one or two children of different ages and attend to their needs; it is simply not physically possible for two parents to do this successfully for seven children of the same age, even if one of the parents is a full-time caregiver. Regardless of the motivation, dedication, love, or stamina of these parents, the sheer limitations of time make it impossible for each of seven identically aged children to receive appropriate parental attention and affection.

8   Just ask yourself: Would you trade being born a healthy single or twin for being born one of the "miraculous" septuplets, even a healthy one? Most of us would probably say "no" because of parental attention we would have lost. And we would be right to think that way.

9   The McCaugheys' experience proves the point. They have been able to raise their septuplets for one year only because they can fall back on a veritable army of volunteers—scores of people with tightly coordinated schedules who assist in the food preparation, feeding, diapering, and care of the seven babies. Few families with quintuplets or more children can expect or rely on such community effort. (Indeed, a Washington, D.C., couple who recently bore quintuplets, had hardly any community help at all until some belated publicity highlighted the family's plight.) And, while the McCaugheys' community-wide effort appears to have worked for the first year of life, it's hardly a sure thing that the assistance will always be there. The first is the year when, despite the demands on time, parents are most

interchangeable and caregiving has the greatest, most unmitigated emotional rewards. The terrible twos and threes will try the patience and dedication of volunteers.

What's more, having multiple caregivers cannot fully substitute for parental time. While it's true that many children do just fine spending large amounts of time in paid day care, where multiple providers care for them, these children at least have the chance to go home and have one-on-one parental time spread among just a few siblings, of different ages. (Having multiple caregivers also becomes more problematic as the children grow, because of child-rearing styles that may differ from those of the parents, particularly on issues like discipline.) This is not possible in the McCaughey or Chukwu families, and it never will be. Spending just 20 minutes a day focusing on each individual child—hardly a lavish amount—will take nearly two and a half hours each day. When competing with sleep, meals, shopping, and all the other demands of basic existence for a family with septuplets, this focused time is likely to disappear.

Remember, too, that, while the McCaughey septuplets seem to have brought together a community to support their care, such children also impose significant costs on the community. It is now estimated that the hospital costs from birth to discharge (or death) for the Chukwu infants will exceed $2 million. And the health care costs don't stop after birth. Any complications—neurological, vision, or other problems—can drive the medical care costs sky-high. Plus, no one knows how much will be required for permanent problems that require ongoing special-education and other accommodations. Yes, there's health insurance. But health insurance exists to cover ill health and problems such as cancer, genetic defects, and accidents that are the result of random chance. The birth of octuplets, by contrast, is not a chance event; it is the result of deliberate actions (or inactions) by physicians, patients, and society. Remember, too, that financial resources are limited; money spent on octuplets is money not spent on other children with special health care and educational needs.

For these reasons, the standard of medical care is not to proceed with such large multiple births. But this raises legitimate ethical problems for many couples. The most common method for interrupting multiple pregnancies is "selective reduction"—that is, doctors abort some of the fetuses for the sake of the mother's health. Many people believe couples who agree to infertility treatments must not only be informed about—but should consent to—the potential need for selective reduction even before beginning the treatments. Yet this is clearly not an option for families like the McCaugheys and the Chukwus, who oppose abortion on religious grounds.

Fortunately, this issue doesn't have to be so morally knotty. In the usual treatment for problems with egg maturation and release (this is what both the McCaughey and Chukwu families were treated for), doctors prescribe drugs such as human menopausal gonadotropin (hMG) or Clomiphene (commonly known as Clomid) to stimulate egg development. Then they administer an additional drug, human chorionic gonadatropin (hCG), to induce ovulation. Using measurements of estrogen and ultrasound monitoring, physicians can assess the number of egg follicles developing in the ovaries. If they observe too many developing follicles, making the likelihood of multiple fertilizations high, physicians can withhold the drugs necessary to stimulate ovulation and advise against intercourse or withhold sperm injection until the next cycle, when they can go through the process again. To be sure, that treatment process can be a little more frustrating for aspiring parents. And many couples are reluctant to skip a cycle because it wastes thousands of dollars on the drugs and treatments, usually out of their own pockets. But carrying septuplets to term has costs, too.

14   In the end, new laws or regulations won't fix this problem. The real solution is leadership by the medical profession and by the media. Reproductive specialists who care for infertile couples are not simply passive technicians following the orders of the parents. They are engaged professionals guiding important technology that can create great joy—but also great pain. Professionalism requires deliberating with the parents about the goals and purposes of the treatments; doctors should draw upon their experience to advise and strongly recommend the best course to the parents, which is to avoid large multiple pregnancies.

15   And the media must stop glorifying the septuplets and octuplets. We live in an era that measures success in terms of quantity, that thinks bigger is necessarily better, where the best is defined by size. The best movie is the one that makes the most money; the best law firm is the one with the highest billings; the best painting is auctioned for the highest price; and the best book is the best-selling book. But, in this case, bigger may not be better—indeed, it may actually be worse. The true miracle of birth is the mysterious process by which the fusing of an egg and a sperm can create in just nine months the complex organism that is an infant with the potential to become an independent, thinking, feeling, socially responsible adult. In this way, the millions of babies born each year are miraculous whether born of singleton, twin, triplet, or octuplet pregnancies. It is the wonder of each infant that we should celebrate.

Critiquing "Eight Is Too Many: The Case against Octuplets"

1. What criteria does Emanuel use in making his case against octuplets? In your own words, summarize his argument.

2. Emanuel's article raises numerous questions of value of the kind we treat in more depth in Chapter 15, "Ethical Arguments." What broad contemporary criteria for value is Emanuel objecting to in this argument? Specifically, what are the popular criteria for "best" (as in "best fertility treatment" or "best professional ethics"), and how does Emanuel hope to change these criteria?

3. Emanuel argues that octuplets are an "error," not a wonder—"the product of fertility technology misused." How convincing is Emanuel's argument? At what points does Emanuel summarize and respond to opposing views? How might defenders of the McCaugheys or the Chukwus and their doctors respond?

14 Proposal Arguments

We Should
(Should Not) Do X

CASE 1

Many cultural commentators are alarmed by a new social disease brought on by addictive spending. Dubbed "affluenza" and "credititis," this disease is spreading through aggressive promotion of credit cards. Economic analysts are particularly concerned at the way credit card companies are deluging teenagers with credit card offers. Some argue that encouraging credit card debt among the young is highly irresponsible corporate behavior. In order to raise public awareness of the problem, a group of legislators proposes that the following warning label be placed prominently on all credit cards: "WARNING: Failure to research interest rates and credit cards may result in personal financial loss or possible bankruptcy."*

CASE 2

In response to the lack of African American, Latino, Asian American, American Indian, and other ethnic characters in new prime-time TV shows, Kweisi Mfume, president and CEO of the National Association for the Advancement of Colored People (NAACP), lobbies Congress and the Federal Communications Commission to correct this racial imbalance. Specifically, he proposes that the NAACP call for congressional hearings on "network ownership, licensing, and programming" to ensure that the four major broadcast networks include a fair representation of minorities in their prime-time TV shows. Mfume asserts that "The airwaves belong to the public. . . . African Americans make up 13 percent of the population; we feel that our presence should be appropriately reflected during prime time."†

---

*"Credit Cards: Wealth Hazard," *Seattle Times* 4 Feb. 1999, B2.

†"NAACP Attacks Four Major Networks," *Seattle Times* 12 July 1999, A3.

AN OVERVIEW OF
PROPOSAL ARGUMENTS

Although proposal arguments are the last type we examine, they are among the most common arguments that you will encounter or be called on to write. Their essence is that they call for action. In reading a proposal, the audience is enjoined to make a decision and then to act on it—to *do* something. Proposal arguments are sometimes called *should* or *ought* arguments because those helping verbs express the obligation to act: "We *should* do X" or "We *ought* to do X."

For instructional purposes, we will distinguish between two kinds of proposal arguments, even though they are closely related and involve the same basic arguing strategies. The first kind we will call *practical proposals*, which propose an action to solve some kind of local or immediate problem. A student's proposal to change the billing procedures for scholarship students would be an example of a practical proposal, as would an engineering firm's proposal for the design of a new bridge being planned by a city government. The second kind we will call *policy proposals*, in which the writer offers a broad plan of action to solve major social, economic, or political problems affecting the common good. An argument that the United States should adopt a national health insurance plan or that the terms for senators and representatives should be limited to twelve years would be examples of policy proposals.

The primary difference is the narrowness versus breadth of the concern. *Practical* proposals are narrow, local, and concrete; they focus on the nuts and bolts of getting something done in the here and now. They are often concerned with the exact size of a piece of steel, the precise duties of a new person to be hired, or a close estimate of the cost of paint or computers to be purchased. *Policy* proposals, in contrast, are concerned with the broad outline and shape of a course of action, often on a regional, national, or even international issue. What government should do about overcrowding of prisons would be a problem addressed by policy proposals. How to improve the security alarm system for the county jail would be addressed by a practical proposal.

Learning to write both kinds of proposals is valuable. Researching and writing a *policy* proposal is an excellent way to practice the responsibilities of citizenship. By researching a complex issue, by attempting to weigh the positive and negative consequences of any policy decision, and then by committing yourself to a course of action, you will be doing the kind of thinking necessary for the survival of a democratic society. Writing *practical* proposals may well be among your most important duties on the job. Writing persuasive practical proposals is the lifeblood of engineering companies and construction firms because through such proposals a company wins bids and creates work. In many companies, employees can initiate improvements in company operations through practical proposals, and it is through grant proposals that innovative people gain funding for research or carry on the work of volunteer and nonprofit organizations throughout our society.

THE GENERAL STRUCTURE
AND STRATEGY
OF PROPOSAL ARGUMENTS

Proposal arguments, whether practical proposals or policy proposals, generally have a three-part structure: (1) description of a problem, (2) proposed solution, and (3) justification for the proposed solution. In the justification section of your proposal argument, you develop *because* clauses of the kinds you have practiced throughout this text.

SPECIAL CONCERNS
FOR PROPOSAL ARGUMENTS

In their call for action, proposal arguments entail certain emphases and audience concerns that you don't generally face with other kinds of arguments. Let's look briefly at some of these special concerns.

The Need for Presence

It's one thing for a person to assent to a value judgment, but it's another thing to act on that judgment. The personal cost of acting may be high for members of your audience. That means that you have to engage not only your audience's intellects but their emotions as well. Thus proposal arguments often require more attention to *pathos* than do other kinds of arguments (see pp. 141–51).

In most cases, convincing people to act means that an argument must have presence as well as intellectual force. An argument is said to have *presence* when the reader senses the immediacy of the writer's words. The reader not only recognizes the truth and consistency of the argument but experiences its very life. An argument with presence includes the reader in the writer's point of view—the writer's emotions, the force of the writer's personal engagement with the issue. It promotes the reader's assent to the writer's conclusions.

How do you achieve presence in an argument? There are a number of ways. For one, you can appeal directly to the reader's emotions through the effective use of details, brief scenes, and compelling examples that show the reader the seriousness of the problem you are addressing or the consequences of not acting on your proposal.

Additionally, writers can use figurative language such as metaphor and analogy to make the problem being addressed more vivid or real to the audience, or they can shift from abstract language to descriptions, dialogs, statistics, and illustrative narratives. Here is how one student used personal experience in the problem section of her proposal calling for redesign of the mathematics department's introductory calculus curriculum:

My own experience in the Calculus 134 and 135 sequence last year showed me that it was not the learning of calculus that was difficult for me. I was able to catch on to the new concepts. The problem for me was in the fast pace. Just as I was assimilating new concepts and feeling the need to reinforce them, the class was on to a new topic before I had full mastery of the old concept. [. . .] Part of the reason for the fast pace is that calculus is a feeder course for computer science and engineering. If prospective engineering students can't learn the calculus rapidly, they drop out of the program. The high dropout rate benefits the Engineering School because they use the math course to weed out an overabundance of engineering applicants. Thus the pace of the calculus course is geared to the needs of the engineering curriculum, not to the needs of someone like me who wants to be a high school mathematics teacher and who believes that my own difficulties with math—combined with my love for it—might make me an excellent math teacher.

By describing the fast pace of the math curriculum from the perspective of a future math teacher rather than an engineering student, this writer turned a non-problem into a problem. What before didn't look like a problem (it is good to weed out weak engineering majors) suddenly became a problem (it is bad to weed out future math teachers). Establishing herself as a serious student genuinely interested in learning calculus, she gave presence to the problem by calling attention to it in a new way.

The Need to Overcome People's
Natural Conservatism

Another difficulty faced by a proposal maker is the innate conservatism of all human beings, whatever their political persuasion. One philosopher refers to this conservatism as the *law of inertia*, the tendency of all things in the universe, including human beings, to remain at rest if possible. The popular adage "If it ain't broke, don't fix it" is one expression of this tendency. Proposers of change face an extraordinary burden of proof. They have to prove that something needs fixing, that it can be fixed, and that the cost of fixing it will be outweighed by the benefits of fixing it.

The difficulty of proving that something needs fixing is compounded by the fact that frequently the status quo appears to be working. So sometimes when writing a proposal, you can't argue that what we have is bad, but only that what we could have would be better. Often, then, a proposal argument will be based not on present evils but on the evils of lost potential. And getting an audience to accept lost potential may be difficult indeed, given the inherently abstract nature of potentiality.

The Difficulty of Predicting
Future Consequences

Further, most proposal makers will be forced to predict consequences of a given act. As we've seen in our earlier discussions of causality, it is difficult enough to argue backward from event Y in order to establish that X caused Y. Think how much harder it is to establish that X will, in the future, cause certain things to occur. We all know enough of history to realize that few major decisions have led neatly to their anticipated results. This knowledge indeed accounts for much of our conservatism. All the things that can go wrong in a causal argument can go wrong in a proposal argument as well; the major difference is that in a proposal argument we typically have less evidence for our conjectures.

The Problem of Evaluating Consequences

A final difficulty faced by all proposal arguments concerns the difficulty of evaluating the consequences of the proposal. In government and industry, managers often turn to a tool known as *cost-benefit analysis* to calculate the potential consequences of a given proposal. As much as possible, a cost-benefit analysis tries to reduce all consequences to a single scale for purposes of comparison. Most often, the scale will be money. Although this scale may work well in some circumstances, it can lead to grotesquely inappropriate conclusions in other situations.

Just how does one balance the money saved by cutting Medicare benefits against the suffering of the people denied benefits? How does one translate the beauty of a wilderness area into a dollar amount? On this score, cost-benefit analyses often run into a problem discussed in the previous chapter: the seductiveness of empirical measures. Because something can't be readily measured doesn't mean it can be safely ignored. And finally, what will be a cost for one group will often be a benefit for others. For example, if Social Security benefits are cut, those on Social Security will suffer, but current workers who pay for it with taxes will take home a larger paycheck.

These, then, are some of the general difficulties facing someone who sets out to argue in favor of a proposal. Although not insurmountable, they are at least daunting.

DEVELOPING A PROPOSAL ARGUMENT

Writers of proposal arguments must focus in turn on three main phases or stages of the argument: showing that a problem exists, explaining the proposed solution, and offering a justification.

Convincing Your Readers That a Problem Exists

There is one argumentative strategy generic to all proposal arguments: awakening in the reader a sense of a problem. Typically, the development of a problem occurs in one of two places in a proposal argument—either in the introduction prior to the presentation of the arguer's proposal claim or in the body of the paper as the first main reason justifying the proposal claim. In the second instance the writer's first *because* clause has the following structure: "We should do X *because* we are facing a serious problem that needs a solution."

At this stage of your argument, it's important to give your problem presence. You must get people to see how the problem affects people, perhaps through examples of suffering or other loss or through persuasive statistics and so forth. Your goal is to awaken your readers to the existence of a problem, a problem they may well not have recognized before.

Besides giving presence to the problem, a writer must also gain the readers' intellectual assent to the depth, range, and potential seriousness of the problem. Suppose, for illustration, that you wanted to propose a special tax to increase funding for higher education in your state. In trying to convince taxpayers in your state that a problem exists, what obstacles might you face? First of all, many taxpayers never went to college and feel that they get along just fine without it. They tend to worry more about the quality of roads, social services, elementary and secondary schools, police and fire protection, and so forth. They are not too convinced that they need to worry about professors' salaries or better-equipped research labs. Thus it's not enough to talk about the importance of education in general or to cite figures showing how paltry your state's funding of higher education is.

To convince your audience of the need for your proposal, you'll have to describe the consequences of low funding levels in terms they can relate to. You'll have to show them that potential benefits to the state are lost because of inadequate funding. Perhaps you can show the cost in terms of inadequately skilled graduates, disgruntled teachers, high turnover, brain drain to other states, inadequate educational services to farmers and businesspeople, lost productivity, and so forth. Or perhaps you can show your audience examples of benefits realized from better college funding in other states. Such examples give life to the abstract notion of lost potential.

All of this is not to say that you can't or shouldn't argue that higher education is inherently good. But until your reader can see low funding levels as "problematic" rather than "simply the way things are," your proposal stands little chance of being enacted.

Showing the Specifics of Your Proposal

Having decided that there is a problem to be solved, you should lay out your thesis, which is a proposal for solving the problem. Your goal now is to stress the feasibility of your solution, including costs. The art of proposal making is the art of the possible. To be sure, not all proposals require elaborate descriptions of the implementation process. If you are proposing, for example, that a local PTA chapter should buy new tumbling mats for the junior high gym classes, the procedures for buying the mats will probably be irrelevant. But in many arguments the specifics of your proposal—the actual step-by-step methods of implementing it— may be instrumental in winning your audience's support.

You will also need to show how your proposal will solve the problem either partially or wholly. Sometimes you may first need to convince your reader that the problem is solvable, not something intractably rooted in "the way things are," such as earthquakes or jealousy. In other words, expect that some members of your audience will be skeptical about the ability of any proposal to solve the problem you are addressing. You may well need, therefore, to "listen" to this point of view in your refutation section and to argue that your problem is at least partially solvable.

In order to persuade your audience that your proposal can work, you can follow any one of several approaches. A typical approach is to lay out a causal argument showing how one consequence will lead to another until your solution is effected. Another approach is to turn to resemblance arguments, either analogy or precedent. You try to show how similar proposals have been successful elsewhere. Or, if similar things have failed in the past, you try to show how the present situation is different.

The Justification: Convincing Your Readers That Your Proposal Should Be Enacted

The justification phase of a proposal argument will need extensive development in some arguments and minimal development in others, again depending on your particular problem and the rhetorical context of your proposal. If your audience already acknowledges the seriousness of the problem you are addressing and has simply been waiting for the right solution to come along, then your argument will be successful so long as you can convince your audience that your solution will work and that it won't cost too much. Such arguments depend on the clarity of your proposal and the feasibility of its being implemented.

But what if the costs are high? What if your readers don't think the problem is serious? What if they don't appreciate the benefits of solving the problem or the bad consequences of not solving it? In such cases you have to develop persuasive reasons for enacting your proposal. You may also have to determine who has the power to act on your proposal and apply arguments directly to that person's or agency's immediate interests. You need to know to whom or to what your power source is beholden or responsive and what values your power source holds that can be appealed to. You're looking, in short, for the best pressure points.

In the next two sections, we explain invention strategies you can use to generate persuasive reasons for proposal arguments and to anticipate your audience's doubts and reservations. We call these the "claim-type strategy" and the "stock issues strategy."

USING THE CLAIM-TYPE STRATEGY TO DEVELOP A PROPOSAL ARGUMENT

In Chapter 9 we explained how claim-type theory can help you generate ideas for an argument. Specifically, we explained how values claims often depend for their supporting reasons on the reality claims of category, cause, or resemblance. This principle leads to a powerful idea-generating strategy that can be schematized as follows:

Overview of Claim-Type Strategy

We should do X (proposal claim)

- because X is a Y (categorical claim)
- because X will lead to good consequences (causal claim)
- because X is like Y (resemblance claim)

With each of those *because* clauses, the arguer's goal is to link X to one or more goods the audience already values. For a specific example, suppose that you wanted insurance companies to pay for long-term psychological counseling for anorexia. The claim-type strategy could help you develop arguments such as these:

Insurance companies should pay for long-term psychological counseling for anorexia (proposal claim)

- because paying for such counseling is a demonstration of commitment to women's health (categorical claim)
- because paying for such counseling might save insurance companies from much more extensive medical costs at a later date (causal claim)
- because paying for anorexia counseling is like paying for alcoholism or drug counseling, which is already covered by insurance (resemblance claim)

Proposal arguments using reality claims as reasons are very common. Here is another example, this time from a famous art exhibit controversy in the early 1990s when conservatives protested government funding for an exhibition of homo-erotic photographs by artist Robert Mapplethorpe:

Taxpayer funding for the Mapplethorpe exhibits should be withdrawn (proposal claim)

- because the photographs are pornographic (a categorical claim linking the photographs to pornography, which the intended audience opposes)
- because the exhibit promotes community acceptance of homosexuality (a causal claim linking the exhibit to acceptance of homosexuality, which the intended audience opposes)
- because the photographs are more like political statements than art (a resemblance claim linking the exhibit to politics rather than art, a situation that the intended audience would consider unsuitable for arts funding)

Whatever you might think of this argument, it shows how the supporting reasons for a proposal claim can be drawn from claims of category, cause, and resemblance. Each of these arguments attempts to appeal to the value system of the audience. Each tries to show how the proposed action is within the class of things that the audience already values, will lead to consequences desired by the audience, or is similar to something the audience already values. The invention procedure can be summarized in the following way.

Argument from Category

To discover reasons by using this strategy, conduct the following kind of search:

We should (should not) do X because X is _____.

Try to fill in the blank with an appropriate adjective (for example, *good, just, ethical, criminal, ugly, violent, peaceful, wrong, inflationary,* or *healing*) or noun (such as *an act of kindness, terrorism, murder, true art,* or *political suicide*). The point is to try to fill in the blank with a noun or adjective that appeals in some way to your audience's values. Your goal is to show that X belongs to the chosen class or category.

Here are examples:

Using a "Category" Search to Generate Reasons

- Our university should abolish fraternities and sororities *because they are elitist* (or "racist" or "sexist" or "an outdated institution" or whatever).

- Our church should start an active ministry to AIDS patients *because doing so would be an act of love* (or "justice" or "an example of spiritual courage" or whatever).

Argument from Consequence

To discover reasons by using this category, conduct the following kind of search:

We should (should not) do X because X leads to these good (bad) consequences: _____, _____, _____, _____.

Then think of consequences that your audience will agree are good (bad) as your argument requires.

Here are examples, using the same claims as before:

Using a "Consequence" Search to Generate Reasons

- Our university should abolish fraternities and sororities *because eliminating the Greek system will improve our school's academic reputation* (or "fill our dormitories," "allow us to experiment with new living arrangements," "replace rush with a better first-year orientation," "reduce the campus drinking problem," and so forth).

- Our church should start an active ministry to AIDS patients *because doing so will help increase community understanding of the disease* (or "reduce fear and prejudice," or "bring comfort to the suffering," and so forth).

Argument from Resemblance

To discover supporting reasons by using this strategy, conduct the following kind of search:

We should (should not) do X because doing X is like _____.

Then think of analogies or precedents that are similar to doing X but currently have greater appeal to your audience. Your task is then to transfer to X your audience's favorable (unfavorable) feelings toward the analogy/precedent.

Here are examples:

Using a "Resemblance" Search to Generate Reasons

- Our university should abolish fraternities and sororities *because other universities that have eliminated the Greek system have reported good results* (or "because eliminating the Greek system is like leveling social classes to promote more democracy and individualism," and so forth).

- Our church should start an active ministry to AIDS patients *because doing so is like Jesus' ministering to the lepers, who were outcasts in their society in the way that AIDS victims are outcasts in ours.*

These three kinds of searches—supporting a proposal claim from the perspectives of category, consequence, and resemblance—are powerful means of invention. In selecting among these reasons, choose those most likely to appeal to your audience's assumptions, beliefs, and values.

▼ FOR CLASS DISCUSSION

1. Working individually or in small groups, use the strategies of principle, consequence, and resemblance to create *because* clauses that support each of the following claims. Try to have at least one *because* clause from each of the categories, but generate as many reasons as possible. Don't worry about whether any individual reason exactly fits the category. The purpose is to stimulate thinking, not fill in the slots.

EXAMPLE

CLAIM:	Pit bulls make bad pets.
REASON FROM CATEGORY:	because they are vicious
REASON FROM CONSEQUENCE:	because owning a pit bull leads to conflicts with neighbors
REASON FROM RESEMBLANCE:	because owning a pit bull is like having a shell-shocked roommate—mostly they're lovely companions but they can turn violent if startled

   a. Marijuana should be legalized.
   b. Division I college athletes should receive salaries.
   c. High schools should pass out free contraceptives.
   d. Violent video games should be made illegal.
   e. Parents should be heavily taxed for having more than two children.

2. Repeat the first exercise, taking a different position on each issue.

USING THE "STOCK ISSUES" STRATEGY TO DEVELOP A PROPOSAL ARGUMENT

An effective way to generate ideas for a proposal argument is to ask yourself a series of questions based on the "stock issues" strategy. Suppose, for example, you wanted to develop the following argument: "In order to solve the problem of students who won't take risks with their writing, the faculty at Weasel College should adopt a pass/fail method of grading in all writing courses." The stock issues strategy invites the writer to consider "stock" ways (that is, common, usual, frequently repeated ways) that such arguments can be conducted.

Stock issue 1: *Is there really a problem here that needs to be solved?* Is it really true that a large number of student writers won't take risks in their writing?

Is this problem more serious than other writing problems such as undeveloped ideas, lack of organization, and poor sentence structure? This stock issue invites the writer to convince her audience that a true problem exists. Conversely, an opponent to the proposal might argue that a true problem does not exist.

Stock issue 2: *Will the proposed solution really solve this problem?* Is it true that a pass/fail grading system will cause students to take more risks with their writing? Will more interesting, surprising, and creative essays result from pass/fail grading? Or will students simply put less effort into their writing? This stock issue prompts a supporter to demonstrate that the proposal will solve the problem; in contrast, it prompts the opponent to show that the proposal won't work.

Stock issue 3: *Can the problem be solved more simply without disturbing the status quo?* An opponent of the proposal might agree that a problem exists and that the proposed solution might solve it. However, the opponent might say, "Are there not less radical ways to solve this problem? If we want more creative and risk-taking student essays, can't we just change our grading criteria so that we reward risky papers and penalize conventional ones?" This stock issue prompts supporters to show that *only* the proposed solution will solve the problem and that no minor tinkering with the status quo will be adequate. Conversely, opponents will argue that the problem can be solved without acting on the proposal.

Stock issue 4: *Is the proposed solution really practical? Does it stand a chance of actually being enacted?* Here an opponent to the proposal might agree that the proposal would work but that it involves pie-in-the-sky idealism. Nobody will vote to change the existing system so radically; therefore, it is a waste of our time to debate it. Following this prompt, supporters would have to argue that pass/fail grading is workable and that enough faculty members are disposed to it that the proposal is worth debating. Opponents might argue that the faculty at Weasel College is so traditional that pass/fail has utterly no chance of being accepted, despite its merits.

Stock issue 5: *What will be the unforeseen positive and negative consequences of the proposal?* Suppose we do adopt a pass/fail system. What positive or negative consequences might occur that are different from what we at first predicted? Using this prompt, an opponent might argue that pass/fail grading will reduce the effort put forth by students and that the long-range effect will be writing of even lower quality than we have now. Supporters would try to find positive consequences—perhaps a new love of writing for its own sake rather than the sake of a grade.

FOR CLASS DISCUSSION

The following collaborative task takes approximately two class days to complete. The exercise takes you through the process of creating a proposal argument.

1. In small groups, identify and list several major problems facing students in your college or university.

2. Decide among yourselves which are the most important of these problems and rank them in order of importance.

3. Take your group's number one problem and explore answers to the following questions. Group recorders should be prepared to present your group's answers to the class as a whole:
   a. Why is the problem a problem?
   b. For whom is the problem a problem?
   c. How will these people suffer if the problem is not solved? (Give specific examples.)
   d. Who has the power to solve the problem?
   e. Why hasn't the problem been solved up to this point?
   f. How can the problem be solved? (That is, create a proposal.)
   g. What are the probable benefits of acting on your proposal?
   h. What costs are associated with your proposal?
   i. Who will bear those costs?
   j. Why should this proposal be enacted?
   k. Why is it better than alternative proposals?

4. As a group, draft an outline for a proposal argument in which you
   a. describe the problem and its significance.
   b. propose your solution to the problem.
   c. justify your proposal by showing how the benefits of adopting that proposal outweigh the costs.

5. Recorders for each group should write their group's outline on the board and be prepared to explain it to the class.

WRITING A PROPOSAL ARGUMENT

WRITING ASSIGNMENT
FOR CHAPTER 14

OPTION 1: *A Practical Proposal Addressing a Local Problem*   Write a practical proposal offering a solution to a local problem. Your proposal should have three main sections: (1) description of the problem, (2) proposed solution, and (3) justification. You may include additional sections or subsections as needed. Longer proposals often include an *abstract* at the beginning of the proposal to provide a summary overview of the whole argument. (Sometimes called the *executive summary*, this abstract may be the only portion of the proposal read by high-level managers.) Sometimes proposals are accompanied by a *letter of transmittal*—a one-page business letter that introduces the proposal to its intended audience and provides some needed background about the writer.

Document design is important in practical proposals, which are aimed at busy people who have to make many decisions under time constraints. Because the writer of a practical proposal usually produces the finished document (practical proposals are seldom submitted to newspapers or magazines for publication), the writer must pay particular attention to the attractive design of the document. An effective design helps establish the writer's *ethos* as a quality-oriented professional and helps make the reading of the proposal as easy as possible. Document design includes effective use of heading and subheadings, attractive typeface and layout, flawless editing, and other features enhancing the visual appearance of the document.

OPTION 2: *A Policy Proposal as a Guest Editorial*   Write a two- to three-page policy proposal suitable for publication as a feature editorial in a college or city newspaper or in some publication associated with a particular group or activity such as a church newsletter or employee bulletin. The voice and style of your argument should be aimed at general readers of your chosen publication. Your editorial should have the following features:

1. The identification of a problem (Persuade your audience that this is a genuine problem that needs solving; give it presence.)
2. A proposal for action that will help alleviate the problem
3. A justification of your solution (the reasons why your audience should accept your proposal and act on it)

OPTION 3: *A Researched Argument Proposing Public Policy*   Write an eight- to twelve-page proposal argument as a formal research paper, using research data for support. Your argument should include all the features of the shorter argument in Option 2 and also a summary and refutation of opposing views (in the form of alternative proposals and/or differing cost-benefit analyses of your proposal.) An example of a researched policy proposal is student writer Stephen Bean's "What Should Be Done about the Mentally Ill Homeless?" on pages 334–42.

Exploring Ideas

Since *should* or *ought* issues are among the most common sources of arguments, you may already have ideas for proposal issues. To think of ideas for practical proposals, try making an idea map of local problems you would like to see solved. For initial spokes, try trigger words such as the following:

- problems at my university (dorms, parking, registration system, financial aid, campus appearance, clubs, curriculum, intramural program, athletic teams)

- problems in my city or town (dangerous intersections, ugly areas, inadequate lighting, parks, police policy, public transportation, schools)

- problems at my place of work (office design, flow of customer traffic, merchandise display, company policies)

- problems related to my future careers, hobbies, recreational time, life as a consumer, life as a homeowner

If you can offer a solution to the problem you identify, you may make a valuable contribution to some phase of public life.

To find a topic for policy proposals, stay in touch with the news, which will keep you aware of current debates on regional and national issues. Also, visit the Web sites of your congressional representatives to see what issues they are currently investigating and debating. You might think of your policy proposal as a white paper for one of your legislators.

Once you have decided on a proposal issue, we recommend you explore it by trying one or more of the following activities:

- *Explore ideas by using the claim-type strategy.* Briefly this strategy invites you to find supporting reasons for your proposal by arguing that (1) X is a Y that the audience values; (2) doing X will lead to good consequences; and (3) doing X has been tried with good results elsewhere, or doing X is like doing Y, which the audience values.

- *Explore ideas by using the "stock issues" strategy.* You will raise vital ideas for your argument by asking the stock questions: (1) Is there really a problem here that has to be solved? (2) Will the proposed solution really solve this problem? (3) Can the problem be solved in a simpler way without disturbing the status quo? (4) Is the proposed solution practical enough that it really stands a chance of being acted on? (5) What will be the positive and negative consequences of the proposal? A fuller version of the stock questions is the eleven questions (a–k) in the third For Class Discussion exercise on page 319.

- *Explore ideas for your argument by completing the ten exploratory tasks in Chapter 3 (pp. 70–71).* These tasks help you generate enough material for a rudimentary rough draft.

Organizing a Proposal Argument

When you write your draft, you may find it helpful to have at hand some plans for typical ways of organizing a proposal argument. What follows are two common methods of organization. Option 1 is the plan most typical for practical proposals. Either Option 1 or Option 2 is effective for a policy proposal.

Option 1

- Presentation of a problem that needs solving:
    Description of problem
    Background, including previous attempts to solve problem
    Argument that the problem is solvable (optional)
- Presentation of writer's proposal:
    Succinct statement of the proposed solution serves as thesis statement
    Explain specifics of proposed solution
- Summary and rebuttal of opposing views (in practical proposals, this section is often a summary and rejection of alternative ways of solving the problem)
- Justification persuading reader that proposal should be enacted:
    Reason 1 presented and developed
    Reason 2 presented and developed
    Additional reasons presented and developed
- Conclusion that exhorts audience to act
    Give presence to final sentences.

Option 2

- Presentation of issue, including background
- Presentation of writer's proposal
- Justification
    Reason 1: Show that proposal addresses a serious problem.

Reason 2: Show that proposal will solve problem.
Reason 3: Give additional reasons for enacting proposal.

- Summary and refutation of opposing views
- Conclusion that exhorts audience to act

Revising Your Draft

As you revise your draft based on peer reviews and on your own assessment of its problems and strengths, consider using a Toulmin analysis to test your argument's persuasiveness. Recall that Toulmin is particularly useful for helping you link each of your reasons to your audience's beliefs, assumptions, and values.

Suppose that there is a debate at Clambake College about whether to banish fraternities and sororities. Suppose further that you are in favor of banishing the Greek system. One of your arguments is that eliminating the Greek system will improve your college's academic reputation. Here is how you might use the Toulmin system to make this line of reasoning as persuasive as possible.

CLAIM:	Clambake College should eliminate the Greek system.
STATED REASON:	because doing so will improve Clambake College's academic reputation
GROUNDS:	*I've got to provide evidence that eliminating the Greek system will improve Clambake's academic reputation. I have shown that last year the GPA of students in fraternities and sororities was 20 percent lower than the GPA of non-Greek students. What else can I add? I can talk about the excessive party atmosphere of some Greek houses, about the emphasis placed on social life rather than studying, about how new pledges have so many house duties that their studies suffer, about how new students think about rush more than about the academic life.*
WARRANT:	It is good for Clambake College to achieve a better academic reputation.
BACKING:	*I see that my draft doesn't have any backing for this warrant. How can I argue that it would be good to have a better academic reputation? Clambake would attract more serious students; its prestige would rise; it might attract and retain better faculty; the college would be a more intellectually interesting place; the long-range careers of our students might improve with a better education.*

CONDITIONS FOR REBUTTAL:	*How would skeptics doubt my reason and grounds? Might they say that I am stereotyping Greeks? Might they argue that some of the brightest and best students on campus are in fraternities and sororities? Might they argue that only a few rowdy houses are at fault? Might they point to very prestigious institutions that have fraternities and sororities? Might they say that the cause of a poor academic reputation has nothing to do with fraternities and sororities and point instead to other causes? How can I respond to these arguments?*
	How could they raise doubts about my warrant and backing? They probably wouldn't argue that it is bad to have a good academic reputation. They will probably argue instead that eliminating sororities and fraternities won't improve the academic reputation of Clambake but will hurt its social life and its wide range of living options. To respond to these arguments, maybe I should do some research into what happened at other colleges when they eliminated the Greek system.
QUALIFIER:	*Should I add a "may" by saying that eliminating the Greek system* may *help improve the academic reputation of Clambake?*

As this example shows, thinking systematically about the grounds, warrant, backing, and conditions of rebuttal for each of your reasons can help you generate additional ideas to strengthen your first draft.

QUESTIONING AND CRITIQUING A PROPOSAL ARGUMENT

As we've suggested, proposal arguments need to overcome the innate conservatism of people, the difficulty of anticipating all the consequences of a proposal, and so forth. What questions, then, can we ask about proposal arguments to help us anticipate these problems?

Will a skeptic deny that my problem is really a problem? The first question to ask of your proposal is "What's so wrong with the status quo that change is necessary?" The second question is "Who loses if the status quo is changed?" Be certain not to overlook this second question. Most proposal makers can demonstrate that some sort of problem exists, but often it is a problem only for certain groups of people. Solving the problem will thus prove a benefit to some people but a cost to others. If audience members examine the problem from the perspective of the potential losers rather than the winners, they can often raise doubts about your proposal.

For example, one state recently held an initiative on a proposed "bottle bill" that would fight litter by permitting the sale of soda and beer only in returnable bottles. Sales outlets would be required to charge a substantial deposit on the bottles in order to encourage people to return them. Proponents of the proposal emphasized citizens as "winners" sharing in the new cleanliness of a landscape no longer littered with cans. To refute this argument, opponents showed consumers as "losers" burdened with the high cost of deposits and the hassle of collecting and returning bottles to grocery stores.

Will a skeptic doubt the effectiveness of my solution? Assuming that you've satisfied yourself that a significant problem exists for a significant number of people, a number of questions remain to be asked about the quality of the proposed solution to solve the problem. First, "Does the problem exist for the reasons cited, or might there be alternative explanations?" Here we return to the familiar ground of causal arguments. A proposal supposedly strikes at the cause of a problem. But perhaps striking at that "cause" won't solve the problem. Perhaps you've mistaken a symptom for a cause, or confused two commonly associated but essentially unlinked phenomena for a cause-effect relationship. For example, will paying teachers higher salaries improve the quality of teaching or merely attract greedier rather than brighter people? Maybe more good teachers would be attracted and retained if they were given some other benefit (fewer students? smaller classes? more sabbaticals? more autonomy? more prestige?).

Another way to test your solution is to list all the uncertainties involved. This might be referred to as "The Devil you know is better than the Devil you don't know" strategy. Remind yourself of all the unanticipated consequences of past changes. Who, for example, would have thought back in the days when aerosol shaving cans were being developed that they might lead to diminished ozone layers, which might lead to more ultraviolet rays getting through the atmosphere from the sun, which would lead to higher incidences of skin cancer? The history of technology is full of such cautionary tales that can be invoked to remind you of the uncertain course that progress can sometimes take.

Will a skeptic think my proposal costs too much? The most commonly asked question of any proposal is simply, "Do the benefits of enacting the proposal outweigh the costs?" As we saw above, you can't foresee all the consequences of any proposal. It's easy, before the fact, to exaggerate both the costs and the benefits of a proposal. So, in asking how much your proposal will cost, we urge you to make an honest estimate. Will your audience discover costs you hadn't anticipated— extra financial costs or unexpected psychological or environmental or aesthetic costs? As much as you can, anticipate these objections.

Will a skeptic suggest counterproposals? Related to all that's been said so far is the counterproposal. Can you imagine an appealing alternative to both the status quo and the proposal that you're making? The more clearly your proposal shows that a significant problem exists, the more important it is that you be able to identify possible counterproposals. Any potential critic of a proposal to remedy an acknowledged problem will either have to make such a counterproposal or have to argue that the problem is simply in the nature of things. So, given the likelihood that you'll be faced with a counterproposal, it only makes sense to anticipate it and to work out a refutation of it before you have it thrown at you. And who knows, you may end up liking the counterproposal better and changing your mind about what to propose!

READINGS

Our first reading, by student writer Jeffrey Cain, is a practical proposal for saving a neighborhood Jewish restaurant in Seattle, Washington. As a practical proposal, it uses headings and subheadings and other elements of document design aimed to give it a finished and professional appearance. When sent to the intended audience, it is accompanied by a single-spaced letter of transmittal following the conventional format of a business letter.

515 West Olympic Pl.
Seattle, Washington 98119

Martin _____
Owner, Bernie's Blintzes Restaurant
1201 10th Avenue
Seattle, Washington 98185

Dear Mr. _____:

    Enclosed is a proposal that addresses Bernie's Blintzes' present economic trouble. It provides an inexpensive alternative to the $60,000 "makeover" plan proposed by the recently hired restaurant consultant. Having been an employee of Bernie's Blintzes for over three years, and having previously been an employee of a catering business, I hope that my observations will be of some interest and help to you.

    In brief, my proposal suggests that investing $60,000 into a complete restaurant upgrade not only exposes you to unnecessary economic risk, but also fails to build on Bernie's Blintzes' strengths and sixteen-year legacy. Instead, I propose that through the production and distribution of Bernie's Blintzes' chocolate chip cookies to area espresso stands and coffee shops, Bernie's Blintzes Restaurant can reestablish itself as a viable money-making business. Unlike the consultant's proposal, this plan recommends that Bernie's Blintzes build on what it has done well for sixteen years, preserving an important part of Seattle's Jewish culture—something I know that is important to you.

    As a member of the Bernie's Blintzes staff, I share your interest in keeping the restaurant economically viable. I hope my thoughts are of some benefit. Thank you for your consideration.

    Sincerely,

    Jeffrey Cain

A Proposal to Save
Bernie's Blintzes Restaurant
Submitted to the Owner, Mr. Martin _____
Jeffrey Cain

Summary

This proposal argues that investing $60,000 in a complete restaurant upgrade not only exposes the owners of Bernie's Blintzes to unnecessary economic risk, it also fails to build on Bernie's Blintzes' strengths and sixteen-year legacy. Instead, I propose that through the production and distribution of Bernie's Blintzes' chocolate chip cookies to area espresso stands and coffee shops, Bernie's Blintzes Restaurant can reestablish itself as a viable money-making business.

Problem

Bernie's Blintzes Restaurant is currently in financial crisis and must either close its doors or substantially increase its sales and profits.

Background on Bernie's Blintzes Restaurant

For over sixteen years Bernie's Blintzes Restaurant has been serving traditional kosher-style food in a family dining atmosphere in Seattle's Queen Anne district. Known for its excellent matzoh ball soup, blintzes, potato latkes, pastrami sandwiches, and giant chocolate chip cookies, Bernie's Blintzes remains one of Seattle's only family-operated ethnic Jewish restaurants. In addition to providing sit-down and take-out dining, Bernie's Blintzes also offers an extensive catering service that has steadily grown since its inception five years ago.

During the past two years, however, a slow but constant decrease in restaurant patronage has led to a decline in Bernie's Blintzes' sales and profits. In an effort to reestablish their restaurant as a money-making business, the owners of Bernie's Blintzes have employed the professional services of a restaurant consultant. After three months of observation and study, the consultant identified three areas that have led to Bernie's Blintzes' decline in patronage: (1) increased competition with the addition of seven new restaurants in the neighborhood over the past three years; (2) menu items that are out of fashion with health-conscious consumers; (3) a lack of marketing and name familiarity—although Bernie's Blintzes is well known around the neighborhood, few in the greater Seattle area would recognize its name. As a remedy, the consultant has recommended a $60,000 restaurant upgrade, including a complete interior remodel, new menu, and an advertising and marketing plan that would include changing the Bernie's Blintzes name and logo. In short, the consultant envisions an entirely new restaurant: rebuilding Bernie's Blintzes from the ground up.

Problems with the Consultant's Proposal

5   A continued loss of patronage would certainly force the owners of Bernie's Blintzes to discontinue their sixteen-year-old labor; yet the prospect of investing $60,000 into a completely "new" restaurant brings economic risk and great uncertainty. A $60,000 investment would require the owners to assume a second home mortgage, and there are certainly no guarantees that their investment would pay off. The owners are rightfully apprehensive. But putting economic considerations aside for the moment, the consultant's "ground-up" proposal also brings great uncertainty because it fails to build on Bernie's Blintzes' strengths in three significant ways.

6   First, increased competition is not necessarily a bad thing. Paragon consultants are correct in observing that new restaurants have brought more competition to Bernie's Blintzes' neighborhood, but these same new restaurants have also brought more potential customers. Bernie's Blintzes' sixteen-year tenure in the neighborhood is a strength that could lure some of the neighborhood's new visitors. A well-established restaurant is a welcome respite from today's ever-changing fast-food culture.

7   Second, a dated menu can be advantageous. While it may be true that consumers have become more health conscious, it is also the case that consumers have become more aware of ethnic cuisine—consider the popularity of Thai food. Bernie's Blintzes' traditional kosher-style menu is a rarity in Seattle and may be a welcome alternative to other more familiar ethnic foods, like Chinese or Mexican.

8   Finally, new isn't always better. The consultant rightfully recognizes that Bernie's Blintzes has poor name familiarity throughout the city; however, it does have strong name familiarity within its neighborhood. Changing Bernie's Blintzes' name, as the consultant's proposal calls for, would take away whatever name familiarity already exists, obscuring what for some is a local landmark.

9   A proposal that builds on Bernie's Blintzes' existing strengths could be less risky and certainly less expensive than the consultant's plan.

Proposal

10   This proposal is offered as a cost-effective, low-risk alternative to the consultant's plan that would utilize Bernie's Blintzes' existing facilities, build on its time-tested strengths, and maintain its traditional ethnic cuisine and character. The nucleus of this proposal involves the production and distribution of Bernie's Blintzes' chocolate chip cookies to area espresso carts and coffee shops. This plan

capitalizes on the popularity of Bernie's Blintzes' cookies and the booming espresso cart and coffee shop industry in Seattle.

Bernie's Blintzes' chocolate chip cookies are well known to customers as "the best coffee cookies in the world." This is because unlike other cookies, Bernie's Blintzes' cookies are a little harder than most, making them excellent for dipping into a hot cup of coffee. It is not unusual for customers to special-order a dozen cookies to have with their coffee at home, and at catering events the cookies quickly disappear when coffee is served.   11

Bernie's Blintzes' chocolate chip cookies are a perfect match for the booming coffee industry in the greater Seattle area. Espresso stands and coffee shops decorate nearly every public place in Seattle, from schools and gas stations to shopping malls and street corners. In addition to selling coffee products, these coffee vendors also sell pastries and sweets. Some carts sell in excess of 200 cookies a week. With very few companies currently distributing quality pastries to espresso carts, the potential for the owners of Bernie's Blintzes to tap into this new and growing market is excellent.   12

Because Bernie's Blintzes already has the means for cookie production, this plan could begin almost immediately. Presently, the restaurant experiences slow hours during the evening and in between lunches when restaurant employees, particularly kitchen staff, have little to do. During this slow time, employees could assist in the production of the chocolate chip cookies, particularly kitchen personnel. Orders for the cookies would be taken via phone or fax by employees who are already being paid. If cookie production exceeded the amount of time that employees who were already on the clock were available, then extended working hours could be offered to existing employees without having to hire new help, at least initially. Delivery would be made the following morning, within twenty-four hours. (The cookies would be delivered, until it became necessary to hire a new employee, by the owner—reducing costs and ensuring positive customer relations.)   13

At least initially, then, the labor cost involved in producing the cookies would be minimal. Therefore, the cookies could continue to sell at their present retail price of $.75, maintaining a $.45 net profit on each cookie. With this scenario, it may be possible to lower the wholesale price of the cookie to $.50. However, it is recommended that Bernie's Blintzes increase the retail price of its cookies to $1.00 instead, with a wholesale price of $.75. A random sampling of area espresso carts reveals that most carts market their cookies for $1.00 to $1.50, some as high as $1.75. In raising the retail cost of the cookie to $1.00 and the wholesale cost to $.75,   14

Bernie's Blintzes would be announcing its cookie as a "high-end" cookie that is competitively priced. Cookies at a wholesale price of $1.00 would realize a $.70 net profit.

15   Distribution to ten coffee carts that each sold 100 cookies a week would yield $700.00, weekly. Given the hundreds of coffee carts in the greater Seattle area, it is likely that Bernie's Blintzes' distribution would far exceed ten coffee carts. Thus, there is a genuine opportunity to make a substantial amount of money from a product that Bernie's Blintzes is already producing. Yet the benefits from such a simple endeavor would far exceed the monetary profit from each cookie.

Justification

16   In several important ways, the production and distribution of Bernie's Blintzes' chocolate chip cookies would help restore Bernie's Blintzes to financial prosperity.

17   First, this proposal builds on existing strengths. Bernie's Blintzes' chocolate chip cookies have already been market-tested—sixteen years of experience shows that Bernie's Blintzes' cookies sell. Moreover, establishing a cookie distribution system would open the door for Bernie's Blintzes to distribute more of its other time-tested items, like its famous matzoh ball soup. Also, distribution need not be limited to Seattle; in time, Bernie's Blintzes' cookies could be distributed throughout the region.

18   Second, initial costs and risks are very low. Because producing chocolate chip cookies takes advantage of existing facilities and labor, the cookies could be distributed and marketed at a very competitive rate, allowing Bernie's Blintzes to establish itself in a citywide market at a nominal cost—producing and distributing cookies would not require a second mortgage.

19   Third, cookie distribution would increase name familiarity. Each cookie would carry a label on one side that would include the Bernie's Blintzes logo, phone number, and address. Coffee drinkers across town will want to visit Bernie's Blintzes Restaurant after they come to appreciate these fine cookies. Curious new visitors to the neighborhood will match the restaurant sign to the label on the cookie they purchased at the espresso cart near their home. Another label on the other side of the cookie could promote Bernie's Blintzes' catering and specialty menu items.

20   Finally, Bernie's Blintzes could continue to do what it does best: serve traditional kosher-style food. Unlike the consultant's proposal, this plan allows Bernie's Blintzes to build on what it has done well for sixteen years, preserving an important part of Seattle's Jewish culture.

Skeptics may criticize a plan such as this because it is simplistic in appearance.   21
After all, it does seem somewhat "starry-eyed" to think that chocolate chip cookies could be the source of economic prosperity. Yet one might consider the millions of dollars made today by Famous Amos Cookies, a company that began on nothing more than a dream and a kitchen in a garage. Sometimes the most effective plans are the simplest ones.

Conclusion

By building on existing strengths and doing what Bernie's Blintzes has   22
been doing well for sixteen years, the owners of Bernie's Blintzes Restaurant can reestablish it as a profitable business. Producing and distributing chocolate chip cookies addresses Bernie's Blintzes' shortcomings while building on its strengths, and in contrast to the Paragon plan, this proposal can be executed immediately with a nominal investment.

Critiquing "A Proposal to Save Bernie's Blintzes Restaurant"

1. Bernie's Blintzes Restaurant (not its real name) was in a state of decline at the time this proposal was written. As a quirky, family-operated business, it seemed out-of-step with new upscale trends in the restaurant business. The owner hired a consultant for advice. What was the consultant's analysis of the problem and recommended solution?

2. Jeffrey Cain's proposal grows out of his personal experience and practical knowledge of a restaurant business. What is Jeffrey's analysis and proposed solution?

3. How does Jeffrey use his experiential knowledge to rebut the consultant's report and support his own ideas? What rhetorical strategies does he use?

4. How effective do you find Jeffrey's proposal argument?

Our second reading, by student writer Stephen Bean, is a policy proposal written for the assignment on pages 320–21. Bean's paper joins a heated social debate about what to do about the mentally ill homeless. In 1988, conservative columnist Charles Krauthammer published an influential article arguing that states should confine the mentally ill homeless—involuntarily if necessary—in state mental hospitals. Krauthammer argued that the huge rise of homeless people in the 1970s and 1980s was the result of the closing of state mental hospitals following court rulings that persons could not be involuntarily committed. In this researched policy argument, Bean aims to refute Krauthammer's argument and offer a counterproposal. Bean's argument is formatted as a formal research paper using the documentation system of the Modern Language Association (MLA). A full explanation of this format is given in Chapter 17.

Stephen Bean

Professor Arness

English 110

June 1, 200–

What Should Be Done about the Mentally Ill Homeless?

1   Winter paints Seattle's streets gray with misting rain that drops lightly
but steadily into pools. Walking to work through one of Seattle's oldest districts,
Pioneer Square, I see an incongruous mixture of people: both successful business
types and a large population of homeless. Some walk to offices or lunches
grasping cups of fresh ground coffee; others slowly push wobbling carts
containing their earthly possessions wrapped carefully in black plastic. These
scenes of homelessness have become common throughout America's urban
centers—so common, perhaps, that despite our feelings of guilt and pity, we
accept the presence of the homeless as permanent. The empty-stomach feeling
of confronting a ragged panhandler has become an often accepted fact of living
in the city. What can we do besides giving a few cents of spare change?

2   Recently, a growing number of commentators have been focusing
on the mentally ill homeless. In response to the violent murder of an elderly
person by a homeless mentally ill man, New York City recently increased its
efforts to locate and hospitalize dangerous homeless mentally ill individuals.
New York's plan will include aggressive outreach—actively going out into the
streets and shelters to locate mentally ill individuals and then involuntarily
hospitalizing those deemed dangerous either to others or to themselves (Dugger,
"Danger" B1). Although the New York Civil Liberties Union has objected to
this action on the grounds that involuntary hospitalization may violate the rights
of the mentally ill, many applaud the city's action as a first step in dealing
with a problem which the nation has grossly ignored. One highly influential
commentator, Charles Krauthammer, has recently called for widescale involuntary
reinstitutionalization of the mentally ill homeless—a seemingly persuasive
proposal until one begins to do research on the mentally ill homeless. Adopting
Krauthammer's proposal would be a dangerous and wrong-headed policy for
America. Rather, research shows that community-based care in which psychiatrists
and social workers provide coordinated services in the community itself is a more

effective solution to the problems of the mentally ill homeless than widescale
institutionalization.

    In his article "How to Save the Homeless Mentally Ill," Charles Krauthammer   3
argues that the federal government should assist the states in rebuilding a national
system of asylums. He proposes that the criteria for involuntary institutionalization
be broadened: The state should be permitted to institutionalize mentally ill persons
involuntarily not only if they are deemed dangerous to others or themselves (the
current criterion for institutionalization) but also if they are "degraded" or made
helpless by their illness. He points to the large number of patients released from
state institutions in the 1960s and 1970s who, finding no support in communities,
ended up on the streets. Arguing that the mentally ill need the stability and
supervision that only an institution can provide, Krauthammer proposes substantial
increases in federal taxes to fund rebuilding of asylums. He argues that the
mentally ill need unique solutions because of their unique problems; their
homelessness, he claims, stems from mental illness not poverty. Finally,
Krauthammer rebuts the argument that involuntary hospitalization violates civil
liberties. He argues that "liberty" has no meaning to someone suffering from
severe psychosis. To let people suffer the pains of mental illness and the pains
of the street when they could be treated and recover is a cruel right indeed. He
points to the project HELP program where less than a fifth of those involuntarily
hospitalized protested their commitment; most are glad, he claims, for a warm
bed, nutritious food, and a safe environment.

    Krauthammer's argument, while persuasive on first reading, is based on four   4
seriously flawed assumptions. His first assumption is the widely accepted notion
that deinstitutionalization of state mental hospitals in the 1960s and 1970s is a
primary cause of the current homelessness problem in America. Krauthammer
talks about the hundreds of thousands released from the hospitals who have
become "an army of grate-dwellers" (24). However, recent research has shown
that the relationship of deinstitutionalization to homelessness is vastly overstated.
Ethnologist Kim Hopper argues that while deinstitutionalization has partly
contributed to increased numbers of mentally ill homeless its influence is far
smaller than popularly believed. She argues that the data many used to support
this claim were methodologically flawed and that researchers who found symptoms

of mental illness in homeless people didn't try to ascertain whether these symptoms were the cause or effect of living on the street. Finally, she points out that a lag time of five years existed between the major release of state hospital patients and the rise of mentally ill individuals in shelters. This time lag suggests that other social and economic factors might have come into play to account for the rise of homelessness (156–57). Carl Cohen and Kenneth Thompson also point to this time lag as evidence to reject deinstitutionalization as the major cause of mentally ill homelessness (817). Jonathan Kozol argues that patients released from state hospitals in the late sixties and early seventies didn't go directly to the streets but went to single-room occupancy housing, such as cheap hotels or boarding houses. Many of these ex-patients became homeless, he argues, when almost half of single-room occupancy housing was replaced by more expensive housing between 1970 and 1980 (18). The effects of this housing shortage might account for the lag time that Hopper and Cohen and Thompson cite.

5   Krauthammer's focus on mental illness as a cause of much of the homelessness problem leads to another of the implicit assumptions in his argument: that the mentally ill comprise a large percentage of the homeless population. Krauthammer avoids mentioning specific numbers until the end of his article when he writes:

> The argument over how many of the homeless are mentally ill is endless. The estimates, which range from one-quarter to three-quarters, vary with method, definition, and ideology. But so what if even the lowest estimates are right? Even if treating the mentally ill does not end homelessness, how can that possibly justify not treating the tens, perhaps hundreds of thousands who would benefit from a partial solution? (25)

This paragraph is rhetorically shrewd. It downplays the numbers issue and takes the moral high road. But by citing estimates between one-quarter and three-quarters, Krauthammer effectively suggests that a neutral estimate might place the number around fifty percent—a high estimate reinforced by his leap from "tens" to "perhaps hundreds of thousands" in the last sentence.

6   Close examination of the research, however, reveals that the percentage of mentally ill people on the streets may be even lower than Krauthammer's lowest figure of 25%. In an extensive study conducted by David Snow and colleagues, a team member lived among the homeless for 12 months to collect data on mental

illness. Additionally, the researchers tracked the institutional histories of a random sample of homeless. The study found that only 10% of the street sample and 16% of the tracking sample showed mental illness. The researchers pointed to a number of reasons why some previous estimates and studies may have inflated the numbers of mentally ill homeless. They suggest that the visibility of the mentally ill homeless (their odd behaviors make them stand out) combined with the widespread belief that deinstitutionalization poured vast numbers of mentally ill onto the streets caused researchers to bias their data. Thus researchers would often interpret behavior such as socially inappropriate actions, depression, and sleeping disorders as indications of mental illness, when in fact these actions may simply be the natural response to living in the harsh environment of the street. Additionally, the Snow study points to the medicalization of homelessness. This phenomenon means that when doctors and psychiatrists treat the homeless they focus on their medical and psychological problems while ignoring their social and economic ones. Because studies of the mentally ill homeless have been dominated by doctors and psychologists, these studies tend to inflate the numbers of mentally ill on the streets (419–21).

Another persuasive study showing low percentages of mentally ill homeless— 7 although not as low as Snow's estimates—comes from Deborah Dennis and colleagues, who surveyed the past decade of research on mentally ill homeless. The combined findings of all these research studies suggest that the mentally ill comprise between 28% and 37% of the homeless population (Dennis et al. 1130). Thus we see that while the mentally ill make up a significant proportion of the homeless population they do not approach a majority as Krauthammer and others would have us believe.

Krauthammer's third assumption is that the causes of homelessness among 8 the mentally ill are largely psychological rather than socioeconomic. By this thinking, the solutions to their problems involve the treatment of their illnesses rather than the alleviation of poverty. Krauthammer writes, "Moreover, whatever solutions are eventually offered the non-mentally ill homeless, they will have little relevance to those who are mentally ill" (25). Closer examination, however, shows that other factors play a greater role in causing homelessness among the mentally ill than mental illness. Jonathan Kozol argues that housing and the economy played the largest role in causing homelessness among the mentally ill. He points to two million jobs lost every year since 1980, an increase in poverty, a massive shortage in low-income housing, and a drop from 500,000 subsidized private housing units to 25,000 during the Reagan era (17–18). Cohen and Thompson also place primary emphasis on poverty and housing shortages:

> Data suggest that most homeless mentally ill persons lost their rooms in single-room-occupancy hotels or low-priced apartments not because of psychoticism but because they 1) were evicted because of renewal projects and fires, 2) were victimized by unscrupulous landlords or by other residents, or 3) could no longer afford the rent. (818)

Douglas Mossman and Michael Perlin cite numerous studies which show that mental illness itself is not the primary factor causing homelessness among the mentally ill; additionally, they point out that the severity of mental illness itself is closely linked to poverty. They argue that lack of private health care increases poor health and the frequency of severe mental illness. They conclude, "Homelessness is, if nothing else, a condition of poverty, and poor individuals in general are at increased risk for episodes of psychiatric illness" (952). Krauthammer's article conveniently ignores the role of poverty, suggesting that much of the homeless problem could be solved by moving the mentally ill back into institutions. But the evidence suggests that symptoms of mental illness are often the <u>results</u> of being homeless and that any efforts to treat the psychological problems of the mentally ill must also address the socioeconomic problems.

9   Krauthammer's belief that the causes of mentally ill homelessness are psychological rather than social and economic leads to a fourth assumption that the mentally ill homeless are a distinct subgroup who need different treatment from the other homeless groups. Krauthammer thus divides the homeless into three primary groups: (1) the mentally ill; (2) those who choose to live on the street; and (3) "the victims of economic calamity, such as family breakup or job loss" (25). By believing that the mentally ill homeless are not also victims of "economic calamity," Krauthammer greatly oversimplifies their problems. As Cohen and Thompson show, it is difficult to separate the mentally ill homeless and the non–mentally ill homeless. "On closer examination, 'not mentally ill' homeless people have many mental health problems; similarly, the 'mentally ill' homeless have numerous nonpsychiatric problems that arise from the sociopolitical elements affecting all homeless people" (817). Because the two groups are so similar, it is counterproductive to insist on entirely different solutions for both groups.

Krauthammer's proposal thus fails on a number of points. It won't solve nearly   10
as much of the homelessness problem as he leads us to believe. It would commit
valuable taxpayer dollars to building asylums rather than attacking the underlying
causes of homelessness in general. And perhaps most importantly, its emphasis on
involuntary confinement in asylums is not the best long-range method to treat the
mentally ill homeless. Instead of moving the mentally ill homeless away from
society into asylums, we would meet their needs far more effectively through
monitored community-based care. Instead of building expensive institutions, we
should focus on finding alternative low-cost housing for the mentally ill homeless
and meet their needs through teams of psychiatrists and social workers who could
oversee a number of patients' treatments, monitoring such things as taking
medications and receiving appropriate counseling. Involuntary hospitalization may
still be needed for the most severely deranged, but the majority of mentally ill
homeless people can be better treated in their communities.

From a purely financial perspective, perhaps the most compelling reason to   11
prefer community-based care is that it offers a more efficient use of taxpayer
dollars. In a letter to the <u>New York Times</u> on behalf of the Project for Psychiatric
Outreach to the Homeless, Drs. Katherine Falk and Gail Albert give us the following
statistics:

> It costs $105,000 to keep someone in a state hospital for a year. But it
> costs only $15,000 to $35,000 (depending on the intensity of services) to
> operate supported residences in the community with the necessary
> onsite psychiatrists, case workers, case managers, drug counselors, and
> other rehabilitation services. (A30)

It can be argued, in fact, that the cost of maintaining state hospitals for the
mentally ill actually prevents large numbers of mentally ill from receiving
treatment. When large numbers of mentally ill persons were released from state
hospitals during the deinstitutionalization movement of the 1960s and 1970s, the
original plan was to convert resources to community-based care. Even though the
number of patients in state institutions has dramatically decreased over the past
two decades, institutions have continued to receive large shares of state funding.
According to David Rothman of Columbia University, "Historically, the dollars have
remained locked in the institutions and did not go into community mental health"
(qtd. in Dugger, "Debate" B2). In fact, cutting New York's state hospital budget

would provide enough money for over 20,000 units in supported community residences (Falk and Albert A30). Furthermore, Linda Chafetz points out that having the money to pay for such resources as clothes, bathing facilities, meals, and housing is the most urgent concern among caregivers in treating the mentally ill homeless. According to Chafetz, "The immediate and urgent nature of the resource dilemma can make other issues appear almost frivolous by comparison" (451). With such an obvious shortage of resources, pouring what money we have into the high-cost institutional system would be a grave disservice to the majority of the mentally ill homeless population and to the homeless population as a whole.

12   A second reason to adopt community-based care over widescale institutionalization is that the vast majority of the homeless mentally ill do not need the tight control of the hospital system. Cohen and Thompson cite a number of studies which show "that only 5%–7% of single adult homeless persons are in need of acute inpatient care" (820). Involuntarily hospitalizing a large number of homeless who don't demand institutionalized care is not only a waste of resources but also an unnecessary assault on individual freedom for many.

13   Finally, the community-based care system is preferable to institutionalization because it most often gives the best treatment to its patients. Although Krauthammer claims that less than a fifth of involuntarily hospitalized patients have legally challenged their confinement (25), numerous studies indicate there is widespread resistance to institutional care by the homeless mentally ill. Mossman and Perlin cite multiple sources indicating that many mentally ill have legitimate reasons to fear state hospitals. Moreover, they provide evidence that many would rather suffer the streets and their mental illness than suffer the conditions of state hospitals and the side effects of medications. The horrible track record of conditions of state hospitals supports the logic of this thinking. Mossman and Perlin also point out that many mentally ill homeless persons will accept treatment from the type of alternative settings community-based care offers (953). Powerful evidence showing the success of community-based care comes from early evaluation reports of ACCESS (Access to Community Care and Effective Services), a community-based program of the Center for Mental Health. More than 11,000 mentally ill homeless have received services through this program, which reports "significant

improvements in almost all outcome measures," such as "a 66 percent decrease in minor criminal activity" and "a 46 percent decrease in reported psychotic symptoms" ("Articles"). Given that institutionalization can leave mentally ill persons feeling humiliated and disempowered (Cohen and Thompson 819), community-based solutions such as ACCESS seem the best approach.

Given the advantages of community-based care, what is the appeal of Krauthammer's proposal? Involuntary institutionalization appeals to our common impulse to lock our problems out of sight. As crime increases, we want to build more prisons; when we see ragged men and women mumbling in the street, we want to shut them up in institutions. But the simple solutions are not often the most effective ones. Institutionalization is tempting, but alternative methods have shown themselves to be more effective. Community-based care works better because it's based on a better understanding of the problem. Community-based care, by allowing the psychiatrist and social worker to work together, attacks both the mental and social dimensions of the problem: The client receives not only psychological counseling and medication but also help on how to find affordable housing, how to manage money and shop effectively, and how to live in a community. Without roots in a community, a patient released from a mental asylum will quickly return to the streets. To pour scarce resources into the expensive project of rebuilding asylums—helping the few while ignoring the many—would be a terrible misuse of taxpayer dollars.

14

Krauthammer's argument appeals in another way also. By viewing the homeless as mentally ill, we see them as inherently different from ourselves. We needn't see any connection to those mumbling bag ladies and those ragged men lying on the grates. When we regard them as mentally ill, we see ourselves as largely unresponsible for the conditions that led them to the streets. Those professional men and women carrying their espresso Starbuck's coffees to their upscale offices in Seattle's Pioneer Square don't have to be reminded that this historic district used to contain a number of single-occupancy boarding houses. The professionals work where the homeless used to live. The rich and the poor are thus interconnected, reminding us that homelessness is primarily a social and economic problem, not a mental health problem. And even the most deranged of the mentally ill homeless are messengers of a nationwide scourge of poverty.

15

Works Cited

"Articles to Focus on National Effort to Help People Who Are Homeless and
    Have Mental Illness." Press release. National Mental Health Services
    Knowledge Exchange Network (KEN) 3 Mar. 1997. 23 Apr. 1998
    <http://www.mentalhealth.org./resource/praccess.htm>.

Chafetz, Linda. "Withdrawal from the Homeless Mentally Ill." Community Mental
    Health Journal 26 (1990): 449–61.

Cohen, Carl I., and Kenneth S. Thompson. "Homeless Mentally Ill or Mentally Ill
    Homeless?" American Journal of Psychiatry 149 (1992): 816–23.

Dennis, Deborah L., et al. "A Decade of Research and Services for Homeless
    Mentally Ill Persons: Where Do We Stand?" American Psychologist 46 (1991):
    1129–38.

Dugger, Celia W. "A Danger to Themselves and Others." New York Times 24
    Jan. 1993: B1+.

---. "A Debate Unstilled: New Plan for Homeless Mentally Ill Does Not Address
    Larger Questions." New York Times 22 Jan. 1993: B2.

Falk, Katherine, and Gail Albert. Letter. New York Times 11 Feb. 1993: A30.

Hopper, Kim. "More Than Passing Strangers: Homelessness and Mental Illness in
    New York City." American Ethnologist 15 (1988): 155–57.

Kozol, Jonathan. "Are the Homeless Crazy?" Harper's Sept. 1988: 17–19.

Krauthammer, Charles. "How to Save the Homeless Mentally Ill." New Republic 8
    Feb. 1988: 22–25.

Mossman, Douglas, and Michael L. Perlin. "Psychiatry and the Homeless Mentally
    Ill: A Reply to Dr. Lamb." American Journal of Psychiatry 149 (1992): 951–56.

Snow, David A., et al. "The Myth of Pervasive Mental Illness among the Homeless."
    Social Problems 33 (1986): 407–23.

Critiquing "What Should Be Done about the Mentally Ill Homeless?"

1. In your own words, summarize Charles Krauthammer's argument for re-opening mental hospitals and reinstitutionalizing the mentally ill homeless. How does Stephen Bean attempt to refute Krauthammer's argument? What is Stephen's own proposal for solving the problem of the mentally ill homeless? What reasons does Stephen give in support of his proposal?

2. What rhetorical strategies does Stephen use to make his argument as compelling as possible? How does he try to create presence? How does he appeal to *ethos* and *pathos* as well as *logos*?

3. How effective do you find Stephen's argument?

Our last reading is an op-ed piece by professional columnist E. J. Dionne Jr. Dionne joins an ongoing public conversation about how to improve the academic performance of public schools. Many politicians advocate strengthening standards and ending the social promotion of poorly performing students. (Social promotion is the practice of letting a student advance to the next grade even if he or she flunked the previous grade.) In his 1999 State of the Union speech, President Clinton proposed ending all social promotion in the schools. Dionne's purpose in this argument is to raise doubts about Clinton's proposal.

Ending Social Promotion Means Fixing Failing Schools

E. J. Dionne Jr.

WASHINGTON—If a politician wants applause for a speech on improving the schools, all it takes are a few magic words. President Clinton knows this. In his State of the Union address, he declared: "All schools must end social promotion." On cue, members of Congress stood up and cheered.

The craze to end social promotion—the practice of moving children on to the next grade whether or not they've passed the previous grade—is national in scope and as bipartisan as you can get. Last Thursday, the Texas State Senate unanimously approved Gov. George W. Bush's plan to end social promotion.

Bush, the undeclared front-runner for the Republican presidential nomination, pronounced the bill "a strong message that no child will be left behind in our state—that when a child is identified with reading deficiency, we'll correct it early, before it's too late."

Hartford, Conn., welcomed a new school superintendent last Wednesday. "We will be relentless on literacy," Anthony Amato declared. Part of that relentlessness, reported *The Hartford Courant,* includes an end to social promotion.

5   On the same day, across the country in Escondido, Calif., school administrators announced a summer-school program for 360 students who were not making the grade.

6   Interim superintendent David Jenkins told the *San Diego Union-Tribune* reporter Anna Cearley that remedial help was part of his effort to end social promotion. "Each year that goes by makes it more difficult for these students to be successful in high school," he said. California's new Democratic governor, Gray Davis, has made a statewide campaign against—you guessed it—social promotion, a key part of his education reform package.

7   Now it's hard to defend social promotion, which is one reason why politicians have latched onto the war against it. When Clinton declares "we do our children no favors when we allow them to pass from grade to grade without mastering the material," everybody nods.

8   But you needn't be a cynic to see that this cause has a certain advantage for those who run schools: It moves the burden of failing systems from the adults who run them to the children who aren't making it.

9   "Simply pounding the kids on the head is not going to get the result we need," says Kati Haycock, president of The Education Trust, a group that battles for better teachers and more accountability. If students fail "there are already serious consequences for the kids, but not for the adults."

10   Writing last year in the American Association of School Administrators magazine, Linda Darling-Hammond pointed to "dozens of studies" showing that holding kids back "actually contributes to greater academic failure, higher levels of dropping out, and greater behavioral difficulties."

11   "Instead of looking carefully at classroom or school practices when students are not achieving, schools typically send students back to repeat the same experience," said Darling-Hammond, executive director of the National Commission on Teaching and America's Future. "Little is done to ensure that the experience will be either more appropriate for the individual needs of the child, or higher quality."

12   It's true, of course, that those who advocate an end to social promotion know that by itself, it's not a solution. Both Clinton and Bush would link its abolition to a variety of remedial and summer-school programs—and, in Bush's case, to teacher training and to a broader program to demand results from teachers and administrators.

13   In Texas, state Sen. Royce West, a Dallas Democrat, insisted on an amendment under which the ban on social promotion would stay in effect only if the state put up the money for the remedial programs. West's worry—a sensible one—is that the current eagerness to hold kids back when they fail tests might be just a "legislative fad."

14   If you want to be an optimist (and I certainly do), you might see the campaign against social promotion as part of a larger effort to ensure accountability by schools, teachers and students alike. It holding kids back focuses attention on how and why schools are failing, if kids get the help they need to move forward and if the practice leads to the hiring of better teachers—if all these things happen, it might work.

15   What the schools don't need is another gimmick, something that sounds tough in a politician's speech but doesn't produce reform. "The federal government's job is to help educate poor kids, not to add more pain," says Haycock of Clinton's program. "The way for the federal government to do that is to help poor kids have the best teachers not the worst."

Critiquing "Ending Social Promotion
Means Fixing Failing Schools"

1. Dionne's argument is not itself a proposal but instead a critique of a proposal. Explain in your own words, why the cry to "end social promotion" has become so popular among politicians.

2. What is Dionne's chief concern about social promotion? What motivates him to write this op-ed piece? In your own words, summarize Dionne's argument.

3. Which of the strategies for questioning and challenging a proposal argument (see pp. 324–26) does Dionne employ to raise doubts about social promotion?

4. How effective is Dionne's argument?

5. If you were to join this argumentative conversation by developing a proposal of your own, what specific aspects of the problem, costs, and consequences would you need to explore first?

15 Ethical Arguments

The line between ethical arguments ("Is X morally good?") and other kinds of values disputes is often pretty thin. Many apparently straightforward practical values issues can turn out to have an ethical dimension. For example, in deciding what kind of car to buy, most people would base their judgments on criteria such as cost, reliability, safety, comfort, and stylishness. But some people might feel morally obligated to buy the most fuel-efficient car, or not to buy a car from a manufacturer whose investment or labor policies they found morally repugnant. Depending on how large a role ethical considerations played in the evaluation, we might choose to call this an *ethical argument* as opposed to a simpler kind of values argument. In any case, we here devote a separate chapter to ethical arguments because we believe they represent special difficulties to the student of argumentation. Let's take a look now at some of those special difficulties.

SPECIAL DIFFICULTIES OF ETHICAL ARGUMENTS

One crucial difficulty with ethical arguments concerns the role of purpose in defining criteria for judgment. In Chapter 13, we assumed that every class of beings has a purpose, that the purpose should be defined as narrowly as possible, and that the criteria for judgment derive directly from that purpose. For example, the purpose of a computer repairperson is to analyze the problem with my computer, to fix it, and to do so in a timely and cost-efficient manner. Once I formulate this purpose, it is easy for me to define criteria for a good computer repairperson.

In ethics, however, the place of purpose is much fuzzier. Just what is the purpose of human beings? Before I can begin to determine what ethical duties I have to myself and to others, I'm going to have to address this question; and because the chance of reaching agreement on that question remains remote, many ethical arguments are probably unresolvable. In ethical discussions we don't ask what a "manager" or a "judge" or a "point guard" is supposed to do in situations relevant to the respective classes; we're asking what John Doe is supposed to be or what Jane Doe is supposed to do with her life. Who they are or what their social function is makes no difference to our ethical assessment of their actions or traits of character. A morally bad person may be a good judge and a morally good person may be a bad manager.

As the discussion so far has suggested, disagreements about ethical issues often stem from different systems of belief. We might call this problem the problem of warrants. That is, people disagree because they do not share common assumptions on which to ground their arguments.

If, for example, you say that good manners are necessary for keeping us from reverting to a state of raw nature, your implied warrant is that raw nature is bad. But if you say that good manners are a political tool by which a ruling class tries to suppress the natural vitality of the working class, then your warrant is that liberation of the working classes from the corrupt habits of the ruling class is good. It would be difficult, therefore, for people representing these opposing belief systems to carry on a reasonable discussion of etiquette—their assumptions about value, about the role of the natural self, and about political progress are different. This is why ethical arguments are often so acrimonious—they frequently lack shared warrants to serve as starting places for argument.

It is precisely because of the problem of warrants, however, that you should try to confront issues of ethics with rational deliberation. The arguments you produce may not persuade others to your view, but they should lay out more clearly the grounds and warrants of your own beliefs. Such arguments serve the purpose of clarification. By drafting essays on ethical issues, you begin to see more clearly what you believe and why you believe it. Although the arguments demanded by ethical issues require rigorous thought, they force us to articulate our most deeply held beliefs and our richest feelings.

AN OVERVIEW OF MAJOR ETHICAL SYSTEMS

When we are faced with an ethical issue, such as the issue of whether terrorism can be justified, we must move from arguments of good or bad to arguments of right or wrong. The terms *right* and *wrong* are clearly different from the terms *good* and *bad* when the latter terms mean simply "effective" (meets purposes of class, as in "This is a good stereo system") or "ineffective" (fails to meet purposes of class, as in "This is a bad cookbook"). But *right* and *wrong* often also differ from what seems to be a moral use of the terms *good* and *bad*. We might say, for example, that sunshine is good because it brings pleasure and that cancer is bad because it brings pain and death, but that is not quite the same thing as saying that sunshine is "right" and cancer is "wrong." It is the problem of "right" and "wrong" that ethical arguments confront.

Thus it is not enough to say that terrorism is "bad"; obviously everyone, including most terrorists, would agree that terrorism is "bad" because it causes suffering and anguish. If we want to condemn terrorism on ethical grounds, we have to say that it's also "wrong" as well as "bad." In saying that something's wrong, we're saying that all people ought to refrain from doing it. We're also saying that acts that are morally "wrong" are in some way blameworthy and deserve censure, a conclusion that doesn't necessarily follow a negative nonethical judgment, which might lead simply to our not buying something or not hiring someone. From a nonethical standpoint, you may even say that someone is a "good" terrorist in that he fully realizes the purposes of the class "terrorist": He causes great damage with a minimum of resources, brings a good deal of attention to his cause, and doesn't get caught. The ethical question here, however, is not whether this person is a good member of the class, but whether it is wrong for such a class to exist.

In asking the question "Ought the class 'terrorist' to exist?" or, to put it more colloquially, "Are there ever cases where terrorism is justified?" we need to seek some consistent approach or principle. In the phrase used by some philosophers, ethical judgments are typically "universalizable" statements. That is, when we oppose a terrorist act, our ethical argument (assuming it's a coherent one) should be capable of being generalized into an ethical principle that will hold for all similar cases. Ethical disputes usually involve clashes between such principles. For example, a pro-terrorist might say, "My ends justify my means," whereas an anti-terrorist might say, "The sanctity of human life is not to be violated for any reason." The differences in principles such as these account for different schools of ethical thought.

There are many different schools of ethical thought—too many to present in this chapter. But to help you think your way through ethical issues, we'll look at some of the most prevalent methods of resolving ethical questions. The first of these methods, "naive egoism," is really less a method than a retreat from method. It doesn't represent a coherent ethical view, but it is a position that many people lapse into on given issues. It represents, in short, the most seductive alternative to rigorous ethical thought.

Naive Egoism

Back in Chapter 1, we touched on the morality of the Sophists and suggested that their underlying maxim was something like "Might makes right." That is, in ethical terms, they were essentially egoists who used other people with impunity to realize their own ends. The appeal of this position, however repugnant it may sound when laid out like this, is that it rationalizes self-promotion and pleasure seeking: If we all follow the bidding of our egos, we'll be happy.

On examination, this philosophy proves to be incoherent. It should be noted, however, that philosophers don't reject naive egoism simply because they believe "selfishness is bad." Rather, philosophers tend to assess ethical systems according to such factors as their scope (how often will this system provide principles to guide our moral action?) and their precision (how clearly can we analyze a given situation using the tools of the system?) rather than their intuition about whether the system is right or wrong. Although naive egoism has great scope (you can always ask, "What's in it for me?"), it is far from precise, as we'll try to show.

Take the case of young Ollie Unger, who has decided that he wants to quit living irrationally and to join some official school of ethical thought. The most appealing school at the moment—recommended to him by a philosophy major over at the Phi Upsilon Nu house—is the "I'm Number One!" school of scruples. He heads downtown to the school's opulent headquarters and meets with the school's guru, Dr. Pheelgood.

"What's involved in becoming a member of your school?" Ollie inquires.

"Ahhh, my apple-cheeked chum, that's the beauty of it. It's so simple. You just give me all your worldly possessions and do whatever I tell you to do."

Ollie is puzzled. He had in mind something a bit more, well, gratifying. He was hoping for something closer to the philosophy of eat, drink, and make merry—all justified through rational thought.

"You seem disappointed," Pheelgood observes. "What's the matter?"

"Well, gee, it just doesn't sound like I'm going to be number one here. I thought that was the idea. To look out for *numero uno*."

"Of course not, silly boy. This is after all the "I'm Number One School of Scruples." And I, *moi*, am the I who's number one.

"But I thought the idea of your school was for everyone to have the maximum amount of enjoyment in life."

Peevishness clouds Pheelgood's face. "Look here, Unger, if I arrange things for you to have a good time, it's going to cost me. Next you'll be asking me to open soup kitchens. If I'm to look out for number one, then you've got to act entirely differently from me. I take, you give. *Capiche?*"

As should be obvious by now, it's very difficult to systematize egoism. You have two sets of demands in constant conflict—the demands of your own personal ego and those of everyone else's. Thus it's impossible to universalize a statement that all members of the school could hold equally without contradicting all other members of the school.

Some egoists try to get around this problem by conceding that we must limit our self-gratification either by entering into contracts or institutional arrangements with others or by sacrificing short-term interests for long-term ones. We might, for example, give to the poor now in order to avoid a revolution of the masses later. But once they've let the camel's nose of concern for others into the tent, it's tough to hang onto egoistic philosophy. Having considered naive egoism, let's turn to a pair of more workable alternatives.

In shifting to the two most common forms of ethical thought, we shift point of view from "I" to "us." Both groups, those who make ethical judgments according to the consequences of any act and those who make ethical judgments according to the conformity of any act with a principle, are guided by their concern for the whole of humanity rather than simply the self.

Consequences as the Base of Ethics

Perhaps the best-known example of evaluating acts according to their ethical consequences is utilitarianism, a down-to-earth philosophy that grew out of nineteenth-century British philosophers' concern to demystify ethics and make it work in the practical world. Jeremy Bentham, the originator of utilitarianism, developed the goal of the greatest good for the greatest number, or "greatest happiness," by which he meant the most pleasure for the least pain. John Stuart Mill, another British philosopher, built on Bentham's utilitarianism, using predicted consequences to determine the morality of a proposed action.

Mill's consequentialist approach allows you readily to assess a wide range of acts. You can apply the principle of utility—which says that an action is morally right if it produces a greater net value (benefits minus costs) than any available alternative action—to virtually any situation and it will help you reach a decision. Obviously, however, it's not always easy to make the calculations called for by the principle, since, like any prediction of the future, an estimate of consequences is conjectural. In particular, it's often very hard to assess the long-term consequences of any action. Too often, utilitarianism seduces us into a short-term analysis of a moral problem simply because long-term consequences are very difficult to predict.

Principles as the Base of Ethics

Any ethical system based on principles will ultimately rest on one or two moral tenets that we are duty bound to uphold, no matter what the consequences. Sometimes the moral tenets come from religious faith—for example, the Ten Commandments. At other times, however, the principles are derived from philosophical reasoning, as in the case of German philosopher Immanuel Kant. Kant held that no one should ever use another person as a means to his own ends and that everyone should always act as if his acts were the basis of universal law. In other words, Kant held that we were duty bound to respect other people's sanctity and to act in the same way that we would want all other people to act. The great advantage of such a system is its clarity and precision. We are never overwhelmed by a multiplicity of contradictory and difficult-to-quantify consequences; we simply make sure we are not violating a principle of our ethical system and proceed accordingly.

The Two Systems Compared

In the eyes of many people, a major advantage of a system such as utilitarianism is that it impels us to seek out the best solution, whereas systems based on principle merely enjoin us not to violate a principle by our action. In turn, applying an ethical principle will not always help us resolve necessarily relativistic moral dilemmas. For instance, what if none of our available choices violates our moral principles? How do we choose among a host of permissible acts? Or what about situations where none of the alternatives is permitted by our principles? How might we choose the least bad alternative?

To further our comparison of the two systems, let's ask what a Mill or a Kant might say about the previously mentioned issue of terrorism. Here the Kantian position is clear: To kill another person to realize your own ends is palpably evil and forbidden.

A follower of Mill will face a less clear choice. A utilitarian could not automatically rule out terrorism or any other means so long as it led ultimately to the greatest good for the greatest number. If a nation is being slowly starved by those around it, if its people are dying, its institutions crumbling, and its future disappearing, who is to say that the aggrieved nation is not justified in taking a few hundred lives to improve the lot of hundreds of thousands? The utilitarian's first concern is to determine whether terrorism will most effectively bring about that end. So long as the desired end represents the best possible net value and the means are effective at bringing about the end, the utilitarian can, in theory anyway, justify almost any action.

Given the shared cultural background and values of most of us, not to mention our own vulnerability to terrorism, the Kantian argument is probably very appealing here. Indeed, Kantian ethical arguments have overwhelming appeal for us when the principle being invoked is already widely held within our culture, and when the violation of that principle will have clear and immediate negative consequences for us. But in a culture that doesn't share that principle and for whom the consequences of violation are positive rather than negative, the argument will undoubtedly appear weaker, a piece of fuzzy-headed idealism.

FOR CLASS DISCUSSION

Working as individuals or in small groups:

1. Try to formulate a utilitarian argument to persuade terrorist leaders in the Mideast, the Balkans, Ireland, or elsewhere to stop terrorist action.

2. Try to formulate an ethical principle or rule that would permit terrorism.

Some Compromise Positions between Consequences and Principles

In the end, most of us would not be entirely happy with an ethic that forced us to ignore either principles or consequences. We all have certain principles that we simply can't violate no matter what the consequences. Thus, for example, some of us would not have dropped the bomb on Hiroshima even if it did mean saving many lives ultimately. And certainly, too, most of us will compromise our principles in certain situations if we think the consequences justify it. For instance, how many of us would not deceive, harm, or even torture a kidnapper to save the life of a stolen child? Indeed, over the years, compromise positions have developed on both sides to accommodate precisely these concerns.

Some "consequentialists" have acknowledged the usefulness of general rules for creating more human happiness over the long run. To go back to our terrorism example, a consequentialist might oppose terrorist action on the grounds that "Thou shalt not kill another person in the name of greater material happiness for the group." This acknowledgment of an inviolable principle will still be based on a concern for consequences—for instance, a fear that terrorist acts may lead to World War III—but having such a principle allows the consequentialist to get away from a case-by-case analysis of acts and to keep more clearly before himself the long-range consequences of acts.

Among latter-day ethics of principle, meanwhile, the distinction between absolute obligation and what philosophers call *prima facie* obligation has been developed to take account of the force of circumstances. An *absolute* obligation would be an obligation to follow a principle at all times, no matter what. A *prima facie* obligation, in contrast, is an obligation to do something "other things being equal," that is, in a normal situation. Hence, to use a classic moral example, you would not, other things being equal, cannibalize an acquaintance. But if there are three of you in a lifeboat, one is dying and the other two will surely die if they don't get food, your *prima facie* obligation not to eat another might be waived. (However, the Royal Commission, which heard the original case, took a more Kantian position and condemned the action of the seamen who cannibalized their mate.)

These, then, in greatly condensed form, are the major alternative ways of thinking about ethical arguments. Let's now briefly summarize the ways you can use your knowledge of ethical thought to develop your arguments and critique those of others.

DEVELOPING AN ETHICAL ARGUMENT

To help you see how familiarity with these systems of ethical thought can help you develop an ethical argument, let's take an example case. How, for example, might we go about developing an argument in favor of abolishing the death penalty?

Our first task is to examine the issue from the two points of view just discussed. How might a utilitarian or a Kantian argue that the death penalty should be abolished? The argument on principle, as is usually the case, would appear to be the simpler of the two. Taking another life is difficult to justify under most ethical principles. For Kant, the sanctity of human life is a central tenet of ethics. Under Judeo-Christian ethics, meanwhile, one is told that "Vengeance is Mine, saith the Lord" and "Thou shalt not kill."

Unfortunately for our hopes of simplicity, Kant argued in favor of capital punishment:

> There is no sameness of kind between death and remaining alive even under the most miserable conditions, and consequently there is no equality between the crime and the retribution unless the criminal is judicially condemned and put to death.*

Kant is here invoking an important principle of justice—that punishments should be proportionate to the crime. Kant appears to be saying that this principle must take precedence over his notion of the supreme worth of the individual. Some philosophers think he was being inconsistent in taking this position. Certainly, in establishing your own position, you could support a case against capital punishment based on Kant's principles, even if Kant himself did not reach the same conclusion. But you'd have to establish for your reader why you are at odds with Kant in this case. Kant's apparent inconsistency here illustrates how powerfully our intuitive judgments can affect our ethical judgment.

Likewise, with the Judeo-Christian position, passages can be found in the Bible that would support capital punishment, notably, the Old Testament injunction to take "an eye for an eye and a tooth for a tooth." The latter principle is simply a more poetic version of "Let the punishment fit the crime." Retribution should be of the same kind as the crime. And the commandment "Thou shalt not kill" is often interpreted as "Thou shalt not commit murder," an interpretation that not only permits just wars or killing in self-defense but is also consistent with other places in the Bible that suggest that people have not only the right but the obligation to punish wrongdoers and not leave their fate to God.

So, there appears to be no clearcut argument in support of abolishing capital punishment on the basis of principle. What about an argument based on consequences? How might abolishing capital punishment result in a net good that is at least as great as allowing it?

A number of possibilities suggest themselves. First, in abolishing capital punishment, we rid ourselves of the possibility that someone may be wrongly executed. To buttress this argument, we might want to search for evidence of how many people have been wrongly convicted of or executed for a capital crime. In making arguments based on consequence, we must, whenever possible, offer

---

*From Immanuel Kant, *The Metaphysical Elements of Justice.*

empirical evidence that the consequences we assert exist—and exist to the degree we've suggested.

There are also other possible consequences that a utilitarian might mention in defending the abolition of capital punishment. These include leaving open the possibility that the person being punished will be reformed, keeping those charged with executing the murderer free from guilt, and putting an end to the costly legal and political process of appealing the conviction.

But in addition to calculating benefits, you will need also to calculate the costs of abolishing the death penalty and to show that the net result favors abolition. Failure to mention such costs is a serious weakness in many arguments of consequence. Moreover, in the issue at hand, the consequences that favor capital punishment—deterrence of further capital crimes, cost of imprisoning murderers, and so forth—are well known to most members of your audience.

In our discussion of capital punishment, then, we employed two alternative ways of thinking about ethical issues. In pursuing an argument from *principle,* we looked for an appropriate rule that permitted or at least did not prohibit our position. In pursuing an argument from *consequence,* we moved from what's permissible to what brings about the most desirable consequences. Most ethical issues, argued thoroughly, should be approached from both perspectives, so long as irreconcilable differences don't present themselves.

Should you choose to adopt one of these perspectives to the exclusion of the other, you will find yourself facing many of the problems mentioned here. This is not to say that you can't ever go to the wall for a principle or focus solely on consequences to the exclusion of principles; it's simply that you will be hard-pressed to convince those of your audience who happen to be of the other persuasion and demand different sorts of proof. For the purpose of developing arguments, we encourage you to consider both the relevant principles and the possible consequences when you evaluate ethical actions.

TESTING ETHICAL ARGUMENTS

Perhaps the first question you should ask in setting out to analyze your draft of an ethical argument is "To what extent is the argument based on consequences or on ethical principles?" If it's based exclusively on one of these two forms of ethical thought, then it's vulnerable to the sorts of criticism discussed here. A strictly principled argument that takes no account of the consequences of its position is vulnerable to a simple cost analysis. What are the costs in the case of adhering to this principle? There will undoubtedly be some, or else there would be no real argument. If the argument is based strictly on consequentialist grounds, we should ask if the position violates any rules or principles, particularly such commandments as the Golden Rule—"Do unto others as you would have others do unto you"—which most members of our audience adhere to. By failing to mention these alternative ways of thinking about ethical issues, we undercut not only our argument but our credibility as well.

Let's now consider a more developed examination of the two positions, starting with some of the more subtle weaknesses in a position based on principle. In practice people will sometimes take rigidly "principled" positions because they live in fear of "slippery slopes"; that is, they fear setting precedents that might lead to ever more dire consequences. Consider, for example, the slippery slope leading from birth control to euthanasia if you have an absolutist commitment to the sanctity of human life. Once we allow birth control in the form of condoms or pills, the principled absolutist would say, then we will be forced to accept birth control "abortions" in the first hours after conception (IUDs, "morning after" pills), then abortions in the first trimester, then in the second or even the third trimester. And once we have violated the sanctity of human life by allowing abortions, it is only a short step to euthanasia and finally to killing off all undesirables.

One way to refute a slippery-slope argument of this sort is to try to dig a foothold into the side of the hill to show that you don't necessarily have to slide all the way to the bottom. You would thus have to argue that allowing birth control does not mean allowing abortions (by arguing for differences between a fetus after conception and sperm and egg before conception), or that allowing abortions does not mean allowing euthanasia (by arguing for differences between a fetus and a person already living in the world).

Consequentialist arguments have different kinds of difficulties. As discussed before, the crucial difficulty facing anyone making a consequentialist argument is to calculate the consequences in a clear and reliable way. Have you considered all significant consequences? If you project your scenario of consequences further into the future (remember, consequentialist arguments are frequently stronger over the short term than over the long term, where many unforeseen consequences can occur), can you identify possibilities that work against the argument?

As also noted, consequentialist arguments carry a heavy burden of empirical proof. What evidence can you offer that the predicted consequences will in fact come to pass? Do you offer any evidence that alternative consequences won't occur? And just how do you prove that the consequences of any given action are a net good or evil?

In addition to the problems unique to each of the two positions, ethical arguments are vulnerable to the more general sorts of criticism, including consistency, recency, and relevance of evidence. Obviously, however, consequentialist arguments will be more vulnerable to weaknesses in evidence, whereas arguments based on principle are more open to questions about consistency of application.

READING

In the following essay, "The Case for Torture," philosopher Michael Levin argues that torture not only can be justified but is positively mandated under certain circumstances.

The Case for Torture

Michael Levin

1   It is generally assumed that torture is impermissible, a throwback to a more brutal age. Enlightened societies reject it outright, and regimes suspected of using it risk the wrath of the United States.

2   I believe this attitude is unwise. There are situations in which torture is not merely permissible but morally mandatory. Moreover, these situations are moving from the realm of imagination to fact.

3   **Death:**   Suppose a terrorist has hidden an atomic bomb on Manhattan Island which will detonate at noon on July 4 unless . . . (here follow the usual demands for money and release of his friends from jail). Suppose, further, that he is caught at 10 A.M. of the fateful day, but—preferring death to failure—won't disclose where the bomb is. What do we do? If we follow due process—wait for his lawyer, arraign him—millions of people will die. If the only way to save those lives is to subject the terrorist to the most excruciating possible pain, what grounds can there be for not doing so? I suggest there are none. In any case, I ask you to face the question with an open mind.

4   Torturing the terrorist is unconstitutional? Probably. But millions of lives surely outweigh constitutionality. Torture is barbaric? Mass murder is far more barbaric. Indeed, letting millions of innocents die in deference to one who flaunts his guilt is moral cowardice, an unwillingness to dirty one's hands. If *you* caught the terrorist, could you sleep nights knowing that millions died because you couldn't bring yourself to apply the electrodes?

5   Once you concede that torture is justified in extreme cases, you have admitted that the decision to use torture is a matter of balancing innocent lives against the means needed to save them. You must now face more realistic cases involving more modest numbers. Someone plants a bomb on a jumbo jet. He alone can disarm it, and his demands cannot be met (or if they can, we refuse to set a precedent by yielding to his threats). Surely we can, we must, do anything to the extortionist to save the passengers. How can we tell 300, or 100, or 10 people who never asked to be put in danger, "I'm sorry, you'll have to die in agony, we just couldn't bring ourselves to . . . ."

6   Here are the results of an informal poll about a third, hypothetical, case. Suppose a terrorist group kidnapped a newborn baby from a hospital. I asked four mothers if they would approve of torturing kidnappers if that were necessary to get their own newborns back. All said yes, the most "liberal" adding that she would like to administer it herself.

7   I am not advocating torture as punishment. Punishment is addressed to deeds irrevocably past. Rather, I am advocating torture as an acceptable measure for preventing future evils. So understood, it is far less objectionable than many extant punishments. Opponents of the death penalty, for example, are forever insisting that executing a murderer will not bring back his victim (as if the purpose of capital punishment were supposed to be resurrection, not deterrence or retribution). But torture, in the cases described, is intended not to bring anyone back but to keep innocents from being dispatched. The most powerful argument against using torture as a punishment or to secure confessions is that such prac-

tices disregard the rights of the individual. Well, if the individual is all that important—and he is—it is correspondingly important to protect the rights of individuals threatened by terrorists. If life is so valuable that it must never be taken, the lives of the innocents must be saved even at the price of hurting the one who endangers them.

Better precedents for torture are assassination and pre-emptive attack. No Allied leader   8
would have flinched at assassinating Hitler, had that been possible. (The Allies did assassinate Heydrich.) Americans would be angered to learn that Roosevelt could have had Hitler killed in 1943—thereby shortening the war and saving millions of lives—but refused on moral grounds. Similarly, if nation A learns that nation B is about to launch an unprovoked attack, A has a right to save itself by destroying B's military capability first. In the same way, if the police can by torture save those who would otherwise die at the hands of kidnappers or terrorists, they must.

Idealism: There is an important difference between terrorists and their victims that   9
should mute talk of the terrorists' "rights." The terrorist's victims are at risk unintentionally, not having asked to be endangered. But the terrorist knowingly initiated his actions. Unlike his victims, he volunteered for the risks of his deed. By threatening to kill for profit or idealism, he renounces civilized standards, and he can have no complaint if civilization tries to thwart him by whatever means necessary.

Just as torture is justified only to save lives (not extort confessions or recantations), it   10
is justifiably administered only to those *known* to hold innocent lives in their hands. Ah, but how can the authorities ever be sure they have the right malefactor? Isn't there a danger of error and abuse? Won't We turn into Them?

Questions like these are disingenuous in a world in which terrorists proclaim them-   11
selves and perform for television. The name of their game is public recognition. After all, you can't very well intimidate a government into releasing your freedom fighters unless you announce that it is your group that has seized its embassy. "Clear guilt" is difficult to define, but when 40 million people see a group of masked gunmen seize an airplane on the evening news, there is not much question about who the perpetrators are. There will be hard cases where the situation is murkier. Nonetheless, a line demarcating the legitimate use of torture can be drawn. Torture only the obviously guilty, and only for the sake of saving innocents, and the line between Us and Them will remain clear.

There is little danger that the Western democracies will lose their way if they choose   12
to inflict pain as one way of preserving order. Paralysis in the face of evil is the greater danger. Some day soon a terrorist will threaten tens of thousands of lives, and torture will be the only way to save them. We had better start thinking about this.

Critiquing "The Case for Torture"

1. Most people think of torture as an abhorrently barbarian practice that civilized society has outgrown. Yet Levin argues that in some cases torture is not only justified but mandated. In your own words, summarize Levin's argument.

2. Analyze Levin's argument in terms of our distinction between arguments from *principle* and arguments from *consequence.*

3. In "The Case for Torture," Levin mentions the possibility of some "murkier" cases in which it is difficult to draw a line demarcating legitimate from illegitimate use of torture. Try to come up with several examples of these "murkier" cases and explain what makes them murky.

part four

Writing from Sources

The Argument as a Formal Research Paper

16 Finding and Selecting Sources

The Library and the Internet

Although the "research paper" is a common writing assignment in college, students are often baffled by their professor's expectations. The problem is that students often think of research writing as presenting information rather than as creating an argument. One of our business school colleagues calls these sorts of research papers "data dumps": The student backs a truckload full of fresh data up to the professor's desk, dumps it, and says: "Here's your load of info on 'world poverty,' Prof. You make sense of it."

But a research paper shouldn't be a data dump. Like any other argument, it should use its information to support a contestable claim. Formal researched arguments have much in common with arguments that freelancers might write in a popular magazine. Consider the following passage from a science writer arguing that male aggression has a strong biological component:

Preliminary work shows that fetal boys are a little more active than fetal girls. It's pretty difficult to argue socialization at this point. There is a strong suspicion that testosterone may create the difference.

And there are a couple of relevant animal models to emphasize the point. Back in the 1960s, Robert Goy, a psychologist at the University of Wisconsin at Madison, first documented that young male monkeys play much more roughly than young females. Goy went on to show that if you manipulate testosterone level—raising it in females, damping it down in males—you can reverse those effects, creating sweet little male monkeys and rowdy young females. [. . .] Studies have found that girls with congenital adrenal hypoplasia—who run high in testosterone—tend to be far more fascinated by trucks and weaponry than most little girls are. They lean toward rough-and-tumble play too.*

This article shares many features of a good research paper. It makes a contestable claim ("Testosterone levels account for much of the difference between male and female behavior"), and the author's supporting data come from external sources rather than personal experiences—in this case, scientific research.

However, there is one major difference between this article and a formal academic research paper—absence of citations. Because readers can't track down the author's sources, they have no way to judge the reliability of her information or to see whether the experiments being cited are open to different interpretations. (From our own research on gender identity, we know that many scientists would contest her claim; they would cite studies showing that cultural conditioning is a far greater factor than biology in creating gender differences.) In academic research, the purpose of in-text citations and a complete bibliography is to enable readers to follow the trail of the author's research. The proper formats for citations and bibliographic entries are simply conventions within an academic discipline to facilitate the reader's retrieval of the original sources.

Fortunately, you will find that writing an argument as a formal research paper draws on the same argumentation skills you have been using all along—the ability to pose a good question at issue within a community, to formulate a contestable claim, and to support your claim with audience-based reasons and evidence. What special skills are required? The main ones are these:

- The ability to use your research effectively to frame your issue and to support your claim, revealing your reputable ethos and knowledge of the issue. Sources should be woven seamlessly into your argument, which is written in your own voice throughout. Writers should avoid a pastiche of block quotations.

- The ability to tap the resources of libraries, online databases, Internet forums, and the World Wide Web.

- The ability to evaluate sources for credibility, bias, and accuracy. Special care is needed to evaluate anything retrieved from the "free access" portion of the World Wide Web.

- The ability to summarize, quote, or paraphrase sources and to avoid plagiarism through citations and attributive tags such as "according to Jones" or "Peterson says."

- The ability to cite and document sources according to appropriate conventions.

This chapter and the next should help you to develop these skills. In Chapter 16 we focus on posing a research question and on unlocking the resources of your

---

*Deborah Blum, "The Gender Blur," *Utne Reader* Sept.–Oct. 1998, 47–48.

library and the Internet. In Chapter 17 we explain the more nitty-gritty details of how to incorporate that information into your writing and how to document it properly.

FORMULATING A RESEARCH QUESTION

The best way to avoid writing a data dump is to begin with a good research question—the formulation of a problem or issue that your essay will address. The research question, usually in the form of an issue question, will give you a guiding purpose in doing your library research. Let's say you are interested in how toys affect the development of gender identity in children. You can see that this topic is big and unfocused. Your library research will be much easier if you give yourself a clear direction through a focused research question. For example, you might formulate a specific question like one of these:

- Why have Barbie dolls been so continuously popular?
- Does the Barbie doll reinforce traditional ideas of womanhood or challenge them?
- Is culture or biology the stronger force in making little boys interested in trucks and guns?
- Do boys' toys such as video games, complex models, electronic gadgets, and science sets develop intellectual and physical skills more than girls' toys do?

The sooner you can settle on a research question, the easier it will be to find the source materials you need in a time-saving, efficient manner. The exploration methods we suggested in Chapter 3 can help you find a research topic that interests you.

A good way to begin formulating a research question is to freewrite for ten minutes or so, reflecting on recent readings that have stimulated your interest, on recent events that have sparked arguments, or on personal experiences that might open up onto public issues. If you have no idea for a topic, try starting with the trigger question "What possible topics am I interested in?" If you already have an idea for a topic area, explore why you are interested in it. Search for the personal connections or the particular angles that most intrigue you. Here is how Lynnea, a student writer, began exploring a topic related to police work. She chose this topic because she had a friend who was a patrol officer.

LYNNEA'S FIRST FREEWRITE

Why am I attracted to this issue? What personal connections do I have?

My friend is a police officer and has been telling me about some of the experiences he has had while walking "the beat" downtown. The people he has to deal with are mostly street people: bums, gang members, drug dealers, etc. He tells me how he just harasses them to get them to move on and to leave the area, or he looks for a reason to give them a ticket so that eventually they will accumulate a few unpaid tickets, and they will have to go to jail. My friend told me about an experience where an alcoholic tramp started kicking his feet against the patrol car after he and his partner had walked about a block away to begin their night shift. The man started yelling at them to come back and kept hitting and throwing himself against the car. "OK, what are you doing that for?" they asked. The man stammered that he wanted to go to "detox." They told the guy that they would not take him to detox, so he kept on banging the car. What can be done about these people? Not only the alcoholics and vagrants, but what about the gang members, prostitutes, drug dealers, etc.? The police forces out on the streets at night seem to be doing little more than just ruffling a few feathers, but what else can they do under the circumstances?

On finishing this freewrite, Lynnea was certain that she wanted to write her research argument on something related to police work. The topic interested her, and having a patrol officer as a friend gave her an opportunity for interview data. She decided she was most interested in gangs and called her friend to get some more insights. Several days later, she met her friend at a local restaurant during his lunch break. After that meeting, she again did a freewrite.

LYNNEA'S SECOND FREEWRITE

Today I went with my friend for a cup of coffee to discuss some possible topics for my paper. He took me to a coffee shop where several of the officers in the area meet for lunch. I had wanted to ask Bob specific questions about gangs in the area, but when we joined the rest of the officers, I didn't have the chance. However, something they brought into the discussion *did* interest me. They were talking about a woman who had recently graduated from the academy and was now trying to pass the student officer's phase. This woman, I was informed, was 4'9" and weighed about 90 pounds. Apparently, at the academy she couldn't perform many of the physical exercises that her fellow trainees could. Where most of the men could pull a trigger between 80 and 90 times during the allotted time, she could pull the trigger of her police issue .38 revolver only once. And she was so tiny that they had to make a booster seat for the patrol car. One of the instructors said that her being in the academy was a joke. Well, it does seem that way to me. I can imagine this woman trying to handle a situation. How could she handcuff someone who resisted arrest? It seems dangerous that someone who is so weak should be allowed to be on patrol duty. I wouldn't want her as my back-up.

Lynnea now knew she had a topic that interested her. She wanted to research women patrol officers, especially the success rate of small women. She formulated her initial research question this way: "Can a small, physically weak woman, such as this 4'9" police candidate, make a good patrol officer?" Her initial thesis was that small, physically weak women could not make good patrol officers, but she wanted to keep an open mind, using argument as a means of clarification. As this chapter progresses, we will return occasionally to Lynnea's research project. (Her final argument essay is reproduced in full at the end of Chapter 17.)

EXPLORING ON THE INTERNET

Besides freewriting and sharing ideas with friends, today's researchers have the vast resources of the Internet and the World Wide Web as sources of ideas and help. Throughout a project, many researchers get invaluable assistance from listserv discussions, Usenet newsgroups, or real-time chat groups.

Listserv Discussions

A potentially productive way to use e-mail is to join a listserv interest group. A listserv compiles any number of e-mail accounts into a mailing list and forwards copies of messages to all people on the list. There are thousands of well-established listservs about a wide variety of topics. You need to know the address of a list in order to join. Specific information about joining various listservs and an index of active lists can be found by entering either the Uniform Resource Locator (URL) address "http://tile.net/lists/" or "http://www.liszt.com" once you are on the World Wide Web in a browser.* Once you have subscribed to a listserv, you receive all messages sent to the list and any message you send to the list address will be forwarded to the other members.

A message sent to a listserv interest group is sure to find a responsive audience because all members on the list have chosen to take part in an ongoing discussion of the list's specific topic. Such lists often archive and periodically post important messages or frequently asked questions (FAQs) for you to study. Most lists are for serious students of the list's topic, so to avoid offending any list members, learn the conventions for posting a message before you jump in.

Although you may find all kinds of interactions on a listserv, many users expect thoughtful, well-organized statements. If you are posting a message that introduces a new thread of discussion, you should clearly state your position (or question) and summarize those of others. Here is a sample posting to a listserv on the environment.

```
To: environL@brahms.usdg.org
From: alanw@armadillo.edu (Alan Whigum)
Subject: Acid Rain and Action

I've been doing research on acid rain and am
troubled by some of the things I've found. For
instance, I've learned that washing coal gases with
```

---

*Each file on the World Wide Web has a unique address, or URL, that allows writers to link to information on the Web and lets users move to specific sites.

```
limestone before they are released could reduce
sulfur emissions. I know that the government has
the power to mandate such devices, but the real
problem seems to be lack of public pressure on
the government. Why don't people push for better
legislation to help end acid rain? I suppose it's
an economic issue.
```

In turn, you can expect cogent, thoughtful responses from the list members. Here's a possible reply to the preceding message.

```
To: environL@brahms.usdg.org
From: bboston@armadillo.edu
Subject: Re Acid Rain and Action

I think you are right in pointing out that it is
ultimately public pressure that will need to be
applied to reduce acid rain. I've heard the
argument that it is cost that prevents steps from
being taken; people will pay more for goods and
services if these measures are taken, so they
resist. However, judging from the people I've
talked to about the subject, I would say that a
bigger problem may be knowledge. Most of them
said they would be willing to pay a little bit
more for their electricity if it meant a safer
environment. People aren't aware that action
needs to be taken now, because the problem seems
remote.
```

When you join a listserv, you are granted instant access to a discourse community that is committed and knowledgeable about its topic. You can join one of the discussions already taking place on the list or post a request to get information and clarification about your own interests.

Listservs can take your ideas through a productive dialectic process as your message is seconded, refuted, complicated, and reclarified by the various list members. They also afford valuable opportunities to practice your summarizing skills as you respond to messages or provide additional information in a second posting. For example, suppose you take issue with a long message that placed the blame for youth violence on the music industry. Rather than reproducing that entire message, you might provide a brief summary of the main points. The summary not only would give the readers enough background information to appreciate fully your response, it also would help you determine the main points of the original message and pinpoint the issues on which you disagree.

Usenet Newsgroups

Among the most useful sections of the Internet for writers are the bulletin-board-like forums of Usenet newsgroups. Newsgroups are electronic forums that allow you to post or respond to messages about nearly any topic imaginable. Newsgroups can be powerful tools for exploring problems and considering alternative viewpoints. The news server at your school determines the organization and number of groups available to you. Some schools carry groups that provide articles from professional news services, such as AP, Reuters, and UPI. Others provide topic-centered discussion groups. Your campus system may also offer class newsgroups for exchanging messages and drafts with others at your school.

The majority of newsgroups are used by members of the larger Internet community. Although some groups are devoted to subjects that don't lend themselves directly to the work you are probably undertaking in the composition class, many are frequented by regulars who are professionals in their fields or individuals deeply interested in the topic of the newsgroup. One key to successfully interacting on newsgroups, then, is finding a group that is appropriate to your work. Most of the newsreading programs that are built into Web browsers have a search function that can help you select appropriate groups. Another strategy is to spend some time searching through the archives of newsgroup postings at the DejaNews site (http://www.dejanews.com). Using keywords, you can comb through postings either to tap into preexisting conversations or to pinpoint newsgroups that seem to take up the issues that you are interested in.

Once you find an appropriate group, you will need to work through the logistics of accessing the newsgroup, reading messages and, perhaps, posting messages of your own. Check with your instructor or computer center to find out how to access and interact with the groups available to you.

Although you may be tempted to begin participating in a group immediately, you should familiarize yourself with some of the style conventions and the audience for that particular newsgroup before jumping in. Take time to "lurk"— read and listen in to the group's postings. Debate on Usenet can become fairly heated, and a message that ignores previous postings can elicit angry responses ("flames"). In addition, a message that doesn't consider the newsgroup's audience or its favored style will likely be challenged. For example, if you want to post something in the "alt.fan.rush-limbaugh" group, you should be cautious about composing a message that openly contradicts Rush Limbaugh's brand of politics. If you send a message to the newsgroup "soc.history," you might be able to tread less carefully—this list is more politically diverse—although members of this group might take offense if asked an obvious factual question.

Regardless of their makeup, most groups resent being asked questions that have already been answered. Some groups provide an archive of frequently asked questions (FAQs). If your interest is in something practical that is likely to be covered in the FAQ files, refer to them before posting a query. You should use the expertise of the group to find information that you might not be able to uncover otherwise.

When you are ready to post a message, use some of the strategies outlined for composing a message to a listserv: Try to summarize and synthesize your own position as well as the positions of others; highlight what you see as the most problematic or murky aspects of the topic. Carefully constructed messages are most likely to receive useful responses.

When you do receive feedback, evaluate it with special care. The unfiltered nature of all Internet media makes critical reading an essential skill. Because anyone with an Internet connection can take part in a discussion or post a message or article, you need to evaluate this information differently than you would articles from national newsmagazines, which are professionally written, edited for clarity, and checked for accuracy.

Although most postings are thoughtful, you will also find carelessly written messages that misconstrue an argument, personal rants that offer few (if any) stated reasons for their claims, and propaganda and offensive speech of many kinds in certain newsgroups. It is your responsibility, and unique opportunity, to read newsgroup messages critically, looking for their various biases and making decisions about their relative authority.

Of course, printed sources are marked by their own biases. Deadlines and space constraints may limit the depth and accuracy of printed coverage, and first-hand insights may be screened by authors and editors. If you were studying attitudes toward the Middle East peace process, a newsgroup exchange between a conservative Jew in Israel and a Palestinian student in the United States might provide better insight than a news article for your work. As you read through newsgroup messages, take time to evaluate the users' personal investments in the issue. Compare their comments to those in traditional sources, check for accuracy, and look for differing perspectives. Work these perspectives into your own thinking and writing about the topic. Treat information and points of view gathered from the Internet as primary rather than as secondary material; many of the people who contribute such material care passionately about an issue. It is up to you to place this material in context and edit it for your own audience.

Real-Time Discussion or Chat

Real-time discussions, or chat, are *synchronous* exchanges that take place on a network—meaning that messages are transferred instantly back and forth among members taking part in the discussion. We focus on real-time interactions that take place on the Internet, but you can apply many of the strategies outlined here to local chat programs in your writing class. One of the most popular forms of real-time interaction takes place in the various channels of Internet Relay Chat (IRC). Additionally, many course Web sites now incorporate a chat function. As with newsgroup and listserv communications, in chat you compose messages on your own computer and send them through the chat program to other users on the network. Since the specifics for connecting and issuing the various commands vary, you will need to check with your instructor or an experienced user for information about using chat resources at your school.

Like other Internet forums, chat groups are organized around common interests, but real-time sessions are more spontaneous and informal than is communication through newsgroups or listservs because they consist of exchanges from people who are logged on at the same time. In these conversations, typographical and spelling errors are mostly overlooked, and abbreviations are an acceptable part of real-time style. The pace can be extremely fast, so users generally focus on getting their thoughts out rather than on producing highly polished messages.

Chat sessions and many other real-time exchanges also allow users to act as characters and to include scripted actions in the conversations. Imagine three users discussing flag burning:

```
William: I'm studying the constitutionality of
flag-burning amendments. Does anybody have any
opinions?

Pat Buchanan: I think that if you are an American,
you should respect the country enough not to deface
her symbols.

*Thomas Jefferson takes out a match and sets fire
to the corner of an old thirteen star flag. It's
probably more important to respect the underlying
principles of our country than its symbols.
```

The asterisk denotes that the user Thomas Jefferson has issued an "Action" or "Emote" command. By putting his name at the beginning of the message, other users see whatever follows as an action performed by that character. Users can construct a third-person narrative by mixing speech with the actions of their characters. You may use this feature in role-playing exercises or to explore some open-ended thinking about your topic.

Perhaps even more than newsgroup or listserv discussions, chat sessions tend to heat up easily. Many real-time forums on the Internet allow users to take on pseudonyms, and some people use the opportunity to become irresponsible in what they say and write.

Real-time interactions give rise to many ethical issues. In these uncensored forums, you will at times encounter discussions and materials that aren't appropriate for your assignments and classwork. You may be challenged to assess your own feelings about censorship, pornography, hate speech, and free speech. And you will need to consider the impact of your persona and words on others as you take on a character or act out an idea.

Perhaps the most useful function of chat sessions is that they promote brainstorming and freewriting. When you are writing in a real-time environment, treat the activity as an exploratory one. Expect the message that you send to be challenged, seconded, or modified by the other writers in the session. Keep an open mind about the various messages that fly back and forth, and be sure to respond to points that you find particularly useful or problematic. If you are interacting with classmates, you will be talking to people you know, so the conversation will be more predictable. When it's over, you might ask your instructor for a transcript of a chat session; reading it later will help solidify the free thinking that goes into a real-time discussion.

LOCATING SOURCES IN THE LIBRARY OR ONLINE

To be a good researcher, you need to unlock the resources of your college's or university's library. Today, most researchers are also using the vast resources of the Internet and the World Wide Web to find materials.

In addition to books, libraries have a wealth of other resources, such as articles in magazines and journals, statistical reports from government agencies, articles and editorials in newspapers (often on microfilm or microfiche), and congressional records. Books, of course, are important, but they tend to be less current than periodical sources. The key is to become skilled at using all of a library's resources.

Using the Online Catalog

Most libraries have converted their card catalogs to online computer-based systems, making card catalogs obsolete. The library online catalog is now your first source of information about the library's holdings. Indexed by subject, title, and author, the online catalog identifies most of the library's holdings: books, magazines, and journals (but not the titles of articles in them), newspapers, theses and dissertations, major government documents (but not minor ones), and most multimedia items including records, cassettes, and filmstrips.

To find the book, magazine, or journal in the stacks, you will need to know the two major systems for shelving books—the Dewey decimal system, which uses a series of numbers and decimals, and the Library of Congress system, which uses letters followed by numbers. Most college and university libraries use the Library of Congress system, although they may have an older book collection still classified using the Dewey decimal system. The following lists show the major categories in each system:

Dewey Decimal System

000   General Works
100   Philosophy and Related Disciplines
200   Religion

300	Social Sciences
400	Language
500	Pure Science
600	Technology and Applied Science
700	The Arts
800	Literature and Rhetoric
900	General Geography and History

Library of Congress System

A	General Works, Polygraphy
B	Philosophy, Psychology, and Religion
C	Auxiliary Sciences of History
D	General and Old World History (except America)
E–F	American History
G	Geography, Anthropology, Manners and Customs, Folklore, Recreation
H	Social Science, Statistics, Economics, Sociology
J	Political Science
K	Law
L	Education
M	Music
N	Fine Arts
P	Language and Literature
Q	Science
R	Medicine
S	Agriculture, Plant and Animal Industry, Fish Culture, Fisheries, Hunting, Game Protection
T	Technology
U	Military Science
V	Naval Science
Z	Bibliography and Library Science

Each of these headings is further subdivided according to an elaborate system of subclassifications. For example, in the Library of Congress system the book by William C. Grimm called *Familiar Trees of America* is filed under QK481 (Q = Science; K = Botany; 481 = North American trees). Knowing something of the system's logic helps you browse.

Figure 16.1 shows how one library's online catalog presents a book entry. Your library's online catalog will probably look similar.

```
                    ITEM REPORT
   Personal author: Owings, Chloe.
              Title: Women police; a study of the
                     development and status of the
                     women police movement.
  Publication info: Montclair, N.J., Patterson Smith,
                     1969.
Physical description: xxii, 337 p. 22 cm.
             Series: (Patterson Smith reprint series
                     in criminology, law enforcement,
                     and social problems, no. 28)
      General note: Reprint of the 1925 ed.
            Subject: Policewomen.

                      COPY MATERIAL      LOCATION
1)363.22 OW3W            1 BOOK           STACKS
```

FIGURE 16.1   Book entry in online catalog

Accessing Online Databases

Often the best sources of information to support a researched argument come from periodicals (magazines, scholarly journals, and newspapers). Today most libraries use major online indexes called "general databases" to catalog such articles. Although the general databases available and the methods for accessing them vary from institution to institution, we offer a few guidelines that are widely applicable. Reference librarians at your institution can show you the specific commands you will need. Note also that online databases can often be accessed from anywhere in the world through your library's World Wide Web site. (Students, faculty, and staff usually have passwords or personal identification numbers for accessing the databases.)*

Most likely your library will have one or more of the following general databases online. Many of these databases indicate that they include not just abstracts of articles but the entire articles (full text).

EBSCOhost: Includes interdisciplinary citations and abstracts as well as the full text of many articles from over 3,000 journals; its *Academic Search Elite* function covers back to the early 1980s.

---

*The general databases discussed in this section are sometimes called "licensed databases" because libraries have to pay a substantial fee to have access to them. The information in these databases is substantially different from that contained in the "free-access" part of the World Wide Web that one surfs with search engines such as Infoseek, Yahoo, or Lycos.

UMI Proquest Direct: Gives access to the full text of articles from journals in a variety of subject areas; includes the full text of articles from newspapers.

Infotrac: Is often called Expanded Academic Index; similar to EBSCOhost and UMI Proquest in its coverage of interdisciplinary subjects.

FirstSearch Databases: Includes multiple specialized databases in many subject areas; includes WorldCat, which contains records of books, periodicals, and multimedia formats in libraries worldwide.

Lexis-Nexis Academic Universe: Is primarily a full-text database covering current events and business and financial news; includes company profiles and legal, medical, and reference information.

Britannica Online: Includes the complete *Encyclopedia Britannica.*

Your first task when using these online resources is to choose which database to search. Sometimes, as with FirstSearch Databases, you will also have to choose from a list of databases contained within the general one. For example, in some libraries, ERIC, an important database that lists articles on education, is found within FirstSearch Databases. The reference librarians in your college or university library will be able to direct you to the most useful General Database for your purpose. For instance, for our purposes we found EBSCOhost and Lexis-Nexis particularly fruitful in helping us find many of the arguments used as readings in this textbook.

To use an online database—or most electronic research technology—effectively, you need to be adept at keyword searching. Figure 16.2 shows a page from a Results List for a search under the keyword "policewomen" in the database EBSCOhost. The page icon in the second left-hand column indicates that the full text of the article is available on the database. The "Note" under each entry indicates whether your particular library subscribes to the magazine. If you click on a specific article in the article listings, you get a full display page showing complete publishing information about that article. Figure 16.3 shows a full display page for the article "A Municipal Mother: Portland's Lola Greene Baldwin, America's First Policewoman." Note that this page provides an abstract of the article—useful for helping you decide whether you want to read the entire text.

When using online databases to find articles, you need to be persistent and flexible in your keyword searches. For example, if you are trying to find information on the economic influence of the timber industry in South America, you might enter the keywords "timber AND economics." If these keywords produce numerous entries on the spotted owl controversy in the Pacific Northwest, you might alter your keywords to "timber AND economics NOT owl" to free your screen of owl references. Most online catalogs allow you to refine keyword searches in a similar way, but you should check the options available before you begin working with an unfamiliar system. Again, your reference librarians can help you narrow down your searches or find other possible keywords to make your searches efficient.

Mark	Full Text	Select Result For More Detail
☐	📄	Who Are the New Beat Poets? Hint: They're Blue.; By: Grace, Julie., Time, 09/13/99, Vol. 154 Issue 11, p20, 1/5p, 1c **Note:** We subscribe to this magazine.
☐		Officer Charged in Sexual Abuse of Ex-Companion.; By: Cooper, Michael., New York Times, 08/31/99, Vol. 148 Issue 51631, pB4, 0p **Note:** We subscribe to this magazine.
☐		Ban on Skirts For Guards Is Challenged.; By: Herszenhorn, David M.., New York Times, 08/26/99, Vol. 148 Issue 51626, pB6, 0p **Note:** We subscribe to this magazine.
☐	📄	Women face 'blue wall' of resistance. (cover story); By: Marks, Alexandra., Christian Science Monitor, 08/18/99, Vol. 91 Issue 184, p1, 0p, 1c **Note:** We subscribe to this magazine.
☐	📄	Affirmative Action, Political Representation, Unions, and Female Police Employment.; By: Sass, Tim R., and Troyer, Jennifer L.., Journal of Labor Research, Fall99, Vol. 20 Issue 4, p571, 17p, 4 charts **Note:** We do not subscribe to this magazine.
☐	📄	Do women make better peacekeepers?; By: DeGroot, Gerard J.., Christian Science Monitor, 07/14/99, Vol. 91 Issue 159, p9, 0p, 1 cartoon **Note:** We subscribe to this magazine.
☐	📄	She goes 'mano a mano' with drug lords. (cover story); By: Marks, Alexandra., Christian Science Monitor, 06/01/99, Vol. 91 Issue 129, p1, 0p, 1c **Note:** We subscribe to this magazine.
☐		Iran to Train *Policewomen.*, New York Times, 05/27/99, Vol. 148 Issue 51535, pA5, 0p **Note:** We subscribe to this magazine.
☐	📄	News Digest., Workforce, May99, Vol. 78 Issue 5, p18, 1/3p **Note:** We do not subscribe to this magazine.
☐		A municipal mother: Portland's Lola Greene Baldwin, America's first policewoman.; By: Myers, Gloria E., Peace Research Abstracts Journal, 2/1/99, Vol. 36, Issue 1, p0, 0p **Note:** We subscribe to this magazine.

FIGURE 16.2 Sample results list for a search using EBSCOhost

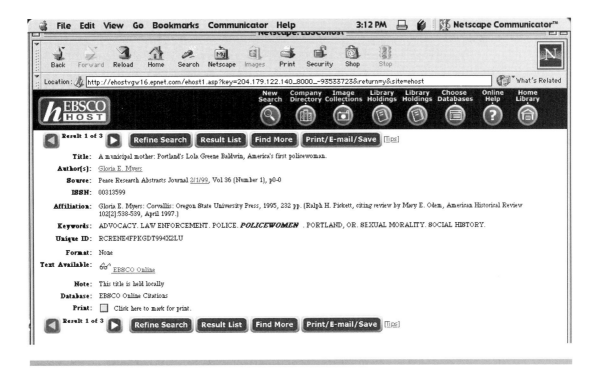

FIGURE 16.3 Sample full display for an article listing on EBSCOhost

Although the full texts of many articles are available online, you should always locate the original magazine or scholarly journal if possible. Articles printed online are decontextualized, giving you no clues about the author, the intended audience, the political bias of the original publication, and so forth. When you look at the original publication—its format, its table of contents, the advertisements it contains, the length and range and style of its articles—you have a rhetorical context for analyzing the article. Therefore if your library has the magazine, newspaper, or scholarly journal—or if it provides quick access to interlibrary loan—jot down all the key information given in the database: name of the magazine or journal, the volume, year, and page numbers. You will need this information to find the article in your library's periodical collection or to order it through interlibrary loan.

Using Specialized Indexes

Depending on the subject area of your research, you may find that specialized indexes can give you more useful information than general databases. Formerly, specialized indexes, which list articles in more narrow and specific areas than do general databases, appeared as hard-copy volumes housed in the reference area of libraries. Today many of these specialized indexes are online as well as in print, and the online versions are substantially easier to use. In the following list, we briefly describe some of the specialized indexes that writers of arguments might find useful. The information given after each index title indicates whether the index exists in both book (noted as "print") and online form:

ABI/Inform. (Online). Includes citations on business and management topics in U.S. and international publications.

America: History and Life. (Print and online). Includes abstracts and scholarly articles on the history of the United States and Canada.

ERIC Database. (Online). Consists of references to thousands of educational topics and includes journal articles, books, theses, curricula, conference papers, and standards and guidelines.

General Science Abstracts. (Print and online). Includes journals and magazines from the United States and Great Britain, covering such subjects as anthropology, astronomy, biology, computers, earth sciences, medicine, and health; includes articles, reviews, biographical sketches, and letters to the editor.

Historical Abstracts. (Print and online). Includes abstracts of scholarly articles on world history (excluding the United States and Canada) from 1775 to 1945.

Humanities Abstracts. (Print and online). Includes periodicals in archaeology, art, classics, film, folklore, journalism, linguistics, music, the performing arts, philosophy, religion, world history, and world literature.

Medline. (Online). Includes journals published internationally covering all areas of medicine.

MLA (Modern Language Association) Bibliography. (Print and online). Indexes scholarly articles on literature, languages, linguistics, and folklore published worldwide.

New York Times Index. (Print and online). Covers international, national, business, and New York regional news as well as sciences, medicine, arts, sports, and lifestyle news; makes the full text of articles available for the last ninety days.

Public Affairs Information Service (PAIS) International. (Print and online). Consists of articles, books, conference proceedings, government documents, book chapters, and statistical directories about public affairs.

Social Sciences Abstracts. (Print and online). Covers international, English-language periodicals in sociology, anthropology, geography, economics, political science, and law; concentrates on articles published in scholarly journals aimed at professional scholars rather than the general audience.

UMI Newspaper Abstracts. (Online). Covers national and regional newspapers; includes the *Wall Street Journal.*

Awareness of these specialized indexes may increase the efficiency of your research as well as expand your skill and power as a researcher.

Using Other Library Sources

Besides being a storehouse for books and periodicals, your library has a wealth of material in the reference section that may be useful to you in finding background information, statistics, and other kinds of evidence. Here are some sources that we have found particularly useful in our own research.

1. *Encyclopedias.* For getting quick background information on a topic, you will often find that a good encyclopedia is your best bet. Besides the well-known general-purpose encyclopedias such as the *Encyclopedia Britannica*, there are excellent specialized encyclopedias devoted to in-depth coverage of specific fields. Among the ones you might find most useful are these:

The International Encyclopedia of the Social Sciences

Dictionary of American History

Encyclopedia of World Art

McGraw-Hill Encyclopedia of Science and Technology

2. *Facts on File.* These interesting volumes give you a year-by-year summary of important news stories. If you wish to assemble a chronological summary of a news event such as Hillary Clinton's task force on national health coverage, ethnic wars in the Balkan countries, or the end of apartheid in South Africa, *Facts on File* gives you a summary of the events along with information about exact dates so that you can find the full stories in newspapers. A special feature is a series of excellent maps in the back of each volume, allowing you to find all geographical place names that occur in the year's news stories. The front cover of each volume explains how to use the series.

3. *Statistical Abstracts of the United States.* Don't even consider picking up one of these volumes if you don't have some spare time. You will get hooked on the fascinating graphs, charts, and tables compiled by the Bureau of Statistics. For statistical data about birth rates and abortions, marriages and divorces, trends in health care, trends in employment and unemployment, nutritional habits, and a host of other topics, these yearly volumes are a primary source of quantitative information about life in the United States.

4. *Congressional Abstracts.* For people working on current or historical events related to politics or any controversy related to the public sector, this index can guide you to all debates about the topic in the Senate or the House of Representatives.

5. *Book Review Digest.* For writers of argument, this series can be a godsend because it provides not only a brief summary of a book but also excerpts from a variety of reviews of the book, allowing the writer to size up quickly the conversation surrounding the book's ideas. To use *Book Review Digest,* you need to know the publishing date of the book for which you want to find reviews. Generally, reviews first appear in the same year the book was published and for several years thereafter. If you want to read reviews, for example, of a book appearing in 1992, you would probably find them in the 1992, 1993, and (if the book was very popular or provocative) 1994 volumes of *Book Review Digest.*

LOCATING AND EVALUATING SOURCES ON THE WORLD WIDE WEB

Another valuable resource for writers of argument is the network of linked computers known broadly as the Internet and more narrowly as the World Wide Web. In this section we begin by explaining briefly the logic of the Internet—the difference between restricted, licensed databases of the kind we discussed in the previous section and the amorphous, ever-changing "free-access" portion of the Internet commonly called the World Wide Web. Then we explain common methods of searching the Web. Finally, we suggest strategies for evaluating Web sites, which can vary enormously in their reliability, accuracy, and usefulness.

The Logic of the Internet

To learn the logic of Internet search engines, you should realize that the Internet is divided into a restricted section open only to those with special access rights (for example, the library online catalogs and general databases discussed in the previous section of this chapter) and a free-access section. Web search engines such as Yahoo or Infoseek search only the free-access portion of the Web; they do not have access to licensed databases or the holdings of libraries. When you search a topic through a licensed database such as EBSCOhost, for example, you retrieve the titles of articles (and often full texts) that originally appeared in magazines, newspapers, and scholarly journals. When you search the same topic through a Web search engine such as Yahoo, you retrieve information posted to the Web by users of the world's networked computers—government agencies, corporations, advocacy groups, information services, individuals with their own Web sites, and hosts of others.

The following example will quickly show you the difference. When we entered the keyword "policewomen" into EBSCOhost, we received 67 "hits"—the titles of 67 recent articles on the subject of policewomen (see Figure 16.2). In contrast, when we entered the same keyword into the Web search engine Infoseek, we received 3,941 "hits"—all the Web sites available to Infoseek that had the word "policewomen" appear somewhere in the site. When we plugged the same word into AltaVista, we received 2,704 hits, and only two of the first ten from AltaVista matched the first ten from Infoseek.

FOR CLASS DISCUSSION

The figures on pages 380 and 381 show the first seven "hits" for the keyword "policewomen" retrieved by the search engine GoTo (Figure 16.4) and the first five hits retrieved by AltaVista (Figure 16.5). Working in small groups or as a whole class, compare these items with those retrieved from a search for "policewomen" in the licensed database EBSCOhost (Figure 16.2).

1. Explain in your own words why the results for the Web searches are different both from each other and from the licensed database search.

2. Which of the Web sites from AltaVista and GoTo might prove useful for Lynnea's research project on whether a physically weak woman can make a good police officer?

Using Search Engines

Although the World Wide Web contains everything from gold to garbage, its resources for writers of argument are breathtaking. At your fingertips you have access to government documents and statistics, legislative white papers, court cases, persuasive appeals of advocacy groups—the list seems endless. Moreover, the hypertext structure of Web sites lets Web designers create links to other sites so that users can read an argument from an advocacy group in one Web site and then have instant links to the argument's sources at other Web sites.

The World Wide Web can be searched with a variety of powerful browsers, which collect and categorize a large number of Internet files and search them for keywords. Most of these search engines will find not only text files but also graphical, audio, and video files. Some look through the titles of files; others scan the entire text of documents. Different search engines can scan different resources, so it is important that you try a variety of searches when you look for information. Although the Web is evolving rapidly, some of the best search engines are fairly stable. For starters, you might try the following:

Hotbot (http://www.hotbot.com)   Webcrawler (http://www.webcrawler.com)

Yahoo (http://www.yahoo.com)   AltaVista (http://www.altavista.com)

Lycos (http://www.lycos.com)   GoTo (http://www.goto.com)

If you are in doubt, your reference librarians can help you choose the most productive search engine for your needs.

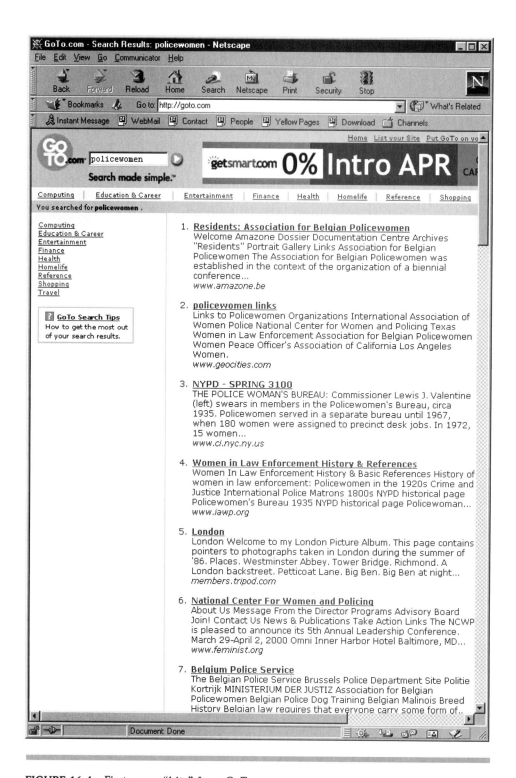

FIGURE 16.4 First seven "hits" from GoTo

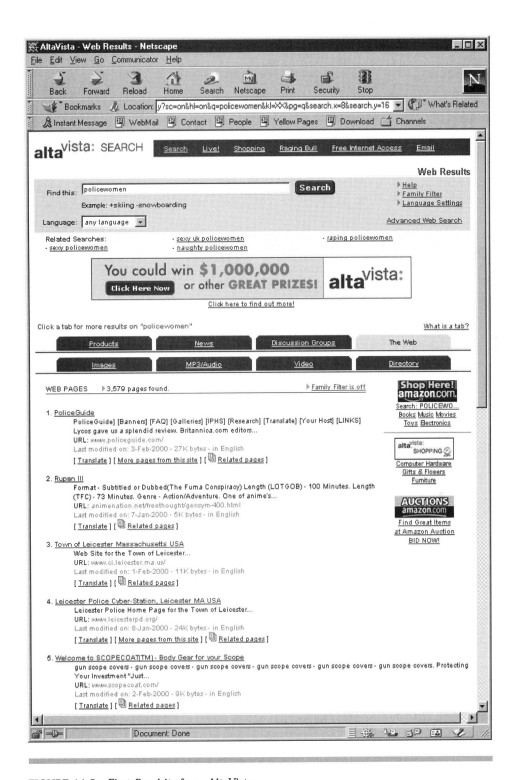

FIGURE 16.5 First five hits from AltaVista

Browsing the Web is an excellent way to help focus your thinking about an issue or topic and scout for resources. Some of the links that you follow will be dead ends; others will lead to new discoveries and useful collections of subject-related sources. Always be aware that anybody can put practically anything on the Web. The next section will help you learn to evaluate Web sites.

Evaluating Web Sites

Although the Web is an exciting, inexhaustible source of information, it also contains lots of junk, and therefore you need to evaluate Web material carefully. Anyone with hypertext skills can put up a Web page that furthers his or her own agenda. Flashy graphics and other design elements can sometimes overwhelm the information that is being presented or lend an air of authority to an otherwise suspect argument or position.

When you look at a Web site, begin by asking the following two questions:

- *What kind of Web site is it?* Web sites can have distinctly different purposes. Business/marketing Web sites are aimed at attracting and serving customers as well as creating a favorable public image. Informational/ government Web sites are aimed at providing basic data ranging from traffic information to bills being debated in Congress. News Web sites supplement coverage in other media. Advocacy Web sites (often indicated by *.org* at the end of their URL address) attempt to influence public opinion on disputed issues. Special interest Web sites are aimed at connecting users with common interests ranging from recent film reviews to kayaking. Personal home pages are created by individuals for their own purposes.

- *What is my purpose in using this Web site?* Am I trying to get an initial understanding of the various points of view on an issue, looking for reliable data, or seeking expert testimony to support my thesis? Joe's Web page— let's say Joe wants California to secede from the United States—may be a terrible source for reliable data about the federal government but an excellent source for helping you understand the views of fringe groups.

One of the most challenging parts of using the Web is determining whether a site offers gold or glitter. Sometimes the case may not be clear-cut. How do you sort out reliable, worthwhile sites from unreliable ones? We offer the following criteria developed by scholars and librarians as points to consider when you are using Web sites.

Criterion 1: Authority

- Is the author or sponsor of the Web site clearly identified?
- Does the site identify the occupation, position, education, experience, and credentials of the site's authors?

- Does the introductory material reveal the author's or sponsor's motivation for publishing this information on the Web?
- Does the site provide contact information for the author or sponsor such as an e-mail or organization address?

Criterion 2: Objectivity or Clear Disclosure of Advocacy

- Is the site's purpose (to inform, explain, or persuade) clear?
- Is the site explicit about declaring its author's or sponsor's point of view?
- Does the site indicate whether authors are affiliated with a specific organization, institution, or association?
- Does the site indicate whether it is directed toward a specific audience?

Criterion 3: Coverage

- Are the topics covered by the site clear?
- Does the site exhibit suitable depth and comprehensiveness for its purpose?
- Is sufficient evidence provided to support the ideas and opinions presented?

Criterion 4: Accuracy

- Are the sources of information stated? Can you tell whether this information is original or taken from someplace else?
- Does the information appear to be accurate? Can you verify this information by comparing this source with other sources in the field?

Criterion 5: Currency

- Are dates included in the Web site?
- Do the dates apply to the material itself or to its placement on the Web? Is the site regularly revised and updated?
- Is the information current, or at least still relevant, for the site's purpose?

To illustrate how these criteria can help you deal with the good points and the deficiencies of Web material, we give an example of how to use the criteria to assess the value of Web information. We wanted to investigate the United States' involvement in exploitation of workers in sweatshops. We specifically wanted to investigate this question: "To what extent are caps and shirts with university logos produced under sweatshop conditions?"

To start our investigation of the link between university-licensed clothing and sweatshops, we entered the keyword "sweatshop" into Yahoo, our selected search engine. We discovered a vast anti-sweatshop movement with a number of promising sites for our first-step initiation into the issues. We decided to investigate the site of "NMASS," which we discovered was the abbreviation for "National Mobilization against Sweatshops" (http://www.nmass.org). Figure 16.6 shows the initial Web page of this site. Using the criteria for evaluating Web sites, we were able to identify the strengths and weaknesses of this site in the light of our question and purpose.

This site does well when measured against the criteria "authority" and "clear disclosure of advocacy." On the home page, the organization's title, "National Mobilization Against Sweatshops," boldly announces its perspective. Information in the bulleted list openly declares its purpose: "Become a sweatshop buster!" The links then provide more detailed information on the goals of the organization. In the "Mission Statement" link, the site forthrightly declares:

> The National Mobilization Against Sweatshops (NMASS) is a grassroots educational effort by and for working people and youth of all backgrounds and communities. NMASS was first started by members and supporters of the Chinese Staff and Workers' Association, an independent workers' center in New York's Chinatown.

Links mentioned on the home page indicate that this site is directed toward both members and prospective members; it seeks to rally the members of the organization and to win new supporters. The site does provide contact information by giving an address for comments and suggestions: nmass@yahoo.com.

We found that this site provides good coverage of material for its purpose, even though it does not specifically address our research question. Particularly, the link called "8 Myths about Sweatshops" introduced us to important sweatshop issues such as the existence of sweatshops in the United States, the exploitation of immigrant workers, the level of government involvement in addressing the problem, and the ineffectiveness of unions. Several of these links identify industries involved with sweatshops, but the site does not give specific information about university-licensed clothing and sweatshops.

The fourth criterion ("accuracy") enabled us to identify some problems with the accuracy of the site's information for our purposes. The links called "Global Sweatshop" and "8 Myths about Sweatshops" offer a number of facts and figures about the origin and history of sweatshops and about current working - conditions, yet no specific sources are cited. These statements are startling and compelling, but are they accurate? And what opposing information should be considered?

Finally, the site seemed satisfactory, but a little vague, with regard to currency. Although the links revealed sources with recent, up-to-date copyright dates, the site itself does not indicate how often it is updated.

In short, we found this site helpful as a first stop to acquaint us with the stakes in the anti-sweatshop movement, but we concluded that this site's information is too broad for our purposes. Furthermore, this site could not stand as a major, unverified source. Using the evaluation criteria helped us recognize our need for more

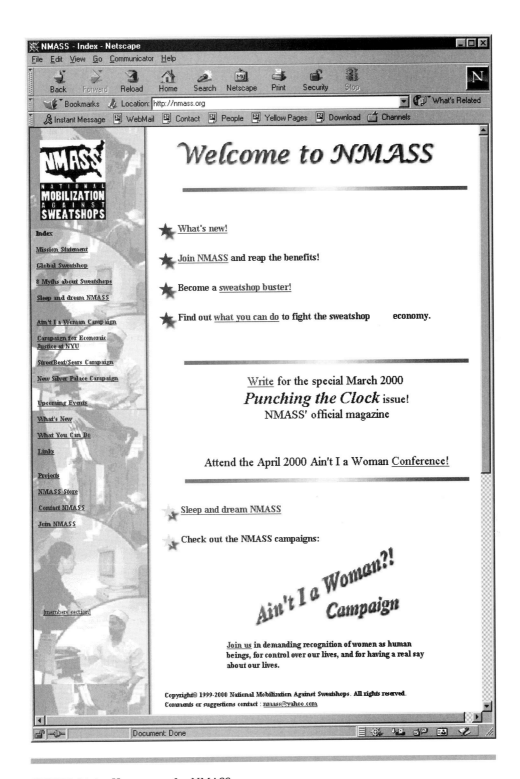

FIGURE 16.6   Home page for NMASS

in-depth research and follow-up investigations. We realized, particularly, that we would need to investigate sweatshops from the perspective of industry (such as the American Apparel Manufacturers Association at www.americanapparel.org) and government regulatory agencies (such as the Bureau of International Labor Affairs at www.dol.gov/dol/ilab).

USING YOUR SOURCES: SITTING DOWN TO READ

Once you have developed a working bibliography of books and articles and have gathered a collection of materials, how do you go about reading and note-taking? There is no easy answer. At times you need to read articles carefully, fully, and empathically—reading as a believer and as a doubter, as discussed in Chapter 2, trying to understand various points of view on your issue, seeing where the disagreements are located, and so forth. Your goal at this time is to clarify your own understanding of the issue in order to join responsibly the ongoing conversation.

At other times you need to read quickly, skimming an article in search of a needed piece of information, an alternative view, or a timely quotation. All these considerations and others—how to get your ideas focused, how to take notes, how to incorporate source material into your own writing, and how to cite and document your sources—are the subjects of the next chapter.

17 Using and Documenting Sources

The previous chapter helped you pose a good research question and begin unlocking some of the resources of your library and the Internet. This chapter helps you see what to do with your sources once you have found them—how to use them to clarify your own thinking and how to incorporate them into your writing through effective use of quotations, paraphrases, and summaries along with appropriate conventional formats for citations and documentation.

CLARIFYING YOUR OWN THINKING: THE CASE OF LYNNEA

In the previous chapter, we followed Lynnea's progress as she posed her research question on the effectiveness of policewomen and began her search for sources. Once Lynnea located several articles on policewomen, she found a quiet spot in the library and began to read. She was guided by two related questions: What physical requirements must someone meet in order to be an effective patrol officer? How successful have policewomen been when assigned to patrol duty? After reading some recent articles, Lynnea noticed that writers often referred to significant earlier studies, particularly a 1984 study called *Policewomen on Patrol, Final Report* by P. B. Bloch and D. Anderson. Lynnea tracked down this study as well as several others referred to in the first articles she read.

Both Lynnea's experience and her research strategy are typical. As a researcher becomes familiar with the ongoing conversation on an issue, she will notice that recent writers frequently refer to the same earlier studies or to the same earlier voices in the conversation. In scientific writing, this background reading is so important that the introductions to scientific studies usually include a "review of the literature" section, wherein writers summarize important research done to date on the question under investigation and identify areas of consensus and disagreement.

Therefore, during the first hours of her research project, Lynnea conducted her own "review of the literature" concerning women on patrol. During an early visit to her university's writing center, she reported that she had found three kinds of studies:

1. *Studies attempting to identify the attitude of the police establishment (overwhelmingly male) toward women entering the police profession and the attitude of the general public toward women patrol officers.* Although the findings weren't entirely consistent, Lynnea reported that male police officers generally distrusted women on patrol and felt that women didn't have the required physical strength or stamina to be patrol officers. The public, however, was more accepting of women patrol officers.

2. *Studies attempting to evaluate the success of women on patrol by examining a variety of data such as arrests made, use of force, firing of weapons, interviews with persons involved in incidents, and evaluation reports by superiors.* Lynnea reported that these studies were generally supportive of women police officers and showed that women cops were as successful as men cops.

3. *Studies examining the legal and political battles fought by women to gain access to successful careers in police work.* Lynnea reported being amazed at how much prejudice against women was evident in the police establishment.

At a writing center conference Lynnea confessed that, as a result of her readings, she was beginning to change her mind: She was now convinced that women could be effective patrol officers. But she wasn't convinced that *all* women could be effective officers any more than *all* men could be. She still felt that minimum size and strength requirements should be necessary. The problem was, she reported, that she couldn't find any information related to size and strength issues. Moreover, the research on women police officers did not mention anything about the size or strength of the women being studied. Were these successful patrol officers "big, husky" women, Lynnea asked, or "petite" women, or both? She left the writing center in pursuit of more data.

Lynnea's dilemma is again typical. As we discussed in Chapter 2, the search for clarification often leads to uncertainty. As you immerse yourself in the conversation surrounding an issue, you find that the experts often disagree and that no easy answers emerge. Your goal under these circumstances is to find the best reasons available and to support them with the best evidence you can muster. But the kind of uncertainty Lynnea felt is both healthy and humbling. If your own research leads to similar feelings, we invite you to reread Strategy 4 in Chapter 2 (pp. 44–47) where, in our discussion of the pay equity controversy, we suggest our own methods for coping with ambiguity.

We'll leave Lynnea at this point to take up the technical side of writing research arguments. Besides using research to clarify your own thinking, you also need to have strategies for note taking and for incorporating the results of your reading into your own writing through proper citations and documentation.

DEVELOPING A GOOD SYSTEM OF NOTE TAKING

There is no one right way to take notes. For short research papers, many students keep all their notes in a spiral notebook; others use a system of 3-by-5 cards (for bibliographic information) and 5-by-8 cards (for actual notes). Increasingly, researchers use database software on their personal computers. Whatever system you use, the key is to take notes that are complete enough so that you don't have to keep going back to the library to reread your sources. Some students try to get around this problem by photocopying all articles they might use in their essays or printing complete texts from online databases, but this is an expensive habit that doesn't help you synthesize information or make it your own.

It is much easier to take good notes for a research project if you have your issue question clearly formulated. When you know your issue question, you can anticipate how information from books and articles is likely to get incorporated into your essay. Sometimes you will need to write an accurate summary of a whole article as part of your research notes. At other times you may want to jot down only some facts or figures from an article. At still other times you may want to copy a passage word for word as a potential quotation. There is no way to know what kind of notes you will need to take on each book or article unless you can predict what kind of thesis you will be supporting. We therefore continue our comments on the art of note taking as we discuss ways information can be used in a research essay.

INCORPORATING SOURCES INTO YOUR ARGUMENT: SOME GENERAL PRINCIPLES

To illustrate different ways that you can use a source, we will use the following brief article from the magazine *Science '86.*

Reading, Writing, and (Ugh!) You Know What

ANN ARBOR, Mich.—Not only are American high school students worse at mathematics than their Japanese and Chinese peers, they start falling behind in kindergarten. [1]

That's one conclusion of a five-year study done by psychologist Harold Stevenson and graduate student Shin-ying Lee, both of the University of Michigan, and psychologist James [2]

Stigler of the University of Chicago. The study also shows for the first time that parents must share the blame.

3   More than 2,000 children in kindergarten and the first and fifth grades were tested and interviewed in Minneapolis, in Sendai, Japan, and in Taipei, China. The researchers composed the test for each grade from math problems found in textbooks in all three cities.

4   All the children in each grade performed equally well on reading and general intelligence tests, but math scores differed from the start. While average scores for U.S. and Chinese kindergarten students were the same, Japanese kindergartners scored about 10 percent higher. First graders in the U.S. were surpassed by their peers in both China and Japan by an average of 10 percent. Then the gap widened. The top U.S. fifth-grade class scored below the lowest Japanese class and the second lowest Chinese class. Of the 100 highest scoring fifth graders, one was American.

5   A crucial difference is time: Chinese and Japanese students spend more hours in math class and attend school some 240 days a year, Americans about 180. But another difference, the researchers found, is parental influence. Chinese and Japanese parents give their children more help with math homework than U.S. parents, who tended to believe that "ability" was the premier reason for academic success, according to the researchers' interviews. Chinese and Japanese parents, in contrast, most often said "effort" was most important. And more than 90 percent of U.S. parents believed the schools did an "excellent" job teaching math and other subjects; most Japanese and Chinese parents said the schools did a "fair" job.

6   "American parents are very involved in teaching reading," says Stigler. "But they seem to think that teaching math is the school's job. It's as if it gets them off the hook."

Citing Information

Sometimes the complete argument of an article may not be relevant to your essay. Often you will use only a piece of information from the article. For example, let's suppose you are writing an argument claiming that American society, as a whole, values individual creativity more than does Japanese society. You plan to contrast an open classroom in an American grade school with a more regimented Japanese classroom. At the end of the passage, you might write something like this:

> Not only is education in Japan more regimented than it is in the United States, it continues through a much longer school year. A typical Japanese grade school student attends classes 240 days a year compared with 180 days a year in the United States ("Reading" 7). Although such a system might produce more academic achievement, it provides little time for children to be children, to play and daydream—essential ingredients for nurturing creativity.*

---

*The material in parentheses ("Reading" 7) cites the source of the information in MLA format. This citation directs the reader to look in the Works Cited list at the end of the essay and find the entry listed alphabetically by its title as "Reading, Writing, and (Ugh!) You Know What" for complete bibliographic information. The cited information is found on page 7 of that article. Ordinarily, the author's name rather than the shortened title would be cited in the parenthetical reference, but in this case no author's name was mentioned in the source.

Here the total argument of the *Science '86* article isn't relevant to the writer's essay. He has borrowed only the small detail about the length of the school year (which, of course, the writer documents by means of a citation in parentheses). In his original note cards, the writer would not have had to summarize the whole *Science '86* article. By knowing his research question, he would have known that only this piece of information was relevant.

Summarizing an Argument: Different Contexts Demand Different Summaries

On other occasions, however, you may need to summarize the entire argument of an essay, or at least a major portion of the argument. How you summarize it depends once again on the context of your own essay because your summary must focus on your own thesis. To illustrate how context influences a summary, we will examine passages by two different writers, Cheryl and Jeff, each of whom uses the *Science '86* article, "Reading, Writing, and (Ugh!) You Know What," but in the context of different arguments. Cheryl is writing on the issue of heredity versus environment in the determination of scholastic achievement. She is making the causal claim that environment plays a key role in scholastic high achievement. Jeff is writing on American mathematics education. He is making the evaluation claim that American mathematics education is in a dangerous shambles. Both writers include a summary of the *Science '86* article,* but their summaries are written in different ways in order to emphasize different aspects of the article.

PASSAGE FROM CHERYL'S ESSAY ON HEREDITY VERSUS ENVIRONMENT

Another argument showing the importance of environment on scholastic achievement comes from a research study done by psychologists at the University of Chicago and the University of Michigan ("Reading" 7). These researchers compared the mathematics achievement of 2000 kindergartners, first graders, and fifth graders from the United States, Japan, and China. At the beginning of the study the researchers determined that the comparison groups were equal in terms of reading ability and general intelligence. But the American students were far behind in mathematics achievement. At the first grade level, the researchers reported, American students were 10 percent behind Japanese and Chinese students and considerably further behind by the end of the fifth grade. In fact, only one American student scored in the top 100 of all students.

What is significant about this study is that heredity seems to play no factor in accounting for the differences between American students and their Japanese and Chinese counterparts since the comparison groups were shown to be of equal intelligence at the beginning of the study. The researchers attribute the differences between the groups to the time they spent on math (Japanese students go to class

_____
*The citations follow the MLA format described later in this chapter.

240 days per year while Americans are in class only 180 days per year) and to parental influence. According to the study, American parents believe that native "ability" is the key factor in math achievement and don't seem to push their children as much. Japanese and Chinese parents, however, believe that "effort" is the key factor and spend considerably more time than American parents helping their children with their math homework (8). Thus, it is the particular environment created by Chinese and Japanese societies, not inherited intelligence, that accounts for the greater math achievement of children in those cultures.

PASSAGE FROM JEFF'S ESSAY ON THE FAILURE
OF MATHEMATICS EDUCATION IN THE UNITED STATES

Further evidence of the disgraceful nature of mathematics education in the United States is the dismal performance of American grade school students in mathematics achievement tests as compared to children from other cultures. One study, reported in the magazine *Science '86,* revealed that American kindergarten students scored 10 percent lower on mathematics knowledge than did kindergartners from Japan. This statistic suggests that American parents don't teach arithmetical skills in the home to preschoolers the way Japanese parents do.

But the most frightening part of the study showed what happens by the fifth grade. The best American class in the study scored below the worst Chinese or Japanese class, and of the top 100 students only one was an American ("Reading" 8). The differences between the American students and their Chinese and Japanese counterparts cannot be attributed to intelligence because the article reports that comparison groups were matched for intelligence at the beginning of the study. The difference can be accounted for only by the quality of education and the effort of students. The researchers who did this study attributed the difference first of all to time. According to the study, Chinese and Japanese students spend 240 days per year in school while Americans spend only 180. The second reason for the difference is parental influence, since Japanese and Chinese parents spend much more time than American parents helping their children with mathematics. The study suggests that if we are to do anything about mathematics education in the United States we need a revolution not only in the schools but in the home.

FOR CLASS DISCUSSION

Although both of the preceding passages summarize the *Science '86* article, "Reading, Writing, and (Ugh!) You Know What," they use the article to support somewhat different claims. Working as individuals or in groups, prepare short answers to the following questions. Be ready to elaborate on your answers in class if called on to defend them.

1. What makes each passage different from a data dump?

2. In what ways are the summaries different? (Compare the summaries to each other and to the original article.)

3. How does the difference between the summaries reflect a different purpose in each passage?

Article Summaries as a Note-Taking Tool

Both Cheryl's passage and Jeff's summarize the *Science '86* article accurately. To be able to write summaries such as these when you compose your rough drafts, you need to have the articles at hand (by photocopying them from the library or printing them online), or you need to have written summaries of the articles in your note cards. We strongly recommend the second practice—writing summaries of articles in your note cards when their arguments seem relevant to your research project. Taking notes this way is time-consuming in the short run but time-efficient in the long run. The act of summarizing forces you to read the article carefully and to perceive its whole argument. It also steers you away from the bad habit of noting facts or information from an article without perceiving how the information supports a meaning. Because summary writing is a way of reading as a believer (see Chapter 2), it helps you listen to the various voices in the conversation about your issue.

Paraphrasing Portions of an Argument

Whereas a summary places a whole argument in a nutshell by leaving out supporting details but keeping the main argument, a paraphrase is about the same length as the original but places the ideas of the original in the writer's own words. Paraphrase often includes pieces of quotation worked neatly into the writer's passage. When you are summarizing a short article, such as the *Science '86* article used in the previous section, parts of your summary can blend into paraphrase. The distinction isn't important. What is important is that you avoid plagiarism by making sure you are restating the original argument in your own words. Generally you should avoid paraphrasing a lengthy passage because then you will simply be turning someone else's argument into your own words. A good research argument weaves together supporting material from a variety of sources; it doesn't paraphrase someone else's argument.

Quoting

Inexperienced writers tend to quote too much material and at too great a length. To see a skillful use of quotations, look again at the *Science '86* article we have been using as an illustration. That article is actually a summary of a much longer and more technical research study written by the researchers Stevenson,

Shin-ying Lee, and Stigler. Note that the summary includes only two kinds of quotation: quotation of the single words *ability, effort, excellent,* and *fair;* and a brief quotation from Stigler to conclude the article.

The first kind of quotation—quoting individual words or short phrases—is a matter of accuracy. The writer summarizing the original research study wanted to indicate the exact terms the researchers used at key points in their argument. The second kind of quotation—quoting a brief passage from an article—has a different purpose. Sometimes writers want to give readers a sense of the flavor of their original source, particularly if the source speaks in a lively, interesting style. At other times a writer might wish to quote a source exactly on an especially important point, both to highlight the point and to increase readers' confidence that the writer has elsewhere been summarizing or paraphrasing accurately. The ending quotation in the *Science '86* article serves both purposes.

As a general rule, avoid too much quotation, especially long quotations. Remember that a research essay, like any other essay, should present *your* argument in *your* voice. When you use summary and to a lesser extent paraphrase, you are in command because you are fitting the arguments of your sources to your own purposes. But when you quote, you are lifting material from a different context with a different purpose and plunking it into an alien home, inevitably mixing voices and styles. Too much quotation is the hallmark of a data dump essay; the writer strings together other people's words instead of creating his own argument.

INCORPORATING SOURCES INTO YOUR ARGUMENT: TECHNICAL ADVICE ON SUMMARIZING, PARAPHRASING, AND QUOTING

As a research writer, you need to be able to move back and forth gracefully between conducting your own argument and using material from your research in the form of summary, paraphrase, or quotation. Let's suppose that you are investigating the following question: "Is terrorism ever ethically justifiable?" As part of your research, you encounter a short argument by philosopher Michael Levin entitled "The Case for Torture." Levin's argument, which originally appeared in *Newsweek,* is reprinted in Chapter 15 on ethical arguments (pp. 356–57). We will use Levin's argument to illustrate summary, paraphrase, and quotation, so you should read the argument before proceeding to the explanations that follow.

Once you have read Levin's argument on torture, suppose that you would like to incorporate some of his ideas into your own argument on terrorism. You have a number of options: summary, paraphrase, long block quotation, short quotations inserted into your own sentences, and inserted quotations modified slightly to fit the grammar of your own sentence. Let's look at each in turn.

Summary

When you wish to include a writer's complete argument (or a large sustained portion of it) in your own essay, you will need to summarize it. For a detailed explanation of how to summarize, see Chapter 2. Summaries can be quite long or very short. The following condensation of Levin's essay illustrates a short summary.

> Levin believes that torture can be justifiable if its purpose is to save innocent lives and if it is certain that the person being tortured has the power to save those lives. Torture is not justifiable as punishment. Levin likens the justified use of torture to the justified use of assassination or preemptive strikes in order to preclude or shorten a war.

This short passage summarizes the main points of the Levin argument in a few sentences. As a summary, it condenses the whole down to a small nutshell. For an example of a somewhat longer summary, see Chapter 2, pages 34–35.

Paraphrase

Unlike summary, which is a condensation of an essay, a paraphrase is a "translation" of an essay into the writer's own words. It is approximately the same length as the original but converts the original into the writer's own voice. Be careful when you paraphrase to avoid both the original writer's words and the original writer's grammatical structure and syntax. If you follow the original sentence structure while replacing occasional words with synonyms, you are cheating: That practice is plagiarism, not paraphrase. Here is a paraphrase of paragraph 4 in Levin's essay:

> Levin asks whether it is unconstitutional to torture a terrorist. He believes that it probably is, but he argues that saving the lives of millions of innocent people is a greater good than obeying the Constitution. Although torture is brutal, so is letting innocent people die. In fact, Levin believes that we are moral cowards if we don't torture a guilty individual in order to save millions of lives.

This paraphrase of paragraph 4 is approximately the same length as the original paragraph. The purpose of a paraphrase is not to condense the original, but to turn the original into one's own language. Even though you are not borrowing any language, you will still need to cite the source to indicate that you are borrowing ideas.

Block Quotation

Occasionally, you will wish to quote an author's words directly. You must be meticulous in copying down the words *exactly* so that you make no changes. You must also be fair to your source by not quoting out of context. When the quoted material takes up more than three lines in your original source, use the following block quotation method:

> In his argument supporting torture under certain circumstances, Levin is careful to insist that he doesn't see torture as punishment but solely as a way of preventing loss of innocent lives:
>
>> I am not advocating torture as punishment. Punishment is addressed to deeds irrevocably past. Rather, I am advocating torture as an acceptable measure for preventing future evils. So understood, it is far less objectionable than many extant punishments.

Here the writer wants to quote Levin's words as found in paragraph 7. Because the passage to be quoted is longer than three lines, the writer uses the block quotation method. Note that the quotation is introduced with a colon and is not enclosed in quotation marks. The indented block format takes the place of quotation marks.

Inserted Quotation

If the passage you wish to quote is less than three lines, you can insert it directly into your own paragraph by using quotation marks instead of the block method:

> In his argument favoring torture, Levin is careful to distinguish between torture and punishment. "I am not advocating torture as punishment," Levin asserts. "Punishment is addressed to deeds irrevocably past. Rather, I am advocating torture as an acceptable measure for preventing future evils."

Here the writer breaks the quotation into parts so that no part is longer than three lines. Thus the writer is able to use quotation marks rather than the indented block format.

If the inserted quotation is a complete sentence in your own essay, then it should begin with a capital letter. The quotation is usually separated from preceding explanatory matter by a colon or comma. However, if the quotation is not a complete sentence in your own essay, then you insert it using quotation marks only and begin the quotation with a small letter.

QUOTATION AS INDEPENDENT SENTENCE
According to Levin, "Punishment is addressed to deeds irrevocably past."

QUOTATION AS CLAUSE OR PHRASE THAT IS NOT AN INDEPENDENT SENTENCE
Levin claims that punishment is concerned with "deeds irrevocably past," while torture is aimed at "preventing future evils."

In the first example, the quotation begins with a capital *P* because the quotation comprises an independent sentence. Note that it is separated from the preceding phrase by a comma. In the second example the quotations do not comprise independent sentences. They are inserted directly into the writer's sentence, using quotation marks only.

Shortening or Modifying Quotations

Sometimes you wish to quote the exact words from a source, but in order to make the quotation fit gracefully into your own sentence you need to alter it in some way, either by shortening it, by changing it slightly, or by adding explanatory material to it. There are several ways of doing so: through judicious selection of phrases to be quoted or through use of ellipses and brackets.

SHORTEN A PASSAGE BY SELECTING ONLY KEY PHRASES FOR QUOTING

In his argument favoring torture, Levin is careful to distinguish between torture and punishment. "I am not advocating torture as punishment," Levin asserts, but only "as an acceptable measure for preventing future evils."

Here the writer quotes only selected pieces of the longer passage and weaves them into her own sentences.

USE ELLIPSES TO OMIT MATERIAL FROM A QUOTATION

Levin continues by distinguishing torture from capital punishment:

> Opponents of the death penalty [. . .] are forever insisting that executing a murderer will not bring back his victim. [. . .] But torture [. . .] is intended not to bring anyone back but to keep innocents from being dispatched.

In this block quotation from paragraph 7, the writer uses ellipses in three places. Made with three spaced periods, an ellipsis indicates that words have been omitted. Note that the second ellipsis in this passage seems to contain four periods. The first period ends the sentence; the last three periods are the ellipsis. The square brackets around the ellipses show that they were inserted by you, the writer, rather than being in the original work.

USE SQUARE BRACKETS TO MAKE SLIGHT CHANGES
IN A QUOTATION OR TO ADD EXPLANATORY MATERIAL

According to Levin, "By threatening to kill for profit or idealism, he [the terrorist] renounces civilized standards."

The writer puts "the terrorist" in brackets to indicate the antecedent of the quoted pronoun "he." This passage is from paragraph 9.

According to Levin, "[T]orture [is] an acceptable measure for preventing future evils."

This passage, from paragraph 7, changes the original slightly: a small *t* has been raised to a capital *T*, and the word *as* has been changed to *is*. These changes are indicated by brackets. You don't usually have to indicate when you change a small letter to a capital or vice versa. But it is important to do so here because the writer is actually changing the grammar of the original by converting a phrase into a sentence.

Using Quotations within Quotations

Sometimes you may wish to quote a passage that already has quotation marks within it. If you use the block quotation method, keep the quotation marks exactly as they are in the original. If you use the inserted quotation method, then use single quotation marks (' ') instead of double marks (" ") to indicate the quotation within the quotation.

> Levin is quick to dismiss the notion that a terrorist has rights:
>
>> There is an important difference between terrorists and their victims that should mute talk of the terrorists' "rights." The terrorist's victims are at risk unintentionally, not having asked to be endangered. But the terrorist knowingly initiated his actions.

Because the writer uses the block quotation method, the original quotation marks around *rights* remain. See the original passage in paragraph 9.

> Levin claims that "an important difference between terrorists and their victims . . . should mute talk of the terrorists' 'rights.' "

Here the writer uses the inserted quotation method. Therefore the original double quotation marks (" ") around *rights* have been changed to single quotation marks (' '), which on a keyboard are made with an apostrophe.

An Extended Illustration: Martha's Argument

To help you get a feel for how a writer integrates brief quotations into paraphrases or summaries, consider the following passage written by Martha, a student who was disturbed by a class discussion of Levin's essay. Several classmates argued that Levin's justification of torture could also be used to justify terrorism. Martha did not believe that Levin's argument could be applied to terrorism. Here is the passage from Martha's argument that summarizes Levin. (Page references in Martha's passage refer to the original *Newsweek* source that she used—part of the MLA citation system to be described shortly.)

> Now it may seem that if terrorism is always wrong then torture should always be wrong also since torture, even more so than terrorism, is a barbaric practice

from a pre-civilized age. But philosopher Michael Levin shows a flaw in this reasoning. Torture is justifiable, says Levin, but only in some cases. First of all, he says that torture should be applied only to those *"known* to hold innocent lives in their hands" and only if the person being tortured is clearly guilty and clearly can prevent a horrible act from occurring (13). Levin uses the example of using torture on a captured terrorist to find the location of an atomic bomb set to go off on Manhattan Island. The principle here is that you are saving the lives of millions of innocent bystanders by applying systematic pain to one person who "renounc[ed] civilized standards" (13) when becoming a terrorist. For Levin, saving the lives of innocent bystanders is a higher moral imperative than refusing to torture the person who can prevent the deaths. In fact, Levin claims, refusal to torture the terrorist is "moral cowardice, an unwillingness to dirty one's hands" (13). "If life is [. . .] valuable," Levin argues, then "the lives of the innocents must be saved even at the price of hurting the one who endangers them" (13).

We can now return to the problem I posed earlier. If Levin is able to justify torture under some conditions, why can't we also justify terrorism under some conditions? The answer is that . . . [Martha's argument continues].

FOR CLASS DISCUSSION

Working as individuals or as small groups, prepare brief answers for the following questions:

1. How is Martha's passage different from a data dump?

2. Without being able to read her whole essay, can you determine Martha's purpose for summarizing Levin within her own argument on terrorism? If so, what is her purpose?

3. Why did the writer use square brackets [ ] within one quotation and bracketed ellipses ([. . .]) within another?

4. What effects did Martha achieve by using only short quotations instead of longer block quotations from Levin's argument?

Signaling Directions:
The Use of Attributive Tags

In all of our examples of citing, summarizing, paraphrasing, and quoting, the writers have used attributive tags to signal to readers which ideas are the writer's own and which ideas are being taken from another source. Attributive tags are phrases such as the following: "according to the researchers . . . ," "Levin claims that . . . ," "the author continues . . . ." Such phrases signal to the reader that the material immediately following is from the cited source. Parenthetical citations are used only to give readers follow-up information on where the source can be found, not to indicate that the writer is using a source. The source being cited should always be mentioned in the text. Note how confusing a passage becomes if these attributive tags are omitted.

CONFUSING ATTRIBUTION

Now it may seem that if terrorism is always wrong then torture should always be wrong also since torture, even more so than terrorism, is a barbaric practice from a pre-civilized age. But there is a flaw in this reasoning. Torture should be applied only to those *"known* to hold innocent lives in their hands" (Levin 13) and only if the person being tortured is clearly guilty and clearly can prevent a terrorist act from occurring. A good example is using torture on a captured terrorist to find the location of an atomic bomb set to go off on Manhattan Island.

Although this writer cites Levin as the source of the quotation, it is not clear just when the borrowing from Levin begins or ends. For instance, is the example of the captured terrorist on Manhattan Island the writer's own or does it come from Levin? As the following revision shows, the use of attributive tags within the text makes it clear exactly where the writer's ideas leave off and a borrowed source begins or ends. In the following example of clear attribution, attributive tags are printed in boldface:

CLEAR ATTRIBUTION

Now it may seem that if terrorism is always wrong then torture should always be wrong also since torture, even more so than terrorism, is a barbaric practice from a pre-civilized age. But **philosopher Michael Levin shows** a flaw in this reasoning. Torture is justifiable, **says Levin,** but only in some cases. First, **he says that** torture should be applied only to those *"known* to hold innocent lives in their hands" and only if the person being tortured is clearly guilty and clearly can prevent a horrible act from occurring (13). **Levin uses** the example of using torture on a captured terrorist to find the location of an atomic bomb set to go off on Manhattan Island.

AVOIDING PLAGIARISM

Plagiarism, a form of academic cheating, is always a serious academic offense. You can plagiarize in one of two ways: (1) by borrowing another person's ideas without indicating the borrowing with attributive tags in the text and a proper citation or (2) by borrowing another person's language without putting the borrowed language in quotation marks or using a block indentation. The first kind of plagiarism is usually outright cheating; the writer usually knows he is stealing material and tries to disguise it.

The second kind of plagiarism, however, often begins in a hazy never-never land between paraphrasing and copying. We refer to it in our classes as "lazy cheating" and still consider it a serious offense, like stealing from your neighbor's vegetable garden because you are too lazy to do your own planting, weeding, and harvesting. Anyone who appreciates how hard it is to write and revise even a short passage will appreciate why it is wrong to take someone else's language ready-made. Thus, in our classes, we would fail a paper that included the following passage. (Let's call the writer Lucy.)

> Another argument showing the importance of environment on scholastic achievement comes from a research study done by psychologists at the University of Chicago and the University of Michigan (*Science '86* 7, 8). The study shows that parents must share the blame for the poor math performance of American students. In this study more than 2,000 children in kindergarten and the fifth grade were tested and interviewed in Minneapolis, in Sendai, Japan, and in Taipei, China. The researchers made up a test based on math problems found in textbooks used in all three cities. All the children in each grade performed equally well on reading and general intelligence tests, but their math scores differed from the start. The kindergartners from Japan scored about 10 percent higher than American kindergartners. The gap widened by the fifth grade. The top U.S. fifth-grade class scored below the lowest Japanese class and the second lowest Chinese class. Of the 100 highest scoring fifth graders, one was American (*Science '86* 8).

FOR CLASS DISCUSSION

Do you think it was fair to flunk Lucy's essay? She claimed she wasn't cheating since she gave two different parenthetical citations accurately citing the *Science '86* article as her source. Before answering this question, compare the passage above with the original article on pp. 389–90; also compare the passage above with the opening paragraph from Cheryl's summary (pp. 391–92) of the *Science '86* article. What justification could a professor use for giving an A to Cheryl's essay while flunking Lucy's?

Note Taking to Avoid Plagiarism

When you take notes on books or articles, be extremely careful to put all borrowed language in quotation marks. If you write summaries of arguments, as we strongly recommend you do, take time at the note-taking stage to put the summaries in your own words. If you wish to paraphrase an important passage, make sure you either copy the original into your notes word for word and indicate that you have done so (so that you can paraphrase it later), or paraphrase it entirely in your language when you take the notes. Inadvertent plagiarism can occur if you copy something in your notes word for word and then later assume that what you copied was actually a paraphrase.

DOCUMENTING YOUR SOURCES

To many students, the dreariest aspect of research writing is documenting their sources—that is, getting citations in the proper places and in the correct forms. As we noted at the beginning of the previous chapter, however, documentation of sources is a service to readers who may want to follow up on your research. Documentation in the proper form allows them to find your sources quickly.

There are two questions that you must answer to ensure proper documentation: "When do I cite a source?" and "Which format do I use?"

When to Cite Sources

As a general rule, cite everything you borrow. Some students take this rule to unnecessary extremes, arguing that everything they "know" comes from somewhere. They end up citing lectures, conversations with a friend, notes from an old high school class, and so forth. Use common sense. If you successfully avoid writing a data dump essay, then your research will be used to support a thesis, which will reflect your own individual thinking and synthesis of material. You will know when you are using evidence from your own personal experience as source material and when you are using evidence you got from doing library research. Document all the material you got from the library or from another external source.

Which Format to Use

Formats for citations and bibliographies vary somewhat from discipline to discipline. At the present time, footnotes have almost entirely disappeared from academic writing as a means of citing sources. Rather, citations for quotations or paraphrased material are now usually made in the text itself by putting brief identifying symbols inside parentheses.

AN OVERVIEW OF THE MLA AND APA
SYSTEMS OF DOCUMENTATION

The two main systems used today for academic essays aimed at general college audiences are the MLA (Modern Language Association) system, generally favored in the humanities, and the APA (American Psychological Association) system, generally favored in the social sciences. Other general systems are sometimes encountered—for example, the *Chicago Manual of Style*—and many specialized disciplines such as biology or chemistry have their own style manuals. But familiarity with the MLA and APA systems should serve you well throughout college.

The sample research argument written by Stephen Bean (pp. 334–42) follows the MLA style. The sample research argument written by Lynnea Clark (pp. 424–30) follows the APA style.

Neither the MLA nor the APA system uses footnotes to document sources. In both systems a source is cited by means of a brief parenthetical reference following the quotation or the passage in which the source is used. Complete bibliographic information on each source is then included in an alphabetical list at the end of the text. Let us now turn to a more complete discussion of these two features.

Feature 1: Place a Complete Bibliographic List at the End of the Text

In both the MLA and the APA styles, a list of all the sources you have cited is included at the end of the research paper. In the MLA system, this bibliographic list is called Works Cited. In the APA system this list is called References. In both systems, entries are listed alphabetically by author (if no author is given for a particular source, then that source is alphabetized by title).

Let's look at how the two style systems would have you cite the Levin article on torture. The article appears in the June 7, 1982, issue of *Newsweek* on page 13. In the MLA style the complete bibliographic reference would be placed at the end of the paper under Works Cited, where it would appear as follows:

MLA: Levin, Michael. "The Case for Torture." Newsweek 7 June 1982: 13.

In the APA system, the complete bibliographic reference would be placed at the end of the paper under References, where it would appear as follows:

APA: Levin, M. (1982, June 7). The case for torture. Newsweek, p. 13.

When you refer to this article in the text—using either system—you place a brief citation in parentheses.

Feature 2: Cite Sources in the Text by Putting Brief References in Parentheses

Both the MLA and the APA systems cite sources through brief parenthetical references in the text. However, the two systems differ somewhat in the way these citations are structured.

In-Text Citation: MLA System

In the MLA system, you place the author's name and the page number of the cited source in parentheses. (If the author's name is mentioned in a preceding attributive tag, only the page number should be placed in parentheses.)

Torture, claims one philosopher, should be applied only to those "<u>known</u> to hold innocent lives in their hands" and only if the person being tortured is clearly guilty and clearly can prevent a terrorist act from occurring (Levin 13).

or

Torture, claims Michael Levin, should be applied only to those "<u>known</u> to hold innocent lives in their hands" and only if the person being tortured is clearly guilty and clearly can prevent a terrorist act from occurring (13).

If your readers wish to follow up on this source, they will look up the Levin article in the Works Cited list at the end of your essay. If more than one work by Levin has been used as sources in the essay, then you would include in the in-text citation an abbreviated title of the article following Levin's name.

(Levin, "Torture" 13)

Once Levin has been cited the first time and it is clear that you are still quoting from Levin, then you need put only the page number in parentheses and eliminate the author's name.

In-Text Citation: APA System

In the APA system, you place the author's name and the date of the cited source in parentheses. If you are quoting a particular passage or citing a particular table, include the page number where the information is found. Use a comma to separate each element of the citation and use the abbreviation *p.* or *pp.* before the page number. (If the author's name is mentioned in a preceding attributive tag, then only the date needs to be placed in parentheses.)

Torture, claims one philosopher, should be applied only to those "<u>known</u> to hold innocent lives in their hands" and only if the person being tortured is clearly guilty and clearly can prevent a terrorist act from occurring (Levin, 1982, p. 13).

or

Torture, claims Michael Levin, should be applied only to those "<u>known</u> to hold innocent lives in their hands" and only if the person being tortured is clearly guilty and clearly can prevent a terrorist act from occurring (1982, p. 13).

If your readers wish to follow up on this source, they will look for the 1982 Levin article in the References at the end of your essay. If Levin had published more than one article in 1982, the articles would be distinguished by small letters placed alphabetically after the date:

(Levin, 1982a)

or

(Levin, 1982b)

In the APA style, if an article or book has more than one author, the word *and* is used to join them in the text but the ampersand (&) is used to join them in the parenthetical reference:

Smith and Peterson (1983) found that . . .

More recent data (Smith & Peterson, 1983) have shown . . .

Citing a Quotation or Other Data from a Secondary Source

Occasionally, you may wish to use a quotation or other kinds of data from a secondary source. For example, suppose you are writing an argument that the United States should reconsider its trade policies with China. You read an article entitled "China's Gilded Age" by Xiao-huang Yin appearing in the April 1994 issue of the *Atlantic*. This article contains the following passage appearing on page 42:

> Dual ownership has in essence turned this state enterprise into a private business. Asked if such a practice is an example of China's "socialist market economy," a professor of economics at Nanjing University, where I taught in the early 1980's, replied, "Nobody knows what the concept means. It is only rhetoric, and it can mean anything but socialism."

In citing material from a secondary source, it is always best, when possible, to locate the original source and cite your data directly. But in the above case, no other source is likely available. Here is how you would cite it in both the MLA and APA systems.

MLA: According to an economics professor at Nanjing University, the term "socialist market economy" has become confused under capitalistic influence: "Nobody knows what the concept means. It is only rhetoric, and it can mean anything but socialism" (qtd. in Yin 42)

APA: According to an economics professor at Nanjing University, the term "socialist market economy" has become confused under capitalistic influence: "Nobody knows what the concept means. It is only rhetoric, and it can mean anything but socialism" (cited in Yin, 1994, p. 42).

In both systems you would place the Yin article in the end-of-text bibliographic list. What follows is a description of the format for the end-of-text bibliographic entries under Works Cited in the MLA system and under References in the APA System.

BIBLIOGRAPHIC LISTINGS AT THE END OF YOUR PAPER

Both the MLA and the APA systems specify a complete list of all items cited, placed at the end of the paper. The list should comprise all sources from which you gathered information, including articles, books, videos, letters, and electronic sources. The list should not include works you read but did not cite. In both systems, all works are listed alphabetically by author, or by title if there is no author.

In the MLA system, the words *Works Cited*, in uppercase and lowercase letters, are centered one inch from the top of the page. Sources are listed alphabetically, the first line flush with the left margin and succeeding lines indented one-half inch (or five spaces if you are using a typewriter). Here is a typical example of a work cited in MLA form.

Karnow, Stanley. In Our Image: America's Empire in the Philippines. New York: Random, 1989.

The same information with a slightly different arrangement is used in the APA system. The word *References* is typed in uppercase and lowercase letters at the top of the page. Entries for sources are listed alphabetically. After the first line, which is flush at the left margin, succeeding lines are indented five spaces.

Karnow, S. (1989). In our image: America's empire in the Philippines. New York: Random House.

The remaining pages in this section show examples of MLA and APA formats for different kinds of sources, including electronic sources. Following these examples are typical pages from a Works Cited list and a References list featuring formats for the most commonly encountered kinds of sources.

General Format for Books

MLA: Author. Title. City of Publication: Publisher, year of publication.

APA: Author. (Year of Publication). Title. City of Publication: Publisher.

Note these important differences between the two systems:

- In MLA style, author entries include first names and middle initials. In APA style, only the initials of the first and middle names are given, unless full names are needed to distinguish persons with the same initials.

- In MLA style, the first word and all important words are capitalized in the title. In APA style, only the first word, proper nouns, and the first word after a dash or a colon are capitalized in the title.

- In MLA style, the year of publication comes last, after the publisher. In APA style, the year of publication follows in parentheses immediately after the author's name.

- In MLA style, names of publishers have standardized abbreviations, listed in section 6.5 of the *MLA Handbook for Writers of Research Papers*, 5th ed. In APA style, names of publishers are not usually abbreviated except for the elimination of unnecessary words such as *Inc., Co.,* and *Publishers.*

- In MLA style, punctuation following the underlined title is not underlined. In APA style, punctuation following the underlined title *is* underlined.

One Author

MLA: Coles, Robert. The Youngest Parents: Teenage Pregnancy As It
            Shapes Lives. New York: Norton, 1997.

APA: Coles, R. (1997). The youngest parents: Teenage pregnancy as it
            shapes lives. New York: W. W. Norton.

Two or More Listings for One Author

MLA: Hass, Robert. Human Wishes. New York: Ecco, 1989.

            ---, ed. Rock and Hawk: A Selection of Shorter Poems by Robinson
            Jeffers. New York: Random, 1987.

            ---. Sun under Wood. New York: Ecco, 1996.

            ---, ed. Tomas Tranströmer: Selected Poems, 1954–1986. New York:
            Ecco, 1987.

In the MLA style, when two or more works by one author are cited, the works are listed in alphabetical order by title. For the second and all additional entries, type three hyphens and a period in place of the author's name. Then type the title. If the person named edited, translated, or compiled the book, place a comma (not a period) after the three hyphens and write the appropriate abbreviation (*ed., trans.,* or *comp.*) before giving the title.

APA: Hass, R. (Ed.). (1987a). <u>Rock and hawk: A selection of shorter poems by Robinson Jeffers.</u> New York: Random House.

Hass, R. (Ed.). (1987b). <u>Tomas Transtromer: Selected poems, 1954–1986.</u> New York: Ecco Press.

Hass, R. (1989). <u>Human wishes.</u> New York: Ecco Press.

Hass, R. (1996). <u>Sun under wood.</u> New York: Ecco Press.

In APA style, when an author has more than one entry in the References list, the author's name is repeated and the entries are listed chronologically (oldest to newest) rather than alphabetically. When two entries by the same author have the same date, they are then listed in alphabetical order. Lowercase letters are added after the year of publication to distinguish them from each other when cited by date in the text.

Two or More Authors of a Single Work

MLA: Ciochon, Russell, John Olsen, and Jamie James. <u>The Search for the Giant Ape in Human Prehistory.</u> New York: Bantam, 1990.

APA: Ciochon, R., Olsen, J., & James, J. (1990). <u>The search for the giant ape in human prehistory.</u> New York: Bantam Books.

Note that APA style uses the ampersand (&) to join the names of multiple authors in the Reference list.

Using et al. for Works with Several Authors

MLA: Maimon, Elaine P., et al. <u>Writing in the Arts and Sciences.</u> Cambridge: Winthrop, 1981.

In the MLA system, if there are four or more authors, you have the option of using the form *et al.* (meaning "and others") after the name of the first author listed on the title page.

APA: Maimon, E. P., Belcher, G. L., Hearn, G. W., Nodine, B. F., & O'Connor, F. W. (1981). <u>Writing in the arts and sciences.</u> Cambridge, MA: Winthrop.

APA style calls for you to write out the names of all authors for one work in your References list, no matter how many.

Edited Anthology

MLA: Gates, Henry Louis, Jr., and Nellie Y. McKay, eds. The Norton
            Anthology of African American Literature. New York: Norton,
            1997.

APA: Gates, H. L., Jr., & McKay, N. Y. (Eds.). (1997). The Norton anthology
            of African American literature. New York: W. W. Norton.

Essay in an Anthology or Other Collection

MLA: Thomson, Peter. "Playhouses and Players in the Time of Shakespeare."
            The Cambridge Companion to Shakespeare Studies. Ed. Stanley
            Wells. Cambridge, Eng.: Cambridge UP, 1986. 67–83.

In the MLA system, the words *University Press* are always abbreviated as *UP*. If
several cities are listed in the book as the place of publication, list only the first.
For cities outside the United States, add an abbreviation of the country (or
province in Canada) if the name of the city is ambiguous or unfamiliar.

APA: Thomson, P. (1986). Playhouses and players in the time of Shakespeare.
            In S. Wells (Ed.), The Cambridge companion to Shakespeare
            studies (pp. 67–83). Cambridge, England: Cambridge University
            Press.

Book in a Later Edition or Revised Edition

MLA: Burns, E. Bradford. Latin America: A Concise Interpretive History. 6th
            ed. Englewood Cliffs: Prentice, 1994.
            Schmidt, Rick. Feature Filmmaking at Used-Car Prices: How to
            Write, Produce, Direct, Film, Edit, and Promote a Feature-Length
            Film for Less than $10,000. Rev. ed. New York: Penguin,
            1995.

APA: Burns, E. B. (1994). Latin America: A concise interpretive history (6th
            ed.). Englewood Cliffs, NJ: Prentice Hall.
            Schmidt, R. (1995). Feature filmmaking at used-car prices: How to
            write, produce, direct, film, edit, and promote a feature-length
            film for less than $10,000 (Rev. ed.). New York: Penguin Books.

Multivolume Work

Cite the whole work when you have used more than one volume of the work.

MLA: Churchill, Winston S. A History of the English-Speaking Peoples.
          4 vols. New York: Dodd, 1956–58.

APA: Churchill, W. S. (1956–1958). A history of the English-speaking
          peoples (Vols. 1–4). New York: Dodd, Mead.

Include the volume number when you have used only one volume of a multi-volume work.

MLA: Churchill, Winston S. The Great Democracies. New York: Dodd, 1957.
          Vol. 4 of A History of the English-Speaking Peoples. 4 vols.
          1956–58.

APA: Churchill, W. S. (1957). A history of the English-speaking peoples:
          Vol. 4. The great democracies. New York: Dodd, Mead.

Reference Work with Frequent Editions

MLA: Pei, Mario. "Language." World Book Encyclopedia. 1976 ed.

In citing familiar reference works under the MLA system, you don't need to include all the normal publication information.

APA: Pei, M. (1976). Language. In World book encyclopedia (Vol. 12,
          pp. 62–67). Chicago: Field Enterprises.

Less Familiar Reference Work without Frequent Editions

MLA: Ling, Trevor O. "Buddhism in Burma." Dictionary of Comparative
          Religion. Ed. S. G. F. Brandon. New York: Scribner's, 1970.

APA: Ling, T. O. (1970). Buddhism in Burma. In S. G. F. Brandon (Ed.),
          Dictionary of comparative religion. New York: Scribner's.

Edition in Which Original Author's Work
Is Prepared by an Editor

MLA: Brontë, Emily. Wuthering Heights. 1847. Ed. V. S. Pritchett. Boston:
          Houghton, 1956.

APA: Brontë, E. (1956). <u>Wuthering Heights</u> (V. S. Pritchett, Ed.). Boston:
Houghton Mifflin. (Original work published 1847)

Translation

MLA: Camus, Albert. <u>The Plague</u>. Trans. Stuart Gilbert. New York: Modern
Lib., 1948. Trans. of <u>La Peste</u>. Paris: Gallimard, 1947.

In MLA style, some or all of the original publication information may be added
at the end of the entry. Though it is not required, adding the date avoids the
suggestion that the original work was written in the same year that it was
translated.

APA: Camus, A. (1948). <u>The plague</u> (S. Gilbert, Trans.). New York: Modern
Library. (Original work published 1947)

In APA style, the date of the translation is placed after the author's name; the date
of original publication of the work is placed in parentheses at the end of the reference. In text, this book would be cited as follows:

(Camus, 1947/1948)

Corporate Author (a Commission, Committee,
or Other Group)

MLA: American Red Cross. <u>Standard First Aid</u>. St. Louis: Mosby, 1993.

APA: American Red Cross. (1993). <u>Standard first aid</u>. St. Louis: Mosby
Lifeline.

Anonymous Work

MLA: <u>The New Yorker Cartoon Album: 1975–1985</u>. New York: Penguin, 1987.

APA: <u>The New Yorker cartoon album: 1975–1985</u>. (1987). New York:
Penguin Books.

Republished Work (For Example, a Newer Paperback
Published after the Original Edition)

MLA: Wollstonecraft, Mary. <u>A Vindication of the Rights of Woman, with
Strictures on Political and Moral Subjects</u>. 1792. Rutland: Tuttle,
1995.

APA: Wollstonecraft, M. (1792/1995). <u>A vindication of the rights of woman, with strictures on political and moral subjects.</u> Rutland, VT: Tuttle and Company.

General Format for Articles

Scholarly Journals

MLA: Author. "Article Title." <u>Journal Title</u> volume number (year): inclusive page numbers.

APA: Author. (year). Article title. <u>Journal Title, volume number,</u> inclusive page numbers.

Magazines and Newspapers

MLA: Author. "Article Title." <u>Magazine or Newspaper Title</u> day month year: inclusive page numbers.

APA: Author. (year, month day). Article title. <u>Magazine or Newspaper Title,</u> volume number, inclusive page numbers.

Note these important details about the two systems:

- MLA and APA styles change slightly between scholarly and popular media sources. Scholarly journals are cited by volume number with the year given in parentheses, while citations for popular media sources do not use the volume number and give all details of the date without parentheses.

- Titles of articles in MLA style are placed in quotation marks (with the period *inside* the closing quotation mark). APA style does not place quotation marks around titles.

- In MLA style, the date is followed by a colon, followed by the inclusive page numbers. The APA system uses a comma to separate the title and volume number from the inclusive page numbers.

- As in book citations, the two styles differ in underlining. MLA style underlines only the title (not the punctuation or volume number). APA style calls for the title, the volume number (if there is one), and the comma to be underlined, unless there is an issue number. In that case, neither the issue number nor the comma is underlined (see the example that follows).

Scholarly Journal with Continuous Annual Pagination

MLA: Barton, Ellen L. "Evidentials, Argumentation, and Epistemological Stance." <u>College English</u> 55 (1993): 745–69.

APA: Barton, E. L. (1993). Evidentials, argumentation, and epistemological stance. <u>College English, 55,</u> 745–769.

Scholarly Journal with Each Issue Paged Separately

MLA: Pollay, Richard W., Jung S. Lee, and David Carter-Whitney. "Separate, but Not Equal: Racial Segmentation in Cigarette Advertising." <u>Journal of Advertising</u> 21.1 (1992): 45–57.

APA: Pollay, R. W., Lee, J. S., & Carter-Whitney, D. (1992). Separate, but not equal: Racial segmentation in cigarette advertising. <u>Journal of Advertising, 21</u>(1), 45–57.

Note that in both systems when each issue is paged separately, both the volume number (in this case, 21) and the issue number (in this case, 1) are given.

Magazine Article

MLA: Fallows, James. "Vietnam: Low-Class Conclusions." <u>Atlantic</u> Apr. 1993: 38–44.

APA: Fallows, J. (1993, April). Vietnam: Low-class conclusions. <u>Atlantic Monthly,</u> 38–44.

Note that this form is for a magazine published each month. The next entry shows the form for a magazine published each week.

Anonymous Article

MLA: "The Rebellious Archbishop." <u>Newsweek</u> 11 July 1988: 38.

APA: The rebellious archbishop. (1988, July 11). <u>Newsweek,</u> 38.

Review

MLA: Lakey, Jennifer. "Exploring Native American Traditions with Children." Rev. of <u>She Who Watches</u>, by Willa Holmes. <u>Writers NW</u> Winter 1997: 7.

For both movie and book reviews, if the reviewer's name is not given, begin with the title of the reviewed work, preceded by "Rev. of" in the MLA system or "[Review of *title*]" in the APA system. Begin with the title of the review if the review is titled but not signed.

> APA: Lakey, J. (1997, Winter). Exploring Native American traditions with
>   children [Review of the book She Who Watches]. Writers NW, 7.

Newspaper Article

> MLA: Henriques, Diana B. "Hero's Fall Teaches Wall Street a Lesson."
>   Seattle Times 27 Sept. 1998: A1+.

The *A1+* indicates that the article begins on page 1 but continues later in the newspaper on a later page or pages.

> APA: Henriques, D. B. (1998, September 27). Hero's fall teaches Wall Street
>   a lesson. The Seattle Times, pp. A1, A24.

The *pp. A1, A24* indicates that the article begins on section A, page 1, and ends on section A, page 24. Note that for both systems, the newspaper section is indicated if each section is paged separately.

Newspaper Editorial

> MLA: Dowd, Maureen. "Legacy of Lust." Editorial. New York Times
>   23 Sept. 1998: A31.

> APA: Dowd, M. (1998, September 23). Legacy of lust [Editorial]. The New
>   York Times, p. A31.

Letter to the Editor of a Magazine or Newspaper

> MLA: Tomsovic, Kevin. "Culture Clash." Letter. New Yorker 13 July 1998: 7.

> APA: Tomsovic, K. (1998, July 13). Culture clash [Letter to the editor].
>   The New Yorker, p. 7.

Include a title if one is given to the letter in the publication.

Information Service such as ERIC (Educational Resources Information Center) or NTIS (National Technical Information Service)

> MLA: Eddy, P. A. The Effects of Foreign Language Study in High School on
>   Verbal Ability as Measured by the Scholastic Aptitude Test—
>   Verbal. Washington: Center for Applied Linguistics, 1981. ERIC
>   ED 196 312.

APA: Eddy, P. A. (1981). <u>The effects of foreign language study in high</u>
<u>school on verbal ability as measured by the Scholastic Aptitude</u>
<u>Test—Verbal.</u> Washington, DC: Center for Applied Linguistics.
(ERIC Document Reproduction Service No. ED 196 312)

General Format for Electronic Sources

While rules for formatting electronic sources are still being developed, the principle that governs electronic citations is the same as for print sources: *Give enough information so that the reader can find the source you used.* If the reader cannot relocate the Web page, listserv, or other electronic source from your citation, then you haven't given enough details. It is also important to give the date that you accessed the material as part of your citation, since Web sites are fluid—frequently updated, altered, or dropped. The reader will know from the date of your citation whether a cite may be inaccessible because it has not been updated, or whether the information on the page is different from your data because it has been updated.

The MLA and APA have developed general guidelines for citing electronic sources, which are applied here to specific examples. Nevertheless, you have more freedom of judgment in this area than in the area of print media citations, because electronic sources are in constant development and flux. When in doubt, always make entries as clear and informative as possible. Also, when you write an electronic citation, use your own citation to relocate the data just to make sure your address is accurate. If you cannot duplicate your own path to the material, give a simpler citation to the site's home page directory that will lead the reader to the original source. (See the example that follows.)

Books, Pamphlets, or Texts in Online Databases
or CD-ROMs That Are Also Available in Print

MLA: Melville, Herman. <u>Moby-Dick, or The White Whale.</u> 1851. Ed. Luther
S. Mansfield and Howard P. Vincent. New York: Hendricks,
1952. 27 Sept. 1998 <http://etext.lib.virginia.edu/modeng/
modeng0.browse. html>.

MLA style uses the book citation format followed by the date of access and the URL (Uniform Resource Locator) enclosed in angle brackets. In this case, the URL is so long that the reader is directed to the browser at the University of Virginia Electronic Text Center. The reader can easily access *Moby-Dick* from there. If you must divide the URL to go to another line, break after a punctuation mark other than a period.

APA: Melville, H. (1851). <u>Moby-Dick, or the white whale.</u> University of
Virginia Electronic Text Center. Retrieved September 27, 1998

from the World Wide Web: http://etext.lib.virginia.edu/modeng/
modeng0.browse.html

APA style calls for the Web site that provides the text, the word *Retrieved* followed
by the access date and the phrase *from the World Wide Web,* and the URL. Note that
the URL is not followed by a period in APA style.

*Journals or Periodicals in Databases or CD-ROMs
That Are Also Available in Print*

MLA: Kowaleski-Wallace, Beth. "Women, China, and Consumer Culture in
Eighteenth-Century England." Eighteenth Century Studies 29.2
(1995–96): 153–67. 1 Feb. 1999 <http://direct.press.jhu.edu/
journals/eighteenth-century_studies/toc/ecsv029.html#v029.2>.

APA: Kowaleski-Wallace, B. (1995–1996). Women, China, and consumer
culture in eighteenth-century England. Eighteenth-Century
Studies, 29(2), 153–167. Retrieved February 1, 1999 from
the World Wide Web: http://direct.press.jhu.edu/journals/
eighteenth-century_studies/toc/ ecsv029.html#v029.2

*Books, Journals, or Periodicals in Online Databases
or CD-ROMs That Are Not Available in Print*

MLA: Lal, Vinay. "Indians and The Guinness Book of World Records:
The Political and Cultural Contours of a National Obsession."
Suitcase: A Journal of Transcriptural Traffic 3 (1998). 2 Oct. 1998
<http:// www.suitcase.net/lai.html>.

APA: Lal, V. (1998). Indians and The Guinness book of world records: The
political and cultural contours of a national obsession. Suitcase:
A journal of transcriptural traffic, 3, Retrieved October 2, 1998
from the World Wide Web: http://www.suitcase.net/lai.html

Computer Disks That Are Not Available in Print

MLA: Microsoft Age of Empires. CD-ROM. Redmond: Microsoft, 1998.

APA: Microsoft age of empires [Computer software]. (1998). Redmond, WA:
Microsoft Software.

For both MLA and APA, include the medium, city of issue, vendor name, and date of issue. APA style follows the specifications for online books available in print.

Scholarly Project, Web Site, or Database

MLA: Starr, Kenneth W. "Report of the Independent Counsel." <u>Thomas:</u> <u>Legislative Information on the Internet.</u> 9 Sept. 1998. Lib. of Congress, Washington. 2 Oct. 1998 <http://icreport.loc.gov/ icreport/1cover.htm>.

For MLA, include the title of the scholarly project, Web site, or database (under-lined), the name of the editor of the project if there is one, and the electronic pub-lication information, including date of last update, date of access, and URL.

APA: Starr, K. W. (1998, September 9). Report of the Independent Counsel. Washington, DC: Library of Congress. Retrieved October 2, 1998 from the World Wide Web: http://icreport.loc.gov/icreport/ 1cover.htm

For APA, omit the name of the project, Web site, or database. The access date and URL follow the same format as in an entry for an online book or article.

E-mail, Listservs, and Other Nonretrievable Sources

MLA: Rushdie, Salman. "My Concern about the Fatwa." E-mail to the author. 1 May 1995.

Note that this format specifies that the document is an e-mail letter, to whom it was addressed, and the date of transmission.

In APA style, this material is not listed in the References. You should, however, acknowledge it in in-text citations.

The novelist has repeated this idea recently (Salman Rushdie, personal communication, May 1, 1995).

Bulletin Board or Newsgroup Posting

MLA: MacDonald, James C. "Suggestions for Promoting Collaborative Writing in College Composition." Online posting. 10 Nov. 1994. NCTE Forum/current topics/bulletin posting. 12 Mar. 1995. America Online.

Include the date of transmission or posting, the medium, network name, location information, an address or path for electronic access, and date of access.

In APA style, this material is acknowledged in in-text citations only. See the specifications for e-mail, listservs, and other nonretrievable sources on page 417.

General Format for Miscellaneous Materials

Films, Filmstrips, Slide Programs, and Videotapes

MLA: Chagall. Dir. Kim Evans. Videocassette. London Weekend Television, 1985.

APA: Evans, K. (Director). (1985). Chagall [Videocassette]. London: London Weekend Television.

Television and Radio Programs

MLA: Korea: The Forgotten War. Narr. Robert Stack. KCPQ, Seattle. 27 June 1988.

APA: Stack, R. (Narrator). (1988, June 27). Korea: The forgotten war. Seattle: KCPQ.

Interview

MLA: Deltete, Robert. Personal interview. 27 Feb. 1994.

APA: Deltete, R. (1994, February 27). [Personal interview].

The APA *Publication Manual* says to omit nonrecoverable material—such as personal correspondence, personal interviews, and lectures—from the References. However, in college research papers, professors usually like to have such information included.

Lecture, Address, or Speech

MLA: North, Oliver. Speech. Washington Policy Council. Seattle. 20 July 1988.

APA: North, O. (1988, July 20). Speech presented to Washington Policy Council, Seattle, WA.

In the MLA system, if the title of the speech is known, give the title in quotation marks instead of the word *Speech.* The APA *Publication Manual* has no provisions for citing lectures, addresses, or speeches because these are nonrecoverable items. However, the manual gives authors leeway to design citations for instances not covered explicitly in the manual. This format is suitable for college research papers.

For more complicated entries, consult the *MLA Handbook for Writers of Research Papers,* fifth edition, or the *Publication Manual of the American Psychological Association,* fourth edition. Both books should be available in your library or bookstore. For additional help in citing online sources, see the Web sites for these organizations, http://www.mla.org and http://www.apa.org.

Quick Check Reference: MLA and APA Bibliographic Entries

As a handy reference to the most commonly encountered kinds of entries in college research papers, see pages 420–21. These two pages illustrate a Works Cited list (MLA format) and a References list (APA format). These lists give you a quick summary of the formats for the most commonly used sources.

FORMATTING A RESEARCH PAPER

College instructors usually ask students to follow standard academic conventions for formatting research papers. Although conventions vary from discipline to discipline, the most common formatting styles are the MLA or the APA. The MLA formatting style is illustrated in Stephen Bean's paper on pages 334–42. The APA formatting style is illustrated in Lynnea Clark's paper on pages 424–30.

Formatting Features Common to Both MLA and APA

- Double-space the text throughout, including quotations and notes.
- Use one-inch margins top and bottom, left and right.
- Indent five spaces at the beginning of every paragraph.
- Number pages consecutively throughout the manuscript including the bibliographic section at the end.
- Begin the bibliographic section (called Works Cited in MLA and References in APA) on a separate page.

Distinctive Formatting Features for MLA

- Do not include a cover page. Type your name, professor's name, course number, and date in the upper left-hand corner of your paper (all double-spaced) beginning one inch from the top of the page; then double-space and type your title, centered, without underlines, boldface, or all caps

Works Cited: MLA Style Sheet for the Most Commonly Used Sources

Ross 27

Works Cited

Adler, Freda. Sisters in Crime. New York: McGraw, 1975.

Andersen, Margaret L. Thinking about Women:
Sociological Perspectives on Sex and Gender.
3rd ed. New York: Macmillan, 1993.

Bart, Pauline, and Patricia O'Brien. Stopping Rape:
Successful Survival Strategies. New York:
Pergamon, 1985.

Durkin, Kevin. "Social Cognition and Social Context
in the Construction of Sex Differences." Sex
Differences in Human Performances. Ed. Mary
Anne Baker. New York: Wiley, 1987. 45–60.

Fairburn, Christopher G., et al. "Predictors of Twelve-
Month Outcome in Bulimia Nervosa and the
Influence of Attitudes to Shape and Weight."
Journal of Consulting and Clinical Psychology 61
(1993): 696–98.

Kantrowitz, Barbara. "Sexism in the Schoolhouse."
Newsweek 24 Feb. 1992: 62.

Langewiesche, William. "The World in Its Extreme."
Atlantic Nov. 1991: 105–40.

National Law Center. "Selected Rights of Homeless
Persons." National Law Center on Homelessness
and Poverty 19 Apr. 1998 <http://www.nlchp.org/
rights2.htm>.

Taylor, Chuck. "After Cobain's Death: Here Come
the Media Ready to Buy Stories." Seattle Times
10 Apr. 1994: A1+.

Writer's last name and page number in upper right corner.

Book entry, one author. Use standard abbreviations for common publishers.

Book entry in a revised edition.

Book by two or three authors. With four or more authors, name only the first and use *et al.*, as in Jones, Peter, et al.

Article in anthology; author heads the entry; editor cited after the book title. Inclusive page numbers come after the period following the year.

Article in scholarly journal paginated consecutively throughout year. This article has four or more authors.

Weekly or biweekly popular magazine; abbreviate all months except May, June, and July.

Monthly, bimonthly, or quarterly magazine.

Online document with corporate author; title in quotation marks; Web site underlined; date of access; Web address in angle brackets.

Newspaper article with identified author; if no author, begin with title.

References: APA Style Sheet for the Most Commonly Used Sources

Women, Health, and Crime   27

References

Adler, F. (1975). Sisters in crime. New York: McGraw-Hill.

Andersen, M. L. (1993). Thinking about women: Sociological perspectives on sex and gender (3rd ed.). New York: Macmillan.

Bart, P., & O'Brien, P. (1985). Stopping rape: Successful survival strategies. New York: Pergamon Press.

Durkin, K. (1987). Social cognition and social context in the construction of sex differences. In M. A. Baker (Ed.), Sex differences in human performances (pp. 45–60). New York: Wiley & Sons.

Fairburn, C. G., Pevaler, R. C., Jones, R., & Hope, R. A. (1993). Predictors of 12-month outcome in bulimia nervosa and the influence of attitudes to shape and weight. Journal of Consulting and Clinical Psychology, 61, 696–698.

Kantrowitz, B. (1992, February 24). Sexism in the schoolhouse. Newsweek, 62.

Langewiesche, W. (1991, November). The world in its extreme. The Atlantic Monthly, 105–140.

National Law Center. Selected rights of homeless persons. (n.d.) Retrieved April 19, 1998 from the World Wide Web: http://www.nlchp.org./rights2.htm

Taylor, C. (1994, April 10). After Cobain's death: Here come the media ready to buy stories. The Seattle Times, pp. A1+.

Running head and page number separated by five spaces.

Book entry, one author. Don't abbreviate publisher but omit unnecessary words.

Book entry in a revised edition.

Book with multiple authors; uses ampersand instead of *and* before last name. Authors' names listed last name first.

Article in anthology; no quotation marks around article title. Name of editor comes before book title.

Article in scholarly journal paginated consecutively throughout year. APA lists all authors in the References rather than using *et al.*

Weekly or biweekly popular magazine; do not abbreviate months.

Monthly, bimonthly, or quarterly magazine.

Online document with corporate author; roman title; access date; no period after Web address. (No date is available for this source.)

Newspaper article with identified author; if no author, begin with title.

(capitalize first word and important words only); then double-space and begin your text (see p. 334 for an example).

- Page numbers go in the upper right-hand corner flush with the right margin and one-half inch from the top of the page. The page number should be preceded by your last name (see pp. 334–42). The text begins one inch from the top of the page.

- Start a new page for your bibliography, which is titled Works Cited (centered, one inch from top of page, without underlining, quotation marks, bold face, or all caps). Format each entry according to the instructions on pages 406–22 (see p. 342 for an example; also see p. 420).

Distinctive Formatting Features for APA

- Has a separate title page, numbered page 1, and a 100-to-150-word abstract, numbered page 2 (the main body of your text begins with page 3). Papers for undergraduate courses often omit the abstract. Approximately one-third from the top of the page, type your title centered and double-spaced, without underlines or all caps (capitalize first word and important words only). Two spaces below the title type your name (centered). Two spaces below your name, type your course number (centered), and two spaces below that type the date (for an example of an APA title page, see p. 424).

- Page numbers go in the upper right-hand corner, flush with the right margin. Five spaces to the left of your page number, type your running head (a short version of your title), capitalizing only the first letters. Note that the first page of the main text is numbered either 2 or 3, depending on whether the paper includes an abstract (see p. 425).

- Start a new page for your bibliography, which is titled References (centered, one inch from top of page, without underlining, quotation marks, bold face, or all caps). Format each entry according to the instructions on pages 406–22 (see p. 430 for an example; also see p. 421).

▼ FOR CLASS DISCUSSION

Now that you have reviewed the formats of the most commonly used kinds of sources, consider the differences between the MLA and the APA systems. The MLA system is used most frequently in the humanities, while the APA system is used in the social sciences. Why do you suppose the MLA system gives complete first names of authors as well as middle initials, while the APA system uses only initials for the first and middle names? Why does the APA system emphasize date of publication by putting dates prominently near the front of an entry just after the author's name? On the basis of the MLA and APA formats, could you make some observations about differences in values between the humanities and the social sciences?

CONCLUSION

This chapter has shown that research writing is a variation on the thesis-governed writing with which you are already familiar. We have discussed how to focus and refine your research question, suggesting that you remain flexible throughout your research process so that your purpose and thesis can evolve as you discover new information. The chapter has explained purposeful strategies for reading, thinking, and note taking to help you avoid random inclusion of data and keep all research information focused on your own thesis. The chapter has also discussed methods of summarizing, paraphrasing, and quoting through the effective use of attributive tags, quotation marks, and block indentation. These methods enable you to work research sources smoothly into your own writing, distinguish your ideas from those of your sources, and avoid plagiarism. Finally, the chapter has explained how to use the MLA and the APA systems to cite and document your sources.

STUDENT EXAMPLE OF A RESEARCHED ARGUMENT PAPER (APA STYLE)

We conclude with a sample of a successful effort: Lynnea Clark's researched argument on policewomen. She uses the APA system for citing and documenting her sources.

Women Police Officers:

Should Size and Strength Be Criteria for Patrol Duty?

Lynnea Clark

English 301

15 November 199X

This research paper follows the APA style for format and documentation.

Women Police Officers:

Should Size and Strength Be Criteria for Patrol Duty?

A marked patrol car turns the corner at 71st and Franklin Avenue and [1]
cautiously proceeds into the parking lot of an old shopping center. About a dozen
gang members, dressed in their gang colors, stand alert, looking down the alley
that runs behind the store. As the car moves toward the gathering, they suddenly
scatter in all directions. Within seconds, several shots are fired from the alley.
Switching on the overhead emergency lights, the officer bolts from the car when
he sees two figures running past him. "Freeze! Police!" the officer yells. The men
dart off in opposite directions. Chasing one, the policeman catches up to him, and,
observing no gun, tackles him. After a violent struggle, the officer manages to
handcuff the man, just as the backup unit comes screeching up.

This policeman is my friend. The next day I am with him as he sits at a cafe [2]
with three of his fellow officers, discussing the incident. One of the officers
comments, "Well, at least you were stronger than he was. Can you imagine if
Connie Jones was on patrol duty last night?" "What a joke," scoffs another officer.
"How tall is she anyway?" "About 4'10" and 90 pounds," says the third officer. "She
could fit in my backpack." Connie Jones (not her real name) has just completed
police academy training and has been assigned to patrol duty in _____. Because
she is so small, she has to have a booster seat in her patrol car and has been given
a special gun, since she can barely manage to pull the trigger of a standard police-
issue .38 revolver. Although she passed the physical requirements at the academy,
which involved speed and endurance running, situps, and monkey bar tests, most
of the officers in her department doubt her ability to perform competently as a
patrol officer. But nevertheless she is on patrol because men and women receive
equal assignments in most of today's police forces. But is this a good policy? Can a
person who is significantly small and weak make an effective patrol officer?

Because the "small and weak" people in question are almost always women, [3]
the issue becomes a woman's issue. Considerable research has been done on
women in the police force, and much of it suggests that women, who are on the
average smaller and weaker than men, can perform competently in law enforcement,
regardless of their size or strength. More specifically, most research concludes that
female police workers in general perform just as well as their fellow officers in
patrolling situations. A major study by Bloch and Anderson (1984), commissioned

by the Urban Institute, revealed that in the handling of violent situations, women performed well. In fact, women and men received equally satisfactory evaluation ratings on their overall performances.

4   In another more recent study (Grennan, 1987) examining the relationship between outcomes of police-citizen confrontations and the gender of the involved officers, female officers were determined to be just as productive as male officers in the handling of violent situations. In his article on female criminal justice employment, Potts (1982) reviews numerous studies on evaluation ratings of policewomen and acknowledges that "the predominant weight of evidence is that women are equally capable of performing police work as are men" (p. 11). Additionally, female officers score higher on necessary traits for leadership (p. 10), and it has been often found that women are better at dealing with rape and abuse victims. Again, a study performed by Grennan (1987), concentrating on male and female police officers' confrontations with citizens, revealed that the inborn or socialized nurturing ability possessed by female police workers makes them "just as productive as male officers in the handling of a violent confrontation" (p. 84).

5   This view has been strengthened further by the recent achievement of Katherine P. Heller, who was honored by receiving the nation's top award in law enforcement for 1990 (Proctor, 1990). Heller, a United States park policewoman, risked her life by stepping in the open to shoot dead an assailant while he leveled his gun to shoot at her fellow police officer. Five feet three inches and 107 pounds, Heller is not only the first woman to be awarded with Police Officer of the Year, but she is also the smallest recipient ever. Maybe Heller's decisiveness will help lay to rest doubts about many women's abilities as police workers.

6   However, despite the evidence provided by the above-cited research, I am not convinced. Although these studies show that women make effective police officers, I believe the studies must be viewed with skepticism. My concern is public safety. In light of that concern, the evidence suggests that police departments should set stringent size and strength requirements for patrol officers, even if these criteria exclude many women.

7   First of all, the research studies documenting the success of women as patrol officers are marred by two major flaws: The amount of evidence gathered is scanty and the way that the data have been gathered doesn't allow us to study factors of size and strength. Because of minimal female participation in patrol work prior to

the past decade, limited amounts of research and reports exist on the issue. And of the research performed, many studies have not been based on representative samples. Garrison, Grant, and McCormick (1988) found that

> [l]iterature on women in patrol or nontraditional police roles tends to be idiosyncratic. . . . Many of the observations written about a relatively small number of women performing successfully in a wider range of police tasks support the assumption that they are exceptions rather than the norm. (p. 32)

Similarly, Bloch and Anderson (1984) note that in the course of their study

> it was not possible to observe enough incidents to be sure that men and women are equally capable in all such situations. It is clear from the incidents which were described that women performed well in the few violent situations which did arise. (p. 61)

Another problem with the available research is that little differentiation has been made within the large group of women being considered; all women officers seem to be grouped and evaluated based on only two criteria: that they are on the police force and that they are female. But like men, women come in all shapes and sizes. To say that women as a class make effective or ineffective police workers is to make too general a claim. The example of women officers such as Katherine Heller proves that some women make excellent patrol cops. But, presumably, some women probably would not make good patrol cops just as some men would not. The available data do not allow us to determine whether size and strength are factors. Because no size differentiation has been made within the groups of women officers under observation in the research studies, it is impossible to conclude whether or not smaller, weaker women performed patrol duties as well as larger, stronger women did. In fact, for Bloch and Anderson's study (which indicates that, from a performance viewpoint, it is appropriate to hire women for patrol assignments on the same basis as men) both men and women had to meet a minimum height requirement of 5'7". Therefore, the performance of smaller, weaker women in handling violent situations remained unevaluated. Thus the data show that many women are great cops; the data do not show that many small women with minimal strength make great cops.

The case of Katherine Heller might seem to demonstrate that smaller women can perform patrol duties successfully. Heller acknowledged in an interview in Parade magazine that ninety percent of her adversaries will be bigger than she

(Proctor, 1990, p. 5). But she is no fluttering fluffball; rather, she has earned the reputation for being an extremely aggressive cop and has compensated for her size by her bearing. But how many women (or men) of Heller's size or smaller could maintain such "officer presence"? How can we be certain that Heller is in fact representative of small women rather than being an exception?

10   This question leads to my second reason for supporting stringent size and strength requirements: Many police officers, both male and female, have real doubts about the abilities of small and physically weak patrol workers, most of whom are women. For example, police officer Elizabeth Demetriou, a six-year veteran of the New York Police Department, said in an interview, "Women on the job still depend on men to help them during confrontations, more so than men do. Male police officers want their partners to be 'tough' or big so that automatically excludes women" (Kennedy, 1996). In a study done by Vega and Silverman (1982), almost 75% of male police officers felt that women were not strong enough to handle the demands of patrol duties, and 42% felt women lacked the needed assertiveness to enforce the law vigorously (p. 32). Unfortunately, however, because of frequent media reports of discrimination and sexism among police personnel and because of pressure from the Equal Employment Opportunity Commission (EEOC) on police agencies and other employers (Vega & Silverman, 1982; Lord, 1986), these reservations and attitudes have not been seriously taken into account.

11   The valid concerns and opinions of police workers who feel that some women officers are not strong enough to deal effectively with violent situations have been asphyxiated by the smoldering accusations of civil rights activists and feminists, who see only layers of chauvinism, conservatism, cynicism, and authoritarianism permeating our law enforcement agencies. These activists view the problem as being only a "women" issue rather than a "size" issue. But the fact remains that both male and female officers think that many patrol workers are incapable of handling violent situations because of small stature and lack of physical strength. Another policewoman belonging to the same department as Connie Jones explained, "She [Jones] doesn't have the authoritarian stance needed to compensate for her size. She's not imposing and is too soft spoken. Once she responded to a call and was literally picked up and thrown out the door" (anonymous personal communication, October 6, 1990).

Finally, patrol duties, unlike other areas of police work, constitute one of the   12
few jobs in our society that may legitimately require above-average strength.
Because the job involves great personal risk and danger, the concern for public
safety overrides the concern for equal rights in this instance. Patrolling is a
high-visibility position in police departments as opposed to jobs such as radio
dispatching, academy training, or clerical duties. Patrol workers directly face the
challenges presented by the public, and violence is always a threat for officers on
patrol (Vega & Silverman, 1982; Grennan, 1987). Due to the nature of patrol work,
officers many times must cope with violent situations by using physical force, such
as that needed for subduing individuals who resist arrest. However, pressure from
liberal groups has prevented special consideration being given to these factors of
patrol duty. As long as student officers pass the standard academy Physical Ability
Test (in addition to the other academy requirements), then they are eligible for
patrol assignments; in fact, everyone out of the academy <u>must</u> go on patrol. But
the minimum physical requirements are not challenging. According to Lord
(1986), police agencies "struggle to find a nondiscriminatory, empirically valid
entry level physical agility test which does not discriminate against women by
overemphasizing upper body strength" (p. 91). In short, the liberal agenda leading
to women on patrol has forced the lowering of strength requirements.

Without establishing minimum size and strength requirements for patrol   13
workers, police departments are not discharging their duties with maximum
competency or effectiveness. Police training programs stress that police officers
should be able to maintain an authoritarian presence in the face of challenges and
possess the ability to diffuse a situation just by making an appearance. But some
individuals who are able to pass basic training programs still lack the size needed to
maintain an imposing physical stance. And as many citizens obviously do not respect
the uniform, police workers must possess the strength to efficiently handle violent
encounters. Even if size and strength requirements have a disproportionate impact
on women, these physical standards are lawful, so long as they relate to the demands
of the job and "constitute valid predictors of an employee's performance on the job"
(Steel & Lovrich, 1987, p. 53). Patrol duties demand highly capable and effective
workers, and in order to professionalize law-enforcement practices and to maintain
the degree of order necessary for a free society, police agencies must maintain a high
level of competency in their street-patrol forces.

References

Bloch, P., & Anderson, D. (1984). Police women on patrol: Final report. Washington, DC: Police Foundation.

Garrison, C., Grant, N., & McCormick, K. (1988). Utilization of police women. The Police Chief, 55(9), 32–73.

Grennan, S. (1987). Findings on the role of officer gender in violent encounters with citizens. Journal of Police Science and Administration, 15(1), 78–84.

Kennedy, E. A. (1996, Spring). Defensive tactics and the female officer. WomenPolice. Retrieved May 4, 1996 from the World Wide Web; http://www.mwarrior.com/DT-fem2.htm

Lord, L. (1986). A comparison of male and female peace officers' stereotypic perceptions of women and women peace officers. Journal of Police Science and Administration, 14(2), 83–91.

Potts, L. (1981). Equal employment opportunity and female criminal justice employment. Police Studies, 4(3), 9–19.

Proctor, P. (1990, September 30). "I didn't have time to taste the fear." Parade, pp. 4–5.

Steel, B., & Lovrich, N., Jr. (1987). Equality and efficiency tradeoffs in affirmative action--real or imagined? The case of women in policing. The Social Science Journal, 24(1), 53–67.

Vega, M., & Silverman, I. (1982). Female police officers as viewed by their male counterparts. Police Studies, 5(1), 31–39.

a p p e n d i x   o n e

Informal Fallacies

In this appendix, we look at ways of testing the legitimacy of an argument. Sometimes, there are fatal logical flaws hiding in the heart of a perfectly respectable-looking argument, and if we miss them, we may find ourselves vainly defending the indefensible. Take, for example, the following cases. Do they seem persuasive to you?

Creationism must be a science because hundreds of scientists believe in it.

I am opposed to a multicultural curriculum because it will lead to ethnic separatism similar to what is happening in eastern Europe.

Smoking must cause cancer because a higher percentage of smokers get cancer than do nonsmokers.

Smoking doesn't cause cancer because my grandfather smoked two packs per day for fifty years and died in his sleep at age ninety.

An abnormal percentage of veterans who were marched to ground zero during atomic tests in Nevada died of leukemia and lung cancer. Surely their deaths were caused by the inhalation of radioactive isotopes.

THE PROBLEM OF CONCLUSIVENESS IN AN ARGUMENT

Although it may distress us to think so, none of the arguments listed above is conclusive. But that doesn't mean they're false, either. So what are they? Well, they are, to various degrees, "persuasive" or "unpersuasive." The problem is that some people will mistake arguments such as those above for "conclusive" or airtight arguments. A person may rest an entire argument on them and then fall right through the holes that observant logicians open in them. Although few people will mistake an airtight case for a fallacious one, lots of people mistake logically unsound arguments for airtight cases. So let's see how to avoid falling into specious reasoning.

Some arguments are flawed because they fail to observe certain formal logical rules. In constructing syllogisms, for example, there are certain formal laws that must be followed if we are to have a valid syllogism. The following argument is beyond doubt invalid and inconclusive:

No Greeks are bald.

No Lithuanians are Greek.

Therefore, all Lithuanians are bald.

But to say the argument is invalid isn't to say that its conclusion is necessarily untrue. Perhaps all Lithuanians really are bald. The point is, if the conclusion were true, it would be by coincidence, not design, because the argument is invalid. All invalid arguments are inconclusive. And, by the same token, a perfectly valid syllogism may be untrue. Just because the premises follow the formal laws of logic doesn't mean that what they say is true. For a syllogistic argument to be absolutely conclusive, its form must be valid and its premises must be true. A perfectly conclusive argument would therefore yield a noncontroversial truth—a statement that no one would dispute.

This is a long way around to reach one point: The reason we argue about issues is that none of the arguments on any side of an issue is absolutely conclusive; there is always room to doubt the argument, to develop a counterargument. We can only create more or less persuasive arguments, never conclusive ones.

We have examined some of these problems already. In Chapter 11 on causal arguments we discussed the problem of correlation versus causation. We know, for example, that smoking and cancer are correlated but that further arguments are needed in order to increase the conclusiveness of the claim that smoking *causes* cancer.

In this appendix we explore the problem of conclusiveness in various kinds of arguments. In particular, we use the *informal fallacies* of logic to explain how inconclusive arguments can fool us into thinking they are conclusive.

AN OVERVIEW OF INFORMAL FALLACIES

The study of informal fallacies remains the murkiest of all logical endeavors. It's murky because informal fallacies are as unsystematic as formal fallacies are rigid and systematized. Whereas formal fallacies of logic have the force of laws, informal fallacies have little more than explanatory power. Informal fallacies are quirky; they identify classes of less conclusive arguments that recur with some frequency, but they do not contain formal flaws that make their conclusions illegitimate no matter what the terms may say. Informal fallacies require us to look at the meaning of the terms to determine how much we should trust or distrust the conclusion. The most common mistake one can make with informal fallacies is to assume that they have the force of laws like formal fallacies. They don't. In evaluating arguments with informal fallacies, we usually find that arguments are "more or less" fallacious, and determining the degree of fallaciousness is a matter of judgment.

Knowledge of informal fallacies is most useful when we run across arguments that we "know" are wrong, but we can't quite say why. They just don't "sound right." They look reasonable enough, but they remain unacceptable to us. Informal fallacies are a sort of compendium of symptoms for arguments flawed in this way. We must be careful, however, to make sure that the particular case before us "fits" the descriptors for the fallacy that seems to explain its problem. It's much easier, for example, to find informal fallacies in a hostile argument than in a friendly one simply because we are more likely to expand the limits of the fallacy to make the disputed case fit.

Not everyone agrees about what to include under the heading "informal fallacies." In selecting the following set of fallacies, we left out far more candidates than we included. Since Aristotle first developed his list of thirteen *elenchi* (refutations) down to the present day, literally dozens of different systems of informal fallacy have been put forward. Although there is a good deal of overlap among these lists, the terms are invariably different, and the definition of fallacy itself shifts from age to age. In selecting the following set of fallacies, we left out a number of other candidates. We chose the following because they seemed to us to be the most commonly encountered.

In arranging the fallacies, we have, for convenience, put them into three categories derived from classical rhetoric: *pathos*, *ethos*, and *logos*. Fallacies of *pathos* rest on a flawed relationship between what is argued and the audience for the argument. Fallacies of *ethos* rest on a flawed relationship between the argument and the character of those involved in the argument. Fallacies of *logos* rest on flaws in the relationship among statements of an argument.

Fallacies of *Pathos*

Argument to the People (Appealing to Stirring Symbols)

This is perhaps the most generic example of a *pathos* fallacy. Argument to the people appeals to the fundamental beliefs, biases, and prejudices of the audience in order to sway opinion through a feeling of solidarity among those of the group. For example, when a politician says, "My fellow Americans, I stand here, draped in this flag from head to foot, to indicate my fundamental dedication to the values and principles of these sovereign United States," he's redirecting to his own person our allegiance to nationalistic values by linking himself with the prime symbol of those values, the flag. The linkage is not rational, it's associative. It's also extremely powerful—which is why arguments to the people crop up so frequently.

Appeal to Ignorance (Presenting Evidence the Audience Can't Examine)

Those who commit this fallacy present assumptions, assertions, or evidence that the audience is incapable of judging or examining. If, for example, a critic were to praise the novel *Clarissa* for its dullness on the grounds that this dullness was the intentional effect of the author, we would be unable to respond because we have no idea what was in the author's mind when he created the work.

Appeal to Irrational Premises (Appealing to Reasons That May Have No Basis in Logic)

This mode of short-circuiting reason may take one of three forms:

1. Appeal to common practice. (It's all right to do X because everyone else does it.)

2. Appeal to traditional wisdom. (It's all right because we've always done it this way.)

3. Appeal to popularity—the bandwagon appeal. (It's all right because lots of people like it.)

In all three cases, we've moved from saying something is popular, common, or persistent to saying it is right, good, or necessary. You have a better chance of rocketing across the Grand Canyon on a motorcycle than you have of going from "is" to "ought" on a *because* clause. Some examples of this fallacy would include (1) "Of course I borrowed money from the company slush fund. Everyone on this floor has done the same in the last eighteen months"; (2) "We've got to require everyone to read *Hamlet* because we've always required everyone to read it"; and (3) "You should buy a Ford Escort because it's the best-selling car in the world."

Provincialism (Appealing to the Belief That the Known Is Always Better Than the Unknown)

Here is an example from the 1960s: "You can't sell small cars in America. In American culture, automobiles symbolize prestige and personal freedom. Those cramped little Japanese tin boxes will never win the hearts of American consumers." Although we may inevitably feel more comfortable with familiar things, ideas, and beliefs, we are not necessarily better off for sticking with them.

Red Herring (Shifting the Audience's Attention from a Crucial Issue to an Irrelevant One)

A good example of a red herring showed up in a statement by Secretary of State James Baker that was reported in the November 10, 1990, *New York Times*. In response to a question about the appropriateness of using American soldiers to defend wealthy, insulated (and by implication, corrupt) Kuwaiti royalty, Baker told an anecdote about an isolated encounter he had with four Kuwaitis who had suffered; he then made a lengthy statement on America's interests in the Persian Gulf. Although no one would argue that America is unaffected by events in the Middle

East, the question of why others with even greater interests at stake had not contributed more troops and resources went unanswered.

Fallacies of *Ethos*

Appeal to False Authority (Appealing to the Authority of a Popular Person Rather Than a Knowledgeable One)

Appeals to false authority involve relying on testimony given by a person incompetent in the field from which the claims under question emerge. Most commercial advertisements are based on this fallacy. Cultural heroes are paid generously to associate themselves with a product without demonstrating any real expertise in evaluating that product. In at least one case, consumers who fell victim to such a fallacy made a legal case out of it. People bilked out of their life savings by a Michigan mortgage company sued the actors who represented the company on TV. Are people fooled by such appeals to false authority entitled to recover assets lost as a result?

The court answered no. The judge ruled that people gullible enough to believe that George Hamilton's capped-tooth smile and mahogany tan qualify him as a real estate consultant deserve what they get. Their advice to consumers? "Buyers beware," because even though sellers can't legally lie, they can legally use fallacious arguments—all the more reason to know your fallacies.

Keep in mind, however, that occasionally the distinction between a false authority fallacy and an appeal to legitimate authority can blur. Suppose that Tiger Woods were to praise a particular company's golf club. Because he is an expert on golf, it is possible that Woods actually speaks from authority and that the golf club he praises is superior. But it might also be that he is being paid to advertise the golf club and is endorsing a brand that is no better than its competitors'. The only way we could make even a partial determination of Woods's motives would be if he presented an *ad rem* ("to the thing") argument showing us scientifically why the golf club in question is superior. In short, appeals to authority are legitimate when the authority knows the field and when her motive is to inform others rather than profit herself.

*Appeal to the Person/*Ad Hominem *(Attacking the Character of the Arguer Rather Than the Argument Itself)*

Literally, *ad hominem* means "to the man" or "to the person." Any argument that focuses on the character of the person making the argument rather than the quality of the reasoning qualifies as an *ad hominem* argument. Ideally, arguments are supposed to be *ad rem*, or "to the thing," that is, addressed to the specifics of the case itself. Thus an *ad rem* critique of a politician would focus on her voting record, the consistency and cogency of her public statements, her responsiveness to constituents, and so forth. An *ad hominem* argument would shift attention from her record to irrelevant features of her personality or personal life. Perhaps an *ad hominem* argument would suggest that she had a less than stellar undergraduate academic record.

But not all *ad hominem* arguments are *ad hominem* fallacies. It's not always fallacious to address your argument to the arguer. There are indeed times when the credibility of the person making an opposing argument is at issue. Lawyers, for example, when questioning expert witnesses who give damaging testimony, will often make an issue of their credibility, and rightfully so. And certainly it's not that clear, for instance, that an all-male research team of social scientists would observe and interpret data in the same way as a mixed-gender research group. An *ad hominem* attack on an opponent's argument is not fallacious so long as (1) personal authority is what gives the opposing argument much of its weight, and (2) the critique of the person's credibility is fairly presented.

An interesting example of an *ad hominem* argument occurred in the 1980s in context of the Star Wars antiballistic missile system debate. Many important physicists around the country signed a statement in which they declared their opposition to Star Wars research. Another group of physicists supportive of that research condemned them on the grounds that none of the protesting physicists stood to get any Star Wars research funds anyway. This attack shifted attention away from the reasons given by the protesting physicists for their convictions and put it instead on the physicists' motives. To some extent, of course, credibility is an issue here, because many of the key issues raised in the debate required some degree of expertise to resolve. Hence, the charges meet the first test for nonfallacious reasoning directed to the arguer.

But we must also ask ourselves if the charges being made are fair. If you'll recall from earlier discussions of fairness, we said that fairness requires similar treatment of similar classes of things. Applying this rule to this situation, we can simply reverse the charge being levied against the anti–Star Wars group and say of its supporters: "Because you stand to gain a good deal of research money from this project, we can't take your support of the Star Wars initiatives seriously." The Star Wars supporters would thus become victims of their own logic. *Ad hominem* attacks are often of this nature: The charges are perfectly reversible—for example, "Of course you support abortion; all your friends are feminists." "Of course you oppose abortion; you've been a Catholic all your life." *Ad hominem* debates resemble nothing so much as mental quick-draw contests. Whoever shoots first wins because the first accuser puts the burden of proof on the opposition.

It's important to see here that an *ad hominem* argument, even if not fallacious, can never be definitive. Like analogies, they are simply suggestive; they raise doubts and focus our attention. Catholic writers can produce reasonable arguments against abortion, and feminists can produce reasonable ones for it. *Ad hominem* attacks don't allow us to discount arguments; but they do alert us to possible biases, possible ways the reasoned arguments themselves are vulnerable.

Several subcategories of *ad hominem* argument that are almost never persuasive include

1. Name calling (referring to a disputant by unsavory names)
2. Appeal to prejudice (applying ethnic, racial, gender, or religious slurs to an opponent)
3. Guilt by association (linking the opposition to extremely unpopular groups or causes)

Name calling is found far more often in transcripts of oral encounters than in books or essays. In the heat of the moment, speakers are more likely to lapse into verbal abuse than are writers who have time to contemplate their words. The *Congressional Record* is a rich source for name calling. Here, for example, one finds a duly elected representative referring to another duly elected representative as "a pimp for the Eastern establishment environmentalists." One of the biggest problems with such a charge is that it's unlikely to beget much in the way of reasoned response. It's far easier to respond in kind than it is to persuade people rationally that one is not a jackass of *that* particular sort.

When name calling is "elevated" to include slighting reference to the opponent's religion, gender, race, or ethnic background, we have encountered an appeal to prejudice. When it involves lumping an opponent with unsavory, terminally dumb, or extremely unpopular causes and characters, it constitutes guilt by association.

Straw Man (Greatly Oversimplifying an Opponent's Argument to Make It Easier to Refute or Ridicule)

Although typically less inflammatory than the preceding sorts of *ethos* fallacies, the straw man fallacy changes the character of the opposition in order to suit the arguer's own needs. In committing a straw man fallacy, you basically make up the argument you *wish* your opponents had made and attribute it to them because it's so much easier to refute than the argument they actually made. Some political debates consist almost entirely of straw man exchanges such as: "You may think that levying confiscatory taxes on homeless people's cardboard dwellings is the surest way out of recession, but I don't." Or: "While my opponent would like to empty our prisons of serial killers and coddle kidnappers, I hold to the sacred principles of compensatory justice."

Fallacies of *Logos*

Logos fallacies comprise flaws in the relationships among the statements of an argument. Thus, to borrow momentarily from the language of the Toulmin schema discussed earlier, you can think of *logos* fallacies as breakdowns between arguments' warrants and their claims, between their warrants and their backing, or between their claims and their reasons and grounds.

Begging the Question (Supporting a Claim with a Reason That Is Really a Restatement of the Claim in Different Words)

Question begging is probably the most obvious example of a *logos* fallacy in that it involves stating a claim as though it warranted itself. For example, the statement "Abortion is murder because it involves the intentional killing of an unborn human being" is tantamount to saying "Abortion is murder because it's murder." The warrant "If something is the intentional killing of a human life, it is murder" simply repeats the claim; murder is *by definition* the intentional killing of another human being. Logically, the statement is akin to a statement like "That fellow is fat because he's considerably overweight." The crucial issue in the abortion debate is whether a fetus is a human being in the legal sense. This crucial issue is avoided in the argument that begins by assuming that the fetus is a legal human being. That argument goes in an endless circle from claim to warrant and back again.

Or consider the following argument: "How can you say Minnie Minoso belongs in the Hall of Fame? He's been eligible for over a decade, and the Selection Committee turned him down every year. If he belonged in the Hall of Fame, the Committee would already have chosen him." Because the point at issue is whether the Hall of Fame Selection Committee *should* elect Minnie Minoso (it should, we think), the use of the committee's vote as proof of the contention that it should not elect him is wholly circular and begs the question.

In distinguishing valid reasoning from fallacious examples of question begging, some philosophers say that a question has been begged when the premises of an argument are at least as uncertain as the claim. In such cases, we are not making any movement from some known general principle toward some new particular conclusion; we are simply asserting an uncertain premise in order to give the appearance of certainty to a shaky claim.

To illustrate the preceding observation, consider the controversy that arose in the late 1980s over whether to impose economic sanctions against South Africa in order to pressure the South Africans into changing their racial policies. One argument against economic sanctions went like this: "We should not approve economic sanctions against South Africa (claim) because economic sanctions will hurt blacks as much as whites" (premise or stated reason). The claim ("We should not impose economic sanctions") is only as certain as the premise from which it was derived ("because blacks will suffer as much as whites"), but many people argued that that premise was extremely uncertain. They thought that whites would suffer the most under sanctions and that blacks would ultimately benefit. The question would no longer be begged if the person included a documented defense of the premise. But without such a defense, the arguer's claim is grounded on a shaky premise that sounds more certain than it is.

Complex Question (Confronting the Opponent
with a Question That Will Put Her in a Bad Light
No Matter How She Responds)

A complex question is one that requires, in legal terms, a self-incriminating response. For example, the question "When did you stop abusing alcohol?" requires the admission of alcohol abuse. Hence the claim that a person has abused alcohol is silently turned into an assumption.

False Dilemma/Either–Or (Oversimplifying
a Complex Issue So That Only Two Choices
Appear Possible)

A good extended analysis of this fallacy is found in sociologist Kai Erikson's analysis of President Truman's decision to drop the A-bomb on Hiroshima. His analysis suggests that the Truman administration prematurely reduced numerous options to just two: Either drop the bomb on a major city, or sustain unacceptable losses in a land invasion of Japan. Erikson, however, shows there were other alternatives. Typically, we encounter false dilemma arguments when people are trying to justify a questionable action by creating a false sense of necessity, forcing us to choose between two options, one of which is clearly unacceptable. Hence, when someone orders us to "Do it my way or hit the highway" or to "Love it or leave it," it's probably in response to some criticism we made about the "way" we're supposed to do it or the "it" we're supposed to love.

But of course not all dilemmas are false. People who reject all binary oppositions (that is, thinking in terms of pairs of opposites) are themselves guilty of a false dilemma. There are times when we might determine through a rational process of elimination that only two possible choices exist. Deciding whether a dilemma is truly a dilemma or only an evasion of complexity often requires a difficult judgment. Although we should initially suspect any attempt to convert a complex problem into an either/or choice, we may legitimately arrive at such a choice through thoughtful deliberation.

Equivocation (Using to Your Advantage
at Least Two Different Definitions of the
Same Term in the Same Argument)

For example, if we're told that people can't "flourish" unless they are culturally literate, we must know which of the several possible senses of *flourish* are being used before we can test the persuasiveness of the claim. If by *flourishing* the author means acquiring great wealth, we'll look at a different set of grounds than if *flourishing* is synonymous with moral probity, recognition in a profession, or simple contentment. To the extent that we're not told what it means to flourish, the relationship between the claim and the grounds and between the claim and the warrant remains ambiguous and unassailable.

*Confusing Correlation for Cause/*Post Hoc, Ergo
Propter Hoc *(After This, Therefore Because of This)*
(Assuming That Event X Causes Event Y
Because Event X Preceded Event Y)

Here are two examples in which this fallacy may be at work:

Cramming for a test really helps. Last week I crammed for a psychology test and I got an A on it.

I am allergic to the sound of a lawn mower because every time I mow the lawn I start to sneeze.

We've already discussed this fallacy in Chapter 11, particularly in our discussion of the difference between correlation and causation. This fallacy occurs when a sequential relationship is mistaken for a causal relationship. To be sure, when two events occur frequently in conjunction with each other in a particular sequence, we've got a good case for a causal relationship. But until we can show how one causes the other, we cannot be certain that a causal relationship is occurring. The conjunction may simply be a matter of chance, or it may be attributable to some as-yet-unrecognized other factor. For example, your A on the psych test may be caused by something other than your cramming. Maybe the exam was easier, or perhaps you were luckier or more mentally alert.

Just when an erroneous causal argument becomes an example of the *post hoc* fallacy, however, is not cut-and-dried. Many reasonable arguments of causality later turn out to have been mistaken. We are guilty of the *post hoc* fallacy only when our claim of causality seems naively arrived at, without reflection or consideration of alternative hypotheses. Thus in our lawn mower argument, it is probably not the sound that creates the speaker's sneezing but all the pollen stirred up by the spinning blades.

We arrived at this more likely argument by applying a tool known as Occam's Razor—the principle that "What can be explained on fewer principles is explained needlessly by more," or "Between two hypotheses, both of which will account for a given fact, prefer the simpler." If we posit that sound is the cause of our sneezing, all sorts of intermediate causes are going to have to be fetched from afar to make the explanation persuasive. But the blades stirring up the pollen will cause the sneezing more directly. So, until science connects lawn mower noises to human eardrums to sneezing, the simpler explanation is preferred.

Slippery Slope

The slippery slope fallacy is based on the fear that once we take a first step in a direction we don't like we will have to keep going.

We don't dare send weapons to eastern Europe. If we do so, we will next send in military advisers, then a special forces battalion, and then large numbers of troops. Finally, we will be in all-out war.

Look, Blotnik, no one feels worse about your need for open-heart surgery than I do. But I still can't let you turn this paper in late. If I were to let you do it, then I'd have to let everyone turn in papers late.

We run into slippery slope arguments all the time, especially when person A opposes person B's proposal. Those opposed to a particular proposal will often foresee an inevitable and catastrophic chain of events that would follow from taking a first, apparently harmless step. In other words, once we put a foot on that slippery slope, we're doomed to slide right out of sight. Often, such arguments are fallacious insofar as what is seen as an inevitable effect is in fact dependent on some intervening cause or chain of causes to bring it about. Will smoking cigarettes lead inevitably to heroin addiction? Overwhelming statistical evidence would suggest that it doesn't. A slippery slope argument, however, would lovingly trace a teenager's inevitable descent from a clandestine puff on the schoolground through the smoking of various controlled substances to a degenerate end in some Needle Park somewhere. The power of the slippery slope argument lies as much as anything in its compelling narrative structure. It pulls us along irresistibly from one plausible event to the next, making us forget that it's a long jump from plausibility to necessity.

One other common place to find slippery slope arguments is in confrontations between individuals and bureaucracies or other systems of rules and laws. Whenever individuals ask to have some sort of exception made for them, they risk the slippery slope reply. "Sorry, Mr. Jones, if we rush your order, then we will have to rush everyone else's order also."

The problem, of course, is that not every slippery slope argument is an instance of the slippery slope fallacy. We all know that some slopes are slippery and that we sometimes have to draw the line, saying, "To here, but no farther." And it is true also that making exceptions to rules is dangerous; the exceptions soon get established as regular procedures. The slippery slope becomes a fallacy, however, when we forget that some slopes don't *have* to be slippery unless we let them be slippery. Often we do better to imagine a staircase with stopping places all along the way. The assumption that we have no control over our descent once we take the first step makes us unnecessarily rigid.

Hasty Generalization (Making a Broad Generalization on the Basis of Too Little Evidence)

Typically, a hasty generalization occurs when someone reaches a conclusion on the basis of insufficient evidence. But what constitutes "sufficient" evidence? No generalization arrived at through empirical evidence would meet a logician's strict standard of certainty. And generally acceptable standards of proof in any given field are difficult to determine.

The Food and Drug Administration (FDA), for example, generally proceeds very cautiously before certifying a drug as "safe." However, whenever doubts arise about the safety of an FDA-approved drug, critics accuse the FDA of having made a hasty generalization. At the same time, patients eager to have access to a new drug and manufacturers eager to sell a new product may lobby the FDA to "quit dragging its feet" and get the drug to market. Hence, the point at which a hasty generalization about drug safety passes over into the realm of a prudent generalization is nearly always uncertain and contested.

A couple of variants of hasty generalization that deserve mention are

1. Pars pro toto/*Mistaking the part for the whole (assuming that what is true for a part will be true for the whole).*   *Pars pro toto* arguments often appear in the critiques of the status quo. If, say, individuals wanted to get rid of the National Endowment for the Arts, they might focus on several controversial grants they've made over the past few years and use them as justification for wiping out all NEA programs.

2. *Suppressed evidence (withholding contradictory or unsupportive evidence so that only favorable evidence is presented to an audience).*   The flip side of *pars pro toto* is suppressed evidence. If the administrator of the NEA were to go before Congress seeking more money and conveniently forgot about those controversial grants, he would be suppressing damaging but relevant evidence.

Faulty Analogy (Claiming That Because X Resembles Y in One Regard, X Will Resemble Y in All Regards)

Faulty analogies occur whenever a relationship of resemblance is turned into a relationship of identity. For example, the psychologist Carl Rogers uses a questionable analogy in his argument that political leaders should make use of discoveries about human communication derived from research in the social sciences. "During the war when a test-tube solution was found to the problem of synthetic rubber, millions of dollars and an army of talent was turned loose on the problem of using that finding. [. . .] But in the social science realm, if a way is found of facilitating communication and mutual understanding in small groups, there is no guarantee that the finding will be utilized."

Although Rogers is undoubtedly right that we need to listen more carefully to social scientists, his analogy between the movement from scientific discovery to product development and the movement from insights into small group functioning to political change is strained. The laws of cause and effect at work in a test tube are much more reliable and generalizable than the laws of cause and effect observed in small human groups. Whereas lab results can be readily replicated in different times and places, small group dynamics are altered by a whole host of factors, including the cultural background, gender, and age of participants. The warrant that licenses you to move from grounds to claim in the realm of science runs up against a statute of limitation when it tries to include the realm of social science.

Non Sequitur *(Making a Claim That Doesn't Follow Logically from the Premises, or Supporting a Claim with Irrelevant Premises)*

The *non sequitur* fallacy (literally, "it does not follow") is a miscellaneous category that includes any claim that doesn't follow logically from its premises or that is supported with irrelevant premises. In effect, any fallacy is a kind of *non sequitur* because what makes all fallacies fallacious is the absence of a logical connection between claim and premises. But in practice the term *non sequitur* tends to be restricted to problems like the following:

A completely illogical leap: "Clambake University has one of the best faculties in the United States because a Nobel Prize winner used to teach there." (How does the fact that a Nobel Prize winner used to teach at Clambake University make its present faculty one of the best in the United States?)

A clear gap in the chain of reasoning: "People who wear nose rings are disgusting. There ought to be a law against wearing nose rings in public." (This is a *non sequitur* unless the arguer is willing to state and defend the missing premise: "There ought to be a law against anything that I find disgusting.")

Use of irrelevant reasons to support a claim: "I should not receive a C in this course because I have received B's or A's in all my other courses (here is my transcript for evidence) and because I worked exceptionally hard in this course (here is my log of hours worked)." (Even though the arguer has solid evidence to support each premise, the premises themselves are irrelevant to the claim. Course grades should be based on actual performance in the class, not on performance in other classes or on amount of effort devoted to the material.)

FOR CLASS DISCUSSION

Working individually or in small groups, determine the potential persuasiveness of each argument. If the arguments are nonpersuasive because of one or more of the fallacies discussed in this appendix, identify the fallacies and explain how they render the argument nonpersuasive.

1. a. All wars are not wrong. The people who say so are cowards.
   b. Either we legalize marijuana or we watch a steady increase in the number of our citizens who break the law.
   c. The Bible is true because it is the inspired word of God.
   d. Mandatory registration of handguns will eventually lead to the confiscation of hunting rifles.
   e. All these tornadoes started happening right after they tested the A-bombs. The A-bomb testing has changed our weather.

    f. Most other progressive nations have adopted a program of government-provided health care. Therefore, it is time the United States abandoned its outdated practice of private medicine.

    g. The number of Hollywood movie stars who support liberal policies convinces me that liberalism is the best policy. After all, they are rich and will not benefit from better social services.

    h. Society has an obligation to provide housing for the homeless because people without adequate shelter have a right to the resources of the community.

    i. I have observed the way the two renters in our neighborhood take care of their rental houses and have compared that to the way homeowners take care of their houses. I have concluded that people who own their own homes take better care of them than those who rent. [This argument goes on to provide detailed evidence about the house-caring practices of the two renters and of the homeowners in the neighborhood.]

    j. Since the universe couldn't have been created out of nothing, it must have been created by a divine being.

2. Consider the following statements. Note places where you think the logic is flawed. If you were asked by writers or speakers to respond to their statements, what advice would you give to those who wrote or said them to rescue them from charges of fallaciousness? What would each of these speakers/writers have to show, in addition to what's given, to render the statement cogent and persuasive?

    a. "America has had the luxury throughout its history of not having its national existence directly threatened by a foreign enemy. Yet we have gone to war. Why?

        "The United States of America is not a piece of dirt stretching mainly from the Atlantic to the Pacific. More than anything else, America is a set of principles, and the historical fact is that those principles have not only served us well, but have also become a magnet for the rest of the world, a large chunk of which decided to change course last year.

        "Those principles are not mere aesthetic ideas. Those principles are in fact the distillation of 10,000 years of human social evolution. We have settled on them not because they are pretty; we settled on them because they are the only things that work. If you have trouble believing that, ask a Pole." (novelist Tom Clancy)

    b. "What particularly irritated Mr. Young [Republican congressman from Alaska] was the fact that the measure [to prohibit logging in Alaska's Tongass National Forest] was initiated by . . . Robert Mrazek, a Democrat from Long Island. 'Bob Mrazek never saw a tree in his entire life until he went to Alaska' said Mr. Young." (*New York Times,* November 10, 1990)

    c. "When Senator Tim Wirth . . . was in Brazil earlier this year on behalf of an effort to save the tropical rain forest of the Amazon basin, the first thing Brazilian President Jose Sarney asked him was, 'What about the Tongass?' " (*New York Times,* November 10, 1990)

a p p e n d i x   t w o

The Writing Community
Working in Groups

In Chapter 1 we stressed that today truth is typically seen as a product of discussion and persuasion by members of a given community. Instead of seeing "truth" as grounded in some absolute and timeless realm such as Plato's forms or the unchanging laws of logic, many modern thinkers assert that truth is the product of a consensus among a group of knowledgeable peers. Our own belief in the special importance of argumentation in contemporary life follows from our assumption that truth arises out of discussion and debate rather than dogma or pure reason.

In this appendix, we extend that assumption to the classroom itself. We introduce you to a mode of learning often called *collaborative learning.* It involves a combination of learning from an instructor, learning independently, and learning from peers. Mostly it involves a certain spirit—the same sort of inquiring attitude that's required of a good arguer.

FROM CONFLICT TO CONSENSUS: HOW TO GET THE MOST OUT OF THE WRITING COMMUNITY

Behind the notion of the writing community lies the notion that thinking and writing are social acts. At first, this notion may contradict certain widely accepted stereotypes of writers and thinkers as solitary souls who retreat to cork-lined studies where they conjure great thoughts and works. But although we agree that every writer at some point in the process requires solitude, we would point out that most writers and thinkers also require periods of talk and social interchange before they retreat to solitude. Poets, novelists, scientists, philosophers, and technological innovators tend to belong to communities of peers with whom they share their ideas, theories, and work. In this section, we try to provide you with some practical advice on how to get the most out of these sorts of communities in developing your writing skills.

445

Avoiding Bad Habits of Group Behavior

Over the years, most of us have developed certain bad habits that get in the way of efficient group work. Although we use groups all the time to study and accomplish demanding tasks, we tend to do so spontaneously and unreflectively without asking why some groups work and others don't. Many of us, for example, have worked on committees that just didn't get the job done and wasted our time, or else got the job done because one or two tyrannical people dominated the group. Just a couple of bad committee experiences can give us a healthy skepticism about the utility of groups in general. "A committee," according to some people, "is a sort of centipede. It has too many legs, no brain, and moves very slowly."

At their worst, this is indeed how groups function. In particular, they have a tendency to fail in two opposite directions, failures that can be avoided only by conscious effort. Groups can lapse into "clonethink" and produce a safe, superficial consensus whereby everyone agrees with the first opinion expressed in order to avoid conflict or to get on to something more interesting. At the other extreme is a phenomenon we'll call "egothink." In egothink, all members of the group go their own way and produce a collection of minority views that have nothing to do with each other and would be impossible to act on. Clonethinkers view their task as conformity to a norm; egothinkers see their task as safeguarding the autonomy of individual group members. Both fail to take other people and other ideas seriously.

Successful groups avoid both extremes and achieve unity out of diversity. This means that any successful community of learners must be willing to endure creative conflict. Creative conflict results from an initial agreement to disagree respectfully with each other and to focus that disagreement on ideas, not people. For this reason, we say that the relationship among the members of a learning community is not so much interpersonal or impersonal as *transpersonal*, or "beyond the personal." Each member is personally committed to the development of ideas and does whatever is necessary to achieve that development.

The Value of Group Work for Writers

Because we are basically social animals, we find it natural, pleasurable even, to deal with problems in groups. Proof of this fact can be found on any given morning in any given student union in the country. Around the room you will find many students working in groups. Math, engineering, and business majors will be solving problems together, comparing solutions and their ways of arriving at solutions. Others will be comparing their class notes and testing their understanding of concepts and terms by explaining them to each other and comparing their explanations. To be sure, their discussions will occasionally drift off the topic to encompass pressing social issues such as what they're going to do next weekend, or why they like or dislike the class they're working on, but much of the work of college students seems to get done in convivial conversation over morning coffee or late-night popcorn. Why not ease into the rigors of writing in a similar fashion?

A second major advantage of working on writing in a group is that it provides a real and immediate audience for people's work. Too often, when students write in a school setting, they get caught up in the writing-for-teacher racket, which may distort their notion of audience. Argumentative writing is best aimed either at opponents or at a neutral "jury" that will be weighing both sides of a controversy. A group of peers gives you a better sense of a real-world audience "out there" than does a single teacher.

There's danger, of course, in having several audiences consider your writing. Your peer audience may well respond differently to your writing than your instructor. You may feel misled if you are praised for something by a peer and then criticized for the same thing by your instructor. These things can and will happen, no matter how much time you spend developing universally accepted criteria for writing. Grades are not facts but judgments, and all judgments involve uncertainty. Students who are still learning the criteria for making judgments will sometimes apply those criteria differently than an instructor who has been working with them for years. But you should know too that two or more instructors might give you conflicting advice also, just as two or more doctors might give you different advice on what to do about the torn ligaments in your knee. In our view, the risks of misunderstanding are more than made up for by gains in understanding of the writing process, an understanding that comes from working in writing communities where everyone functions both as a writer and as a writing critic.

A third advantage to working in writing communities is closely related to the second advantage. The act of sharing your writing with other people helps you get beyond the bounds of egocentrism that limit all writers. By egocentrism, we don't mean pride or stuck-upness; we mean the failure to consider the needs of your readers. Unless you share your writing with another person, your audience is always a "mythical group," a fiction or a theory that exists only in your head. You must always try to anticipate the problems others will have in reading your work. But until others actually read it and share their reactions to it with you, you can never be fully sure you have understood your audience's point of view. Until another reads your writing critically, you can't be sure you aren't talking to yourself.

FORMING WRITING COMMUNITIES: SKILLS AND ROLES

Given that there are advantages to working in groups, just how do we go about forming writing communities in the classroom? We first have to decide how big to make the groups. From our experience, the best groups consist of either five to seven people or simply two people. Groups of three or four tend to polarize and become divisive, and larger groups tend to be unmanageable. Because working in five- to seven-person groups is quite different from working in pairs, we discuss each of these different-size groups in turn.

Working in Groups of Five to Seven People

The trick to successful group work is to consider the maximum number of viewpoints and concerns without losing focus. Because these two basic goals frequently conflict, you need some mechanisms for monitoring your progress. In particular, it's important that each group member is assigned to perform those tasks necessary to effective group functioning. (Some teachers assign roles to individual students, shifting the roles from day to day. Other teachers let the groups themselves determine the roles of individuals.) That is, the group must recognize that it has two objectives at all times: the stated objectives of a given task and the objective of making the group work well. It is very easy to get so involved with the given task that you overlook the second objective, generally known as "group maintenance."

The first role is group leader. We hesitate to call persons who fill this role "leaders" because we tend sometimes to think of leaders as know-it-alls who take charge and order people about. In classroom group work, however, being a group leader is a role you play, not a fixed part of your identity. The leader, above all else, keeps the group focused on agreed-on ends and protects the right of every group member to be heard. It's an important function, and group members should share the responsibility from task to task. Here is a list of things for the leader to do during a group discussion:

1. Ensure that everyone understands and agrees on the objectives of any given task and on what sort of final product is expected of the group (for example, a list of criteria, a brief written statement, or an oral response to a question).

2. Ask that the group set an agenda for completing the task, and have some sense of how much time the group will spend at each stage. (Your instructor should always make clear what time limits you have to operate within and when he or she expects your task to be completed. If a time limit isn't specified, you should request a reasonable estimate.)

3. Look for signs of getting off the track, and ask individual group members to clarify how their statements relate to agreed-on objectives.

4. Actively solicit everyone's contributions, and take care that all viewpoints are listened to and that the group does not rush to incomplete judgment.

5. Try to determine when the task has been adequately accomplished.

In performing each of these functions, the leader must be concerned to turn criticisms and observations into questions. Instead of saying to one silent and bored-looking member of the group, "Hey, Gormley, you haven't said diddly-squat here so far; say something relevant or take a hike," the leader might ask, "Irwin, do you agree with what Beth just said about this paper being disorganized?" Remember, every action in nature is met with an equal and opposite reaction—commands tend to be met with resistance, questions with answers.

A second crucial role for well-functioning groups is that of recorder. The recorder's function is to provide the group with a record of their deliberations so they can measure their progress. It is particularly important that the recorder write down the agenda and the solution to the problem in precise form. Because the recorder must summarize the deliberations fairly precisely, he must ask for clarifications. In doing this, he ensures that group members don't fall into the "ya know?" syndrome (a subset of clonethink) in which people assent to statements that are in fact cloudy to them. (Ya know?) At the completion of the task, the recorder should also ask whether there are any significant remaining disagreements or unanswered questions. Finally, the recorder is responsible for reporting the group's solutions to the class as a whole.*

If these two roles are conscientiously filled, the group should be able to identify and solve problems that temporarily keep it from functioning effectively. Maybe you are thinking that this sounds dumb. Whenever you've been in a group, everyone has known whether there were problems without leaders or recorders. Too often, however, a troubled group may sense that there is a problem without being perfectly clear about the nature of the problem or the solution. Let's say you are in a group with Elwood Lunt Jr., who is very opinionated and dominates the discussions. (For a sample of Elwood's cognitive style, see his essay "Good Writing and Computers for Today's American Youth of America," in Task 1 on page 454.) Group members may represent their problem privately to themselves with a statement such as "Lunt's such a jerk nobody can work with him. He talks constantly and none of the rest of us can get a word in." The group may devote all of its energies to punishing Lunt with ridicule or silence rather than trying to solve the problem. Although this may make you feel better for a short time, Lunt is unlikely to get any better, and the group is unlikely to get much done.

If Lunt is indeed bogging the group down by airing his opinions at great length, it is the leader's job to limit his dominance without excluding him. Because group members all realize that it is the group leader's role to handle such problems, the leader has a sort of license that allows her or him to deal directly with Lunt. Moreover, the leader also has the explicit responsibility to do so, so that each member is not forced to sit, silently seething and waiting for someone to do something.

The leader might control Lunt in one of several ways: (1) by keeping to the agenda ("Thanks, Elwood, hate to interrupt, but we're a bit behind schedule and we haven't heard from everyone on this point yet. Jack, shall we move on to you?"); (2) by simply asking Lunt to demonstrate how his remarks are relevant to the topic at hand. ("That's real interesting, Elwood, that you got to see Kurt Cobain in his last performance, but can you tell us how you see that relating to Melissa's point about ending welfare?"); or (3) by introducing more formal procedures such

---

*There is a debate among experts who study small-group communications about whether the roles of leader and recorder can be collapsed into one job. Your group may need to experiment until it discovers the structure that works best for bringing out the most productive discussions.

as asking group members to raise their hands and be called on by the chair. These procedures might not satisfy your blood lust, your secret desire to stuff Lunt into a Dumpster; however, they are more likely to let the group get its work done and perhaps, just maybe, to help Lunt become a better listener and participant.

The rest of the group members, though they have no formally defined roles, have an equally important obligation to participate fully. To ensure full participation, group members can do several things. They can make sure that they know all the other group members by their first names and speak to them in a friendly manner. They can practice listening procedures wherein they try not to dissent or disagree without first charitably summarizing the view with which they are taking issue. Most importantly, they can bring to the group as much information and as many alternative points of view as they can muster. The primary intellectual strength of group work is the ability to generate a more complex view of a subject. But this more complex view cannot emerge unless all individuals contribute their perspectives.

One collaborative task for writers that requires no elaborate procedures or any role playing is reading your essays aloud within the group. A good rule for this procedure is that no one responds to any one essay until all have been read. This is often an effective last step before handing in any essay. It's a chance to share the fruits of your labor with others and to hear finished essays that you may have seen in the draft stages. Hearing everyone else's final draft can also help you get a clearer perspective on how your own work is progressing. Listening to the essays read can both reassure you that your work is on a par with other people's and challenge you to write up to the level of the best student writing in your group.

Many of you may find this process a bit frightening at first. But the cause of your fright is precisely the source of the activity's value. In reading your work aloud, you are taking responsibility for that work in a special way. Writing specialist Kenneth Bruffee, whose work on collaborative learning introduced us to many of the ideas in this chapter, likens the reading of papers aloud to reciting a vow, of saying "I do" in a marriage ceremony. You are taking public responsibility for your words, and there's no turning back. The word has become deed. If you aren't at least a little nervous about reading an essay aloud, you probably haven't invested much in your words. Knowing that you will take public responsibility for your words is an incentive to make that investment—a more real and immediate incentive than a grade.

Working in Pairs

Working in pairs is another effective form of community learning. In our classes we use pairs at both the early-draft and the late-draft stages of writing. At the early-draft stage, it serves the very practical purpose of clarifying a student's ideas and sense of direction at the beginning of a new writing project. The interaction best takes place in the form of pair interviews. When you first sit down to interview each other, each of you should have done a fair amount of exploratory writing and thinking about what you want to say in your essay and how you're going to say it. Here is a checklist of questions you can use to guide your interview:

1. "What is your issue?" Your goal here is to help the writer focus an issue by formulating a question that clearly has alternative answers.

2. "What is your position on the issue, and what are alternative positions?" After you have helped your interviewee formulate the issue question, help her clarify this issue by stating her own position and show how that position differs from opposing ones. Your interviewee might say, for example, that "many of my friends are opposed to building more nuclear power plants, but I think we need to build more of them."

3. "Can you walk me through your argument step by step?" Once you know your interviewee's issue question and intended position, you can best help her by having her walk you through her argument talking out loud. You can ask prompting questions such as "What are you going to say first?" "What next?" and so on. At this stage your interviewee will probably still be struggling to discover the best way to support the point. You can best help by brainstorming along with her, both of you taking notes on your ideas. Often at this stage you can begin making a schematic plan for the essay and formulating supporting reasons as *because* clauses. Along the way give your interviewee any information or ideas you have on the issue. It is particularly helpful at this stage if you can provide counter-arguments and opposing views.

The interview strategy is useful before writers begin their rough drafts. After the first drafts have been written, there are a number of different ways of using pairs to evaluate drafts. One practice that we've found helpful is simply to have writers write a one-paragraph summary of their own drafts and of their partner's. In comparing summaries, writers can often discover which, if any, of their essential ideas are simply not getting across. If a major idea is not in the reader's summary, writer and reader need to decide whether it's due to a careless reading or to problems within the draft. The nice thing about this method is that the criticism is given indirectly and hence isn't as threatening to either party. At other times, your instructor might also devise a checklist of features for you to consider, based on the criteria you have established for the assignment.

FOR CLASS DISCUSSION

1. As a group, consider the following quotation and then respond to the questions that follow: "In most college classrooms there is a reluctance to assume leadership. The norm for college students is to defer to someone else, to refuse

to accept the position even if it is offered. There is actually a competition in humility and the most humble person usually ends up as the leader."*
   a. Do you think this statement is true?
   b. On what evidence do you base your judgment of its truthfulness?
   c. As a group, prepare an opening sentence for a paragraph that would report your group's reaction to this quotation.

2. Read the following statements about group interaction and decide as a group whether these statements are true or false.
   a. Women are less self-assertive and less competitive in groups than are men.
   b. There is a slight tendency for physically superior individuals to become leaders in a group.
   c. Leaders are usually more intelligent than nonleaders.
   d. Females conform to majority opinion more than males in reaching group decisions.
   e. An unconventional group member inhibits group functioning.
   f. An anxious group member inhibits group functioning.
   g. Group members with more power are usually better liked than low-power group members.
   h. Groups usually produce more and better solutions to problems than do individuals working alone.

With the assistance of the group, the recorder should write a four- to five-sentence description of the process your group used to reach agreement on the true-false statements. Was there discussion? Disagreement? Did you vote? Did every person give an opinion on each question? Were there any difficulties?

A SEVERAL-DAYS' GROUP PROJECT: DEFINING "GOOD ARGUMENTATIVE WRITING"

The problem we want you to address in this sequence of tasks is how to define and identify "good argumentative writing." This is a particularly crucial problem for developing writers insofar as you can't begin to measure your growth as a writer until you have some notion of what you're aiming for. To be sure, it's no easy task defining good argumentative writing. In order for even experienced teachers to reach agreement on this subject, some preliminary discussions

---

*Gerald Philips, Douglas Pederson, and Julia Wood, *Group Discussion: A Practical Guide to Participant Leadership* (Boston: Houghton Mifflin, 1979).

and no small amount of compromise are necessary. By the end of this task you will most certainly not have reached a universally acceptable description of good argumentative writing. (Such a description doesn't exist.) But you will have begun a dialog with each other and your instructor on the subject. Moreover, you will have developed a vocabulary for sharing your views on writing with each other.

For this exercise, we give you a sequence of four tasks, some homework, and other in-class group tasks. Please do the tasks in sequence.

Task 1 (Homework):
Preparing for the Group Discussion

Freewrite for five minutes on the question "What is good argumentation writing?" After finishing your freewrite, read fictional student Lunt's argument that follows and, based on the principles that Lunt seems to break, develop a tentative list of criteria for good argumentative writing.

Explanation   Before you come together with a group of people to advance your understanding and knowledge collectively, you first need to explore your own thoughts on the matter. Too often, groups collapse not because the members lack goodwill but because they lack preparation. To discharge your responsibility as a good group member, you must therefore begin by doing your homework. By using a freewriting exercise, you focus your thinking on the topic, explore what you already know or feel about it, and begin framing questions and problems.

To help you establish a standard for good argumentative writing, we've produced a model of bad arguing by a fictional student, one Elwood P. Lunt Jr. If you can figure out what's bad about Lunt's argument, then you can formulate the principles of good argument that he violates. Of course, no student of our acquaintance has ever written anything as bad as Lunt's essay. That's the virtue of this contrived piece. It's an easy target. In going over it critically, you may well find that Lunt violates principles of good writing you hadn't thought of in your freewrite. (We tried to ensure that he violated as many as possible.) Thus you should be sure to go back and modify your ideas from your freewrite accordingly.

A couple of important points to keep in mind here as you prepare to critique another person's work: (1) Remember the principle of charity. Try to look past the muddied prose to a point or intention that might be lurking in the background. Your critique should speak as much as possible to Lunt's failure to realize this intent. (2) Direct your critique to the prose, not the writer. Don't settle for "He just doesn't make sense" or "He's a dimwit." Ask yourself why he doesn't make sense and point to particular places where he doesn't make sense. In sum, give Lunt the same sort of reading you would like to get: compassionate and specific.

Good Writing and Computers for Today's Modern American Youth of America

(A partial fulfillment of writing an argument in the course in which I am attending)

1   In todays modern fast paced world computers make living a piece of cake. You can do a lot with computers which in former times took a lot of time and doing a lot of work. Learning to fly airplanes, for example. But there are no such things as a free lunch. People who think computers will do all the work for you need to go to the Iron Curtain and take a look around, that's the place for people who think they can be replaced by computers. The precious computer which people think is the dawn of a new civilization but which is in all reality a pig in a poke makes you into a number but can't even add right! So don't buy computers for two reasons.

2   The first reason you shouldn't buy a computer is writing. So what makes people think that they won't have to write just because they have a computer on his desk. "Garbage in and garbage out one philosopher said." Do you want to sound like garbage? I don't. That's why modern American fast paced youth must conquer this affair with computers and writing by ourselves is the answer to our dreams and not just by using a computer for that aforementioned writing. A computer won't make you think better and that's the problem because people think a computer will do your thinking for you. No way, Jose.

3   Another thing is grammar. My Dad Elwood P. Lunt Sr. hit the nail on the head; when he said bad grammar can make you sound like a jerk. Right on Dad. He would be so upset to think of all the jerks out there who wasted their money on a computer so that the computer could write for them. But do computers know grammar? So get on the bandwagon and write good and get rich with computers. Which can make you write right. You think any computer could catch the errors I just made? Oh, sure you do. Jerk. And according to our handbook on writing writing takes intelligence which computers don't have. Now I'm not against computers. I am just saying that computers have there place.

4   In conclusion there are two reasons why you shouldn't buy a computer. But if you want to buy one that is all right as long as you understand that it isn't as smart as you think.

Task 2 (In-Class Group Work): Developing a Master List of Criteria

As a group, reach a consensus on at least six or seven major problems with Lunt's argumentative essay. Then use that list to prepare a parallel list of criteria for a good written argument. Please have your list ready in thirty minutes.

Explanation   Your goal for this task is to reach consensus about what's wrong with Lunt's argument. As opposed to a "majority decision," in which more people agree than disagree, a "consensus" entails a solution that is generally acceptable to all members of the group. In deciding what is the matter with Lunt's essay, you should be able to reach consensus also on the criteria for a good argument. After each group has completed its list, recorders should report each group's consensus to the class as a whole. Your instructor will facilitate a discussion leading to the class's "master list" of criteria.

Task 3 (Homework):
Applying Criteria to Student Essays

At home, consider the following five samples of student writing. (This time they're real examples.) Rank the essays "1" through "5," with 1 being the best and 5 the worst. Once you've done this, develop a brief rationale for your ranking. This rationale should force you to decide which criteria you rank highest and which lowest. For example, does "quality of reasons" rank higher than "organization and development"? Does "colorful, descriptive style" rank high or low in your ranking system?

Explanation   The following essays were written as short arguments developing two or three reasons in support of a claim. Students had studied the argumentative concepts in Chapters 1–6 but had not yet studied refutation strategies. Although the students were familiar with classical argument structure, this introductory assignment asked them to support a claim/thesis with only two or three reasons. Summarizing and responding to opposing views was optional.

Bloody Ice

It is March in Alaska. The ocean-side environment is full of life and death. Man and animal share this domain but not in peace. The surrounding iceflows, instead of being cold and white, are steaming from the remains of gutted carcasses and stained red. The men are hunters and the animals are barely six weeks old. A slaughter has just taken place. Thousands of baby Harp seals lie dead on the ice and thousands more of adult mothers lay groaning over the death of their babies. Every year a total limit of 180,000 seals set by the U.S. Seal Protection Act is filled in a terrifying bloodbath. But Alaska with its limit of 30,000 is not alone. Canadians who hunt seals off the coast of Northern Newfoundland and Quebec are allowed 150,000 seals. The Norwegians are allowed 20,000 and native Eskimos of Canada and Greenland are allowed 10,000 seals per year. Although this act appears heartless and cruel, the men who hunt have done this for 200 years as a tradition for survival. They make many good arguments supporting their traditions. They feel the seals are in no immediate danger of extinction. Also seal furs can be used to line boots and gloves or merely traded for money and turned into robes or fur coats. Sometimes the meat is even used for food in the off hunting months when money is scarce. But are these valid justifications for the unmerciful killings? No, the present limit on Harp seal killings should be better regulated because the continued hunting of the seals will lead to eventual extinction and because the method of slaughter is so cruel and inhumane.

2   The Harp seal killing should be better regulated first because eventual extinction is inevitable. According to *Oceans* magazine, before the limit of 180,000 seals was established in 1950, the number of seals had dwindled from 3,300,000 to 1,250,000. Without these limitations hundreds of thousands were killed within weeks of birth. Now, even with this allotment, the seals are being killed off at an almost greater rate than they can remultiply. Adult female seals give birth once every year but due to pollution, disease, predation, whelping success and malnutrition they are already slowly dying on their own without being hunted. Eighty percent of the seals slaughtered are pups and the remaining twenty percent are adult seals and even sometimes mothers who try attacking the hunters after seeing their babies killed. The hunters, according to the Seal Protection Act, have this right.

3   Second, I feel the killing should be better regulated because of the inhumane method used. In order to protect the fur value of the seals, guns are not used. Instead, the sealers use metal clubs to bludgeon the seal to death. Almost immediately after being delivered a direct blow, the seals are gutted open and skinned. Although at this stage of life the seal's skull is very fragile, sometimes the seals are not killed by the blows but merely stunned; thus hundreds are skinned alive. Still others are caught in nets and drowned, which according to *America* magazine, the Canadian government continues to deny. But the worst of the methods used is when a hunter gets tired of swinging his club and uses the heel of his boot to kick the seal's skull in. Better regulation is the only way to solve this problem because other attempts seem futile. For example, volunteers who have traveled to hunting sites trying to dye the seals to ruin their fur value have been caught and fined heavily.

4   The plight of the Harp seals has been long and controversial. With the Canadian hunters feeling they have the right to kill the seals because it has been their industry for over two centuries, and on the other hand with humane organizations fearing extinction and strongly opposing the method of slaughter, a compromise must be met among both sides. As I see it, the solution to the problem is simple. Since the Canadians do occasionally use the whole seal and have been sealing for so long they could be allowed to continue but at a more heavily regulated rate. Instead of filling the limit of 180,000 every year and letting the numbers of seals decrease, Canadians could learn to ranch the seals as Montanans do cattle or sheep. The United States has also offered to help them begin farming their land for a new livelihood. The land is adequate for crops and would provide work all year round instead of only once a month every year. As a result of farming, the number of seals killed would be drastically cut down because Canadians would not be so dependent on the seal industry as before. This would in turn lead back to the ranching aspect of sealing and allow the numbers to grow back and keeping the tradition alive for future generations and one more of nature's creatures to enjoy.

RSS Should Not Provide Dorm Room Carpets

1   Tricia, a University student, came home exhausted from her work-study job. She took a blueberry pie from the refrigerator to satisfy her hunger and a tall glass of milk to quench her thirst. While trying to get comfortable on her bed, she tipped her snack over onto the

floor. She cleaned the mess, but the blueberry and milk stains on her brand new carpet could not be removed. She didn't realize that maintaining a clean carpet would be difficult and costly. Tricia bought her own carpet. Some students living in dorm rooms want carpeted rooms provided for them at the expense of the University. They insist that since they pay to live on campus, the rooms should reflect a comfortable home atmosphere. However, Resident Student Services (RSS) should not be required to furnish the carpet because other students do not want carpets. Furthermore, carpeting all the rooms totals into a very expensive project. And lastly, RSS should not have to provide the carpet because many students show lack of respect and responsibility for school property.

Although RSS considers the carpeting of all rooms a strong possibility, students like Tricia oppose the idea. They feel the students should buy their own carpets. Others claim the permanent carpeting would make dorm life more comfortable. The carpet will act as insulation and as a sound proofing system. These are valid arguments, but they should not be the basis for changing the entire residence hall structure. Those students with "cold feet" can purchase house footwear, which cost less than carpet. Unfortunately carpeting doesn't muffle all the noise; therefore, some students will be disturbed. Reasonable quietness should be a matter of respect for other students' privacy and comfort. Those opposed to the idea reason out the fact that students constantly change rooms or move out. The next person may not want carpet. Also, if RSS carpets the rooms, the students will lose the privilege they have of painting their rooms any color. Paint stains cannot be removed. Some students can't afford to replace the carpet. Still another factor, carpet color may not please everyone. RSS would provide a neutral color like brown or gray. With tile floors, the students can choose and purchase their own carpets to match their taste.

Finally, another reason not to have carpet exists in the fact that the project can be expensive due to material costs, installation cost, and the maintenance cost caused mainly by the irresponsibility of many students. According to Rick Jones, Asst. Director of Housing Services, the cost will be $300 per room for the carpet and installation. RSS would also have to purchase more vacuum cleaners for the students use. RSS will incur more expense in order to maintain the vacuums. Also, he claims that many accidents resulting from shaving cream fights, food fights, beverage parties, and smoking may damage the carpet permanently. With floor tiles, accidents such as food spills can be cleaned up easier than carpet. The student's behavior plays an important role in deciding against carpeting. Many students don't follow the rules of maintaining their rooms. They drill holes into the walls, break mirrors, beds, and closet doors, and leave their food trays all over the floor. How could they be trusted to take care of school carpet when they violate the current rules? Many students feel they have the "right" to do as they please. This irresponsible and disrespectful behavior reflects their future attitude about carpet care.

In conclusion, the university may be able to afford to supply the carpets in each room, but maintaining them would be difficult. If the students want carpets, they should pay and care for the carpets themselves. Hopefully, they will be more cautious and value it more. They should take the initiative to fundraise or find other financial means of providing this "luxury." They should not rely on the school to provide unnecessary room fixtures such as carpets. Also, they must remember that if RSS provides the carpet and they don't pay for the damages, they and future students will endure the consequences. What will happen???? Room rates will skyrocket!!!!!

Sterling Hall Dorm Food

1   The quality of Sterling Hall dorm food does not meet the standard needed to justify the high prices University students pay. As I watched a tall, medium-built University student pick up his Mexican burrito from the counter it didn't surprise me to see him turn up his nose. Johnny, our typical University student, waited five minutes before he managed to make it through the line. After he received his bill of $4.50 he turned his back to the cash register and walked away displeased with his meal.

2   As our neatly groomed University student placed his ValiDine eating card back into his Giorgio wallet, he thought back to the balance left on his account. Johnny had $24 left on his account and six more weeks left of school. He had been eating the cheapest meals he could and still receive a balanced meal, but the money just seemed to disappear. No student, not even a thrifty boy like Johnny, could possibly afford to live healthfully according to the University meal plan system.

3   Johnny then sat down at a dirty table to find his burrito only half way cooked. Thinking back to the long-haired cook who served him the burrito, he bit into the burrito and noticed a long hair dangling from his lips. He realized the cook's lack of preparation when preparing his burrito.

4   Since the food costs so much, yet the quality of the food remains low, University students do not get the quality they deserve. From the information stated I can conclude that using the ValiDine service system University students would be jeopardizing their health and wasting their hard-earned money. University students deserve something more than what they have now.

ROTC Courses Should Not Get College Credit

1   One of the most lucrative scholarships a student can receive is a four-year ROTC scholarship that pays tuition and books along with a living allowance. It was such a scholarship that allowed me to attend an expensive liberal arts college and to pursue the kind of well rounded education that matters to me. Of course, I am obligated to spend four years on active duty—an obligation that I accept and look forward to. What I am disappointed in, however, is the necessity to enroll in Military Science classes. Strong ROTC advocates argue that Military Science classes are essential because they produce good citizens, teach leadership skills, and provide practical experience for young cadets. Maybe so. But we could get the same benefits without having to take these courses for credit. Colleges should make ROTC training an extracurricular activity, not a series of academic courses taken for academic credit.

2   First of all, ROTC courses, unlike other college courses, do not stress inquiry and true questioning. The ROTC program has as its objective the preparation of future officers committed to the ideals and structure of the military. The structure of the military is based upon obediently following the orders of military superiors. Whereas all my other teachers stress

critical thinking and doing independent analysis, my ROTC instructors avoid political or so-cial questions saying it is the job of civilian leaders to debate policies and the job of the mil-itary to carry them out. We don't even debate what role the military should play in our country. My uncle, who was an ROTC cadet during the Vietnam war, remembers that not only did ROTC classes never discuss the ethics of the war but that cadets were not allowed to protest the war outside of their ROTC courses. This same obedience is demanded in my own ROTC courses, where we are not able to question administration policies and exam-ine openly the complexity of the situation in Iraq and Kuwait.

A second reason that Army ROTC courses do not deserve academic credit is that the classes are not academically strenuous, thus giving cadets a higher GPA and an unfair advantage over their peers. Much of what a cadet does for academic credit involves non-academic activities such as physical training for an hour three days a week so that at least some of a cadet's grade is based on physical activity, not mental activity. In conducting an informal survey of 10 upper-classmen, I found out that none of them has ever gotten any-thing lower than an A in a Military Science class and they do not know of anyone who got anything lower than an A. One third-year cadet stated that "the classes are basic. A mon-key coming out of the zoo could get college credit for a Military Science class." He went on to say that most of the information given in his current class is a brush-up to 8th grade U.S. history. In contrast, a typical liberal arts college class requires much thought, questioning, and analysis. The ROTC Military Science class is taught on the basis of "regurgitated knowl-edge," meaning that once you are given a piece of information you are required to know it and reproduce it at any time without thought or question. A good example is in my class Basic Officership. Our first assignment is to memorize and recite in front of the class the Preamble to the Constitution of the United States. The purpose of doing so doesn't seem to be to understand or analyze the constitution because we never talk about that. In fact, I don't know what the purpose is. I just do it because I am told to. Because the "A" is so easy to get in my ROTC class, I spend all my time studying for my other classes. I am a step ahead of my peers in the competition for a high GPA, even though I am not getting as good an education.

Finally, having to take ROTC classes means that I can't take other liberal arts courses which would be more valuable. One of the main purposes for ROTC is to give potential of-ficers a liberal education. Many cadets have the credentials to get into an armed forces acad-emy, but they chose ROTC programs because they could combine military training with a well-rounded curriculum. Unfortunately, by taking Military Science classes each quarter, cadets find that their electives are all but eaten up by the time they are seniors. If ROTC classes were valuable in themselves, I wouldn't complain. But they aren't, and they keep me from taking upper division electives in philosophy, literature, and the humanities.

All of these reasons lead me to believe that Army ROTC cadets are getting short-changed when they enroll for Military Science classes. Because cadets receive a lucrative scholarship, they should have to take the required military science courses. But these courses should be treated as extracurricular activities, like a work-study job or like athlet-ics. Just as a student on a full-ride athletic scholarship does not receive academic credit for football practices and games, so should a student on a full-ride ROTC scholarship have to participate in the military education program without getting academic credit. By treating

ROTC courses as a type of extracurricular activity like athletics, students can take more elective credits that will expand their minds, better enabling them to have the knowledge to make moral decisions and to enjoy their world more fully.

Legalization of Prostitution

1   Prostitution . . . It is the world's oldest profession. It is by definition the act of offering or soliciting sex for payment. It is, to some, evil. Yet the fact is it exists.

2   Arguments are not necessary to prove the existence of prostitution. Rather, the argument arises when trying to prove something must be done to reduce the problems of this profession. The problems which exist are in the area of crime, of health, and of environment. Crime rates are soaring, diseases are spreading wildly, and the environment on the streets is rapidly decaying. Still, it has been generally conceded that these problems cannot be suppressed. However, they can be reduced. Prostitution should be legalized because it would reduce the wave of epidemics, decrease high crime rates, provide good revenue by treating it like other businesses, and get girls off the streets where sexual crimes often occur.

3   Of course, there are those who would oppose the legalization of prostitution stating that it is one of the main causes for the spread of venereal diseases. Many argue that it is inter-related with drug-trafficking and other organized crimes. And probably the most controversial is the moral aspect of the subject; it is morally wrong, and legalizing it would be enforcing, or even justifying, such an existence.

4   These points propose good arguments, but I shall counter each point and explain the benefits and advantages of legalizing prostitution. In the case of prostitution being the main cause for the spread of epidemics, I disagree. By legalizing it, houses would be set up which would solve the problem of girls working on the streets and being victims of sexual crimes. It would also provide regular health checks, as is successfully done in Nevada, Germany, and other parts of the U.S. and Europe, which will therefore cut down on diseases spreading unknowingly.

5   As for the increase of organized crime if prostitution is legalized, I disagree again. Firstly, by treating it like businesses, then that would make good state revenue. Secondly, like all businesses have regulations, so shall these houses. That would put closer and better control in policing the profession, which is presently a problem. Obviously, if the business of prostitution is more closely supervised, that would decrease the crime rates.

6   Now, I come to one of the most arguable aspects of legalizing prostitution: the moral issue. Is it morally wrong to legalize prostitution? That is up to the individual. To determine whether anything is "right or wrong" in our society is nearly impossible to do since there are various opinions. If a person were to say that prostitution is the root of all evil, that will not make it go away. It exists. Society must begin to realize that fear or denial will not make the "ugliness" disappear. It still exists.

7   Prostitution can no longer go ignored because of our societal attitudes. Legalizing it is beneficial to our society, and I feel in time people may begin to form an accepting attitude.

It would be the beginning of a more open-minded view of what is reality. Prostitution . . . it is the world's oldest profession. It exists. It is a reality.

Task 4 (In-Class Group Work):
Reaching Consensus on Ranking of Essays

Working again in small groups, reach consensus on your ranking of the five essays. Groups should report both their rankings and their justification for the rankings based on the criteria established in Task 2 or as currently modified by your group.

Explanation   You are now to reach consensus on how you rank the papers and why you rank them the way you do. Feel free to change the criteria you established earlier if they seem to need modification. Be careful in your discussions to distinguish between evaluation of the writer's written product and your own personal position on the writer's issue. In other words, there is a crucial difference between saying, "I don't like Pete's essay because I disagree with his ideas," and "I don't like Pete's essay because he didn't provide adequate support for his ideas." As each group reports back the results of its deliberations to the class as a whole, the instructor will highlight discrepancies among the groups' decisions and collate the criteria as they emerge. If the instructor disagrees with the class consensus or wants to add items to the criteria, he or she might choose to make these things known now. By the end of this stage, everyone should have a list of criteria for good argumentative writing established by the class.

A CLASSROOM DEBATE

In this exercise, you have an opportunity to engage in a variant of a formal debate. Although debates of this nature don't always lead to truth for its own sake, they are excellent forums for the development of analytical and organizational skills. The format for the debate is as follows.

First Hour   Groups will identify and reach consensus on "the most serious impediment to learning at this institution." Participants should have come to class prepared with their own individual lists of at least three problems. Once the class has reached consensus on the single most serious impediment to learning on your campus, your instructor will write it out as a formal statement. This statement constitutes the preliminary topic, which will eventually result in a proposition for your debate.

The instructor will then divide the class into an equal number of Affirmative and Negative teams (three to five members per team). Homework for all the Affirmative team members is to identify proposals for solving the problem identified by the class. Negative team members, meanwhile, will concentrate on reasons that the problem is not particularly serious and/or that the problem is "in the nature of things" and simply not solvable by any sort of proposal.

Second Hour   At the beginning of the period, the instructor will pair up each Affirmative team with a Negative team. The teams will be opponents during the actual debate, and there will be as many debates as there are paired teams. Each Affirmative team will now work on choosing the best proposal for solving the problem, while the Negative team pools its resources and builds its case against the seriousness and solvability of the problem. At the end of the period, each Affirmative team will share its proposal with its corresponding Negative team. The actual topic for each of the debates is now set: "Resolved: Our campus should institute Z (the Affirmative team's proposal) in order to solve problem X (the class's original problem statement)."

Homework for the next class is for each team to conduct research (interviewing students, gathering personal examples, polling students, finding data or expert testimony from the library, and so forth) to support its case. Each Affirmative team's research will be aimed at showing that the problem is serious and that the solution is workable. Each Negative team will try to show that the proposal won't work or that the problem isn't worth solving.

Third Hour   At this point each Affirmative team and each Negative team will select two speakers to represent their sides. During this hour each team will pool its ideas and resources to help the speakers make the best possible cases. Each team should prepare an outline for a speech supporting its side of the debate. Team members should then anticipate the arguments of the opposition and prepare a rebuttal.

Fourth (and Fifth) Hour(s)   The actual debates. (There will be as many debates as there are paired Affirmative and Negative teams.) Each team will present two speakers. Each speaker is limited to five minutes. The order of speaking is as follows:

FIRST AFFIRMATIVE:	Presents best case for the proposal
FIRST NEGATIVE:	Presents best case against the proposal
SECOND NEGATIVE:	Rebuts argument of First Affirmative
SECOND AFFIRMATIVE:	Rebuts argument of First Negative

Those team members who do not speak will be designated observers. Their task is to take notes on the debate, paying special attention to the quality of support for each argument and to those parts of the argument that are not rebutted by the opposition. By the next class period (fifth or sixth), they will have prepared a brief, informal analysis titled "Why Our Side Won the Debate."

Fifth or Sixth Hour   The observers will report to the class on their perceptions of the debates by using their prepared analysis as the basis of the discussion. The instructor will attempt to synthesize the main points of the debates and the most telling arguments for either side. At this point, your instructor may ask each of you to write an argument on the debate topic, allowing you to argue for or against any of the proposals presented.

p a r t   f i v e

An Anthology of Arguments

AN OVERVIEW OF THE ANTHOLOGY

Up to this point, we've concentrated mostly on how to write arguments. In Part Five of this text, we present a number of finished arguments on eleven important social issues. As we discussed in Chapter 3, writers engage in argument from multiple social contexts, from within many communities in society: as lobbyists and advocacy groups, as average citizens, as media commentators and professional staff writers for magazines and newspapers, and as scholars and academics. Writers of arguments also differ in their commitment to persuasion versus truth seeking in pursuit of the most responsible solution to a problem. In assembling this anthology, we have been reminded of how many forms arguments take. This fascinating array of genres will be apparent to you as you read these arguments: short opinion-editorials, scholarly academic research-based arguments, advocacy web sites, speeches delivered to academic institutions, and white papers prepared to influence legislators.

In creating this anthology, we have searched for articles that represent distinctly divergent voices on issues. These voices reveal the complexity of the issues and often speak passionately about the stakes involved in them. Further, in expressing a wide range of views, these writers often frame the issues in different terms, direct their claims and proposals at different audiences, and employ different argumentative strategies to influence readers' views and to win over decision makers.

To help you understand the ongoing conversation that these arguments are participating in, we have provided short headnotes that give original publication data and, in most cases, a brief identification of the writer. It is important that you continue this contextualizing process by asking key questions: Is this magazine or journal liberal or conservative? What audience is this writer addressing, and what are the writer's assumptions about the audience's beliefs and values? Is this writer's purpose mainly to redefine the issue or to propose a specific plan for change?

463

As you read through the arguments in Part Five, you might want to keep in mind the question of where each of them fits into a larger context of issues—those recurrent questions and dilemmas that we struggle with in different guises all the time. No matter what the specific issue is, certain recurring patterns of concern keep cropping up, such as the conflict between principles and consequences in ethical arguments, or between spiritual and material values, individual rights and public duties, duties to self and duties to others, short-range consequences and long-range consequences, and commitment to tradition and commitment to progress. For example, whether you are considering a proposal for mandatory drug testing or for a new zoning regulation to prevent homeowners from building too high a fence, you are dealing with the conflict between "rights of the individual" and "rights of the society." One advantage of an anthology of arguments is that in reading through them you can see for yourself how frequently these large issues recur in different guises.

As we discussed in Chapter 2, reading arguments often functions as a bridge to writing arguments. Instead of standing as the last word on some problematical subject, these arguments are presented as positions on an issue. However eloquent and persuasive they may be, each should be recognized as one voice in a conversation. Indeed, after responsibly weighing the alternative views, you may well decide that one of the arguments is right and another wrong. But even then, the position you choose will be understood differently by virtue of your having considered another point of view. After reading divergent points of view on a given subject, you are left with the responsibility to synthesize what's given and to create your own new argument for a new context. Challenging claims, enlarging perspectives—the process of dissent and synthesis—is the very lifeblood of argument. The arguments in this anthology, then, can function to draw you into these argumentative conversations.

The arguments in this anthology may also be useful to you in another way. As writers within your own communities on issues that matter to you, you can benefit from looking at arguments constructed in different contexts and from studying a wide variety of argumentative strategies. These readings are not intended to be "model" arguments for imitation but a means to expand your repertoire as an arguer. What typically makes these arguments worthy of our attention is the writers' commitment to and knowledge of their subjects and their ability to find a form appropriate to their audience and purpose. Every argument has a specific occasion, a set of circumstances that gave rise to the writer's choice of voice, structure, and evidence. In approaching these written arguments, you should ask questions like these: What works or doesn't work to make this argument persuasive? Why might it work for its intended audience but not for the audience I am addressing? What can I learn about successful or weak uses of evidence or analogies from this argument? One of the benefits of examining arguments is that this experience acquaints you as a writer with multiple options, which you can then adapt to your own needs and audiences: Reading these arguments can empower you as a writer of arguments.

GUIDE QUESTIONS FOR THE ANALYSIS AND EVALUATION OF ARGUMENTS

As you read various arguments from this anthology, we hope that you will internalize habits of analysis and evaluation that we believe are essential for arguers. These habits derive from the principles of argument analysis covered throughout this text, so what follows is simply a summary and review of concepts you have already studied.

Questions for Analyzing and Evaluating a Conversation

Whenever you read two or more arguments addressing the same issue, we recommend that you follow the principles of reading described in Chapter 2.

1. *What does each argument say?* (Reading as a believer, be able to summarize each argument, stating its main claim and supporting reasons in a single sentence, if possible.)

2. *How can each argument be doubted?* (Reading as a doubter, search for weaknesses in the argument and for important questions that you would like to raise if you could talk to the author.)

3. *Why do the disputants disagree?* (Do they disagree at the level of truth or facts? At the level of values, assumptions, and beliefs?)

4. *Which arguments appear to be stronger?* (Which arguments seem most persuasive to you? Before you could take a stand on the issue yourself, what further questions would you need to have answered? Which of your own assumptions, values, and beliefs would you have to examine further and clarify?)

Questions for Analyzing and Evaluating an Individual Argument

The previous questions ask you to examine arguments in the context of the conversations to which they belong. This next set of questions asks you to look closely at a single argument, examining in detail its structure, its argumentative strategies, and its rhetorical force.

1. *How effective is the writer at creating logical appeals?*

   - What is the claim?

   - What reasons support the claim?

   - What are the ground and warrants for each of the reasons?

- How effective is the argument, particularly its use of evidence (grounds) and its support of its basic assumptions (warrants)?
- Does the argument exhibit any of the *logos* fallacies explained in Appendix 1?

2. *How effective is the writer at creating ethical appeals?*
   - What *ethos* does the writer project? What is the writer's stance toward the audience?
   - Is the writer's *ethos* effective?
   - Does the writer commit any of the *ethos* fallacies explained in Appendix 1?

3. *How effective is the writer at creating pathetic appeals?*
   - How effective is the writer at using audience-based reasons?
   - How effective is the writer's use of concrete language, word choice, powerful examples, and analogies for enhancing the pathetic appeal of the argument?

4. *How could the writer's argument be refuted?*
   - Can the writer's grounds be called into question?
   - Can the writer's warrants be called into question?

SOCIAL CAUSES OF TEEN VIOLENCE

*Kill-for-Kicks Video Games
Desensitizing Our Children*

John Leo

This article by syndicated columnist John Leo appeared as an op-ed piece in the Seattle Times *on April 27, 1999.*

Was it real life or an acted-out video game? 1

Marching through a large building using various bombs and guns to pick off victims is 2
a conventional video game scenario. In the Colorado massacre, Dylan Klebold and Eric Harris used pistol-grip shotguns, as in some video arcade games. The pools of blood, screams
of agony and pleas for mercy must have been familiar; they are featured in some of the
newer and more realistic kill-for-kicks games.

"With each kill," the *Los Angeles Times* reported, "the teens cackled and shouted as 3
though playing one of the more morbid video games they loved." And they ended their
spree by shooting themselves in the head, the final act in the game Postal, and in fact, the
only way to end it.

Did the sensibilities created by the modern video kill games play a role in the Little- 4
ton massacre? Apparently so. Note the cool and casual cruelty, the outlandish arsenal of
weapons, the cheering and laughing while hunting down victims one by one. All of this
seems to reflect the style and feel of the video killing games they played so often.

No, there isn't any direct connection between most murderous games and most mur- 5
ders. And yes, the primary responsibility for protecting children from dangerous games lies
with parents, many of whom like to blame the entertainment industry for their own failings.

But there is a larger problem here: We are now a culture in which the chief form of
play for millions of youngsters is making large numbers of people die. Hurting and maim-
ing others is the central fun activity in video games played so addictively by the young. A
widely cited survey of 900 fourth- through eighth-grade students found that almost half of
the children said their favorite games involve violence. Can it be that all this constant training in make-believe killing has no social effects?

The conventional argument is that this is a harmless activity among children who know 6
the difference between fantasy and reality. But the games are often played by unstable
youngsters who are unsure about the difference. Many have been maltreated or rejected
and left alone most of the time (a precondition for playing the games obsessively). Adolescent feelings of resentment, powerlessness and revenge pour into the killing games. In
these children, the games can become dress rehearsal for the real thing.

7   Psychologist David Grossman of Arkansas State University, a retired Army officer, thinks "point and shoot" video games have the same effect as military strategies used to break down a soldier's aversion to killing. During World War II, only 15 percent to 20 percent of all American soldiers fired their weapons in battle. Shooting games in which the target is a man-shaped outline, the Army found, made recruits more willing to "make killing a reflex action."

8   Video games are much more powerful versions of the military's primitive discovery about overcoming the reluctance to shoot. Grossman says Michael Carneal, the schoolboy shooter in West Paducah, Ky., showed the effects of video-game lessons in killing. Carneal coolly shot nine times, hitting eight people, five of them in the head or neck. Head shots pay a bonus in many video games. Now, the Marine Corps is adapting a version of Doom, the hyperviolent game played by one of the Littleton killers, for its own training purposes.

9   More realistic touches in video games help blur the boundary between fantasy and reality—carefully modeled real guns, accurate-looking wounds, screams and other sound effects, even the recoil of a heavy rifle.

10   Some newer games seem intent on erasing children's empathy and concern for others. Once, the intended victims of video slaughter were mostly gangsters or aliens. Now, some games invite players to blow away ordinary people who have done nothing wrong—pedestrians, marching bands, an elderly woman with a walker. In these games, the shooter is not a hero, just a violent sociopath. One ad for a SONY game says: "Get in touch with your gun-toting, testosterone-pumping, cold-blooded murdering side."

11   These killings are supposed to be taken as harmless over-the-top jokes. But the bottom line is that the young are being invited to enjoy the killing of vulnerable people picked at random. This looks like the final lesson in a course to eliminate any lingering resistance to killing.

12   SWAT teams and cops now turn up as the targets of some video-game killings. This has the effect of exploiting resentments toward law enforcement and making real-life shooting of cops more likely. The sensibility turns up in the hit movie *Matrix:* world-saving hero Keanu Reeves, in a mandatory Goth-style long black coat packed with countless heavy-duty guns, is forced to blow away huge numbers of uniformed law-enforcement people.

13   "We have to start worrying about what we are putting into the minds of our young," says Grossman. "Pilots train on flight simulators, drivers on driving simulators, and now we have our children on murder simulators." If we want to avoid more Littleton-style massacres, we will begin taking the social effects of the killing games more seriously.

Stop Blaming Kids and TV

Mike Males

Mike Males is the author of The Scapegoat Generation: America's War on Adolescents *(1996). This article was originally published in the October 1997 issue of* the Progressive.

Children have never been very good at listening to their elders," James Baldwin wrote   1
in *Nobody Knows My Name.* "But they have never failed to imitate them." This basic truth
has all but disappeared as the public increasingly treats teenagers as a robot-like population
under sway of an exploitative media. White House officials lecture film, music, Internet,
fashion, and pop-culture moguls and accuse them of programming kids to smoke, drink,
shoot up, have sex, and kill.

So do conservatives, led by William Bennett and Dan Quayle. Professional organiza-   2
tions are also into media-bashing. In its famous report on youth risks, the Carnegie Corporation devoted a full chapter to media influences.

Progressives are no exception. *Mother Jones* claims it has "proof that TV makes kids   3
violent." And the Institute for Alternative Media emphasizes, "the average American child
will witness . . . 200,000 acts of [TV] violence" by the time that child graduates from high
school.

None of these varied interests note that during the eighteen years between a child's   4
birth and graduation from high school, there will be fifteen million cases of *real* violence
in American homes grave enough to require hospital emergency treatment. These assaults
will cause ten million serious injuries and 40,000 deaths to children. In October 1996,
the Department of Health and Human Services reported 565,000 serious injuries that abusive parents inflicted on children and youths in 1993. The number is up four-fold since
1986.

The Department of Health report disappeared from the news in one day. It elicited   5
virtually no comment from the White House, Republicans, or law-enforcement officials. Nor
from Carnegie scholars, whose 150-page study, "Great Transitions: Preparing Adolescents
for a New Century," devotes two sentences to household violence. The left press took no
particular interest in the story, either.

All sides seem to agree that fictional violence, sex on the screen, Joe Camel, beer-   6
drinking frogs, or naked bodies on the Internet pose a bigger threat to children than do actual beatings, rape, or parental addictions. This, in turn, upholds the Clinton doctrine that
youth behavior is the problem, and curbing young people's rights the answer.

Claims that TV causes violence bear little relation to real behavior. Japanese and   7
European kids behold media as graphically brutal as that which appears on American
screens, but seventeen-year-olds in those countries commit murder at rates lower than
those of American seventy-year-olds.

Likewise, youths in different parts of the United States are exposed to the same media   8
but display drastically different violence levels. TV violence does not account for the fact
that the murder rate among black teens in Washington, D.C., is twenty-five times higher
than that of white teens living a few Metro stops away. It doesn't explain why, nationally,
murder doubled among nonwhite and Latino youth over the last decade, but declined
among white Anglo teens. Furthermore, contrary to the TV brainwashing theory, Anglo
sixteen-year-olds have lower violent-crime rates than black sixty-year-olds, Latino forty-year-
olds, and Anglo thirty-year-olds. Men, women, whites, Latinos, blacks, Asians, teens, young
adults, middle-agers, and senior citizens in Fresno County—California's poorest urban
area—display murder and violent-crime rates double those of their counterparts in Ventura
County, the state's richest.

9   Confounding every theory, America's biggest explosion in felony violent crime is not street crime among minorities or teens of any color, but domestic violence among aging, mostly white baby boomers. Should we arm Junior with a V-chip to protect him from Mom and Dad?

10   In practical terms, media-violence theories are not about kids, but about race and class: If TV accounts for any meaningful fraction of murder levels among poorer, nonwhite youth, why doesn't it have the same effect on white kids? Are minorities inherently programmable?

11   The newest target is Channel One, legitimately criticized by the Unplug Campaign—a watchdog sponsored by the Center for Commercial-Free Public Education—as a corporate marketing ploy packaged as educational TV. But then the Unplug Campaign gives credence to claims that "commercials control kids" by "harvesting minds," as Roy Fox of the University of Missouri says. These claims imply that teens are uniquely open to media brainwashing.

12   Other misleading claims come from Johns Hopkins University media analyst Mark Crispin Miller. In his critique of Channel One in the May edition of *Extra!*, Miller invoked such hackneyed phrases as the "inevitable rebelliousness of adolescent boys," the "hormones raging," and the "defiant boorish behavior" of "young men." Despite the popularity of these stereotypes, there is no basis in fact for such anti-youth bias.

13   A 1988 study in the *Journal of Youth and Adolescence* by psychology professors Grayson Holmbeck and John Hill concluded: "Adolescents are *not* in turmoil, *not* deeply disturbed, *not* at the mercy of their impulses, *not* resistant to parental values, and *not* rebellious."

14   In the November 1992 *Journal of the American Academy of Child and Adolescent Psychiatry,* Northwestern University psychiatry professor Daniel Offer reviewed 150 studies and concluded, in his article "Debunking the Myths of Adolescence," that "the effects of pubertal hormones are neither potent nor pervasive."

15   If anything, Channel One and other mainstream media reinforce young people's conformity to—not defiance of—adult values. Miller's unsubstantiated claims that student consumerism, bad behaviors, and mental or biological imbalances are compelled by media ads and images could be made with equal force about the behaviors of his own age group. Binge drinking, drug abuse, and violence against children by adults over the age of thirty are rising rapidly.

16   The barrage of sexually seductive liquor ads, fashion images, and anti-youth rhetoric, by conventional logic, must be influencing those hormonally unstable middle-agers.

17   I worked for a dozen years in youth programs in Montana and California. When problems arose, they usually crossed generations. I saw violent kids with dads or uncles in jail for assault. I saw middle-schoolers molested in childhood by mom's boyfriend. I saw budding teen alcoholics hoisting forty-ouncers alongside forty-year-old sots. I also saw again and again how kids start to smoke. In countless trailers and small apartments dense with blue haze, children roamed the rugs as grownups puffed. Mom and seventh-grade daughter swapped Dorals while bemoaning the evils of men. A junior-high basketball center slept outside before a big game because a dozen elders—from her non-inhaling sixteen-year-old brother to her grandma—were all chain smokers. Two years later, she'd given up and joined the party.

As a rule, teen smoking mimicked adult smoking by gender, race, locale, era, and   18
household. I could discern no pop-culture puppetry. My survey of 400 Los Angeles middle
schoolers for a 1994 *Journal of School Health* article found children of smoking parents
three times more likely to smoke by age fifteen than children of nonsmokers. Parents were
the most influential but not the only adults kids emulated. Nor did youngsters copy elders
slavishly. Youths often picked slightly different habits (like chewing tobacco, or their own
brands).

In 1989, the Centers for Disease Control lamented, "75 percent of all teenage smok-   19
ers come from homes where parents smoke." You don't hear such candor from today's put-
politics-first health agencies. Centers for Disease Control tobacco chieftain Michael Eriksen
informed me that his agency doesn't make an issue of parental smoking. Nor do anti-
smoking groups. Asked Kathy Mulvey, research director of INFACT: "Why make enemies of
fifty million adult smokers" when advertising creates the real "appeal of tobacco to youth?"

Do ads hook kids on cigarettes? Studies of the effects of the Joe Camel logo show only   20
that a larger fraction of teen smokers than veteran adult smokers choose the Camel brand.
When asked, some researchers admit they cannot demonstrate that advertising causes kids
to smoke who would not otherwise. And that's the real issue. In fact, surveys found smoking declining among teens (especially the youngest) during Joe's advent from 1985 to 1990.

The University of California's Stanton Glantz, whose exposure of 10,000 tobacco   21
documents enraged the industry, found corporate perfidy far shrewder than camels and
cowboys.

"As the tobacco industry knows well," Glantz reported, "kids want to be like adults."   22
An industry marketing document advises: "To reach young smokers, present the cigarette
as one of the initiations into adult life . . . the basic symbols of growing up."

The biggest predictor of whether a teen will become a smoker, a drunk, or a druggie   23
is whether or not the child grows up amid adult addicts. Three-fourths of murdered kids
are killed by adults. Suicide and murder rates among white teenagers resemble those of
white adults, and suicide and murder rates among black teens track those of black adults.
And as far as teen pregnancy goes, for minor mothers, four-fifths of the fathers are adults
over eighteen, and half are adults over twenty.

The inescapable conclusion is this: If you want to change juvenile behavior, change   24
adult behavior. But instead of focusing on adults, almost everyone points a finger at kids—
and at the TV culture that supposedly addicts them.

Groups like Mothers Against Drunk Driving charge, for instance, that Budweiser's frogs   25
entice teens to drink. Yet the 1995 National Household Survey found teen alcohol use declining. "Youths aren't buying the cute and flashy beer images," an in-depth *USA Today* survey found. Most teens found the ads amusing, but they did not consume Bud as a result.

By squabbling over frogs, political interests can sidestep the impolitic tragedy that   26
adults over the age of twenty-one cause 90 percent of America's 16,000 alcohol-related traffic deaths every year. Clinton and drug-policy chief Barry McCaffrey ignore federal reports
that show a skyrocketing toll of booze and drug-related casualties among adults in their thir-
ties and forties—the age group that is parenting most American teens. But both officials get
favorable press attention by blaming alcohol ads and heroin chic for corrupting our kids.

Progressive reformers who insist kids are so malleable that beer frogs and Joe Camel   27
and Ace Ventura push them to evil are not so different from those on the Christian right

who claim that *Our Bodies, Ourselves* promotes teen sex and that the group Rage Against the Machine persuades pubescents to roll down Rodeo Drive with a shotgun.

28   America's increasingly marginalized young deserve better than grownup escapism. Millions of children and teenagers face real destitution, drug abuse, and violence in their homes. Yet these profound menaces continue to lurk in the background, even as the frogs, V-chips, and Mighty Morphins take center stage.

Supremacy Crimes

Gloria Steinem

Gloria Steinem is a feminist, politician, and consulting editor for Ms. *magazine. This article appeared in the August/September 1999 issue of* Ms.

1   You've seen the ocean of television coverage, you've read the headlines: "How to Spot a Troubled Kid," "Twisted Teens," "When Teens Fall Apart."

2   After the slaughter in Colorado that inspired those phrases, dozens of copycat threats were reported in the same generalized way: "Junior high students charged with conspiracy to kill students and teachers" (in Texas); "Five honor students overheard planning a June graduation bombing" (in New York); "More than 100 minor threats reported statewide" (in Pennsylvania). In response, the White House held an emergency strategy session titled "Children, Violence, and Responsibility." Nonetheless, another attack was soon reported: "Youth with 2 Guns Shoots 6 at Georgia School."

3   I don't know about you, but I've been talking back to the television set, waiting for someone to tell us the obvious: it's not "youth," "our children," or "our teens." It's our sons—and "our" can usually be read as "white," "middle class," and "heterosexual."

4   We know that hate crimes, violent and otherwise, are overwhelmingly committed by white men who are apparently straight. The same is true for an even higher percentage of impersonal, resentment-driven, mass killings like those in Colorado; the sort committed for no economic or rational gain except the need to say, "I'm superior because I can kill." Think of Charles Starkweather, who reported feeling powerful and serene after murdering ten women and men in the 1950s; or the shooter who climbed the University of Texas Tower in 1966, raining down death to gain celebrity. Think of the engineering student at the University of Montreal who resented females' ability to study that subject, and so shot to death 14 women students in 1989, while saying "I'm against feminism." Think of nearly all those who have killed impersonally in the workplace, the post office, McDonald's.

5   White males—usually intelligent, middle class, and heterosexual, or trying desperately to appear so—also account for virtually all the serial, sexually motivated, sadistic killings, those characterized by stalking, imprisoning, torturing, and "owning" victims in death. Think of Edmund Kemper, who began by killing animals, then murdered his grandparents, yet was released to sexually torture and dismember college students and other young women until he himself decided he "didn't want to kill *all* the coeds in the world." Or David

Berkowitz, the Son of Sam, who murdered *some* women in order to feel in control of *all* women. Or consider Ted Bundy, the charming, snobbish young would-be lawyer who tortured and murdered as many as 40 women, usually beautiful students who were symbols of the economic class he longed to join. As for John Wayne Gacy, he was obsessed with maintaining the public mask of masculinity, and so hid his homosexuality by killing and burying men and boys with whom he had sex.

These "senseless" killings begin to seem less mysterious when you consider that they were committed disproportionately by white, non-poor males, the group most likely to become hooked on the drug of superiority. It's a drug pushed by a male-dominant culture that presents dominance as a natural right; a racist hierarchy that falsely elevates whiteness; a materialist society that equates superiority with possessions, and a homophobic one that empowers only one form of sexuality.   6

As Elliot Leyton reports in *Hunting Humans: The Rise of the Modern Multiple Murderer,* these killers see their behavior as "an appropriate—even 'manly'—response to the frustrations and disappointments that are a normal part of life." In other words, it's not their life experiences that are the problem, it's the impossible expectation of dominance to which they've become addicted.   7

This is not about blame. This is about causation. If anything, ending the massive cultural cover-up of supremacy crimes should make heroes out of boys and men who reject violence, especially those who reject the notion of superiority altogether. Even if one believes in a biogenetic component of male aggression, the very existence of gentle men proves that socialization can override it.   8

Nor is this about attributing such crimes to a single cause. Addiction to the drug of supremacy is not their only root, just the deepest and most ignored one. Additional reasons why this country has such a high rate of violence include the plentiful guns that make killing seem as unreal as a video game; male violence in the media that desensitizes viewers in much the same way that combat killers are desensitized in training; affluence that allows maximum access to violence-as-entertainment; a national history of genocide and slavery; the romanticizing of frontier violence and organized crime; not to mention extremes of wealth and poverty and the illusion that both are deserved.   9

But it is truly remarkable, given the relative reasons for anger at injustice in this country, that white, non-poor men have a near-monopoly on multiple killings of strangers, whether serial and sadistic or mass and random. How can we ignore this obvious fact? Others may kill to improve their own condition—in self-defense, or for money or drugs; to eliminate enemies; to declare turf in drive-by shootings; even for a jacket or a pair of sneakers—but white males addicted to supremacy kill even when it worsens their condition or ends in suicide.   10

Men of color and females are capable of serial and mass killing, and commit just enough to prove it. Think of Colin Ferguson, the crazed black man on the Long Island Railroad, or Wayne Williams, the young black man in Atlanta who kidnapped and killed black boys, apparently to conceal his homosexuality. Think of Aileen Carol Wuornos, the white prostitute in Florida who killed abusive johns "in self-defense," or Waneta Hoyt, the upstate New York woman who strangled her five infant children between 1965 and 1971, disguising their cause of death as sudden infant death syndrome. Such crimes are rare enough to leave a   11 haunting refrain of disbelief as evoked in Pat Parker's poem "jonestown": "Black folks do not / Black folks do not / Black folks do not commit suicide." And yet they did.

12   Nonetheless, the proportion of serial killings that are not committed by white males is about the same as the proportion of anorexics who are not female. Yet we discuss the gender, race, and class components of anorexia, but not the role of the same factors in producing epidemics among the powerful.

13   The reasons are buried deep in the culture, so invisible that only by reversing our assumptions can we reveal them.

14   Suppose, for instance that young black males—or any other men of color—had carried out the slaughter in Colorado. Would the media reports be so willing to describe the murderers as "our children"? Would there be so little discussion about the boys' race? Would experts be calling the motive a mystery, or condemning the high school cliques for making those young men feel like "outsiders"? Would there be the same empathy for parents who gave the murderers luxurious homes, expensive cars, even rescued them from brushes with the law? Would there be as much attention to generalized causes, such as the dangers of violent video games and recipes for bombs on the Internet?

15   As for victims, if racial identities had been reversed, would racism remain so little discussed? In fact, the killers themselves said they were targeting blacks and athletes. They used a racial epithet, shot a black male student in the head, and then laughed over the fact that they could see his brain. What if *that* had been reversed?

16   What if these two young murderers, who were called "fags" by some of the jocks at Columbine High School, actually had been gay? Would they have got the same sympathy for being gay-baited? What if they had been lovers? Would we hear as little about their sexuality as we now do, even though only their own homophobia could have given the word "fag" such power to humiliate them?

17   Take one more leap of the imagination: suppose these killings had been planned and executed by young women—of any race, sexuality, or class. Would the media still be so disinterested in the role played by gender-conditioning? Would journalists assume that female murderers had suffered from being shut out of access to power in high school, so much so that they were pushed beyond their limits? What if dozens, even hundreds of young women around the country had made imitative threats—as young men have done—expressing admiration for a well-planned massacre and promising to do the same? Would we be discussing their youth more than their gender, as is the case so far with these male killers?

18   I think we begin to see that our national self-examination is ignoring something fundamental, precisely because it's like the air we breathe: the white male factor, the middle-class and heterosexual one, and the promise of superiority it carries. Yet this denial is self-defeating—to say the least. We will never reduce the number of violent Americans, from bullies to killers, without challenging the assumptions on which masculinity is based: that males are superior to females, that they must find a place in a male hierarchy, and that the ability to dominate *someone* is so important that even a mere insult can justify lethal revenge. There are plenty of studies to support this view. As Dr. James Gilligan concluded in *Violence: Reflections on a National Epidemic,* "If humanity is to evolve beyond the propensity toward violence . . . then it can only do so by recognizing the extent to which the patriarchal code of honor and shame generates and obligates male violence."

I think the way out can only be found through a deeper reversal: just as we as a society have begun to raise our daughters more like our sons—more like whole people—we must begin to raise our sons more like our daughters—that is, to value empathy as well as hierarchy; to measure success by other people's welfare as well as their own.   19

But first, we have to admit and name the truth about supremacy crimes.   20

Littleton Massacre Seems So . . . American

Charlie James

Charlie James is publisher of the African-American Business and Employment Journal *and an activist in the African American community. This article appeared on the editorial page of the* Seattle Times *on April 29, 1999.*

Now the smoke clears from another shooting, now we sing, precious Lord take my hand! Now we cry for the innocence lost, for the new scars that may never go away. Now we pray; while asking why, while knowing that there is something in who we have become as Americans that seems to make this so natural, so American.   1

Our love of guns, our worship of the rights of individuals to confront the larger society—finally, our history of racism has left a terrible legacy on all of us: Young, white, angry males who will never have the power over their lives and the lives of women and minorities that their grandfathers and fathers enjoyed and will always resent it.   2

Freedom is a tricky thing, and everyone will not use the responsibilities that come with freedom wisely. Being young and disenfranchised is also a tricky thing. We are at an age where every slight takes on huge proportions. Your hormones are raging and rejection of any kind is hard to take, and people in your peer group will not let you forget.   3

They are young men far from mature who are still close enough to Superman or Batman to visualize themselves as superheroes who can right the wrongs done to them. They see people on TV and in movies taking a gun, getting even, and are willing to take their own lives and call it an "honorable death."   4

Kurt Cobain kills himself and becomes immortalized, Jimmy Dean dies a violent death and becomes a cult hero. If that's the only door they find open to becoming somebody, some of them will walk through it, put on a long trench coat and take a walk toward infamy and history.   5

We can gnash our teeth all we want. We can go out and find all of the psychiatrists and psychoanalysts we can find and somone will do something similar next month, somewhere else, and again we ask: "Why?"   6

Yet, we fail to see the blood-stained hands of our American heroes. The slaveowning Founding Fathers, the people who massacred Native Americans and became American heroes, elected officials, even presidents. Wyatt Earp, Wild Bill Hickok or Audie Murphy glorified the gun and man's right to bear and use weapons. Hollywood has kept these heroes and their philosophy alive. We have added the mobsters, the pimps and pushers to this group. They are so . . . American.   7

8   Shall we do something? Yes!

9   What? I don't know.

10 But turning the schools into miniature prison camps is surely not the answer. As long as there are guns and bombs available, disenfranchised youth and a glorified culture of violence, armed guards will not stop the carnage.

11 We must fix this element in our social fabric as we make a transition from the America we were to the America we must become. We need to go back and clean up America's history and call a thug a thug, a killer a killer, an outlaw and crook an outlaw and a crook.

12 We must not allow Hollywood or anyone else to make them something else and clean up their deeds because they are white males who "made America what it is."

13 This is not going to be easy, but we must purge our culture of this myth of violence and these violent mythical heroes or it will be impossible to stop the children from becoming what we have glorified and immortalized.

14 It was hard for the young white men in Colorado to accept that African American, Hispanic male athletes, or any athlete, could be more popular and desirable among whites than they were. It's easy to reach out and embrace Hitler and white supremacy or male supremacy if that's the only place you can find a philosophy that makes you feel good about yourself.

15 It's hard to create a culture that proclaims and enforces equality and creates an even playing field for everyone. But you can't play games with this. If you go half the way and retreat, you are leaving the impression that real equality is really not where we need to go.

16 Let's do what we say we are about. Let's take the final step and say clearly that we are building a new environment where being a white male is no different than being a black male, and not stop because the country is going through *Happy Days* withdrawal.

17 We have not fully committed ourselves to a fully equal America. We hold on to the vestiges of white privilege while denying they even exist. We are giving mixed messages to our youth and we react in horror when they embrace the America we once were rather than the America we say we are trying to become—or are we?

When White Boys Kill, White Dads Fail

Chuck Shelton

Chuck Shelton is a diversity consultant and CEO of Diversity Management Inc., a company based in western Washington. This article appeared as an op-ed piece in the Seattle Times *on June 25, 1999.*

1   Hillary Rodham Clinton got it right—it does take a village to raise a child. And some of the children we're raising are killers.

2   America's village-wide soul search since the Colorado carnage prioritizes four interventions with young people: improve our parenting, handle at-risk adolescents better, control their access to guns, and decrease the availability of violence via the Web, TV, movies and video games.

But our finely wrought angst overlooks the obvious: 100 percent of the recent school   3
shooters were young white men, while only 35 percent of Americans are white males. So
what?

Those of us who are white men are singularly obliged to raise white boys right. White   4
boys look to white men as fathers and friends for protection, love, fun and the confidence
to achieve in life.

Granted, girls use guns sometimes, and people of color have also committed horrific   5
violence. Yes, mothers and other diverse villagers nurture healthy young men. But boys
won't be boys—they will be men. It is indisputably true that, to succeed as men themselves,
white boys need white men. And when any white boy kills his classmates, many white men
have failed.

Blaming white men for all manner of social ills, of course, has ripened into a perverse   6
national pastime. Formerly a white boy myself, I'm sick of how white men are caricatured
and stereotyped. In a 1988 study of 1,000 random advertisements, men were 100 percent
of the jerks singled out in male/female relationships.

As a diversity consultant, I observe white women and people of color diagnosing   7
"power and privilege" like some secret disease infecting only white guys. This revictim-
ization yields a fearful silence among white men: perched on eggshells about offending with
our words, anxious that a coworker will claim sexual harassment or racial discrimination,
worried about our opportunities because the job we want is "slotted for a diverse candidate." The blame and shame game erodes the ability of white men to summon in their boys
the self-esteem and ambition every young man needs.

Will we learn to tell our truths to one another without accusation? Let me try it out   8
with my own kind: As white men, it is our duty to shape our boys' opinions about human
differences. For example:

- The Colorado killings marked the birthday of Adolf Hitler, the prototypical twisted
  white man. Take your son to the U.S. Holocaust Museum in Washington, D.C.,
  when he's old enough. Face the evils of prejudice together.

- Three young white men in Texas dismembered James Lee Byrd—with their pickup
  truck. Read *By the Color of Our Skin: The Illusion of Integration and the Reality of
  Race* (by Leonard Steinhorn and Barbara Diggs-Brown). Discuss it with your son.
  An enduring commitment to inter-racial relationships may replace any inclination
  to whine about reverse discrimination.

American men of European ancestry should redefine whiteness and masculinity as a   9
matter of integrity. As white men, we are answerable like no other villager for thwarting
the hateful ideologies of racism and sexism. The lethality of our white sons demonstrates
the danger in assuming our own normativity: White guys are normal, everyone else is *different,* and different is bad. Presumed superiority is a not-so-little white lie fueling violence
in some of our young men. The white male antidote to this poison: equip our sons to engage diversity with candor and compassion.

Such empathy and honesty about race and gender will spring from loving your son and   10
befriending his buddies with disciplined intention. Listen to them without your motor running, talk with them, not at them, help them avoid school clique conflicts, learn a video game,

fix the car together, take a hike. If you are a dad at a distance, e-mail constantly and rack up an absurd phone bill.

11   White men, teach your children well. Befriend the boys around you—particularly the boys at the margins of village life. A few of them are making the village green run red. The white man's burden is to raise white boys right.

The Crackdown on Kids

Annette Fuentes

This article was first published in the June 15–22, 1998, issue of the Nation. *At the time of writing this article, Annette Fuentes had recently completed a Prudential Fellowship on Children and the News at Columbia University.*

1   When Kipland Kinkel, Mitchell Johnson and Andrew Golden reportedly unloaded mini arsenals of guns at their classmates, they fulfilled the worst fears about young people that now dominate the nation's adult consciousness. Kinkel, 15, of Springfield, Oregon, allegedly is responsible for the deaths of two students as a result of an incident on May 21, as well as for the deaths of his parents. Johnson, 13, and Golden, 11, were charged in connection with the March 24 deaths of four students and a teacher in Jonesboro, Arkansas. All were instantly transformed from average American boys, perhaps a bit on the wild side, into evil incarnate. Forget that Mitchell sobbed next to his mother in court, or that Drew learned to sling a shotgun from Dad and Grandpa the way many boys learn to swing a bat. "Let 'em have it" was the sentiment, with catchy phrases like "adult crime, adult time."

2   After the Arkansas incident, Attorney General Janet Reno scoured federal laws for some way to prosecute Johnson and Golden so they could be locked up till age 21 if convicted, a stiffer sentence than the state could mete out. One *Washington Post* Op-Ed called for states to adopt a national uniform minimum age for juveniles to be tried as adults for violent crimes.

3   The three boys are believed to have committed terrible deeds, no question. But twenty years ago, a Greek chorus would have been clamoring to understand why they went bad. The events themselves would have been seen as aberrations. Redemption might have been mentioned, especially since these were not career delinquents. Instead, we have proposals like the one from Texas legislator Jim Pitts, who wants his state to use the death penalty on children as young as 11. And he's got plenty of support, because this is the era of crime and punishment and accountability for all constituencies without wealth or power to shield them. And the young are such a class of people.

4   In the past two decades, our collective attitude toward children and youth has undergone a profound change that's reflected in the educational and criminal justice systems as well as in our daily discourse. "Zero tolerance" is the mantra in public schools and juvenile courts, and what it really means is that to be young is to be suspect. Latino and black youth have borne the brunt of this growing criminalization of youth. But the trend has spilled over racial and ethnic boundaries—even class boundaries, to a degree. Youth, with all its innocence and vulnerability, is losing ground in a society that exploits both.

In fact, youth crime has not changed as dramatically as our perceptions of it. Data from   5
the National Center for Juvenile Justice show that between 1987 and 1996, the number of
juvenile arrests increased 35 percent. Juvenile violent-crime arrests were up 60 percent, but
they represent a sliver of all juvenile arrests—about 5 percent of the 1996 total of 135,100.
A 1997 study by the center found that "today's violent youth commits the same number of
violent acts as his/her predecessor of 15 years ago." As to whether criminals are getting
younger, a 1997 report from the Justice Department answers clearly: "Today's serious and
violent juvenile offenders are not significantly younger than those of 10 or 15 years ago."

What's more, from 1994 to 1995 there was a 3 percent decline in juvenile arrests for   6
violent crime, and from 1995 to 1996 there was a 6 percent decline. "I have people call
me up and ask, 'Why is juvenile crime down?' " says Robert Shepherd Jr., a law professor
at the University of Richmond in Virginia. "I say, 'Why was it up?' It could be just one of
history's cycles. Over the thirty years I've been involved in juvenile justice issues, I've seen
very little change in the incidence of violent crime by kids."

One thing that *has* changed is the prominence of guns and their role in violence. A   7
1997 Justice Department report looked at homicides by youths aged 13 and 14 with and
without guns. In 1980 there were 74 murders committed with guns and 68 without by that
age group. In 1995 gun-related murders totaled 178; there were 67 nongun murders.

Exaggerated claims about juvenile crime would be a hard sell if people weren't ready   8
to believe the worst about young people. A 1997 report from Public Agenda, a nonprofit
policy group, called "Kids These Days: What Americans Really Think about the Next Generation," found that 58 percent of those surveyed think children and teens will make the
world a worse place or no different when they grow up. Even kids aged 5 to 12 weren't
spared, with 53 percent of respondents characterizing them in negative terms. Only 23 percent had positive things to say about children. What America really thinks about its kids,
in short, is: not much.

The generation gap is old news, but this sour, almost hateful view of young people is   9
different. Adults aren't merely puzzled by young people; they're terrified of them. It can't
be a coincidence that the shift in adult attitudes began roughly a generation after the height
of political and social movements created by young people of all colors. Policy-makers now
propelling anti-youth agendas remember how effective young people can be as a force for
change. Demographics and the shifting nature of U.S. families also foster the anti-youth bias.
According to census statistics, the number of people under age 65 has tripled since 1900,
while the population aged 65 or over has increased elevenfold. One-quarter of all households are people living alone. And children are no longer integral to family structure: In
51 percent of all families there are no children under 18 living at home. Young people are
easily demonized when their worlds don't coincide with ours. The sense of collective responsibility in raising children disappears as the building blocks of community change.

To an older America in a postindustial world, children have become more of a liability   10
than an asset. Middle-class parents calculate the cost of raising kids, including an overpriced
college education, as they would a home mortgage. Low-income parents are bludgeoned by
policies designed to discourage having children, from welfare reform to cuts in higher-
education assistance. Young people's place in the economic order is uncertain, and a threat
to those elders who are scrambling for the same jobs at McDonald's or in Silicon Valley. Says
Barry Feld, professor at the University of Minnesota Law School and author of the upcoming

Bad Kids: Race and the Transformation of Juvenile Court, "Parents raised kids so they could take care of them when they're old. As caring for the old has shifted to the public sector, the elderly no longer have that fiscal investment in their kids. They know Social Security will be there for them."

11   Another reason adults are willing to condemn children is that it saves them from taking responsibility when kids go wrong. Take this statistical nugget: From 1986 to 1993, roughly the same period of the youth crime "explosion," the number of abused and neglected children doubled to 2.8 million, according to the Justice Department. And just three years later, the total of all juvenile arrests was 2.8 million. What goes around comes around.

12   Historically, U.S. criminal law followed the definitions of adulthood and childhood laid down by William Blackstone in his *Commentaries on the Laws of England* (1765–69). Children up to 7 were considered incapable of criminal responsibility by dint of their immaturity. At 14, they could be held as responsible as adults for their crimes; the years in between were a gray area of subjective judgment on culpability. But by 1900, reformers had created a separate system of juvenile courts and reform schools based on the principles that delinquency had social causes and that youth should not be held to adult standards. Eighteen was generally held as the entryway to adulthood.

13   The current transformation in juvenile justice is no less radical than the one 100 years ago. This time, though, we are marching backward to a one-size-fits-all system for youth and adults in which punishment, not reform, is the goal. From 1992 to 1995, forty-one states passed laws making it easier to prosecute juveniles in adult criminal court, and today all fifty states have such laws. In more than half the states, children under 14 can be tried in adult court for certain crimes. In thirteen states, there is no minimum age at which a child can be tried in adult court for felonies. New York permits prosecution of a 7-year-old as an adult for certain felonies. The Hatch-Sessions bill now in the U.S. Senate continues the assault on youthful offenders. It would use block grants to encourage states to toughen further their juvenile justice procedures. One provision eliminates the longstanding mandate to separate incarcerated juveniles and adults. "You're going to see more suicides and assaults if that happens," says Robert Shepherd.

14   Violent crimes like those in Oregon and Arkansas are a rarity, but they've become the rationale for a widespread crackdown on youth at school and on the streets. If Dennis the Menace were around, he'd be shackled hand and foot, with Mr. Wilson chortling as the cops hauled his mischievous butt off to juvenile hall. In Miami recently, a 10-year-old boy was handcuffed, arrested and jailed overnight because he kicked his mother at a Pizza Hut. His mother protested the police action—it was a waitress who turned him in. The boy now faces domestic battery charges in juvenile court.

15   Last October at the Merton Intermediate School in Merton, Wisconsin, four boys aged 12 and 13 were suspended for three days and slapped with disorderly conduct citations and fines (later dropped) by the local sheriff after they yanked up another boy's underwear "wedgie style." "The boys were playing, wrestling around in the schoolyard, and there was a pile-on," says Kevin Keane, an attorney who represented one of the boys. "One kid was on the ground and the others gave him a wedgie. He wasn't hurt or upset, and they all went back to class." But the principal learned about the incident and termed it a sexual assault.

16   Anti-youth analysts prefer to think more juvenile arrests means more kids are behaving recklessly. But it's just as plausible to argue that the universe of permissible behavior has

shrunk. Look at curfews, which were virtually unknown twenty years ago. Curfews generated 185,000 youth arrests in 1996—a 113 percent increase since 1987. Disorderly conduct arrests of youth soared 93 percent between 1987 and 1996, with 215,000 arrests in 1996 alone.

Public schools are at ground zero in the youth crackdown. A report released in March   17
by the National Center for Education Statistics surveyed 1,234 public schools on crime and security measures. Three-fourths have "zero tolerance" policies on drugs, alcohol and weapons, which means ironclad punishment for any transgression. Six percent of the schools surveyed use police or other law enforcement on campus at least thirty hours a week, while 19 percent of high schools have stationed cops full time. Public schools are even using dogs to search for illegal drugs. The Northern California A.C.L.U. filed suit in March 1997 against the Galt, California, school district on behalf of two students and a teacher who were subjected to dog searches during a course on criminal justice. "It's a real state police-prison element introduced into the schools," says A.C.L.U lawyer Ann Bick. "It tells kids, 'We don't trust you.' And they'll live down to those expectations."

If the goal is to change behavior, draconian policies aimed at young people have been   18
a dismal failure. Half a dozen studies have shown that transferring juveniles to adult courts not only doesn't deter crime, it's more likely to spur recidivism. But if the goal of the crackdown on youth is to divert attention from the real crimes plaguing the nation—child poverty, failing educational systems, 15 million kids without health insurance—then it's a success. New York City Mayor Rudolph Giuliani uses that strategy brilliantly: In January a child was killed by a brick falling from a badly managed school construction site, and reading scores were once again abysmally low. What were Giuliani's issues? Uniforms for students and deployment of police in the schools.

The criminalization of young people makes no sense, of course. Kids are a national trea-   19
sure and natural resource, the bearers of our collective dreams and hopes. But logic and humanity don't often determine public policies or opinion. We are sowing the seeds, the dragon's teeth, of our own comeuppance. Erasing the line between youth and adulthood without granting youths the same constitutional protections and rights of citizenship as adults sets up a powerful contradiction. And sooner or later, to paraphrase Malcolm X, the chickens will come home to roost.

Children in a Violent World
A Metaphysical Perspective
James Garbarino

James Garbarino is the director of the Family Life Development Center and a professor of human development and family studies at Cornell University. He has written widely on children and class, poverty, and violence. This article originally appeared in the July 1998 issue of Family and Conciliation Courts Review.

For the past twenty-five years, I have sought to understand the meaning of violence in   1
the lives of children, youths, and families. This has taken me to many of the world's war zones—to Mozambique, to Nicaragua, to Cambodia, to Kuwait, to Croatia, to Iraq, and to

the streets of America's inner cities (cf. Garbarino, Kostelny, and Dubrow 1991; Garbarino et al. 1992). Out of these experiences have come the beginnings of an understanding of what it means to live in a violent world, what it means for a child's development and for the life course to come.

2   For me, commentary on war zones at home and abroad begins and ends with personal reflection. A few years ago, while watching the news in Chicago, a local news story made a personal connection with me. The report concerned a teenager who had been shot because he had angered a group of his male peers. This act of violence caused me to recapture a memory from my own adolescence because of an instructive parallel in my own life with this boy who had been shot. When I was a teenager some thirty-five years ago in the New York metropolitan area, I wrote a regular column for my high school newspaper. One week, I wrote a column in which I made fun of the fraternities in my high school. As a result, I elicited the anger of some of the most aggressive teenagers in my high school. A couple of nights later, a car pulled up in front of my house, and the angry teenagers in the car dumped garbage on the lawn of my house as an act of revenge and intimidation.

3   In today's language, you could say I was a victim of a "drive-by littering." What I had seen on the television news in Chicago a few years ago was a boy who had done much the same thing that I did thirty years earlier (i.e., make his peers angry with him), but who had experienced something far more serious than I almost three decades earlier. When his peers responded in anger, the result was not a drive-by littering, but a drive-by shooting. For me, this juxtaposition captured something very disturbing about changes in American society.

4   Over the thirty plus years that intervened between the drive-by littering and the drive-by shooting, the social environment had changed such that the consequences of peer conflict had changed, as part of a broader change in the "terms of engagement" for adolescents in general. And the direction of that change was negative; now, you could get killed for behavior that a generation ago might only expose you to frightening experiences with limited long-term risks (I lived to recall the story of the drive-by littering at my thirtieth high school reunion). Out of that insight came the concept of "social toxicity," the idea that just as the quality of the physical environment can become so negative that it is justifiably called "toxic," the same thing can happen in the social environment.

5   The concept of social toxicity refers to the idea that there can be cultural and social poisons abroad in a society that shorten life and that bring about a deterioration of well-being, and that these poisons include and interact with violence (Garbarino 1995). With physical toxicity, we know that there are individual and group differences in vulnerability. For example, if there is an air pollution problem in a city, we would worry first and most about old people with emphysema or children with asthma. I believe that this is an analogy to what we see among children and youths in the social environment: there is a kind of psychological asthma that some children and youths have that makes them particularly vulnerable to whatever social toxins are in their environment.

6   I thought of this when I went to visit a day-treatment program for emotionally disturbed children in Chicago, a program that had been in operation for over twenty-five years. By all accounts this program once worked, but it now no longer does because these children, these highly vulnerable children, these psychologically asthmatic children, now bring with them into the school a level of aggression and nastiness and violence that overwhelms the

program. We need to understand that these psychologically asthmatic kids exist in every society. They exist particularly when home has become empty or hostile. These children whose homes are empty and hostile are likely to become socially and psychologically asthmatic and show us the worst that is going in society.

We know, for example, from research in the United States, that all children are affected by watching violent television but children who are otherwise at risk because of psychological or emotional vulnerability are the ones who are most affected (National Research Council 1993). We ourselves have done research in the Middle East that demonstrates that Palestinian children involved in the Intifada are most affected by political violence when their homes are abusive or neglectful (Garbarino and Kostelny 1996).   7

I think that there is a natural merging of the interests of those among us who have a primary focus on family with those of us who are concerned principally with community because those who fall victim to violence and social toxicity within the community are particularly those who have been hurt or neglected at home. And, more than even that, we have come to understand in child development research that the presence or absence of any single risk factor tells us very little about the outcome for a child. Rather, it is the accumulation of risk factors (Sameroff et al. 1987). This emerges over and over again in research when it is designed to reveal it. It may be accurate to say that runaways and drug addicts and sexually abused children come from all strata of society, but it is not to the point because the point is that victimization, when coupled with other risk factors, is what really does the damage.   8

One of the things I have learned from time spent talking with children and adults in war zones at home and abroad is that there are three dark secrets that children learn, three dark secrets that children learn from exposure to violent trauma. The first of these I call "Snowden's secret," and it refers to a book by Joseph Heller, *Catch-22* (1961). During the course of war-time combat on an American airplane, a character comes to understand what happens to human bodies when they are exposed to human violence. He witnesses the effect of shrapnel on the human body, in the form of another crew member, Snowden. Snowden's secret is that the human body, which appears strong and tough, is really just a fragile bag filled with gooey stuff and lumps. This knowledge is itself traumatic; it changes you forever, as anyone who has worked in an emergency room or visited with victims of war comes to understand. This is one of the dark secrets that children have to contend with. How do you rebuild your understanding of human life once you have learned Snowden's secret up close and personal?   9

A second dark secret that children learn I call "Dantrell's secret." The reference here is to a little boy in Chicago, seven-year-old Dantrell Davis, who was walked to school by his mother one day in a dangerous neighborhood. When they got to school, there were policemen on either corner, and there were teachers standing on the front steps of the school. But when his mother let go of his hand and he walked the last seventy-five feet from her hand to the teacher's hand, he was shot in the back of the head and killed. What do other children learn from his death? What other children learned from his death is that adults cannot protect you. And this is one of the darkest secrets of all that violent trauma can teach, that you as a child are alone. And if children understand that they are alone, they naturally turn to each other and to themselves to replace the adults gone missing in action.   10

So a nine-year-old boy living in a dangerous area, when I asked him what it would take to make him feel safer, told me "if I had a gun of my own." A boy in Michigan said to me, "If I join a gang I am 50 percent safe; if I don't join a gang I am zero percent safe."

11   Adults don't enter into the equation. As we think about violence, we also have to think about the messages of strength and competence that we as adults send children and youths. The issue is our capacity and willingness to protect them. This is why a program like Mad Dads (begun in Omaha, Nebraska) makes sense. Mad Dads is a program in which adult men go out on the streets of their community with green jackets on to send a physical message that says to children, "We the adults of your community are in charge, not fifteen-year-olds with guns." This brave foolish act is essential to address the damage done by Dantrell's secret.

12   A third dark secret that children learn I call "Milgram's secret" from research conducted by psychologist Stanley Milgram many years ago on what he called the Eichmann Effect. In Milgram's study, normal people were put in a situation in which they were encouraged to behave barbarously, violently—to inflict horrible pain on a defenseless victim. They did it. When it comes to violence, "anything is possible." That is the secret unlocked by Milgram's research, the secret that victims and perpetrators share. None of us is immune from finding the wrong situation. Any of us can commit acts of atrocity. Children in Mozambique learned the secret when they saw their parents beheaded and then cooked in a pot. Children in Guatemala learned the secret when they saw their villages burned and their neighbors executed.

13   We made a film some years ago at Cornell called *I Still Can't Say It* about a child abuse prevention program. In the course of the film, one of the teachers discloses that she herself was a victim of abuse as a child. And she illustrates Milgram's secret. She says, "When I was a little girl my mama used to beat me. One day the police were called and they came to my house and they interviewed me and they said is your mama beating you. And I said no and they went away." Now thirty years later she looks into the camera and she says, "Later that day my mama came home and she said to me, 'Why didn't you tell the police that I beat you?' And I looked her in the eye and I said, 'cause you could kill me.'" Because you could kill me. As a child, she understood Milgram's secret, that when it comes to violence, anything is possible.

14   As I meditate upon these secrets and how to understand them, I am constantly drawn to the fact that there are at least three voices that we can use to make sense of violence in human experiences, three voices to help us understand and to develop efforts to prevent and to treat and to intervene. The first voice is the voice of social science. It is the voice of statistics, of empirical research, of epidemiology. It focuses on the social toxicity of images of viciousness in the life of children and asks us to understand posttraumatic stress disorder as Robert Pynoos (Pynoos and Nader 1988) has led us to understand it. It asks us to understand what Bruce Perry and his colleagues (1995) has been finding in his research on the impact of violence, trauma, and deprivation on brain development and the eventual impact of that damage on the very ability to think and reason morally. It is really about the psychological wounds of violent trauma, and we have come to understand it pretty well. We have come to understand that experiencing the psychological wounds of violent trauma creates risk for future development, and, by the same token, we have come to understand

that this knowledge can lead to programs. For example, Kellam and his colleagues (1994) developed a program called "The Good Behavior Game" that demonstrates its ability to reduce aggressive behavior in children starting at age six and continuing to a later age. In our own work, we have developed a book for children called *Let's Talk about Living in a World with Violence* (Garbarino 1993), and recently our research has shown that it too can reduce aggressive behavior in young children (Bolger et al. 1997). This emphasis on young children is important, because one of the conclusions of various longitudinal studies (e.g., National Research Council 1993) is that by age eight, patterns of aggression and violence become so well established, crystallized, and stabilized that without intervention they begin to predict onto adulthood. So we have to act early in this social science voice to understand the early origins of violence and to intervene to prevent it from continuing.

But this is not the only voice for understanding and intervening. There is a second, 15 deeper voice that Bert Cohler (1991) at the University of Chicago calls "Human Studies." What he means is that there is an individual narrative account, a life story, a life history that each of us tells. And this act of making sense of life experience is a very important influence in the outcome of that experience. In fact, Cohler goes so far as to say it is not the experience of bad things early in life that predicts later difficulties but the quality of the story one can tell about that life, the making sense of it. Bessel Van der Kolk (1994), a psychiatrist working in Boston, has found that if children who are exposed to violent trauma early in life cannot make sense of it, they are in for a lifetime of difficulty. He finds, for example, that among his patients who have experienced violent trauma before the age of five when he asks the question, "Have you given up all hope of finding meaning in your life?" 75 percent answer "Yes."

This is what I would call the philosophical wound of violent trauma. The threat that it 16 poses, the injury that it produces, is to our sense of meaningfulness. The social toxicity that perpetuates this is the shallow materialistic culture in which more and more people around the world live—what is now being called "affluenza."

I think traumatized American children are particularly at risk in this regard because 17 of the shallowness of the culture around them, culture that we are exporting to the world with growing rapidity. The fact that there is nothing more to life than shopping and material acquisition is linked to nihilism in a culture that has no depth. And without any depth, where can children and youths at risk draw a compelling life story? But even these human studies, these narrative accounts, are not the whole story and not the only voice that we can use to understand what living in a world of violence means to children and youths.

There is a third voice, a voice I would call "soul-searching." This is the voice that be- 18 gins from the fact that we are not best understood as animals with complicated brains but we humans are first and foremost to be understood as spiritual beings having a physical experience in the world. Once this is recognized, we see that the third wound of violent trauma is not so much an injury but a spiritual challenge. The spiritual challenge of violent trauma is that it diverts us from the path of enlightenment (Garbarino and Bedard 1997), It diverts us from the path of being fully in touch with our nature as spiritual beings.

Violent trauma tends to divert us from this path to a series of dead ends. For example, 19 it may divert us to the quest for revenge which is fundamentally against the human spirit.

Some cultures contain the proverb, "If you begin a journey of revenge start by digging two graves; one for your enemy and one for yourself." That is a very spiritual message which I think is grounded in psychological realities. For inspiration, for intervention, for a basis for soul-searching, we can look to something like Joe Marshall's book *Street Soldier* (1996) in which he recognizes that without this spiritual depth to an intervention program with violently traumatized children, there is very little hope of their recovery because they have experienced the psychological wounds, the philosophical wounds, and the unmet spiritual challenge of trauma.

20   Here, too, American culture and increasingly world culture is toxic for the victims of violent trauma. Increasingly, the Western view of the world predominates. What is at the heart of that worldview? Our Native American colleagues from the earliest days of their contacts with Euro-American culture were very cognizant of the puzzling facts that European Americans thought of the world as being dead, that the trees were simply standing wood, that the animals were simply walking flesh. They were puzzled and often disturbed and depressed by this deadness in the way we looked at the world, when they saw the world as alive, with spirits everywhere.

21   I think particularly now we need to understand the aliveness of the entire universe, the spiritual unity of all of existence because indeed we are spiritual beings. I see this now particularly as I interview boys who are incarcerated in a maximum security institution because of murder and other acts of severe violence. It is a peculiar kind of maximum security institution, because unlike most of them, the boys are safe. This is unusual for a maximum security facility. But this one functions so well, the boys feel safe usually for the first time in their life. So, on the one hand, they are safe, but on the other hand, they are immobilized so that their energy cannot be diverted into guns or drugs or girls or cars or jewelry or gold or money. So they are immobilized. They are safe and immobilized. They need to be in a place like this that encourages reflection and discipline, without the "temptations" of the socially toxic environments from which they come (and to which most will return eventually). I think the model for such a setting is not the power-oriented "boot camp," which has garnered so much attention recently, but rather the reflection-oriented "monastery," where the vows of "obedience, chastity, and poverty" are coupled with meditation, reflection, study, and soul-nourishing work. This is what the most traumatized violent youths need, because all that is left for them is to go inward to their deepest core and upward, to make touch with the grandest spiritual realities that they can discover and as a result grow in wisdom in ways that were previously unavailable to them.

22   I would like to close by reminding each of us that whatever our religious allegiance or cultural traditions, we share a common spiritual ancestry and a common spiritual aspiration. Therefore, we can find common ground in dealing with violence-related trauma. Each and every day, each of us as professionals and advocates should take a moment to meditate and to reflect on how well we are prepared for the spiritual journey that it will take to transform the world, because as Mahatma Gandhi said, "You must be the change you wish to see in the world." Our professional training teaches to think and act, but the foundation for that thinking and action must be a solid spiritual and metaphysical base. Breathe and reflect, then think and act.

REFERENCES

Bolger, K., C. Collins, J. Darcy, and J. Garbarino. 1997. *Evaluation of a violence prevention program.* Ithaca, NY: Family Life Development Center, Cornell University.

Cohler, B. 1991. The life story and the study of resilience and response to adversity. *Journal of Narrative and Life History* 1:169–200.

Garbarino, J. 1993. *Let's talk about living in a world with violence.* Chicago, IL: Erikson Institute for Advanced Study in Child Development.

———. 1995. *Raising children in a socially toxic environment.* San Francisco: Jossey-Bass.

Garbarino, J., and C. Bedard. 1997. The spiritual challenges to children facing violent trauma. *Childhood 3:*467–478.

Garbarino, J., N. Dubrow, K. Kostelny, and C. Pardo. 1992. *Children in danger: Coping with the consequences of community violence.* San Francisco: Jossey-Bass.

Garbarino, J., and K. Kostelny. 1996. The effects of political violence on Palestinian children: An accumulation of risk model. *Child Development 67:*33–45.

Garbarino, J., K. Kostelny, and N. Dubrow. 1991. *No place to be a child: Growing up in a war zone.* New York: Lexington Books.

Heller, J. 1961. *Catch-22.* New York: Simon and Schuster.

Kellam, S. G., G. W. Rebok, N. Lalongo, and L. S. Mayer. 1994. The course and malleability of aggressive behavior from early first grade into middle school: Results of a developmental epidemiology-based preventive trial. *Journal of Child Psychology and Psychiatry and Allied Disciplines 35:*259–81.

Marshall, J. 1996. *Street soldier.* New York: Delacorte.

National Research Council. 1993. *Understanding and preventing violence.* Washington, DC: National Academy Press.

Perry, B., R. Pollard, T. Blakley, W. Baker, and D. Vigilante. 1995. Childhood trauma, the neurobiology of adaptation, and "use-dependent" development of the brain: How "states" become traits. *Infant Mental Health Journal 16:*271–91.

Pynoos, R., and K. Nader. 1988. Psychological first aid and treatment approach to children exposed to community violence: Research implications. *Journal of Traumatic Stress 1:*445–73.

Sameroff, A., R. Seifer, R. Barocas, M. Zax, and S. Greenspan. 1987. Intelligence quotient scores of 4-year-old children: Socio-environmental risk factors. *Pediatrics 79:*343–50.

Van der Kolk, B. 1994, October. *Meaning and trauma.* Presentation to the Rochester Symposium on Developmental Psychopatholgy, University of Rochester, Rochester, NY.

FOR CLASS DISCUSSION

1. Analyze and evaluate the sources of disagreement among these writers concerning the causes of teen violence by applying the first set of guide questions on page 465. What kinds of causal reasoning and evidence do these articles incorporate in their efforts to make their case? Which article do you think offers the most convincing causal analysis? Which article helped you to see the problem of teen violence in a new way?

2. Often it is easier to cast blame than it is to propose constructive means for dealing with a problem. How do some of these articles frame their proposals for grappling with teen violence? Which proposals seem to be the most promising?

3. Choose one of the arguments for closer analysis, applying the second set of guide questions on pages 465–66.

OPTIONAL WRITING ASSIGNMENT   A local school board is holding open meetings to discuss ways to prevent school violence and keep children safe. Attended by city council members, school administrators, teachers, business leaders, parents, and other interested residents, these meetings are considering such proposals as encouraging parents to restrict their kids' television viewing and the amount of time they spend playing violent video games, having schools institute rules that all students wear identification tags and report all violent threats, and having the community offer more after-school and weekend programs for kids. Drawing on your reading, personal experience, and any other research you may have done, compose a speech that proposes a workable plan for addressing what you see as a major contributing factor to the violence. What course of action do you propose? You may choose to emphasize preventative measures or security.

THE SOCIAL IMPACT
OF POPULAR CULTURE

From "A Sickness in the Soul"

Michael Medved

This reading is an excerpt from the opening chapter of a controversial book by the film critic Michael Medved, Hollywood vs. America: Popular Culture and the War on Traditional Values *(1992). This book helped start the "cultural wars against Hollywood"—a largely middle-class movement aimed at attacking the values of popular media. When Medved showed an outline of his proposed book to a movie industry friend, the friend replied: "[I]f you insist on going forward with something like this, you're going to become the most hated man in Hollywood."*

ALIENATING THE AUDIENCE

1   America's long-running romance with Hollywood is over.

2   As a nation, we no longer believe that popular culture enriches our lives. Few of us view the show business capital as a magical source of uplifting entertainment, romantic in-spiration, or even harmless fun. Instead, tens of millions of Americans now see the enter-

tainment industry as an all-powerful enemy, an alien force that assaults our most cherished values and corrupts our children. The dream factory has become the poison factory.

The leaders of the industry refuse to acknowledge this rising tide of alienation and hostility. They dismiss anyone who dares to question the impact of the entertainment they produce as a "right-wing extremist" or a "religious fanatic." They self-righteously assert their own right to unfettered free expression while condemning as "fringe groups" all organizations that plead for some sense of restraint or responsibility. In the process, Hollywood ignores the concerns of the overwhelming majority of the American people who worry over the destructive messages so frequently featured in today's movies, television, and popular music.   3

Dozens of recent studies demonstrate the public's deep disenchantment. In 1989, for instance, an Associated Press/Media General poll showed that 82 percent of a scientifically selected sample felt that movies contained too much violence; 80 percent found too much profanity; and 72 percent complained of too much nudity. By a ratio of more than three to one, the respondents believed that "overall quality" of movies had been "getting worse" as opposed to "getting better."   4

In 1990, a *Parents* magazine poll revealed similar attitudes toward television. Seventy-one percent of those surveyed rated today's TV as "fair, poor, or terrible." Seventy-two percent of this sample supported strict prohibitions against "ridiculing or making fun of religion" on the air, while 64 percent backed restrictions on "ridiculing or making fun of traditional values, such as marriage and motherhood." A Gallup Poll in 1991 turned up additional evidence of the public's suspicious and resentful attitude toward televised entertainment. Fifty-eight percent of Americans said that they are "offended frequently or occasionally" by prime-time programming; only three percent believed that TV portrayed "very positive" values.   5

This widespread concern over the messages of the popular culture stems from an increasingly common conviction that mass entertainment exacerbates our most serious social problems. A *Time*/CNN survey in 1989 showed that 67 percent believe that violent images in movies are "*mainly* to blame" for the national epidemic of teenage violence; 70 percent endorse "greater restraints on the showing of sex and violence" in feature films. A *Los Angeles Times* survey of the same year reported 63 percent who assert that television "encourages crime," while a 1991 *Newsweek*/Gallup Poll showed 68 percent who hold that today's movies have a "considerable" or "very great" effect in causing real-life violence. . . .   6

While searching for scapegoats, the entertainment industry ignores the obvious: that Hollywood's crisis is, at its very core, a crisis of values. It's not "mediocrity and escapism" that leave audiences cold, but sleaze and self-indulgence. What troubles people about the popular culture isn't the competence with which it's shaped, but the messages it sends, the view of the world it transmits.   7

Hollywood no longer reflects—or even respects—the values of most American families. On many of the important issues in contemporary life, popular entertainment seems to go out of its way to challenge conventional notions of decency. For example: 8

- Our fellow citizens cherish the institution of marriage and consider religion an important priority in life; but the entertainment industry promotes every form of sexual adventurism and regularly ridicules religious believers as crooks or crazies.

- In our private lives, most of us deplore violence and feel little sympathy for the criminals who perpetrate it; but movies, TV, and popular music all revel in graphic brutality, glorifying vicious and sadistic characters who treat killing as a joke.

- Americans are passionately patriotic, and consider themselves enormously lucky to live here; but Hollywood conveys a view of the nation's history, future, and major institutions that is dark, cynical, and often nightmarish.

- Nearly all parents want to convey to their children the importance of self-discipline, hard work, and decent manners; but the entertainment media celebrate vulgar behavior, contempt for all authority, and obscene language—which is inserted even in "family fare" where it is least expected.

9   As a working film critic, I've watched this assault on traditional values for more than a decade. Not only have I endured six or seven movies every week, year after year, but I've also received a steady stream of letters from moviegoers who are upset by one or another of Hollywood's excesses. At times, they blame me for failing to warn them ardently enough about avoiding a particular film; in other cases they are writing to express their pent-up frustration with an industry that seems increasingly out of control and out of touch. My correspondents frequently use words such as "disgusting" or "pathetic" to describe the sorry state of today's films. In 1989 a young woman from Westport, Connecticut, expressed these sentiments with memorable clarity. "The problem is that whenever I take a chance and go against my better judgment and venture back into a movie theater," she wrote, "I always feel like a worse person when I come out. I'm embarrassed for the people who made this trash, and I'm embarrassed for myself. It's like watching the stuff that I've just watched has made me a smaller human being. Isn't that sad?"

10   It *is* terribly sad, especially in view of the technical brilliance that turns up in so many of Hollywood's most recent productions. When people express their disappointment at the generally low level of contemporary films, they seldom indict the camera work, the editing, the set design, or even the acting. In fact, these components of moviemaking have reached a level of consistent competence—even artistry—that would be the envy of Hollywood's vaunted Golden Age. I regularly marvel at gorgeous and glowing visual images, captured on screen in the service of some pointless and heartless waste of celluloid, or sympathize with an ensemble of superbly talented performers, acting their hearts out, and trying to make the most of empty material that is in no way worthy of them. If Robert De Niro and Dustin Hoffman have failed to inspire the sort of devoted and consistent following once enjoyed by Jimmy Stewart or John Wayne, it is not because they are less capable as actors. What ails today's films has nothing to do with the prowess or professionalism of the filmmakers. The true sickness is in the soul.

"A PERFORMANCE PIECE BY MICHAEL JACKSON"

11   This heartbreaking combination of dazzling technique wedded to a puerile and degrading purpose recently shocked the country in one of the most heavily hyped entertainment "events" in history: the world premiere of the music video "Black or White," from Michael Jackson's album *Dangerous.*

On November 14, 1991, Fox Network, MTV, and Black Entertainment Television simul- 12
taneously broadcast the first showing of this eleven-minute extravaganza, which had been
created by director John Landis at an unprecedented cost of $7.2 million. To prepare the
public for the momentous occasion of the televised premiere, Epic Records released the
song (without the accompanying images) to radio stations just two days in advance. Within
twenty-four hours, "Black or White," described by the record company as "a rock 'n' roll
dance song about racial harmony," had been added to the playlists of 96 percent of America's 237 Top 40 radio stations. This broke the previous record for a first-day release—
94 percent—which had been set by Madonna's "Like a Prayer" in 1989.

On the fateful Thursday night of the televised premiere, an estimated 40 million indi- 13
viduals tuned in—helping Fox Network score the highest ratings of any night in its five-
year history. To insure maximum exposure to the children and preteens who make up such
an important part of Michael Jackson's core audience, the video featured well-advertised
cameo appearances by both TV favorite Bart Simpson and diminutive movie star Macaulay
(*Home Alone*) Culkin.

The video begins, in fact, with a tender domestic scene between Culkin and George 14
Wendt (of TV's *Cheers*), playing his irritable dad. Macaulay is upstairs in his room, happily
listening to music, when his father orders him to turn it down, threatening the child with
a wagging finger. In response, the adorable boy hauls some huge amplifiers and speakers
downstairs, tells Dad to "Eat this!" and proceeds to blast the music at such an ear-shattering
level that he literally blows his parent through the roof.

The video proceeds to a display of a dizzying succession of more or less random im- 15
ages, including dancing Cossacks in the Kremlin, whooping Native Americans in feathers
and paint, and Michael and a partner hoofing their way through hundreds of speeding cars
on a busy freeway. The most memorable sequence involves a series of fifteen magical transformations in the course of little more than a minute, using the costly computer-generated
special effect called "morphing" and made popular by *Terminator 2.*

The most troublesome transformation comes near the end of this incoherent epic, as 16
the song concludes and the soundtrack falls silent except for a selection of jungle growls,
screeches, and roars. A stalking black panther turns miraculously into Michael Jackson as
we've never seen him before—attempting a feeble impersonation of a sulky, menacing,
inner-city tough guy, tap-dancing down a wet, deserted street. As if to prove his manliness,
Michael grabs repeatedly at his crotch, with close-ups showing our hero pulling the zipper
of his pants suggestively up and down. *Entertainment Weekly* magazine later counted thirteen instances in which the superstar touched his "private parts," and at one point he per-
forms an exaggerated simulation of masturbation. Finally, this inane episode reaches its
creepy climax, as Jackson picks up a garbage can to shatter a store window, and uses a crowbar to savagely bust up a parked car, for no apparent reason whatever. As director John Landis helpfully explained in an interview prior to the premiere broadcast: "The epilogue is
really a performance piece by Michael Jackson that can stand totally on its own. It's essentially an improvisation of Michael's."

The national television audience failed to appreciate that improvisation. Immediately 17
following the telecast, switchboards at MTV, Fox Network, and all the network affiliates lit
up with outraged complaints. One Fox official commented: "In all my years of television,
I never saw anything like it. We couldn't believe the volume, and we couldn't believe the

intensity. It was like a tidal wave." A spokesman for Jackson's production company confirmed that negative feedback was coming at them "from all directions."

18   Within twenty-four hours, the chagrined superstar agreed to delete the controversial four-minute epilogue from all future versions of his video and issued an elaborate apology to his fans. "It upsets me to think that 'Black or White' could influence any child or adult to destructive behavior, either sexual or violent," his statement read. "I've always tried to be a good role model and therefore have made these changes to avoid any possibility of affecting any individual's behavior. I deeply regret any pain or hurt that the final segment of 'Black or White' has caused children, their parents, or any other viewers."

19   Fox Network issued a lame apology of its own, admitting that "based on calls we've received, the strong symbolism used in one sequence overshadowed the film's message about racial harmony. We apologize to anyone who interpreted that sequence as sexually suggestive or violent and was offended."

20   It is impossible to imagine how anyone could possibly interpret the sequence as anything *other* than "sexually suggestive or violent"—after all, toying with your fly in intense close-up and using a crowbar to shatter a parked car amount to the sort of "symbolism" that is hardly ambiguous.

21   The unanswerable question about this entire affair is how the experienced executives at the network, the record company, and Jackson's PR agency could seem to be so sincerely surprised by the public's outraged response. Did it never occur to them that people might find it more than a bit distasteful to use Macaulay Culkin and Bart Simpson to promote a video freak show that unequivocally encouraged vandalism and crotch-grabbing as forms of self-expression? With so many tens of millions of dollars riding on the outcome, with Michael's album setting all-time records for both its production and promotional costs, how could they afford to be so blind?

22   The lessons of this astonishing affair mirror three of the major arguments that I am advancing in this book.

23   First, the Michael Jackson fiasco shows that some of the most powerful, highly paid, and widely respected titans in Hollywood are hopelessly out of touch with the public they are trying to reach. They don't begin to understand the values of the average American family, or the special concerns of the typical parents who worry about unwholesome influences on their children.

24   Second, the Jackson affair clearly demonstrates that the American people understand that media images influence real-life behavior. The entertainment industry may deny its own impact, but ordinary citizens know better. They know perfectly well that if tens of millions of kids watch repeatedly as Michael Jackson gleefully smashes a car with a crowbar, then their own car is that much more likely to get smashed someday—and their own kids are that much more likely to try some smashing. The logic of this assumption is so obvious and inescapable that only the most shameless entertainment executives and their hired academic experts would even attempt to argue against it.

25   Third, the outcome of the "Black or White" controversy proves that an outraged audience can force changes on even the most powerful figures in show business. As a result of the spontaneous public outcry, Michael Jackson and his associates agreed to the uncomfortable and expensive expedient of cutting four questionable minutes from their eleven-

minute video. Similar pressure, applied in a sustained and coordinated manner on a range of issues in American entertainment, could alter the entire direction of the popular culture.

The Artist as Citizen

Barbra Streisand

Singer, actor, and political activist Barbra Streisand delivered this speech at the John F. Kennedy School of Government at Harvard University. Streisand takes a stand in the cultural wars, arguing for public money to support the arts, protesting right-wing censorship, and defending moviemakers and artists as responsible, socially progressive voices. The speech was published in New Perspectives Quarterly *in Spring 1995.*

A year ago, I was much more optimistic than I am today. We had seven women in the Senate, bringing the hope of full representation for more than half the population. And we had a President who judged our ethnic, cultural and artistic diversity as a source of strength rather than weakness.   1

Then came the election of 1994, and suddenly the progress of the recent past seemed threatened by those who hunger for the "good old days" when women and minorities knew their place. In this resurgent reactionary mood, artists derided as the "cultural elite" are convenient objects of scorn; and those institutions that have given Americans access to artistic works—such as the National Endowment for the Arts (NEA) and the Corporation for Public Broadcasting (PBS)—are in danger of being abolished.   2

Part of the profound conflict is between those who would widen freedom and those who would narrow it; those who defend tolerance and those who view it as a threat.   3

All great civilizations have supported the arts. However, the new Speaker of the House, citing the need to balance the budget, insists that the arts programs should be the first to go. But the government's contribution to the NEA and PBS is actually quite meager. To put it in perspective, the entire budget of the NEA is equal to one F-22 fighter jet—a plane that some experts say may not even be necessary—yet the Pentagon is planning to buy 442 of them. One less plane could fund the whole arts budget! Seventy-two billion dollars for fighterjets—that is real money. On the other hand, PBS costs each taxpayer less than one dollar a year and National Public Radio, 29 cents annually.   4

Perhaps, then, balancing the budget is not at issue; maybe it's about shutting the minds and mouths of artists who might have something thought-provoking to say.   5

William Bennett, the former United States education secretary who called recently for the elimination of the arts agencies, charged that they were corrupt for supporting artists whose work undermines "mainstream American values." Art does not exist only to entertain—but also to challenge one to think, to provoke, even to disturb, in a constant search for the truth. To deny artists, or any of us, free expression and free thought—or worse, to force us to conform to some rigid notion of "mainstream American values"—is to weaken the very foundation of our democracy.   6

7   The far right is waging a war for the soul of America by making art a partisan issue; by trying to cut these arts programs, which bring culture, education and joy into the lives of ordinary Americans, they are hurting the very people they claim to represent.

8   I find it ironic that Newt Gingrich claims that "the NEA and PBS are protected by a bunch of rich upper-class people." Isn't it hypocritical to lobby for tax cuts for these same rich upper-class people, but resent them when they try to protect the arts?

9   The persistent drumbeat of cynicism on the talk shows and in the new Congress reeks of disrespect for the arts and artists. But what else is new? Even Plato said that artists were nothing but troublemakers and wanted to ban poets from his perfect republic. In Victorian times there were signs requiring actors and dogs to eat in the kitchen. As recently as last year, artists who have spoken out politically have been derided as airheads, bubble-heads and nitwits—and this is not just by someone like Rush Limbaugh, who has called people in my industry the "spaced-out Hollywood left"—it is also the rhetoric of respectable publications.

10   The editor of *The New Republic* wrote of actors: "In general, they are an excruciating bunch of egomaniacs. They have little to say for themselves . . . and their politics are uniformly idiotic." To me, this is about jealousy. He specifically singled out Paul Newman, Whoopi Goldberg and Tom Hanks as subjects for his wrath after last year's Academy Awards.

11   What is the sin? Is it caring about your country? Why should the actor give up his role as citizen just because he's in show business? For his role in the movie *Philadelphia,* Tom Hanks had to learn quite a bit about being a gay man with AIDS. Should he have remained silent on this issue? For 30 years, Paul Newman has been an outspoken defender of civil liberties and a major philanthropist. Would it be better if he just made money and played golf? Should Whoopi Goldberg retreat into her home and not do anything for the homeless? Or is Robert Redford a bubblehead because he knows more about the environment than most members of Congress?

12   Imagine talking about the leaders of any other group in our society this way—say, leaders of the steelworkers union, agribusiness, or chief executives of the automobile industry. Imagine having this kind of contempt for an industry that is second only to aerospace in export earnings abroad. According to *Business Week,* Americans spent $340 billion on entertainment in 1993. Maybe policy makers could learn something from an industry that makes billions while the government owes trillions.

13   The presumption is that people in my profession are too insulated, too free-thinking, too subversive. One can almost hear the question—are you now or have you ever been a member of the Screen Actors Guild? Never mind that the former president of our guild did become President of the United States. The Hollywood smear seems to apply only to liberals.

14   Ironically, contempt for the artist as citizen is often expressed by those most eager to exploit the celebrity of the entertainer. Both journalists and politicians feed off the celebrity status of the successful artist. We can attract a crowd and raise astounding amounts of money for the politicians—and make good copy for the journalists. Which is precisely why we are courted and resented by both. I recall various leading newspapers and magazines trying to entice Hollywood celebrities to join their tables at the White House correspondents' dinner, only to trash them afterward. One can almost hear them thinking—you make money, you're famous, you have to have political opinions, too?

But we, as people, are more than what we do as performers, professors or plumbers; we also are—and we also should be—participants in the larger life of society.   15

In the past, in the days of the dominant movie studios, an artist wasn't allowed to express political opinions. But with the breakup of the studio system, creative people gained independence. And with the rise of the women's, environmental and gay rights movements, there has been an increase in artists who support liberal causes.   16

Most artists are on the humanist, compassionate side of public debate because it is consistent with the work we do. The basic task of the artist is to explore the human condition. In order to do what we do well, the writer, the director, the actor has to inhabit other people's psyches, understand other people's problems. We have to walk in other people's shoes and live in other people's skins. This does tend to make us more sympathetic to politics that are more tolerant. In our work, in our preparation and in our research, we are continuously trying to educate ourselves. And with learning comes compassion. Education is the enemy of bigotry and hate. It's hard to hate someone you truly understand.   17

Our participation in politics is a natural outgrowth of what we do, and it can and should be a responsible use of celebrity. Since we do have the ability to raise issues, reach people and influence opinion, as with Charlton Heston lobbying against gun control and, thank God, for the NEA, we do have a greater responsibility to be informed.   18

I will not defend everything that comes out of the entertainment industry. A lot of junk is produced; gratuitously violent, sexist, exploitive and debasing of the human spirit. I don't like it and I won't defend it. This is a profit-driven industry that produces the best and the worst in its attempt to find a market.   19

Further, the far right rarely attacks the violent movies—in fact, their candidates campaign alongside some of the major practitioners of this so-called art form. What disturbs them is often the best work of the mass media. They have attacked programming, beginning with *All in the Family* because it dealt with the controversial issues of racism and sexism. They attacked *Murphy Brown* which is a thoughtful attempt to deal with American lives that, for better or for worse, are very different from the lives of Ozzie and Harriet.   20

Art is the signature of a generation; artists have a way of defining the times. Marian Anderson, singing on the steps of the Lincoln Memorial because, as a black woman, she was forbidden to sing at Constitution Hall, forced Americans to confront the outrageousness of segregation. Art can illuminate, enlighten, inspire. Art finds a way to be constructive. It becomes heat in cold places; it becomes light in dark places.   21

When there was chaos in the 1960s, Bob Dylan said it was like "Blowin' in the Wind." During the riots of the 1960s, when people tried to explain the inexplicable, Aretha Franklin sang simply what was being asked for, "R-E-S-P-E-C-T."   22

Then there are the movies that spoke for their times. The movie version of John Steinbeck's *The Grapes of Wrath* brought the sad reality of the Depression home to those who wanted to ignore it. In the 1940s, a movie called *Gentleman's Agreement* raised the issue of anti-semitism in America. *In the Heat of the Night* was named Best Picture of 1967 and is remembered for its unsparing look at the issue of race. *Mr. Smith Goes to Washington* focused on buying votes and favors—a problem we still haven't solved. A generation ago, *Inherit the Wind* took on the Scopes trial and the subordination of science to one narrow   23 religious view—and the movie is powerfully relevant today in light of the Christian Coalition's efforts to reintroduce creationism into the public school curriculum.

24   Just last year, we saw a motion picture called *Schindler's List* bring the subject of the Holocaust to millions of people around the world. Steven Spielberg rescued it from fading newsreels and recast it in black and white that made it vivid, real and undeniable.

25   Moviemakers can be late to a subject, or afraid, but often they are brave and ahead of their time. Artists were criticized for their involvement in the civil rights struggle and their early opposition to the Vietnam War. In those cases at least, I would suggest that the painters and performers were wiser than most pundits and politicians.

26   I am not suggesting that actors run the country; we have already tried that. I am suggesting, for example, that on the issue of AIDS, I would rather have America listen to Elizabeth Taylor, who had the courage to sponsor the first major fund-raiser against this dreaded disease, than to Jesse Helms, who has consistently fought legislation that would fund AIDS research.

27   Our role as artist is more controversial now because there are those, claiming the absolute authority of religion, who detest much of our work as much as they detest most of our politics. Instead of rationally debating subjects such as abortion or gay rights, they condemn as immoral those who favor choice and tolerance. They disown their own dark side and magnify everyone else's until, at the extreme, doctors are murdered in the name of protecting life. Who is this God they invoke, who is so petty and mean? Is God really against gun control and food stamps for poor children?

28   All people need spiritual values in their lives. But we can't reduce the quest for eternal meaning to a right-wing political agenda. What is dangerous about the far right is not that it takes religion seriously—most of us do—but rather that it condemns all other spiritual choices—the Buddhist, the Jew, the Muslim and many others who consider themselves to be good Christians. The wall of separation between church and state is needed precisely because religion, like art, is too important a part of the human experience to be choked by the hands of censors.

29   Artists have long felt the stranglehold of censorship by officially established religions. A 16th-century Pope ordered loincloths painted on the figures in Michelangelo's "Last Judgement"; 19th-century clerics damned Walt Whitman. Tolstoy was viewed as a heretic; and today, Islamic extremists, sanctioned by governments, are still hunting down Salman Rushdie.

30   It is interesting that Americans applaud artists in other parts of the world for speaking out, in China, for example. It is very often the artist who gives a voice to the voiceless by speaking up when no one else will. The playwright Vaclav Havel went to jail because of that. Now he is the president of his country.

31   Fortunately, there are reasonable Republicans. But I am worried about the direction in which the new Congress now seeks to take the country. I am worried about the name calling, the stereotypical labeling. I want to believe that these people have good intentions, but I think it was dangerous when Newt Gingrich developed a strategy in the last campaign of pitting President Clinton against so-called "normal Americans." The Speaker attacked again more recently when he said, "I fully expect Hollywood to have almost no concept of either normal American behavior, in terms of healthy families, healthy structures, religious insti-

tutions, conservative politics or the free enterprise system." This from a politician who held up a Hollywood movie, *Boy's Town,* as his answer to welfare reform. And, how can he say that Hollywood doesn't know anything about free enterprise?

32   Most of all, I deeply resent the notion that one politician or political party owns the franchise on family values, personal responsibility, traditional values and religion.

33   We are all normal Americans, even with our problems and complexities, including people in my community. We were not born in movie studios. We come from every part of this country and most of us are self-made. We have worked hard to get where we are and we do not forget where we came from, whether it's Iowa, Cincinnati or Brooklyn.

34   The notion of "normal Americans" has a horrible historical echo. It presupposes that there are "abnormal" Americans who are responsible for all that is wrong. The new scapegoats are members of what Gingrich calls the "counterculture McGoverniks."

35   I did a concert for George McGovern in 1972, and I still think that he would have made a better President than Richard Nixon. I am disappointed that I have read so little in defense of McGovern. Was McGovern countercultural? This son of a Republican Methodist minister has been married to the same woman for 51 years and flew 35 combat missions in World War II. Isn't it odd that his patriotism be disputed by a person who never served in the military and whose own family can hardly be called exemplary? But then again no one should have to conform to some mythical concept of the ideal family—not even Mr. Gingrich.

36   I am also very proud to be a liberal. Why is that so terrible these days? The liberals were liberators—they fought slavery, fought for women to have the right to vote, fought against Hitler, Stalin, fought to end segregation, fought to end apartheid. Thanks to liberals we have Social Security, public education, consumer and environmental protection, Medicare and Medicaid, the minimum wage law, unemployment compensation. Liberals put an end to child labor and they even gave us the five-day workweek! Such a record should be worn as a badge of honor!

37   Liberals have also always believed in public support for the arts. At the height of the Depression, Franklin Delano Roosevelt created the Works Progress Administration, which helped struggling artists. Willem de Kooning, Jackson Pollock and John Cage were among those who benefited from the support of the WPA.

38   Art was a way out for me. I represent a generation of kids who happened to benefit from government support of the arts in public schools. I was a member of the choral club at Erasmus Hall High School in Brooklyn. Sadly, the current generation of young people does not have the same opportunities.

39   How can we accept a situation in which there are no longer orchestras, choruses, libraries or art classes to nourish our children? We need more support for the arts, not less—particularly to make this rich world available to young people whose vision is choked by a stark reality. How many children, who have no other outlet in their lives for their grief, have found solace in an instrument to play or a canvas to paint on? When you take into consideration the development of the human heart, soul and imagination, the arts take on just as much importance as math or science.

40   As the difference between the elections of 1992 and 1994 shows, the outcome is not pre-ordained; progress, whatever one's definition of it, is not inevitable. I thought the current administration was doing a good job: reducing the deficit by $700 billion, creating

six million jobs, downsizing government and passing a significant amount of important legislation.

41   We also need to keep in mind some words spoken by President John F. Kennedy who said he valued what artists could give because they "knew the midnight as well as the high noon (and) understood the ordeal as well as the triumph of the human spirit." He also said, "In serving his vision of the truth, the artist best serves his nation." President Kennedy was also the first to suggest the creation of the National Endowment for the Arts.

42   Well aware that art can be controversial, he concluded, "(the artist) must often sail against the currents of his time. This is not a popular role."

43   In 1995 I continue to believe it is an indispensable role. Artists, especially those who have had success, and have won popularity in their work, not only have the right, but the responsibility, to risk the unpopularity of being committed and active. And until women are treated equally with men, until gays and minorities are not discriminated against and until children have their full rights, artists must continue to speak out. I will be one of them. Sorry, Rush, Newt and Jesse, but the artist as citizen is here to stay.

Adults Watching Children Watch South Park

Helen Nixon

Helen Nixon is a lecturer at the Language and Literacy Research Center at the University of South Australia. This article was published in the September 1999 issue of the Journal of Adolescent and Adult Literacy.

1   Like the British television series *Teletubbies,* discussed in this column by David Buckingham (Dec./Jan. 1998–99), it is clear that the U.S. series *South Park* now has the same kind of "popularity—and a notoriety—that goes well beyond its target audience" (p. 292). Although it was designed as a satirical cartoon for adults, *South Park* has clearly established a strong following with much younger viewers than its original audience of mainly 18- to 39-year-old males. As has been the case with *The Simpsons,* the language and other semiotic codes associated with *South Park* have entered the everyday lives of young people the world over.

2   In Australia, my school teacher colleagues report that their students can be overheard using such common *South Park* expressions as "holy crap, dude!" and "kick ***!" (albeit with ironic overtones and in fake American accents). I would want to argue that precisely because of its level of popularity with its child audience, and the degree of censure this has aroused in parents and teachers, *South Park* too requires serious consideration for the significant questions it raises about the relations between childhood and adulthood.

"LET'S GO DOWN TO SOUTH PARK AND HAVE OURSELVES A TIME!"

3   *South Park* is an animated series set in the small village of South Park, Colorado. Unlike its popular counterpart *The Simpsons,* whose storylines are built around the lives of

the Simpson family, *South Park* is not a variation on that United States television staple, the sitcom. Rather, the series focuses on the seasonal lives of an isolated rural community, with a particular focus on four 8-year-old boys. These characters, described by *Time* magazine as having grating voices and feeble minds, are the fat and self-centred Eric Cartman, the wussy Stan Marsh, the Jewish Kyle Broslofski, and the poverty-stricken Kenny McCormick. As these descriptions suggest, the characters are in many ways stereotypical, a fact that is emphasised by the naive, two-dimensional style of *South Park*'s animation.

Other regular characters in the *South Park* cartoon include key members of the South   4
Park Elementary School community: the children's strange teacher, Mr. Garrison; the school's grouchy bus driver, Mrs. Crabtree; and the town's only African American, the lovable school chef known simply as Chef. Some of the more unusual characters in the series include Mr. Hankey, the Christmas poo; Mr. Garrison's talking glove puppet, Mr. Hat (replaced in several episodes by Mr. Twig); Sparky, the gay dog; and Jesus, the host of the public access cable program Jesus and Pals. The names of these characters, the recurring storylines of Kenny's weekly and often violent death, and Mr. Garrison's possible mental instability and homosexuality together point to some of the sources of controversy surrounding what has been called *South Park*'s political incorrectness.

Reportedly made for about US$300,000 an episode, a third of the cost of *The Simp-*   5
sons, *South Park* was created by Trey Parker and Matt Stone, young Americans then in their mid-20s. *Newsweek* reported that Parker and Stone turned down development deals by major studios such as New Line, Warner Brothers, and Dreamworks before signing over the screening rights to cable channel Comedy Central, which guaranteed them creative control of the series. Still heavily involved in production, Parker voices the characters of Cartman, Stan, and Mr. Garrison; Stone voices the characters of Kyle, Kenny, Jesus, and Jimbo.

In one of the most outrageous but amusing twists in the series, musician and record   6
producer Isaac Hayes provides the voice of the Chef, a character who regularly bursts into sexually suggestive blues tunes while cooking such specialties as Chef's Chocolate Salty Balls and advising the children of South Park about life, love, and growing up. It is Chef who often educates the children about such realities as "Life isn't fair, children. Get used to it."

WHO IN THE WORLD WATCHES *SOUTH PARK*?

Considered by its reviewers as "too hot for mainstream television," *South Park* first   7
aired in the U.S. in August 1997 on cable TV's Comedy Central channel in a late night time slot. There it has been an outstanding ratings success, regularly producing viewing figures of up to triple the previous records set by such programs as *Absolutely Fabulous* (from Britain). In Australia, Special Broadcasting Service (SBS) began screening *South Park* in December 1997. SBS is a usually low-rated, free-to-air, minority public television channel. There, with screening in an established cult cartoon slot at 8:00 P.M. on Saturday nights, the size of the audience soon doubled and had reached more than half a million for the final episode of the first series.

By mid-1998, *South Park* became the station's second most watched program after the   8
World Cup Soccer finals. When several episodes from the second series were classified M (suitable for audiences over 15), SBS was forced to move the program to a later time slot where its ratings continued to soar.

9   It is a measure of *South Park*'s success in Australia that all three commercial, free-to-air television stations vied with SBS for rights to broadcast the third and fourth series. Recent research for SBS by market researcher A. C. Nielsen shows that *South Park* has attracted more than a million viewers, the channel's largest audience since SBS was established in 1980. Of these viewers, 60% are teens (13–17) and young adults (18–24), and 30% have never previously tuned in to the minority multicultural and multilingual broadcaster.

10   By early 1999, repeat first- and second-series episodes of *South Park* screened on SBS as well as on Foxtel pay TV's The Comedy Channel. Similarly, in the U.K. *South Park* is broadcast in a late night time slot on satellite pay TV, as well as on Channel 4, a minority television channel.

11   Across the U.S., the U.K., and Australia, therefore, *South Park* is clearly marked out in its programming as something other than child or family viewing. This means the series cannot easily be compared with such mainstream counterparts as *The Simpsons.* Clearly *South Park* is very differently positioned, both by the nature of its broadcast outlets and by the timing of its programming. Although it is not so well placed to attract the large advertising investments that come with mainstream success, *South Park* nonetheless appeals to a large viewing population that appreciates its absurd humour and originality. In the U.S., Canada, and Australia this audience includes a significant number of children as young as 8 years old, as well as teenagers and young adults. Not surprisingly this information has made the series attractive to advertisers who support popular cultural forms other than television.

THE CULT APPEAL OF *SOUTH PARK*

12   At the time of writing, Australian *South Park* viewers eagerly anticipate the screening of the third TV series and are beginning to read press reports of the release in the U.S. of trailers of *South Park: The Movie.* As the show's popularity grows, *South Park* viewers and nonviewers alike have been increasingly exposed to intertextual references to the series and other information about it. In February of 1999 alone, the character Chef was featured in a *Who Weekly* cover story about TV's most fascinating faces, cover stories about the real South Park (Fairfield, Colorado) were featured in the style magazine *The Face* and the youth music magazine *Juice,* and *South Park* stickers and posters were featured in the teen magazines *big hit* and *TV Hits.*

13   Meanwhile, the Australian Yahoo! Web guide reported that *South Park* ranked fourth in the list of most frequently searched terms and topics on the World Wide Web, and a *South Park* Does Mardi Gras float—complete with Kenny deaths—was featured in the 1999 Sydney Gay and Lesbian Mardi Gras; a fact that warranted national attention in the Australian press.

14   March 1999 saw the release of a *South Park* computer game designed for the Nintendo 64 and PCs using Windows 95/98, surely an indication of investor faith that *South Park* merchandise remains potentially lucrative in what is a mainly male youth market. At the same time, SBS reported that *South Park* has sold AUS$38 million worth of merchandise in Australia, with $11 million of that spent on T-shirts alone. Further, *South Park* mer-

chandise reportedly outsells all comparable products, including those associated with *The Simpsons,* by a ratio of 10:1. Thus despite its language and content—which make the show more likely to be classified as an adult rather than a children's program—*South Park* was quickly established as what my local press described as the hippest, hottest TV viewing for university students, children, and older folk alike. This seemed to hold true in Britain and Canada as well.

WATCHING CHILDREN WHO WATCH *SOUTH PARK*

There is no doubt, then, that children and young people the world over are now regularly tuned in to *South Park*. However, for some adults at least, the fact that children want to watch such a satirical, adult cartoon is cause for concern. Parents whose children do watch *South Park* report delicate domestic negotiations about which family members may watch which episodes in their households. Nonetheless, despite its late night time slot, children's access to the program becomes less and less possible to monitor as the series is repeated and videotaped by family and friends. It would seem valuable, therefore, for parents and teachers to give serious consideration to the reasons why some children might enjoy watching *South Park* as much as some adults do. Watching children who watch *South Park* may provide some clues.   15

My bemused colleagues report that their children's and students' talk now includes such terms from *South Park* (and *Beavis and Butthead* before that) as "cool," "dude," and "that sucks!" I had firsthand evidence of the extent of children's take-up of *South Park* language and mannerisms when I was recently entertained in rural South Australia by a friend's 8- and 12-year-old daughters. They performed for me improvised routines in the personae of Terrance and Phillip, the cartoon characters who star in the *South Park* children's favourite TV program. The girls' improvisations skillfully combined satirical comments about their daily school lives with the characters' two trademarks of high-pitched mono-tone laughter and an obsession with flatulence. Similarly, a Canadian colleague reports that the *South Park* character Kenny is frequently the subject of schoolyard chat and improvised conversations among his 14-year-old students.   16

"OH MY GOD! THEY KILLED KENNY."

Adolescents' reported fascination with the *South Park* character Kenny raises interesting questions for parents and teachers. Obviously part of that character's appeal lies in the fantasy elements of the recurring storyline with which he is associated. The predictable pattern, as well as fantasy element of the storyline, is that although Kenny is killed in nearly every episode he reappears in the following episode as if nothing had happened. Some adults understandably express concern at this supposed emphasis on killing and death, as well as the implied violence of some of the deaths.   17

However, I would want to argue that there might also be productive ways of thinking about the appeal of Kenny's death for children. It is possible, for example, to see this pattern as a contemporary, if somewhat bizarre, illustration of that well-known mythic pattern   18 of the literary hero's death, rebirth, and renewal. It is also possible to understand children's enjoyment of it as an example of an age-old narrative pleasure: the delightful anticipation of something inevitable and the gradual revelation of details about when and how it will happen. While it is true that Kenny often dies in a very gruesome cartoon fashion, with lots of associated blood and gore (as well as the immediate attention of scavenging rats), his despatch can also be very low-key. One time he was killed by a falling cart of underpants. Such variations, however silly, provide an element of surprise and suspense that children enjoy and that is comfortingly familiar to them from other popular cultural forms.

19   Another source of pleasure when Kenny dies is the anticipation of how his death will be registered by the other three boys. More often than not, each death elicits from Stan the now predictable cry of "Oh my God! They killed Kenny. You bastards!" The occasional variations on this response, designed to match an episode's particular narrative line, provide high points of dramatic and humorous contrast with previous episodes. Hence the cry sometimes changes to "Oh my God! I found a penny," or "Oh my God! They videotaped killing Kenny!"

20   On the one hand, it may be disturbing for adults to see children take pleasure in predicting when and how an 8-year-old child, albeit a cartoon character, meets his untimely death. After all, the children's pleasure challenges some of the salient features of dominant social constructions of childhood, such as its supposed vulnerability and innocence.

21   On the other hand, surely these kinds of pleasures of prediction, as well as children's delight in rhyme and repetition, are not very far removed from the socially sanctioned pleasures experienced by adults and children alike during the reading of nursery rhymes and bedtime stories.

22   A second key characteristic of the Kenny character is that what he says cannot be clearly heard by the viewer. His dialogue is always muffled and only partially audible, largely because of the orange parka hood that closely circles his face. However, although viewers cannot hear Kenny's exact words, they are nonetheless able to deduce something of their meaning. Thus teenagers' reported schoolyard imitation of Kenny's mostly incomprehensible dialogue has pedagogic potential. It has the potential, for example, to be used to illustrate a key sociolinguistic point that meaning is made by an utterance's tone and inflection working in concert with its linguistic and social context.

23   For teachers, the fact that Kenny's playmates find what he says hilariously crude raises a particular dilemma associated with the use of *South Park* as a starting point for teaching. How can teachers justify opening up for discussion what it is that Kenny might really be saying? Can they risk asking students to repeat what they are saying to each other in "Kenny code" in the school yard?

24   Indeed, one difficulty for those wishing to think seriously or write about *South Park*—whether as a potential teaching resource or not—is that much of the show, which is funny when watched, cannot be put in print. In addition, when voiced, the content is so outrageously silly, sexist, racist, or crude that you can't easily justify repeating it. When translated literally, much of *South Park* must at best be described as nonsensical and in extremely bad taste. As one Australian newspaper put it, even mass media reviews of *South*

Park simply dared not allude to most of the show's dialogue, double entendres, and sight gags. In its view, this was hysterical adults-only viewing that simply had to be seen to be believed.

Here we have, I think, at least part of the explanation for the popularity of *South Park* among school-aged children. First, like most children's cartoons, *South Park* relies heavily on spectacle. Much of the humour is conveyed in silly sounds, sight gags, and frequent pregnant pauses when the children stare blankly at the viewer, nonplussed by the silly antics of the mostly adult people around them. This is immediate, visual, and visceral entertainment that is not easily translated.   25

Second, *South Park* is not easily translated into a socially acceptable text. Nor is it easily summarised in terms of its themes or social comment. Hence, when the series was released, *Time* magazine (August 18, 1997) lamented what it saw as *South Park*'s inferiority to *The Simpsons,* claiming that "unlike *The Simpsons* and *Beavis and Butthead, South Park* is devoid of subtext—it isn't really about the emptiness of suburban life or the ugliness of youthful nihilism or the perniciousness of pop culture" (p. 74). That is, the anarchic randomness of its humour keeps the show outside the bounds of mainstream discussion and analysis. *South Park* is therefore found wanting by serious adult critics.   26

Of course, this is part of the program's appeal for young people. It successfully provides children's enjoyment with a transgressive edge. Just as watching *The Simpsons* did in the early 1990s, watching *South Park* operates as a sign among today's children and teens. It signifies their subscription to a particular antiauthoritarian and contemporary attitude. Like Kenny's muffled street-wise talk, familiarity with *South Park* operates as a shared code between peers that effectively marks them out against parents and other adults. Put simply, there is a very youthful and naughty pleasure in being complicit with a program that, according to reviewers, is an obnoxious and offensive cartoon that takes bad taste to jaw-dropping extremes.   27

All this, I suggest, points to the reason many adults feel uncomfortable about watching *South Park.* The knowledge that this often crude, shocking, and humorously offensive satire is also a cartoon being watched and enjoyed by children serves to foreground for adults both their similarity with, and yet ambivalence towards, children. As an SBS spokesperson puts it, young people enjoy the program because it is "subversive, cutting edge, and intensely realistic," while the broader audience likes it "because they know that this is what little kids can be like."   28

Of course, creators Parker and Stone are well able to anticipate such audience responses. Hence *South Park* has been described using publicity similar to that Parker and Stone provide for their fictional *Jesus and Pals* program: "Too hot for TV—this is stuff you can't see on TV." In one episode the title characters in the Canadian cartoon *Terrance and Phillip* sit down to watch American television; they find themselves watching *South Park,* only to dismiss it as "That's so juvenile!" Further, the silliness of the *Terrance and Phillip* cartoon stirs up as much controversy in the *South Park* fictional community as the *South Park* cartoon has stirred up in real life.   29

In a rebellion against *Terrance and Phillip* by South Park parents, Mrs. Broslofski leads the South Park Parent Teacher Association in a campaign against Cartoon Central for the   30 provision of better TV for South Park's children. Mr. Garrison cautions his students that "Shows like *Terrance and Phillip* are what we call toilet humour. They don't expand your minds. You see children, these kinds of shows are senseless, vile trash." Further, he is concerned that "you all seem to enjoy the show even if it isn't based on reality."

31   Hilariously, of course, regular viewers of *South Park* know that showing the TV program *Barnaby Jones* is a staple of Mr. Garrison's teaching method. Moreover, when challenged by his students about how much class time is given over to this pursuit, Mr. Garrison's defence has been that they won't get very far in life unless they pay attention to the lessons learned from TV. Adults' patronising attitude towards children, as well as their blatant hypocrisy, is yet again glaringly exposed by *South Park*'s creators, much to the delight of youthful viewers and the discomfort of some older ones.

32   Finally in this same episode, while their parents successfully protest to get *Terrance and Phillip* taken off air—only for it to be replaced by an adult program that is similarly crude and sexist—the *South Park* boys get into some serious trouble when Death comes to town. The failure of their distracted parents to heed the boys' requests for assistance leads young Stan Marsh to add some platitudes of his own: "You know, I think if parents spent less time worrying about what their kids are watching on TV, and more time worrying about what's going on in kids' lives, the world would be a better place." As on many other occasions, this adult at least has to admit that Stan does have a point.

Movie Review: "South Park *Movie Revels in Its Really Bad Behavior*"

Ron Weiskind

This article by Pittsburgh Post-Gazette *movie editor Ron Weiskind appeared at the Web site www.post-gazette.com/magazine on June 30, 1999.*

1   I was talking on the telephone to someone who had just seen *South Park: Bigger, Longer and Uncut* and who still seemed a bit shellshocked.

2   "So you don't think I should take my kids to the screening?" I said, as if I were that stupid.

3   "Don't take them even if you think they're old enough," came the reply.

4   Good advice. It will come as no surprise to anyone familiar with the TV cartoon that the movie version, freed from whatever content restrictions may still exist on cable, allows *South Park* third-graders Kyle, Stan, Kenny and Cartman to let loose with a barrage of foul language that would make longshoremen blush.

5   But there's method to this madness. The agent provocateurs behind *South Park*, co-creators Matt Stone and Trey Parker, use their regressively juvenile property as an anti-censorship screed that appears on the nation's movie screens with exquisite timing, smack dab in the middle of the post-Columbine furor over Hollywood's role in corrupting America's minors.

Parker, who directed the movie and co-wrote it with Stone, all but pleads guilty to   6
the charge and not only wears it as a badge of honor but, with typical insouciance, uses
it as justification for their actions. They're out to shock you as much as they can—and
then to make you think about why it shocks you and about what doesn't shock you but
should.

Then again, this is a pair of filmmakers who employ the most primitive animation—   7
the characters and settings are little more than paper cutouts—and snigger like adolescents
who have just discovered how much attention they can get by telling poo-poo jokes, showing irreverence toward virtually anything adults hold sacred, just plain acting gross and
demonstrating that kids really do say the darnedest things, none of them as bland as
"darnedest."

Again, their offensiveness works as a kind of defense. America could have just ignored   8
South Park. Instead, the show became for a time the hottest ticket on television and a mer-
chandising juggernaut. Some of its biggest fans are adolescents who, if movie theaters are
serious about enforcing the age limit on R movies, won't get in to see it—which won't stop
them from trying or from conning a parent into taking them.

Parents? Listen. Think of every possible permutation of the F-word. Hyphenate these   9
to words representing various members of the family, including species of pet. Imagine an
audience of cartoon 8-year-olds attending a movie where they hear all of these epithets,
then realize how many real-life under-17s want to see the movie. Once the film's characters start repeating the words at home, in school, in church, then you'll understand why
you should just say no.

Of course, you needn't go as far as the adults in the movie. They find out their kids   10
learned the words from a Canadian movie (darned foreigners) and wind up declaring war
on our northern neighbors.

To be fair, the cinematic *South Park* can boast its share of humor so goofy that one al-   11
most has to laugh. Imagine Satan and Saddam Hussein as squabbling lovers in Hell, using
the U.S.–Canada war as a springboard for taking over the world. All Saddam can think about
is sex and world domination. Satan turns out to be the sensitive one, wishing for time to
smell the roses.

The movie takes its share of potshots against the censors, the critics and celebrities   12
ranging from Winona Ryder to Brooke Shields. And amid all the swearing, the *South Park*
kids punctuate the film with nimble parodies of Broadway show anthems, of all things, the
better to heighten the absurdity of the proceedings.

To Parker and Stone, nothing is more absurd than our hysteria over bad words (or   13
sexual images) as opposed to the way Americans not only tolerate but encourage graphic
violence.

They have a point. But they conveniently forget that words have power and can hurt.   14
And even anti-censorship crusaders will acknowledge that children are not ready to see
pornography. Just watch how the *South Park* youngsters react in the scene where they
cruise sex sites on the Internet. Heck, Stan throws up every time he merely talks to the girl
he likes.

Not everything is for kids. That includes *South Park: Bigger, Longer and Uncut.*   15

Put on a Happy Face: Masking Differences between Blacks and Whites

Benjamin DeMott

This article by the well-known media and film critic Benjamin DeMott was originally published in the September 1995 issue of Harper's. *DeMott is the author of* The Trouble with Friendship: Why Americans Can't Think Straight about Race *(1995).*

1   At the movies these days, questions about racial injustice have been amicably resolved. Watch *Pulp Fiction* or *Congo* or *A Little Princess* or any other recent film in which both blacks and whites are primary characters and you can, if you want, forget about race. Whites and blacks greet one another on the screen with loving candor, revealing their common humanity. In *Pulp Fiction,* an armed black mobster (played by Samuel L. Jackson) looks deep into the eyes of an armed white thief in the middle of a holdup (played by Tim Roth) and shares his version of God's word in Ezekiel, whereupon the two men lay aside their weapons, both more or less redeemed. The moment inverts an earlier scene in which a white boxer (played by Bruce Willis) risks his life to save another black mobster (played by Ving Rhames), who is being sexually tortured as a prelude to his execution.

2   *Pulp Fiction* (gross through July: $107 million) is one of a series of films suggesting that the beast of American racism is tamed and harmless. Close to the start of *Die Hard with a Vengeance* (gross through July: $95 million) the camera finds a white man wearing sandwich boards on the corner of Amsterdam Avenue and 138th Street in Harlem. The boards carry a horrific legend: I HATE NIGGERS. A group of young blacks approach the man with murderous intent, bearing guns and knives. They are figures straight out of a national nightmare—ugly, enraged, terrifying. No problem. A black man, again played by Jackson, appears and rescues the white man, played by Willis. The black man and white man come to know each other well. In time the white man declares flatly to the black, "I need you more than you need me." A moment later he charges the black with being a racist—with not liking whites as much as the white man likes blacks—and the two talk frankly about their racial prejudices. Near the end of the film, the men have grown so close that each volunteers to die for the other.

3   *Pulp Fiction* and *Die Hard with a Vengeance* follow the pattern of *Lethal Weapon 1, 2, and 3,* the Danny Glover/Mel Gibson buddy vehicles that collectively grossed $357 million, and *White Men Can't Jump,* which, in the year of the L.A. riots, grossed $76 million. In *White Men Can't Jump,* a white dropout, played by Woody Harrelson, ekes out a living on black-dominated basketball courts in Los Angeles. He's arrogant and aggressive but never in danger because he has a black protector and friend, played by Wesley Snipes. At the movie's end, the white, flying above the hoop like a stereotypical black player, scores the winning basket in a two-on-two pickup game on an alley-oop pass from his black chum, whereupon the two men fall into each other's arms in joy. Later, the black friend agrees to find work for the white at the store he manages.

WHITE (*helpless*):   I gotta get a job. Can you get me a job?   4

BLACK (*affectionately teasing*):   Got any references?   5

WHITE (*shy grin*):   You.   6

Such dialogue is the stuff of romance. What's dreamed of and gained is a place where whites are unafraid of blacks, where blacks ask for and need nothing from whites, and where sameness of the races creates a common fund of sweet content.[1] The details of the dream matter less than the force that makes it come true for both races, eliminating the constraints of objective reality and redistributing resources, status, and capabilities. That cleansing social force supersedes political and economic fact or policy; that force, improbably enough, is friendship.   7

Watching the beaming white men who know how to jump, we do well to remind ourselves of what the camera shot leaves out. Black infants die in America at twice the rate of white infants. (Despite the increased number of middle-class blacks, the rates are diverging, with black rates actually rising.) One out of every two black children lives below the poverty line (as compared with one out of seven white children). Nearly four times as many black families exist below the poverty line as white families. More than 50 percent of African American families have incomes below $25,000. Among black youths under age twenty, death by murder occurs nearly ten times as often as among whites. Over 60 percent of births to black mothers occur out of wedlock, more than four times the rate for white mothers. The net worth of the typical white household is ten times that of the typical black household. In many states, five to ten times as many blacks as whites age eighteen to thirty are in prison.   8

The good news at the movies obscures the bad news in the streets and confirms the Supreme Court's recent decisions on busing, affirmative action, and redistricting. Like the plot of *White Men Can't Jump,* the Court postulates the existence of a society no longer troubled by racism. Because black-white friendship is now understood to be the rule, there is no need for integrated schools or a congressional Black Caucus or affirmative action. The Congress and state governors can guiltlessly cut welfare, food assistance, fuel assistance, Head Start, housing money, fellowship money, vaccine money. Justice Anthony Kennedy can declare, speaking for the Supreme Court majority last June, that creating a world of genuine equality and sameness requires only that "our political system and our society cleanse themselves . . . of discrimination."   9

The deep logic runs as follows: *Yesterday white people didn't like black people, and accordingly suffered guilt, knowing that the dislike was racist and knowing also that as*   10

---

[1] I could go on with examples of movies that deliver the good news of friendship: *Regarding Henry, Driving Miss Daisy, Forrest Gump, The Shawshank Redemption, Philadelphia, The Last Boy Scout, 48 Hours I–II, Rising Sun, Iron Eagle I–II, Rudy, Sister Act, Hearts of Dixie, Betrayed, The Power of One, White Nights, Clara's Heart, Doc Hollywood, Cool Runnings, Places in the Heart, Trading Places, Fried Green Tomatoes, Q & A, Platoon, A Mother's Courage: The Mary Thomas Story, The Unforgiven, The Air Up There, The Pelican Brief, Losing Isaiah, Smoke, Searching for Bobby Fischer, An Officer and a Gentleman, Speed, etc.*

moral persons they would have to atone for the guilt. They would have to ante up for welfare and Head Start and halfway houses and free vaccine and midnight basketball and summer jobs for schoolkids and graduate fellowships for promising scholars and craft-union apprenticeships and so on, endlessly. A considerable and wasteful expense. But at length came the realization that by ending dislike or hatred it would be possible to end guilt, which in turn would mean an end to redress: no more wasteful ransom money. There would be but one requirement: the regular production and continuous showing forth of evidence indisputably proving that hatred has totally vanished from the land.

11   I cannot tell the reader how much I would like to believe in this sunshine world. After the theater lights brighten and I've found coins for a black beggar on the way to my car and am driving home through downtown Springfield, Massachusetts, the world invented by *Die Hard with a Vengeance* and America's highest court gives way only slowly to the familiar urban vision in my windshield—homeless blacks on trash-strewn streets, black prostitutes staked out on a corner, and signs of a not very furtive drug trade. I know perfectly well that most African Americans don't commit crimes or live in alleys. I also know that for somebody like myself, downtown Springfield in the late evening is not a good place to be.

12   The movies reflect the larger dynamic of wish and dream. Day after day the nation's corporate ministries of culture churn out images of racial harmony. Millions awaken each morning to the friendly sight of Katie Couric nudging a perky elbow into good buddy Bryant Gumbel's side. My mailbox and millions of demographically similar others are choked with flyers from companies (Wal-Mart, Victoria's Secret) bent on publicizing both their wares and their social bona fides by displaying black and white models at cordial ease with one another. A torrent of goodwill messages about race arrives daily—revelations of corporate largesse, commercials, news features, TV specials, all proclaiming that whites like me feel strongly positive impulses of friendship for blacks and that those same admirable impulses are effectively eradicating racial differences, rendering blacks and whites the same. Bell-South TV commercials present children singing "I am the keeper of the world"—first a white child, then a black child, then a white child, then a black child. Because Dow Chemical likes black America, it recruits young black college grads for its research division and dramatizes, in TV commercials, their tearful-joyful partings from home. ("Son, show 'em what you got," says a black lad's father.) American Express shows an elegant black couple and an elegant white couple sitting together in a theater, happy in one another's company. (The couples share the box with an oversized Gold Card.) During the evening news I watch a black mom offer Robitussin to a miserably coughing white mom. Here's *People* magazine promoting itself under a photo of John Lee Hooker, the black bluesman. "We're these kinds of people, too," *People* claims in the caption. In the current production of *Hamlet* on Broadway, Horatio is played by a black actor. On *The 700 Club,* Pat Robertson joshes Ben Kinchlow, his black sidekick, about Ben's far-out ties.

13   What counts here is not the saccharine clumsiness of the interchanges but the bulk of them—the ceaseless, self-validating gestures of friendship, the humming, buzzing background theme: *All decent Americans extend the hand of friendship to African Americans; nothing but nothing is more auspicious for the African American future than this extended hand.* Faith in the miracle cure of racism by change-of-heart turns out to be so familiar as

to have become unnoticeable. And yes, the faith has its benign aspect. Even as they nudge me and others toward belief in magic (instant pals and no-money-down equality), the images and messages of devoted relationships between blacks and whites do exert a humanizing influence.

Nonetheless, through these same images and messages the comfortable majority tells itself a fatuous untruth. Promoting the fantasy of painless answers, inspiring groundless self-approval among whites, joining the Supreme Court in creating "cleansing" as *inevitable,* the new orthodoxy of friendship incites culture-wide evasion, justifies one political step backward after another, and greases the skids along which, tomorrow, welfare block grants will slide into state highway-resurfacing budgets. Whites are part of the solution, says this orthodoxy, if we break out of the prison of our skin color, say hello, as equals, one-on-one, to a black stranger, and make a black friend. We're part of the problem if we have an aversion to black people or are frightened of them, or if we feel that the more distance we put between them and us the better, or if we're in the habit of asserting our superiority rather than acknowledging our common humanity. Thus we shift the problem away from politics—from black experience and the history of slavery—and perceive it as a matter of the suspicion and fear found within the white heart; solving the problem asks no more of us than that we work on ourselves, scrubbing off the dirt of ill will. 14

The approach miniaturizes, personalizes, and moralizes; it removes the large and complex dilemmas of race from the public sphere. It tempts audiences to see history as irrelevant and to regard feelings as decisive—to believe that the fate of black Americans is shaped mainly by events occurring in the hearts and minds of the privileged. And let's be frank: the orthodoxy of friendship feels *nice.* It practically *consecrates* self-flattery. The "good" Bill Clinton who attends black churches and talks with likable ease to fellow worshipers was campaigning when Los Angeles rioted in '92. "White Americans," he said, "are gripped by the isolation of their own experience. Too many still simply have no friends of other races and do not know any differently." Few black youths of working age in South-Central L.A. had been near enough to the idea of a job even to think of looking for work before the Rodney King verdict, but the problem, according to Clinton, was that whites need black friends. 15

Most of the country's leading voices of journalistic conscience (editorial writers, television anchorpersons, syndicated columnists) roundly endorse the doctrine of black-white friendship as a means of redressing the inequalities between the races. Roger Rosenblatt, editor of the *Columbia Journalism Review* and an especially deft supplier of warm and fuzzy sentiment, published an essay in *Family Circle* arguing that white friendship and sympathy for blacks simultaneously make power differentials vanish and create interracial identity between us, one by one. The author finds his *exemplum* in an episode revealing the personal sensitivity, to injured blacks, of one of his children. 16

"When our oldest child, Carl, was in high school," he writes, "he and two black friends were standing on a street corner in New York City one spring evening, trying to hail a taxi. The three boys were dressed decently and were doing nothing wild or threatening. Still, no cab would pick them up. If a driver spotted Carl first, he might slow down, but he would take off again when he saw the others. Carl's two companions were familiar with this sort of abuse. Carl, who had never observed it firsthand before, burned with anger and embarrassment that he was the color of a world that would so mistreat his friends." 17

18   Rosenblatt notes that when his son "was applying to colleges, he wrote his essay on that taxi incident with his two black friends. . . . He was able to articulate what he could not say at the time—how ashamed and impotent he felt. He also wrote of the power of their friendship, which has lasted to this day and has carried all three young men into the country that belongs to them. To all of us."

19   In this homily white sympathy begets interracial sameness in several ways. The three classmates are said to react identically to the cabdrivers' snub; i.e., they feel humiliated. "[Carl] could not find the words to express his humiliation and his friends *would* not express theirs."

20   The anger that inspires the younger Rosenblatt's college-admission essay on racism is seen as identical with black anger. Friendship brings the classmates together as joint, equal owners of the land of their birth ("the country that belongs to [all of] them"). And Rosenblatt supplies a still larger vision of essential black-white sameness near the end of his essay: "Our proper hearts tell the truth," he declares, "which is that we are all in the same boat, rich and poor, black and white. We are helpless, wicked, heroic, terrified, and we need one another. We need to give rides to one another."

21   Thus do acts of private piety substitute for public policy while the possibility of urgent political action disappears into a sentimental haze. "If we're looking for a formula to ease the tensions between the races," Rosenblatt observes, then we should "attack the disintegration of the black community" and "the desperation of the poor." Without overtly mocking civil rights activists who look toward the political arena "to erase the tensions," Rosenblatt alludes to them in a throwaway manner, implying that properly adjusted whites look elsewhere, that there was a time for politicking for "equal rights" but we've passed through it. Now is a time in which we should listen to our hearts at moments of epiphany and allow sympathy to work its wizardry, cleansing and floating us, blacks and whites "all in the same boat," on a mystical undercurrent of the New Age.

22   Blacks themselves aren't necessarily proof against this theme, as witness a recent essay by James Alan McPherson in the Harvard journal *Reconstruction.* McPherson, who received the 1977 Pulitzer Prize for fiction for his collection of stories *Elbow Room,* says that "the only possible steps, the safest steps . . . small ones" in the movement "toward a universal culture" will be those built not on "ideologies and formulas and programs" but on experiences of personal connectedness.

23   "Just this past spring," he writes, "when I was leaving a restaurant after taking a [white] former student to dinner, a black [woman on the sidewalk] said to my friend, in a rasping voice, 'Hello, girlfriend. Have you got anything to spare?' " The person speaking was a female crack addict with a child who was also addicted. "But," writes McPherson, when the addict made her pitch to his dinner companion, "I saw in my friend's face an understanding and sympathy and a shining which transcended race and class. Her face reflected one human soul's connection with another. The magnetic field between the two women was charged with spiritual energy."

24   The writer points the path to progress through interpersonal gestures by people who "insist on remaining human, and having human responses. . . . Perhaps the best that can be done, now, is the offering of understanding and support to the few out of many who are capable of such gestures, rather than devising another plan to engineer the many into one."

The elevated vocabulary ("soul," "spiritual") beatifies the impulse to turn away from   25
the real-life agenda of actions capable of reducing racial injustice. Wherever that impulse
dominates, the rhetoric of racial sameness thrives, diminishing historical catastrophes affecting millions over centuries and inflating the significance of tremors of tenderness briefly
troubling the heart or conscience of a single individual—the boy waiting for a cab, the
woman leaving the restaurant. People forget the theoretically unforgettable—the caste history of American blacks, the connection between no schools for longer than a century and
bad school performance now, between hateful social attitudes and zero employment
opportunities, between minority anguish and majority fear.

How could this way of seeing have become conventional, so swiftly? How did the dogmas   26
of instant equality insinuate themselves so effortlessly into courts and mass audiences alike?
How can a white man like myself, who taught Southern blacks in the 1960s, find himself
seduced—as I have been more than once—by the orthodoxy of friendship? In the civil
rights era, the experience for many millions of Americans was one of discovery. A hitherto
unimagined continent of human reality and history came into view, inducing genuine concern and at least a temporary setting aside of self-importance. I remember with utter clarity what I felt at Mary Holmes College in West Point, Mississippi, when a black student of
mine was killed by tailgating rednecks; my fellow tutors and I were overwhelmed with how
shamefully wrong a wrong could be. For a time, we were released from the prisons of moral
weakness and ambiguity. In the year or two that followed—the mid-Sixties—the notion that
some humans are more human than others, whites more human than blacks, appeared to
have been overturned. The next step seemed obvious: society would have to admit that
when one race deprives another of its humanity for centuries, those who have done the
depriving are obligated to do what they can to restore the humanity of the deprived. The
obligation clearly entailed the mounting of comprehensive *long-term* programs of developmental assistance—not guilt-money handouts—for nearly the entire black population. The
path forward was unavoidable.

It was avoided. Shortly after the award of civil rights and the institution, in 1966, of   27
limited preferential treatment to remedy employment and educational discrimination
against African Americans, a measure of economic progress for blacks did appear in census
reports. Not much, but enough to stimulate glowing tales of universal black advance and to
launch the good-news barrage that continues to this day (headline in the *New York Times*,
June 18, 1995: "Moving On Up: The Greening of America's Black Middle Class").

After Ronald Reagan was elected to his first term, the new dogma of black-white same-   28
ness found ideological support in the form of criticism of so-called coddling. Liberal activists
of both races were berated by critics of both races for fostering an allegedly enfeebling psychology of dependency that discouraged African Americans from committing themselves to
individual self-development. In 1988, the charge was passionately voiced in an essay in
these pages, "I'm Black, You're White, Who's Innocent?" by Shelby Steele, who attributed
the difference between black rates of advance and those of other minority groups to white
folks' pampering. Most blacks, Steele claimed, could make it on their own—as voluntary
immigrants have done—were they not held back by devitalizing programs that presented
them, to themselves and others, as somehow dissimilar to and weaker than other Americans.

This argument was all-in-the-same-boatism in a different key; the claim remained that progress depends upon recognition of black-white sameness. Let us see through superficial differences to the underlying, equally distributed gift for success. Let us teach ourselves—in the words of the Garth Brooks tune—to ignore "the color of skin" and "look for . . . the beauty within."

29   Still further support for the policy once known as "do-nothingism" came from points-of-light barkers, who held that a little something might perhaps be done *if* accompanied by enough publicity. Nearly every broadcaster and publisher in America moves a bale of reportage on pro bono efforts by white Americans to speed the advance of black Americans. Example: McDonald's and the National Basketball Association distribute balloons when they announce they are addressing the dropout problem with an annual "Stay in School" scheme that gives schoolkids who don't miss a January school day a ticket to an all-star exhibition. The publicity strengthens the idea that these initiatives will nullify the social context—the city I see through my windshield. Reports of white philanthropy suggest that the troubles of this block and the next should be understood as phenomena in transition. The condition of American blacks need not be read as the fixed, unchanging consequence of generations of bottom-caste existence. Edging discreetly past a beggar posted near the entrance to Zabar's or H&H Bagels, or, while walking the dog, stepping politely around black men asleep on the sidewalk, we need not see ourselves and our fellows as uncaring accomplices in the acts of social injustice.

30   Yet more powerful has been the ceaseless assault, over the past generation, on our knowledge of the historical situation of black Americans. On the face of things it seems improbable that the cumulative weight of documented historical injury to African Americans could ever be lightly assessed. Gifted black writers continue to show, in scene after scene—in their studies of middle-class blacks interacting with whites—how historical realities shape the lives of their black characters. In *Killer of Sheep,* the brilliant black filmmaker Charles Burnett dramatizes the daily encounters that suck poor blacks into will-lessness and contempt for white fairy tales of interracial harmony; he quickens his historical themes with images of faceless black meat processors gutting undifferentiated, unchoosing animal life. Here, say these images, as though talking back to Clarence Thomas, here is a basic level of black life unchanged over generations. Where there's work, it's miserably paid and ugly. Space allotments at home and at work cramp body and mind. Positive expectation withers in infancy. People fall into the habit of jeering at aspiration as though at the bidding of physical law. Obstacles at every hand prevent people from loving and being loved in decent ways, prevent children from believing their parents, prevent parents from believing they themselves know anything worth knowing. The only true self, now as in the long past, is the one mocked by one's own race. "Shit on you, nigger," says a voice in *Killer of Sheep.* "Nothing you say matters a good goddamn."

31   For whites, these words produce guilt, and for blacks, I can only assume, pain and despair. The audience for tragedy remains small, while at the multiplex the popular enthusiasm for historical romance remains constant and vast. During the last two decades, the entertainment industry has conducted a siege on the pertinent past, systematically excising knowledge of the consequences of the historical exploitation of African Americans. Factitious renderings of the American past blur the outlines of black-white conflict, redefine the

ground of black grievances for the purpose of diminishing the grievances, restage black life in accordance with the illusory conventions of American success mythology, and present the operative influences on race history as the same as those implied to be pivotal in *White Men Can't Jump* or a BellSouth advertisement.

Although there was scant popular awareness of it at the time (1977), the television miniseries *Roots* introduced the figure of the Unscathed Slave. To an enthralled audience of more than 80 million the series intimated that the damage resulting from generations of birth-ascribed, semi-animal status was largely temporary, that slavery was a product of motiveless malignity on the social margins rather than of respectable rationality, and that the ultimate significance of the institution lay in the demonstration, by freed slaves, that no force on earth can best the energies of American Individualism. ("Much like the Waltons confronting the depression," writes historian Eric Foner, a widely respected authority on American slavery, "the family in 'Roots' neither seeks nor requires outside help; individual or family effort is always sufficient.") Ken Burns's much applauded PBS documentary *The Civil War* (1990) went even further than *Roots* in downscaling black injury; the series treated slavery, birth-ascribed inferiority, and the centuries-old denial of dignity as matters of slight consequence. (By "implicitly denying the brutal reality of slavery," writes historian Jeanie Attie, Burns's programs crossed "a dangerous moral threshold." To a group of historians who asked him why slavery had been so slighted, Burns said that any discussion of slavery "would have been lengthy and boring.")   32

Mass media treatments of the civil rights protest years carried forward the process, contributing to the "positive" erasure of difference. Big-budget films like *Mississippi Burning,* together with an array of TV biographical specials on Dr. Martin Luther King and others, presented the long-running struggle between disenfranchised blacks and the majority white culture as a heartwarming episode of interracial unity; the speed and caringness of white response to the oppression of blacks demonstrated that broadscale race conflict or race difference was inconceivable.   33

A consciousness that ingests either a part or the whole of this revisionism loses touch with the two fundamental truths of race in America; namely, that because of what happened in the past, blacks and whites cannot yet be the same; and that because what happened in the past was no mere matter of ill will or insult but the outcome of an established caste structure that has only very recently begun to be dismantled, it is not reparable by one-on-one goodwill. The word "slavery" comes to induce stock responses with no vital sense of a grinding devastation of mind visited upon generation after generation. Hoodwinked by the orthodoxy of friendship, the nation either ignores the past, summons for it a detached, correct "compassion," or gazes at it as though it were a set of aesthetic conventions, like twisted trees and fragmented rocks in nineteenth-century picturesque painting—lifeless phenomena without bearing on the present. The chance of striking through the mask of corporate-underwritten, feel-good, ahistorical racism grows daily more remote. The trade-off—whites promise friendship, blacks accept the status quo—begins to seem like a good deal.   34

Cosseted by Hollywood's magic lantern and soothed by press releases from Washington and the American Enterprise Institute, we should never forget what we see and hear for ourselves. Broken out by race, the results of every social tabulation from unemployment   35 to life expectancy add up to a chronicle of atrocity. The history of black America fully explains—to anyone who approaches it honestly—how the disaster happened and why neither guilt money nor lectures on personal responsibility can, in and of themselves, repair the damage. The vision of friendship and sympathy placing blacks and whites "all in the same boat," rendering them equally able to do each other favors, "to give rides to one another," is a smiling but monstrous lie.

Women and Weight: Gendered Messages on Magazine Covers

Amy R. Malkin, Kimberlie Wornian, and Joan C. Chrisler

This article was originally published in the July–August 1999 issue of Sex Roles: A Journal of Research.

Abstract

In this content analysis, the covers of 21 popular women's and men's magazines were examined for gendered messages related to bodily appearance. Magazine covers were divided according to gender of readers and each cover was reviewed using a checklist designed to analyze visual images and text as well as the placement of each on the covers. Analyses showed that 78% of the covers of the women's magazines contained a message regarding bodily appearance, whereas none of the covers of the men's magazines did so. Twenty-five percent of the women's magazine covers contained conflicting messages regarding weight loss and dietary habits. In addition, the positioning of weight-related messages on the covers often implied that losing weight may lead to a better life. Men's magazines focus on providing entertainment and expanding knowledge, hobbies, and activities; women's magazines continue to focus on improving one's life by changing one's appearance.

1   Feminist researchers have repeatedly reported on the significant role that the media play in the construction of the "beauty ideal" that society holds up to women (Faludi, 1991; Freedman, 1986; Wolf, 1991). For the majority of women this ideal is impossible to attain and may lead to feelings of inadequacy. Feelings of inadequacy are also likely to be fed by cosmetic manufacturers and weight management programs whose ad campaigns focus on convincing women that they can ameliorate their bodily flaws and imperfections only by purchasing their products or taking part in their programs (Freedman, 1986).

2   The messages sent out by the media regarding bodily appearance are quite different for women and men. A strong emphasis has been placed on the bodily appearance of women that equates a thin body to beauty, sexuality, and social status; less focus has been placed on the bodily appearance of men (Freedman, 1986). These gendered messages can clearly be seen in magazine articles and advertisements. For example, Anderson and

DiDomenico (1992) examined the 20 most popular magazines read by women and men to see if the number of articles that focused on dieting and body shape would reflect the actual prevalence rates of eating disorders in the general population. The results indicated that the 10 magazines most frequently read by women contained significantly more diet articles and advertisements than the 10 magazines most frequently read by men. The ratio of diet articles in men's and women's magazines was 1 : 10, which is identical to the actual ratio of eating disorders in men and women in the general population. The authors noted that when the men's magazines focused on bodily appearance the articles and advertisements centered on changes in body shape (i.e., "bulking up"), whereas the women's magazines focused on changes in body weight (i.e., "slimming down"). Anderson and DiDomenico suggested that "Instead of simply reflecting the weight and shape ideals of our society, popular media may be, to some extent, imposing gender-related norms, which then lead to sex-related differences in the frequency of critical behaviors" (Anderson & DiDomenico, 1992, p. 286).

Nemeroff, Stein, Diehl, and Smilack (1994) also examined women's and men's magazines to see if different types of magazines contained discrepant messages for men and women and whether this has changed over time. They looked at articles that focused on the behavioral means used to achieve physical ideals, which they placed into four categories: weight loss, beauty, fitness, and health. Based on previous work in the area, Nemeroff et al. chose to examine three categories of general interest magazines (i.e., traditional magazines, fashion magazines, and modern magazines), and they picked magazines with broad circulation and longevity of publication to represent each of the categories over a 12 year duration. They found that, overall, the women's magazines contained far more body-oriented articles than did the magazines that targeted male readers. However, the frequency of weight loss articles increased over the time period for men, but decreased for women, which indicated a gender-related change in trends. In addition, when they compared analyses of gender by magazine category, it appeared that over time the frequency of health articles seemed to increase in men's fashion magazines but not in women's fashion magazines. The authors concluded that at least some concern with the body was now being portrayed in men's fashion magazines. Finally, in comparing the different types of magazines, the researchers noted that fashion magazines were the most body oriented, modern magazines the least so, and traditional magazines fell somewhere in-between.

The purpose of the present study was to examine gendered messages regarding weight and bodily appearance on the covers of popular magazines. We chose to examine magazine covers because often it is the cover that initially attracts the reader to the magazine. Titles, catch phrases, and pictures displayed on magazine covers are usually all that the reader has time to look at in a store. Frequently it is these items that influence the reader to buy the magazine, as is reflected in the following statement by a corporate circulation director in the marketing industry. "The cover is primarily a sales tool . . . the images selected and the way we describe the contents must be provocative, hard-hitting and full of elements that sell—not feature oriented" (Love, 1999, p. 1). For this reason, it is important to explore the messages that are being presented to readers on the covers of popular magazines.

It was hypothesized that, overall, covers of women's magazines would be more likely to contain a message about bodily appearance than covers of magazines targeted at men.

We were interested in examining conflicting messages (i.e., messages with opposite meanings placed in close proximity to each other) that were displayed on magazine covers. It was hypothesized that covers of women's magazines would also be more likely to contain conflicting messages about bodily appearance than would covers of men's magazines.

METHOD

Materials

6   Twenty-one magazines were chosen for the present analysis (see Table I). Of these, 18 were chosen based on the results of the 1987 Simmon's Study of Media and Markets, which rated magazines on the basis of readership by gender and age. These magazines were essentially the same ones used by Anderson and DiDomenico (1992), however two were eliminated (i.e., *Playboy* and *Penthouse*) because they were not available in public libraries, where the rest of the magazines were obtained. Three additional magazines (i.e., *Vogue, Ms.,* and *Esquire*) were chosen based on suggestions from other members of the authors' research team. These magazines were included because it was believed that they were frequently-read magazines that were not included on the Simmon's list.

7   For each magazine title, six monthly issues were reviewed from different seasons throughout the year of 1996. At least one issue from each season was included to account for seasonal variability in topical articles. For one magazine (i.e., *Ms.*) only three issues were obtainable. In total, 69 covers of women's magazines and 54 covers of men's magazines were examined.

TABLE I   Magazines used in this analysis

Women's magazines		
Traditional	**Fashion**	**Modern**
Better Homes and Gardens	Cosmopolitan	Ms.
Family Circle	Glamour	
Good Housekeeping	Seventeen	
Ladies' Home Journal	Vogue	
McCall's		
Redbook		
Women's Day		

Men's magazines		
Traditional	**Fashion**	**Entertainment**
Life	Esquire	Field and Stream
National Geographic	Gentlemen's Quarterly	Jet
Newsweek		Rolling Stone
		Sports Illustrated

Procedure

A checklist was designed to examine the magazine covers; it concerned the content of   8
the visual images and text on the covers, as well as the placement of each. The content
of the text was analyzed to determine whether it contained a diet message (e.g., "Cut 100
Calories a Meal and Lose 10 Pounds"), an exercise message (e.g., "Walk Your Way to Thin"),
a message regarding cosmetic surgery to change the size of the body (e.g., "I Love My New
Thighs: Diary of a Liposuction"), or a general message about weight loss with no specifications about how to lose the weight (e.g., "5 Ways to Lose 5 Pounds"). The position of messages was examined to determine if conflicting messages were placed next to each other
(e.g., a message about losing weight next to a cookie recipe), if the conflicting messages were
separated on the page, and if there were articles about appearance and romance placed ad-
jacent to each other. Magazines were divided by gender of readers, and percentages for each
item of the checklist were obtained for each magazine category. Percentages for each magazine category were calculated by dividing the number of magazine issues that contained each
checklist item by the total number of magazine issues for that magazine category.

Each cover was examined by two of the authors together as they completed each check-   9
list. It was determined beforehand that differences between the authors on which section
a message fell into (i.e., diet, exercise, cosmetic surgery, other) would be discussed until an
agreement was reached. No differences arose, however, and all messages clearly fit into only
one section of the checklist.

RESULTS/DISCUSSION

Table II displays the percentages of each type of message related to bodily appearance   10
found in women's and men's magazines. Of the 12 magazines most frequently read by women,
54 of the 69 covers (78%) contained some message about bodily appearance, whereas none of
the 53 covers of men's magazines contained such messages, $X^2, (1, N - 123) = 49.62, p < .005$.

TABLE II   Percentages of each message type on magazine covers, by gender[a]

Type of message	Women (n = 69) n (%)	Men (n = 54) n (%)	X^2
Diet	23 (33)	0 (0)	
Excercise	16 (23)	0 (0)	
Cosmetic Surgery	4 (6)	0 (0)	
Unspecified	11 (16)	0 (0)	
At least one message (any type)	54 (78)	0 (0)	49.62[b]
Conflicting message	18 (26)	0 (0)	8.59[b]

[a]Percentages may sum to more than 100 because some magazine covers contained more than one type
of message.
[b]$p < .005$.

Therefore, consistent with previous research (Anderson & DiDomenico, 1992; Nemeroff *et al.,* 1994), the analysis showed that women's magazines were more likely to contain messages about diet, exercise, and cosmetic surgery to change body size than were men's magazines. Although the majority of the most popular women's magazines focused on changing and improving one's self, most of the popular men's magazines focused on the outside world, news, politics, hobbies, and activities.

11   An examination of the body types displayed on magazine covers revealed that 94% of the covers of women's magazines showed a thin female model or celebrity in excellent shape, whereas only about 3% showed a male on the cover. Of the covers of men's magazines, however, 28% showed a male model or celebrity, whereas women appeared almost 50% of the time. Again, most women were young, thin, and wore revealing clothing. Overall it seems that visual images on both men's and women's magazine covers tend to portray what women should look like and what men should look for. There is minimal focus on the male body.

12   In addition to examining weight loss messages on magazine covers, visual images and text related to food were also examined to determine the prevalence of conflicting messages about weight loss. Eighteen of the 69 covers of women's magazines contained some type of conflicting message (26%), whereas none of the covers of men's magazines contained such messages, X^2 (1, N = 123) = 8.59, p < .005. Therefore, the hypothesis that women's magazines would contain more conflicting messages than men's was supported. It is interesting that the majority of these conflicting messages (61%) were positioned right next to one another. For example, a magazine might show a picture of an ice-cream cake with a message that says "Ice-cream Extravaganza!" next to an exercise message that says "Trim Your Thighs in 3 Weeks." Recent research (Nemeroff *et al.,* 1994) has suggested that there has been a decrease in the emphasis on weight loss in women's magazines over the last decade, however it is apparent from this study that women are still receiving gendered messages from magazines regarding weight and bodily appearance at a fairly high rate.

13   Because articles on weight loss do not consistently appear in the most popular men's magazines, the rest of this report will focus on the messages displayed in women's magazines. Magazine covers in popular women's magazines were further separated into three magazine categories: Modern magazines (e.g., *Ms.*), Traditional magazines (e.g., *Family Circle*), and Fashion magazines (e.g., *Cosmopolitan*). Table III displays the percentages of each type of message for each magazine category. Although no statistical analyses were calculated, a comparison of the frequencies of messages about weight loss and bodily appearance in each category of magazine revealed a trend in which traditional magazines contained the most messages regarding weight loss and bodily appearance (58%) and contained all of the conflicting messages involving weight loss and fattening foods. Fashion magazines contained a smaller percentage of messages (20%). Finally, modern magazines did not contain any messages related to weight or bodily appearance. Similarly, Nemeroff *et al.* (1994) found that modern magazines contained the least amount of messages related to bodily appearance, however their results suggested that fashion magazines were more body-oriented than traditional magazines. It is interesting that many of the same magazines were used in both studies.

TABLE III   Percentages of each message type on women's magazine covers, by magazine category[a]

Type of message	Traditional (n = 42) n (%)	Fashion (n = 24) n (%)	Modern (n = 3) n (%)
Diet	19 (45)	5 (21)	0 (0)
Exercise	11 (26)	5 (21)	0 (0)
Cosmetic surgery	0 (0)	4 (17)	0 (0)
Unspecified	10 (24)	4 (17)	0 (0)
At least one message (any type)	40 (95)	14 (58)	0 (0)

[a]Percentages may sum to more than 100 because some magazine covers contained more than one type of message.

Perhaps the most alarming finding in this study was the position of weight-related messages in relation to other messages on the magazine covers. By their positioning of messages on magazine covers, magazines may imply that losing weight or changing the shape of one's body will lead to a better life (see Table IV). For example, messages such as "Get the Body You Want" placed next to "How to Get Your Husband to Really Listen" and "Lose 10 Pounds" placed next to "Ways to Make Your Life Easier, Happier, and Better" may give women the false idea that changing the appearance of their bodies will lead to better relationships, stronger friendships, and happier lives.   14

It is possible that different results may have been found if other types of magazines (i.e., men's body-building magazines or health magazines) had been included in this study. However, the magazines in this study were chosen on the basis of popularity and not on specific magazine theme or content. Magazines specifically associated with fitness, health, or appearance were not purposefully chosen for women or men. Instead, magazines that were reported as "frequently read" were selected. One limitation of this study is the sample of magazines chosen. As the authors did not have access to a more recent Simmon's Study of Media and Markets, the 1987 list was used to determine which magazines were   15

TABLE IV   Examples of message positioning that implies that changing bodily appearance will lead to a better life

Text	next to	Text
"Get the Body You Really Want"		"How to Get Your Husband to Really Listen"
"Tighten Your Butt"		"Habits of Confident Women"
"Drop 8 Pounds This Month"		"25 Ways to Make Your Marriage Hot Again"
"Get a Really Firm Body in 30 Days"		"5 Ways to Keep Your Husband Faithful"
"Lose 10 Pounds"		"Ways to Make Your Life Easier, Happier, and Better"
"Stay Skinny"		"What Men Want Most"

most frequently read by women and men in this study. Many new magazines have been introduced in the 1990s, and it is possible that the magazines examined in this study may no longer be the most frequently read. We also used three additional magazines that were perceived to be "popular" but were not on the Simmon's 1987 list. Perhaps it would have been better to use a recent list and not add additional magazines. However, many of the magazines selected in this study have been used in previous research on messages related to bodily appearance (i.e., Anderson & DiDomenico, 1992; Nemeroff *et al.,* 1994). Because the present study builds on this prior work, we believe that the results from the magazines used in this study are meaningful. Finally, it is not our intention to suggest that magazines such as *Newsweek, Life,* or *National Geographic* are exclusively "men's magazines" and that women do not read them. The categories of "women's" and "men's" magazines in this study were based entirely on the outcomes of the 1987 Simmon's Study.

16   In conclusion, it seems that in men's popular magazines the focus is on providing entertainment and improving one's life by expanding knowledge, hobbies, and activities. Women's magazines, however, seem to focus on improving one's life by changing one's appearance, especially by losing weight. It is implied through both images and text that being thin means being happier, sexier, and more lovable. Women's magazines also contain conflicting messages about weight loss strategies and eating behaviors, including the placement of weight loss prescriptions next to recipes and pictures of foods that are extremely high in fat content. The findings from this analysis suggest that women are not only being told that they should focus on obtaining an impossible body shape through dieting and exercising, but they are also being told that they should be able to do so while eating, or at least preparing for others, foods that are high in fat content. These fattening foods, obviously not typical diet foods, may make women think that it is even more impossible for them to obtain the thin ideal that is being presented to them or the ideal life that goes with it. The consequences of striving for these unrealistic ideals may be that an increasing number of women take aggressive means to control and reduce their weight (Wadden, Brown, Foster, & Linowitz, 1991). These dieting efforts can have serious implications, including inadequate nutrition, fatigue, weakness, irritability, depression, social withdrawal, loss of sexual desire, and even sudden death from cardiac arrhythmia (Ciliska, 1990). In addition, dietary restraint increases the likelihood of binge eating, which may initiate the cycle of bulimia in individuals at risk for developing eating disorders (Polivy & Herman, 1985). In short, dieting should never be considered a risk-free activity (Chrisler, 1994). Perhaps editors of popular women's magazines need to be more aware of the implications of gendered messages on magazine covers and the physical and psychological consequences they may have for women.

REFERENCES

Anderson, A. E., & DiDomenico, L. (1992). Diet vs. shape content of popular male and female magazines: A dose-response relationship to the incidence of eating disorders? *International Journal of Eating Disorders, 11,* 283–287.

Chrisler, J. C. (1994). Reframing women's weight: Does thin equal healthy? In A. Dan (Ed.), *Reframing women's health: Multidisciplinary research and practice.* Newbury Park, CA: Sage.

Ciliska, D. (1990). *Beyond dieting: Psychoeducational interventions for chronically obese women—A non-dieting approach.* New York: Brunner/Mazel.

Faludi, S. (1991). *Backlash: The undeclared war against American women.* New York: Crown.

Freedman, T. (1986). *Beauty bound.* Lexington, MA: D. C. Heath.

Love, B. (1999). Make the cover a sales tool. *Folio Special Report, 27* (18), 197. [On-line]. Available: http://web.lexis-nexis.com.

Nemeroff, C. J., Stein, R. I., Diehl, N. S., & Smilack, K. M. (1994). From the Cleavers to the Clintons: Role choices and body orientation as reflected in magazine article content. *International Journal of Eating Disorders, 16,* 167–176.

Polivy, J., & Herman, C. P. (1985). Dieting and bingeing: A causal analysis. *American Psychologist, 40,* 193–201.

Simmon's study of media and markets. (1987). New York: Simmon's Market Research Bureau, Inc.

Wadden, T. A., Brown, G., Foster, G. D., & Linowitz, J. R. (1991). Salience of weight-related worries in adolescent males and females. *International Journal of Eating Disorders, 10,* 407–414.

Wolf, N. (1991). *The beauty myth: How images of beauty are used against women.* New York: William Morrow.

Modern Makeup: Two Cheers for the Beauty Industry

Judith Shulevitz

This article was posted April 29, 1998, on the Web site www.slate.com/BookReview.

In the past five years, my friends and I have taken to getting our nails done—filed, painted—every week. So, it seems, have many other women we see in the subway or office. Is this an improvement in personal grooming (a thesis communitarian philosophers might advance) or yet another imposition on busy professionals by the beauty industry (as feminist pundits might argue)? Well, here's why I do it: Manicures look and feel great, plus they're remarkably cheap and fast these days—$7 plus tip, 20 minutes tops. You used to have to go to a beauty salon, stay twice as long, and pay twice as much. What happened? Enterprising Korean and Vietnamese women, putting ethnic credit unions to good use, opened discount nail salons in every city neighborhood in America. 1

If the goal of feminism is greater economic and social independence for women, then storefront manicure parlors are a feminist success story for the 1990s: They've turned a generation of new female immigrants into small-business owners. But cosmetics and personal care have always been a way for marginalized women to gain entry to the marketplace. That's one lesson of *Hope in a Jar,* a history of American beauty culture from the late-19th to the mid-20th century, a period when the pursuit of improved looks was transformed from a matter of folk recipes whispered from woman to woman to a multibillion dollar industry. In fact, historian Kathy Peiss writes, "the beauty industry may be the only business, at least until recent decades, in which American women achieved the highest levels of success, wealth, and authority." 2

3   For the past three decades, feminists have been accusing the beauty industry of fiendishly sophisticated campaigns to undercut women's self-worth. A century ago, no one could have imagined that beauty could be anything as faceless as an industry, let alone one capable of a broad social agenda. In the late 19th century, beauty, connoting as it did individual service and the laying on of hands, was considered a trade too vulgar for respectable people. It was a low-class, penny ante affair, and therefore an excellent opportunity for immigrants and blacks to begin their climb upward. There were men in the field, but women had the edge. They could claim to use the products themselves, and other women trusted them. The women who rose to the top invented flamboyant personas to go with their step-by-step systems, but they came from distinctly unglamorous backgrounds.

4   Helena Rubinstein was a Polish Jew who embarked on a career as a cold- and vanishing-cream saleswoman only after her parents interrupted her medical education to ship her out of reach of an unsuitable boyfriend. But she claimed to descend from aristocracy and to have advanced scientific degrees. Elizabeth Arden was born Florence Nightingale Graham, the daughter of Canadian tenant farmers. Madame C. J. Walker and Annie Turnbo Malone, two of the best-known entrepreneurs in African-American history, were both daughters of slaves, orphaned as children, who began as purveyors of black women's hair potions. Both defused charges of pandering to the straight-hair, white ideal of beauty by becoming prominent "race women"—hiring only blacks (usually women), giving generously to black causes, and refusing to sell skin bleach, a popular item among African-Americans.

5   The early female cosmetics tycoons faced two problems. One was the lingering Victorian belief that face painting was for hussies. The solution was to tie makeup to the freedoms women were beginning to enjoy: The "New Woman"—who worked in the city or went to college, or just thought of herself as modern—needed and deserved a new face for the world, just as she needed and deserved the right to work and vote.

6   Women eagerly embraced the idea that changing their faces would change their social status. The new consumers of beauty products wrote to manufacturers that they applied rouge, lipstick, and mascara for their own pleasure, not that of their men. Men were more likely to oppose makeup than demand it, and often forbade their wives and girlfriends to use it.

7   The second problem was access to capital and to store shelves. Bankers and distributors were generally loath to do business with the gentler sex. The cosmetics queens solved this problem by exploiting their intimacy with their customers. During the first quarter of the century, the beauty industry advanced new sales techniques emphasizing personal contact: door-to-door and mail-order marketing, beauty schools and correspondence courses, lines of cosmetics tied to salons. Walker and Malone were particularly adept at what is known today as "multilevel marketing": They traveled around the country recruiting black women as sales representatives.

8   The rise of mass production, national advertising, and brand identity—the mainstays of consumer capitalism—sent most small beauty manufacturers out of business and the rest into the hands of men who directed large corporations. (Rubinstein sold out to Lehman Brothers. Later, enraged by their downscale positioning of her upscale products, she bought her company back.) But female founders were kept on as spokeswomen, or new front women were hired. Advertising agencies hired their first women to write beauty copy, then

promoted them to higher positions. Beauty magazines, with scores of editorial jobs for women, emerged out of what had been farm or dress-pattern publications. And some women, such as Estée Lauder and Mary Kay Ash, made the strategic alliances with male financiers required to keep them afloat.

For consumers, the key development of the 1910s, '20s, and '30s was the mass-produced image, which led to the culture of celebrity and unified standards of feminine beauty. Suddenly, there was a look, and everyone had to have it. Whereas once beauty practices had had an appealingly informal kitchen quality, now skin care and makeup regimens were codified—even taught in offices and schools. Women went from being active to passive participants in the rites of beauty. No longer was putting on one's face seen as a matter of individuality, dignity, or even racial advancement (moving to Northern cities in the Great Migration of the 1930s, '40s, and '50s, many former sharecroppers saw applying cosmetics as a step toward participating in the wider American culture). Making up became a mandatory act of conformity and, by the time the women's movement began to address it, of oppression. 9

This is the resentful perception so many mainstream feminists seem stuck in today. When Susan Faludi and Naomi Wolf, for instance, talk about the beauty industry, they sound rather like middle-class ladies suspiciously eyeing a Chanel counter at Saks—they'll resist those foreign wiles! But as Peiss' excellent research demonstrates, the culture of beauty isn't all big corporations and victimized customers. Even during the 1950s, the height of American conformism, women consistently ranked advice from mothers, sisters, and friends as more likely to drive their buying decisions than advertising. Nowadays, lefty female academics dress as "white trash" as a statement of class protest. Lipstick lesbians wear heavier makeup than straight women. Black professionals braid their hair to display their ethnic pride. In other words, using makeup is as complicated an act as it has ever been. 10

Parallel Worlds: The Surprising Similarities (and Differences) of Country-and-Western and Rap

Denise Noe

Journalist Denise Noe originally published this article in the July–August 1995 issue of the Humanist.

In all of popular music today, there are probably no two genres that are more apparently dissimilar than country-and-western and rap: the one rural, white, and southern; the other urban, black, and identified with the two coasts ("New York style" versus "L.A. style"). Yet C&W and rap are surprisingly similar in many ways. In both C&W and rap, for example, lyrics are important. Both types of music tell stories, as do folk songs, and the story is much more than frosting for the rhythm and beat. 1

2   The ideologies espoused by these types of music are remarkably similar as well. We frequently stereotype country fans as simple-minded conservatives—"redneck," moralistic super-patriots à la Archie Bunker. But country music often speaks critically of mainstream American platitudes, especially in such highly charged areas as sexual morality, crime, and the Protestant work ethic.

3   The sexual ethos of C&W and rap are depressingly similar: the men of both genres are champion chauvinists. Country singer Hank Williams, Jr., declares he's "Going Hunting Tonight," but he doesn't need a gun since he's hunting the "she-cats" in a singles bar. Male rappers such as Ice-T, Ice Cube, and Snoop Doggy Dogg are stridently misogynist, with "bitches" and "hos" their trademark terms for half of humanity; their enthusiastic depictions of women raped and murdered are terrifying. Indeed, the sexism of rap group NWA (Niggaz with Attitude) reached a real-life nadir when one member of the group beat up a woman he thought "dissed" them—and was praised for his brutality by the other members.

4   On a happier note, both rap and C&W feature strong female voices as well. Women rappers are strong, confident, and raunchy: "I want a man, not a boy / to approach me / Your lame game really insults me. . . . I've got to sit on my feet to come down to your level," taunt lady rappers Entice and Barbie at Too Short in their duet/duel, "Don't Fight the Feeling." Likewise, Loretta Lynn rose to C&W fame with defiant songs like "Don't Come Home a-Drinkin' with Lovin' on Your Mind" and "Your Squaw Is on the Warpath Tonight,"

5   Country music can be bluntly honest about the realities of sex and money—in sharp contrast to the "family values" rhetoric of the right. "Son of Hickory Hollow's Tramp" by Johnny Darrell salutes a mother who works as a prostitute to support her children. "Fancy" by Bobbie Gentry (and, more recently, Reba McEntire) describes a poverty-stricken woman's use of sex for survival and her rise to wealth on the ancient "gold mine." Both tunes are unapologetic about the pragmatic coping strategies of their heroines.

6   More startling than the resemblances in their male sexism and "uppity" women are the parallels between C&W and rap in their treatment of criminality. Country-and-western music is very far from a rigid law-and-order mentality. The criminal's life is celebrated for its excitement and clear-cut rewards—a seemingly promising alternative to the dull grind of day-to-day labor.

7   "Ain't got no money / Ain't got no job / Let's find a place to rob," sings a jaunty Ricky Van Shelton in "Crime of Passion." In "I Never Picked Cotton," Roy Clark is more subdued but still unrepentant when he says: "I never picked cotton / like my mother did and my sister did and my brother did / And I'll never die young / working in a coal mine like my daddy did." Waylon Jennings' "Good Ole Boys" boast gleefully of having "hot-wired a city truck / turned it over in the mayor's yard."

8   Similarly, rap songs like "Gangsta, Gangsta" and "Dopeman" by NWA and "Drama" by Ice-T tell of the thrill and easy money offered by a life of crime. "Drama" records the dizzying high of the thief; "Gangsta, Gangsta," the rush of adrenaline experienced by a murderer making a quick getaway. Of course, both C&W and rap songs do express the idea that in the long run crime doesn't pay. The sad narrator of Merle Haggard's "Mama Tried" "turned 21 in prison / doing life without parole," while the thief of Ice-T's "Drama" is forced to re-

alize that "I wouldn't be here if I'd fed my brain / Got knowledge from schoolbooks / 'stead of street crooks / Now all I get is penitentiary hard looks."

Though both C&W and rap narrators are often criminals, their attitudes toward law enforcement differ radically. The Irish Rovers' "Wasn't That a Party?" ("that little drag race down on Main Street / was just to see if the cops could run") pokes light-hearted fun at the police, while the Bobby Fuller Four's "I Fought the Law and the Law Won" expresses the most common C&W attitude: an acceptance that criminals must be caught, even if you are one. Neither song displays any anger toward the police, who are, after all, just doing their job. 9

To rappers, on the other hand, cops are the enemy. Two of the most notorious rap songs are Ice-T's "Cop Killer" and NWA's "Fuck tha Police" (which angrily asserts, "Some police think they have the authority to kill a minority"). Despite ample evidence of police brutality in the inner city, "Fuck tha Police" was almost certainly regarded by nonblack America as a paranoid shriek—until the world witnessed the infamous videotape of several of Los Angeles' finest brutally beating Rodney King while a dozen other "peace officers" nonchalantly looked on.

Interestingly, although the C&W view of law enforcement naturally sits better with the general public (certainly with the police themselves), the fact remains that country-and-western music contains a good deal of crime, violence, and casual sex. Yet it is easily accepted by white Americans while rap arouses alarm and calls for labeling. Why? 10

I believe there are three major reasons. The first, and simplest, is language. Rappers say "bitch," "ho," "fuck," and "motherfucker"; C&W artists don't. Country singers may say, "I'm in the mood to speak some French tonight" (Mary Chapin-Carpenter, "How Do") or "There's two kinds of cherries / and two kinds of fairies" (Merle Haggard, "My Own Kind of Hat"), but they avoid the bluntest Anglo-Saxon terms. 11

A second reason is race. African-Americans have a unique history of oppression in this country, and rap reflects the inner-city African-American experience. Then, too, whites expect angry, frightening messages from blacks and listen for them. Many blacks, on the other hand, hope for uplifting messages—and are dismayed when black artists seem to encourage or glorify the drug abuse and violence in their beleaguered communities. Thus, the focus on violence in rap—and the dismissal of same in C&W. 12

While the differing attitudes toward law enforcement are real enough, much of the difference between violence in country-and-western music and in rap lies not in the songs themselves but in the way they are heard. Thus, when Ice Cube says, "Let the suburbs see a nigga invasion / Point-blank, smoke the Caucasian," many whites interpret that as an incitement to violence. But when Johnny Cash's disgruntled factory worker in "Oney" crows, "Today's the day old Oney gets his," it's merely a joke. Likewise, when Ice Cube raps, "I've got a shotgun and here's the plot / Taking niggas out with the fire of buckshot" ("Gangsta, Gangsta"), he sends shudders through many African-Americans heartbroken by black-on-black violence; but when Johnny Cash sings of an equally nihilistic killing in "Folsom Prison Blues"—"Shot a man in Reno / just to watch him die"—the public taps its feet and hums along. . . . It's just a song, after all. 13

There is a third—and ironic—reason why rap is so widely attacked: rap is actually closer to mainstream American economic ideology than country-and-western is. While 14

C&W complains about the rough life of honest labor for poor and working-class people, rap ignores it almost entirely. "Work your fingers to the bone and what do you get?" asks Hoyt Axton in a satirical C&W song, then answers sardonically with its title: "Bony Fingers." Likewise, Johnny Paycheck's infamous "Take This Job and Shove It" is a blue-collar man's bitter protest against the rough and repetitive nature of his life's work. Work in C&W is hard and meaningless; it keeps one alive, but leaves the worker with little time or energy left to enjoy life.

15   Songs by female country singers reinforce this point in a different way; they insist that love (with sex) is more important than affluence. The heroine of Reba McEntire's "Little Rock" says she'll have to "slip [her wedding ring] off," feeling no loyalty to the workaholic husband who "sure likes his money" but neglects his wife's emotional and physical needs. Jeanne Pruett in "Back to Back" lampoons the trappings of wealth and proclaims, "I'd trade this mansion / for a run-down shack / and a man who don't believe in sleeping back to back."

16   Rap's protagonists, on the other hand, are shrewd, materialistic, and rabidly ambitious—although the means to their success are officially proscribed in our society. Not for them a "life that moves at a slower pace" (Alabama, "Down Home"); unlike the languorous hero of country-and-western, "catching these fish like they're going out of style" (Hank Williams, Jr., "Country State of Mind"), rap singers and rap characters alike are imbued with the great American determination to get ahead.

17   Rap's protagonists—drug dealers, burglars, armed robbers, and "gangstas"—live in a society where success is "a fistful of jewelry" (Eazy E, "No More ?s"), "Motorola phones, Sony color TVs" (Ice-T, "Drama"), where "without a BMW you're through" (NWA, "A Bitch Iz a Bitch"). In NWA's "Dopeman," sometimes cited as an antidrug song, the "Dopeman" is the archetypal American entrepreneur: clever, organized, ruthless, and not ruled by impulse—"To be a dopeman you must qualify / Don't get high off your own supply."

18   The proximity of rap to our success ethic arouses hostility because America is torn by a deep ideological contradiction: we proudly proclaim ourselves a moral (even religious) nation and tout our capitalist economic system. But the reality of a successful capitalist system is that it undermines conventional morality. A glance at the history books shows how our supposedly moral nation heaped rewards upon the aptly named "robber barons": the Rockefellers, Vanderbilts, Carnegies, and Morgans. The crack dealer is a contemporary version of the bootlegger—at least one of whom, Joe Kennedy, Sr., founded America's most famous political dynasty. (Indeed; I would not be surprised if history repeated itself and the son—or daughter—of a drug lord becomes this country's first African-American president.)

19   Capitalism is unparalleled in its ability to create goods and distribute services, but it is, like the hero of "Drama," "blind to what's wrong." The only real criterion of a person's worth becomes how much money she or he has—a successful crook is treated better than a poor, law-abiding failure.

20   In short, the laid-back anti-materialism of country-and-western can be dismissed with a shrug, but the rapper is attacked for that unforgivable sin: holding a mirror up to unpleasant truths. And one of them is that amoral ambition is as American as apple pie and the Saturday Night Special.

Warrior Women
Why Are TV Shows like *Buffy the Vampire Slayer,* *La Femme Nikita,* and *Xena: Warrior Princess* So Popular, Especially among Teens?

Michael Ventura

This article was originally published in the November–December 1998 issue of Psychology Today.

You can gauge the public's true feeling by what its entertainment is trying to salve. 1
Television's weekly one-hour shows, known in the trade as "episodics," constitute the bulk
of America's exposure to serious drama. These series mostly depict cops, doctors and
lawyers—professions on the gritty interface between working citizens and the ruling powers, professions that Americans are leery of in real life.

We watch to reassure ourselves that the representatives of Officialdom can be de- 2
pended upon in a pinch. We need to be reassured; deep down, we harbor the nasty notion
that nobody's really looking out for us. These shows soothe our fears. Somebody cares. The
heart of society is good, after all.

I've dubbed these dramas the Priest-and-Nun Shows: characters agonize earnestly 3
and endlessly over moral choices and their own worthiness. *ER, Chicago Hope:* priests and
nuns with stethoscopes. *NYPD Blue, Homicide: Life on the Streets:* priests and nuns
with guns. *Law and Order, The Practice:* priests and nuns with briefcases. *The X-Files:* a
priest and nun (who, unlike most of the other "clerics," seem to be celibate) fight the Dark
Powers, for the truth must be out there somewhere—a moral conviction if ever there was
one. Throw in *Baywatch:* naked priests and nuns. And *Dawson's Creek:* the teen novitiate
hour.

Such fare speaks of a people unsure of what it means to be good or bad. In classic Holly- 4
wood films, moral choice wasn't an issue, wasn't the meat of the drama. The major characters had already drawn a hard line between right and wrong; the drama was in getting
the job done against enormous odds. Now characters anguish over where the line is, or
whether it even exists. They always come out on the side of traditional morality, of course.
That's the point of the exercise, though it can take a while to get there, to reaffirm that the
heart of society is, after all, good.

But there is another breed of show on TV, with a very large and mostly young follow- 5
ing, that takes the opposite stance: the heart of society is demonic. Society is Hell. The
vision is fatalistic, the moral choice made for us before we were born. There may or may
not be a God, but the Devil is the bully in your neighborhood. And to be human is to constantly fight demons.

The X-Files, at first glance, seems to fall in this category. But Fox Mulder and Dana 6
Scully continue, despite all evidence to the contrary, to believe that there's a moral solution
to their dilemma. If only the truth "out there" were known, they'd be victorious.

7   The real society-is-hell shows aren't so optimistic. For one thing, they don't believe there's an end to the struggle. For another, in these shows men aren't much good at demon-fighting. It's up to the women.

8   *Buffy the Vampire Slayer* follows a perky high-school girl (Sarah Michelle Gellar) whom fate has designated the Slayer. Every generation has one, and if you're it, you have no choice. Two students, a boy and a girl, are Buffy's allies, but she's the Slayer. She does all the fighting, mostly kickboxing. Convinced that she'll die young—you can only kickbox for so long—Buffy lives for the moment, though she's kept so busy with her duties, she doesn't get to date much.

9   According to Buffy, the American high school lies right around the corner from the Mouth of Hell, which constantly spews forth demons (mostly teens) intent on disrupting the course of education. With the exception of the school librarian, adults are oblivious to the evil reality. Bizarre events occur with unnerving regularity and Buffy is rarely home nights, but her single Mom remains certain that things will be normal in the morning and that Buffy could finish her homework if only she had the right counseling.

10   The symbolism is dizzying. Drugs, alcohol and gangs are conspicuously absent from Buffy's high school, but it's clear that these are Hell Mouth's vomitus. Demons are the gangs. The surreal transformations in gullible kids victimized by demons—that's your brain on drugs. And the helplessness of grown-ups in the face of this Hell—that's life. Even Buffy's love, Angel, is in the end just another vampire.

11   Done with sly yet generous humor, *Buffy* lets us forget the pain of its premise—which is precisely its appeal. Buffy, the pagan priestess, struggles to turn darkness into light, but the battle is unending. There's always another vampire to fight, every night, every generation. Humor makes it bearable but doesn't change it.

12   Only one show has a bleaker premise: *La Femme Nikita.* With *Buffy,* Hell's around the corner. But Nikita lives in Hell. It's called Section One, and it's even located underground. "I was falsely accused of a hideous crime," intones Nikita in the opening narration of each episode, "and condemned to death." Section One staged her funeral, recruited her, trained her, "and if I don't play by their rules, I die."

13   If Buffy is uncorrupted by her struggle, Nikita has fallen victim to it, accepting corruption and far worse. Nikita herself is a demon, one of the living dead, but darkly on the side of light. Section One fights terrorists. And in fighting terrorists, the ends justify the means. Nikita kills and tortures on order. She resisted the practice at first, but now she breaks fingers with the best of them. The show's horrors are something Buffy would not dare contemplate.

14   But make no mistake: *La Femme Nikita*'s weekly torture session, indulged in by characters with whom viewers are encouraged to identify and empathize, is unconscionable. Torture is disturbing, but the real ugliness here is the stylistic flourish with which it is presented. In *Nikita,* torture is not a horror but a titillation.

15   *Nikita* pushes our preconceptions in other ways as well. While Buffy is a squeaky-clean hetero teen, Nikita (Peta Wilson) is a seductive 20-ish blonde, a fashion plate with a runway walk who sexually swings both ways. In one episode Nikita falls in love with a stunning African-American woman, and their close-up tongue-twining kiss makes the cancelled Ellen's lesbian lip-locks look as tame as a Brady Bunch buss. In most episodes, though,

Nikita's love is a cold control-freak named Michael. A Section One comrade, he's passive-aggressive, effeminate and masculine.

Hell, in other words, knows no boundaries. Butch/femme, straight/gay, good/evil, sweet/bitter, control/chaos—everything's blurred. Hell is just like the Nineties. The ambivalences that frighten Americans so much are taken for granted on *La Femme Nikita.*   16

You want Officialdom to be on your side? OK, it's on your side—sort of. But it's evil. If it has to threaten you and your children to stop a terrorist, it will. Being on society's side doesn't necessarily mean being on your side. *La Femme Nikita* provides no comfort. It assumes we're living in the worst of worlds. As with *Buffy,* there is no future. For every terrorist you kill, you'll have to face another.   17

What Buffy and Nikita have most in common is that they are warriors. Western storytelling hasn't seen their ilk since the legendary female fighters of the Celts. So it's fitting that the most brazen of TV's new warrior women is the Celtic battler Xena (played by the grand Lucy Lawless).   18

Buffy and Nikita inhabit the Devil's kingdom, but Xena frolics in a sorcerer's realm where *Playboy*-foldout witches come and go in puffs of smoke. Xena is never threatening like Nikita or focused like Buffy. She cavorts safely in the legendary past. It's all comic book—except for the look in Xena's eyes.   19

A scantily-clad butch who's still femme enough to please the boys, Xena has a sentimental streak and a fundamental sweetness. But her eyes blaze with rages and fears, bright with paradoxes that belie the silly scripts. The strain of her fierceness wears on her. Where we see a fairy realm, she seems to see a bad dream. A very human face stares from that comic book, and you can't get more Nineties than that surreal mix.   20

Not so long ago, viewers wouldn't follow a woman into such hellish worlds. Now they wouldn't follow a man. (*Hercules,* for all its popularity, is basically a cartoon for little kids; it's *Xena: Warrior Princess* that grabs both teens and adults.) Far from softening the shows, these warrior women make the nightmarish visions all the more stark. Male heroes just aren't flexible enough to handle the conditions that Buffy, Nikita and Xena deal with. To handle, that is, the Nineties.   21

John Wayne would sooner nuke Nikita's world than tolerate it, even if it means blowing up the planet; Humphrey Bogart, trapped in Buffy's high school, would get drunk and stay drunk; Errol Flynn, faced with Xena, would drop his sword and abandon the field. The old dramatic conception of the male hero depends upon strong boundaries and clear choices. In a world increasingly without boundaries, those guys would just look lost—as their descendants usually do on the male-dominated Priest-and-Nun shows.   22

America isn't ready to accept sexual ambivalence in its male action heroes. America still wants them to make clear moral choices, even if they have to struggle to get there. None of this half-angel, half-devil stuff. In a man, that's still seen as somewhat sinister; in a woman, it's seductive.   23

Young America, the big audience for these shows, seems willing to let warrior women lead in the realm of the betwixt-and-between, morally, sexually, every which way. If the women prove survival is possible in such a world, the men may eventually tag along. But they won't be ready until they, like Buffy and Xena, can not only tolerate but learn to relish   24 ambivalence—and, unlike poor fallen Nikita, refuse to let a lack of boundaries demolish their morality.

FOR CLASS DISCUSSION

1. Although popular culture has become a topic of academic study in the last twenty years as well as a site of volatile political contention, many people resist seeing popular culture as anything other than simply entertainment. What arguments do these articles use to persuade readers that a specific part of popular culture should be taken seriously?

2. Theories of popular culture differ concerning whether popular culture merely reflects society or is an active force in constructing society, in actually molding people's behavior. Further, is the individual consumer free of popular culture or does the market co-opt and shape desire? Can you see lines of argument in these articles that employ any of these theories?

3. Which articles represent opposing theoretical positions on popular culture's relation to society? Analyze and evaluate different claims and lines of argument in these articles by comparing the argumentative strategies of these writers. How effective is the evidence that is employed in these interpretive arguments?

4. Choose one of these arguments for closer analysis, applying the second set of guide questions on pages 465–66.

OPTIONAL WRITING ASSIGNMENT   A standard argumentative move in analyses of popular culture is to make a surprising reversal claim in which the writer's surprising view is juxtaposed against a common view. Here are some representative patterns:

- Many people think that [some art form] is just entertainment; however, it really does social harm by promoting [immorality, racism, nonintellectualism, insensitivity toward some group of people, callousness toward violence, or some other negative effect].

- Many people think that [some cultural form] represents social progress; however, a closer examination reveals that it is really reactionary [conservative, backward-looking].

- Many people think that [some cultural form] is traditional and conservative when in actuality it promotes [revolutionary behavior, healthy change, radically new perspectives.]

Choose a cultural form or artifact such as a sitcom, film, or genre of films, a trend or fashion, a musical group or style of music, advertisements for a particular product, or some other aspect of the popular culture, and write an interpretive argument that surprises your chosen audience by presenting a novel, uncommon view of it.

DISTRIBUTION OF WEALTH: WHAT RESPONSIBILITY DO THE RICH HAVE FOR THE POOR?

Lifeboat Ethics
The Case against Aid That Harms
Garrett Hardin

Philosopher Garrett Hardin first published this classic argument in Psychology Today *in 1974.*

Environmentalists use the metaphor of the earth as a "spaceship" in trying to persuade countries, industries and people to stop wasting and polluting our natural resources. Since we all share life on this planet, they argue, no single person or institution has the right to destroy, waste or use more than a fair share of its resources.   1

But does everyone on earth have an equal right to an equal share of its resources? The spaceship metaphor can be dangerous when used by misguided idealists to justify suicidal policies for sharing our resources through uncontrolled immigration and foreign aid. In their enthusiastic but unrealistic generosity, they confuse the ethics of a spaceship with those of a lifeboat.   2

A true spaceship would have to be under the control of a captain, since no ship could possibly survive if its course were determined by committee. Spaceship Earth certainly has no captain; the United Nations is merely a toothless tiger, with little power to enforce any policy upon its bickering members.   3

If we divide the world crudely into rich nations and poor nations, two thirds of them are desperately poor, and only one third comparatively rich, with the United States the wealthiest of all. Metaphorically each nation can be seen as a lifeboat full of comparatively rich people. In the ocean outside each lifeboat swim the poor of the world, who would like to get in, or at least to share some of the wealth. What should the lifeboat passengers do?   4

First, we must recognize the limited capacity of any lifeboat. For example, a nation's land has a limited capacity to support a population and as the current energy crisis has shown us, in some ways we have already exceeded the carrying capacity of our land.   5

ADRIFT IN A MORAL SEA

So here we sit, say fifty people in our lifeboat. To be generous, let us assume it has room for ten more, making a total capacity of sixty. Suppose the fifty of us in the lifeboat see 100 others swimming in the water outside, begging for admission to our boat or for handouts. We have several options: We may be tempted to try to live by the Christian ideal   6 of being "our brother's keeper," or by the Marxist ideal of "to each according to his needs." Since the needs of all in the water are the same, and since they can all be seen as "our brothers," we could take them all into our boat, making a total of 150 in a boat designed for sixty. The boat swamps, everyone drowns. Complete justice, complete catastrophe.

7   Since the boat has an unused excess capacity of ten more passengers, we could admit just ten more to it. But which ten do we let in? How do we choose? Do we pick the best ten, the neediest ten, "first come, first served"? And what do we say to the ninety we exclude? If we do let an extra ten into our lifeboat, we will have lost our "safety factor," an engineering principle of critical importance. For example, if we don't leave room for excess capacity as a safety factor in our country's agriculture, a new plant disease or a bad change in the weather could have disastrous consequences.

8   Suppose we decide to preserve our small safety factor and admit no more to the lifeboat. Our survival is then possible, although we shall have to be constantly on guard against boarding parties.

9   While this last solution clearly offers the only means of our survival, it is morally abhorrent to many people. Some say they feel guilty about their good luck. My reply is simple: "Get out and yield your place to others." This may solve the problem of the guilt-ridden person's conscience, but it does not change the ethics of the lifeboat. The needy person to whom the guilt-ridden person yields his place will not himself feel guilty about his good luck. If he did, he would not climb aboard. The net result of conscience-stricken people giving up their unjustly held seats is the elimination of that sort of conscience from the lifeboat.

10   This is the basic metaphor within which we must work out our solutions. Let us now enrich the image, step by step, with substantive additions from the real world, a world that must solve real and pressing problems of overpopulation and hunger.

11   The harsh ethics of the lifeboat become even harsher when we consider the reproductive differences between the rich nations and the poor nations. The people inside the lifeboats are doubling in numbers every eighty-seven years; those swimming around outside are doubling, on the average, every thirty-five years, more than twice as fast as the rich. And since the world's resources are dwindling, the difference in prosperity between the rich and the poor can only increase.

12   As of 1973, the U.S. had a population of 210 million people, who were increasing by 0.8 percent per year. Outside our lifeboat, let us imagine another 210 million people (say the combined populations of Colombia, Ecuador, Venezuela, Morocco, Pakistan, Thailand and the Philippines), who are increasing at a rate of 3.3 percent per year. Put differently, the doubling time for this aggregate population is twenty-one years, compared to eighty-seven years for the U.S.

MULTIPLYING THE RICH AND THE POOR

13   Now suppose the U.S. agreed to pool its resources with those seven countries, with everyone receiving an equal share. Initially the ratio of Americans to non-Americans in this model would be one-to-one. But consider what the ratio would be after eighty-seven years, by which time the Americans would have doubled to a population of 420 million. By then,

doubling every twenty-one years, the other group would have swollen to 3.54 billion. Each American would have to share the available resource with more than eight people.

But, one could argue, this discussion assumes that current population trends will con-   14
tinue, and they may not. Quite so. Most likely the rate of population increase will decline much faster in the U.S. than it will in the other countries, and there does not seem to be much we can do about it. In sharing with "each according to his needs," we must recognize that needs are determined by population size, which is determined by the rate of reproduction, which at present is regarded as a sovereign right of every nation, poor or not. This being so, the philanthropic load created by the sharing ethic of the spaceship can only increase.

THE TRAGEDY OF THE COMMONS

The fundamental error of spaceship ethics, and the sharing it requires, is that it leads   15
to what I call "the tragedy of the commons." Under a system of private property, the men who own property recognize their responsibility to care for it, for if they don't they will eventually suffer. A farmer, for instance, will allow no more cattle in a pasture than its carrying capacity justifies. If he overloads it, erosion sets in, weeds take over, and he loses the use of the pasture.

If a pasture becomes a commons open to all, the right of each to use it may not be   16
matched by a corresponding responsibility to protect it. Asking everyone to use it with discretion will hardly do, for the considerate herdsman who refrains from overloading the commons suffers more than a selfish one who says his needs are greater. If everyone would restrain himself, all would be well; but it takes only one less than everyone to ruin a system of voluntary restraint. In a crowded world of less than perfect human beings, mutual ruin is inevitable if there are no controls. This is the tragedy of the commons.

One of the major tasks of education today should be the creation of such an acute   17
awareness of the dangers of the commons that people will recognize its many varieties. For example, the air and water have become polluted because they are treated as commons. Further growth in the population or per-capita conversion of natural resources into pollutants will only make the problem worse. The same holds true for the fish of the oceans. Fishing fleets have nearly disappeared in many parts of the world, technological improvements in the art of fishing are hastening the day of complete ruin. Only the replacement of the system of the commons with a responsible system of control will save the land, air, water and oceanic fisheries.

THE WORLD FOOD BANK

In recent years there has been a push to create a new commons called a World Food   18
Bank, an international depository of food reserves to which nations would contribute according to their abilities and from which they would draw according to their needs. This humanitarian proposal has received support from many liberal international groups, and from such prominent citizens as Margaret Mead, U.N. Secretary General Kurt Waldheim, and Senators Edward Kennedy and George McGovern.

19   A world food bank appeals powerfully to our humanitarian impulses. But before we rush ahead with such a plan, let us recognize where the greatest political push comes from, lest we be disillusioned later. Our experience with the "Food for Peace program," or Public Law 480, gives us the answer. This program moved billions of dollars' worth of U.S. surplus grain to food-short, population-long countries during the past two decades. But when P.L. 480 first became law, a headline in the business magazine *Forbes* revealed the real power behind it: "Feeding the World's Hungry Millions: How It Will Mean Billions for U.S. Business."

20   And indeed it did. In the years 1960 to 1970, U.S. taxpayers spent a total of $7.9 billion on the Food for Peace program. Between 1948 and 1970, they also paid an additional $50 billion for other economic-aid programs, some of which went for food and food-producing machinery and technology. Though all U.S. taxpayers were forced to contribute to the cost of P.L. 480, certain special interest groups gained handsomely under the program. Farmers did not have to contribute the grain; the Government, or rather the taxpayers, bought it from them at full market prices. The increased demand raised prices of farm products generally. The manufacturers of farm machinery, fertilizers and pesticides benefited by the farmers' extra efforts to grow more food. Grain elevators profited from storing the surplus until it could be shipped. Railroads made money hauling it to ports, and shipping lines profited from carrying it overseas. The implementation of P.L. 480 required the creation of a vast Government bureaucracy, which then acquired its own vested interest in continuing the program regardless of its merits.

EXTRACTING DOLLARS

21   Those who proposed and defended the Food for Peace program in public rarely mentioned its importance to any of these special interests. The public emphasis was always on its humanitarian effects. The combination of silent selfish interests and highly vocal humanitarian apologists made a powerful and successful lobby for extracting money from taxpayers. We can expect the same lobby to push now for the creation of a world food bank.

22   However great the potential benefit to selfish interests, it should not be a decisive argument against a truly humanitarian program. We must ask if such a program would actually do more good than harm, not only momentarily but also in the long run. Those who propose the food bank usually refer to a current "emergency" or "crisis" in terms of world food supply. But what is an emergency? Although they may be infrequent and sudden, everyone knows that emergencies will occur from time to time. A well-run family, company, organization or country prepares for the likelihood of accidents and emergencies. It expects them, it budgets for them, it saves for them.

LEARNING THE HARD WAY

23   What happens if some organizations or countries budget for accidents and others do not? If each country is solely responsible for its own well-being, poorly managed ones will suffer. But they can learn from experience. They may mend their ways, and learn to budget for infrequent but certain emergencies. For example, the weather varies from year to

year, and periodic crop failures are certain. A wise and competent government saves out of the production of the good years in anticipation of bad years to come. Joseph taught this policy to Pharaoh in Egypt more than 2,000 years ago. Yet the great majority of the governments in the world today do not follow such a policy. They lack either the wisdom or the competence, or both. Should those nations that do manage to put something aside be forced to come to the rescue each time an emergency occurs among the poor nations?

"But it isn't their fault!" some kindhearted liberals argue. "How can we blame the poor   24
people who are caught in an emergency? Why must they suffer for the sins of their governments?" The concept of blame is simply not relevant here. The real question is, what are the operational consequences of establishing a world food bank? If it is open to every country every time a need develops, slovenly rulers will not be motivated to take Joseph's advice. Someone will always come to their aid. Some countries will deposit food in the world food bank, and others will withdraw it. There will be almost no overlap. As a result of such solutions to food shortage emergencies, the poor countries will not learn to mend their ways, and will suffer progressively greater emergencies as their populations grow.

POPULATION CONTROL THE CRUDE WAY

On the average, poor countries undergo a 2.5 percent increase in population each year;   25
rich countries, about 0.8 percent. Only rich countries have anything in the way of food reserves set aside, and even they do not have as much as they should. Poor countries have none. If poor countries received no food from the outside, the rate of their population growth would be periodically checked by crop failures and famines. But if they can always draw on a world food bank in time of need, their populations can continue to grow unchecked, and so will their "need" for aid. In the short run, a world food bank may diminish that need, but in the long run it actually increases the need without limit.

Without some system of worldwide food sharing, the proportion of people in the rich   26
and poor nations might eventually stabilize. The overpopulated poor countries would decrease in numbers, while the rich countries that had room for more people would increase. But with a well-meaning system of sharing, such as a world food bank, the growth differential between the rich and the poor countries will not only persist, it will increase. Because of the higher rate of population growth in the poor countries of the world, 88 percent of today's children are born poor, and only 12 percent rich. Year by year the ratio becomes worse, as the fast-reproducing poor outnumber the slow-reproducing rich.

A world food bank is thus a commons in disguise. People will have more motivation   27
to draw from it than to add to any common store. The less provident and less able will multiply at the expense of the abler and more provident, bringing eventual ruin upon all who share in the commons. Besides, any system of "sharing" that amounts to foreign aid from the rich nations to the poor nations will carry the taint of charity, which will contribute little to the world peace so devoutly desired by those who support the idea of a world food bank.

As past U.S. foreign-aid programs have amply and depressingly demonstrated, interna-   28
tional charity frequently inspires mistrust and antagonism rather than gratitude on the part of the recipient nation.

CHINESE FISH AND MIRACLE RICE

29   The modern approach to foreign aid stresses the export of technology and advice, rather than money and food. As an ancient Chinese proverb goes: "Give a man a fish and he will eat for a day; teach him how to fish and he will eat for the rest of his days." Acting on this advice, the Rockefeller and Ford Foundations have financed a number of programs for improving agriculture in the hungry nations. Known as the "Green Revolution," these programs have led to the development of "miracle rice" and "miracle wheat," new strains that offer bigger harvests and greater resistance to crop damage. Norman Borlaug, the Nobel Prize winning agronomist who, supported by the Rockefeller Foundation, developed "miracle wheat," is one of the most prominent advocates of a world food bank.

30   Whether or not the Green Revolution can increase food production as much as its champions claim is a debatable but possibly irrelevant point. Those who support this well-intended humanitarian effort should first consider some of the fundamentals of human ecology. Ironically, one man who did was the late Alan Gregg, a vice president of the Rockefeller Foundation. Two decades ago he expressed strong doubts about the wisdom of such attempts to increase food production. He likened the growth and spread of humanity over the surface of the earth to the spread of cancer in the human body, remarking that "cancerous growths demand food; but, as far as I know, they have never been cured by getting it."

OVERLOADING THE ENVIRONMENT

31   Every human born constitutes a draft on all aspects of the environment: food, air, water, forests, beaches, wildlife, scenery and solitude. Food can, perhaps, be significantly increased to meet a growing demand. But what about clean beaches, unspoiled forests, and solitude? If we satisfy a growing population's need for food, we necessarily decrease its per-capita supply of the other resources needed by men.

32   India, for example, now has a population of 600 million, which increases by 15 million each year. This population already puts a huge load on a relatively impoverished environment. The country's forests are now only a small fraction of what they were three centuries ago, and floods and erosion continually destroy the insufficient farmland that remains. Every one of the 15 million new lives added to India's population puts an additional burden on the environment, and increases the economic and social costs of crowding. However humanitarian our intent, every Indian life saved through medical or nutritional assistance from abroad diminishes the quality of life for those who remain, and for subsequent generations. If rich countries make it possible, through foreign aid, for 600 million Indians to swell to 1.2 billion in a mere twenty-eight years, as their current growth rate threatens, will future generations of Indians thank us for hastening the destruction of their environment? Will our good intentions be sufficient excuse for the consequences of our actions?

33   My final example of a commons in action is one for which the public has the least desire for rational discussion—immigration. Anyone who publicly questions the wisdom of current U.S. immigration policy is promptly charged with bigotry, prejudice, ethnocentrism, chauvinism, isolationism or selfishness. Rather than encounter such accusations, one would rather talk about other matters, leaving immigration policy to wallow in the

crosscurrents of special interests that take no account of the good of the whole, or the interest of posterity.

Perhaps we still feel guilty about things we said in the past. Two generations ago the popular press frequently referred to Dagos, Wops, Polacks, Chinks and Krauts, in articles about how America was being "overrun" by foreigners of supposedly inferior genetic stock. But because the implied inferiority of foreigners was used then as justification for keeping them out, people now assume that restrictive policies could only be based on such misguided notions. There are no other grounds.   34

A NATION OF IMMIGRANTS

Just consider the numbers involved. Our Government acknowledges a net inflow of 400,000 immigrants a year. While we have no hard data on the extent of illegal entries, educated guesses put the figure at about 600,000 a year. Since the natural increase (excess of births over deaths) of the resident population now runs about 1.7 million per year, the yearly gain from immigration amounts to at least 19 percent of the total annual increase, and may be as much as 37 percent if we include the estimate for illegal immigrants. Considering the growing use of birth-control devices, the potential effect of educational campaigns by such organizations as Planned Parenthood Federation of America and Zero Population Growth, and the influence of inflation and the housing shortage, the fertility rate of American women may decline so much that immigration could account for all the yearly increase in population. Should we not at least ask if that is what we want?   35

For the sake of those who worry about whether the "quality" of the average immigrant compares favorably with the quality of the average resident, let us assume that immigrants and native-born citizens are of exactly equal quality, however one defines that term. We will focus here only on quantity; and since our conclusions will depend on nothing else, all charges of bigotry and chauvinism become irrelevant.   36

IMMIGRATION VS. FOOD SUPPLY

World food banks *move food to the people,* hastening the exhaustion of the environment of the poor countries. Unrestricted immigration, on the other hand, *moves people to the food,* thus speeding up the destruction of the environment of the rich countries. We can easily understand why poor people should want to make this latter transfer, but why should rich hosts encourage it?   37

As in the case of foreign-aid programs, immigration receives support from selfish interests and humanitarian impulses. The primary selfish interest in unimpeded immigration is the desire of employers for cheap labor, particularly in industries and trades that offer degrading work. In the past, one wave of foreigners after another was brought into the U.S. to work at wretched jobs for wretched wages. In recent years, the Cubans, Puerto Ricans and Mexicans have had this dubious honor. The interests of the employers of cheap labor mesh well with the guilty silence of the country's liberal intelligentsia. White Anglo-Saxon Protestants are particularly reluctant to call for a closing of the doors to immigration for fear of being called bigots.   38

39   But not all countries have such reluctant leadership. Most educated Hawaiians, for example, are keenly aware of the limits of their environment, particularly in terms of population growth. There is only so much room on the islands, and the islanders know it. To Hawaiians, immigrants from the other forty-nine states present as great a threat as those from other nations. At a recent meeting of Hawaiian government officials in Honolulu, I had the ironic delight of hearing a speaker, who like most of his audience was of Japanese ancestry, ask how the country might practically and constitutionally close its doors to further immigration. One member of the audience countered: "How can we shut the doors now? We have many friends and relatives in Japan that we'd like to bring here some day so that they can enjoy Hawaii too." The Japanese-American speaker smiled sympathetically and answered: "Yes, but we have children now, and someday we'll have grandchildren too. We can bring more people here from Japan only by giving away some of the land that we hope to pass on to our grandchildren some day. What right do we have to do that?"

40   At this point, I can hear U.S. liberals asking, "How can you justify slamming the door once you're inside? You say that immigrants should be kept out. But aren't we all immigrants, or the descendants of immigrants? If we insist on staying, must we not admit all others?" Our craving for intellectual order leads us to seek and prefer symmetrical rules and morals: a single rule for me and everybody else; the same rule yesterday, today, and tomorrow. Justice, we feel, should not change with time and place.

41   We Americans of non-Indian ancestry can look upon ourselves as the descendants of thieves who are guilty morally, if not legally, of stealing this land from its Indian owners. Should we then give back the land to the now living American descendants of those Indians? However morally or logically sound this proposal may be, I, for one, am unwilling to live by it and I know no one else who is. Besides, the logical consequence would be absurd. Suppose that, intoxicated with a sense of pure justice, we should decide to turn our land over to the Indians. Since all our wealth has also been derived from the land, wouldn't we be morally obliged to give that back to the Indians too?

PURE JUSTICE VS. REALITY

42   Clearly, the concept of pure justice produces an infinite regression to absurdity. Centuries ago, wise men invented statutes of limitations to justify the rejection of such pure justice, in the interest of preventing continual disorder. The law zealously defends property rights, but only relatively recent property rights. Drawing a line after an arbitrary time has elapsed may be unjust, but the alternatives are worse.

43   We are all descendants of thieves, and the world's resources are inequitably distributed. But we must begin the journey to tomorrow from the point where we are today. We cannot remake the past. We cannot safely divide the wealth equitably among all peoples so long as people reproduce at different rates. To do so would guarantee that our grandchildren, and everyone else's grandchildren, would have only a ruined world to inhabit.

44   To be generous with one's own possessions is quite different from being generous with those of posterity. We should call this point to the attention of those who, from a

commendable love of justice and equality, would institute a system of the commons, either in the form of a world food bank, or of unrestricted immigration. We must convince them if we wish to save at least some parts of the world from environmental ruin.

Without a true world government to control reproduction and the use of available re-   45
sources, the sharing ethic of the spaceship is impossible. For the foreseeable future, our survival demands that we govern our actions by the ethics of a lifeboat, harsh though they may be. Posterity will be satisfied with nothing less.

Rich and Poor

Peter Singer

This article, by one of the world's most influential and controversial moral philosophers, appeared in the second edition of his book Practical Ethics (*1993*).

Consider these facts: by the most cautious estimates, 400 million people lack the calo-   1
ries, protein, vitamins and minerals needed for a normally healthy life. Millions are constantly hungry; others suffer from deficiency diseases and from infections they would be able to resist on a better diet. Children are worst affected. According to one estimate, 15 million children under five die every year from the combined effects of malnutrition and infection. In some areas, half the children born can be expected to die before their fifth birthday.

Nor is lack of food the only hardship of the poor. To give a broader picture, Robert   2
McNamara, President of the World Bank, has suggested the term "absolute poverty." The poverty we are familiar with in industrialized nations is relative poverty—meaning that some citizens are poor, relative to the wealth enjoyed by their neighbors. People living in relative poverty in Australia might be quite comfortably off by comparison with old-age pensioners in Britain, and British old-age pensioners are not poor in comparison with the poverty that exists in Mali or Ethiopia. Absolute poverty, on the other hand, is poverty by any standard. In McNamara's words:

> Poverty at the absolute level . . . is life at the very margin of existence.
>
> The absolute poor are severely deprived human beings struggling to survive in a set of squalid and degraded circumstances almost beyond the power of our sophisticated imaginations and privileged circumstances to conceive.
>
> Compared to those fortunate enough to live in developed countries, individuals in the poorest nations have:
>
> An infant mortality rate eight times higher
>
> A life expectancy one-third lower
>
> An adult literacy rate 60% less
>
> A nutritional level, for one out of every two in the population, below acceptable standards; and for millions of infants, less protein than is sufficient to permit optimum development of the brain.

3   Absolute poverty is, as McNamara has said, responsible for the loss of countless lives, especially among infants and young children. When absolute poverty does not cause death it still causes misery of a kind not often seen in the affluent nations. Malnutrition in young children stunts both physical and mental development. It has been estimated that the health, growth and learning capacity of nearly half the young children in developing countries are affected by malnutrition. Millions of people on poor diets suffer from deficiency diseases, like goitre, or blindness caused by a lack of vitamin A. The food value of what the poor eat is further reduced by parasites such as hookworm and ringworm, which are endemic in conditions of poor sanitation and health education.

4   Death and disease apart, absolute poverty remains a miserable condition of life, with inadequate food, shelter, clothing, sanitation, health services and education. According to World Bank estimates which define absolute poverty in terms of income levels insufficient to provide adequate nutrition, something like 800 million people—almost 40% of the people of developing countries—live in absolute poverty. Absolute poverty is probably the principal cause of human misery today. . . .

5   The problem is not that the world cannot produce enough to feed and shelter its people. People in the poor countries consume, on average, 400 lbs of grain a year, while North Americans average more than 2000 lbs. The difference is caused by the fact that in the rich countries we feed most of our grain to animals, converting it into meat, milk and eggs. Because this is an inefficient process, wasting up to 95% of the food value of the animal feed, people in rich countries are responsible for the consumption of far more food than those in poor countries who eat few animal products. If we stopped feeding animals on grains, soybeans and fishmeal the amount of food saved would—if distributed to those who need it—be more than enough to end hunger throughout the world.

6   These facts about animal food do not mean that we can easily solve the world food problem by cutting down on animal products, but they show that the problem is essentially one of distribution rather than production. The world does produce enough food. Moreover the poorer nations themselves could produce far more if they made more use of improved agricultural techniques.

7   So why are people hungry? Poor people cannot afford to buy grain grown by American farmers. Poor farmers cannot afford to buy improved seeds, or fertilizers, or the machinery needed for drilling wells and pumping water. Only by transferring some of the wealth of the developed nations to the poor of the undeveloped nations can the situation be changed.

8   That this wealth exists is clear. Against the picture of absolute poverty that McNamara has painted, one might pose a picture of "absolute affluence." Those who are absolutely affluent are not necessarily affluent by comparison with their neighbors, but they are affluent by any reasonable definition of human needs. This means that they have more income than they need to provide themselves adequately with all the basic necessities of life. After buying food, shelter, clothing, necessary health services and education, the absolutely affluent are still able to spend money on luxuries. The absolutely affluent choose their food for the pleasures of the palate, not to stop hunger; they buy new clothes to look fashionable, not to keep warm; they move house to be in a better neighbourhood or have a play room for the children, not to keep out the rain; and after all this there is still money to spend on books and records, colour television, and overseas holidays.

At this stage I am making no ethical judgments about absolute affluence, merely point-   9
ing out that it exists. Its defining characteristic is a significant amount of income above the
level necessary to provide for the basic human needs of oneself and one's dependents. By
this standard Western Europe, North America, Japan, Australia, New Zealand and the oil-
rich Middle Eastern states are all absolutely affluent, and so are many, if not all, of their citizens. The USSR and Eastern Europe might also be included on this list. To quote McNamara
once more:

> The average citizen of a developed country enjoys wealth beyond the wildest dreams
> of the one billion people in countries with per capita incomes under $200. . . .

These, therefore, are the countries—and individuals—who have wealth which they could,
without threatening their own basic welfare, transfer to the absolutely poor.

At present, very little is being transferred. Members of the Organization of Petroleum   10
Exporting Countries lead the way, giving an average of 2.1% of their Gross National Product. Apart from them, only Sweden, The Netherlands and Norway have reached the modest UN target of 0.7% of GNP. Britain gives 0.38% of its GNP in official development
assistance and a small amount in unofficial aid from voluntary organizations. The total
comes to less than £1 per month per person, and compares with 5.5% of GNP spent on alcohol, and 3% on tobacco. Other, even wealthier nations, give still less: Germany gives
0.27%, the United States 0.22% and Japan 0.21%.

The Obligation to Assist.   The path from the library at my university to the Human-   11
ities lecture theatre passes a shallow ornamental pond. Suppose that on my way to give a
lecture I notice that a small child has fallen in and is in danger of drowning. Would anyone
deny that I ought to wade in and pull the child out? This will mean getting my clothes
muddy, and either cancelling my lecture or delaying it until I can find something dry to
change into; but compared with the avoidable death of a child this is insignificant.

A plausible principle that would support the judgment that I ought to pull the child out   12
is this: if it is in our power to prevent something very bad happening, without thereby sacrificing anything of comparable moral significance, we ought to do it. This principle seems
uncontroversial. It will obviously win the assent of consequentialists; but non-consequentialists should accept it too, because the injunction to prevent what is bad applies only when
nothing comparably significant is at stake. Thus the principle cannot lead to the kinds of
actions of which non-consequentialists strongly disapprove—serious violations of individual rights, injustice, broken promises, and so on. If a non-consequentialist regards any of
these as comparable in moral significance to the bad thing that is to be prevented, he will
automatically regard the principle as not applying in those cases in which the bad thing can
only be prevented by violating rights, doing injustice, breaking promises, or whatever else
is at stake. Most non-consequentialists hold that we ought to prevent what is bad and promote what is good. Their dispute with consequentialists lies in their insistence that this is
not the sole ultimate ethical principle: that it is *an* ethical principle is not denied by any
plausible ethical theory.

Nevertheless the uncontroversial appearance of the principle that we ought to pre-   13
vent what is bad when we can do so without sacrificing anything of comparable moral

significance is deceptive. If it were taken seriously and acted upon, our lives and our world would be fundamentally changed. For the principle applies, not just to rare situations in which one can save a child from a pond, but to the everyday situation in which we can assist those living in absolute poverty. In saying this I assume that absolute poverty, with its hunger and malnutrition, lack of shelter, illiteracy, disease, high infant mortality and low life expectancy, is a bad thing. And I assume that it is within the power of the affluent to reduce absolute poverty, without sacrificing anything of comparable moral significance. If these two assumptions and the principle we have been discussing are correct, we have an obligation to help those in absolute poverty which is no less strong than our obligation to rescue a drowning child from a pond. Not to help would be wrong, whether or not it is intrinsically equivalent to killing. Helping is not, as conventionally thought, a charitable act which it is praiseworthy to do, but not wrong to omit; it is something that everyone ought to do.

14   This is the argument for an obligation to assist. Set out more formally, it would look like this:

FIRST PREMISE:	If we can prevent something bad without sacrificing anything of comparable significance, we ought to do it.
SECOND PREMISE:	Absolute poverty is bad.
THIRD PREMISE:	There is some absolute poverty we can prevent without sacrificing anything of comparable moral significance.
CONCLUSION:	We ought to prevent some absolute poverty.

15   The first premise is the substantive moral premise on which the argument rests, and I have tried to show that it can be accepted by people who hold a variety of ethical positions.

16   The second premise is unlikely to be challenged. Absolute poverty is, as McNamara put it, "beneath any reasonable definition of human decency" and it would be hard to find a plausible ethical view which did not regard it as a bad thing.

17   The third premise is more controversial, even though it is cautiously framed. It claims only that some absolute poverty can be prevented without the sacrifice of anything of comparable moral significance. It thus avoids the objection that any aid I can give is just "drops in the ocean" for the point is not whether my personal contribution will make any noticeable impression on world poverty as a whole (of course it won't) but whether it will prevent some poverty. This is all the argument needs to sustain its conclusion, since the second premise says that any absolute poverty is bad, and not merely the total amount of absolute poverty. If without sacrificing anything of comparable moral significance we can provide just one family with the means to raise itself out of absolute poverty, the third premise is vindicated.

18   I have left the notion of moral significance unexamined in order to show that the argument does not depend on any specific values or ethical principles. I think the third premise is true for most people living in industrialized nations, on any defensible view of what is morally significant. Our affluence means that we have income we can dispose of without giving up the basic necessities of life, and we can use this income to

reduce absolute poverty. Just how much we will think ourselves obliged to give up will depend on what we consider to be of comparable moral significance to the poverty we could prevent: colour television, stylish clothes, expensive dinners, a sophisticated stereo system, overseas holidays, a (second?) car, a larger house, private schools for our children. . . . For a utilitarian, none of these is likely to be of comparable significance to the reduction of absolute poverty; and those who are not utilitarians surely must, if they subscribe to the principle of universalizability, accept that at least *some* of these things are of far less moral significance than the absolute poverty that could be prevented by the money they cost. So the third premise seems to be true on any plausible ethical view—although the precise amount of absolute poverty that can be prevented before anything of moral significance is sacrificed will vary according to the ethical view one accepts.

Taking Care of Our Own.   Anyone who has worked to increase overseas aid will   19
have come across the argument that we should look after those near us, our families and then the poor in our own country, before we think about poverty in distant places.

No doubt we do instinctively prefer to help those who are close to us. Few could stand   20
by and watch a child drown; many can ignore a famine in Africa. But the question is not what we usually do, but what we ought to do, and it is difficult to see any sound moral justification for the view that distance, or community membership, makes a crucial difference to our obligations.

Consider, for instance, racial affinities. Should whites help poor whites before helping   21
poor blacks? Most of us would reject such a suggestion out of hand: people's need for food has nothing to do with their race, and if blacks need food more than whites, it would be a violation of the principle of equal consideration to give preference to whites.

The same point applies to citizenship or nationhood. Every affluent nation has some   22
relatively poor citizens, but absolute poverty is limited largely to the poor nations. Those living on the streets of Calcutta, or in a drought stricken region of the Sahel, are experiencing poverty unknown in the West. Under these circumstances it would be wrong to decide that only those fortunate enough to be citizens of our own community will share our abundance. . . .

The element of truth in the view that we should first take care of our own, lies in the   23
advantage of a recognized system of responsibilities. When families and local communities look after their own poorer members, ties of affection and personal relationships achieve ends that would otherwise require a large, impersonal bureaucracy. Hence it would be absurd to propose that from now on we all regard ourselves as equally responsible for the welfare of everyone in the world; but the argument for an obligation to assist does not propose that. It applies only when some are in absolute poverty, and others can help without sacrificing anything of comparable moral significance. To allow one's own kin to sink into absolute poverty would be to sacrifice something of comparable significance; and before that point had been reached, the breakdown of the system of family and community responsibility would be a factor to weigh the balance in favour of a small degree of preference for family and community. This small degree of preference is, however, decisively outweighed by existing discrepancies in wealth and property.

24   **Property Rights.**   Do people have a right to private property, a right which contradicts the view that they are under an obligation to give some of their wealth away to those in absolute poverty? According to some theories of rights (for instance, Robert Nozick's)[1] provided one has acquired one's property without the use of unjust means like force and fraud, one may be entitled to enormous wealth while others starve. This individualistic conception of rights is in contrast to other views, like the early Christian doctrine to be found in the works of Thomas Aquinas, which holds that since property exists for the satisfaction of human needs, "whatever a man has in superabundance is owed, of natural right, to the poor for their sustenance." A socialist would also, of course, see wealth as belonging to the community rather than the individual, while utilitarians, whether socialist or not, would be prepared to override property rights to prevent great evils. . . .

25   However, I do not think we should accept such an individualistic theory. It leaves too much to chance to be an acceptable ethical view. For instance, those whose forefathers happened to inhabit some sandy wastes around the Persian Gulf are now fabulously wealthy, because oil lay under those sands; while those whose forefathers settled on better land south of the Sahara live in absolute poverty, because of drought and bad harvests. Can this distribution be acceptable from an impartial point of view? If we imagine ourselves about to begin life as a citizen of either Kuwait or Chad—but we do not know which—would we accept the principle that citizens of Kuwait are under no obligation to assist people living in Chad?

26   **Population and the Ethics of Triage.**   Perhaps the most serious objection to the argument that we have an obligation to assist is that since the major cause of absolute poverty is overpopulation, helping those now in poverty will only ensure that yet more people are born to live in poverty in the future.

27   In its most extreme form, this objection is taken to show that we should adopt a policy of "triage." The term comes from medical policies adopted in wartime. With too few doctors to cope with all the casualties, the wounded were divided into three categories: those who would probably survive without medical assistance, those who might survive if they received assistance, but otherwise probably would not, and those who even with medical assistance probably would not survive. Only those in the middle category were given medical assistance. The idea, of course, was to use limited medical resources as effectively as possible. For those in the first category, medical treatment was not strictly necessary; for those in the third category, it was likely to be useless. It has been suggested that we should apply the same policies to countries, according to their prospects of becoming self-sustaining. We would not aid countries which even without our help will soon be able to feed their populations. We would not aid countries which, even with our help, will not be able to limit their population to a level they can feed. We would aid those countries where our help might make the difference between success and failure in bringing food and population into balance.

28   Advocates of this theory are understandably reluctant to give a complete list of the countries they would place into the "hopeless" category; but Bangladesh is often cited as

---

[1]Robert Nozick, *Anarchy, State, and Utopia* (New York, Basic Books, 1974).

an example. Adopting the policy of triage would, then, mean cutting off assistance to Bangladesh and allowing famine, disease and natural disasters to reduce the population of that country (now around 80 million) to the level at which it can provide adequately for all.

In support of this view Garrett Hardin has offered a metaphor: we in the rich nations   29
are like the occupants of a crowded lifeboat adrift in a sea full of drowning people. If we try to save the drowning by bringing them aboard our boat will be overloaded and we shall all drown. Since it is better that some survive than none, we should leave the others to drown. In the world today, according to Hardin, "lifeboat ethics" apply. The rich should leave the poor to starve, for otherwise the poor will drag the rich down with them. . . .

The consequences of triage on this scale are so horrible that we are inclined to reject   30
it without further argument. How could we sit by our television sets, watching millions starve while we do nothing? Would not that (far more than the proposals for legalizing euthanasia) be the end of all notions of human equality and respect for human life? Don't people have a right to our assistance, irrespective of the consequences?

Anyone whose initial reaction to triage was not one of repugnance would be an un-   31
pleasant sort of person. Yet initial reactions based on strong feelings are not always reliable guides. Advocates of triage are rightly concerned with the long-term consequences of our actions. They say that helping the poor and starving now merely ensures more poor and starving in the future. When our capacity to help is finally unable to cope—as one day it must be—the suffering will be greater than it would be if we stopped helping now. If this is correct, there is nothing we can do to prevent absolute starvation and poverty, in the long run, and so we have no obligation to assist. Nor does it seem reasonable to hold that under these circumstances people have a right to our assistance. If we do accept such a right, ir-respective of the consequences, we are saying that, in Hardin's metaphor, we would con-tinue to haul the drowning into our lifeboat until the boat sank and we all drowned.

If triage is to be rejected it must be tackled on its own ground, within the framework   32
of consequentialist ethics. Here it is vulnerable. Any consequentialist ethics must take prob-ability of outcome into account. A course of action that will certainly produce some bene-fit is to be preferred to an alternative course that may lead to a slightly larger benefit, but is equally likely to result in no benefit at all. Only if the greater magnitude of the uncertain benefit outweighs its uncertainty should we choose it. Better one certain unit of benefit than a 10% chance of 5 units; but better a 50% chance of 3 units than a single certain unit. The same principle applies when we are trying to avoid evils.

The policy of triage involves a certain, very great evil: population control by famine and   33
disease. Tens of millions would die slowly. Hundreds of millions would continue to live in absolute poverty, at the very margin of existence. Against this prospect, advocates of the policy place a possible evil which is greater still: the same process of famine and disease, taking place in, say, fifty years time, when the world's population may be three times its present level, and the number who will die from famine, or struggle on in absolute poverty, will be that much greater. The question is: how probable is this forecast that continued as-sistance now will lead to greater disasters in the future?

Forecasts of population growth are notoriously fallible, and theories about the factors   34
which affect it remain speculative. One theory, at least as plausible as any other, is that countries pass through a "demographic transition" as their standard of living rises. When

people are very poor and have no access to modern medicine their fertility is high, but population is kept in check by high death rates. The introduction of sanitation, modern medical techniques and other improvements reduces the death rate, but initially has little effect on the birth rate. Then population grows rapidly. Most poor countries are now in this phase. If standards of living continue to rise, however, couples begin to realize that to have the same number of children surviving to maturity as in the past, they do not need to give birth to as many children as their parents did. The need for children to provide economic support in old age diminishes. Improved education and the emancipation and employment of women also reduce the birthrate, and so population growth begins to level off. Most rich nations have reached this stage, and their populations are growing only very slowly.

35   If this theory is right, there is an alternative to the disasters accepted as inevitable by supporters of triage. We can assist poor countries to raise the living standards of the poorest members of their population. We can encourage the governments of these countries to enact land reform measures, improve education, and liberate women from a purely child-bearing role. We can also help other countries to make contraception and sterilization widely available. There is a fair chance that these measures will hasten the onset of the demographic transition and bring population growth down to a manageable level. Success cannot be guaranteed; but the evidence that improved economic security and education reduce population growth is strong enough to make triage ethically unacceptable. We cannot allow millions to die from starvation and disease when there is a reasonable probability that population can be brought under control without such horrors.

Children and Poverty in America

James Garbarino

James Garbarino is the director of the Family Life Development Center and a professor of human development and family studies at Cornell University. This article appeared in National Forum *in 1996.*

1   What does it mean to be poor in America? In one sense, this question is easy to answer: Sophie Tucker pointed us in the right direction when she said, "I've been rich and I've been poor . . . and rich is better." Good as it is, however, the question and the answer are insufficient. We need more.

2   By official government policy, an objective definition of poverty exists. It is based upon the income needed to meet an agreed-upon minimal standard of living. Thus, the poverty line at a given time and place is defined as X dollars for a family of Y persons. But as with most objective classifications of complex human phenomena, this simple definition masks a host of subtleties and complexities of what poverty means for children.

3   What does being poor mean to a child? We know that being poor means being at statistical risk. Poor children live in the kinds of socially toxic environments that generate multiple threats to development—academic failure, child maltreatment, learning disabilities,

and others. That is one clear meaning of being poor in America. Interestingly, this social toxicity parallels physical toxicity; low-income populations are more likely to be exposed to chemical and radioactive waste and polluted air and water. Being poor means that the odds are stacked against you. Poverty has that meaning in a statistical sense. But what does poverty mean to a child?

The daughter of a colleague once wrote in a composition for school that she was "the   4
poorest kid on her block" because she lived in the smallest house. She did live in the small-est house on the block. However, it was a seven-bedroom house on a block of mansions. What does it mean to children to be poor if they use such a relative standard as poor means having less than others?

When most of the people of the world live on incomes of hundreds of dollars a year,   5
what does it mean when we define the poverty level at $14,000 dollars a year? As Cristina S. Blanc points out in *Urban Children in Distress: Global Predicaments and Innovative Strategies,* India defines poverty as having access to less than 2,100 calories per day. Using that yardstick, 20 percent of the population are poor (a figure roughly the same as ours). If poor children around the world are shoeless, how do we make sense of American poor kids who wear $150 running shoes? Once when I was in China, a man reported to me that be-fore the 1948 Revolution very few people were rich, but that now many people were rich. As evidence he pointed to the fact that he himself owned a wrist watch, a radio, and a bi-cycle. By that standard, poverty is virtually absent in the United States, and we Americans are universally rich.

Analyzing the meaning of poverty for children is not simple. It is not a matter of sim-   6
ple accounting. Rather, it calls for thinking about the relationship between the meaning and meeting of basic needs and the social conditions that shape those meanings. It calls for a look at the economic context of childhood in the United States. Being poor is about being left out of what your society tells people they could expect if they were included. It is a so-cial question at root. Recently a child asked me, "When you were growing up, were you poor or regular?" That is it precisely. Being poor means being different, not meeting the basic standards set by your society, not being "regular." It is not so much a matter of what you have, as what you do not have. And, it is the messages that difference sends.

THE ECONOMICS OF CHILDHOOD

In contrast to most of the societies of Western Europe, we have not put into place the   7
basic elements of a modern social-welfare state—universal access to health care, a livable minimum wage, direct child subsidies. Thus, poverty is the vehicle through which the de-ficiencies in our economic thinking and action are made manifest.

However it is defined, poverty is a risk factor in two ways. First, it reflects terrible ob-   8
stacles to participating fully in the monetarized economy. That problem becomes ever big-ger as monetarization proceeds, and resources in the non-monetarized economy become inaccessible and devalued. Second, it is tied up in feelings of shame.

Both risks have grown in recent decades. Poverty now has messages that were largely   9
absent in the past. This change is one way to understand the many first-person accounts of life in an earlier era that begin, "I never knew we were poor until. . . ." A priest tells the

story of spending a day at school putting together "poor baskets" for Christmas, only to be shocked the next day when one was delivered to his house. "I never knew we were poor until that day," he recounts.

10   The conventional way of looking at the economy confines serious analysis to the monetarized economy, without regard to its relationship with the non-monetarized economy. This deficiency can hide troubling problems. For example, the GNP grew by 2.2 percent in the 1980s. Good news for families? Not really, because in that same period child poverty doubled, so that by the end of the 1980s more children lived in poverty than at the start of the decade. More to the point is the finding that income for the lower 40 percent of Americans declined during the 1980s (and declined 4.4 percent for the bottom 20 percent of the population).

11   What's more, young families suffered the most severe declines in income. These declines were most evident for families in which the breadwinners had a track record of educational failure. In particular, families headed by high-school dropouts suffered a 17.3-percent decline in income during the 1980s.

12   At the same time, income for educationally successful families (for example, those with college-educated breadwinners) increased significantly. For families in the top 20 percent of the income structure, income increased by 28.9 percent, and for the top 1 percent it increased by 74 percent! (Economic Policy Institute, *The State of Working America*, 1989). Tax policies that relieve upper-income taxpayers while increasing the burden of lower-income taxpayers have compounded this problem.

13   At one time (not that long ago in our national history), it made sense to use the unemployment rate as a good indicator of family well-being because it was taken for granted that being employed meant having enough income to meet children's basic needs. But a report prepared for the Congress by the U.S. Census Bureau concluded that half the new jobs created during the 1980s paid a wage that was less than the poverty figure for a family of four, even if held full-time for twelve months out of the year (*Money, Income, and Poverty Studies of Families and Persons in the United States*, 1989). And this trend continues in the 1990s (as does the trend noted earlier in which the minimum wage fails to raise a family above the poverty line). The point is that lowered unemployment rates may mislead us into thinking that things are improving for families. But if holding a full-time job still means poverty for a worker's children, then the numbers are giving us a false picture of what is really going on. This problem is particularly serious for single-parent, female-headed households because women earn on average only 70 percent of what men earn.

14   Some economists argue that the basis used for calculating the poverty level itself is flawed because of the disproportionate rise in the costs of food, housing, and child care—which consume a greater proportion of income at the lower rather than the higher end of the scale. Others contend that this increase in costs is offset by the fact that non-cash medical benefits available to the poor are not included in the standard calculations of the poverty level. Whatever the resolution to these debates, poverty remains a serious psychological and moral problem for American families and for the entire society because of the adverse consequences that poverty brings to children (and for what it indicates about a family).

15   Despite the rosy economic data presented in some quarters in the early 1990s, the real economic news for families is bad and getting worse. For example, fewer and fewer fami-

lies with one income can afford to own a home. Most single parents are priced out of the market entirely, while many two-parent families face the strain of coping with child-care issues and general exhaustion in an effort to participate in the experience of owning a home.

This point is important because home ownership is valuable for the family and for the community both psychologically and socially. It motivates investment in the community and enhances stability. Homeowners have a stake in the well-being of the community. Ownership builds financial equity that can be cashed in or borrowed against to fund important activities (for example, college education for children). It is the bedrock of middle-class economic life, the bedrock of the bedrock.   16

Poverty is social quicksand. It swallows up community. We cannot expect child-welfare services to compensate for our society's deteriorating foundations, to clean up the mess of social toxicity. Right now we are passing the buck until it stops at the door of those who are charged with the responsibility of child-protective services, remedial education, and all other human services that were designed to be a last resort rather than the principal resource base for developing children.   17

WHERE YOU ARE POOR MATTERS

The geographic concentration of poverty is an important indicator of growing toxicity and a challenge to our belief in community. A study by Claudia J. Coulton in Cleveland (*American Behavioral Scientist 35*.3, 1992) revealed that the percentage of that city's poor people living in neighborhoods with concentrated poverty (meaning an area in which more than 40 percent of the residents were poor) increased from 21 percent in 1970 to 61 percent in 1990. Why is that important? It is important because economically mixed areas offer advantages to both the middle class and the poor. For the poor they mean the presence of multiple role models, for concrete alternative answers to the question, "How else might I live?" They also mean that poor kids will have potential access to families with extra resources, resources that can be shared—an extra ticket to the ball game, a visit to the zoo, an inside look at what middle-class life is like and what it takes to move up. For affluent kids, living near poor families is a good antidote for negative stereotypes. Without rubbing shoulders with real poor kids and thus having an opportunity to form authentic relationships, affluent kids must depend upon the news media, social-studies classes, and chance encounters to give poverty a human face.   18

I suspect the growing estrangement of affluent and poor families is one reason why, when an informal survey of middle-class children posed the following question, "Which would be worse, to be poor or to be blind?" a majority of the children chose "poor" as the worse alternative. Why? When asked to explain, one replied that "You could do something about being blind, but you couldn't do anything about being poor."   19

Childish thinking? A distorted value system? Perhaps. But perhaps also these children were on the mark in assessing the life implications of poverty in America today, when poverty is coming to be more and more intractable a problem at both the personal and the social levels, and an affluent person does have many resources to turn to in dealing with blindness.   20

Economic disturbances that occur now are more closely related to social toxicity for many reasons. One is that people must face them in the wake of the economic track record   21 of the post–World War II era that led most Americans, except perhaps the chronically impoverished underclass, to expect material affluence on a mass scale that was unprecedented in human history. Many now take for granted as necessities what were considered previously to be luxuries. Even poor people may now have things that once were considered luxuries (for instance, television). The news media, in particular television, compound this perception by making everyone intimately aware of what is possible (and what someone else has). This combination of knowing what "regular" people have and what you do not have has become increasingly socially toxic for children.

22   Although the federal budget includes a substantial commitment to entitlement programs, most of the budget goes to programs that disproportionately assist affluent adults, while relatively little goes to families with young children in the service of child welfare–related objectives. This may explain why correlations between measures of income or socioeconomic status and basic child outcomes are often higher in the United States than in other modern societies (Urie Bronfenbrenner, *Developmental Psychology 22*.6, 1986). Low income is a better predictor of child-development deficits in the United States than in other countries because our social policies tend to exaggerate rather than minimize the effect of family income on access to preventive and rehabilitative services.

23   What does it take to meet the minimal standards for child care? Any statement of the budget for child care by a family reflects assumptions about the kinds of materials that are necessary. For example, previous generations used cloth diapers and made large investments of time and personal energy to maintain them. Currently, even families with small incomes and very limited prospects for earning have come to think of expensive paper/plastic diapers as a basic necessity. These substitutes cost a great deal, and their environmental impact is insidious.

24   Even a financially affluent social environment may lack the kind of enduring support systems that adolescents need to provide positive role models, caring adult supervision, and a sense of personal validation. The same may be true for the parents of those adolescents who may feel acutely embarrassed to admit difficulty with their adolescents in a community in which there is a presumption of competence and high expectations for achievement. Of course, having said this, I must quickly reassert that the social toxicity that comes from unsupportive communities is seen most clearly among the poor, and particularly among the concentrations of poverty that have come to dominate many inner-city areas.

A MATTER OF VALUES

25   It is one thing for social-class differences to predict matters of style and taste—for example, whether you watch PBS or the Fox network, drink fine white wine or inexpensive red, or wear a blue blazer or overalls. It is quite another when social class—and poverty in particular—predicts who lives and who dies, and who is robust and who is disabled. But understanding the meaning of poverty for children is not simply a matter of calculating the correlations between income and social pathologies such as infant mortality. There is more to poverty than income disparities (although the disparities themselves are implicated in the problem).

26   If a lesson is to be learned from the 1980s, it is that in the current economic situation, without intervention, the rich really do get richer while the poor really do get poorer. The

internal situation in the United States thus mirrors the global choices to be made between more luxuries for the "haves" and more necessities for the "have-nots."

Average income is not the issue. Average income rose 14.5 percent during the 1980s.   27
If we adjust the Bureau of Labor statistics to account for inflation since the data were last compiled in the mid-1980s, for a family of four to live at a "high" level requires about $48,000, while to live at a "lower" ("struggling") level requires about $25,000, and living at the "poverty" level requires about $13,000. How do these numbers compare with the realities of family income? By 1989, half of America's families had an income of $33,974. That is good. But, the average income of the lowest 20 percent was $7,725 at the end of the 1980s—much too little while the average income of the highest 20 percent was $105,209—well above the comfort level.

While each dollar above the affluent range may mean nothing in terms of improved   28
child well-being, each dollar below the struggling level has a negative payoff in the welfare of children. It increases the odds of a child suffering from some form of physical, psychological, or social pathology. Each dollar above the adequate figure has only a marginal payoff in terms of child welfare and development. Expressed statistically, reducing poverty is associated with improved outcomes for children, while increasing affluence is not (Garbarino, *Successful Schools and Competent Students,* 1981).

Conventional economic models of growth do not recognize the critical quality of this   29
distinction. If one billion dollars were to be added to the GNP, conventional economic models would not see any intrinsic reason to be concerned with whether those added dollars come to raise incomes at the bottom or to increase wealth at the top. Conventional thinking about economic growth obscures this important fact. As a character in a recent *New Yorker* cartoon put it: "The poor are getting poorer, but with the rich getting richer it all averages out in the end." This problem is evident in Miringoff's 1995 analysis of "social health indicators" in the United States, *The Index of Social Health.* These data show that until the mid-1970s conventional measures of economic growth were positively correlated with increased social health of the population, but that since then the two measures have tended to be either uncorrelated or negatively correlated.

What should we expect? Along one path lies an increasing return to the Dickensian   30
model: extreme disparities of income and justice, with the lower end of the spectrum being mired in poverty. We can look to other countries—in Central and South America, for example—for case studies of what this would mean now that the United States has become as rife with economic inequality as any former "banana republic" ever was. Brazil is a prime example. Along another path lies a commitment to meet the basic needs of all of the people all of the time, regardless of race, creed, national origin, or income-generating capacity. Put another way, the goal is strengthening middle-class society as the foundation for a more socially benign environment for children.

The challenge is both intellectual and spiritual. The intellectual challenge is to insist   31
upon analytic models that address both the monetarized and the non-monetarized economies. This challenge strains our intellectual resources to their limits, and sometimes beyond. The spiritual challenge is to put our money where our values are, to make reducing poverty and reinforcing middle-class society our number one national priority. Achieving this goal means more than just handing out welfare checks, of course. It means building successful families, competent schools, and positive communities in which good jobs exist to meet the

basic human need to work. It means an accounting system that takes seriously the total wealth of families (in both the monetarized and non-monetarized economies) and their need for affirmation, respect, and regard. It means a commitment to see and deal with poverty in the lives of children as the highest priority in ensuring the basic human rights enshrined in the Declaration of Independence—life, liberty, and the pursuit of happiness.

Solving the Problem of Poverty
Steve Mariotti

Steve Mariotti is president and founder of the National Foundation for Teaching Entrepreneurship. This argument was delivered as a speech in May 1998 at the Shavano Institute for National Leadership seminar in Memphis, Tennessee.

1   I know a secret which, if fully understood by our government, business and community leaders, could have enormous positive implications for the future of our society. Simply put, the secret is this: Children born into poverty have special gifts that prepare them for business formation and wealth creation. They are mentally strong, resilient, and full of chutzpa. They are skeptical of hierarchies and the status quo. They are long-suffering in the face of adversity. They are comfortable with risk and uncertainty. They know how to deal with stress and conflict.

2   These are the attitudes and abilities that make them ideally suited for breaking out of the cycle of dependency that so often comes with poverty and for getting ahead in the marketplace. In short, poor kids are "street smart," or what we at the National Foundation for Teaching Entrepreneurship (NFTE) call "business smart." Precisely because of their poverty—that is, because of their experience surviving in a challenging world—they are able to perceive and pursue fleeting opportunities that others, more content with their lot in life, tend to miss.

3   Children born into poverty have all the characteristics of the classic entrepreneurs like Henry Ford, Andrew Carnegie, and Thomas Edison—the heroes of our capitalist system. It stands to reason, therefore, that as a society we should make special efforts to encourage the development of entrepreneurial skills among low-income youths. But we have done just the opposite, spending over $1.5 trillion since the beginning of the "War on Poverty" in the 1960s on public assistance programs that are actually designed to protect children from the free enterprise system.

4   In today's dollars, $1.5 trillion would be enough to purchase half of all the Fortune 500 companies in America. Such a colossal malinvestment has cost millions of dollars in lost revenue, and it has also discouraged millions of would-be young entrepreneurs from ever entering the marketplace.

5   This is a particular personal tragedy for children born into poverty, for, as the Nobel Prize winning economist F. A. Hayek once noted, the free market offers the most effective way of identifying what we are good at and how our comparative advantages can be developed. Public assistance limits and, in many cases even prevents, its recipients from

engaging in this vital process of self-discovery. As a result, generation after generation of children born into poverty are settling for the security of welfare while missing out on the thrills and challenges of competition. Properly developed, their skills might be highly valued in the marketplace—but they will never find out.

Even more misguided than our national welfare strategy is our 7.5 million-word tax   6
code. Even the most respected tax experts can't claim to understand fully this maze of vague and often contradictory rules that runs no less than 38,000 pages. How can we expect young people who have never even seen a W-2 form to make sense out of the thousands of tax regulations that apply to starting and running a business? The U.S. tax code has been a terrible burden for the business community, but for low-income youths it has been absolutely devastating.

Besides the length of the tax code, there is something even more insidious: The code   7
itself changes all the time. There is no constant body of information that can be regarded as definite and the $1.5 trillion I mentioned earlier has been minimal in comparison with the psychological damage to millions of people who have been told, in effect, by welfare and tax bureaucrats that they are "worthless goods" in the marketplace and that they will be rewarded for unproductive behavior.

I founded the National Foundation for Teaching Entrepreneurship (NFTE) on the   8
premise, which is still a secret to most, that children born into poverty have enormous potential in business. Let me share with you some of the history of NFTE.

After receiving an M.B.A. from the University of Michigan, I won a Liberty Fund fel-   9
lowship to study Austrian economics at the Institute for Humane Studies (IHS) with F. A. Hayek, who had just won the Nobel Peace Prize [sic] in Economics. Although I was well versed in free market principles because of my contacts at places such as Hillsdale College, this fellowship enabled me to increase my knowledge of Austrian trade cycle theory and international finance.

After leaving IHS, I spent the next 30 months at Ford Motor Company as the South   10
African and Latin American treasury analyst. Then I pulled up stakes and moved to New York to open an import-export firm specializing in African small business. This was great fun, and my business was profitable. But, as it happened, in 1981, I was robbed and beaten by a group of young men.

As a way of working through this traumatic event, I began a career as a special educa-   11
tion teacher in New York's most difficult impoverished neighborhoods. My first year was almost as traumatic as the mugging. I was assigned remedial students. In each of my classes, there was a group of six or seven students whose behavior was so disruptive that I had to stop the class every five minutes to get them to quiet down. On one occasion, in my third-period class, I was forced to throw out all the boys.

Ironically, it was these "troublemakers" who provided me with the valuable insight   12
that set me on the road to teaching entrepreneurship. I took them out to dinner one evening and asked them why they had acted so badly in class. They said my class was boring and I had nothing to teach them. I asked if anything I taught in class interested them. One fellow responded that I had caught his attention when I had discussed my import-export business. He rattled off various figures I had mentioned in class, calculated my profit margin, and concluded that my business was doing well.

13   I was dazzled to find such business smarts in a student whom the public schools had labeled "borderline retarded." This was my first inkling that something was wrong not only with my teaching but also with the standard remedial education curriculum.

14   Meanwhile, the situation at school worsened. I began to lose control of my classroom, almost on a daily basis. One student set fire to the back of another student's coat—the student with the coat was as astonished as I was. In a rage, I ordered the arsonist out of class, and he was expelled the same day. Days later, I was locked out of my eighth-period class. The students wouldn't open the door. Finally, just as I was going to admit defeat and find a security guard, one of the girls took pity on me and opened it.

15   I didn't know how to deal with this kind of nightmarish situation. I wanted to walk out of school and call it quits. After a minute or two, I realized that I couldn't do that. I stepped into the hallway to regain my composure. I thought about my dinner with the young men from my third-period class. They had said I was boring—except when I talked about business and about making money. I walked back into the classroom, and without any introductory comments, launched a mock sales pitch, selling my own watch to the class. I enumerated the benefits of the watch. I explained why the students should purchase it from me at the low price of only $6. The students quieted down and became interested in hearing what I had to say. I didn't know it at the time, but this incident, born of desperation, was pointing me toward my real vocation—teaching entrepreneurship to low-income youths.

16   After I had gained the students' attention, I moved from the sales talk into a conventional "buy low/sell high," and on the more advanced concept of "return on investment."

17   Before long, I began offering a special class, "How to Start, Finance, and Manage a Small Business—A Guide for the Urban Entrepreneur." During the next seven years, this course became so successful that even the most challenging and disruptive students settled down and learned a great deal. In my last teaching assignment in the Fort Apache area of the South Bronx, 100 percent of my students started small businesses and reported that they experienced major positive changes in their lives. The difference teaching entrepreneurship seemed to be making in regard to student behavior was incredible; I noticed among my students that chronic problems such as absenteeism, dropping out, pregnancy, drug use, drug dealing and violent behavior seemed to be significantly alleviated.

18   The overwhelming success of this class gave me the confidence to launch the National Foundation for Teaching Entrepreneurship (NFTE) in 1988. NFTE's mission is to teach low-income youths the basics of starting their own businesses by creating a curriculum, training teachers, and providing graduate services. NFTE has year-round programs in eight cities and license agreements in Scotland, Belgium, and soon, Argentina. We have 21,000 graduates, all of whom have learned the basics of the free enterprise economy.

19   In 1993, in conjunction with the Heller School at Brandeis University, we completed a study which found that NFTE program graduates were far more likely than their peers to start a business. Here are some specifics: 32 times more NFTE graduates than nongraduates were running a business, and a post program survey found that 33 percent of those graduates were still running a business. And in 1998, the David H. Koch Charitable Foundation sponsored one of the most comprehensive examinations of entrepreneurship training ever conducted. An organization known as Research & Evaluation for Philanthropy tracked two different randomly selected groups: one comprised of 120 low-income Wash-

ington, D.C., residents between the ages of 18 and 30 who had completed the NFTE program and one comprised of 152 of their peers who had received no training. Here are some of the highlights of the Koch study:

- 91 percent of the NFTE alumni stated that they wanted to start their own business, compared with 75 percent of the comparison group and 50 percent of the U.S. public.
- NFTE alumni were two times more likely to be current business owners (12 percent in the NFTE group vs. 5 percent in the comparison group). In fact, the rate of business formation was substantially higher than the 1–3 percent rate for minority adults nationwide.
- NFTE participation increased the likelihood of starting a business four-fold.
- NFTE increased high school students' exposure to business and entrepreneurship training fourteen-fold.
- 88 percent of NFTE alumni stated that they gave serious consideration to going into business after completing the program.
- 99 percent of NFTE alumni indicated that the program gave them a more positive view of business, and they were two times more likely to predict that they would own a business in five years.
- 68 percent of NFTE alumni were the first in their families to start a business.
- 97 percent of NFTE alumni reported improved business skills and knowledge.
- 100 percent said they would recommend the program to others.
- NFTE alumni were two times less likely to prefer government employment over business ownership and corporate management.

This study demonstrates that teaching about the free enterprise system and encouraging children to start businesses and create wealth are powerful tools that promote independence and self-sufficiency.

Today, we at NFTE are confident that our program is adding significant value to thousands   20
of young people's lives. We plan to "go to scale" and create a national movement in which every low-income child is taught entrepreneurial skills and elementary business principles.

Our plan is two-fold. First, we intend to recruit the best business and academic minds   21
to help us in our efforts. NFTE's board and sponsors now include some of America's leading businessmen and philanthropists.

Second, we intend to use high technology in all of NFTE's teaching models. This will   22
help our students to compete in the 21st century. Through an exciting partnership with Microsoft, NFTE has developed BizTech, a state-of-the-art learning site that offers an on-line curriculum. BizTech lets students anywhere in the world access information on entrepreneurship 24-hours-a-day, seven-days-a-week. Under the direction of NFTE's CEO, Michael J. Caslin III, BizTech will also enable them to begin trading online.

BizTech is currently operating as a pilot program in dozens of schools, and it has gener-   23
ated a huge positive response. Fortunately, we are now able to deliver much of our program

at a fraction of the initial cost. And a great selling point for the program is the fact that the administrative record-keeping function is on-line, which liberates the teacher from cumbersome paperwork and allows him to become a true guide and coach. Perhaps most exciting is the news that NFTE, in cooperation with some of the country's leading educators, is developing state-of-the-art lesson plans that fully integrate information technology into a classroom environment.

24   At NFTE, the future is bright for low-income youths. By combining the most recent technology with the time-tested principles of capitalism, we are developing solutions for one of the most serious threats to our society: poverty. Sure, we are small, but we are growing like a mustard seed.

25   One of our greatest strengths is the unquenchable optimism of the young men and women we serve. As one of NFTE's graduates put it so aptly, "My dream is not to die in poverty, but to have poverty die in me."

FOR CLASS DISCUSSION

1. Analyze and evaluate the controversy over the obligation of the rich to help the poor by applying the first set of guide questions from page 465. How do you account for the disagreement between Hardin and Singer? Which argument do you think employs stronger reasoning? How are the arguments based on different underlying assumptions?

2. Garbarino frames his argument about poverty as a definition argument whereas Mariotti frames his as a proposal argument. How well does each argument achieve its argumentative goal? Do you see these arguments as contradictory or complementary? What audience do you think each writer is particularly trying to influence?

3. Choose one of the arguments for closer analysis, applying the second set of guide questions on pages 465–66.

OPTIONAL WRITING ASSIGNMENT   At last, you've won the lottery. You'll be receiving $250,000 per year for the next twenty years. Ever since you got the news, your phone's been ringing off the hook. Your older brother, Fast Eddie, has called urging you to buy a big house and a fast car and to consider putting a couple of big ones on the Blue Jays for the American League pennant. Your younger sister, Sensible Sarah, has outlined a comprehensive investment strategy for you that will put you into CDs, zero coupon bonds, and a few blue chippers. Then Aunt Teresa calls. "What are your plans for charitable giving?" she wants to know.

"I'm looking into that," you lie. "I have a plan," you lie further.

"Good," she responds. "Send it to me next week in my birthday card."

Your time is running out. What will you tell Aunt Teresa? Just what are your obligations? Some? None? All? Drawing on ideas from the preceding essays, personal experience, and any other research you may have done, write a letter to her justifying your decision.

CIVIL DISOBEDIENCE

"Letter from Birmingham Jail"
in Response to "Public Statement
by Eight Alabama Clergymen"

Martin Luther King Jr.

On April 12, 1963, eight Alabama clergymen signed a public statement urging "outsiders" to halt the racial demonstrations they had instigated. Four days later, while under arrest for instigating the demonstrations, King produced his "Letter from Birmingham Jail."

We the undersigned clergymen are among those who, in January, issued "An Appeal for Law and Order and Common Sense," in dealing with racial problems in Alabama. We expressed understanding that honest convictions in racial matters could properly be pursued in the courts, but urged that decisions of those courts should in the meantime be peacefully obeyed.

Since that time there had been some evidence of increased forbearance and a willingness to face facts. Responsible citizens have undertaken to work on various problems which cause racial friction and unrest. In Birmingham, recent public events have given indication that we all have opportunity for a new constructive and realistic approach to racial problems.

However, we are now confronted by a series of demonstrations by some of our Negro citizens, directed and led in part by outsiders. We recognize the natural impatience of people who feel that their hopes are slow in being realized. But we are convinced that these demonstrations are unwise and untimely.

We agree rather with certain local Negro leadership which has called for honest and open negotiation of racial issues in our area. And we believe this kind of facing of issues can best be accomplished by citizens of our own metropolitan area, white and Negro, meeting with their knowledge and experience of the local situation. All of us need to face that responsibility and find proper channels for its accomplishment.

Just as we formerly pointed out that "hatred and violence have no sanction in our religious and political traditions," we also point out that such actions as incite to hatred and violence, however technically peaceful those actions may be, have not contributed to the resolution of our local problems. We do not believe that these days of new hope are days when extreme measures are justified in Birmingham.

We commend the community as a whole, and the local news media and law enforcement officials in particular, on the calm manner in which these demonstrations have been handled. We urge the public to continue to show restraint should the demonstrations continue, and the law enforcement officials to remain calm and continue to protect our city from violence.

We further strongly urge our own Negro community to withdraw support from these demonstrations, and to unite locally in working peacefully for a better Birmingham. When rights are consistently denied, a cause should be pressed in the courts and in negotiations among local leaders, and not in the streets. We appeal to both our white and Negro citizenry to observe the principles of law and order and common sense.

Signed by:

C. C. J. Carpenter, D.D., LL.D., *Bishop of Alabama*
Joseph A. Durick, D.D., *Auxiliary Bishop, Diocese of Mobile, Birmingham*
Rabbi Milton L. Grafman, *Temple Emanu-El, Birmingham, Alabama*
Bishop Paul Hardin, *Bishop of the Alabama–West Florida Conference of the Methodist Church*
Bishop Nolan B. Harmon, *Bishop of the North Alabama Conference of the Methodist Church*
George M. Murray, D.D., LL.D., *Bishop Coadjutor, Episcopal Diocese of Alabama*
Edward V. Ramage, *Moderator, Synod of the Alabama Presbyterian Church in the United States*
Earl Stallings, *Pastor, First Baptist Church, Birmingham, Alabama*

Following is the letter Martin Luther King Jr. wrote in response to the clergymen's public statement.

April 16, 1963

My Dear Fellow Clergymen:

1   While confined here in the Birmingham city jail, I came across your recent statement calling my present activities "unwise and untimely." Seldom do I pause to answer criticism of my work and ideas. If I sought to answer all the criticisms that cross my desk, my secretaries would have little time for anything other than such correspondence in the course of the day, and I would have no time for constructive work. But since I feel that you are men of genuine good will and that your criticisms are sincerely set forth, I want to try to answer your statement in what I hope will be patient and reasonable terms.

2   I think I should indicate why I am here in Birmingham, since you have been influenced by the view which argues against "outsiders coming in." I have the honor of serving as president of the Southern Christian Leadership Conference, an organization operating in every southern state, with headquarters in Atlanta, Georgia. We have some eighty-five affiliated organizations across the South, and one of them is the Alabama Christian Movement for Human Rights. Frequently we share staff, educational and financial resources with our affiliates. Several months ago the affiliate here in Birmingham asked us to be on call to engage in a nonviolent direct-action program if such were deemed necessary. We readily consented, and when the hour came we lived up to our promise. So I, along with several members of my staff, am here because I was invited here. I am here because I have organizational ties here.

3   But more basically, I am in Birmingham because injustice is here. Just as the prophets of the eighth century B.C. left their villages and carried their "thus saith the Lord" far beyond the boundaries of their home towns, and just as the Apostle Paul left his village of Tarsus and carried the gospel of Jesus Christ to the far corners of the Greco-Roman world, so

am I compelled to carry the gospel of freedom beyond my own home town. Like Paul, I must constantly respond to the Macedonian call for aid.

Moreover, I am cognizant of the interrelatedness of all communities and states. I cannot sit idly by in Atlanta and not be concerned about what happens in Birmingham. Injustice anywhere is a threat to justice everywhere. We are caught in an inescapable network of mutuality, tied in a single garment of destiny. Whatever affects one directly, affects all indirectly. Never again can we afford to live with the narrow, provincial "outside agitator" idea. Anyone who lives inside the United States can never be considered an outsider anywhere within its bounds. 4

You deplore the demonstrations taking place in Birmingham. But your statement, I am sorry to say, fails to express a similar concern for the conditions that brought about the demonstrations. I am sure that none of you would want to rest content with the superficial kind of social analysis that deals merely with effects and does not grapple with underlying causes. It is unfortunate that demonstrations are taking place in Birmingham, but it is even more unfortunate that the city's white power structure left the Negro community with no alternative. 5

In any nonviolent campaign there are four basic steps: collection of the facts to determine whether injustices exist; negotiation; self-purification; and direct action. We have gone through all these steps in Birmingham. There can be no gainsaying the fact that racial injustice engulfs this community. Birmingham is probably the most thoroughly segregated city in the United States. Its ugly record of brutality is widely known. Negroes have experienced grossly unjust treatment in the courts. There have been more unsolved bombings of Negro homes and churches in Birmingham than in any other city in the nation. These are the hard, brutal facts of the case. On the basis of these conditions, Negro leaders sought to negotiate with the city fathers. But the latter consistently refused to engage in good-faith negotiation. 6

Then, last September, came the opportunity to talk with leaders of Birmingham's economic community. In the course of the negotiations, certain promises were made by the merchants—for example, to remove the stores' humiliating racial signs. On the basis of these promises, the Reverend Fred Shuttlesworth and the leaders of the Alabama Christian Movement for Human Rights agreed to a moratorium on all demonstrations. As the weeks and months went by, we realized that we were the victims of a broken promise. A few signs, briefly removed, returned; the others remained. 7

As in so many past experiences, our hopes had been blasted, and the shadow of deep disappointment settled upon us. We had no alternative except to prepare for direct action, whereby we would present our very bodies as a means of laying our case before the conscience of the local and the national community. Mindful of the difficulties involved, we decided to undertake a process of self-purification. We began a series of workshops on nonviolence, and we repeatedly asked ourselves: "Are you able to accept blows without retaliating?" "Are you able to endure the ordeal of jail?" We decided to schedule our direct-action program for the Easter season, realizing that except for Christmas, this is the main shopping period of the year. Knowing that a strong economic-withdrawal program would be the by-product of direct action, we felt that this would be the best time to bring pressure to bear on the merchants for the needed change. 8

9   Then it occurred to us that Birmingham's mayoral election was coming up in March, and we speedily decided to postpone action until after election day. When we discovered that the Commissioner of Public Safety, Eugene "Bull" Connor, had piled up enough votes to be in the run-off, we decided again to postpone action until the day after the run-off so that the demonstrations could not be used to cloud the issues. Like many others, we waited to see Mr. Connor defeated, and to this end we endured postponement after postponement. Having aided in this community need, we felt that our direct-action program could be delayed no longer.

10   You may well ask: "Why direct action? Why sit-ins, marches and so forth? Isn't negotiation a better path?" You are quite right in calling for negotiation. Indeed, this is the very purpose of direct action. Nonviolent direct action seeks to create such a crisis and foster such a tension that a community which has constantly refused to negotiate is forced to confront the issue. It seeks so to dramatize the issue that it can no longer be ignored. My citing the creation of tension as part of the work of the nonviolent-resister may sound rather shocking. But I must confess that I am not afraid of the word "tension." I have earnestly opposed violent tension, but there is a type of constructive, nonviolent tension which is necessary for growth. Just as Socrates felt that it was necessary to create a tension in the mind so that individuals could rise from the bondage of myths and half-truths to the unfettered realm of creative analysis and objective appraisal, so must we see the need for nonviolent gadflies to create the kind of tension in society that will help men rise from the dark depths of prejudice and racism to the majestic heights of understanding and brotherhood.

11   The purpose of our direct-action program is to create a situation so crisis-packed that it will inevitably open the door to negotiation. I therefore concur with you in your call for negotiation. Too long has our beloved Southland been bogged down in a tragic effort to live in monologue rather than dialogue.

12   One of the basic points in your statement is that the action that I and my associates have taken in Birmingham is untimely. Some have asked: "Why didn't you give the new city administration time to act?" The only answer that I can give to this query is that the new Birmingham administration must be prodded about as much as the outgoing one, before it will act. We are sadly mistaken if we feel that the election of Albert Boutwell as mayor will bring the millennium to Birmingham. While Mr. Boutwell is a much more gentle person than Mr. Connor, they are both segregationists, dedicated to maintenance of the status quo. I have hope that Mr. Boutwell will be reasonable enough to see the futility of massive resistance to desegregation. But he will not see this without pressure from devotees of civil rights. My friends, I must say to you that we have not made a single gain in civil rights without determined legal and nonviolent pressure. Lamentably, it is an historical fact that privileged groups seldom give up their privileges voluntarily. Individuals may see the moral light and voluntarily give up their unjust posture; but, as Reinhold Niebuhr has reminded us, groups tend to be more immoral than individuals.

13   We know through painful experience that freedom is never voluntarily given by the oppressor; it must be demanded by the oppressed. Frankly, I have yet to engage in a direct-action campaign that was "well timed" in the view of those who have not suffered unduly from the disease of segregation. For years now I have heard the word "Wait!" It rings in the ear of every Negro with piercing familiarity. This "Wait" has almost always meant

"Never." We must come to see, with one of our distinguished jurists, that "justice too long delayed is justice denied."

We have waited for more than 340 years for our constitutional God-given rights. The nations of Asia and Africa are moving with jetlike speed toward gaining political independence, but we still creep at horse-and-buggy pace toward gaining a cup of coffee at a lunch counter. Perhaps it is easy for those who have never felt the stinging darts of segregation to say, "Wait." But when you have seen vicious mobs lynch your mothers and fathers at will and drown your sisters and brothers at whim; when you have seen hate-filled policemen curse, kick, and even kill your black brothers and sisters; when you see the vast majority of your twenty million Negro brothers smothering in an airtight cage of poverty in the midst of an affluent society; when you suddenly find your tongue twisted and your speech stammering as you seek to explain to your six-year-old daughter why she can't go to the public amusement park that has just been advertised on television, and see tears welling up in her eyes when she is told that Funtown is closed to colored children, and see ominous clouds of inferiority beginning to form in her little mental sky, and see her beginning to distort her personality by developing an unconscious bitterness toward white people; when you have to concoct an answer for a five-year-old son who is asking: "Daddy, why do white people treat colored people so mean?"; when you take a cross-country drive and find it necessary to sleep night after night in the uncomfortable corners of your automobile because no motel will accept you; when you are humiliated day in and day out by nagging signs reading "white" and "colored"; when your first name becomes "nigger," your middle name becomes "boy" (however old you are) and your last name becomes "John," and your wife and mother are never given the respected title "Mrs."; when you are harried by day and haunted by night by the fact that you are a Negro, living constantly at tiptoe stance, never quite knowing what to expect next, and are plagued with inner fears and outer resentments; when you are forever fighting a degenerating sense of "nobodiness"—then you will understand why we find it difficult to wait. There comes a time when the cup of endurance runs over, and men are no longer willing to be plunged into the abyss of despair. I hope, sirs, you can understand our legitimate and unavoidable impatience.

You express a great deal of anxiety over our willingness to break laws. This is certainly a legitimate concern. Since we so diligently urge people to obey the Supreme Court's decision of 1954 outlawing segregation in the public schools, at first glance it may seem rather paradoxical for us consciously to break laws. One may well ask: "How can you advocate breaking some laws and obeying others?" The answer lies in the fact that there are two types of laws: just and unjust. I would be the first to advocate obeying just laws. One has not only a legal but a moral responsibility to obey just laws. Conversely, one has a moral responsibility to disobey unjust laws. I would agree with St. Augustine that "an unjust law is no law at all."

Now, what is the difference between the two? How does one determine whether a law is just or unjust? A just law is a man-made code that squares with the moral law or the law of God. An unjust law is a code that is out of harmony with the moral law. To put it in the terms of St. Thomas Aquinas: An unjust law is a human law that is not rooted in eternal law and natural law. Any law that uplifts human personality is just. Any law that degrades human personality is unjust. All segregation statutes are unjust because segregation distorts the soul and damages the personality. It gives the segregator a false sense of superiority and the segregated a false sense of inferiority. Segregation, to use the terminology of the Jewish philosopher Martin Buber, substitutes an "I–it" relationship for an "I–thou" relationship and ends up relegating persons to the status of things. Hence, segregation is not only politically, economically and sociologically unsound, it is morally wrong and sinful. Paul Tillich has said that sin is separation. Is not segregation an existential expression of man's tragic separation, his awful estrangement, his terrible sinfulness? Thus it is that I can urge men to obey the 1954 decision of the Supreme Court, for it is morally right; and I can urge them to disobey segregation ordinances, for they are morally wrong.

17   Let us consider a more concrete example of just and unjust laws. An unjust law is a code that a numerical or power majority group compels a minority group to obey but does not make binding on itself. This is *difference* made legal. By the same token, a just law is a code that a majority compels a minority to follow and that it is willing to follow itself. This is *sameness* made legal.

18   Let me give another explanation. A law is unjust if it is inflicted on a minority that, as a result of being denied the right to vote, had no part in enacting or devising the law. Who can say that the legislature of Alabama which set up that state's segregation laws was democratically elected? Throughout Alabama all sorts of devious methods are used to prevent Negroes from becoming registered voters, and there are some counties in which, even though Negroes constitute a majority of the population, not a single Negro is registered. Can any law enacted under such circumstances be considered democratically structured?

19   Sometimes a law is just on its face and unjust in its application. For instance, I have been arrested on a charge of parading without a permit. Now, there is nothing wrong in having an ordinance which requires a permit for a parade. But such an ordinance becomes unjust when it is used to maintain segregation and to deny citizens the First-Amendment privilege of peaceful assembly and protest.

20   I hope you are able to see the distinction I am trying to point out. In no sense do I advocate evading or defying the law, as would the rabid segregationist. That would lead to anarchy. One who breaks an unjust law must do so openly, lovingly, and with a willingness to accept the penalty. I submit that an individual who breaks a law that conscience tells him is unjust, and who willingly accepts the penalty of imprisonment in order to arouse the conscience of the community over its injustice, is in reality expressing the highest respect for law.

21   Of course, there is nothing new about this kind of civil disobedience. It was evidenced sublimely in the refusal of Shadrach, Meshach and Abednego to obey the laws of Nebuchadnezzar, on the ground that a higher moral law was at stake. It was practiced superbly by the early Christians, who were willing to face hungry lions and the excruciating pain of chopping blocks rather than submit to certain unjust laws of the Roman Empire. To a degree, academic freedom is a reality today because Socrates practiced civil disobedience. In our own nation, the Boston Tea Party represented a massive act of civil disobedience.

22   We should never forget that everything Adolf Hitler did in Germany was "legal" and everything the Hungarian freedom fighters did in Hungary was "illegal." It was "illegal" to aid and comfort a Jew in Hitler's Germany. Even so, I am sure that, had I lived in Germany at the time, I would have aided and comforted my Jewish brothers. If today I lived in a Com-

munist country where certain principles dear to the Christian faith are suppressed I would openly advocate disobeying that country's antireligious laws.

I must make two honest confessions to you, my Christian and Jewish brothers. First, I must confess that over the past few years I have been gravely disappointed with the white moderate. I have almost reached the regrettable conclusion that the Negro's great stumbling block in his stride toward freedom is not the White Citizen's Counciler or the Ku Klux Klanner, but the white moderate, who is more devoted to "order" than to justice; who prefers a negative peace which is the presence of tension to a positive peace which is the presence of justice; who constantly says, "I agree with you in the goal you seek, but I cannot agree with your methods of direct action"; who paternalistically believes he can set the timetable for another man's freedom; who lives by a mythical concept of time and who constantly advises the Negro to wait for a "more convenient season." Shallow understanding from people of good will is more frustrating than absolute misunderstanding from people of ill will. Lukewarm acceptance is much more bewildering than outright rejection.

I had hoped that the white moderate would understand that law and order exist for the purpose of establishing justice and that when they fail in this purpose they become the dangerously structured dams that block the flow of social progress. I had hoped that the white moderate would understand that the present tension in the South is a necessary phase of the transition from an obnoxious negative peace, in which the Negro passively accepted his unjust plight, to a substantive and positive peace, in which all men will respect the dignity and worth of human personality. Actually, we who engage in nonviolent direct action are not the creators of tension. We merely bring to the surface the hidden tension that is already alive. We bring it out in the open, where it can be seen and dealt with. Like a boil that can never be cured so long as it is covered up but must be opened with all its ugliness to the natural medicines of air and light, injustice must be exposed, with all the tension its exposure creates, to the light of human conscience and the air of national opinion before it can be cured.

In your statement you assert that our actions, even though peaceful, must be condemned because they precipitate violence. But is this a logical assertion? Isn't this like condemning a robbed man because his possession of money precipitated the evil act of robbery? Isn't this like condemning Socrates because his unswerving commitment to truth and his philosophical inquiries precipitated the act by the misguided populace in which they made him drink hemlock? Isn't this like condemning Jesus because his unique God-consciousness and never-ceasing devotion to God's will precipitated the evil act of crucifixion? We must come to see that, as the federal courts have consistently affirmed, it is wrong to urge an individual to cease his efforts to gain his basic constitutional rights because the quest may precipitate violence. Society must protect the robbed and punish the robber.

I had also hoped that the white moderate would reject the myth concerning time in relation to the struggle for freedom. I have just received a letter from a white brother in Texas. He writes: "All Christians know that the colored people will receive equal rights eventually, but it is possible that you are in too great a religious hurry. It has taken Christianity almost two thousand years to accomplish what it has. The teachings of Christ take time to come to earth." Such an attitude stems from a tragic misconception of time, from the strangely irrational notion that there is something in the very flow of time that will inevitably cure all ills. Actually, time itself is neutral; it can be used either destructively or constructively. More and more I feel that the people of ill will have used time much more effectively than have the people of good will. We will have to repent in this generation not merely for the hateful words and actions of the bad people but for the appalling silence of the good people. Human progress never rolls in on wheels of inevitability; it comes through the tireless efforts of men willing to be co-workers with God, and without this hard work, time itself becomes an ally of the forces of social stagnation. We must use time creatively, in the knowledge that the time is always ripe to do right. Now is the time to make real the promise of democracy and transform our pending national elegy into a creative psalm of brotherhood. Now is the time to lift our national policy from the quicksand of racial injustice to the solid rock of human dignity.

27   You speak of our activity in Birmingham as extreme. At first I was rather disappointed that fellow clergymen would see my nonviolent efforts as those of an extremist. I began thinking about the fact that I stand in the middle of two opposing forces in the Negro community. One is a force of complacency, made up in part of Negroes who, as a result of long years of oppression, are so drained of self-respect and a sense of "somebodiness" that they have adjusted to segregation; and in part of a few middle-class Negroes who, because of a degree of academic and economic security and because in some ways they profit by segregation, have become insensitive to the problems of the masses. The other force is one of bitterness and hatred, and it comes perilously close to advocating violence. It is expressed in the various black nationalist groups that are springing up across the nation, the largest and best-known being Elijah Muhammad's Muslim movement. Nourished by the Negro's frustration over the continued existence of racial discrimination, this movement is made up of people who have lost faith in America, who have absolutely repudiated Christianity, and who have concluded that the white man is an incorrigible "devil."

28   I have tried to stand between these two forces, saying that we need emulate neither the "do-nothingism" of the complacent nor the hatred and despair of the black nationalist. For there is the more excellent way of love and nonviolent protest. I am grateful to God that, through the influence of the Negro church, the way of nonviolence became an integral part of our struggle.

29   If this philosophy had not emerged, by now many streets of the South would, I am convinced, be flowing with blood. And I am further convinced that if our white brothers dismiss as "rabble-rousers" and "outside agitators" those of us who employ nonviolent direct action, and if they refuse to support our nonviolent efforts, millions of the Negroes will, out of frustration and despair, seek solace and security in black-nationalist ideologies—a development that would inevitably lead to a frightening racial nightmare.

30   Oppressed people cannot remain oppressed forever. The yearning for freedom eventually manifests itself, and that is what has happened to the American Negro. Something within has reminded him of his birthright of freedom, and something without has reminded him that it can be gained. Consciously or unconsciously, he has been caught up by the *Zeitgeist,* and with his black brothers of Africa and his brown and yellow brothers of Asia, South America and the Caribbean, the United States Negro is moving with a sense of great urgency toward the promised land of racial justice. If one recognizes this vital urge that has engulfed the Negro community, one should readily understand why public demonstrations

are taking place. The Negro has many pent-up resentments and latent frustrations, and he must release them. So let him march; let him make prayer pilgrimages to the city hall; let him go on freedom rides—and try to understand why he must do so. If his repressed emotions are not released in nonviolent ways, they will seek expression through violence; this is not a threat but a fact of history. So I have not said to my people: "Get rid of your discontent." Rather, I have tried to say that this normal and healthy discontent can be channeled into the creative outlet of nonviolent direct action. And now this approach is being termed extremist.

But though I was initially disappointed at being categorized as an extremist, as I continued to think about the matter I gradually gained a measure of satisfaction from the label. Was not Jesus an extremist for love: "Love your enemies, bless them that curse you, and persecute you." Was not Amos an extremist for justice: "Let justice roll down like waters and righteousness like an ever-flowing stream." Was not Paul an extremist for the Christian gospel: "I bear in my body the marks of the Lord Jesus." Was not Martin Luther an extremist: "Here I stand; I cannot do otherwise, so help me God." And John Bunyan: "I will stay in jail to the end of my days before I make a butchery of my conscience." And Abraham Lincoln: "This nation cannot survive half slave and half free." And Thomas Jefferson: "We hold these truths to be self-evident, that all men are created equal. . . ." So the question is not whether we will be extremists, but what kind of extremists we will be. Will we be extremists for hate or for love? Will we be extremists for the preservation of injustice or for the extension of justice? In that dramatic scene on Calvary's hill three men were crucified. We must never forget that all three were crucified for the same crime—the crime of extremism. Two were extremists for immorality, and thus fell below their environment. The other, Jesus Christ, was an extremist for love, truth and goodness, and thereby rose above his environment. Perhaps the South, the nation and the world are in dire need of creative extremists.

31

I had hoped that the white moderate would see this need. Perhaps I was too optimistic; perhaps I expected too much. I suppose I should have realized that few members of the oppressor race can understand the deep groans and passionate yearnings of the oppressed race, and still fewer have the vision to see that injustice must be rooted out by strong, persistent and determined action. I am thankful, however, that some of our white brothers in the South have grasped the meaning of this social revolution and committed themselves to it. They are still all too few in quantity, but they are big in quality. Some—such as Ralph McGill, Lillian Smith, Harry Golden, James McBride Dabbs, Ann Braden and Sarah Patton Boyle—have written about our struggle in eloquent and prophetic terms. Others have marched with us down nameless streets of the South. They have languished in filthy, roach-infested jails, suffering the abuse and brutality of policemen who view them as "dirty nigger-lovers." Unlike so many of their moderate brothers and sisters, they have recognized the urgency of the moment and sensed the need for powerful "action" antidotes to combat the disease of segregation.

32

Let me take note of my other major disappointment. I have been so greatly disappointed with the white church and its leadership. Of course, there are some notable exceptions. I am not unmindful of the fact that each of you has taken some significant stands on this issue. I commend you, Reverend Stallings, for your Christian stand on this past

33

Sunday, in welcoming Negroes to your worship service on a nonsegregated basis. I commend the Catholic leaders of this state for integrating Spring Hill College several years ago.

34   But despite these notable exceptions, I must honestly reiterate that I have been disappointed with the church. I do not say this as one of those negative critics who can always find something wrong with the church. I say this as a minister of the gospel, who loves the church; who was nurtured in its bosom; who has been sustained by its spiritual blessings and who will remain true to it as long as the cord of life shall lengthen.

35   When I was suddenly catapulted into the leadership of the bus protest in Montgomery, Alabama, a few years ago, I felt we would be supported by the white church. I felt that the white ministers, priests and rabbis of the South would be among our strongest allies. Instead, some have been outright opponents, refusing to understand the freedom movement and misrepresenting its leaders; all too many others have been more cautious than courageous and have remained silent behind the anesthetizing security of stained-glass windows.

36   In spite of my shattered dreams, I came to Birmingham with the hope that the white religious leadership of this community would see the justice of our cause and, with deep moral concern, would serve as the channel through which our just grievances could reach the power structure. I had hoped that each of you would understand. But again I have been disappointed.

37   I have heard numerous southern religious leaders admonish their worshipers to comply with a desegregation decision because it is the law, but I have longed to hear white ministers declare: "Follow this decree because integration is morally right and because the Negro is your brother." In the midst of blatant injustices inflicted upon the Negro, I have watched white churchmen stand on the sideline and mouth pious irrelevancies and sanctimonious trivialities. In the midst of a mighty struggle to rid our nation of racial and economic injustice, I have heard many ministers say: "Those are social issues, with which the gospel has no real concern." And I have watched many churches commit themselves to a completely otherworldly religion which makes a strange, un-Biblical distinction between body and soul, between the sacred and the secular.

38   I have traveled the length and breadth of Alabama, Mississippi and all the other southern states. On sweltering summer days and crisp autumn mornings I have looked at the South's beautiful churches with their lofty spires pointing heavenward. I have beheld the impressive outlines of her massive religious-education buildings. Over and over I have found myself asking: "What kind of people worship here? Who is their God? Where were their voices when the lips of Governor Barnett dripped with words of interposition and nullification? Where were they when Governor Wallace gave a clarion call for defiance and hatred? Where were their voices of support when bruised and weary Negro men and women decided to rise from the dark dungeons of complacency to the bright hills of creative protest?"

39   Yes, these questions are still in my mind. In deep disappointment I have wept over the laxity of the church. But be assured that my tears have been tears of love. There can be no deep disappointment where there is not deep love. Yes, I love the church. How could I do otherwise? I am in the rather unique position of being the son, the grandson, and the great-grandson of preachers. Yes, I see the church as the body of Christ. But, oh! How we have blemished and scarred that body through social neglect and through fear of being nonconformists.

There was a time when the church was very powerful—in the time when the early   40
Christians rejoiced at being deemed worthy to suffer for what they believed. In those days
the church was not merely a thermometer that recorded the ideas and principles of popular opinion; it was a thermostat that transformed the mores of society. Whenever the early
Christians entered a town, the people in power became disturbed and immediately sought
to convict the Christians for being "disturbers of the peace" and "outside agitators." But
the Christians pressed on, in the conviction that they were "a colony of heaven," called to
obey God rather than man. Small in number, they were big in commitment. They were too
God-intoxicated to be "astronomically intimidated." By their effort and example they
brought an end to such ancient evils as infanticide and gladiatorial contests.

Things are different now. So often the contemporary church is a weak, ineffectual voice   41
with an uncertain sound. So often it is an archdefender of the status quo. Far from being
disturbed by the presence of the church, the power structure of the average community is
consoled by the church's silent—and often even vocal—sanction of things as they are.

But the judgment of God is upon the church as never before. If today's church does not   42
recapture the sacrificial spirit of the early church, it will lose its authenticity, forfeit the loyalty of millions, and be dismissed as an irrelevant social club with no meaning for the twentieth century. Every day I meet young people whose disappointment with the church has
turned into outright disgust.

Perhaps I have once again been too optimistic. Is organized religion too inextricably   43
bound to the status quo to save our nation and the world? Perhaps I must turn my faith
to the inner spiritual church, the church within the church, as the true *ekklesia* and the
hope of the world. But again I am thankful to God that some noble souls from the ranks
of organized religion have broken loose from the paralyzing chains of conformity and
joined us as active partners in the struggle for freedom. They have left their secure con-
gregations and walked the streets of Albany, Georgia, with us. They have gone down the
highways of the South on tortuous rides for freedom. Yes, they have gone to jail with us.
Some have been dismissed from their churches, have lost the support of their bishops and
fellow ministers. But they have acted in the faith that right defeated is stronger than evil
triumphant. Their witness has been the spiritual salt that has preserved the true meaning
of the gospel in these troubled times. They have carved a tunnel of hope through the dark
mountain of disappointment.

I hope the church as a whole will meet the challenge of this decisive hour. But even if   44
the church does not come to the aid of justice, I have no despair about the future. I have
no fear about the outcome of our struggle in Birmingham, even if our motives are at present misunderstood. We will reach the goal of freedom in Birmingham and all over the nation, because the goal of America is freedom. Abused and scorned though we may be, our
destiny is tied up with America's destiny. Before the pilgrims landed at Plymouth, we were
here. Before the pen of Jefferson etched the majestic words of the Declaration of Independence across the pages of history, we were here. For more than two centuries our forebears
labored in this country without wages; they made cotton king; they built the homes of their
masters while suffering gross injustice and shameful humiliation—and yet out of a bottomless vitality they continued to thrive and develop. If the inexpressible cruelties of slavery
could not stop us, the opposition we now face will surely fail. We will win our freedom

because the sacred heritage of our nation and the eternal will of God are embodied in our echoing demands.

45   Before closing I feel impelled to mention one other point in your statement that has troubled me profoundly. You warmly commended the Birmingham police force for keeping "order" and "preventing violence." I doubt that you would have so warmly commended the police force if you had seen its dogs sinking their teeth into unarmed, nonviolent Negroes. I doubt that you would so quickly commend the policemen if you were to observe their ugly and inhumane treatment of Negroes here in the city jail; if you were to watch them push and curse old Negro women and young Negro girls; if you were to see them slap and kick old Negro men and young boys; if you were to observe them, as they did on two occasions, refuse to give us food because we wanted to sing our grace together. I cannot join you in your praise of the Birmingham police department.

46   It is true that police have exercised a degree of discipline in handling the demonstrators. In this sense they have conducted themselves rather "nonviolently" in public. But for what purpose? To preserve the evil system of segregation. Over the past few years I have consistently preached that nonviolence demands that the means we use must be as pure as the ends we seek. I have tried to make clear that it is wrong to use immoral means to attain moral ends. But now I must affirm that it is just as wrong, or perhaps even more so, to use moral means to preserve immoral ends. Perhaps Mr. Connor and his policemen have been rather nonviolent in public, as was Chief Pritchett in Albany, Georgia, but they have used the moral means of nonviolence to maintain the immoral end of racial injustice. As T. S. Eliot has said: "The last temptation is the greatest treason: To do the right deed for the wrong reason."

47   I wish you had commended the Negro sit-inners and demonstrators of Birmingham for their sublime courage, their willingness to suffer and their amazing discipline in the midst of great provocation. One day the South will recognize its real heroes. They will be the James Merediths, with the noble sense of purpose that enables them to face jeering and hostile mobs, and with the agonizing loneliness that characterizes the life of the pioneer. They will be old, oppressed, battered Negro women, symbolized in a seventy-two-year-old woman in Montgomery, Alabama, who rose up with a sense of dignity and with her people decided not to ride segregated buses, and who responded with ungrammatical profundity to one who inquired about her weariness: "My feets is tired, but my soul is at rest." They will be the young high school and college students, the young ministers of the gospel and a host of their elders, courageously and nonviolently sitting in at lunch counters and willingly going to jail for conscience' sake. One day the South will know that when these disinherited children of God sat down at lunch counters, they were in reality standing up for what is best in the American dream and for the most sacred values in our Judaeo-Christian heritage, thereby bringing our nation back to those great wells of democracy which were dug deep by the founding fathers in their formulation of the Constitution and the Declaration of Independence.

48   Never before have I written so long a letter. I'm afraid it is much too long to take your precious time. I can assure you that it would have been much shorter if I had been writing from a comfortable desk, but what else can one do when he is alone in a narrow jail cell, other than write long letters, think long thoughts and pray long prayers?

If I have said anything in this letter that overstates the truth and indicates an unreasonable impatience, I beg you to forgive me. If I have said anything that understates the truth and indicates my having a patience that allows me to settle for anything less than brotherhood, I beg God to forgive me.   49

I hope this letter finds you strong in faith. I also hope that circumstances will soon make it possible for me to meet each of you, not as an integrationist or a civil-rights leader but as a fellow clergyman and a Christian brother. Let us all hope that the dark clouds of racial prejudice will soon pass away and the deep fog of misunderstanding will be lifted from our fear-drenched communities, and in some not too distant tomorrow the radiant stars of love and brotherhood will shine over our great nation with all their scintillating beauty.   50

Yours for the cause of Peace and Brotherhood
MARTIN LUTHER KING, JR.

Civil Disobedience
Destroyer of Democracy
Lewis H. Van Dusen Jr.

Attorney Lewis H. Van Dusen Jr. is a Rhodes Scholar and graduate of Harvard Law School. This argument was published in the ABA Journal (*American Bar Association*) *in 1969 at the height of the Vietnam War.*

As Charles E. Wyzanski, Chief Judge of the United States District Court in Boston, wrote in the February, 1968, *Atlantic:* "Disobedience is a long step from dissent. Civil disobedience involves a deliberate and punishable breach of legal duty." Protesters might prefer a different definition. They would rather say that civil disobedience is the peaceable resistance of conscience.   1

The philosophy of civil disobedience was not developed in our American democracy, but in the very first democracy of Athens. It was expressed by the poet Sophocles and the philosopher Socrates. In Sophocles's tragedy, Antigone chose to obey her conscience and violate the state edict against providing burial for her brother, who had been decreed a traitor. When the dictator Creon found out that Antigone had buried her fallen brother, he confronted her and reminded her that there was a mandatory death penalty for this deliberate disobedience of the state law. Antigone nobly replied, "Nor did I think your orders were so strong that you, a mortal man, could overrun the gods' unwritten and unfailing laws."   2

Conscience motivated Antigone. She was not testing the validity of the law in the hope that eventually she would be sustained. Appealing to the judgment of the community, she explained her action to the chorus. She was not secret and surreptitious—the interment of her brother was open and public. She was not violent; she did not trespass on another citizen's rights. And finally, she accepted without resistance the death sentence—the penalty for violation. By voluntarily accepting the law's sanctions, she was not a revolutionary   3 denying the authority of the state. Antigone's behavior exemplifies the classic case of civil disobedience.

4   Socrates believed that reason could dictate a conscientious disobedience of state law, but he also believed that he had to accept the legal sanctions of the state. In Plato's *Crito,* Socrates from his hanging basket accepted the death penalty for his teaching of religion to youths contrary to state laws.

5   The sage of Walden, Henry David Thoreau, took this philosophy of nonviolence and developed it into a strategy for solving society's injustices. First enunciating it in protest against the Mexican War, he then turned it to use against slavery. For refusing to pay taxes that would help pay the enforcers of the fugitive slave law, he went to prison. In Thoreau's words, "If the alternative is to keep all just men in prison or to give up slavery, the state will not hesitate which to choose."

6   Sixty years later, Gandhi took Thoreau's civil disobedience as his strategy to wrest Indian independence from England. The famous salt march against a British imperial tax is his best-known example of protest.

7   But the conscientious law breaking of Socrates, Gandhi and Thoreau is to be distinguished from the conscientious law testing of Martin Luther King, Jr., who was not a civil disobedient. The civil disobedient withholds taxes or violates state laws knowing he is legally wrong, but believing he is morally right. While he wrapped himself in the mantle of Gandhi and Thoreau, Dr. King led his followers in violation of state laws he believed were contrary to the Federal Constitution. But since Supreme Court decisions in the end generally upheld his many actions, he should not be considered a true civil disobedient.

8   The civil disobedience of Antigone is like that of the pacifist who withholds paying the percentage of his taxes that goes to the Defense Department, or the Quaker who travels against State Department regulations to Hanoi to distribute medical supplies, or the Vietnam war protester who tears up his draft card. This civil disobedient has been nonviolent in his defiance of the law; he has been unfurtive in his violation; he has been submissive to the penalties of the law. He has neither evaded the law nor interfered with another's rights. He has been neither a rioter nor a revolutionary. The thrust of his cause has not been the might of coercion but the martyrdom of conscience.

WAS THE BOSTON TEA PARTY CIVIL DISOBEDIENCE?

9   Those who justify violence and radical action as being in the tradition of our Revolution show a misunderstanding of the philosophy of democracy.

10   James Farmer, former head of the Congress of Racial Equality, in defense of the mass action confrontation method, has told of a famous organized demonstration that took place in opposition to political and economic discrimination. The protesters beat back and scattered the law enforcers and then proceeded to loot and destroy private property. Mr. Farmer then said he was talking about the Boston Tea Party and implied that violence as a method for redress of grievances was an American tradition and a legacy of our revolutionary heritage. While it is true that there is no more sacred document than our Declaration of Independence, Jefferson's "inherent right of rebellion" was predicated on the tyrannical denial of democratic means. If there is no popular assembly to provide an adjustment of ills, and if there is no court system to dispose of injustices, then there is, indeed, a right to rebel.

The seventeenth century's John Locke, the philosophical father of the Declaration of Independence, wrote in his *Second Treatise on Civil Government:* "Wherever law ends, tyranny begins . . . and the people are absolved from any further obedience. Governments are dissolved from within when the legislative [chamber] is altered. When the government [becomes] . . . arbitrary disposers of lives, liberties and fortunes of the people, such revolutions happen. . . ." 11

But there are some sophisticated proponents of the revolutionary redress of grievances who say that the test of the need for radical action is not the unavailability of democratic institutions but the ineffectuality of those institutions to remove blatant social inequalities. If social injustice exists, they say, concerted disobedience is required against the constituted government, whether it be totalitarian or democratic in structure. 12

Of course, only the most bigoted chauvinist would claim that America is without some glaring faults. But there has never been a utopian society on earth and there never will be unless human nature is remade. Since inequities will mar even the best-framed democracies, the injustice rationale would allow a free right of civil resistance to be available always as a shortcut alternative to the democratic way of petition, debate and assembly. The lesson of history is that civil insurgency spawns far more injustices than it removes. The Jeffersons, Washingtons and Adamses resisted tyranny with the aim of promoting the procedures of democracy. They would never have resisted a democratic government with the risk of promoting the techniques of tyranny. 13

LEGITIMATE PRESSURES AND ILLEGITIMATE RESULTS

There are many civil leaders who show impatience with the process of democracy. They rely on the sit-in, boycott or mass picketing to gain speedier solutions to the problems that face every citizen. But we must realize that the legitimate pressures that won concessions in the past can easily escalate into the illegitimate power plays that might extort demands in the future. The victories of these civil rights leaders must not shake our confidence in the democratic procedures, as the pressures of demonstration are desirable only if they take place within the limits allowed by law. Civil rights gains should continue to be won by the persuasion of Congress and other legislative bodies and by the decision of courts. Any illegal entreaty for the rights of some can be an injury to the rights of others, for mass demonstrations often trigger violence. 14

Those who advocate taking the law into their own hands should reflect that when they are disobeying what they consider to be an immoral law, they are deciding on a possibly immoral course. Their answer is that the process for democratic relief is too slow, that only mass confrontation can bring immediate action, and that any injuries are the inevitable cost of the pursuit of justice. Their answer is, simply put, that the end justifies the means. It is this justification of any form of demonstration as a form of dissent that threatens to destroy a society built on the rule of law. 15

Our Bill of Rights guarantees wide opportunities to use mass meetings, public parades and organized demonstrations to stimulate sentiment, to dramatize issues and to cause change. The Washington freedom march of 1963 was such a call for action. But the rights of free expression cannot be mere force cloaked in the garb of free speech. As the courts have decreed in labor cases, free assembly does not mean mass picketing or sit-down 16 strikes. These rights are subject to limitations of time and place so as to secure the rights of others. When militant students storm a college president's office to achieve demands, when certain groups plan rush-hour car stalling to protest discrimination in employment, these are not dissent, but a denial of rights to others. Neither is it the lawful use of mass protest, but rather the unlawful use of mob power.

17   Justice Black, one of the foremost advocates and defenders of the right of protest and dissent, has said:

> Experience demonstrates that it is not a far step from what to many seems to be the earnest, honest, patriotic, kind-spirited multitude of today, to the fanatical, threatening, lawless mob of tomorrow. And the crowds that press in the streets for noble goals today can be supplanted tomorrow by street mobs pressuring the courts for precisely opposite ends.

18   Society must censure those demonstrators who would trespass on the public peace, as it must condemn those rioters whose pillage would destroy the public peace. But more ambivalent is society's posture toward the civil disobedient. Unlike the rioter, the true civil disobedient commits no violence. Unlike the mob demonstrator, he commits no trespass on others' rights. The civil disobedient, while deliberately violating a law, shows an oblique respect for the law by voluntarily submitting to its sanctions. He neither resists arrest nor evades punishment. Thus, he breaches the law but not the peace.

19   But civil disobedience, whatever the ethical rationalization, is still an assault on our democratic society, an affront to our legal order and an attack on our constitutional government. To indulge civil disobedience is to invite anarchy, and the permissive arbitrariness of anarchy is hardly less tolerable than the repressive arbitrariness of tyranny. Too often the license of liberty is followed by the loss of liberty, because into the desert of anarchy comes the man on horseback, a Mussolini or a Hitler.

20   **Violations of Law Subvert Democracy.**   Law violations, even for ends recognized as laudable, are not only assaults on the rule of law, but subversions of the democratic process. The disobedient act of conscience does not ennoble democracy; it erodes it.

21   First, it courts violence, and even the most careful and limited use of nonviolent acts of disobedience may help sow the dragon-teeth of civil riot. Civil disobedience is the progenitor of disorder, and disorder is the sire of violence.

22   Second, the concept of civil disobedience does not invite principles of general applicability. If the children of light are morally privileged to resist particular laws on grounds of conscience, so are the children of darkness. Former Deputy Attorney General Burke Marshall said: "If the decision to break the law really turned on individual conscience, it is hard to see in law how [the civil rights leader] is better off than former Governor Ross Barnett of Mississippi who also believed deeply in his cause and was willing to go to jail."

23   Third, even the most noble act of civil disobedience assaults the rule of law. Although limited as to method, motive and objective, it has the effect of inducing others to engage in different forms of law breaking characterized by methods unsanctioned and condemned by classic theories of law violation. Unfortunately, the most patent lesson of civil disobedience is not so much nonviolence of action as defiance of authority.

24   Finally, the greatest danger in condoning civil disobedience as a permissible strategy for hastening change is that it undermines our democratic processes. To adopt the tech-

niques of civil disobedience is to assume that representative government does not work. To resist the decisions of courts and the laws of elected assemblies is to say that democracy has failed.

There is no man who is above the law, and there is no man who has a right to break the law. Civil disobedience is not above the law, but against the law. When the civil disobedient disobeys one law, he invariably subverts all law. When the civil disobedient says that he is above the law, he is saying that democracy is beneath him. His disobedience shows a distrust for the democratic system. He is merely saying that since democracy does not work, why should he help make it work. Thoreau expressed well the civil disobedient's disdain for democracy: 25

> As for adopting the ways which the state has provided for remedying the evil, I know not of such ways. They take too much time and a man's life will be gone. I have other affairs to attend to. I came into this world not chiefly to make this a good place to live in, but to live in it, be it good or bad.

Thoreau's position is not only morally irresponsible but politically reprehensible. When citizens in a democracy are called on to make a profession of faith, the civil disobedients offer only a confession of failure. Tragically, when civil disobedients for lack of faith abstain from democratic involvement, they help attain their own gloomy prediction. They help create the social and political basis for their own despair. By foreseeing failure, they help forge it. If citizens rely on antidemocratic means of protest, they will help bring about the undemocratic result of an authoritarian or anarchic state.   26

How far demonstrations properly can be employed to produce political and social change is a pressing question, particularly in view of the provocations accompanying the National Democratic Convention in Chicago last August and the reaction of the police to them. A line must be drawn by the judiciary between the demands of those who seek absolute order, which can lead only to a dictatorship, and those who seek absolute freedom, which can lead only to anarchy. The line, wherever it is drawn by our courts, should be respected on the college campus, on the streets and elsewhere.   27

Undue provocation will inevitably result in overreaction, human emotions being what they are. Violence will follow. This cycle undermines the very democracy it is designed to preserve. The lesson of the past is that democracies will fall if violence, including the intentional provocations that will lead to violence, replaces democratic procedures, as in Athens, Rome and the Weimar Republic. This lesson must be constantly explained by the legal profession.   28

We should heed the words of William James: 29

> Democracy is still upon its trial. The civic genius of our people is its only bulwark and . . . neither battleships nor public libraries nor great newspapers nor booming stocks: neither mechanical invention nor political adroitness, nor churches nor universities nor civil service examinations can save us from degeneration if the inner mystery be lost.
>
> That mystery, at once the secret and the glory of our English-speaking race, consists of nothing but two habits. . . . One of them is habit of trained and disciplined good temper towards the opposite party when it fairly wins its innings. The other is that of fierce and merciless resentment toward every man or set of men who break the public peace. (James, *Pragmatism,* 127–28)

From the Crito

Plato

Plato and his student Aristotle are considered the founders of Western philoso-
phy. Plato is famous for his dialogues in which philosophical issues are debated
in dramatic form, one of the speakers being Plato's teacher Socrates. Plato prob-
ably wrote the Crito *around 400 B.C.E.*

1   SOCRATES: . . . Ought a man to do what he admits to be right, or ought he to betray the right?

2   CRITO: He ought to do what he thinks right.

3   SOCRATES: But if this is true, what is the application? In leaving the prison against the will of the Athenians, do I wrong any? Or rather do I not wrong those whom I ought least to wrong? Do I not desert the principles which are acknowledged by us to be just—what do you say?

4   CRITO: I cannot tell, Socrates; for I do not know.

5   SOCRATES: Then consider the matter in this way:—Imagine that I am about to play truant (you may call the proceeding by any name which you like), and the laws of the government come and interrogate me: "Tell us, Socrates," they say: "what are you about? Are you not going by an act of yours to overturn us—the laws, and the whole state, as far as in you lies? Do you imagine that a state can subsist and not be overthrown, in which the decisions of law have no power, but are set aside and trampled upon by individuals?" What will be our answer, Crito, to these and the like words? Any one, and especially a rhetorician, will have a good deal to say on behalf of the law which requires a sentence to be carried out. He will argue that this law should not be set aside; and shall we reply, "Yes, but the state has in-jured us and given an unjust sentence." Suppose I say that?

6   CRITO: Very good, Socrates.

7   SOCRATES: "And was that our agreement with you?" the law would answer; "or were you to abide by the sentence of the state?" And if I were to express my astonishment at their words, the law would probably add: "Answer, Socrates, instead of opening your eyes—you are in the habit of asking and answering questions. Tell us—What complaint have you to make against us which justifies you in attempting to destroy us and the state? In the first place did we not bring you into existence? Your father married your mother by our aid and begat you. Say whether you have any objection to urge against those of us who regulate marriage?" None, I should reply. "Or against those of us who after birth regulate the nur-ture and education of children, in which you also were trained? Were not the laws, which have the charge of education, right in commanding your father to train you in music and gymnastics?" Right, I should reply. "Well then, since you were brought into the world and nurtured and educated by us, can you deny in the first place that you are our child and slave, as your fathers were before you? And if this is true you are not on equal terms with us; nor can you think that you have a right to do to us what we are doing to you. Would you have any right to strike or revile or do any other evil to your father or your master, if you

had one, because you have been struck or reviled by him, or received some other evil at his hands?—you would not say this? And because we think right to destroy you, do you think that you have any right to destroy us in return, and your country as far as in you lies? Will you, O professor of true virtue, pretend that you are justified in this? Has a philosopher like you failed to discover that our country is more to be valued and higher and holier far than mother or father or any ancestor, and more to be regarded in the eyes of the gods and of men of understanding? Also to be soothed, and gently and reverently entreated when angry, even more than a father, and either to be persuaded, or if not persuaded, to be obeyed? And when we are punished by her, whether with imprisonment or stripes, the punishment is to be endured in silence, and if she leads us to wounds or death in battle, thither we follow as is right; neither may any one yield or retreat or leave his rank, but whether in battle or in a court of law, or in any other place, he must do what his city and his country order him; or he must change their view of what is just: and if he may do no violence to his father or mother, much less may he do violence to his country." What answer shall we make to this, Crito? Do the laws speak truly, or do they not?

CRITO: I think that they do.   8

SOCRATES: Then the laws will say, "Consider, Socrates, if we are speaking truly that in your   9
present attempt you are going to do us an injury. For, having brought you into the world, and nurtured and educated you, and given you and every other citizen a share in every good which we had to give, we further proclaim to any Athenian by the liberty which we allow him, that if he does not like us when he has become of age and has seen the ways of the city, and made our acquaintance, he may go where he pleases and take his goods with him. None of our laws will forbid him or interfere with him. Any one who does not like us and the city, and who wants to emigrate to a colony or to any other city, may go where he likes, retaining his property. But he who has experience of the manner in which we order justice and administer the state, and still remains, has entered into an implied contract that he will do as we command him. And he who disobeys us is, as we maintain, thrice wrong; first, because in disobeying us he is disobeying his parents; secondly, because we are the authors of his education; thirdly, because he has made an agreement with us that he will duly obey our commands; and he neither obeys them nor convinces us that our commands are unjust; and we do not rudely impose them, but give him the alternative of obeying or convincing us—that is what we offer, and he does neither.

"These are the sort of accusations to which, as we were saying, you, Socrates, will   10
be exposed if you accomplish your intentions; you, above all other Athenians." Suppose now I ask, why I rather than anybody else? They will justly retort upon me that I above all other men have acknowledged the agreement. "There is clear proof," they will say, "Socrates, that we and the city were not displeasing to you. Of all Athenians you have been the most constant resident in the city, which, as you never leave, you may be supposed to love. For you never went out of the city either to see the games, except once when you went to the Isthmus, or to any other place unless when you were on military service; nor did you travel as other men do. Nor had you any curiosity to know other states or their laws: your affections did not go beyond us and our state; we were your special favourites, and you acquiesced in our government of you; and here in this city

you begat your children, which is a proof of your satisfaction. Moreover, you might in the course of the trial, if you had liked, have fixed the penalty at banishment; the state which refuses to let you go now would have let you go then. But you pretended that you preferred death to exile, and that you were not unwilling to die. And now you have forgotten these fine sentiments, and pay no respect to us the laws, of whom you are the destroyer; and are doing what only a miserable slave would do, running away and turning your back upon the compacts and agreements which you made as a citizen. And first of all answer this very question: Are we right in saying that you agreed to be governed according to us in deed, and not in word only? Is that true or not?" How shall we answer, Crito? Must we not assent?

11   CRITO: We cannot help it, Socrates.

12   SOCRATES: Then will they not say: "You, Socrates, are breaking the covenants and agreements which you made with us at your leisure, not in any haste or under any compulsion or deception, but after you have had seventy years to think of them, during which time you were at liberty to leave the city, if we were not to your mind, or if our covenants appeared to you to be unfair. You had your choice, and might have gone either to Lacedaemon or Crete, both which states are often praised by you for their good government, or to some other Hellenic or foreign state. Whereas you, above all other Athenians, seemed to be so fond of the state, or, in other words, of us her laws (and who would care about a state which has no laws?), that you never stirred out of her; the halt, the blind, the maimed were not more stationary in her than you were. And now you run away and forsake your agreements. Not so, Socrates, if you will take our advice; do not make yourself ridiculous by escaping out of the city.

13   "For just consider, if you transgress and err in this sort of way, what good will you do either to yourself or to your friends? That your friends will be driven into exile and deprived of citizenship, or will lose their property, is tolerably certain; and you yourself, if you fly to one of the neighboring cities, as, for example, Thebes or Megara, both of which are well governed, will come to them as an enemy, Socrates, and their government will be against you, and all patriotic citizens will cast an evil eye upon you as a subverter of the laws, and you will confirm in the minds of the judges the justice of their own condemnation of you. For he who is a corrupter of the laws is more than likely to be a corrupter of the young and foolish portion of mankind. Will you then flee from well-ordered citizens and virtuous men? and is existence worth having on these terms? Or will you go to them without shame, and talk to them, Socrates? And what will you say to them? What you say here about virtue and justice and institutions and laws being the best things among men? Would that be decent of you? Surely not. But if you go away from well-governed states to Crito's friends in Thessaly, where there is a great disorder and licence, they will be charmed to hear the tale of your escape from prison, set off with ludicrous particulars of the manner in which you were wrapped in a goatskin or some other disguise, and metamorphosed as the manner is of runaways; but will there be no one to remind you that in your old age you were not ashamed to violate the most sacred laws from a miserable desire of a little more life? Perhaps not, if you keep them in a good temper; but if they are out of temper you will hear many degrading things; you will live, but how?—as the flatterer of all men, and the servant of all men; and doing what?—eating and drinking in Thessaly, having gone abroad in order that you may get a dinner. And

where will be your fine sentiments about justice and virtue? Say that you wish to live for the sake of your children—you want to bring them up and educate them—will you take them into Thessaly and deprive them of Athenian citizenship? Is this the benefit which you will confer upon them? Or are you under the impression that they will be better cared for and educated here if you are still alive, although absent from them: for your friends will take care of them? Do you fancy that if you are an inhabitant of Thessaly they will take care of them, and if you are an inhabitant of the other world that they will not take care of them? Nay: but if they who call themselves friends are good for anything, they will—to be sure they will.

"Listen, then Socrates, to us who have brought you up. Think not of life and children   14
first, and of justice afterwards, but of justice first, that you may be justified before the princes of the world below. For neither will you nor any that belong to you be happier or holier or juster in this life, or happier in another, if you do as Crito bids. Now you depart in innocence, a sufferer and not a doer of evil; a victim, not of the laws, but of men. But if you go forth, returning evil for evil, and injury for injury, breaking the covenants and agreements which you have made with us, and wronging those whom you ought least of all to wrong, that is to say, yourself, your friends, your country, and us, we shall be angry with you while you live, and our brethren, the laws in the world below, will receive you as an enemy; for they will know that you have done your best to destroy us. Listen, then, to us and not to Crito."

This, dear Crito, is the voice which I seem to hear murmuring in my ears, like the   15
sound of the flute in the ears of the mystic; that voice, I say, is humming in my ears, and prevents me from hearing any other. And I know that anything more which you may say will be vain. Yet speak, if you have anything to say.

CRITO: I have nothing to say, Socrates.   16

SOCRATES: Leave me then, Crito, to fulfill the will of God, and to follow whither he leads.   17

FOR CLASS DISCUSSION

1. Analyze and evaluate the disagreement between Martin Luther King Jr. and Lewis Van Dusen Jr. over the ethics of civil disobedience by applying the first set of guide questions from page 465. How do you account for their disagreement?

2. To what extent do you think that Van Dusen and Socrates agree on their reasons for disapproving civil disobedience?

3. Choose one of the arguments for closer analysis, applying the second set of guide questions on pages 465–66.

OPTIONAL WRITING ASSIGNMENTS

1. You are a successful civil rights attorney. The principal of your child's junior high school has approached you with a concern. It seems that none of the social studies textbooks discusses the concept of civil disobedience. He wants to provide the social studies teachers with a statement on civil disobedience.

Drawing on the preceding essays, personal experience, and any other research you may have done, write a brief explanation of the role of civil disobedience in a democracy. Before you start writing, believe/doubt the following statement: "There is no place for civil disobedience in a modern democracy." Whatever you decide about that statement, construct a brief explanation of your view that would be appropriate for use in an eighth grade textbook.

2. The aerial bombardment of Iraq at the start of the 1991 war set off waves of student protests on college campuses reminiscent of the Vietnam antiwar movement. Several students at one college missed a midterm exam to join a protest march at the start of the war. When the students showed up the next day asking to take the midterm, the professor refused. He explained that his syllabus specifically stated that students could make up an exam only in cases of illness or personal emergency. Write a letter to the professor either supporting or opposing his decision that political protests do not constitute grounds for missing an exam.

CENSORSHIP ON THE INTERNET

Civility without Censorship
The Ethics of the Internet

Raymond W. Smith

Raymond W. Smith, former chairman of Bell Atlantic Corporation, delivered this argument as a speech to the Simon Wiesenthal Center and Museum of Tolerance in Los Angeles, California, on December 1, 1998. It was reprinted in the January 15, 1999, issue of Vital Speeches of the Day.

1   Thank you, Rabbi Cooper, for the gracious introduction . . . and let me acknowledge the tremendous contributions the Museum and the Center have made toward harmonizing race relations and advancing equality and justice. We're truly honored that you would include us in today's program.

2   For the past two years, I've been using the "bully pulpit" to alert various civil rights leaders and organizations (like Martin Luther King III and the NAACP) of the dangers posed by cyberhate. If not for the early groundbreaking work by the Simon Wiesenthal Center, I doubt whether I would have even known of this growing threat. Thank you for warning us—and now, for showing us—how extremists are using the Internet for their own purposes.

3   When thinking about this morning's topic, I can't help but mention a cartoon that recently appeared in the newspapers. Through the doorway, a mother calls out to her

teenager—who is surrounded by high-tech equipment—"I hope you're not watching sex stuff on the Internet!" To which her son replies, "Naw, I'm getting it on TV!"

Until recently, the chief concern of parents was pornography—kid's access to it over the Web and the fear of sexual predators cruising cyberspace. Now, we're worried about hate mongers reaching out to our children in digital space.   4

As we have just seen and heard, Neo-Nazis and extremists of every political stripe who once terrorized people in the dead of night with burning crosses and painted swastikas are now sneaking up on the public—especially our kids—through the World Wide Web.   5

As cyberhate is nothing less than the attempt to corrupt public discourse on race and ethnicity via the Internet, many people see censorship of web sites and Net content as the only viable way to meet this growing threat.   6

I disagree.   7

Instead of fearing the Internet's reach, we need to embrace it—to value its ability to connect our children to the wealth of positive human experience and knowledge. While there is, to quote one critic, "every form of diseased intelligence" in digital space, we must remember that it comprises only a small fraction of cyberspace. The Internet provides our children unlimited possibilities for learning and education—the great libraries, cities and cultures of the world also await them at just the click of a mouse key.   8

In short, we need to think less about ways to keep cyberhate off the screen, and more about ways to meet it head on: which translates into fighting destructive rhetoric with constructive dialogue—hate speech with truth—restrictions with greater Internet access.   9

This morning then, I would like to discuss with you the options that are available to combat cyberhate that don't endanger our First Amendment guarantees—and that remain true to our commitment to free speech.   10

That people and institutions should call for a strict ban on language over the Web that could be considered racist, anti-Semitic or bigoted is totally understandable. None of us was truly prepared for the emergence of multiple hate-group web sites (especially those geared toward children), or the quick adoption of high-technology by skinheads and others to market their digital cargo across state lines and international date lines at the speed of light.   11

One possible reason some people feel inclined to treat the Internet more severely than other media is that the technology is new and hard to understand. Also, the Internet's global reach and ubiquitous nature makes it appear ominous. As Justice Gabriel Bach, of Israel, noted, this ability makes it especially dangerous. "I'm frightened stiff by the Internet," he said, "billions of people all over the world have access to it."

My industry has seen all this before.   12

The clash between free speech and information technology is actually quite an old one. Nearly a century ago, telephone companies, courts, and the Congress debated whether "common carriers" (public phone companies) were obligated to carry all talk equally, regardless of content. And in the end—though some believed that the phone would do everything from eliminate Southern accents and increase Northern labor unrest—free speech won out in the courts.   13

Whatever the technology, be it the radio or the silver screen, history teaches us that white supremacists, anti-Semites and others will unfortunately come to grasp, relatively early on, a new medium's potential.   14

15   We simply can't condemn a whole technology because we fear that a Father Coughlin or a Leni Riefenstahl (early pioneers in the use of radio and film to advance anti-Semitism or Hitler's Reich) is waiting in the wings to use the latest technology to their own advantage. Nor can we expect the Congress, the federal government or an international regulatory agency to tightly regulate cyberspace content in order to stymie language we find offensive.

16   The wisdom of further empowering such organizations and agencies like the FCC or the United Nations aside, it is highly doubtful even if they had the authority, that they would have the ability to truly stem the flow of racist and anti-Semitic language on the World Wide Web.

17   Anybody with a phone line, computer and Internet connection can set up a web site—even broadcast over the Net.

18   Even if discovered and banned, on-line hate groups can easily jump Internet service providers and national boundaries to avoid accountability. I think cyber guru, Peter Huber, got it right when he said, "To censor Internet filth at its origins, we would have to enlist the Joint Chiefs of Staff, who could start by invading Sweden and Holland."

19   Then there is the whole matter of disguise. Innocent sounding URLs (handles or Web site names) can fool even the most traveled or seasoned "cybernaut."

20   As for efforts on Capitol Hill and elsewhere to legislate all so-called "offensive" language off the Internet, here again, we can expect the courts to knock down any attempts to curtail First Amendment rights on the Internet. As the Supreme Court ruled last year when it struck down legislation restricting the transmission of "indecent" material on-line: (To Quote) "Regardless of the strength of the government's interest, the level of discourse reaching a mailbox simply cannot be limited to what is suitable for a sandbox."

21   In short, although the temptation is great to look to legislation and regulation as a remedy to cyberhate, our commitment to free speech must always take precedence over our fears.

22   So, cyberhate will not be defeated by the stroke of a pen.

23   Now, this is not to say that, because we place such a high value on our First Amendment rights, we can't do anything to combat the proliferation of hate sites on the Internet or protect young minds from such threatening and bigoted language.

24   Law enforcement agencies and state legislators can use existing laws against stalking and telephone harassment to go after those who abuse e-mail . . . parents can install software filtering programs (such as the Anti-Defamation League's HateFilter, or the one Bell Atlantic uses, CyberPatrol) to block access to questionable Internet sites . . . schools and libraries can protect children by teaching them how to properly use the Internet and challenge cyberhate . . . and Internet Service Providers can voluntarily decline to host hate sites. (Bell Atlantic Internet Services, for instance, reserves the right to decline or terminate service which "espouses, promotes or incites bigotry, hatred or racism.")

25   Given that today's panel has representatives from state government, law enforcement, the courts and the Internet industry, we can discuss these initiatives later in more detail. The point is, there are other ways besides empowering national or international oversight agencies, or drafting draconian legislation, to lessen the impact of cyberhate.

26   Freedom, not censorship, is the only way to combat this threat to civility. In short, more speech—not less—is needed on the World Wide Web.

27   In fact, the best answer to cyberhate lies in the use of information technology itself. As a reporter for the *Boston Globe* recently concluded, (quote) "the same technology that pro-

vides a forum for extremists, enables civil rights groups and individuals to mobilize a response in unprecedented ways."

We totally agree. 28

Our prescription to cyberhate is therefore rather simple, but far reaching in its approach: 29

The first component is access: if we're to get to a higher level of national understanding on racial and ethnic issues—and strike at the very roots of cyberhate—we must see that no minority group or community is left out of cyberspace for want of a simple Internet connection or basic computer. 30

At Bell Atlantic, we've been working very hard to provide the minority communities we serve with Internet access. Across our region, thousands of inner-city schools, libraries, colleges and community groups are now getting connected to cyberspace through a variety of our foundation and state grant programs. Also, our employees have been in the forefront of volunteering their time and energy to wire schools to the Internet during specially designated "Net" days. 31

Internet access alone, however, won't build bridges of understanding between people— or level the playing field between cyber-haters and the targets of their hate. 32

The second thing we must do is make sure the Web's content is enriched by minority culture and beliefs, and that there are more Web sites and home pages dedicated to meeting head-on the racist caricatures and pseudo history often found in cyberspace. 33

While cyberhate cannot be mandated or censored out of existence, it can be countered by creating hundreds of chat-lines, home pages, bulletin boards and Web sites dedicated to social justice, tolerance and equality—for all people regardless of race, nationality or sexual orientation. 34

Over the past two years, Bell Atlantic has helped a number of minority and civil rights groups launch and maintain their Web sites (like the NAACP, the Leadership Council on Civil Rights, and the National Council of La Raza), and we've done the same for dozens of smaller cultural organizations (like the Harlem Studio Museum and El Museo del Barrio). 35

We believe that kind of moral leadership can have a tremendous impact. Quite simply, we need more Simon Wiesenthal Centers, Anti-Defamation Leagues, and Southern Poverty Law Centers monitoring and responding to cyberhate. 36

If we're to bring the struggle for human decency and dignity into cyberspace, we must see that the two most powerful revolutions of the 20th century—those of civil rights and information technology—are linked even closer together. 37

Finally, we need to drive real-time, serious dialogue on the religious, ethnic, and cultural concerns that divide us as a nation—a task for which the Internet is particularly suited. 38

Precisely because it is anonymous, the Internet provides a perfect forum to discuss race, sexual orientation and other similar issues. On the Internet, said one user, "you can speak freely and not have fears that somebody is going to attack you for what comes out of your heart." It's this kind of open and heart-felt discussion that we need to advance and sponsor on-line.

Already, a number of small groups and lone individuals are meeting the cyberhate challenge through simple dialogue between strangers. I'm talking about Web sites run by educators to inform parents about on-line hate materials . . . sites operated by "recovering" 39 racists to engage skinheads and other misguided kids in productive debate . . . Web sites run by concerned citizens to bridge the gap in ignorance between ethnic, racial and other communities.

40   The "Y? forum," also known as the National Forum on People's Differences, is a wonderful example of a Web site where readers can safely ask and follow discussions on sensitive cross-cultural topics without having to wade through foul language or "flame wars."

41   As a columnist from the *Miami Herald* described the appeal of these kinds of sites: "As long as we are mysteries, one to another, we face a perpetuation of ignorance and a feeding of fear. I'd rather people ask the questions than try to make up the answers. I'd rather they ask the questions than turn to myth and call it truth."

42   In closing, my company recognizes that the Internet doesn't operate in a vacuum. We agree that those who profit from information technology have a special responsibility to see that its promise is shared across class, race and geographic boundaries.

43   That's why we're working with the public schools and libraries in our region to see that they're all equipped with the pens, pencils and paper of the 21st century . . . why we're helping to further distance learning and telemedicine applications that serve the educational and health needs of the disabled and isolated . . . why we're helping minority groups and civil rights organizations use information technology to spread their vision and their values to the millions of people electronically linked to the global village.

44   And that's the way it should be.

45   Let me leave you with a personal story . . .

46   When growing up, my Jewish friends and I often swapped theology—tales from the Hassidic Masters for stories from the Lives of the Saints. I remember from these discussions that one of the great Rabbis noted that the first word of the Ten Commandments is "I" and the last word is "neighbor." In typical Talmudic fashion, the Rabbi was telling us that if we want to incorporate the Commandments into our lives, we must move from a focus on ourselves to others.

47   At Bell Atlantic, the more we grow—in both scale and scope—the greater the emphasis we place on being a good corporate citizen, and the more we're driven to see that digital technology is used for purposes of enlightenment and education.

48   The Internet will fundamentally transform the way we work, learn, do commerce. It will also, if properly used and rightly taught, help bridge the gap in understanding between communities—becoming not a tool of hate, but one of hope.

49   Thank you again for the invitation to join you this morning.

Internet Censorship
Issues for Teacher-Librarians

Alvin Schrader

In this article, originally published in the May–June 1999 issue of Teacher Librarian, *Dr. Alvin Schrader, director of the School of Library Studies at the Uni-*

versity of Alberta, explores librarians' positions on the accessibility of Internet resources in schools and school libraries.

Converging communication technologies offer mesmerizing potentialities for global access to local culture. However, concerns about controversial images and ideas on the Internet have inspired both political and technological challenges to open access. Over the past three or four years, a bewildering array of software products has appeared on the US and Canadian markets that claim to be able to either "filter" or "rate" Internet-based content. Typical product claims are couched in the rhetoric of child protection and parental guidance.

The purpose of this article is to describe and critique emerging issues about Internet access in schools and school libraries. In the cyberspace universe of instant access to information and images of all kinds, how should school librarians around the world respond to these commercial products? What is the role of school librarians in the Internet content transmission chain? How can they reconcile the sometimes conflicting goals of parental responsibilities with children's educational and developmental interests, media literacy and community standards?

More specifically, what is the purpose of Internet filters? Are they sensible tools for librarians in all sectors to use to identify and describe creative content on the Internet, in the interests of child protection and social responsibility? Or are they merely the latest technologies for censorship?

The topic of Internet filters is an exciting one for librarians in all sectors because it represents the intersection of our roles as advocates for intellectual freedom, as organizers of information and as promoters of media literacy. It gives us the opportunity to share our knowledge and expertise, and to increase our contribution to society at large and around the world.

SOFTWARE PRODUCTS
FOR FILTERING AND RATING
EXPRESSIVE CONTENT ON THE INTERNET

Filtering software products are designed to perform at one or more levels of computer configuration, ranging from the individual computer workstation or local area network, to a remote vendor server, an ISP (Internet service provider), and other arrangements.

These products offer a rather bewildering array of software options for controlling and suppressing expressive content on the Internet, including such things as "bad word," "bad phrase," and "bad syllable" stoplists, "bad site" lists, "bad topic" lists and content rating systems.

The magnitude of the task that the producers of filtering and rating software have undertaken is formidable. With one estimate putting the number of new sites appearing each day at 3,000 in the US alone, the Internet is a dynamic phenomenon that leaves product owners shooting at moving targets—speeding targets, actually. The most recent estimate of the size of the web is 320 million web pages currently accessible to casual browsers, a number expected to grow by 1,000 percent in the next few years.

8   In this rapidly changing technological climate, product manufacturers are targeting widely divergent materials based on widely divergent criteria. This variation is reflected in the number and range of Internet sites that are blocked, with some products reporting as few as 15,000 and others as many as 138,000 sites (Oder 1997, 41). One Internet rating product reports that it has rated 1.5 million URLs (NetShepherd 1997).

9   And they all claim to have qualified staff. Nothing is disclosed, however, about the professional qualifications of this community, how they are selected, who selects them, what they are paid, what sort of quality control over their work is in place, or what sort of retrieval testing is done to ensure accuracy and consistency in the resulting product.

10   The most egregious blocking makes the offending words, sites and topics disappear, utterly invisible to searchers, so that they are completely unaware that suppressed information even exists. For example, targeting "sex" blocks the NASA site marsexplorer.com, the works of poet Anne Sexton, sexual harassment sites and information about sexually transmitted diseases. Also blocked and invisible to the searcher using some filtering products is anything that remotely concerns homosexuality, lesbianism or bisexuality. One product prevented access to the entire library web site of the Archie R. Dykes Medical Library because it blocks homosexuality and therefore the term "dyke" (Chelton 1997).

11   But most products do not stop there. Some also block numerous feminist sites such as NOW, the National Organization for Women feminist newsgroups, and sites such as alt.feminism, soc.support.pregnancy.loss, soc.support.fat-acceptance and Planned Parenthood. One product blocked the important Holocaust archive and anti-revisionist resource site Nizkor for a time, because it contained "hate speech" (Wallace 1997). Another blocks all URLs containing the tilde sign (~). These examples serve to illustrate the variety of problems that are equally inherent in accurately identifying negative targets for Internet blocking programs as in identifying positive targets for conventional retrieval systems.

12   Society is intrinsically complex, and complex concepts do not fit into simple compartments. The word, phrase, and site identification strategies of the blocking products pigeonhole ideas and impose ideological agendas. Is all violence of the same kind? Is a punch the same as an execution? Should nudity and sex be categorized together? Is erotica the same as the sexually explicit?

13   While some of the software products acknowledge the existence of a value system or some sort of ideological agenda in their filtering and rating operations, others resolutely deny the charge. CyberSitter, for example, denies that it has a political agenda and that it blocks only sites "that meet a pre-defined criteria . . . without exception" (CyberSitter 1997). In contrast, CyberPatrol states that it operates on an explicit criterion: "In evaluating a site for inclusion in the [blocking] list, we consider the effect of the site on a typical 12 year old searching the Internet unaccompanied by a parent or educator" (CyberPatrol 1997).

14   In spite of the denials of some producers of these products, any operation that identifies words, phrases, topics and sites for blocking is of necessity imposing an ideological agenda or value system. In the approach followed by these commercial products, context is ignored and one four-letter word becomes more important than 400 pages of story. Margaret Laurence, the great Canadian novelist, is said to have called this "snippet censorship," the practice of basing one's judgment of a work on excerpts, offending words or phrases, and scenes lifted out of context (Carver 1997). How, for example, would the products treat

the Bible? According to what criteria? Would they rate each story individually? Or even individual words within each story?

When blocking and rating decisions are made by unknown third parties with unknown   15
qualifications and unknown ideological agendas, the danger to public debate is palpable.
With a broad sweep, these products indict all representations of violence, sex, hatred and
other targets as equally bad, and as especially bad for young people.

READER RESPONSE THEORY IMPLICATIONS
FOR FILTERING AND RATING INTERNET CONTENT

Since meaning is embedded in the context in which information is used, the root   16
of library policy on Internet use must be the concept that the context of the use of information is critical to how appropriate the information is in a given institutional setting
(Davison 1996). For example, studying hate propaganda sites on the Internet is a much different intellectual and educational activity than adding racial slurs oneself. Reading is not
endorsing.

To a certain degree, therefore, readers participate in creating the meaning of a text   17
based on their own reading history, their own personal filter of cultural, moral and aesthetic
values, and their own reading motivation. In this dynamic, the meaning that a particular
reader ascribes to a text may or may not approximate the author's original conception—or,
for that matter, any other reader's.

According to this view of reader response, then, far from being a fixed and objective   18
thing that every reader perceives identically, a text is somewhat ambiguous, fluid, subjective, susceptible to multiple meanings and contrary interpretations. Reader response theory is captured in a familiar expression: It's in the eye of the beholder.

Reader response theory is especially relevant in considering text for children, taking   19
into account the enormous variation exhibited by children in emotional development and
psychological maturity not only at different stages of growth but at the same age as well.
Maturity is not a simple function of biological age: one 12 year old is nearly an adult, another is closer to childhood.

To accommodate the vast diversity of needs in young people means that each young   20
child must seek out his or her own level of reading, viewing and listening interests, both
individually and continuously, under the guidance of their parents or guardians. Moreover,
most young people who are readers tend to "read up," that is to say, they read above the
reading level designations assigned by publishers, reviewers, and librarians. Internet content is no different. Filtering and rating decisions that treat it as if it were fixed for all
children regardless of age and maturity is an inadequate and flawed approach to child
development.

AMBIGUITIES

Internet filtering and rating technologies are theoretically unworkable. It is not that they   21
are technologically unworkable or technologically limited. It is that the essential ambiguities
of language, text, reader, rating and blocking methods ensure the failure of automated

filtering. The problems of identifying and describing Internet content for purposes of control and prohibition are intractable: new sites, new terms, new issues, the world cacophony of languages, variable interpretations of meaning, variable perceptions of offensiveness, variable perceptions of age appropriateness and variable cultural norms.

22   These ambiguities and dynamics prevent blocking and rating software from ever being successful in controlling the world of ideas in a way that would satisfy critics, reassure parents, and relieve librarians and teachers of unpleasant encounters with complainants. Human language is just too unstable, words and meanings just too indeterminate, too elastic, too mutable, too imperfect. As one critic has put it, "safeonly access can not happen because individual perceptions of safe are as varied as the number of sites on the Internet" (Crosslin 1998, 52).

23   The American Library Association's "Statement on library use of filtering software," an explanatory document accompanying the "Resolution on the use of filtering software in libraries" that was adopted by ALA Council on July 2, 1997, concluded that:

> Library use of blocking/filtering software creates an implied contract with parents that their children will not be able to access material on the Internet that they do not wish their children to read or view. Libraries will be unable to fulfill this implied contract, due to the technological limitations of the software, thus exposing themselves to possible legal liability and litigation. (American Library Association 1997, 120)

24   In response to criticisms of software imperfection, apologists are quick to argue that current technology is "good though not perfect," "reasonably accurate," "extremely effective but not foolproof." One public library director calls WebSense "80 percent effective" (Oder 1997, 41).

25   We need to ask if smoke detectors that worked 75 or 80 percent of the time would be better than nothing—especially when the timing of the operational phase is unknown and unknowable. Moreover, to extend the analogy, we might ask how acceptable such smoke detectors would be if they not only reacted to smoke but also to incense, garlic, sweat, perfume or other unpredicted and unpredictable triggers. Or, more radically yet, what if the detectors promised home safety but disclosed nothing about what that meant or how it would be realized.

26   Yet the very names of the software products—nanny, patrol, shepherd, sitter, watch—conjure up images of unqualified protection, safety, guidance and comfort. NetNanny advertising, for example, says: "NetNanny is watching when parents aren't."

27   But instead of fulfilling these explicit advertising promises, what the new products offer is the illusion of success—an illusion that comes with a high price tag. One price is a false sense of security. Its twin is a false sense of confidence that all appropriate information will still be retrieved when one searches the Internet.

28   Another price is intellectual freedom. The crude, paternalistic strategies adopted by blocking and rating products should serve to remind us that authority control keeps some voices out just as easily as it lets others in. Internet blocking software is like performing brain surgery with a chainsaw.

29   I would like to see librarians in all sectors of service to society enter into the public debate about the Internet through their institutions and associations as well as individually by

virtue of professional training. I would like to see them help refocus public debate around fundamental social policy objectives and the strategies to achieve them, to work to dispel fear and moral panic about the Internet and kids, and to help instead to promote critical thinking and understanding. As Herbert Foerstel told a meeting called in response to complaints about the inclusion of certain materials in a Maryland library collection: "Tell us what you want to read, rather than what you don't want others to read" (Foerstel 1994, 30).

We need to implement acceptable use policies, AUPs, that make explicit the respective rights and responsibilities of students, parents and school officials for acceptable behavior on the Internet. Dillon (1996) and Ingvarson (1996) have described in considerable detail the elements and principles that should go into such policies, and the Internet is full of examples easily retrieved, such as The Internet Advocate site, a web-based resource guide for librarians and educators interested in providing youth access, at http://www.monroe.lib.in.us/Ichampel/netadv.html. Doug Johnson (1998) has also summarized issues that should be considered in developing AUPs.   30

We need to expand school library collection development into Internet sites; to educate parents about child safety issues on the Internet and how to raise "Net smart" children to ensure that school library policies on collection development, intellectual freedom, Internet access and materials reconsideration are understood; to forge alliances among different types of libraries as well as stronger community links; to provide in-house staff training and regular refresher sessions; to participate in the development of professional association policy statements and positions; and to support research efforts that investigate software product claims.   31

Above all, we need to expand information and library literacy into the school curriculum with school librarians in the lead to teach the skills of both information searching and critical thinking. As a recent New *York Times* editorial, critical of a legislative initiative to require antipornography filters on school and school library computers, concluded, "Given the limitations of filtering technology, the best way to protect children is to teach them how to use the Internet. A software program simply cannot do that" (*New York Times* 1998).   32

The Canadian Library Association encourages librarians to incorporate Internet use policies into overall policies on access to library resources and has produced a bestselling brochure entitled "Have a safe trip! A parent's guide to safety on the Internet" (Canadian Library Association 1997, 1998).   33

I do not believe that bad ideas or bad images produce bad kids. Nor do I believe that there is a shred of evidence to support this simplistic argument. We should worry much more about a lack of information than about too much or the wrong kind. There are no reasonable grounds to fear contagion or uncritical acceptance of ideas if children have strong family values. What should concern librarians is young people who have access to only one view of the world, young people brought up with no knowledge of choice, no awareness of diversity.   34

By way of postscript, I would like to see school librarians caution parents and individuals about the serious shortcomings of Internet software products that promise protection and monitoring, shortcomings that are not merely technological but more importantly moral, for blocking and rating systems do not help young people learn how to assume the responsibilities of adulthood, how to make independent critical judgments, how to say no,   35 how to live vicariously through story rather than dangerously through experience. As one librarian has asked rather rhetorically, do parents really want to turn their children's value systems over to a software vendor? (Crosslin 1998, 52). "What drives the filtering debate," wrote one recent correspondent to *American Libraries,* "is the question of who will control access to information. Will it be the government, or the individual? (Taylor 1999).

36   Outsourcing moral authority to faceless and anonymous Internet guardians is no alternative to family responsibility, librarian and teacher guidance, and individual critical awareness. As Meeks and McCullagh (1996) have so eloquently written, "Technology is no substitute for conscience." If the analysis presented in this article is accurate, it is irresponsible of institutions such as schools and libraries to use taxpayer money to buy products that do not work as advertised and that do not advance pedagogical goals: first we pay to obtain Internet access, and then we pay again to get rid of it. And when administrators install filters without discussion and debate, they miss an opportunity to facilitate and promote critical thinking in action. They disempower everyone.

37   My final word goes, fittingly, to a twelve-year-old girl—the typical young person for whom one of the filtering products is explicitly marketed—who wrote a letter to the local newspaper opposing censorship of the Internet at the Dundas Public Library in Ontario, Canada. She said:

> I am twelve years old and I go on the Internet all the time, on average ½ hour per day. Of all the time that I have been using it, (more than four years now), I have never seen or heard about any pornography pages or sites. . . . To me, the Internet is a way to explore the world without going anywhere. When I am on the Internet, it is my responsibility to pick and choose which pages are appropriate for me.

38   If you are worried about your child's choices, explore it together (Blonski 1997).

REFERENCES

American Library Association (1997). Statement on library use of filtering software. *Newsletter on Intellectual Freedom,* September, 119–120.
Blonski, Jackie (1997). "The Internet is an important place to learn and explore" (letter to the editor). *Dundas Review,* June 15, 4. http://insight.mcmaster.ca/org . . . dia,Dundasreview.15jun97.html
Canadian Library Association (1997). Statement on Internet access. http://www.cla.amlibs.ca/internet.htm
——— (1998). Have a safe trip! A parent's guide to safety on the Internet. http://www.cla.amlibs.ca/safetrip.htm
Carver, Peter (1997). Battle over novel (letter to the editor). *Globe and Mail*, February 7, A14.
Chelton, Mary K. (1997). Internet names and filtering software. E-mail message from cheltonm@esumail.emporia.edu (March 4).
Crosslin, Donna (1998). Unsafe at any modem speed (letter to the editor). *American Libraries, 29,* 52.
CyberPatrol (1997). Overview: The CyberNOT Block List. http://www.cyberpatrol.corn/cp_block.htm (May 11)
CyberSitter (1997). Frequently asked questions about CyberSITTER. http://www.solidoak.com/cyberfaq.htm

Davison, Phil (1996). Censorship and the need to develop policy. In Lyn Hay and James Henri (eds.), *A meeting of the minds: ITEC virtual conference '96 proceedings* (p. 9). Belconnen, ACT: Australian School Library Association.

Dillon, Ken (1996). Management of student access to the Internet: Issues and responsibilities. In Lyn Hay and James Henri (eds.), *A meeting of the minds: ITEC virtual conference '96 proceedings* (pp. 16–23). Belconnen, ACT: Australian School Library Association.

Foerstel, Herbert (1994). Conflict and compromise over homosexual literature. *Emergency Librarian, 22,* 30.

Ingvarson, Daniel (1996). Censorship: Planning a safe ride on the superhighway. In Lyn Hay and James Henri (eds.), *A meeting of the minds: ITEC virtual conference '96 proceedings* (pp. 3–6). Belconnen, ACT: Australian School Library Association.

Johnson, Doug (1998). Internet filters: Censorship by any other name? *Emergency Librarian, 25,* 11–13.

Meeks, Brock N., and Declan B. McCullagh (1996). Keys to the kingdom. CyberWire Dispatch. (July). http://www.eff.orgipubiPublications/DeclanMcCullagh/cwd.keys.to.the.kingdom.0796.article

NetShepherd (1997). NetShepherd responds to the EPIC report "Faulty Filters." http://www.netshepherd.com/fsEpicResponse.htm (December 2).

New York Times (1998). Filtering the Internet (Editorial). *New York Times,* March 16, A24.

Oder, Norman (1997). Filtering and its contradictions. *Library Journal, 122,* 41–42.

Schrader, Alvin M. (1998). Internet censorship: Access issues for school librarians in a cyberspace world. Education for all: Culture, reading and information. Selected papers. 27th International Conference of the International Association of School Librarianship, Ramat-Gan, Israel, July 5–10, 1998. Eds. Snunith Shham and Moshe Yitzhaki. IASL, 1998, pp. 189–210.

Taylor, Paul (1999). "Let unfiltered freedom ring" (letter to the editor). *American Libraries, 30,* 34.

Wallace, Jonathan D. (1997). Purchase of blocking software by public libraries is unconstitutional. *The Ethical Spectacle.* November 9. http://www.spectacle/org/cs/library.html

This article is based on a longer research paper presented at the 1998 annual conference of the International Association of School Librarianship in Ramat-Gan, Israel.

Fahrenheit 451.2
Is Cyberspace Burning?

Ann Beeson and Chris Hansen

This article is a white paper written by Ann Beeson and Chris Hansen of the American Civil Liberties Union (ACLU) Legal Department and ACLU Associate Director Barry Steinhardt and mounted on the ACLU Web site, www.aclu.org, in 1997.

EXECUTIVE SUMMARY

In the landmark case *Reno v. ACLU,* the Supreme Court overturned the Communications Decency Act, declaring that the Internet deserves the same high level of free speech protection afforded to books and other printed matter.   [1]

2   But today, all that we have achieved may now be lost, if not in the bright flames of censorship then in the dense smoke of the many ratings and blocking schemes promoted by some of the very people who fought for freedom.

3   The ACLU and others in the cyber-liberties community were genuinely alarmed by the tenor of a recent White House summit meeting on Internet censorship at which industry leaders pledged to create a variety of schemes to regulate and block controversial online speech.

4   But it was not any one proposal or announcement that caused our alarm; rather, it was the failure to examine the longer-term implications for the Internet of rating and blocking schemes.

5   The White House meeting was clearly the first step away from the principle that protection of the electronic word is analogous to protection of the printed word. Despite the Supreme Court's strong rejection of a broadcast analogy for the Internet, government and industry leaders alike are now inching toward the dangerous and incorrect position that the Internet is like television, and should be rated and censored accordingly.

6   Is Cyberspace burning? Not yet, perhaps. But where there's smoke, there's fire.

INTRODUCTION

7   In his chilling (and prescient) novel about censorship, *Fahrenheit 451,* author Ray Bradbury describes a futuristic society where books are outlawed. "Fahrenheit 451" is, of course, the temperature at which books burn.

8   In Bradbury's novel—and in the physical world—people censor the printed word by burning books. But in the virtual world, one can just as easily censor controversial speech by banishing it to the farthest corners of cyberspace using rating and blocking programs. Today, will Fahrenheit, version 451.2—a new kind of virtual censorship—be the temperature at which cyberspace goes up in smoke?

9   The first flames of Internet censorship appeared two years ago, with the introduction of the Federal Communications Decency Act (CDA), outlawing "indecent" online speech. But in the landmark case *Reno v. ACLU,* the Supreme Court overturned the CDA, declaring that the Internet is entitled to the highest level of free speech protection. In other words, the Court said that online speech deserved the protection afforded to books and other printed matter.

10   Today, all that we have achieved may now be lost, if not in the bright flames of censorship then in the dense smoke of the many ratings and blocking schemes promoted by some of the very people who fought for freedom. And in the end, we may find that the censors have indeed succeeded in "burning down the house to roast the pig."

IS CYBERSPACE BURNING?

11   The ashes of the CDA were barely smoldering when the White House called a summit meeting to encourage Internet users to self-rate their speech and to urge industry leaders to develop and deploy the tools for blocking "inappropriate" speech. The meeting was "voluntary," of course: the White House claimed it wasn't holding anyone's feet to the fire.

The ACLU and others in the cyber-liberties community were genuinely alarmed by   12
the tenor of the White House summit and the unabashed enthusiasm for technological
fixes that will make it easier to block or render invisible controversial speech. (Note: see
pp. 601–02] for detailed explanations of the various technologies.)

Industry leaders responded to the White House call with a barrage of announcements: 13

- Netscape announced plans to join Microsoft—together the two giants have 90% or more of the web browser market—in adopting PICS (Platform for Internet Content Selection), the rating standard that establishes a consistent way to rate and block online content;

- IBM announced it was making a $100,000 grant to RSAC (Recreational Software Advisory Council) to encourage the use of its RSACi rating system. Microsoft Explorer already employs the RSACi rating system, Compuserve encourages its use and it is fast becoming the de facto industry standard rating system;

- Four of the major search engines—the services which allow users to conduct searches of the Internet for relevant sites—announced a plan to cooperate in the promotion of "self-regulation" of the Internet. The president of one, Lycos, was quoted in a news account as having "thrown down the gauntlet" to the other three, challenging them to agree to exclude unrated sites from search results;

- Following announcement of proposed legislation by Sen. Patty Murray (D-Wash.), which would impose civil and ultimately criminal penalties on those who mis-rate a site, the makers of the blocking program Safe Surf proposed similar legislation, the "Online Cooperative Publishing Act."

But it was not any one proposal or announcement that caused our alarm; rather, it was the failure to examine the longer-term implications for the Internet of rating and blocking schemes.

What may be the result? The Internet will become bland and homogenized. The major   14
commercial sites will still be readily available, they will have the resources and inclination
to self-rate, and third-party rating services will be inclined to give them acceptable ratings.
People who disseminate quirky and idiosyncratic speech, create individual home pages, or
post to controversial news groups, will be among the first Internet users blocked by filters
and made invisible by the search engines. Controversial speech will still exist, but will only
be visible to those with the tools and know-how to penetrate the dense smokescreen of industry "self-regulation."

As bad as this very real prospect is, it can get worse. Faced with the reality that, al-   15
though harder to reach, sex, hate speech and other controversial matter is still available on
the Internet, how long will it be before governments begin to make use of an Internet already configured to accommodate massive censorship? If you look at these various proposals in a larger context, a very plausible scenario emerges. It is a scenario which in some
respects has already been set in motion:

- First, the use of PICS becomes universal; providing a uniform method for content rating.

- Next, one or two rating systems dominate the market and become the de facto standard for the Internet.

- PICS and the dominant rating(s) system are built into Internet software as an automatic default.

- Unrated speech on the Internet is effectively blocked by these defaults.

- Search engines refuse to report on the existence of unrated or "unacceptably" rated sites.

- Governments frustrated by "indecency" still on the Internet make self-rating mandatory and mis-rating a crime.

16   The scenario is, for now, theoretical—but inevitable. It is clear that any scheme that allows access to unrated speech will fall afoul of the government-coerced push for a "family friendly" Internet. We are moving inexorably toward a system that blocks speech simply because it is unrated and makes criminals of those who mis-rate.

17   The White House meeting was clearly the first step in that direction and away from the principle that protection of the electronic word is analogous to protection of the printed word. Despite the Supreme Court's strong rejection of a broadcast analogy for the Internet, government and industry leaders alike are now inching toward the dangerous and incorrect position that the Internet is like television, and should be rated and censored accordingly.

18   Is Cyberspace burning? Not yet, perhaps. But where there's smoke, there's fire.

FREE SPEECH ONLINE: A VICTORY UNDER SIEGE

19   On June 26, 1997, the Supreme Court held in *Reno v. ACLU* that the Communications Decency Act, which would have made it a crime to communicate anything "indecent" on the Internet, violated the First Amendment. It was the nature of the Internet itself, and the quality of speech on the Internet, that led the Court to declare that the Internet is entitled to the same broad free speech protections given to books, magazines, and casual conversation.

20   The ACLU argued, and the Supreme Court agreed, that the CDA was unconstitutional because, although aimed at protecting minors, it effectively banned speech among adults. Similarly, many of the rating and blocking proposals, though designed to limit minors' access, will inevitably restrict the ability of adults to communicate on the Internet. In addition, such proposals will restrict the rights of older minors to gain access to material that clearly has value for them.

RETHINKING THE RUSH TO RATE

21   This paper examines the free speech implications of the various proposals for Internet blocking and rating. Individually, each of the proposals poses some threat to open and robust speech on the Internet; some pose a considerably greater threat than others.

22   Even more ominous is the fact that the various schemes for rating and blocking, taken together, could create a black cloud of private "voluntary" censorship that is every bit as

threatening as the CDA itself to what the Supreme Court called "the most participatory form of mass speech yet developed."

We call on industry leaders, Internet users, policy makers and parents groups to en-   23
gage in a genuine debate about the free speech ramifications of the rating and blocking schemes being proposed.

To open the door to a meaningful discussion, we offer the following recommendations   24
and principles:

RECOMMENDATIONS AND PRINCIPLES

- *Internet users know best.* The primary responsibility for determining what speech to access should remain with the individual Internet user; parents should take primary responsibility for determining what their children should access.

- *Default setting on free speech.* Industry should not develop products that require speakers to rate their own speech or be blocked by default.

- *Buyers beware.* The producers of user-based software programs should make their lists of blocked speech available to consumers. The industry should develop products that provide maximum user control.

- *No government coercion or censorship.* The First Amendment prevents the government from imposing, or from coercing industry into imposing, a mandatory Internet ratings scheme.

- *Libraries are free speech zones.* The First Amendment prevents the government, including public libraries, from mandating the use of user-based blocking software.

SIX REASONS WHY SELF-RATING SCHEMES
ARE WRONG FOR THE INTERNET

To begin with, the notion that citizens should "self-rate" their speech is contrary to the   25
entire history of free speech in America. A proposal that we rate our online speech is no less offensive to the First Amendment than a proposal that publishers of books and magazines rate each and every article or story, or a proposal that everyone engaged in a street corner conversation rate his or her comments. But that is exactly what will happen to books, magazines, and any kind of speech that appears online under a self-rating scheme.

In order to illustrate the very practical consequences of these schemes, consider the   26
following six reasons, and their accompanying examples, illustrating why the ACLU is against self-rating:

Reason #1: Self-Rating Schemes Will Cause Controversial
Speech to Be Censored.

Kiyoshi Kuromiya, founder and sole operator of Critical Path AIDS Project, has a web   27
site that includes safer sex information written in street language with explicit diagrams, in order to reach the widest possible audience. Kuromiya doesn't want to apply the rating

"crude" or "explicit" to his speech, but if he doesn't, his site will be blocked as an unrated site. If he does rate, his speech will be lumped in with "pornography" and blocked from view. Under either choice, Kuromiya has been effectively blocked from reaching a large portion of his intended audience—teenage Internet users—as well as adults.

28   As this example shows, the consequences of rating are far from neutral. The ratings themselves are all pejorative by definition, and they result in certain speech being blocked.

29   The White House has compared Internet ratings to "food labels"—but that analogy is simply wrong. Food labels provide objective, scientifically verifiable information to help the consumer make choices about what to buy, e.g., the percentage of fat in a food product like milk. Internet ratings are subjective value judgments that result in certain speech being blocked to many viewers. Further, food labels are placed on products that are readily available to consumers—unlike Internet labels, which would place certain kinds of speech out of reach of Internet users.

30   What is most critical to this issue is that speech like Kuromiya's is entitled to the highest degree of Constitutional protection. This is why ratings requirements have never been imposed on those who speak via the printed word. Kuromiya could distribute the same material in print form on any street corner or in any bookstore without worrying about having to rate it. In fact, a number of Supreme Court cases have established that the First Amendment does not allow government to compel speakers to say something they don't want to say—and that includes pejorative ratings. There is simply no justification for treating the Internet any differently.

Reason #2: Self-Rating Is Burdensome, Unwieldy, and Costly.

31   Art on the Net is a large, non-profit web site that hosts online "studios" where hundreds of artists display their work. The vast majority of the artwork has no sexual content, although there's an occasional Rubenesque painting. The ratings systems don't make sense when applied to art. Yet Art on the Net would still have to review and apply a rating to the more than 26,000 pages on its site, which would require time and staff that they just don't have. Or, they would have to require the artists themselves to self-rate, an option they find objectionable. If they decline to rate, they will [be] blocked as an unrated site even though most Internet users would hardly object to the art reaching minors, let alone adults.

32   As the Supreme Court noted in *Reno v. ACLU,* one of the virtues of the Internet is that it provides "relatively unlimited, low-cost capacity for communication of all kinds." In striking down the CDA, the Court held that imposing age-verification costs on Internet speakers would be "prohibitively expensive for noncommercial—as well as some commercial—speakers." Similarly, the burdensome requirement of self-rating thousands of pages of information would effectively shut most noncommercial speakers out of the Internet marketplace.

33   The technology of embedding the rating is also far from trivial. In a winning ACLU case that challenged a New York state online censorship statute, *ALA v. Pataki,* one long-time Internet expert testified that he tried to embed an RSACi label in his online newsletter site but finally gave up after several hours.

34   In addition, the ratings systems are simply unequipped to deal with the diversity of content now available on the Internet. There is perhaps nothing as subjective as a viewer's

reaction to art. As history has shown again and again, one woman's masterpiece is another woman's pornography. How can ratings such as "explicit" or "crude" be used to categorize art? Even ratings systems that try to take artistic value into account will be inherently subjective, especially when applied by artists themselves, who will naturally consider their own work to have merit.

The variety of news-related sites on the Web will be equally difficult to rate. Should explicit war footage be labeled "violent" and blocked from view to teenagers? If a long news article has one curse word, is the curse word rated individually, or is the entire story rated and then blocked?   35

Even those who propose that "legitimate" news organizations should not be required to rate their sites stumble over the question of who will decide what is legitimate news.   36

Reason #3: Conversation Can't Be Rated.

You are in a chat room or a discussion group—one of the thousands of conversational areas of the Net. A victim of sexual abuse has posted a plea for help, and you want to respond. You've heard about a variety of ratings systems, but you've never used one. You read the RSACi web page, but you can't figure out how to rate the discussion of sex and violence in your response. Aware of the penalties for mis-labeling, you decide not to send your message after all.   37

The burdens of self-rating really hit home when applied to the vibrant, conversational areas of the Internet. Most Internet users don't run web pages, but millions of people around the world send messages, short and long, every day, to chat rooms, news groups and mailing lists. A rating requirement for these areas of the Internet would be analogous to requiring all of us to rate our telephone or streetcorner or dinner party or water cooler conversations.   38

The only other way to rate these areas of cyberspace would be to rate entire chat rooms or news groups rather than individual messages. But most discussion groups aren't controlled by a specific person, so who would be responsible for rating them? In addition, discussion groups that contain some objectionable material would likely also have a wide variety of speech totally appropriate and valuable for minors—but the entire forum would be blocked from view for everyone.   39

Reason #4: Self-Rating Will Create "Fortress America" on the Internet.

You are a native of Papua, New Guinea, and as an anthropologist you have published several papers about your native culture. You create a web site and post electronic versions of your papers, in order to share them with colleagues and other interested people around the world. You haven't heard about the move in America to rate Internet content. You don't know it, but since your site is unrated none of your colleagues in America will be able to access it.   40

People from all corners of the globe—people who might otherwise never connect because of their vast geographical differences—can now communicate on the Internet both easily and cheaply. One of the most dangerous aspects of ratings systems is their   41 potential to build borders around American- and foreign-created speech. It is important to remember that today, nearly half of all Internet speech originates from outside the United States.

42   Even if powerful American industry leaders coerced other countries into adopting American ratings systems, how would these ratings make any sense to a New Guinean? Imagine that one of the anthropology papers explicitly describes a ritual in which teenage boys engage in self-mutilation as part of a rite of passage in achieving manhood. Would you look at it through the eyes of an American and rate it "torture," or would you rate it "appropriate for minors" for the New Guinea audience?

Reason #5: Self-Ratings Will Only Encourage, Not Prevent, Government Regulation.

43   The webmaster for Betty's Smut Shack, a web site that sells sexually explicit photos, learns that many people won't get to his site if he either rates his site "sexually explicit" or fails to rate at all. He rates his entire web site "okay for minors." A powerful Congressman from the Midwest learns that the site is now available to minors. He is outraged, and quickly introduces a bill imposing criminal penalties for mis-rated sites.

44   Without a penalty system for mis-rating, the entire concept of a self-ratings system breaks down. The Supreme Court that decided *Reno v. ACLU* would probably agree that the statute theorized above would violate the First Amendment, but as we saw with the CDA, that won't necessarily prevent lawmakers from passing it.

45   In fact, as noted earlier, a senator from Washington state—home of Industry giant Microsoft, among others—has already proposed a law that creates criminal penalties for mis-rating. Not to be outdone, the filtering software company Safe Surf has proposed the introduction of a virtually identical federal law, including a provision that allows parents to sue speakers for damages if they "negligently" mis-rate their speech.

46   The example above shows that, despite all good intentions, the application of ratings systems is likely to lead to heavy-handed government censorship. Moreover, the targets of that censorship are likely to be just the sort of relatively powerless and controversial speakers, like the groups Critical Path AIDS Project, Stop Prisoner Rape, Planned Parenthood, Human Rights Watch, and the various gay and lesbian organizations we represented in *Reno v. ACLU*.

Reason #6: Self-Ratings Schemes Will Turn the Internet into a Homogenized Medium Dominated by Commercial Speakers.

47   Huge entertainment conglomerates, such as the Disney Corporation or Time Warner, consult their platoons of lawyers who advise that their web sites must be rated to reach the widest possible audience. They then hire and train staff to rate all of their web pages. Everybody in the world will have access to their speech.

48   There is no question that there may be some speakers on the Internet for whom the ratings systems will impose only minimal burdens: the large, powerful corporate speakers with the money to hire legal counsel and staff to apply the necessary ratings. The com-

mercial side of the Net continues to grow, but so far the democratic nature of the Internet has put commercial speakers on equal footing with all of the other non-commercial and individual speakers.

Today, it is just as easy to find the Critical Path AIDS web site as it is to find the Dis-   49
ney site. Both speakers are able to reach a worldwide audience. But mandatory Internet self-rating could easily turn the most participatory communications medium the world has yet seen into a bland, homogenized, medium dominated by powerful American corporate speakers.

IS THIRD-PARTY RATING THE ANSWER?

Third-party ratings systems, designed to work in tandem with PICS labeling, have been   50
held out by some as the answer to the free speech problems posed by self-rating schemes. On the plus side, some argue, ratings by an independent third party could minimize the burden of self-rating on speakers and could reduce the inaccuracy and mis-rating problems of self-rating. In fact, one of the touted strengths of the original PICS proposal was that a variety of third-party ratings systems would develop and users could pick and choose from the system that best fit their values. But third party ratings systems still pose serious free speech concerns.

First, a multiplicity of ratings systems has not yet emerged on the market, probably due   51
to the difficulty of any one company or organization trying to rate over a million web sites, with hundreds of new sites—not to mention discussion groups and chat rooms—springing up daily.

Second, under third-party rating systems, unrated sites still may be blocked.   52

When choosing which sites to rate first, it is likely that third-party raters will rate the   53
most popular web sites first, marginalizing individual and non-commercial sites. And like the self-rating systems, third-party ratings will apply subjective and value-laden ratings that could result in valuable material being blocked to adults and older minors. In addition, available third-party rating systems have no notification procedure, so speakers have no way of knowing whether their speech has received a negative rating.

The fewer the third-party ratings products available, the greater the potential for   54
arbitrary censorship. Powerful industry forces may lead one product to dominate the marketplace. If, for example, virtually all households use Microsoft Internet Explorer and Netscape, and the browsers, in turn, use RSACi as their system, RSACi could become the default censorship system for the Internet. In addition, federal and state governments could pass laws mandating use of a particular ratings system in schools or libraries. Either of these scenarios could devastate the diversity of the Internet marketplace.

Pro-censorship groups have argued that a third-party rating system for the Internet is   55
no different from the voluntary Motion Picture Association of America ratings for movies that we've all lived with for years. But there is an important distinction: only a finite number of movies are produced in a given year. In contrast, the amount of content on the Internet is infinite. Movies are a static, definable product created by a small number of producers; speech on the Internet is seamless, interactive, and conversational. MPAA ratings also don't come with automatic blocking mechanisms.

THE PROBLEMS WITH USER-BASED
BLOCKING SOFTWARE IN THE HOME

56   With the explosive growth of the Internet, and in the wake of the recent censorship battles, the marketplace has responded with a wide variety of user-based blocking programs. Each company touts the speed and efficiency of its staff members in blocking speech that they have determined is inappropriate for minors. The programs also often block speech based on keywords. (This can result in sites such as www.middlesex.gov or www.SuperBowlXXX.com being blocked because they contain the keywords "sex" and "XXX.").

57   In *Reno v. ACLU,* the ACLU successfully argued that the CDA violated the First Amendment because it was not the least restrictive means of addressing the government's asserted interest in protecting children from inappropriate material. In supporting this argument, we suggested that a less restrictive alternative was the availability of user-based blocking programs, e.g., Net Nanny, that parents could use in the home if they wished to limit their child's Internet access.

58   While user-based blocking programs present troubling free speech concerns, we still believe today that they are far preferable to any statute that imposes criminal penalties on online speech. In contrast, many of the new ratings schemes pose far greater free speech concerns than do user-based software programs.

59   Each user installs the program on her home computer and turns the blocking mechanism on or off at will. The programs do not generally block sites that they haven't rated, which means that they are not 100 percent effective.

60   Unlike the third-party ratings or self-rating schemes, these products usually do not work in concert with browsers and search engines, so the home user rather than an outside company sets the defaults. (However, it should be noted that this "standalone" feature could theoretically work against free speech principles, since here, too, it would be relatively easy to draft a law mandating the use of the products, under threat of criminal penalties.)

61   While the use of these products avoids some of the larger control issues with ratings systems, the blocking programs are far from problem-free. A number of products have been shown to block access to a wide variety of information that many would consider appropriate for minors. For example, some block access to safer sex information, although the Supreme Court has held that teenagers have the right to obtain access to such information even without their parent's consent. Other products block access to information of interest to the gay and lesbian community. Some products even block speech simply because it criticizes their product.

62   Some products allow home users to add or subtract particular sites from a list of blocked sites. For example, a parent can decide to allow access to "playboy.com" by removing it from the blocked sites list, and can deny access to "powerrangers.com" by adding it to the list. However most products consider their lists of blocked speech to be proprietary information which they will not disclose.

63   Despite these problems, the use of blocking programs has been enthusiastically and uncritically endorsed by government and industry leaders alike. At the recent White House summit, Vice President Gore, along with industry and non-profit groups, announced the

creation of www.netparents.org, a site that provides direct links to a variety of blocking programs.

The ACLU urges the producers of all of these products to put real power in users' hands   64
and provide full disclosure of their list of blocked speech and the criteria for blocking.

In addition, the ACLU urges the industry to develop products that provide maximum   65
user control. For example, all users should be able to adjust the products to account for the varying maturity level of minors, and to adjust the list of blocked sites to reflect their own values.

It should go without saying that under no set of circumstances can governments con-   66
stitutionally require anyone—whether individual users or Internet Service Providers—to run user-based blocking programs when accessing or providing access to the Internet.

WHY BLOCKING SOFTWARE SHOULD NOT
BE USED BY PUBLIC LIBRARIES

The "never-ending, worldwide conversation" of the Internet, as one lower court judge   67
called it, is a conversation in which all citizens should be entitled to participate—whether they access the Internet from the library or from the home. Just as government cannot require home users or Internet Service Providers (ISPs) to use blocking programs or self-rating programs, libraries should not require patrons to use blocking software when accessing the Internet at the library. The ACLU, like the American Library Association (ALA), opposes use of blocking software in public libraries.

Libraries have traditionally promoted free speech values by providing free books and   68
information resources to people regardless of their age or income. Today, more than 20 percent of libraries in the United States are offering free access to the Internet, and that number is growing daily. Libraries are critical to realizing the dream of universal access to the Internet, a dream that would be drastically altered if they were forced to become Internet censors.

In a recent announcement stating its policy, the ALA said: 69

> Libraries are places of inclusion rather than exclusion. Current blocking/filtering software prevents not only access to what some may consider "objectionable" material, but also blocks information protected by the First Amendment. The result is that legal and useful material will inevitably be blocked.

Librarians have never been in the business of determining what their patrons should   70
read or see, and the fact that the material is now found on Internet is no different. By installing inaccurate and unreliable blocking programs on library Internet terminals, public libraries—which are almost always governmental entities—would inevitably censor speech that patrons are constitutionally entitled to access.

It has been suggested that a library's decision to install blocking software is like other   71
legitimate selection decisions that libraries routinely make when they add particular books to their collections. But in fact, blocking programs take selection decisions totally out of the hands of the librarian and place them in the hands of a company with no experience in

library science. As the ALA noted, "(F)ilters can impose the producer's viewpoint on the community."

72   Because, as noted above, most filtering programs don't provide a list of the sites they block, libraries won't even know what resources are blocked. In addition, Internet speakers won't know which libraries have blocked access to their speech and won't be able to protest.

73   Installing blocking software in libraries to prevent adults as well as minors from accessing legally protected material raises severe First Amendment questions. Indeed, that principle—that governments can't block adult access to speech in the name of protecting children—was one of the key reasons for the Supreme Court's decision in *Reno v. ACLU.*

74   If adults are allowed full access, but minors are forced to use blocking programs, constitutional problems remain. Minors, especially older minors, have a constitutional right to access many of the resources that have been shown to be blocked by user-based blocking programs.

75   One of the virtues of the Internet is that it allows an isolated gay teenager in Des Moines, Iowa, to talk to other teenagers around the globe who are also struggling with issues relating to their sexuality. It allows teens to find out how to avoid AIDS and other sexually transmitted diseases even if they are too embarrassed to ask an adult in person or even too embarrassed to check out a book.

76   When the ACLU made this argument in *Reno v. ACLU,* it was considered controversial, even among our allies. But the Supreme Court agreed that minors have rights too. Library blocking proposals that allow minors full access to the Internet only with parental permission are unacceptable.

77   Libraries can and should take other actions that are more protective of online free speech principles. First, libraries can publicize and provide links to particular sites that have been recommended for children. Second, to avoid unwanted viewing by passersby (and to protect the confidentiality of users), libraries can install Internet access terminals in ways that minimize public view. Third, libraries can impose "content-neutral" time limits on Internet use.

CONCLUSION

78   The ACLU has always favored providing Internet users, especially parents, with more information. We welcomed, for example, the American Library Association's announcement at the White House summit of *The Librarian's Guide to Cyberspace for Parents and Kids*, a "comprehensive brochure and Web site combining Internet terminology, safety tips, site selection advice and more than 50 of the most educational and entertaining sites available for children on the Internet."

79   In *Reno v. ACLU,* we noted that Federal and state governments are already vigorously enforcing existing obscenity, child pornography, and child solicitation laws on the Internet. In addition, Internet users must affirmatively seek out speech on the Internet; no one is caught by surprise.

80   In fact, many speakers on the Net provide preliminary information about the nature of their speech. The ACLU's site on America Online, for example, has a message on its home

page announcing that the site is a "free speech zone." Many sites offering commercial transactions on the Net contain warnings concerning the security of Net information. Sites containing sexually explicit material often begin with a statement describing the adult nature of the material. Chat rooms and news groups have names that describe the subject being discussed. Even individual e-mail messages contain a subject line.

The preliminary information available on the Internet has several important components that distinguish it from all the ratings systems discussed above: (1) it is created and provided by the speaker; (2) it helps the user decide whether to read any further; (3) speakers who choose not to provide such information are not penalized; (4) it does not result in the automatic blocking of speech by an entity other than the speaker or reader before the speech has ever been viewed. Thus, the very nature of the Internet reveals why more speech is always a better solution than censorship for dealing with speech that someone may find objectionable.   81

It is not too late for the Internet community to slowly and carefully examine these proposals and to reject those that will transform the Internet from a true marketplace of ideas into just another mainstream, lifeless medium with content no more exciting or diverse than that of television.   82

Civil libertarians, human rights organizations, librarians and Internet users, speakers and providers all joined together to defeat the CDA. We achieved a stunning victory, establishing a legal framework that affords the Internet the highest constitutional protection. We put a quick end to a fire that was all but visible and threatening. The fire next time may be more difficult to detect—and extinguish.   83

APPENDIX: INTERNET RATINGS SYSTEMS—HOW DO THEY WORK?

The Technology: PICS, Browsers, Search Engines, and Ratings

The rating and blocking proposals discussed below all rely on a few key components of current Internet technology. While none of this technology will by itself censor speech, some of it may well enable censorship to occur.   84

PICS.   The Platform for Internet Content Selection (PICS) is a rating standard that establishes a consistent way to rate and block online content. PICS was created by a large consortium of Internet industry leaders, and became operational last year. In theory, PICS does not incorporate or endorse any particular rating system—the technology is an empty vessel into which different rating systems can be poured. In reality, only three third-party rating systems have been developed for PICS: Safe Surf, Net Shepherd, and the de facto industry standard RSACi.[1]   85

Browsers.   Browsers are the software tool that Internet users need in order to access information on the World Wide Web. Two products, Microsoft's Internet Explorer and Netscape, currently control 90% of the browser market. Microsoft's Internet Explorer is now compatible with PICS. That is, the Internet Explorer can now be configured to block speech that has been rated with PICS-compatible ratings. Netscape has announced that it   86 will soon offer the same capability. When the blocking feature on the browser is activated, speech with negative ratings is blocked. In addition, because a vast majority of Internet sites remain unrated, the blocking feature can be configured to block all unrated sites.

87   **Search Engines.**   Search engines are software programs that allow Internet users to conduct searches for content on a particular subject, using a string of words or phrases. The search result typically provides a list of links to sites on the relevant topic. Four of the major search engines have announced a plan to cooperate in the move toward Internet ratings. For example, they may decide not to list sites that have negative ratings or that are unrated.

88   **Ratings Systems.**   There are a few PICS-compatible ratings systems already in use. Two self-rating systems include RSACi and Safe Surf. RSACi, developed by the same group that rates video games, attempts to rate certain kinds of speech, like sex and violence, according to objective criteria describing the content. For example, it rates levels of violence from "harmless conflict; some damage to objects" to "creatures injured or killed." Levels of sexual content are rated from "passionate kissing" to "clothed sexual touching" to "explicit sexual activity; sex crimes." The context in which the material is presented is not considered under the RSACi system; for example, it doesn't distinguish educational materials from other materials.

89   Safe Surf applies a complicated ratings system on a variety of types of speech, from profanity to gambling. The ratings are more contextual, but they are also more subjective and value-laden. For example, Safe Surf rates sexual content from "artistic" to "erotic" to "explicit and crude pornographic."

90   Net Shepherd, a third-party rating system that has rated 300,000 sites, rates only for "maturity" and "quality."

NOTES

1. While PICS could be put to legitimate use with adequate free speech safeguards, there is a very real fear that governments, especially authoritarian governments, will use the technology to impose severe content controls.

<hr>

It's Time to Tackle Cyberporn

John Carr

John Carr, Internet consultant to NCH Action for Children, challenges the anti-censorship position in the debate between free speech and self-protection from undesirable Internet material. Specifically, Carr responds to the ACLU's protest against ratings systems for the Internet. This article originally appeared in the February 2, 1998, issue of New Statesman.

The Great Internet Freedom Debate is rolling forward. At issue is the balance to be   1
struck between "free speech" and the ability of families, employers, schools or other or-
ganisations to protect themselves against the receipt of material that is unwanted, illegal or
both. The responsibility for striking the balance and providing mechanisms to enforce it—
is, however, increasingly seen not as a job for governments, legislatures or police forces,
but for private citizens and the private companies that own and run the Internet industry.

There is a tenacious cyber-myth that the Internet is a vast, anarchic forum, beyond the   2
reach of any government or authority, uncontrolled and uncontrollable. The reality is that
for all parts of the Internet there are several potential points of control, and for the typical
UK cybernaut one of them has been in operation for a while. So this debate is not about
whether some sacred principle of non-regulation or freedom from censorship should be
breached: that point was passed some time ago. Now we are discussing practical questions
of degree: the ways in which intervention or regulation might occur; the level at which a
censorship option might be feasible or appropriate.

If you link up to the Internet with any of the big UK-based Internet service providers   3
(ISPs), such as AOL, MSN, Compuserve, Poptel or LineOne, you already do not enjoy full
and unrestricted access to the superhighway. Even Demon, the ISP that represents the liberal wing in this debate, does not allow its subscribers to access everything that is "out
there." Most of what is kept from you is illegal material, principally child pornography.
There are ways of circumventing the barriers, but you have to know first that you are being
"deprived"; second, how to get around the obstacles; and third, you have to find an unrestricted source that will let you in. The last bit in particular is not easy.

It is only in the past two years that the ISPs operating in Britain have chosen to restrict   4
what they provide as part of their standard service. They have done so as a result of a combination of threats from police and the last government, administrative convenience and
their own sense of civic responsibility (all foreign-owned ISPs come within the jurisdiction
of UK courts for their operation in this country).

The UK Internet industry also established the Internet Watch Foundation (IWF), on   5
whose policy board I sit as an unpaid member. The IWF runs a hotline facility, which allows people who find potentially illegal material on the Internet to report it. Once a report
is verified two things will happen: if the material is housed on a server owned by a British-
based ISP it will be removed forthwith and the police will be notified. The deal between
the industry, the IWF and police, however, is that, whereas possession of certain types of
illegal material is normally a crime, if the material is removed promptly the police will not
prosecute the service provider.

The IWF's remit covers all illegal material on all parts of the Net, but it has prioritised   6
child pornography, which is principally exchanged through newsgroups, occasionally is
found on Web sites, and increasingly is being spread and procured through chat rooms.

Similar hotlines are springing up all over the world and the EU recently announced its   7
intention to support their development as part of an ambitious package of measures aimed
at making the Internet a safer, more congenial place.

However, the IWF and the police are powerless to do anything about a huge body of   8
material which, though not illegal, is highly offensive to some (hardcore pornography, for

instance) or else dangerous or undesirable (say, information about bomb-making). It is not simply a matter of overprotecting the frail or faint-hearted: anyone may by accident or through curiosity stumble on unwanted matter. Debate is now focused on what might be done about this type of material: in the US it is a topic of urgent public concern.

9   There is no legal basis for banning these categories; neither will the newsagents' answer to printed pornography work: the physical barrier a "top shelf" policy offers to children and customers who don't want to stand and stare at porn mags simply cannot be replicated on the Net.

10   Instead the buzz phrase is "ratings systems," a concept akin to film or video classification, although necessarily rather more complex. A ratings system is an agreed set of criteria for describing material to be published on the Internet. The originator or publisher of the material provides the rating, which appears as a label attached to the article or site, giving a brief standardised description of its content. As the system is based on self-assessment, there may eventually need to be a set of sanctions for migrating and methods for policing, but these are not yet in place. The idea is that the ratings labels are picked up and read by filtering programmes that work with your browser. The user will have told the filtering programme what to allow through and what to block. Those who do not want any material filtered will still be able to set that option on their computer.

11   There is no jurisprudentially savvy software available on the market that would filter out only illegal material. You have to describe categories or types of material you do not want to see. Thus if you do not want to access anything with violent images or bad language, you could programme accordingly; alternatively you might find "PG"-type levels acceptable.

12   It is easy to foresee the emergence of third-party ratings systems; so for instance if you are a devout Catholic, you might put your trust in "Vatican Net," a subscription service which, if it is ever formed, will only allow material through that would not trouble the Pontiff. Different ratings levels can also be set for different users of the same computer or network, allowing parents to set different access levels for their children than for themselves.

13   There is already one type of ratings system in widespread use, built into Internet Explorer. That system was established and is managed by RSACi (Recreational Software Advisory Council on the Internet), a not-for-profit body linked to the Massachusetts Institute of Technology. However, the current RSACi criteria are too narrowly American and their system is too crude. The UK's IWF has been trying to work out a better alternative and will shortly be consulting on its proposals, with a view to co-operating eventually with RSACi and other interests in the formulation of a global system. Some day a Baptist minister in the US Bible Belt, a liberal atheist in Amsterdam and a party official in Peking should all be able to use the same means to decide whether or not their nine year olds can visit this or that Web site or newsgroup.

14   Not everyone welcomes the prospect, however. There is vocal opposition to the development of ratings systems, most forcibly expressed by the American Civil Liberties Union (ACLU) in its paper "Fahrenheit 451.2:—Is Cyberspace Burning?" In ratings systems the cyber-libertarians see not enhanced consumer choice but new tools being fashioned to allow authoritarian interests to "lock out" unpopular views, or otherwise to control the content of the Internet by requiring all ISPs, for example, to run it on their servers. They fear that minority opinions or tastes will be excluded.

These anxieties about illiberal abuse of the Internet through ratings and similar tech-   15
nologies are, I believe, at best misplaced and at worst paranoid, reckless or self-serving. The
days are over when the Internet was the private preserve of academics and computer geeks.
Now that its trajectory is to become an integral part of our living-room mass media (with a
projected 200 million users worldwide by 2001), the rules simply have to change.

If we do nothing to curb some of the more rampant excesses, the Internet as we know   16
it will cease to exist in the not-too-distant future. It will be replaced by (at least) two In-
ternets: one which is safe, homogenised, dull, highly commercialised and accessible by subscription only, and another which will be for the poor: free and wild, but most definitely a
place to go only at your own risk.

The anti-censorship lobby has had an early but significant victory in this battle. In 1996   17
the US government tried to legislate against offensive Internet material. The Communications Decency Act (CDA) was fatally undermined during its passage through Congress when
the religious right sought to widen its ambit. The ACLU sued and in June last year the
Supreme Court struck down the relevant provisions as being contrary to the first amendment protection of free speech.

Its strategy in tatters, in July the White House reiterated its intention to make the Inter-   18
net "family-friendly," but stressed that it would look to the industry to take the initiative.
Self-regulation was the new approach, but with the clear warning that inaction would
lead to renewed legislative efforts. As Al Gore said at the time, "Hands off does not mean
indifference."

In December the US Internet industry gathered in Washington, DC, to deliver its   19
response. Many in the industry fully share their government's aims. Steve Case, president
of AOL, declared: "Let's face it, many of us are parents and we want to work in an industry we can feel proud of."

All the major ISPs announced they were supporting ratings systems. The owners of   20
some of the bigger Internet search services—Yahoo, Lycos and Excite—said they were considering in future allowing into their directories only material that had been rated. The ISPs
also announced that they are going to amend their standard terms of contract to allow them
to withdraw service from anyone found misusing their Internet connection by, for instance,
soliciting or offering child pornography.

The conference also announced other initiatives being researched, notably to place   21
greater requirements on distributors of hardcore porn not to sell to underage viewers; to
make it easier to identify visitors to chat rooms; and to try to end the practice of anonymous e-mailing.

Disney and Time Warner announced they are establishing "whitelisting services": In-   22
ternet subscription services that give you access not to the whole of the Net but only to the
parts they have vetted. For "Vatican Net" read "Donald Duck Net." We are soon likely to
see an explosion of similar whitelists here, especially aimed at the schools audience. BT's
"Campus World" already exists and is being marketed as a safe haven.

Janet Reno, the US Attorney General, told the Washington conference that last year   23
alone there were roughly 200 convictions for child pornography and other forms of paedo-
phile activity where the Internet played a major part. She did not tell us how many arrests
there had been, how many cases were awaiting trial or how many perpetrators escaped

prosecution on technical grounds. The UK's IWF, in its first, underpublicised year of operation, received more than a thousand complaints, of which 300-plus were adjudged to contain illegal material, the great bulk of them relating to child pornography.

24   The Internet is far from a stable or mature technology. Advances are made almost daily, some of which can have profound and immediate consequences for the medium. It serves no one's interests to pretend we are on the brink of some last-ditch defence of democracy and free speech when we engage in this debate. Instead we should all recognise that almost all of us are looking, in good faith, for new answers to the new problems thrown up by the new technology.

25   In doing so I trust we will all give at least equal weight to the right of a child to grow up unmolested by paedophiles as we do to the rights of the rugged cyberfrontiersmen who pose as defenders of liberty in a medium that almost no one had even heard of six years ago.

FOR CLASS DISCUSSION

1. Much of the disagreement over censoring the Internet concerns who should be responsible for filtering out unwanted or dangerous material. According to these different writers, where does the responsibility lie for preventing unwanted material from reaching children or others? With the government? With regulatory agencies? With private organizations? With companies producing filtering software? With schools and librarians? With parents? With individual users? Analyze and evaluate the differing positions of these writers by applying the first set of guide questions from page 465.

2. How does the job or organizational affiliation of each of the writers of these articles influence the stand that each takes on Internet censorship?

3. Articles on Internet censorship usually include proposals. Several of the writers claim that increased access to the Internet rather than filtering devices to limit access to material is the answer to problems like cyberhate. Which proposal argument do you think is the strongest and why?

4. Choose one of the arguments for closer analysis, applying the second set of guide questions on pages 465–66.

OPTIONAL WRITING ASSIGNMENT   A bombing incident in your city has leveled a local church, injuring several people. Two suspects are subsequently captured, tried, and convicted of the bombing. During the course of that trial, it is learned that the two young men who planted the bomb got the "recipe" for their device off the Internet. They are, it turns out, subscribers to a list called "alt.Nazi.pranks" that calls for a return to "the mastery of the white race" through such strategies as hate speech against minorities, sharing intelligence about those federal office buildings with lax security, and explaining how to make explosive devices out of ordinary household items like lawn fertilizer.

The members of your quiet little community are outraged to learn about the ready availability of such dangerous information, not to mention the vile and offensive language used by subscribers to support their widely discredited theories of racial superiority. Many of these people are equally outraged by the easy availability of pornography on the Net. Letters begin flooding in to the paper calling for censorship of the Internet, including removal of the Nazi list. Some go so far as to demand the criminal prosecution of the list's subscribers.

Having just read all about this issue in your college writing course, you feel that you have something to add to the debate. So you repair to your word processor and begin writing two responses. The first is a letter to the editor, aimed at the outraged citizenry of your town; the second is directed to Congressman Ralph Pangloss, your district's congressional representative and long-time foe of censorship of any sort. Whichever side in the debate you support, your letters should be responsive to your two different audiences.

SEXUAL HARASSMENT: WHEN IS OFFENSIVENESS A CIVIL OFFENSE?

Gender Dilemmas in Sexual Harassment Policies and Procedures

Stephanie Riger

Stephanie Riger is a psychology professor. This article originally appeared in American Psychologist *in 1991.*

Sexual harassment—unwanted sexually oriented behavior in a work context—is the   1
most recent form of victimization of women to be redefined as a social rather than a personal problem, following rape and wife abuse. A sizeable proportion of women surveyed in a wide variety of work settings reported being subject to unwanted sexual attention, sexual comments or jokes, offensive touching, or attempts to coerce compliance with or punish rejection of sexual advances. In 1980 the U.S. Merit Systems Protection Board (1981) conducted the first comprehensive national survey of sexual harassment among federal employees: About 4 out of 10 of the 10,648 women surveyed reported having been the target of sexual harassment during the previous 24 months. A recent update of this survey found that the frequency of harassment in 1988 was identical to that reported earlier: 42%

of all women surveyed in 1988 reported that they had experienced some form of unwanted and uninvited sexual attention compared to exactly the same percentage of women in 1980 (U.S. Merit Systems Protection Board, 1988).

2   Women ranging from blue-collar workers (LaFontaine & Tredeau, 1986; Maypole & Skaine, 1982) to lawyers (Burleigh & Goldberg, 1989) to airline personnel (Littler-Bishop, Seidler-Feller, & Opaluch, 1982) have reported considerable amounts of sexual harassment in surveys. Among a random sample of private sector workers in the Los Angeles area, more than one half of the women surveyed by telephone reported experiencing at least one incident that they considered sexual harassment during their working lives (Gutek, 1985). Some estimate that up to about one third of women in educational institutions have experienced some form of harassment (Kenig & Ryan, 1986). Indeed, Garvey (1986) stated that "Unwanted sexual attention may be the single most widespread occupational hazard in the workplace today" (p. 75).

3   It is a hazard faced much more frequently by women than men. About 40% of the women in the original U.S. Merit Systems Protection Board survey reported having experienced sexual harassment, compared with only 15% of the men (U.S. Merit Systems Protection Board, 1981). Among working people surveyed in Los Angeles, women were nine times more likely than men to report having quit a job because of sexual harassment, five times more likely to have transferred, and three times more likely to have lost a job (Konrad & Gutek, 1986). Women with low power and status, whether due to lower age, being single or divorced, or being in a marginal position in the organization, are more likely to be harassed (Fain & Anderton, 1987; LaFontaine & Tredeau, 1986; Robinson & Reid, 1985).

4   Sex differences in the frequency of harassment also prevail in educational environments (Fitzgerald et al., 1988). A mailed survey of more than 900 women and men at the University of Rhode Island asked about a wide range of behavior, including the frequency of respondents' experience of sexual insult, defined as an "uninvited sexually suggestive, obscene or offensive remark, stare, or gesture" (Lott, Reilly, & Howard, 1982, p. 309). Of the female respondents, 40% reported being sexually insulted occasionally or often while on campus, compared with 17% of the men. Both men and women reported that women are rarely the source of such insults. Similar differences were found in a survey of social workers, with 2½ times as many women as men reporting harassment (Maypole, 1986).

5   Despite the high rates found in surveys of sexual harassment of women, few complaints are pursued through official grievance procedures. Dzeich and Weiner (1984) concluded, after reviewing survey findings, that 20% to 30% of female college students experience sexual harassment. Yet academic institutions averaged only 4.3 complaints each during the 1982–1983 academic year (Robertson, Dyer, & Campbell, 1988), a period roughly consecutive with the surveys cited by Dzeich and Weiner. In another study conducted at a university in 1984, of 38 women who reported harassment, only 1 reported the behavior to the offender's supervisor and 2 reported the behavior to an adviser, another professor, or employer (Reilly, Lott, & Gallogly, 1986). Similar findings have been reported on other college campuses (Adams, Kottke, & Padgitt, 1983; Benson & Thomson, 1982; Brandenburg, 1982; Cammaert, 1985; Meek & Lynch, 1983; Schneider, 1987).

6   Low numbers of complaints appear in other work settings as well. In a survey of federal workers, only about 11% of victims reported the harassment to a higher authority, and

only 2.5% used formal complaint channels (Livingston, 1982). Similarly, female social workers reacted to harassment by avoiding or delaying the conflict or attempting to defuse the situation rather than by adopting any form of recourse such as filing a grievance (Maypole, 1986). The number of complaints alleging sexual harassment filed with the Equal Employment Opportunity Commission in Washington, DC, has declined since 1984, despite an increase in the number of women in the workforce during that time (Morgenson, 1989), and surveys suggest that the rate of sexual harassment has remained relatively stable (U.S. Merit Systems Protection Board, 1981, 1988).

It is the contention of this article that the low rate of utilization of grievance procedures   7
is due to gender bias in sexual harassment policies that discourages their use by women. Policies are written in gender-neutral language and are intended to apply equally to men and women. However, these policies are experienced differently by women than men because of gender differences in perceptions of harassment and orientation toward conflict. Although victims of all forms of discrimination are reluctant to pursue grievances (Bumiller, 1987), women, who are most likely to be the victims of sexual harassment, are especially disinclined to pursue sexual harassment grievances for at least two reasons. First, the interpretation in policies of what constitutes harassment may not reflect women's viewpoints, and their complaints may not be seen as valid. Second, the procedures in some policies that are designed to resolve disputes may be inimical to women because they are not compatible with the way that many women view conflict resolution. Gender bias in policies, rather than an absence of harassment or lack of assertiveness on the part of victims, produces low numbers of complaints.

GENDER BIAS IN THE DEFINITION OF SEXUAL HARASSMENT

The first way that gender bias affects sexual harassment policies stems from differences   8
between men and women in the interpretation of the definition of harassment. Those writing sexual harassment policies for organizations typically look to the courts for the distinction between illegal sexual harassment and permissible (although perhaps unwanted) social interaction (see Cohen, 1987, for a discussion of this distinction in legal cases). The definition of harassment in policies typically is that provided by the U.S. Equal Employment Opportunity Commission (1980) guidelines:

> Unwelcome sexual advances, requests for sexual favors, and other verbal or physical conduct of a sexual nature constitute sexual harassment when (1) submission to such conduct is made either explicitly or implicitly a term or condition of an individual's employment, (2) submission to or rejection of such conduct by an individual is used as the basis for employment decisions affecting such individual, or (3) such conduct has the purpose or effect of unreasonably interfering with an individual's work performance or creating an intimidating, hostile, or offensive working environment. (p. 74677)

The first two parts of the definition refer to a quid pro quo relationship involving people in positions of unequal status, as superior status is usually necessary to have control over another's employment. In such cases bribes, threats, or punishments are used. Incidents of this type need happen only once to fall under the definition of sexual harassment. However, courts have required that incidents falling into the third category, "an intimidating, hostile, or offensive working environment," must be repeated in order to establish that such an environment exists (Terpstra & Baker, 1988); these incidents must be both pervasive and so severe that they affect the victim's psychological well-being (Trager, 1988). Harassment of this type can come from peers or even subordinates as well as superiors.

9   In all three of these categories, harassment is judged on the basis of conduct and its effects on the recipient, not the intentions of the harasser. Thus, two typical defenses given by accused harassers—"I was just being friendly," or "I touch everyone, I'm that kind of person"—do not hold up in court. Yet behavior may have an intimidating or offensive effect on some people but be inoffensive or even welcome to others. In deciding whose standards should be used, the courts employ what is called the *reasonable person rule,* asking whether a reasonable person would be offended by the conduct in question. The dilemma in applying this to sexual harassment is that a reasonable woman and a reasonable man are likely to differ in their judgments of what is offensive.

10   Definitions of sexual harassment are socially constructed, varying not only with characteristics of perceiver but also those of the situational context and actors involved. Behavior is more likely to be labelled harassment when it is done by someone with greater power than the victim (Gutek, Morasch, & Cohen, 1983; Kenig & Ryan, 1986; Lester et al., 1986; Popovich, Licata, Nokovich, Martelli, & Zoloty, 1987); when it involves physical advances accompanied by threats of punishment for noncompliance (Rossi & Weber-Burdin, 1983); when the response to it is negative (T. S. Jones, Remland, & Brunner, 1987); when the behavior reflects persistent negative intentions toward a woman (Pryor & Day, 1988); the more inappropriate it is for the actor's social role (Pryor, 1985); and the more flagrant and frequent the harasser's actions (Thomann & Wiener, 1987). Among women, professionals are more likely than those in secretarial-clerical positions to report the more subtle behaviors as harassment (McIntyre & Renick, 1982).

11   The variable that most consistently predicts variation in people's definition of sexual harassment is the sex of the rater. Men label fewer behaviors at work as sexual harassment (Kenig & Ryan, 1986; Konrad & Gutek, 1986; Lester et al., 1986; Powell, 1986; Rossi & Weber-Burdin, 1983). Men tend to find sexual overtures from women at work to be flattering, whereas women find similar approaches from men to be insulting (Gutek, 1985). Both men and women agree that certain blatant behaviors, such as sexual assault or sexual bribery, constitute harassment, but women are more likely to see as harassment more subtle behavior such as sexual teasing or looks or gestures (Adams et al., 1983; Collins & Blodgett, 1981; Kenig & Ryan, 1986; U.S. Merit Systems Protection Board, 1981). Even when they do identify behavior as harassment, men are more likely to think that women will be flattered by it (Kirk, 1988). Men are also more likely than women to blame women for being sexually harassed (Kenig & Ryan, 1986; Jensen & Gutek, 1982).

12   These gender differences make it difficult to apply the reasonable person rule. Linenberger (1983) proposed 10 factors that permit an "objective" assessment of whether behavior constitutes sexual harassment, regardless of the perception of the victim and the intent of the perpetrator. These factors range from the severity of the conduct to the number and frequency of encounters, and the relationship of the parties involved. For example, behavior is less likely to be categorized as harassment if it is seen as a response to provocation from the victim. But is an objective rating of provocation possible? When gender dif-

ferences are as clear-cut and persistent as they are in the perception of what behavior constitutes sexual harassment, the question is not one of objectivity, but rather of which sex's definition of the situation will prevail. Becker (1967) asserted that there is a "hierarchy of credibility" in organizations, and that credibility and the right to be heard are differentially distributed: "In any system of ranked groups, participants take it as given that members of the highest group have the right to define the way things really are" (p. 241). Because men typically have more power in organizations (Kanter, 1977), Becker's analysis suggests that in most situations the male definition of harassment is likely to predominate. As MacKinnon (1987) put it, "objectivity—the nonsituated, universal standpoint, whether claimed or aspired to—is a denial of the existence or potency of sex inequality that tacitly participates in constructing reality from the dominant point of view" (p. 136). "The law sees and treats women the way men see and treat women" (p. 140). This means that men's judgments about what behavior constitutes harassment, and who is to blame, are likely to prevail. Linenberger's 10 factors thus may not be an objective measure, but rather a codification of the male perspective on harassment. This is likely to discourage women who want to bring complaints about more subtle forms of harassment.

SEX DIFFERENCES IN THE ATTRIBUTION OF HARASSMENT

Attribution theory provides an explanation for the wider range of behaviors that women define as harassment and for men's tendency to find women at fault (Kenig & Ryan, 1986; Pryor, 1985; Pryor & Day, 1988). Attribution theory suggests that people tend to see their own behaviors as situationally determined, whereas they attribute the behaviors of others to personality characteristics or other internal causes (E. E. Jones & Nisbett, 1971). Those who see sexual harassment through the eyes of the actor are likely to be male. As actors are wont to do, they will attribute their behaviors to situational causes, including the "provocations" of the women involved. They will then not perceive their own behaviors as harassment. In fact, those who take the perspective of the victim do see specific behaviors as more harassing than those who take the perspective of the actor (Pryor & Day, 1988). Women are more likely to view harassment through the eyes of the victim; therefore they will label more behaviors as harassment because they attribute them to men's disposition or personality traits. Another possibility is that men, as potential harassers, want to avoid blame in the future, and so shift the blame to women (Jensen & Gutek, 1982) and restrict the range of behaviors that they define as harassment (Kenig & Ryan, 1986). Whatever the cause, a reasonable man and a reasonable woman are likely to differ in their judgments of whether a particular behavior constitutes sexual harassment. 13

Men tend to misinterpret women's friendliness as an indication of sexual interest (Abbey, 1982; Abbey & Melby, 1986; Saal, Johnson, & Weber, 1989; Shotland & Craig, 1988). Acting on this misperception may result in behavior that is harassing to women. Tangri, Burt, and Johnson (1982) stated that "Some sexual harassment may indeed be clumsy or insensitive expressions of attraction, while some is the classic abuse of organizational power" (p. 52). Gender differences in attributional processes help explain the first type of harassment, partially accounting for the overwhelming preponderance of sexual harassment incidents that involve a male offender and a female victim. 14

GENDER BIAS IN GRIEVANCE PROCEDURES

15   Typically, procedures for resolving disputes about sexual harassment are written in gender-neutral terms so that they may apply to both women and men. However, men and women may react quite differently to the same procedures.

16   Analyzing this problem requires looking at specific policies and procedures. Educational institutions will serve as the context for this discussion for three reasons. First, they are the most frequent site of surveys about the problem, and the pervasive nature of harassment on campuses has been well documented (Dzeich & Weiner, 1984). Second, although sexual harassment is harmful to women in all occupations, it can be particularly devastating to those in educational institutions, in which the goal of the organization is to nurture and promote development. The violation of relationships based on trust, such as those between faculty and students, can leave long-lasting and deep wounds, yet many surveys find that those in positions of authority in educational settings are often the sources of the problem (Benson & Thomson, 1982; Fitzgerald et al., 1988; Glaser & Thorpe, 1986; Kenig & Ryan, 1986; Maihoff & Forrest, 1983; Metha & Nigg, 1983; Robinson & Reid, 1985; K. R. Wilson & Kraus, 1983). Third, educational institutions have been leaders in the development of sexual harassment policies, in part because of concern about litigation. In *Alexander v. Yale University* (1977) the court decided that sexual harassment constitutes a form of sex discrimination that denies equal access to educational opportunities, and falls under Title IX of the Educational Amendments of 1972. The Office of Civil Rights in the U.S. Department of Education now requires institutions that receive Title IX funds to maintain grievance procedures to resolve complaints involving sexual discrimination or harassment (M. Wilson, 1988). Consequently, academic institutions may have had more experience than other work settings in developing procedures to combat this problem. A survey of U.S. institutions of higher learning conducted in 1984 (Robertson et al., 1988) found that 66% of all responding institutions had sexual harassment policies, and 46% had grievance procedures specifically designed to deal with sexual harassment complaints, with large public schools more likely to have them than small private ones. These percentages have unquestionably increased in recent years, given the government funding regulations. Although the discussion here is focused on educational contexts, the problems identified in sexual harassment policies exist in other work settings as well.

17   Many educational institutions, following guidelines put forward by the American Council on Education (1986) and the American Association of University Professors (1983), have established policies that prohibit sexual harassment and create grievance procedures. Some use a formal board or hearing, and others use informal mechanisms that protect confidentiality and seek to resolve the complaint rather than punish the offender (see, e.g., Brandenburg, 1982; Meek & Lynch, 1983). Still others use both types of procedures. The type of procedure specified by the policy may have a great impact on victims' willingness to report complaints.

Comparison of Informal and Formal Grievance Procedures

18   Informal attempts to resolve disputes differ from formal procedures in important ways (for a general discussion of dispute resolution systems, see Brett, Goldberg, & Ury, 1990).

First, their goal is to solve a problem, rather than to judge the harasser's guilt or innocence. The assumptions underlying these processes are that both parties in a dispute perceive a problem (although they may define that problem differently); that both share a common interest in solving that problem; and that together they can negotiate an agreement that will be satisfactory to everyone involved. Typically, the goal of informal processes is to end the harassment of the complainant rather than judge (and punish, if appropriate) the offender. The focus is on what will happen in the future between the disputing parties, rather than on what has happened in the past. Often policies do not specify the format of informal problem solving, but accept a wide variety of strategies of reconciliation. For example, a complainant might write a letter to the offender (Rowe, 1981), or someone might talk to the offender on the complainant's behalf. The offender and victim might participate in mediation, in which a third party helps them negotiate an agreement. Many policies accept a wide array of strategies as good-faith attempts to solve the problem informally.

In contrast, formal procedures generally require a written complaint and have a specified procedure for handling cases, usually by bringing the complaint to a group officially designated to hear the case, such as a hearing board. The informal process typically ends when the complainant is satisfied (or decides to drop the complaint); the formal procedure ends when the hearing board decides on the guilt or innocence of the alleged harasser. Thus, control over the outcome usually rests with the complainant in the case of informal mechanisms, and with the official governance body in the case of a hearing. Compliance with a decision is usually voluntary in informal procedures, whereas the decision in a formal procedure is binding unless appealed to a higher authority. Formal procedures are adversarial in nature, with the complainant and defendant competing to see whose position will prevail.   19

A typical case might proceed as follows: A student with a complaint writes a letter to the harasser (an informal procedure). If not satisfied with the response, she submits a written complaint to the sexual harassment hearing board, which then hears both sides of the case, reviews available evidence, and decides on the guilt or innocence of the accused (a formal procedure). If the accused is found guilty, the appropriate officer of the institution decides on punishment.   20

Gender Differences in Orientation to Conflict

Women and men may differ in their reactions to dispute resolution procedures for at least two reasons. First, women typically have less power than men in organizations (Kanter, 1977). Using a grievance procedure, such as appearing before a hearing board, may be inimical because of the possibility of retaliation for a complaint. Miller (1976) suggested that differences in status and power affect the way that people handle conflict: 21

> As soon as a group attains dominance it tends inevitably to produce a situation of conflict and . . . it also, simultaneously, seeks to suppress conflict. Moreover, subordinates who accept the dominant's conception of them as passive and malleable do not openly engage in conflict. Conflict . . . is forced underground (p. 127).

This may explain why some women do not report complaints at all. When they do complain, however, their relative lack of power or their values may predispose women to   22 prefer informal rather than formal procedures. Beliefs about the appropriate way to handle disputes vary among social groups (Merry & Silbey, 1984). Gilligan's (1982) distinction between an orientation toward rights and justice compared with an emphasis on responsibilities to others and caring is likely to be reflected in people's preferences for ways of handling disputes (Kolb & Coolidge, 1988). Neither of these orientations is exclusive to one sex, but according to Gilligan, women are more likely to emphasize caring. Women's orientation to caring may be due to their subordinate status (Miller, 1976). Empirical support for Gilligan's theories is inconclusive (see, e.g., Mednick, 1989, for a summary of criticisms). Yet the fact that most victims of sexual harassment state that they simply want an end to the offending behavior rather than punishment of the offender (Robertson et al., 1988) suggests a "caring" rather than "justice" perspective (or possibly, a fear of reprisals).

23   In the context of dispute resolution, an emphasis on responsibilities and caring is compatible with the goals of informal procedures to restore harmony or at least peaceful coexistence among the parties involved, whereas that of justice is compatible with formal procedures that attempt to judge guilt or innocence of the offender. Thus women may prefer to use informal procedures to resolve conflicts, and indeed most cases in educational institutions are handled through informal mechanisms (Robertson et al., 1988). Policies that do not include an informal dispute resolution option are likely to discourage many women from bringing complaints.

Problems with Informal Dispute Resolution Procedures

24   Although women may prefer informal mechanisms, they are problematic for several reasons (Rifkin, 1984). Because they do not result in punishment, offenders suffer few negative consequences of their actions and may not be deterred from harassing again. In institutions of higher learning, the most common form of punishment reported is a verbal warning by a supervisor, which is given only "sometimes" (Robertson et al., 1988). Dismissal and litigation are almost never used. It seems likely, then, that sexual harassment may be viewed by potential harassers as low-risk behavior, and that victims see few incentives for bringing official complaints.

25   The confidentiality usually required by informal procedures prevents other victims from knowing that a complaint has been lodged against a multiple offender. If a woman knows that another woman is bringing a complaint against a particular man who has harassed both of them, then she might be more willing to complain also. The secrecy surrounding informal complaint processes precludes this information from becoming public and makes it more difficult to identify repeat offenders. Also, complaints settled informally may not be included in reports of the frequency of sexual harassment claims, making these statistics underestimate the scope of the problem. Yet confidentiality is needed to protect the rights of the accused and may be preferred by those bringing complaints.

26   These problems in informal procedures could discourage male as well as female victims from bringing complaints. Most problematic for women, however, is the assumption in informal procedures that the complainant and accused have equal power in the process of resolving the dispute. This assumption is likely to put women at a disadvantage. Parties involved in sexual harassment disputes may not be equal either in the sense of formal position within the organization (e.g., student versus faculty) or status (e.g., female versus

male students), and position and status characteristics that reflect levels of power do not disappear simply because they are irrelevant to the informal process. External status characteristics that indicate macrolevel social stratification (e.g., sex and age) help explain the patterns of distribution of sexual harassment in the workplace (Fain & Anderton, 1987). It seems likely that these external statuses will influence the interpersonal dynamics within a dispute-resolution procedure as well. Because women are typically lower than men in both formal and informal status and power in organizations, they will have less power in the dispute resolution process.

When the accused has more power than the complainant (e.g., a male faculty member accused by a female student), the complainant is more vulnerable to retaliation. Complainants may be reluctant to use grievance procedures because they fear retaliation should the charge be made public. For example, students may fear that a faculty member will punish them for bringing a complaint by lowering their grades or withholding recommendations. The person appointed to act as a guide to the informal resolution process is usually expected to act as a neutral third party rather than advocate for the complainant, and may hold little formal power over faculty: "Relatively few institutions have persons empowered to be (nonlegal) advocates for the complainants; a student bringing a complaint has little assurance of stopping the harassment and avoiding retaliation" (Robertson et al., 1988, p. 801). The victim then is left without an advocate to face an opponent whose formal position, age, and experience with verbal argument is often considerably beyond her own. The more vulnerable a woman's position is in her organization, the more likely it is that she will be harassed (Robinson & Reid, 1985); therefore sexual harassment, like rape, involves dynamics of power and domination as well as sexuality. The lack of an advocate for the complainant who might equalize power between the disputing parties is particularly troubling. However, if an advocate is provided for the complainant in an informal process, fairness and due process require that the defendant have an advocate as well. The dilemma is that this seems likely to transform an informal, problem-solving process into a formal, adversarial one.

OTHER OBSTACLES TO REPORTING COMPLAINTS

Belief That Sexual Harassment of Women Is Normative

Because of differences in perception of behavior, men and women involved in a sexual harassment case are likely to have sharply divergent interpretations of that case, particularly when a hostile environment claim is involved. To women, the behavior in question is offensive, and they are likely to see themselves as victims of male actions. The requirement that an attempt be made to mediate the dispute or solve it through informal processes may violate their perception of the situation and of themselves as victims of a crime. By comparison, a victim of a mugging is not required to solve the problem with the mugger through mediation (B. Sandler, personal communication, 1988). To many men, the behavior is not offensive, but normative. In their eyes, no crime has been committed, and there is no problem to be solved.

Some women may also consider sexual harassment to be normative. Women may believe that these sorts of behaviors are simply routine, a commonplace part of everyday life, and thus not something that can be challenged. Younger women—who are more likely to be victims (Fain & Anderton, 1987; LaFontaine & Tredeau, 1986; McIntyre & Renick, 1982)—are more tolerant of harassment than are older women (Lott et al., 1982; Reilly et al., 1986). Indeed, Lott et al. concluded that "younger women in particular have accepted the idea that prowling men are a 'fact of life'" (p. 318). This attitude might prevent women from labelling a negative experience as harassment. Surveys that ask women about sexual harassment and about the frequency of experiencing specific sexually harassing behaviors find discrepancies in responses to these questions (Fitzgerald et al., 1988). Women report higher rates when asked if they have been the target of specific harassing behaviors than when asked a general question about whether they have been harassed. Women are also more willing to report negative reactions to offensive behaviors than they are to label those behaviors as sexual harassment (Brewer, 1982).

30   Normative beliefs may deter some male victims of harassment from reporting complaints also, because men are expected to welcome sexual advances if those advances are from women.

Negative Outcome for Victims Who Bring Complaints

31   The outcome of grievance procedures does not appear to provide much satisfaction to victims who bring complaints. In academic settings, despite considerable publicity given to a few isolated cases in which tenured faculty have been fired, punishments are rarely inflicted on harassers, and the punishments that are given are mild, such as verbal warnings (Robertson et al., 1988). Among federal workers, 33% of those who used formal grievance procedures to protest sexual harassment found that it "made things worse" (Livingston, 1982). More than 65% of the cases of formal charges of sexual harassment filed with the Illinois Department of Human Rights involved job discharge of the complainant (Terpstra & Cook, 1985). Less than one third of those cases resulted in a favorable settlement for the complainant, and those who received financial compensation got an average settlement of $3,234 (Terpstra & Baker, 1988). Similar findings in California were reported by Coles (1986), with the average cash settlement there of $973, representing approximately one month's pay. Although a few legal cases have resulted in large settlements (Garvey, 1986), these studies suggest that typical settlements are low. Formal actions may take years to complete, and in legal suits the victim usually must hire legal counsel at considerable expense (Livingston, 1982). These small settlements seem unlikely to compensate victims for the emotional stress, notoriety, and financial costs involved in filing a public complaint. Given the consistency with which victimization falls more often to women than men, it is ironic that one of the largest settlements awarded to an individual in a sexual harassment case ($196,500 in damages) was made to a man who brought suit against his female supervisor (Brewer & Berk, 1982), perhaps because sexual aggression by a woman is seen as especially egregious.

Emotional Consequences of Harassment

32   In academic settings, harassment can adversely affect students' learning, and therefore their academic standing. It can deprive them of educational and career opportunities be-

cause they wish to avoid threatening situations. Students who have been harassed report that they consequently avoid taking a class from or working with a particular faculty member, change their major, or leave a threatening situation (Adams et al., 1983; Lott et al., 1982). Lowered self-esteem follows the conclusion that rewards, such as a high grade, may have been based on sexual attraction rather than one's abilities (McCormack, 1985). Decreased feelings of competence and confidence and increased feelings of anger, frustration, depression, and anxiety all can result from harassment (Cammaert, 1985; Crull, 1982; Hamilton, Alagna, King & Lloyd, 1987; Livingston, 1982; Schneider, 1987). The psychological stress produced by harassment is compounded when women are fired or quit their jobs in fear or frustration (Coles, 1986).

Meek and Lynch (1983) proposed that victims of harassment typically go through several stages of reaction, at first questioning the offender's true intentions and then blaming themselves for the offender's behavior. Women with traditional sex-role beliefs are more likely to blame themselves for being harassed (Jensen & Gutek, 1982). Victims then worry about being believed by others and about possible retaliation if they take formal steps to protest the behavior. A victim may be too frightened or confused to assert herself or punish the offender. Psychologists who work with victims of harassment would do well to recognize that not only victims' emotional reactions but also the nature of the grievance process as discussed in this article may discourage women from bringing formal complaints.   33

PREVENTION OF SEXUAL HARASSMENT

Some writers have argued that sexual harassment does not occur with great frequency, or if it once was a problem, it has been eliminated in recent years. Indeed, Morgenson (1989), writing in the business publication *Forbes,* suggested that the whole issue had been drummed up by professional sexual harassment counselors in order to sell their services. Yet the studies cited in this article have documented that sexual harassment is a widespread problem with serious consequences.   34

Feminists and union activists have succeeded in gaining recognition of sexual harassment as a form of sex discrimination (MacKinnon, 1979). The law now views sexual harassment not as the idiosyncratic actions of a few inconsiderate males but as part of a pattern of behaviors that reflect the imbalance of power between women and men in society. Women in various occupations and educational settings have sought legal redress for actions of supervisors or coworkers, and sexual harassment has become the focus of numerous organizational policies and grievance procedures (Brewer & Berk, 1982).   35

Well-publicized policies that use an inclusive definition of sexual harassment, include an informal dispute resolution option, provide an advocate for the victim (if desired), and permit multiple offenders to be identified seem likely to be the most effective way of addressing claims of sexual harassment. However, even these modifications will not eliminate all of the problems in policies. The severity of the consequences of harassment for the victim, coupled with the problematic nature of grievance procedures and the mildness of punishments for offenders, makes retribution less effective than prevention of sexual harassment. Organizational leaders should not assume that their job is completed when   36 they have established a sexual harassment policy. Extensive efforts at prevention need to be mounted at the individual, situational, and organizational level.

37   In prevention efforts aimed at the individual, education about harassment should be provided (e.g., Beauvais, 1986). In particular, policymakers and others need to learn to "think like a woman" to define which behaviors constitute harassment and recognize that these behaviors are unacceptable. Understanding that many women find offensive more subtle forms of behavior such as sexual jokes or comments may help reduce the kinds of interactions that create a hostile environment. Educating personnel about the punishments involved for offensive behavior also may have a deterring effect.

38   However, education alone is not sufficient. Sexual harassment is the product not only of individual attitudes and beliefs, but also of organizational practices. Dzeich and Weiner (1984, pp. 39–58) described aspects of educational institutions that facilitate sexual harassment, including the autonomy afforded the faculty, the diffusion of authority that permits lack of accountability, and the shortage of women in positions of authority. Researchers are beginning to identify the practices in other work settings that facilitate or support sexual harassment, and suggest that sexual harassment may be part of a pattern of unprofessional and disrespectful attitudes and behaviors that characterizes some workplaces (Gutek, 1985).

39   Perhaps the most important factor in reducing sexual harassment is an organizational culture that promotes equal opportunities for women. There is a strong negative relationship between the level of perceived equal employment opportunity for women in a company and the level of harassment reported (LaFontaine & Tredeau, 1986): Workplaces low in perceived equality are the site of more frequent incidents of harassment. This finding suggests that sexual harassment both reflects and reinforces the underlying sexual inequality that produces a sex-segregated and sex-stratified occupational structure (Hoffman, 1986). The implementation of sexual harassment policies demonstrates the seriousness of those in authority; the language of the policies provides some measure of clarity about the types of behavior that are not acceptable; and grievance procedures may provide relief and legitimacy to those with complaints (Schneider, 1987). But neither policies nor procedures do much to weaken the structural roots of gender inequalities in organizations.

40   Reforms intended to ameliorate women's position sometimes have unintended negative consequences (see Kirp, Yudof, & Franks, 1986). The presence of sexual harassment policies and the absence of formal complaints might promote the illusion that this problem has been solved. Assessment of whether organizational policies and practices promote or hinder equality for women is required to insure that this belief does not prevail. A long-range strategy for organizational reform in academia would thus attack the chilly climate for women in classrooms and laboratories (Project on the Status and Education of Women, 1982), the inferior quality of athletic programs for women, differential treatment of women applicants, the acceptance of the masculine as normative, and a knowledge base uninfluenced by women's values or experience (Fuehrer & Schilling, 1985). In other work settings, such a long-range approach would attack both sex-segregation of occupations and sex-stratification within authority hierarchies. Sexual harassment grievance procedures alone are not sufficient to insure that sexual harassment will be eliminated. An end to this problem requires gender equity within organizations.

REFERENCES

Abbey, A. (1982). Sex differences in attributions for friendly behavior: Do males misperceive females' friendliness? *Journal of Personality and Social Psychology, 42,* 830–838.

Abbey, A., & Melby, C. (1986). The effects of nonverbal cues on gender differences in perceptions of sexual intent. *Sex Roles, 15,* 283–298.

Adams, J. W., Kottke, J. L., & Padgitt, J. S. (1983). Sexual harassment of university students. *Journal of College Student Personnel, 23,* 484–490.

Alexander et al. v. Yale University, 459 F. Supp. 1 (D. Conn. 1977), affirmed 631 F. 2d 178 (2nd Cir. 1980).

American Association of University Professors. (1983). Sexual harassment: Suggested policy and procedures for handling complaints. *Academe, 69,* 15a–16a.

American Council on Education. (1986). *Sexual harassment on campus: Suggestions for reviewing campus policy and educational programs.* Washington, DC: Author.

Beauvais, K. (1986). Workshops to combat sexual harassment: A case study of changing attitudes. *Signs: Journal of Women in Culture and Society, 12,* 130–145.

Becker, H. S. (1967). Whose side are we on? *Social Problems, 14,* 239–247.

Benson, D. J., & Thomson, G. (1982). Sexual harassment on a university campus: The confluence of authority relations, sexual interest and gender stratification. *Social Problems, 29,* 236–251.

Brandenburg, J. B. (1982). Sexual harassment in the university: Guidelines for establishing a grievance procedure. *Signs: Journal of Women in Culture and Society, 8,* 320–336.

Brett, J. M., Goldberg, S. B., & Ury, W. L. (1990). Designing systems for resolving disputes in organizations. *American Psychologist, 45,* 162–170.

Brewer, M. (1982). Further beyond nine to five: An integration and future directions. *Journal of Social Issues, 38,* 149–157.

Brewer, M. B., & Berk, R. A. (1982). Beyond nine to five: Introduction. *Journal of Social Issues, 38,* 1–4.

Bumiller, K. (1987). Victims in the shadow of the law: A critique of the model of legal protection. *Signs: Journal of Women in Culture and Society, 12,* 421–439.

Burleigh, N., & Goldberg, S. (1989). Breaking the silence: Sexual harassment in law firms. *ABA Journal, 75,* 46–52.

Cammaert, L. P. (1985). How widespread is sexual harassment on campus? *International Journal of Women's Studies, 8,* 388–397.

Cohen, C. F. (1987, November). Legal dilemmas in sexual harassment cases. *Labor Law Journal,* 681–689.

Coles, F. S. (1986). Forced to quit: Sexual harassment complaints and agency response. *Sex Roles, 14,* 81–95.

Collins, E. G. C., & Blodgett, T. B. (1981). Some see it . . . some won't. *Harvard Business Review, 59,* 76–95.

Crull, P. (1982). The stress effects of sexual harassment on the job. *American Journal of Orthopsychiatry, 52,* 539–543.

Dzeich, B., & Weiner, L. (1984). *The lecherous professor.* Boston: Beacon Press.

Fain, T. C., & Anderton, D. L. (1987). Sexual harassment: Organizational context and diffuse status. *Sex Roles, 5/6,* 291–311.

Fitzgerald, L. F., Schullman, S. L., Bailey, N., Richards, M., Swecker, J., Gold, Y., Ormerod, M., & Weitzman, L. (1988). The incidence and dimensions of sexual harassment in academia and the workplace. *Journal of Vocational Behavior, 32,* 152–175.

Fuehrer, A., & Schilling, K. M. (1985). The values of academe: Sexism as a natural consequence. *Journal of Social Issues, 41,* 29–42.

Garvey, M. S. (1986). The high cost of sexual harassment suits. *Labor Relations, 65,* 75–79.

Gilligan, C. (1982). *In a different voice: Psychological theory and women's development.* Cambridge, MA: Harvard University Press.

Glaser, R. D., & Thorpe, J. S. (1986). Unethical intimacy: A survey of sexual contact and advances between psychology educators and female graduate students. *American Psychologist, 41,* 43–51.

Gutek, B. A. (1985). *Sex and the workplace.* San Francisco: Jossey-Bass.

Gutek, B. A., Morasch, B., & Cohen, A. G. (1983). Interpreting social-sexual behavior in a work setting. *Journal of Vocational Behavior, 22,* 30–48.

Hamilton, J. A., Alagna, S. W., King, L. S., & Lloyd, C. (1987). The emotional consequences of gender-based abuse in the workplace: New counseling programs for sex discrimination. *Women and Therapy, 6,* 155–182.

Hoffman, F. L. (1986). Sexual harassment in academia: Feminist theory and institutional practice. *Harvard Educational Review, 56*(2), 107–121.

Jensen, I. W., & Gutek, B. A. (1982). Attributions and assignment of responsibility in sexual harassment. *Journal of Social Issues, 38,* 121–136.

Jones, E. E., & Nisbett, R. E. (1971). *The actor and the observer: Divergent perceptions of the causes of behavior.* Morristown, NJ: General Learning Press.

Jones, T. S., Remland, M. S., & Brunner, C. C. (1987). Effects of employment relationship, response of recipient and sex of rater on perceptions of sexual harassment. *Perceptual and Motor Skills, 65,* 55–63.

Kanter, R. M. (1977). *Men and women of the corporation.* New York: Basic Books.

Kenig, S., & Ryan, J. (1986). Sex differences in levels of tolerance and attribution of blame for sexual harassment on a university campus. *Sex Roles, 15,* 535–549.

Kirk, D. (1988, August). *Gender differences in the perception of sexual harassment.* Paper presented at the Academy of Management National Meeting, Anaheim, CA.

Kirp, D. L., Yudof, M. G., & Franks, M. S. (1986). *Gender justice.* Chicago: University of Chicago Press.

Kolb, D. M., & Coolidge, G. G. (1988). *Her place at the table: A consideration of gender issues in negotiation* (Working paper series 88-5). Harvard Law School, Program on Negotiation.

Konrad, A. M., & Gutek, B. A. (1986). Impact of work experiences on attitudes toward sexual harassment. *Administrative Science Quarterly, 31,* 422–438.

LaFontaine, E., & Tredeau, L. (1986). The frequency, sources, and correlates of sexual harassment among women in traditional male occupations. *Sex Roles, 15,* 433–442.

Lester, D., Banta, B., Barton, J., Elian, N., Mackiewicz, L., & Winkelried, J. (1986). Judgments about sexual harassment: Effects of the power of the harasser. *Perceptual and Motor Skills, 63,* 990.

Linenberger, P. (1983, April). What behavior constitutes sexual harassment? *Labor Law Journal,* 238–247.

Littler-Bishop, S., Seidler-Feller, D., & Opaluch, R. E. (1982). Sexual harassment in the workplace as a function of initiator's status: The case of airline personnel. *Journal of Social Issues, 38,* 137–148.

Livingston, J. A. (1982). Responses to sexual harassment on the job: Legal, organizational, and individual actions. *Journal of Social Issues, 38*(4), 5–22.

Lott, B., Reilly, M. E., & Howard, D. R. (1982). Sexual assault and harassment: A campus community case study. *Signs: Journal of Women in Culture and Society, 8,* 296–319.

MacKinnon, C. A. (1979). *Sexual harassment of working women: A case of sex discrimination.* New Haven, CT: Yale University Press.

MacKinnon, C. A. (1987). Feminism, Marxism, method and the state: Toward feminist jurisprudence. In S. Harding (Ed.), *Feminism and methodology: Social science issues.* Bloomington: Indiana University Press.

Maihoff, N., & Forrest, L. (1983). Sexual harassment in higher education: An assessment study. *Journal of the National Association for Women Deans, Administrators, and Counselors, 46*, 3–8.

Maypole, D. E. (1986). Sexual harassment of social workers at work: Injustice within? *Social Work, 31*, 29–34.

Maypole, D. E., & Skaine, R. (1982). Sexual harassment of blue-collar workers. *Journal of Sociology and Social Welfare, 9*, 682–695.

McCormack, A. (1985). The sexual harassment of students by teachers: The case of students in science. *Sex Roles, 13*, 21–32.

McIntyre, D. I., & Renick, J. C. (1982). Protecting public employees and employers from sexual harassment. *Public Personnel Management Journal, 11*, 282–292.

Mednick, M. T. (1989). On the politics of psychological constructs: Stop the bandwagon, I want to get off. *American Psychologist, 44*, 1118–1123.

Meek, P. M., & Lynch, A. Q. (1983). Establishing an informal grievance procedure for cases of sexual harassment of students. *Journal of the National Association for Women Deans, Administrators, and Counselors, 46*, 30–33.

Merry, S. E., & Silbey, S. S. (1984). What do plaintiffs want? Reexamining the concept of dispute. *Justice System Journal, 9*, 151–178.

Metha, J., & Nigg, A. (1983). Sexual harassment on campus: An institutional response. *Journal of the National Association for Women Deans, Administrators, and Counselors, 46*, 9–15.

Miller, J. B. (1976). *Toward a new psychology of women.* Boston: Beacon Press.

Morgenson, G. (1989, May). Watch that leer, stifle that joke. *Forbes*, 69–72.

Popovich, P. M., Licata, B. J., Nokovich, D., Martelli, T., & Zoloty, S. (1987). Assessing the incidence and perceptions of sexual harassment behaviors among American undergraduates. *Journal of Psychology, 120*, 387–396.

Powell, G. N. (1986). Effects of sex role identity and sex on definitions of sexual harassment. *Sex Roles, 14*, 9–19.

Project on the Status and Education of Women. (1982). *The campus climate: A chilly one for women?* Washington, DC: Association of American Colleges.

Pryor, J. B. (1985). The lay person's understanding of sexual harassment. *Sex Roles, 13*, 273–286.

Pryor, J. B., & Day, J. D. (1988). Interpretations of sexual harassment: An attributional analysis. *Sex Roles, 18*, 405–417.

Reilly, M. E., Lott, B., & Gallogly, S. (1986). Sexual harassment of university students. *Sex Roles, 15*, 333–358.

Rifkin, J. (1984). Mediation from a feminist perspective: Promise and problems. *Mediation, 2*, 21–31.

Robertson, C., Dyer, C. E., & Campbell, D. (1988). Campus harassment: Sexual harassment policies and procedures at institutions of higher learning. *Signs: Journal of Women in Culture and Society, 13*, 792–812.

Robinson, W. L., & Reid, P. T. (1985). Sexual intimacy in psychology revisited. *Professional Psychology: Research and Practice, 16*, 512–520.

Rossi, P. H., & Weber-Burdin, E. (1983). Sexual harassment on the campus. *Social Science Research, 12*, 131–158.

Rowe, M. P. (1981, May–June). Dealing with sexual harassment. *Harvard Business Review*, 42–46.

Saal, F. E., Johnson, C. B., & Weber, N. (1989). Friendly or sexy? It may depend on whom you ask. *Psychology of Women Quarterly, 13*, 263–276.

Schneider, B. E. (1987). Graduate women, sexual harassment, and university policy. *Journal of Higher Education, 58*, 46–65.

Shotland, R. L., & Craig, J. M. (1988). Can men and women differentiate between friendly and sexually interested behavior? *Social Psychology Quarterly, 51*, 66–73.

Tangri, S. S., Burt, M. R., & Johnson, L. B. (1982). Sexual harassment at work: Three explanatory models. *Journal of Social Issues, 38,* 33–54.

Terpstra, D. E., & Baker, D. D. (1988). Outcomes of sexual harassment charges. *Academy of Management Journal, 31,* 185–194.

Terpstra, D. E., & Cook, S. E. (1985). Complainant characteristics and reported behaviors and consequences associated with formal sexual harassment charges. *Personnel Psychology, 38,* 559–574.

Thomann, D. A., & Wiener, R. L. (1987). Physical and psychological causality as determinants of culpability in sexual harassment cases. *Sex Roles, 17,* 573–591.

Trager, T. B. (1988). Legal considerations in drafting sexual harassment policies. In J. Van Tol (Ed.), *Sexual harassment on campus: A legal compendium* (pp. 181–190). Washington, DC: National Association of College and University Attorneys.

U.S. Equal Employment Opportunity Commission. (1980, November 10). Final amendment to guidelines on discrimination because of sex under Title VII of the Civil Rights Act of 1964, as amended. 29 CFR Part 1604. *Federal Register, 45,* 74675–74677.

U.S. Merit Systems Protection Board. (1981). *Sexual harassment in the federal workplace: Is it a problem?* Washington, DC: Government Printing Office.

U.S. Merit Systems Protection Board. (1988). *Sexual harassment in the federal government: An update.* Washington, DC: U.S. Government Printing Office.

Wilson, K. R., & Krause, L. A. (1983). Sexual harassment in the university. *Journal of College Student Personnel, 24,* 219–224.

Wilson, M. (1988). Sexual harassment and the law. *The Community Psychologist, 21,* 16–17.

Harassment Blues

Naomi Munson

This article first appeared in Commentary *in 1992.*

1   When I was graduated from college in the early '70s, I had the good fortune to land a job at a weekly newsmagazine. It was a wonderful place to work, financially lucrative, intellectually demanding but not overwhelming, and, above all, fun.

2   There was, actually, a sort of hierarchy of fun at the office. Ranking lowest were the hard-news departments; although (or perhaps because) they offered the excitement of late-breaking news and fast-developing stories, both the national- and the foreign-affairs sections were socially rather staid. Next up the scale came the business section, where the people were lively enough but where the general tone nevertheless reflected the serious nature of the subject matter. Then there was the culture department, a barrel of laughs in its own way, though the staff did seem to spend a certain amount of time at the opera. At the top of the scale stood the department where I wound up, which included science, sports, education, religion, and the like. Though there might be the occasional breaking news, these sections generally called more for long thought and thorough research, which led to a very laidback atmosphere and a lot of down time. Drinking at nearby bars, dining at the finest restaurants, and dancing at local discos occupied a great deal of that time. And sex played

a major role in all of this. (It did throughout the magazine, of course, but nowhere so openly and unselfconsciously as here.)

The men were a randy lot, dedicated philanderers, and foul-mouthed to boot; the   3
women, having vociferously demanded—and been granted—absolutely equal status, were considered fair game (though there were a couple of secretaries whose advancing age and delicate sensibilities consigned them to the sidelines).

Imagine my surprise, then, when one day a young woman who worked with me   4
flounced into my office, cheeks flushed, eyes flashing, to announce that she had just been subjected to sexual harassment. (It was a fairly new concept back then, at the end of the '70's, but being in the vanguard of social trends, we had heard of it.) When she explained that the offense had occurred not in our own neck of the woods but in the national-affairs section, I was truly shocked. When she identified the offender, however—sexually, one of the least lively types on the premises—I began to be skeptical. And when she described his crime—which was having said something to the effect that he longed for the good old days of miniskirts when a fellow had a real chance to see great legs like hers—I scoffed. "Oh, come on," I said. "That's not sexual harassment; that's just D. trying to pay you a compliment." To myself, after she had calmed down and left, I said, "She's even dimmer than I thought. She thinks *that's* what they mean by sexual harassment."

If I was convinced that this woman's experience did not constitute sexual harassment,   5
I, like the vast majority of people at that time, had rather vague notions of what did. Whatever it was, however, it already seemed clear that the charge of sexual harassment would serve as a perfect instrument of revenge for disgruntled female employees. This was borne out by the story I came to know, years later, about a man at another office who had had several formal harassment charges brought against him by women who worked for him. The man was someone who would, as his coworkers saw it, "nail" anything that moved. He had, in fact, had longstanding affairs—which he had ended in order to move on to fresh conquests—with the women now accusing him of having offered financial inducements in exchange for sexual favors. The women claimed to have declined the offers and consequently suffered the loss of promotions.

Disgruntlement aside, however, it still seemed obvious to me that in a case of sexual   6
harassment, something *sexual* might be supposed to have occurred. That quaint notion of mine was finally laid to rest during the Clarence Thomas–Anita Hill debacle. Professor Hill's performance convinced me of nothing save that if she told me the sun was shining, I would head straight for my umbrella and galoshes. The vast outpouring of feminist outrage that accompanied the event did, however, succeed in opening my eyes to the sad fact that it was I, way back when, who had been the dim one; my erstwhile colleague had merely been a bit ahead of her time. For, it now turns out, what she described is precisely what they *do* mean by sexual harassment.

During the course of the hearing, story after story appeared in the media supporting   7
the claim that men out there are abusive to their female employees. It was declared, over and over, that virtually every woman in the country had either suffered sexual harassment herself or knew someone who had (I myself, I realize, figure in that assessment). The abuse, it appeared, had been going on since time immemorial and was so painful to some of the women involved that they had repressed it for decades.

8   It became clear amid all the hand-wringing that we were not talking here about bosses exacting sexual favors in exchange for promotions, raises, or the like. Even Professor Hill never claimed that Judge Thomas promised to promote her if she succumbed to his charms, or that he threatened to fire her if she failed to do so. What she said, as all the world now knows, was that he pestered her for dates; that he boasted of his natural endowments and of his sexual prowess; that he used obscene language in her presence; that he regaled her with the details of porno flicks; and that he discussed the joys of, as Miss Hill so expressively put it, "(gulp) oral sex." The closest anyone at the hearing came to revealing anything like direct action was a Washington woman who was horrified when a member of Congress played footsie with her under the table at an official function, and a friend of Anita Hill who announced that she had been "touched in the workplace."

9   What we—or, to be more precise, they—were talking about was sexual innuendo, ogling, obscenity, unwelcome importuning, nude pin-ups; about an "unpleasant atmosphere in the workplace"; about male "insensitivity." One columnist offered behavioral guidelines to men who had been reduced to "whining" that they no longer knew what was appropriate— something to the effect that though it is OK to say, "Gee, I bet you make the best blackened redfish in town," it is not OK to say, "Wow, I bet you're really hot between the sheets." Even Judge Thomas himself declared that if he *had* said the things the good professor was accusing him of, it *would* have constituted sexual harassment.

10   Yet in response to all of this it also emerged very plainly that the American public just was not buying it. Single women were heard to worry that putting a lid on sex at the office might hurt their chances of finding a husband; one forthright woman was even quoted by a newspaper as saying that office sex was the spice of life. Rather more definitively, polls showed that most people, black and white, male and female, thought Judge Thomas should be confirmed, *even if the charges against him were true.*

11   How can it be that the majority of Americans were dismissing the significance of sexual harassment (as now defined) even as their elected representatives were declaring it just the most hideous, heinous, gosh-awful stuff they had ever heard of? How is it possible that, at the very moment newspapers and TV were proclaiming that American women were mad as hell and weren't going to take it anymore, most of these women themselves—and their husbands—were responding with a raised eyebrow and a small shrug of the shoulders?

12   For one thing, most Americans—unlike the ideologues who brought us sexual harassment in the first place, and who have worked a special magic on pundits and politicos for more than two decades now—have a keen understanding of life's realities. Having had no choice but to work, in order to feed and clothe and doctor and educate their children, they have always known that, while work has its rewards, financial and otherwise, "an unpleasant atmosphere in the workplace" is something they may well have to put up with. That, where women are concerned, the unpleasantness might take on sexual overtones gives it no more weight than the uncertainties, the frustrations, and the humiliations, petty and grand, encountered by men.

13   Most people, furthermore, have a healthy respect for the ability of women to hold their own in the battle of the sexes. They know that women have always managed to deal perfectly well with male lust: to evade it, to quash it, even to be flattered by it. The bepaunched

and puffing boss, chasing his buxom secretary around the desk, is, after all, a figure of fun—because we realize that he will never catch her, and that even if he did, she would know very well how to put him in his place.

The women's movement and its fellow travelers, on the other hand, have never had any such understanding or any such respect. On the contrary, rage against life's imperfections, and a consequent revulsion against men, has been the bone and sinew of that movement.   14

The feminists came barreling into the workforce, some twenty years ago, not out of necessity, but with the loud assertion that here was to be found something called fulfillment. Men, they claimed, had denied them access to this fulfillment out of sheer power-hungry selfishness. Women, they insisted, were no different from men in their talents or their dispositions; any apparent differences had simply been manufactured, as a device to deprive mothers, wives, and sisters of the excitement and pleasure to which men had had exclusive title for so long, and which they had come to view as their sole privilege.   15

No sooner had these liberated ladies taken their rightful place alongside men at work, however, than it began to dawn on them that the experience was not quite living up to their expectations. They quickly discovered, for example, what their fathers, husbands, and brothers had always known: that talent is not always appreciated, that promotions are not so easy to come by, that often those most meritorious are inexplicably passed over in favor of others. But rather than recognizing this as a universal experience, they descried a "glass ceiling," especially constructed to keep them in their place, and they called for the hammers.   16

Feminists had insisted that child-bearing held no more allure for them than it did for men. That insistence quickly began to crumble in the face of a passionate desire for babies. But rather than recognizing that life had presented them with a choice, they demanded special treatment. They reserved the right to take leave from their work each time the urge to procreate came upon them. And they insisted that husbands, employers, and even the government take equal responsibility with them for the care and upbringing of the little bundles of joy resulting from that urge.   17

And as for sex in the workplace, well, that was pretty much what it had always been everywhere: an ongoing battle involving, on the one side, attentions both unwelcome and welcome, propositions both unappealing and appealing, and compliments both unpleasing and pleasing, and on the other, evasive action, outright rejection, or happy capitulation. Having long ago decided that the terms of this age-old battle were unacceptable to them, the women of the movement might have been expected to try to eliminate them. With the invention of sexual harassment, they have met that expectation, and with a vengeance. Laws have been made, cases have been tried and, in the Clarence Thomas affair, a decent man was pilloried.   18

Having, in other words, finally been permitted to play with the big boys, these women have found the game not to their liking. But rather than retiring from the field, they have called for a continuous and open-ended reformation of the rules. Indeed, like children in a temper, who respond to maternal placating with a rise in fury, they have met every accommodating act of the men in their lives with a further escalation of demand. The new insistence that traditional male expressions of sexual interest be declared taboo, besides being the purest revelation of feminist rage, is the latest arc in that vicious cycle.   19

Watch That Leer, Stifle That Joke

Gretchen Morgenson

Gretchen Morgenson, a writer for the business magazine Forbes, *published this article in 1989.*

1   It's been almost ten years since the Equal Employment Opportunity Commission wrote its guidelines defining sexual harassment as a form of sex discrimination and, therefore, illegal under Title VII of the Civil Rights Act of 1964.

2   During that time, women have transformed the workplace, taken on untraditional jobs, excelled in male-oriented businesses, started their own firms and garnered new power on corporate boards.

3   Have women been harassed every inch of the way by leering, lascivious male chauvinists? It sometimes sounds that way. Following the Equal Employment Opportunity Commission's lead, an estimated three out of four companies nationwide have instituted strict policies against harassment; millions of dollars are dutifully spent each year educating employees in Title VII etiquette.

4   What are the boundaries? Where does good-humored kidding cease and harassment begin? How deeply should the courts concern themselves with personal behavior and good manners? Requests or demands for sexual favors are clear-cut cases of behavior that lie beyond the pale. Sleep-with-me-and-you'll-get-promoted propositions are clearly illegal. Where the law gets hazy and goes beyond where some reasonable people think the law should go is in what is known as hostile environment harassment—the hazing, joking, sexually suggestive talk between men and the women who work alongside them.

5   Both types of behavior are increasing? That's the story you get from the media, which loves a salacious issue, and from employee relations consultants who make money telling corporations how to protect themselves from costly harassment claims. These are the loudest voices in the din. Loud but not persuasive.

6   The peddlers of sex harassment advice have, of course, their own moneymaking agenda. Equally suspect are those extremists who would politicize all of American life and seek to regulate human behavior to suit their private prejudices. These people want to impose stringently moralistic standards on private industry that are not met in any other environment. It's all part of the transformation taking place today in employment law in which employers' responsibilities to their workers seem to grow just as workers' responsibilities to the bosses seem to diminish.

7   A growth industry has sprung up to dispense harassment advice to worried companies in the form of seminars, videos and group gropes.

8   The deeper *Forbes* delved, the more we became convinced that the alleged increase in sexual harassment was more a product of propaganda from self-interested parties. "At least 35% and as many as 90% of women get harassed," contends Linda Krystal Doran, president of Krystal & Kalan Associates, a sex harassment consultant in Issaquah, Wash. Doran conjures up images of a major portion of the work force wolfishly and lustfully abused by another portion. If her figures are taken seriously, as many as 49 million women are getting pinched, propositioned or annoyed on the job.

But why then is the number of federal cases alleging harassment on the job actually de-   9
clining? This, in spite of a growing female work force. According to the EEOC, where anyone bringing a federal sex harassment case must first file a complaint, the number of
Title VII complaints in which sexual harassment was mentioned peaked at 6,342 five years
ago; last year there were 4,984 cases.

Sound like a lot? It's not. It's 0.0091% of the female work force—one in every 11,000.   10
And that's cases filed, not cases proven. Furthermore, these cases may primarily involve
other forms of discrimination: race, national origin, color and religion.

Forbes consulted human rights commissions that compile such figures in four populous,   11
regionally diverse states: California, Michigan, New York and Texas. Excepting California,
where there has been a modest increase, sex harassment cases in these states are down.

Yet the money to be made these days advising corporations on the issue of harassment   12
is not insubstantial. Susan Webb, president of Pacific Resource Development Group, a Seattle consultant, says she spends 95% of her time advising on sex harassment. Like most of
the consultants, Webb acts as an expert witness in harassment cases, conducts investigations for companies or municipalities and teaches seminars. She charges clients $1,495 to
buy her 60-minute sex harassment video program and handbooks. Webb, who's worked for
350 companies or municipalities, is one of a dozen such consultants, and her prices are typical. Solving the problem is supposed to be their business, but hyping the problem is very
much in their personal interests.

Michael Connolly, former general counsel to the EEOC, and now a partner at Cross   13
Wrock in Detroit, says: "There are a lot of bad consultants taking advantage of the fact that
harassment is in vogue." There are even consultants who act as agents for other consultants. Jennifer Coplon of Resource Group–Videolearning in Boston represents some 15 sex
harassment video producers, connecting them with corporations, universities and government agencies. "Among all employment issues, sexual harassment is the biggest concern
among companies," she reports happily.

Sexual harassment became a serious legal issue in the early 1980s, just after the Equal   14
Employment Opportunity Commission published its first guidelines. But it was *Mentor
Savings Bank v. Vinson,* a harassment case that made it to the Supreme Court in 1986, that
really acted as a full employment act for sex harassment consultants. In *Vinson,* the
Supreme Court conveyed the idea that employers could limit their liability to harassment
claims by implementing antiharassment policies and procedures in the workplace. And so
the antiharassment industry was born. Even today corporate attorneys are sometimes the
best salespeople for the sexual harassment prevention industry. They tell their bosses that
the existence of a corporate program should be part of a company's legal defenses.

No surprise then that sexual harassment consultants like to claim the problem is get-   15
ting worse, not better.

What about those bothersome EEOC numbers? The consultants say that there is a more   16
than offsetting increase in private suits. Really? There's simply no proof that huge or increasing numbers of private actions are being filed and litigated. The San Francisco law firm
of Orrick, Herrington & Sutcliffe has monitored private sex harassment cases filed in California since 1984. From 1984 to March 1989, the number of sexual harassment cases in
California that were litigated through to a verdict totaled 15. That's in a litigation-happy
state with 5.8 million working women.

17   Those sex harassment actions that do get to a jury are the ones that really grab headlines. A few scary awards have been granted recently—five plaintiffs were awarded $3.8 million by a jury in a North Carolina case against a Texas S&L, Murray Savings Association—but mammoth awards are often reduced in subsequent court proceedings. In California the median jury verdict for all sex harassment cases litigated since 1984 is $183,000. The top verdict in the state was just under $500,000, the lowest was $45,000. California, known for its sympathetic jurors, probably produces higher awards than most states.

18   Paul Tobias, a partner at the Cincinnati law firm of Tobias & Kraus and executive director of the Plaintiffs Employment Lawyers Association, for the past decade has focused on individual employees' problems, including sex harassment. His experience? "During a year, 10 or 15 people may come in and complain; maybe one of those cases is winnable."

19   Of the dozen or so labor lawyers *Forbes* interviewed—from both plaintiffs' and defendants' bars—most feel that job-related harassment, though not gone, occurs much less frequently now than it did ten years ago.

20   Well, maybe, the sex harassment industry replies, but that's only because women are afraid or ashamed to complain. Bringing a sex harassment case is similar to filing a rape case, consultants and lawyers say; both are nasty proceedings that involve defamation, possible job loss and threats to family harmony. "More people are experiencing harassment, but they may not want to bring a case," says Webb, the Seattle trainer.

21   Maybe so, but there is no evidence of this. After reading cases and talking to the lawyers who litigate them, it becomes clear that women have become much more aggressive in filing sex harassment claims.

22   According to the New York State Division of Human Rights, more than half of the complaint outcomes from 1980 through 1986 were dismissed for lack of probable cause. Actual number: 521, or 52%. Compare this with the cases in which probable cause was found and a conciliation was reached: 39, or 4% of the total.

23   One explanation for the large percentage of dismissed cases is that hostile environment harassment is difficult to define. Asking a subordinate to perform sexual favors in exchange for a raise is clearly illegal. But a dirty joke? Behavior that one woman may consider harassment could be seen by another as a nonthreatening gag. Whose standards should be used?

24   Under tort law, the standard that must be met is called the reasonable person rule. This means that the behavior that has resulted in a case—such as an assault or the intent to cause emotional distress—must be considered objectionable by a "reasonable person." The EEOC follows this lead and in its guidelines defines environmental harassment as that which "unreasonably interferes with an individual's job performance."

25   How to define that? Says Freada Klein of Klein Associates, a Boston consulting firm: "My goal is to create a corporate climate where every employee feels free to object to behavior, where people are clear about their boundaries and can ask that objectionable behavior stop." Objectionable to whom? By what standards?

26   Can rudeness and annoying behavior really be legislated out of existence? Can women really think they have the right to a pristine work environment free of rude behavior? These are permissive times: Mrs. Grundy has been laughed out of most areas of our life. Should she be allowed to flourish in the workplace alone? Says Susan Hartzoge Gray, an employ-

ment lawyer at Haworth, Riggs, Kuhn & Haworth in High Point, N.C.: "We condone sexual jokes and innuendo in the media—a movie might get a PG rating—yet an employer can be called on the carpet because the same thing bothers someone in an office."

In a curious way, the news stories, the harassment seminars, the showing of video- 27 tapes—even if educational—can act to perpetuate the woman-as-victim mentality. There is even a kind of backlash at work. Increasing numbers of wrongful discharge cases are brought by men who believe they were fired because of a false harassment claim.

Yet the noise will probably continue for a long time to come. The demand by some 28 women for a perfect work climate is part of a larger trend in society. Many people feel they are entitled not only to jobs but to work conditions that suit their tastes.

Some of those higher standards, as far as sex harassment is concerned, are approach- 29 ing the unreasonable. To combat incidents of hostile environment harassment, management is effectively being told to shoulder two new and onerous responsibilities. First, provide a pristine work environment, and second, police it as well.

But if women want a level corporate playing field on which they can compete with 30 men, should they expect to be coddled and protected from rudeness or boors? Why can't they be expected to take care of themselves?

Women do themselves and their careers no favors by playing victim. Sexual harassment 31 is not about sex, it is about power. If women act powerless at work, they'll almost certainly be taken advantage of. Women are more powerful than the sex harassment peddlers will have you believe. A woman's power is not in her ability to bring a harassment claim, it's in her ability to succeed on her merits. And to be able to say, "Back off, bub."

As more and more women recognize this, sex harassment will likely become even less 32 of a real problem in the years ahead than it is today. But don't expect the sex harassment specialists to go out of business. They'll only stop levying their special tax on U.S. business and consumers when demand for their services dries up.

A Wink Here, a Leer There: It's Costly

Susan Crawford

Susan Crawford's article appeared in the New York Times *on March 28, 1993.*

Did the Anita Hill–Clarence Thomas hearings serve as a cautionary tale? For many 1 employers, yes; for many others, regrettably, no. Sexual harassment in the workplace continues to be an insidious problem, as well as a degrading and career-limiting experience for many women. Research indicates that 50 to 85 percent of all female employees experience some form of harassment during their careers, and 15 percent in any given year. Similarly, 90 percent of Fortune 500 companies have received complaints of sexual harassment, more than a third have been sued and nearly a quarter have been sued repeatedly.

It is unrealistic to think we can eradicate harassment in a single generation. But huge 2 strides can be made if it is viewed as an *economic* problem.

3   With more women in the workplace, we must realize that their abilities—and productivity—are critical to our nation's economic health. It is imperative that companies grasp an essential fact: sexual harassment damages the bottom line.

4   As we evolve from an industrial economy toward one based on information and services, human resources are becoming the true engine of added value. Skilled, experienced and committed employees frequently provide a company its competitive edge. But many companies fail to understand that valuable human capital can be squandered by tolerance of harassment.

5   A 1988 study of 160 Fortune 500 companies reached a striking conclusion: harassment costs the average big company, with 23,750 employees, $6.7 million a year. The study calculated losses linked to absenteeism, low productivity and turnover; it did not count the hard-to-measure costs of legal defense, time lost and tarnished public image. Recent research by the author, Freada Klein, a Cambridge, Mass., analyst, confirmed that the data are still valid; anecdotal evidence suggests the costs may be even higher now.

6   How can a company lose $6.7 million a year?

7   First, sexual harassment results in a costly tax on employee performance. At the least, the victim is forced to waste time parrying unwanted attention or enduring improper comments. At the same time, the transgressor is devoting work time to activities that are in no way good for business.

8   Typically, victims retreat into a passive or even sullen acceptance: 12 percent of women who face harassment report stress-related health problems, 27 percent report undermined self-confidence and 13 percent see long-term career damage.

9   Second, harassment breeds resentment and mistrust. Tension can spread to others, breeding widespread cynicism—and limiting productivity.

10   Third, harassment contributes to costly turnover. Women are nine times as likely as men to quit because of harassment, five times as likely to transfer and three times as likely to lose jobs. Fully 25 percent of women who believe they have been harassed have been dismissed or have quit.

11   Every woman who leaves because of harassment represents a large loss of investment, which is compounded by employee replacement costs.

12   To attack the problem, many forward-thinking companies are using awareness-training programs to help employees understand the pain and indignity of harassment. Such programs, if they are comprehensive and used aggressively, can be highly effective. The cost ranges from $5,000 for a small company to $200,000 for a large one.

13   Thus, for that Fortune 500 company facing a $6.7 million liability, it is 34 times as costly to ignore the problem as to take steps to eradicate it. Looked at another way, a sexual-harassment program can be cost-effective if it averts the loss of one key employee—or prevents one lawsuit.

14   We are failing to exploit the full potential of half the nation's work force. And the cost to business is increasingly burdensome. As competition intensifies, managers and directors cannot afford sexual harassment. Corporations—indeed, all organizations—should take aggressive action to eliminate it. Not just to avoid litigation, not just because it is "politically correct" or "the right thing to do," but also because such programs can yield a startlingly positive return on investment.

15   It's an opportunity we can't afford to miss.

Universal Truth and Multiple Perspectives
Controversies on Sexual Harassment
Martha Chamallas

Law professor Martha Chamallas published this article in 1992 in Et Cetera, *a scholarly journal published by the International Society for General Semantics.*

The question I wish to pose has to do with whether the Constitution and the Bill of Rights will prove up to the challenge of a postmodern world. The term "postmodern" is an overused but nonetheless useful way of describing contemporary society—a society that is marked by diversity, contradiction, and complicated interrelationships. In such a postmodern world, invocations of shared values and fundamental rights are not likely to go unchallenged—in almost every conversation, someone will first want to know just who shares these values and who considers these interests to be fundamental? In a postmodern world it makes sense to speak in the plural—to talk about truths rather than a single truth and to think in terms of American cultures rather than the American culture.

In a variety of disciplines, feminist and postmodern scholars have changed their fields by their persistence in investigating the relationship between knowledge and power. There is now a rich body of scholarship demonstrating how particular views of the world come to dominate the discourse, how our knowledge is far less diverse than our people. A central feature of these new critical inquiries is their skepticism about claims of "objectivity" and "neutrality" and of statements that purport to have "universal" applicability. The take home message of much of this work is that frequently what passes for the whole truth is instead a representation of events from the perspective of those who possess the power to have their version of reality accepted. The search is on for multiple meanings and multiple perspectives, whether attached to language, texts, or human events.

One area of the law in which the postmodern challenge to objectivity is the most visible is anti-discrimination law and discourse. I am using anti-discrimination law and discourse here broadly to include specific constitutional protections such as the fifth and fourteenth amendment protections of equality; specific statutory provisions, including the various civil rights legislation prohibiting discrimination based on race, ethnicity, sex, religion, disability and age; as well as public debate on matters such as race and gender equality which highlight the legal dimension of the issues.

These days even law professors must of necessity go beyond the cases decided by appellate courts and become conversant in what is sometimes referred to as "cultural politics." It has occurred to me that the most celebrated sexual harassment case of our time—Professor Anita Hill's accusation of sexual harassment by Clarence Thomas—was not a lawsuit at all. However, Hill's statements generated the most thorough and diverse public discussion of the intersection of gender and race and of the harms caused by sexual harassment that I have ever witnessed. What was most striking for me was the variety of viewpoints from which the controversy was viewed. Opinion about the Thomas matter did not break down neatly along gender lines, nor along racial lines. The response to the hearings dramatically demonstrated that women are not a monolithic group who think alike, nor are African-Americans all of the same mindset.

5   But this acknowledgment of diversity of opinion among women and among African-American men and women does not mean that perspective was not important to one's understanding of the Thomas hearings. Instead I regard the voluminous commentary generated by the Thomas hearing to be an excellent example of multiple realities and multiple perspectives operating in public debate. It was not just a matter of how inclined a person was to believe that either Hill or Thomas was telling the truth. Rather it seemed that for many people what Hill described as her experience readily fit into a coherent and familiar pattern of behavior for them. There was an immediate sense of recognition. Other people had great difficulty making sense of Hill's story. For them, it just did not seem to add up.

6   Hill's revelations prompted many women to tell about their own encounters with sexually harassing behavior—both in private and in public. The day after the hearings ended I sat at a public hearing in Des Moines as a member of a statewide taskforce investigating racial and gender bias in the Iowa judicial system. One of the witnesses that day was a woman who is now a United States Magistrate. She told about an incident that happened to her many years before when she was a young attorney. A man who then served as bailiff for the local courthouse had known this young woman since she was in grade school—in fact, he had been the bus driver for her elementary school. At the end of one day, the woman attorney asked the bailiff to get her a file. He walked over to her, put his arm around her, said he'd do anything for her, and kissed her on the lips. The woman attorney was stunned and humiliated and rushed out of the courtroom. She never reported the incident, never told her friends or family, and spent considerable emotional energy trying to avoid the bailiff while she worked in that area. As she told her experiences to the taskforce, she expressed her empathy for Anita Hill. In her assessment, Hill's account had no holes in it. Hill was not simply a credible witness (or, as one of the Senators on the Judiciary Committee put it, Hill did not just "present" herself well). Instead, she shared a similar "victim's perspective" with Anita Hill. For this woman, Hill's story possessed an internal logic and expressed a reality about the working lives of women.

7   In some feminist groups I have participated in, we talk about being "of the experience." This means being part of a group who has experienced a certain type of discrimination first-hand or supporting close friends through such a period of victimization. And I think it is experiences like these that give people a certain perspective on the world. Only some women and some men share a victim's perspective on sexual harassment.

8   When those in a position to judge insist that the victim respond as they imagine they would in such circumstances, the perspective of the victim most often is erased.

9   If anti-discrimination law and discourse is to respond to a postmodern world, we need to find ways to reach out for and to give weight to suppressed perspectives in the decisional rules that structure legal definitions of equality. We seldom find victims' perspectives embraced in the law. For example, the leading equal protection case—*Washington v. Davis* (1)—requires that plaintiff prove that defendant intended to discriminate. This means that the perspective that determines whether a constitutional violation has occurred is the per-

spective of the defendant. Although like all legal standards, the intent requirement is highly manipulable, it symbolizes that the viewpoint of the defendant—not the victim—is the one that should control. It is not surprising that critical race scholars such as Charles Lawrence have renewed their criticism of *Washington v. Davis* and have urged the courts in constitutional cases to go beyond the motivations of lawmakers and judge the race-based nature of an action by its "cultural meaning" (2). For Lawrence, the cultural meaning of an action is more likely to take into account the perspectives of suppressed minorities than would the intent of those elected to Congress or state legislatures.

One area of the law in which we can begin to glimpse the victim's perspective being taken into account is in Title VII sexual harassment cases involving claims of a hostile or intimidating work environment—the kind of claim Anita Hill might have brought against EEOC had she filed suit. In these cases the plaintiff must prove that the harassing conduct "had the purpose or effect of unreasonably interfering with an individual's work performance or creating an intimidating, hostile or offensive working environment" (3). This standard is more victim-friendly than the current constitutional standard. Because there is no requirement to prove bad intent on the part of the defendant, the perpetrator's perspective is not necessarily determinative.   10

Recently, courts have recognized that events can look very different from the standpoint of plaintiff or defendant—and a few courts have opted to credit plaintiff's version of reality in an effort to uncover and validate a formerly suppressed perspective. An important recent case is *Ellison v. Brady* (4), decided by a panel of the Ninth Circuit in 1991. Depending on your perspective you could call this case either the "love letters" case or the "delusional romance" case. The plaintiff in the case, Kerry Ellison, received two letters from Sterling Gray, a man in her office with whom she had had only casual contact as a co-employee. They both worked as trainees for the IRS. The letters described Gray's intense feelings for Ellison. In one note, for example, he wrote: "I cried over you last night and I'm totally drained today. I've never been in such constant term oil [sic]." They also contained several statements that seemed to assume that the two had formed a genuine and mutual relationship. In one single-spaced, three-page letter, Gray wrote to Ellison "I know you are worth knowing with or without sex . . . Leaving aside the hassles and disasters of recent weeks. I have enjoyed you so much over these past months. Watching you. Experiencing you from O so far away. Admiring your style and your elan . . . Don't you think it odd that two people who have never even talked together alone are striking off such intense sparks . . . I will write another letter in the near future" (5).   11

This pursuit frightened Ellison because as far as she was concerned there was no such relationship: she had rejected several of Gray's invitations to lunch and had asked a male colleague to inform Gray that she had no interest in him and to leave her alone. Ellison then complained about Gray's conduct to her supervisor and insisted that something be done to make Gray stop.   12

Ellison's perspective was that this was a case of "delusional romance." She saw Gray's actions as a nontrivial threat of sexual coercion. From Ellison's perspective, through no action of her own, she had been made the object of a man's fantasies who had ignored her   13 clear requests to stop his aggressive behavior towards her. This victim's perspective differed sharply from the perspective expressed by the district court which dismissed Ellison's claim as stating no cause of action under Title VII. The district court saw Gray's letters as harmless love letters designed to win over Ellison's affections, and stressed that there had been no explicit threats or physically aggressive conduct.

14   On appeal to the Ninth Circuit, Ellison won. The plurality consisting of Judge Beezer and Judge Kozinsky held that Ellison had stated a cause of action and that the case ought to be judged from the perspective of a "reasonable woman" in the position of plaintiff who had received such letters. I'll save for another day the very interesting discussion of whether it is best to describe the victim perspective in sexual harassment litigation in terms of the "reasonable woman." What I think is most important about *Ellison* is the adoption of a perspective other than the perspective of either the accused or the administrators who handled the complaint.

15   I applaud the result in *Ellison* because it validates my own perspective on such matters. On more than one occasion I have been consulted by women students who have received similar, one-sided "love" notes from men in their class. In those cases, the men refused to stop their pursuit of these women, despite warnings from administrators. These "delusional romances" interfered with the women's education. They were afraid to go to class, to go to the library, and they worried when the phone rang when they were alone in their apartments. In my view these were not harmless love letters; they were forms of sexual harassment.

16   Taking the victim's perspective in anti-discrimination law would mean a profound change and I do not expect the courts to go far in this direction until I am way too old to teach employment discrimination. I do believe, however, that suppressed perspectives are now being publicly expressed with greater clarity and with greater frequency. The days of universal truth are numbered.

NOTES

I have explored some of the ideas in this essay in greater depth in Martha Chamallas, "Feminist Constructions of Objectivity: Multiple Perspectives in Sexual and Racial Harassment Litigation," 1. *Texas Journal of Women & the Law* 95 (1992).

1. 426 U.S. 229 (1976).
2. Charles Lawrence, "The Id, the Ego and Equal Protection: Reckoning with Unconscious Racism," 39. *Stan. Law Review* 317 (1987).
3. EEOC Guidelines on Discrimination Because of Sex, 29. C.F.R., §1604.11(a)(3) (1982).
4. 924 F.2d 872 (9th Cir. 1991).
5. Id. at 874.

FOR CLASS DISCUSSION

1. According to the writers of these articles, is sexual harassment primarily a feminist issue, a woman's issue, a business and financial issue, or an employee's issue?

2. A number of these articles address the problem of the differences between the way men view sexual harassment and the way women view it. Which writer's treatment of this difference is the most convincing? Do you see evidence that a writer's stand on how serious a problem sexual harassment is and what should be done about it has any relation to the politics of the writer? In other words, is there an identifiable liberal and conservative stand on sexual harassment?

3. Analyze and evaluate the disagreements among these writers concerning sexual harassment by applying the first set of guide questions from page 465.

4. Choose one of the arguments for closer analysis, applying the second set of guide questions on pages 465–66.

OPTIONAL WRITING ASSIGNMENT   The following story recently appeared in a local newspaper. It was told originally by a former high federal official at a meeting of bankers:

> There was a woman, an old maid, who was looking for some adventure in her life and decided to take a cruise. These are her journal entries.
>
> Day 1:   Glorious morning. It's great to be alive.
>
> Day 2:   Perfect weather. Having a wonderful time.
>
> Day 3:   Sat at the captain's table at dinner. Captain propositioned me. Turned him down.
>
> Day 4:   Captain insisted I sleep with him and said that if I didn't, he'd run the ship into rocks and drown all the passengers.
>
> Day 5:   Saved 600 lives last night.

A columnist who reprinted the story called two sexual harassment consultants and asked them if telling the story in the workplace would constitute sexual harassment. They gave the columnist markedly different answers. Drawing on your reading of the preceding arguments, write your own response to the question "Does telling this story constitute an act of sexual harassment?"

SOCIAL POLICY TOWARD
THE MENTALLY ILL HOMELESS

Crazy in the Streets

Paul S. Appelbaum

Paul S. Appelbaum is the A. F. Zeleznik Professor of Psychiatry and director of the Law and Psychiatry Program at the University of Massachusetts Medical School. This article appeared in Commentary *in May 1987.*

1   They are an inescapable presence in urban America. In New York City they live in subway tunnels and on steam grates, and die in cardboard boxes on windswept street corners. The Los Angeles City Council has opened its chambers to them, allowing them to seek refuge from the Southern California winter on its hard marble floors. Pioneer Square in Seattle, Lafayette Park in Washington, the old downtown in Atlanta have all become places of refuge for these pitiable figures, so hard to tell apart: clothes tattered, skins stained by the streets, backs bent in a perpetual search for something edible, smokable, or tradable that may have found its way to the pavement below.

2   Riddled by psychotic illnesses, abandoned by the systems that once pledged to care for them as long as they needed care, they are the deinstitutionalized mentally ill, the detritus of the latest fashion in mental-health policy. The lucky ones live in board-and-care homes where they can be assured of their next meal; perhaps they have a place to go a few hours a week for support, coffee, even an effort at restoring their productive capacity. Those less fortunate live in our public places, existing on the beneficence of their fellow men and God. It is extraordinary how quickly we have become immune to their presence. Where we might once have felt compassion, revulsion, or fear, now we feel almost nothing at all.

3   There are times, of course, when the reality of the deinstitutionalized breaks through our defenses. Three days after the Statue of Liberty extravaganza in New York harbor last July, in the shadow of the icon of huddled masses, a psychotic man ran amok on the Staten Island ferry, slashing at enemies in a war entirely of his own imagining. Two victims died. Investigations ensued. For a moment we became aware of the world of shelters and emergency rooms, a world where even those willing to accept help and clearly in need of it are turned away because the state has deliberately dismantled the system where they might once have received care. Briefly, the curious wondered, how did this come to be?

4   Like its victims, the policy of deinstitutionalization has been taken for granted. It is difficult to recall that mentally ill persons ever were treated differently. Yet the process that came to be called deinstitutionalization (no one knows when the term was coined) only began in the mid-1950's, and did not move into high gear until a decade later. Although the term itself suggests a unitary policy, deinstitutionalization has had complex roots, and

at different times has sought diverse goals. Its failure, however, was all but preordained by several of the forces that gave it birth. Any attempt to correct the debacle that has attended the contraction—some might say implosion—of our public mental-health systems will require an understanding of those forces.

II

The idea that the states bear some responsibility for the care of the mentally ill was not immediately obvious to the founders of this country. Through the colonial and federalist periods, care of psychotic and other dependent persons was the responsibility of local communities. They responded then as many of them do today. Almshouses and jails were overrun with the mentally ill, who, though thrown together with the criminal, tubercular, and mendicant, were often treated with a cruelty visited on none of the others.   5

Change came in the second quarter of the 19th century. New interest was stimulated among a small number of physicians in a system of treatment of the mentally ill begun in a Quaker hospital in England and called "moral" care. The name—with its ironic allusion to the immorality that had governed most other efforts to deal with the mentally ill—denoted a therapeutic system based on the radical idea that the mentally ill were more like us than unlike. If they were treated with kindness, encouraged to establish order in their lives, given the opportunity to work at productive trades, and provided with models of behavior, their mental illnesses might dissipate.   6

The belief that the mentally ill could be treated, and thus need not be relegated to the cellars of local jails, was championed by Dorothea Dix, a spinster Sunday-school teacher from Massachusetts, who traversed the country, cataloging the barbarities inflicted on mentally ill persons and petitioning legislatures to establish facilities where moral treatment might be applied. Her efforts and those of others resulted in the creation of a network of state-operated hospitals. As the states assumed ever wider responsibility for the mentally ill, the hospitals grew in size, absorbing the denizens of the jails and poorhouses.   7

In the wake of the Civil War, as the burdens created by waves of immigration stood unrelieved by increases in funding, the public hospitals surrendered the goal of active treatment. They continued to expand, but changed into enormous holding units, to which the mentally ill were sent and from which many never emerged. Once again sliding to the bottom of the list of social priorities, the mentally ill were often treated with brutality. At best, they suffered from benign indifference to anything more than their needs for shelter and food.   8

Such had been the condition of public mental hospitals for nearly eighty years as World War II came to a close. Periodic efforts at reform had left them largely untouched. Over one-half million patients languished in their wards, accounting for half of all the occupants of hospital beds in the country. The state hospitals had swelled to bloated proportions. Pilgrim State Hospital on Long Island, New York's largest, held nearly 20,000 patients. St. Elizabeths in Washington, D.C., the only mental hospital operated directly by the federal government, had its own railroad and post office. Most facilities, located away from major population centers, used patients to work large farms on their grounds, thus defraying a good part of the costs of running the institution.   9

10   A new generation of psychiatrists, returning from the war, began to express their disquiet with the system as it was. They had seen how rapid-treatment models in hospitals close to the front and the introduction of group therapy had drastically cut the morbidity of psychiatric conditions evident earlier in World War I. With the belief that patients need not spend their lives sitting idly in smoky, locked wards, they determined to tackle a situation which Albert Deutsch had described as the "shame of the states."

11   These psychiatrists and their disciples, emphasizing the desirability of preparing patients for return to the community, began to introduce reforms into the state systems. Wards that had been locked for nearly a century were opened; male and female patients were allowed to mix. Active treatment programs were begun, and many patients, particularly elderly ones, were screened prior to admission, with efforts made to divert them where possible to more appropriate settings. The effects soon became evident. More than a century of inexorable growth in state-hospital populations began to reverse itself in 1955, when the number of residents peaked at just over 558,000. The first phase of deinstitutionalization was under way.

12   A second factor was introduced at this point. In 1952, French scientists searching for a better antihistamine discovered chlorpromazine, the first medication with the power to mute and even reverse the symptoms of psychosis. Introduced in this country in 1954 under the trade name Thorazine (elsewhere the medication was called Largactil, a name that better conveys the enormous hope that accompanied its debut), the drug rapidly and permanently altered the treatment of severe mental illness. The ineffective treatment of the past, from bleedings and purgings, cold baths and whirling chairs, to barbiturates and lobotomies, were supplanted by a genuinely effective medication. Thorazine's limitations and side-effects would become better known in the future; for now the emphasis was on its ability to suppress the most flagrant symptoms of psychosis.

13   Patients bedeviled by hallucinatory voices and ridden by irrational fears, who previously could have been managed only in inpatient units, now became tractable. They still suffered from schizophrenia, still manifested the blunted emotions, confused thinking, odd postures that the disease inflicts. But the symptoms which had made it impossible for them to live outside the hospital could, in many cases, be controlled.

14   Psychiatrists still argue over whether the new ideas of hospital and community treatment or the introduction of Thorazine provided the initial push that lowered state-hospital censuses. The truth is that both factors probably played a role, with the medications allowing the new psychiatric enthusiasm for community-based care to be applied to a larger group of patients than might otherwise have been the case. The effects of the first stage of deinstitutionalization can be seen in the figures for patients resident in state psychiatric facilities. By 1965 that number had decreased gradually but steadily to 475,000.

III

15   Until the mid-1960's, deinstitutionalization had been a pragmatic innovation; its driving force was the conviction that some patients could be treated and maintained in the community. Although large-scale studies supporting this belief were lacking, psychiatrists' everyday experiences confirmed its validity. Further, control of the process of discharging patients

was solidly in the hands of mental-health professionals. By the end of the first decade of deinstitutionalization, however, the process was in the midst of being transformed.

What had begun as an empirical venture was now about to become a movement. 16 Deinstitutionalization was captured by the proponents of a variety of ideologies, who sensed its value for their causes. Although their underlying philosophies were often at odds, they agreed on what seemed a simple statement of mission: all patients should be treated in the community or in short-term facilities. The state hospitals should be closed.

Some of the earliest advocates of this position were themselves psychiatrists. Unlike 17 their predecessors, who first let light and air into the back wards, these practitioners were not content to whittle away at the number of patients in state hospitals. They sought systemic changes. The pragmatism of the psychiatrists, persuaded on their return from the war that many patients could be treated without long-term hospitalization, was transmuted into a rigid credo. No patient should be confined in a massive state facility, it was now declared. All treatment should take place in the community.

These advocates, who saw themselves as part of a new subspecialty of community psy- 18 chiatry, were heavily influenced by the sociologists of institutional life, notable Erving Goffman, the author of *Asylums.* That book, based on a year of observing patients and staff at St. Elizabeths Hospital in Washington, D.C., catalogued the ways, subtle and blatant, in which patients were forced by the demands of a large institution into an unthinking conformity of behavior and thought. The rules that constrained their behavior, Goffman wrote, derived not from a consideration of therapeutic needs, but from the desires of hospital staff members to simplify their own tasks. From Goffman's work a new syndrome was defined— "institutionalism": the progressive loss of functional abilities caused by the denial of opportunities to make choices for oneself, and leading to a state of chronic dependency. Robbed of their ability to function on their own, state-hospital patients had no alternative but to remain in an environment in which their lives were directed by others.

Community psychiatry embellished Goffman's charges. Articles in professional journals 19 began to allege that the chronic disability accompanying psychiatric illnesses, particularly schizophrenia, was not a result of the disease process itself, but an effect of archaic treatment methods in which patients were uprooted from their own communities. With the attachments of a lifetime severed, often irretrievably, patients lost the incentive and then the will to maintain their abilities to relate to others and function in social environments. Thus, state hospitals, in addition to subjecting patients to abominable physical conditions—the stuff of exposés since the 1860's—were exacerbating and embedding the very symptoms they purported to treat. The only way to prevent the development of a new generation of dysfunctional chronic patients was to close the hospitals.

Of course, alternative places of treatment would have to be created. In 1963, the new 20 community psychiatrists persuaded a President already interested in mental-health issues and a receptive Congress that, with a new approach, chronicity could be averted. The consensus that emerged was embodied in the Community Mental Health Center Act of 1963. With seed money from the federal government, the law encouraged the development of outpatient clinics in every area of the country. Ultimately, it was hoped, no citizen would live outside one of the 2,000 designated "catchment areas" in which community-based treatment could be provided.

21   Psychiatric proponents of closing the state hospitals found unlikely allies in a group of civil-libertarian attorneys who were now turning their attention to the mentally ill. Fresh from victories in the civil-rights movement, and armed with potent new constitutional interpretations that restricted the power of the state to infringe personal liberties, these lawyers sought the dismantling of state hospitals as the first step in eliminating all coercive treatment of the mentally ill. They sought this end not simply because they believed that encouraging autonomy reduced chronicity, as the community psychiatrists claimed, but because in their own hierarchy of values individual autonomy was paramount.

22   Mentally ill persons seemed particularly appropriate targets for a crusade against governmental power, for the state was depriving them of liberty—with ostensibly benevolent aims, yet in conditions that belied the goal of treatment. It appeared to these critics that ultimately the state was concerned most with maintaining imbalances of power that favored the privileged classes and with suppressing dissent. By confining and discrediting the more obstreperous members of the lower classes, the mental-health system served as a pillar of the ruling elite.

23   Critiques of this sort were not rare in the late 1960's, when skepticism of established power was, for many, a prerequisite of intellectual discourse. Its application to psychiatry was encouraged, however, by the writings of iconoclastic psychiatrists like Thomas Szasz, who maintained that mental illness was a "myth," perpetuated only as a mechanism for social control, and R. D. Laing, whose books touted the value of the psychotic experience for elevating one's perceptions of the meaning of life. Additional academic support for Szasz's views came from sociologists known as labeling theorists who believed that deviance was a creation of the person with the power so to name it.

24   Whereas the community psychiatrists initially sought to achieve their ends through a legislative reconstruction of the mental-health system, the civil-libertarian attorneys favored the judicial route. They attacked the major mechanism for entry into the public mental-health system, the statutes governing involuntary commitment. These laws, they charged, were unconstitutionally broad in allowing any mentally ill person in need of treatment to be hospitalized against his will. Surely individual liberty could not legitimately be abridged in the absence of a substantial threat to a person's life or to the life of others. In addition, they alleged that the wording of the statutes, many little changed for one hundred years, was impermissibly vague; particularly problematic for the civil libertarians were the definitions of mental illness and the circumstances that rendered one committable.

25   In an era of judicial activism, many courts, both federal and state, agreed. Involuntary commitment came to be limited to persons exhibiting danger to themselves or others; strict, criminal-law-style procedures came to be required, including judicial hearings with legal representation. As the trend in the courts became apparent, many legislatures altered their statutes in anticipation of decisions in their own jurisdictions, or in emulation of California, where civil libertarians won legislative approval of a tightened statute even without the threat of court action.

26   The final common pathway of this complex set of interests led through the state legislatures. Although concerns about better treatment for chronic patients and the enhancement of individual liberty were not foreign here, more mundane concerns made themselves felt as well. The old state mental hospitals took up a significant proportion of most state

budgets, in some jurisdictions the largest single allocation. Advocates of closing the old facilities were not reticent in claiming enormous cost savings if patients were transferred to community-based care. And even if real costs remained constant, the availability of new federal entitlement programs such as Supplemental Security Income and Medicaid, to which outpatients but not inpatients would have access, promised a shift in the cost of supporting these people from the states to the federal government.

In many states, this was the final straw. The possibility that patients could be cared for   27 in the community at less expense, perhaps with better results, and certainly with greater liberty, was an irresistible attraction. Deinstitutionalization was too valuable a tool of social policy to remain a discretionary option of state-hospital psychiatrists. It now became an avowed goal of the states. Quotas were set for reductions in state-hospital populations; timetables were drawn up for the closure of facilities. Individual discretion in the release of patients was overridden by legislative and administrative fiat. Patients were to be released at all costs. New admissions were to be discouraged, in some cases prohibited. In the words of Joseph Morrissey, if the first phase of deinstitutionalization reflected an opening of the back wards, the second phase was marked by a closing of the front door.[1]

Thus did deinstitutionalization assume the form in which we know it today.   28

IV

If a decrease in patient population is the sole measure for gauging the outcome of   29 deinstitutionalization, the success of the policy is unquestionable. From 1965 to 1975, inpatient populations in state hospitals fell from 475,000 to 193,000. By 1980, the figure was 137,000, and today all indications are that the number is even smaller. Relatively few of the state hospitals closed. The majority shrank from bustling colonies with thousands of patients to enclaves of a few hundred patients, clustered in a few buildings in largely abandoned campuses.

Yet by the mid-1970's professionals in the field and policy analysts had begun to ask   30 whether the underlying goals espoused by the advocates of deinstitutionalization were really being met. Are the majority of the mentally ill, by whatever measure one chooses to apply, better off now than before the depopulation of the state hospitals? The inescapable answer is that they are not.

A large part of the reason for the movement's failure stems from its overly optimistic   31 belief in the ability of many mentally ill persons to function on their own, without the much-maligned structure of state-hospital care. Rather than liberating patients from the constraints of institutional life, the movement to reduce the role of state hospitals merely shifted the locus of their regimented existences. Indeed, *trans*institutionalization may be a better term to describe the process that occurred. It is estimated that 750,000 chronic mentally ill persons now live in nursing homes, a figure nearly 50 percent higher than the

---

[1]A good comprehensive history of deinstitutionalization has yet to be written. The best of the existing, essay-length works is Joseph Morrissey's "Deinstitutionalizing the Mentally Ill: Process, Outcomes, and New Directions," in W. R. Grove, ed., *Deviance and Mental Illness* (Beverly Hills: Sage Publications, 1982). Morrissey focuses in particular on the experiences in Massachusetts, New York, and California.

state-hospital population at its 1955 apogee. Additional hundreds of thousands live in board-and-care homes or other group residences. Many of these facilities, particularly the nursing homes, have locked wards nearly indistinguishable from the old state hospitals. They are, in psychiatrist H. Richard Lamb's evocative phrase, the asylums in the community.

32   Many of the mentally ill, of course, have drifted away entirely from any form of care. Given the freedom to choose, they have chosen to live on the streets; according to various estimates they comprise between 40 and 60 percent of homeless persons. They filter into overcrowded shelters—as Juan Gonzalez did before becoming the agent of his fantasies on the Staten Island ferry—where they may experience fleeting contact with mental-health personnel. The lack of external structure is reflected in their internal disorganization. Whatever chance they had to wire together their shattered egos has been lost.

33   What of the hopes of the community psychiatrists that liberating patients from state hospitals would prevent the development of the chronic dependency which stigmatizes the mentally ill and inhibits their reintegration into the community? They learned a sad lesson suspected by many of their colleagues all along. The withdrawal, apathy, bizarre thinking, and oddities of behavior which Goffman and his students attributed to "institutionalism" appear even in populations maintained outside of institutions. They are the effects of the underlying psychiatric illnesses, usually schizophrenia, not of the efforts to treat those conditions. And contrary to the claims of the labeling theorists, it is the peculiar behavior of severely psychotic persons, not the fact that they were once hospitalized and "labeled" ill, that stigmatizes and isolates them in the community. Studies of discharged patients demonstrate that those who continue to display the signs of their illnesses and disrupt the lives of others are the ones who suffer social discrimination.

34   To some extent, the community psychiatrists never had a chance to test their theories. The community mental-health centers in which they envisioned care taking place were, for the most part, never built. Fewer than half of the projected 2,000 centers reached operation. Of those that did, many turned from the severely ill to more desirable patients, less disturbed, easier to treat, more gratifying, and above all, as federal subsidies were phased out, able to pay for their own care. A few model programs, working with a selected group of cooperative patients, are all the community psychiatrists have to show for their dreams. But the evidence suggests that even optimal levels of community care cannot enable many mentally ill persons to live on their own.

35   The goals of the civil libertarians, except in the narrowest sense, have fared little better. If one conceives that liberty is enhanced merely by the release of patients from the hospitals to the streets, then perhaps one might glean some satisfaction from the course of deinstitutionalization to date. But if individual autonomy implies the ability to make reasoned choices in the context of a coherent plan for one's life, then one must conclude that few of the deinstitutionalized have achieved autonomy. One study found fewer than half the residents of a large board-and-care home with a desire to change anything at all about their lives, no matter how unrealistic their objectives might be. If the façade of autonomy has been expanded, the reality has suffered.

36   Finally, and with fitting irony, not even the hope that deinstitutionalization would save money has been realized. It was originally anticipated that the closing of state hospitals would allow the transfer of their budgetary allocations to community facilities. But state

hospitals proved difficult to close. As many hospitals existed in 1980 as in 1955, despite a fourfold reduction in patients. Even with current, broad definitions of who can survive in the community, tens of thousands of patients nationwide continue to require institutional care, often long-term. They are so regressed, self-destructive, violent, or otherwise disruptive that no community can tolerate them in its midst. Moreover, the communities that derive jobs from the facilities have fought hard to preserve them. As censuses have fallen, per-capita costs of care have increased, pushed up even further by pressure to improve the level of care for those who remain. Many costs for the treatment of outpatients have been redistributed, with the federal and local governments bearing heavier burdens; but no one has ever demonstrated overall savings. Even as the quality of life for many mentally ill persons has fallen, state mental-health budgets have continued to expand.

V

Both the failure of deinstitutionalization and our seeming paralysis in correcting it stem   37
from the same source: the transformation of deinstitutionalization from a pragmatic enterprise to an ideological crusade. The goal of the first phase of the process—to treat in the community all mentally ill persons who did not require full-time supervision and might do equally well or better in alternate settings—was hardly objectionable. Had state-hospital populations been reduced in a deliberate manner, with patients released no faster than treatment, housing, and rehabilitative facilities became available in the community, the visions of psychiatry's Young Turks of the 1950's might well have been realized.

Once the release of state-hospital patients became a matter of faith, however, this in-   38
dividualized approach was thrown to the winds. In the Manichean view that soon predominated, confinement in state hospitals came to be seen as invariably bad. Freedom was always to be preferred, both for its own sake and because it had a desirable, albeit mysterious therapeutic value. Further, we came to doubt our own benevolent impulses, yielding to those who claimed that any effort to act for the welfare of others was illegitimate and doomed to end with their oppression. Thus, although we may now recognize the failure of deinstitutionalization, we as a society have been unable to reverse course; these same ideologies continue to dominate our policies not by the power of logic but by the force of habit.

It is time to rethink these presuppositions. That freedom *per se* will not cure mental   39
illness is evident from the abject condition of so many of the deinstitutionalized. More difficult to deal with is the belief that, even if the lives of hundreds of thousands of mentally ill persons have been made objectively more miserable by the emptying of our state hospitals, we have no right to deprive people of liberty, even for their own benefit. In the currently fashionable jargon of bioethics, the value of autonomy always trumps the value of beneficence.

Interestingly, this position is now being challenged by a number of our leading public   40
philosophers, who have called attention to its neglected costs. Robert Burt of the Yale Law School and Daniel Callahan of the Hastings Center, for example, have taken aim at the belief that the freedom to do as we please should be our primary societal value. This emphasis on individual autonomy, they point out, has come to mean that in making our choices, as long as we do not actively infringe on the prerogatives of others, we face no obligation

to consider them and their needs. The result has been the creation of an atomistic community in which, relieved of the duty to care for others, we pursue our goals in disregard of the suffering that surrounds us. This lack of an obligation to care for others has been transmuted in some cases into an actual duty to ignore their suffering, lest we act in such a way as to limit their autonomy.

41   Although Burt and Callahan have not addressed themselves to mental-health policy *per se,* there is no better illustration of their thesis. The right to liberty has become an excuse for failing to address, even failing to recognize, the needs of the thousands of abandoned men and women we sweep by in our streets, in our parks, and in the train and bus stations where they gather for warmth. We have persuaded ourselves that it is better to ignore them—that we have an obligation to ignore them—because their autonomy would be endangered by our concern.

42   But the impulse to act for the benefit of others is the adhesive substance that binds human communities together. A value system that looses those bonds by glorifying individual autonomy threatens the cohesion of the polity. Nobody wants to live in a society characterized by unrestrained intervention (even with benevolent intent), but that does not mean we must reject altogether the notion that doing good for others, despite their reluctance, is morally appropriate under some conditions.

43   Meaningful autonomy does not consist merely in the ability to make choices for oneself. Witness the psychotic ex-patients on the streets, who withdraw into rarely used doorways, rigidly still for hours at a time, hoping, like chameleons on the forest floor, that immobility will help them fade into the grimy urban background, bringing safety and temporary peace from a world which they envision as a terrifying series of threats. Can the choices they make, limited as they are to the selection of a doorway for the day, be called a significant embodiment of human autonomy? Or is their behavior rather to be understood on the level of a simple reflex—autonomous only in a strictly formal sense?

44   Far from impinging on their autonomy, treatment of such psychotics, even coercive treatment, would not only hold out some hope of mitigating their condition but might simultaneously increase their capacity for more sophisticated autonomous choices. To adopt the typological scheme of the philosopher Bruce Miller, patients might thereby be enabled to move from mere freedom of action to choices that reflect congruence with personal values, effective rational deliberation, and moral reflection. Our intervention, though depriving them of the right to autonomy in the short term, may enhance that quality in the long run. In such circumstances, benevolence and autonomy are no longer antagonistic principles.

VI

45   Deinstitutionalization is a remnant of a different era in our political life, one in which we sought broadly framed solutions to human problems that have defied man's creativity for millennia. In the 1960's and 70's we declared war on poverty, and we determined to wipe out injustice and bigotry; government, we believed, had the tools and resources to accomplish these ends; all that was needed was the will.

46   This set of beliefs, applied to the mentally ill, allowed us to ignore the failure of a century-and-a-half of mental-health reform in this country, in the conviction that this time

we had the answer. The problem, as it was defined, was the system of large state hospitals. Like a cancer, it could be easily excised. And the will was there.

Unfortunately, the analysis was wrong. The problems of severe mental illness have 47 proved resistant to unitary solutions. For some patients, discharge from the state hospitals was a blessing. For all too many others, it was the ultimate curse. Far from a panacea, the policy created as many problems as it solved, perhaps more. To be sure, it is never easy to admit that massive social initiatives have been misconceived. The time has come, however, to lay deinstitutionalization to rest.

It would not be difficult to outline a reasonable program to restore some sense to the 48 care of the mentally ill: moderate expansion of beds in state facilities, especially for the most severely ill patients; good community-based services for those patients—and their number is not small—who could prosper outside of an institution with proper supports; and greater authority for the state to detain and treat the severely mentally ill for their own benefit, even if they pose no immediate threat to their lives or those of others.

Deinstitutionalization has been a tragedy, but it need not be an irreversible one. 49

Are the Homeless Crazy?

Jonathan Kozol

Jonathan Kozol, author of Rachel and Her Children *(1988), published this excerpt from his book in* Harper's *in 1992.*

It is commonly believed by many journalists and politicians that the homeless of Amer- 1 ica are, in large part, former patients of large mental hospitals who were deinstitutionalized in the 1970s—the consequence, it is sometimes said, of misguided liberal opinion that favored the treatment of such persons in community-based centers. It is argued that this policy, and the subsequent failure of society to build such centers or to provide them in sufficient number, is the primary cause of homelessness in the United States.

Those who work among the homeless do not find that explanation satisfactory. While 2 conceding that a certain number of the homeless are or have been mentally unwell, they believe that, in the case of most unsheltered people, the primary reason is economic rather than clinical. The cause of homelessness, they say with disarming logic, is the lack of homes and of income with which to rent or acquire them.

They point to the loss of traditional jobs in industry (2 million every year since 1980) 3 and to the fact that half of those who are laid off end up in work that pays a poverty-level wage. They point out that since 1968 the number of children living in poverty has grown by 3 million, while welfare benefits to families with children have declined by 35 percent.

And they note, too, that these developments have occurred during a time in which the 4 shortage of low-income housing has intensified as the gentrification of our major cities has accelerated. Half a million units of low-income housing are lost each year to condominium conversion as well as to arson, demolition, or abandonment. Between 1978 and 1980, median rents climbed 30 percent for people in the lowest income sector, driving many of these families into the streets. Since 1980, rents have risen at even faster rates.

5   Hard numbers, in this instance, would appear to be of greater help than psychiatric labels in telling us why so many people become homeless. Eight million American families now use half or more of their income to pay their rent or mortgage. At the same time, federal support for low-income housing dropped from $30 billion (1980) to $7.5 billion (1988). Under Presidents Ford and Carter, 500,000 subsidized private housing units were constructed. By President Reagan's second term, the number had dropped to 25,000.

6   In our rush to explain the homeless as a psychiatric problem even the words of medical practitioners who care for homeless people have been curiously ignored. A study published by the Massachusetts Medical Society, for instance, has noted that, with the exceptions of alcohol and drug use, the most frequent illnesses among a sample of the homeless population were trauma (31 percent), upper-respiratory disorders (28 percent), limb disorders (19 percent), mental illness (16 percent), skin diseases (15 percent), hypertension (14 percent), and neurological illnesses (12 percent). Why, we may ask, of all these calamities, does mental illness command so much political and press attention? The answer may be that the label of mental illness places the destitute outside the sphere of ordinary life. It personalizes an anguish that is public in its genesis; it individualizes a misery that is both general in cause and general in application.

7   There is another reason to assign labels to the destitute and single out mental illness from among their many afflictions. All these other problems—tuberculosis, asthma, scabies, diarrhea, bleeding gums, impacted teeth, etc.—bear no stigma, and mental illness does. It conveys a stigma in the United States. It conveys a stigma in the Soviet Union as well. In both nations the label is used, whether as a matter of deliberate policy or not, to isolate and treat as special cases those who, by deed or word or by sheer presence, represent a threat to national complacence. The two situations are obviously not identical, but they are enough alike to give Americans reason for concern.

8   The notion that the homeless are largely psychotics who belong in institutions, rather than victims of displacement at the hands of enterprising realtors, spares us from the need to offer realistic solutions to the deep and widening extremes of wealth and poverty in the United States. It also enables us to tell ourselves that the despair of homeless people bears no intimate connection to the privileged existence we enjoy—when, for example, we rent or purchase one of those restored town houses that once provided shelter for people now huddled in the street.

9   What is to be made, then, of the supposition that the homeless are primarily the former residents of mental hospitals, persons who were carelessly released during the 1970s? Many of them are, to be sure. Among the older men and women in the streets and shelters, as many as one-third (some believe as many as one-half) may be chronically disturbed, and a number of these people were deinstitutionalized during the 1970s. But to operate on that assumption in a city such as New York—where nearly half the homeless are small children whose average age is six—makes no sense. Their parents, with an average age of twenty-seven, are not likely to have been hospitalized in the 1970s, either.

10   A frequently cited set of figures tells us that in 1955 the average daily census of non-federal psychiatric institutions was 677,000, and that by 1984 the number had dropped to

151,000. But these people didn't go directly from a hospital room to the street. The bulk of those who had been psychiatric patients and were released from hospitals during the 1960s and early 1970s had been living in low-income housing, many in skid-row hotels or boardinghouses. Such housing—commonly known as SRO (single-room occupancy) units—was drastically diminished by the gentrification of our cities that began in the early '70s. Almost 50 percent of SRO housing was replaced by luxury apartments or office buildings between 1970 and 1980, and the remaining units have been disappearing even more rapidly.

Even for those persons who are ill and were deinstitutionalized during the decades before 1980, the precipitating cause of homelessness in 1987 is not illness but loss of housing. SRO housing offered low-cost sanctuaries for the homeless, providing a degree of safety and mutual support for those who lived within them. They were a demeaning version of the community health centers that society had promised; they were the de facto "halfway houses" of the 1970s. For these people too—at most half of the homeless single persons in America—the cause of homelessness is lack of housing.   11

Even in those cases where mental instability is apparent, homelessness itself is often the precipitating factor. For example, many pregnant women without homes are denied prenatal care because they constantly travel from one shelter to another. Many are anemic. Many are denied essential dietary supplements by recent federal cuts. As a consequence, some of their children do not live to see their second year of life. Do these mothers sometimes show signs of stress? Do they appear disorganized, depressed, disordered? Frequently. They are immobilized by pain, traumatized by fear. So it is no surprise that when researchers enter the scene to ask them how they "feel," the resulting reports tell us that the homeless are emotionally unwell. The reports do not tell us that we have *made* these people ill. They do not tell us that illness is a natural response to intolerable conditions. Nor do they tell us of the strength and the resilience that so many of these people retain despite the miseries they must endure.   12

A writer in the *New York Times* describes a homeless woman standing on a traffic island in Manhattan. "She was evicted from her small room in the hotel just across the street," and she is determined to get revenge. Until she does, "nothing will move her from that spot. . . . Her argumentativeness and her angry fixation on revenge, along with the apparent absence of hallucinations, mark her as a paranoid." Most physicians, I imagine, would be more reserved in passing judgment with so little evidence, but this reporter makes his diagnosis without hesitation. "The paranoids of the street," he says, "are among the most difficult to help."   13

Perhaps so. But does it depend on who is offering the help? Is anyone offering to help this woman get back her home? Is it crazy to seek vengeance for being thrown into the street? The absence of anger, some psychiatrists believe, might indicate much greater illness.   14

"No one will be turned away," says the mayor of New York City, as hundreds of young mothers with their infants are turned from the doors of shelters season after season. That may sound to some like a denial of reality. "Now you're hearing all kinds of horror stories," says the President of the United States as he denies that anyone is cold or hungry or unhoused. On another occasion he says that the unsheltered "are homeless, you might say, by choice." That sounds every bit as self-deceiving.   15

16   The woman standing on the traffic island screaming for revenge until her room has been restored to her sounds relatively healthy by comparison. If 3 million homeless people did the same, and all at the same time, we might finally be forced to listen.

How to Save the Homeless Mentally Ill

Charles Krauthammer

Charles Krauthammer, a psychiatrist who changed careers to become a nationally syndicated political columnist, published this article in the New Republic *in 1988.* *

1   Hard cases make bad law. Joyce Brown is a hard case. She was one of the first persons locked up in Bellevue Hospital when New York City decided to begin sweeping the homeless mentally ill off the streets. And she was first to challenge in court her forcible hospitalization. She won, but an appeals court reversed the decision. Now that a court has upheld her right to refuse treatment, the city will release her any day now. The case, like Brown herself, is a muddle and making a muddle of the law. But it dramatically illustrates what is wrong with the current debate about the homeless mentally ill and with the limits of benevolence that our society permits itself to accord them.

2   Everything about Brown allows contradictory explanations. Court documents refer not to Joyce Brown but to Billie Boggs, the name of a local TV personality and one of the several false names Brown adopted. Is she delusional or did she choose new names the better to hide from her sisters who in the past had tried to get her hospitalized? She cut up and publicly urinated on paper money. Is that crazy or, as her lawyers claim, was she symbolically demonstrating disdain for the patronizing solicitude of strangers who gave her money? She shouted obscenities in the street. Is that the result of demented rage or was it her only effective means of warding off the busybodies of the city's Project HELP (Homeless Emergency Liaison Project) who might take her away to a hospital?

3   In sum, was she living on a grate at 2nd and East 65th because she is mentally ill or because she has chosen the life of a professional (her word) street person?

4   "A lucid and rational woman who is down on her luck," Brown's ACLU lawyer calls her. Being down on one's luck can just be that. But it can be a sign of something graver, namely the downward social mobility that is characteristic of schizophrenia and that is caused by the gradual disintegration of the personality that marks its course. The classic picture is: brilliant physics major drops out, becomes cabbie, becomes unemployed, drifts, becomes homeless. Brown was a secretary, lost her job, did drugs, wandered from sister's house to sister's house, then ended up a bag lady.

5   She is a puzzle. The first judge thought the ACLU's psychiatrists correct. The appeals court bought the city's diagnosis. Dr. Francine Cournos, the most recent court-appointed

(and thus disinterested) psychiatrist, determined that she did suffer from "a serious mental illness," that she "would benefit from medication," but that, since she refused, forcing it upon her would do more harm than good.

My guess is that Dr. Cournos is right. Brown most likely is a chronic schizophrenic. 6 But that is a condition more reliably diagnosed by observing a patient's course than by a snapshot observation. The symptoms can remit for a time. When Brown was cleaned up, dressed up, and given attention, she appeared lucid and rational in court. Left on her own, however, her course had been relentlessly downhill. The proof will come if, as is likely, she ends up back at the hospital.

But the lawyers' duel was not just over whether Brown is mentally ill. Mental illness 7 is a necessary, but not a sufficient, condition for involuntary commitment. The other condition is dangerousness: a person must also be a danger to himself or to others before he may be forcibly taken care of.

Brown's ACLU lawyers argued for the now traditional standard of dangerousness: 8 imminent danger, meaning harm—suicide or extreme neglect leading to serious injury or death—within hours or days. The city was pushing for a broader standard: eventual danger, meaning that Brown's life was such that she inevitably would come to grief, even if it could not now be foreseen exactly when and how. Maureen McLeod, one of the city's lawyers, protested having "to wait until something happens to her. It is our duty to act before it is too late."

Is it? Generally speaking, the answer is no. We don't permit preventive detention even 9 for criminals who we "know" are going to commit crimes. We have to wait and catch them. If involuntary commitment requires that dangerousness be shown, then it is not enough to say that something awful will happen eventually. By that standard, heavy smoking ought to be a criterion for commitment.

The city, trying desperately to stretch the dangerousness criterion to allow the forced 10 hospitalization of Joyce Brown, had to resort to a very strained logic. After all, Brown had spent a year on the grate without any apparent physical harm from illness, malnutrition, or exposure. As the appeals court dissent pointed out, the city's case came down to a claim that Brown would ultimately be assaulted if she continued living and acting as provocatively as she was. But there is hardly a New Yorker who is not subject to assault merely by passing through the streets of New York. It is odd to blame the pathology of the city on her and lock her up to protect her from it.

The idea of eventual harm as opposed to imminent harm is slippery and arbitrary. Brown 11 had already been exposed to all the things that the city said would do her in—traffic, disease, strangers, the elements—and had survived quite nicely. The city was reduced to arguing that her luck was going to run out. It had to make this claim because it had to prove dangerousness. But why should a civilized society have to prove that a person's mental incapacity will lead to death before it is permitted to save that person? Should not degradation be reason enough?

The standard for the involuntary commitment of the homeless mentally ill is wrong. It 12 should not be dangerousness but helplessness. We have a whole array of laws (e.g., on drug abuse and prostitution) that prohibit certain actions not primarily because they threaten life but because they degrade the person. In order to override the liberty of the severely mentally ill, one should not be forced to claim—as the city disingenuously claimed in the Brown case—that life is at stake, but that a minimal human dignity is at stake.

13   Joyce Brown is a tough case because it is at least possible that she is, in fact, not mentally ill at all, only unlucky, eccentric and willful. Fine. But you cannot make that case for thousands of other homeless people. Helen Phillips, for example, picked up in the same New York City round-up as Brown, lives in Pennsylvania Station and is convinced that plutonium is poisoning the water. For the homeless who are clearly mentally ill, why should it be necessary to convince a judge that, left alone, they will die? The vast majority won't. It should be enough to convince a judge that, left alone, they will suffer.

14   Moreover, the suffering is needless. It can be mitigated by a society that summons the courage to give the homeless mentally ill adequate care, over their objections if need be. In a hospital they will at the very least get adequate clothing and shelter. And for some, medication will relieve the torment of waking dreams.

15   What prevents us from doing this is the misguided and pernicious civil libertarian impulse that holds liberty too sacred to be overridden for anything other than the preservation of life. For the severely mentally ill, however, liberty is not just an empty word but a cruel hoax. Free to do what? To defecate in one's pants? To wander around Grand Central Station begging for sustenance? To freeze to death in Central Park? The week that Joyce Brown won her reprieve from forced medication, three homeless men were found frozen dead in New York. What does freedom mean for a paranoid schizophrenic who is ruled by voices commanded by his persecutors and rattling around in his head?

16   What to do? The New York City sweep is only the first temporary step. It yields a bath, a check-up, a diagnosis, and the beginning of treatment. The sicker patients will need long-term custodial care in a psychiatric hospital. Others might respond to treatment and graduate to the less restrictive environment of a local clinic or group home. Many of these people will fall apart and have to be swept up and cycled through the system again.

17   A sensible approach to the problem begins with the conviction that those helpless, homeless, and sick are the responsibility of the state. Society must be willing to assert control even if protection and treatment have to be given involuntarily. These people are owed asylum. Whether the asylums should be large or small, rural or urban is a matter for debate. (In my view a mix of asylum size and location would serve the widest spectrum of patients' needs.) What should by now be beyond debate is that the state must take responsibility for the homeless mentally ill. And that means asserting control over their lives at least during their most severe incapacity.

18   In 1963 President Kennedy helped launch the community mental health revolution that emptied America's state mental hospitals. Kennedy said in his message to Congress, "Reliance on the cold mercy of custodial isolation will be supplanted by the open warmth of community concern." It wasn't. In the turbulence of urban life even the mentally well have trouble finding community, let alone deriving from it any warmth. The mentally ill are even less likely to find it. Everyone is for community mental health care—until it comes to his community. This may be deplorable but it is a fact. And it is cruel to allow the mentally ill to suffer neglect pending rectification of that fact, under the assumption that until the community is ready to welcome the mentally ill, the street is better than the asylum. It is not.

19   In 1955 state psychiatric hospitals had 559,000 patients. Today there are about 130,000, a decline of 75 percent. Now, the incidence of severe mental illness has not changed. (Schizo-

phrenia, for example, afflicts about one percent of the population.) Nor have drugs and modern treatment yielded a cure rate of 75 percent. Many of the 75 percent discharged from the state hospitals have simply been abandoned. They have become an army of grate-dwellers.

Helping them will require, first, rebuilding the mental hospital system. These hospitals   20
do not have to be rural, they do not have to be massive, and they do not have to be rundown. The entire American medical care system runs on incentives. Psychiatry, social work, and nursing are not immune to the inducement that good money would offer to work with the severely ill.

Second, a new asylum system will require support for a string of less restrictive halfway   21
environments and for the personnel to run them. New York State has just announced a program to supply another element of psychiatric care: a new cadre of case workers to supervise intensively the most severely ill. They would follow the mentally ill through all parts of the system, even back onto the streets, and offer supervision, advice, and some services. But facilitators cannot be enough. If there are no beds in a state mental hospital when the patient is severely delusional or self-destructive, if there are no halfway houses during recovery or remission, then the case worker is left helpless. Anybody who has worked with the mentally ill knows that all the goodwill in the world is insufficient if the institutions are not there. Intensive case management can guide a patient through a rebuilt asylum system. Without such a system, however, they can only provide the most superficial succor. The basic facts of the homeless mentally ill, destitution and degradation, will remain unchanged.

Rebuilding an asylum system is one problem we can and should throw money at. It   22
will take a lot. The way to do it is to say to Americans: You are pained and offended by homelessness. We propose to get the most wretched, confused, and disruptive of the homeless off the streets and into clean and humane asylums. We need to pay for them. We propose capping the mortgage interest deduction: less of a tax break on your house so that others can be housed. (A cap at $20,000 would yield $1 billion of revenues annually.) A new asylum system begins with concern for the elementary dignity of the homeless mentally ill. But it does not end there. The rest of us need it too. Not just, as the cynics claim, for reasons of cleanliness, so that the comfortable bourgeois does not have his daily routine disturbed by wretchedness. Getting the homeless mentally ill off the streets is an exercise in morality, not aesthetics.

It is not our aesthetic but our moral sensibilities that are most injured by the spectacle   23
of homelessness. The city, with its army of grate-dwellers, is a school for callousness. One's natural instincts to help are suppressed every day. Moreover, they have to be suppressed if one is to function: there are simply too many homeless. Thirty years ago if you saw a person lying helpless on the street, you ran to help him. Now you step over him. You know that he is not an accident victim. He lives there. Trying to get him out of his cardboard house is not a simple act of mercy of which most people are quite capable. It is a major act of social work that only the professional and the saintly can be expected to undertake. To expect saintliness of the ordinary citizen is bad social policy. Further, to expose him hourly to a wretchedness far beyond his power to remedy is to make moral insensitivity a requirement of daily living. Society must not leave the ordinary citizen with no alternative between ignoring the homeless and playing Mother Teresa. A civilized society ought to offer its people some communal act that lies somewhere in between, such as contributing to the public treasury to build an asylum system to care for these people.

24   Project HELP, the necessary first stage in such a system, is already under attack. First, because it curtails civil liberties. Second, because it sets up a revolving door: off the street, into a hospital for 21 days, then to some lightly supervised home, then back on the streets. In fact, those picked up in Project HELP have been given a high priority for scarce state hospital and other psychiatric beds. (Of the 29 New York patients who have thus far left Bellevue, 21 went to a special 50-bed unit at Creedmoor Psychiatric Center and eight have been discharged to family or adult homes.) It is hard to place the rest in state hospitals or in existing community services because there are few of either: the first as a matter of conscious policy, the second as a matter of political neglect. The way to avert the revolving-door problem is not by leaving the homeless mentally ill on the streets, but by building a long-term psychiatric care system that can accommodate them.

25   Third, charge the critics, Project HELP deals only with the very tip of the iceberg, so far 70 out of thousands. True. But those 70 are, after all, real suffering people. Moreover, as proper long-term facilities are built, there is no reason why Project HELP cannot become their triage service, assigning the homeless mentally ill to appropriate care.

26   Still, it will not do to have illusions about what can be achieved. After winning the appeal in the Brown case, Mayor Ed Koch declared himself eager "to treat her medically. I want this woman to get well, as quickly as possible." Unfortunately, chronic schizophrenics do not get well quickly. Some never get well. This is not a question of getting them off the street, giving them an injection, and letting them go. It is a question of getting people permanently off the street and into a system of comprehensive long-term care.

27   Rebuilding that system is a question of money. But being prepared to pick people up and send them into it—and keep them in it, if necessary—is a question of political will. It requires relinquishing the illusions of community and the phony promise of liberty that led to the dismantling of the system over the last 30 years. It requires a new consensus that a life of even minimal dignity is preferable to a wretchedness the homeless endure in the name of rights from which, like the world around them, they have long been alienated. Most of the homeless mentally ill picked up so far seem to share, as far as they can, that view. They have not protested the city's efforts. Less than a fifth of those hospitalized thus far have lodged legal challenges against their commitment. Two challenges, including Brown's, have met with some success. Most are grateful for a safe and warm hospital bed. What they seem to fear is being carted off to one of the wretched emergency shelters, where they feel—rightly—more endangered than they do on the street.

28   A new asylum system will not solve the homeless problem. Obviously the mentally ill are not the only category of homeless people in America. There are at least two others. Some of the homeless are not helpless but defiantly indigent. This is Joyce Brown, as she depicts herself: a professional street person, a lucid survivor who has chosen a life of drift. "It was my choice to live on the streets," she says. "It was an experience." Such people used to be called hoboes. Then there are the victims of economic calamity, such as family breakup or job loss. Often these are single mothers with children. Unlike the hoboes, they hate the street and want to get off, but lack the money, skills, and social supports. Some nonetheless try very hard: two homeless mothers who testified recently at a House hearing are actually working and putting kids through school.

We can debate for years what to do for these people. Should the hoboes who prefer   29
street life be forced off the street in the name of order? And how best to help the homeless
who are simply too poor to buy decent housing in the city? Whatever the answers to these
questions, it is both cruel and dishonest to defer addressing the mentally ill homeless—for
whom choice is not an issue and for whom poverty is a symptom, not the cause, of their
misery—until we have figured out a solution to the rest.

When the mentally ill infiltrate the ranks of another deviant group, criminals, we try   30
to segregate them and treat them differently. We do not await a cure for psychopathy or a
solution to criminality before applying different standards of treatment for the criminally in-
sane. There is no reason to defer saving the homeless mentally ill until the solution to the
rest of homelessness is found. Moreover, whatever solutions are eventually offered the non-
mentally ill homeless, they will have little relevance to those who are mentally ill. Housing
vouchers, counseling, and job training won't do much for Helen Phillips until we get the
plutonium out of the water. And since we may never succeed, she will need more than
housing vouchers, counseling, job training. She will need constant care.

The argument over how many of the homeless are mentally ill is endless. The esti-   31
mates, which range from one-quarter to three-quarters, vary with method, definition, and
ideology. But so what if even the lowest estimates are right? Even if treating the mentally
ill does not end homelessness, how can that possibly justify not treating the tens, perhaps
hundreds of thousands who would benefit from a partial solution?

In the end, the Brown case boils down to a problem of category, not a problem of prin-   32
ciple. Is she a schizophrenic or a hobo? There is inevitably some blurring of the lines between categories. (Studies of homeless families in New York have shown that many heads
of these families exhibit signs of mental illness.) But even the judge who ruled in her favor
on the grounds that she was not mentally ill upheld the city's program.

In Brown's case, we will not know which category she really belongs to until her ill-   33
ness, if it is there, plays itself out. We will find out soon enough if she is a professional street
person or a chronic schizophrenic. But there are others for whom there is no need to wait.
The diagnosis is clear, and treatment, or at least care, is available. In their cases, to wait is
a dereliction of social duty bordering on criminal neglect.

Who Goes Homeless?

E. Fuller Torrey

*E. Fuller Torrey is a clinical and research psychiatrist who has done volunteer work
in clinics for homeless mentally ill women. This article was published in* National
Review *in August 1991.*

Should the homeless be included in the statement, "Ye have the poor always with   1
you"? Given the array of individuals who have become permanent fixtures on the streets
of every American city in the last decade, the answer would appear to be yes. In fact,

however, homelessness has evolved from being a homogeneous, sphinx-like problem to being a heterogeneous cluster of interrelated problems for which many of the solutions are known. The mystery no longer is what to do, but rather why do we not do it.

2   One change in homelessness has been the perceived magnitude of the problem. Until 1987 some advocates were claiming that more than two million Americans were homeless. A 1987 study by the Urban Institute initially estimated the number to be between 567,000 and 600,000; the primary author later revised this downward to between 355,000 and 445,000. Peter H. Rossi, in his 1989 book, *Down and Out in America,* concluded that "the most believable national estimate is that at least 300,000 people are homeless each night in this country, and possibly as many as 400,000 to 500,000." In 1990, Census takers claimed to have found 228,621 homeless on the night of March 20, including 49,793 persons "visible at preidentified street locations." If it is assumed that only one-third of those actually living on the streets were counted by the Census, the total number of homeless persons would be 328,207, a number consistent with the estimates by both the Urban Institute and Rossi.

CHANGING CLIMATES

3   Another change is a decrease in the public's tolerance for the homeless. In New York City, labeled by one newspaper as "Calcutta on the Hudson," police evicted the homeless from Penn Station and razed their temporary shelters in Tompkins Square Park. In Washington, D.C., a right-to-shelter law was rescinded in a 1990 referendum, and local police began enforcing a city ordinance against begging. Atlanta's Mayor Maynard Jackson in 1991 asked the City Council to impose stiff penalties, including up to sixty days in jail, for aggressive begging or sleeping in vacant buildings.

4   Perhaps most surprising has been the decreased sympathy for the homeless in towns and cities traditionally thought of as bastions of liberalism. In Santa Monica, which serves free meals daily on the City Hall lawn, a 1990 poll showed voters favoring tougher law enforcement against the homeless. In Berkeley, police regularly make sweeps of People's Park, and across the Bay, San Franciscans overwhelmingly picked homelessness as the city's biggest problem—bigger than drugs, crime, or AIDS—in a newspaper poll. Indeed, according to *San Francisco Chronicle* columnist Cyra McFadden, "You could get rich in this town right now by selling T-shirts reading, 'Eat the homeless.'" Decreasing public tolerance does not by itself produce any more solutions to the homelessness problem than did the earlier indulgences of public guilt, but it does tend to force harder thinking about solutions. Shelters and soup kitchens provide short-term respite from serious thinking about long-term solutions.

5   Probably the most significant shift in debates about the homeless has been a growing consensus that they are not a monolithic group, but rather composed of three distinct groups. Eliciting the most sympathy from the public are the down-on-my-luck individuals and families, especially children. Economic recession, shrinking availability of low-income housing, and marginal job skills have affected this group. Eliciting somewhat less sympathy are homeless individuals with serious mental illnesses especially schizophrenia, because

many people are frightened of them and do not realize that they have a brain disease that places them in the same category as people with Alzheimer's disease. It has been estimated that there are now twice as many schizophrenics living in public shelters and on the streets as there are in all state and county psychiatric hospitals. Eliciting by far the least public sympathy are the alcoholics and drug abusers. Many of them use public shelters and soup kitchens in order to save their money to feed their addiction, and they panhandle the most aggressively.

It is widely agreed that approximately half of all the homeless have an alcohol and/or   6
drug problem; some of these are also mentally ill and/or have marginal job skills. The mentally ill account for approximately one-third; this percentage is lower in cities with relatively good public psychiatric services (e.g., Salt Lake City) and higher in cities where such services are abysmal (e.g., Los Angeles, Houston, Miami). The pure down-on-my-luck group is relatively small (about 15 per cent) although very visible in stories about the homeless; advocates learned long ago that this group most effectively elicits support for their cause.

SEPARATING THE STRANDS

Henry J. Kaiser once wrote that "problems are only opportunities in work clothes."   7
This is certainly true for homelessness, which is really three separate problems corresponding to these three groups.

The easiest of the three problems is what to do with the mentally ill. Their homeless-   8
ness is a consequence of deinstitutionalization and the subsequent breakdown of public psychiatric services. A 1983 study of discharges from Metropolitan State Hospital in Boston, for example, found that 27 per cent of all discharged patients became at least intermittently homeless within six months of discharge. A similar study in 1986 of discharges from Columbus State Hospital in Ohio reported that 36 per cent were homeless within six months. Furthermore, the number of beds in state mental hospitals was reduced from 552,000 in 1955 to 108,000 in 1986. As was pointed out in *The 1990 Annual Report of the Interagency Council on the Homeless,* given the 41 per cent increase in the population of the United States since 1955, if there had been no deinstitutionalization there would be 800,000 state psychiatric beds today, nearly eight times the actual number.

The major reason for the failure of public psychiatric services has been a fiscal one. It   9
is not, however, a question of *how much* is being spent, as is commonly supposed; the approximately $20 billion in public funds currently being spent each year is probably sufficient to buy first-class services if it were utilized properly. Rather, the problem is *how these services are funded.* Until the early 1960s, approximately 96 per cent of public psychiatric services were funded by the states, with the other 4 per cent split between federal and local sources. As deinstitutionalization got under way, the released patients were made eligible for federal Supplemental Security Income (SSI), Social Security Disability Income (SSDI), Medicaid, Medicare, food stamps, and other federal subsidies. By 1985 it was estimated that the states' share of the cost for the mentally ill had fallen to 53 per cent of the total, while the federal share had risen to 38 per cent (it is undoubtedly several percentage points higher by now).

10   The shift of the fiscal burden from the states to the Federal Government was not, by itself, a disaster. The problems arose out of how the various fiscal supports were related to each other. For example, the patients in Metropolitan State Hospital and Columbus State Hospital mentioned above were primarily the fiscal responsibilities of the states of Massachusetts and Ohio as long as they were in the hospitals. Once discharged, they became primarily the responsibility of the Federal Government. If such patients relapse and need rehospitalization, as most of them do, they typically are sent to the psychiatric ward of a general hospital, where Medicaid pays most of the bill. Elderly psychiatric patients were similarly transferred from state hospitals to nursing homes not because the care was necessarily better (often it was worse) but rather because such a transfer made them eligible for Medicare and Medicaid. Even with the states coming up with Medicaid matching funds, it was extremely cost-effective, from the point of view of state government, to shift the fiscal burden to the Federal Government.

11   The fiscal organization of public psychiatric services in the United States is more thought-disordered than most of their patients. The incentives all lead to discharging psychiatric patients from state facilities as quickly as possible; there is no incentive to worry about where they go, whether they get aftercare, or whether they become homeless. Indeed, if you tried to set up a system for funding public psychiatric services in a way which would guarantee its failure, you would set up just such a system as we have created.

12   The solution is to meld federal and state funding streams into a single stream with responsibility placed at the state level, unless states wish to delegate to the county level (as do California, Minnesota, and Wisconsin). All incentives to shift the fiscal burden to the Federal Government must be removed. States would rapidly learn that it is cost-effective to provide good psychiatric aftercare, because the costs of repeated rehospitalizations are very high. Continuity of care between inpatient and outpatient programs would become the rule rather than the exception. Existing model programs for the homeless mentally ill such as Seattle's El Rey Residential Treatment Facility or the widely praised Weingart Center in Los Angeles, which combine treatment, housing, and rehabilitation, would spread quickly. State laws making it difficult to hospitalize obviously impaired individuals would be amended as it became apparent that good psychiatric care does not cost more in the long run than not-so-benign neglect. And the homeless mentally ill, including the emblematic bag ladies, would become a thing of the past.

NOW FOR THE HARDER ONES

13   The problem of the homeless mentally ill is easy to solve compared with the problems of the other groups. Alcoholics have always made up a significant percentage of the homeless population, from the days of the early American almshouses to the hobos who rode the rails in the years before World War II. When one is addicted to alcohol or drugs the highest priority is to save as much money as possible to feed that addiction. Present homeless policies, which in some cities have guaranteed free beds and food for everyone who asks, have probably exacerbated rather than relieved the problem of homeless substance abusers.

Although there is no policy which can force a person to help himself, it stands to rea-   14
son that public programs should not make alcohol and drug problems worse. All substance
abusers who have any income should be required to pay a certain proportion of it for shelter and food and should also be required to attend regular meetings of Alcoholics Anonymous or Narcotics Anonymous. Rehabilitation programs including vocational training
should be readily available, but abstinence should be a requirement for participation. For
those who refuse to meet minimal requirements for such publicly funded programs, there
is a network of private and church-run shelters (such as the Salvation Army's) which have
provided exemplary care for alcoholics and drug abusers for many years.

Solutions to the down-on-my-luck homeless are both easy and difficult at the same   15
time. Many of them are victims of reduced stocks of low-income housing. It does not take
a PhD to realize that when single-room-occupancy (SRO) hotel units were reduced from
127,000 to 14,000, as happened in New York City between 1970 and 1983, or from 1,680
to 15, as happened in Nashville between 1970 and 1990, some people would be left with
nowhere to live.

But housing is the easy half of solving the down-on-my-luck problem. Many of these   16
people have a poor education and marginal job skills. As the workplace demands increasing technological skills for even entry-level positions, this group is likely to continue to
grow. Solutions require the whole panoply of often discussed but rarely available services
from remedial education to vocational training, job coaching, transitional employment, supported employment, and counseling. This is certainly the most difficult and most expensive
segment of the homeless population to rehabilitate, but not rehabilitating them is also
expensive.

As long as programs for the mentally ill, substance abusers, and consumers of low-   17
income housing are part of the ongoing political tug-of-war between federal and state governments, solutions to the problems of the homeless will be elusive. The homeless are, in
one sense, daily reminders of the lack of resolution of this issue.

In the area of public psychiatric and substance-abuse services, the Federal Government   18
has a miserable record of achievement. Exhibit A is the federally funded Community Mental Health Centers program, which wasted over $3 billion setting up 769 centers, most of
which never did what they were intended to do. It seems likely that service programs conceived by federal officials, who are too far removed from the real world, will almost inevitably fail.

What, then, should be the Federal Government's role? The setting of minimal standards   19
and enforcement of such standards through fiscal incentives and disincentives is necessary,
e.g., expecting states to reduce the mentally ill homeless to a specified level and reducing
federal subsidies if they fail. The enforcement function should probably be vested in the Office of Inspector General in departments such as Health and Human Services (HHS) or Housing and Urban Development (HUD). Model programs such as those under the McKinney
Act, the HHS-HUD collaborative program to improve housing and services for the homeless
mentally ill, or Senator Pete Domenici's recently introduced "Projects to Aid the Transition
from Homelessness" bill, should be encouraged. The problem is that from most states' point
of view, such programs are not regarded merely as models, but rather as an ongoing federal
commitment to replace the efforts of the states themselves.

20   The homeless, then, will be with us until we are able to resolve the issue of federal versus state responsibility for social programs. Hallucinating quietly next to vacant buildings, lying under bushes in the park, or aggressively accosting strangers on the street, the homeless represent not only a failure of social programs, but more broadly a failure of government at all levels.

FOR CLASS DISCUSSION

1. Analyze and evaluate the debate on the mentally ill homeless by applying the first set of guide questions from page 465. How do you account for the disagreements among the disputants? This is a particularly good controversy for examining disagreements based on disputes about facts as well as values.

2. Many of these arguments turn on knotty definitional questions: When is a person mentally ill? When is a person homeless? At what point does a person lose his or her rights as a free, autonomous individual? Which articles manage the definition part of their argument the most effectively?

3. Which proposals for handling the mentally ill homeless are the most persuasively supported?

4. Choose one of the arguments for closer analysis, applying the second set of guide questions on pages 465–66.

OPTIONAL WRITING ASSIGNMENT   You are a newly hired research assistant to Senator Sarah Goodperson. For the past several weeks Senator Goodperson has been lobbied intensely by the National Coalition for the Homeless. The lobbyists are urging her to support new legislation calling for the construction of 2.5 million low-cost, subsidized housing units in major cities across the United States. The senator also has been lobbied with almost equal force by organizations devoted to reducing federal taxes and trimming what they see as a huge welfare bureaucracy. In addition, a coalition of big-city mayors, in partnership with an association of psychiatrists, has been calling for the rebuilding of state mental hospitals to provide treatment for the mentally ill homeless. These persons have sent Senator Goodperson copies of Charles Krauthammer's "How to Save the Homeless Mentally Ill" (pp. 648–53) and are urging her to support Krauthammer's proposal.

Senator Goodperson writes you a memo asking you to research the issue of the mentally ill homeless. "Should I support Krauthammer's proposal?" she asks. "Are there alternative approaches? Based on your research, which approach do you most recommend and why?"

Your task: Write a white paper for Senator Goodperson, giving your argument for or against Krauthammer's proposal.

SAME-SEX MARRIAGE*

Here Comes the Groom
A (Conservative) Case for Gay Marriage
Andrew Sullivan

Andrew Sullivan is a former editor of the New Republic. *This article appeared in the* New Republic *in August 1989.*

Last month in New York, a court ruled that a gay lover had the right to stay in his deceased partner's rent-control apartment because the lover qualified as a member of the deceased's family. The ruling deftly annoyed almost everybody. Conservatives saw judicial activism in favor of gay rent control: three reasons to be appalled. Chastened liberals (such as the *New York Times* editorial page), while endorsing the recognition of gay relationships, also worried about the abuse of already stretched entitlements that the ruling threatened. What neither side quite contemplated is that they both might be right, and that the way to tackle the issue of unconventional relationships in conventional society is to try something both more radical and more conservative than putting courts in the business of deciding what is and is not a family. That alternative is the legalization of civil gay marriage.

The New York rent-control case did not go anywhere near that far, which is the problem. The rent-control regulations merely stipulated that a "family" member had the right to remain in the apartment. The judge ruled that to all intents and purposes a gay lover is part of his lover's family, inasmuch as a "family" merely means an interwoven social life, emotional commitment, and some level of financial interdependence.

It's a principle now well established around the country. Several cities have "domestic partnership" laws, which allow relationships that do not fit into the category of heterosexual marriage to be registered with the city and qualify for benefits that up till now have been reserved for straight married couples. San Francisco, Berkeley, Madison, and Los Angeles all have legislation, as does the politically correct Washington, D.C., suburb, Takoma Park. In these cities, a variety of interpersonal arrangements qualify for health insurance, bereavement leave, insurance, annuity and pension rights, housing rights (such as rent-control apartments), adoption and inheritance rights. Eventually, according to gay lobby groups, the aim is to include federal income tax and veterans' benefits as well. A recent

---

*For an additional argument on this issue, see student writer Sam Isaacson's essay on pages 294–96.

case even involved the right to use a family member's accumulated frequent-flier points. Gays are not the only beneficiaries; heterosexual "live-togethers" also qualify.

4   There's an argument, of course, that the current legal advantages extended to married people unfairly discriminate against people who've shaped their lives in less conventional arrangements. But it doesn't take a genius to see that enshrining in the law a vague principle like "domestic partnership" is an invitation to qualify at little personal cost for a vast array of entitlements otherwise kept crudely under control.

5   To be sure, potential DPs have to prove financial interdependence, shared living arrangements, and a commitment to mutual caring. But they don't need to have a sexual relationship or even closely mirror old-style marriage. In principle, an elderly woman and her live-in nurse could qualify. A couple of uneuphemistically confirmed bachelors could be DPs. So could two close college students, a pair of seminarians, or a couple of frat buddies. Left as it is, the concept of domestic partnership could open a Pandora's box of litigation and subjective judicial decision-making about who qualifies. You either are or are not married; it's not a complex question. Whether you are in a "domestic partnership" is not so clear.

6   More important, the concept of domestic partnership chips away at the prestige of traditional relationships and undermines the priority we give them. This priority is not necessarily a product of heterosexism. Consider heterosexual couples. Society has good reason to extend legal advantages to heterosexuals who choose the formal sanction of marriage over simply living together. They make a deeper commitment to one another and to society; in exchange, society extends certain benefits to them. Marriage provides an anchor, if an arbitrary and weak one, in the chaos of sex and relationships to which we are all prone. It provides a mechanism for emotional stability, economic security, and the healthy rearing of the next generation. We rig the law in its favor not because we disparage all forms of relationship other than the nuclear family, but because we recognize that not to promote marriage would be to ask too much of human virtue. In the context of the weakened family's effect upon the poor, it might also invite social disintegration. One of the worst products of the New Right's "family values" campaign is that its extremism and hatred of diversity has disguised this more measured and more convincing case for the importance of the marital bond.

7   The concept of domestic partnership ignores these concerns, indeed directly attacks them. This is a pity, since one of its most important objectives—providing some civil recognition for gay relationships—is a noble cause and one completely compatible with the defense of the family. But the decision to go about it is not to undermine straight marriage; it is to legalize old-style marriage for gays.

8   The gay movement has ducked this issue primarily out of fear of division. Much of the gay leadership clings to notions of gay life as essentially outsider, anti-bourgeois, radical. Marriage, for them, is co-optation into straight society. For the Stonewall generation, it is hard to see how this vision of conflict will ever fundamentally change. But for many other gays—my guess, a majority—while they don't deny the importance of rebellion 20 years ago and are grateful for what was done, there's now the sense of a new opportunity. A need to rebel has quietly ceded to a desire to belong. To be gay and to be bourgeois no longer seems such an absurd proposition. Certainly, since AIDS, to be gay and to be responsible has become a necessity.

9   Gay marriage squares several circles at the heart of the domestic partnership debate. Unlike domestic partnership, it allows for recognition of gay relationships, while casting no

aspersions on traditional marriage. It merely asks that gays be allowed to join in. Unlike domestic partnership, it doesn't open up avenues for heterosexuals to get benefits without the
responsibilities of marriage, or a nightmare of definitional litigation. And unlike domestic
partnership, it harnesses to an already established social convention the yearnings for stability and acceptance among a fast-maturing gay community.

Gay marriage also places more responsibilities upon gays: it says for the first time that   10
gay relationships are not better or worse than straight relationships, and that the same is
expected of them. And it's clear and dignified. There's a legal benefit to a clear, common
symbol of commitment. There's also a personal benefit. One of the ironies of domestic partnership is that it's not only more complicated than marriage, it's more demanding, requiring an elaborate statement of intent to qualify. It amounts to a substantial invasion of
privacy. Why, after all, should gays be required to prove commitment before they get married in a way we would never dream of asking of straights?

Legalizing gay marriage would offer homosexuals the same deal society now offers het-   11
erosexuals: general social approval and specific legal advantages in exchange for a deeper
and harder-to-extract-yourself-from commitment to another human being. Like straight marriage, it would foster social cohesion, emotional security, and economic prudence. Since
there's no reason gays should not be allowed to adopt or be foster parents, it could also help
nurture children. And its introduction would not be some sort of radical break with social
custom. As it has become more acceptable for gay people to acknowledge their loves publicly, more and more have committed themselves to one another for life in full view of their
families and their friends. A law institutionalizing gay marriage would merely reinforce a
healthy social trend. It would also, in the wake of AIDS, qualify as a genuine public health
measure. Those conservatives who deplore promiscuity among some homosexuals should
be among the first to support it. Burke could have written a powerful case for it.

The argument that gay marriage would subtly undermine the unique legitimacy of   12
straight marriage is based upon a fallacy. For heterosexuals, straight marriage would remain
the most significant—and only legal—social bond. Gay marriage could only delegitimize
straight marriage if it were a real alternative to it, and this is clearly not true. To put it
bluntly, there's precious little evidence that straights could be persuaded by any law to have
sex with—let alone marry—someone of their own sex. The only possible effect of this sort
would be to persuade gay men and women who force themselves into heterosexual marriage (often at appalling cost to themselves and their families) to find a focus for their family instincts in a more personally positive environment. But this is clearly a plus, not a
minus: gay marriage could both avoid a lot of tortured families and create the possibility for
many happier ones. It is not, in short, a denial of family values. It's an extension of them.

Of course, some would claim that any legal recognition of homosexuality is a de facto   13
attack upon heterosexuality. But even the most hardened conservatives recognize that gays
are a permanent minority and aren't likely to go away. Since persecution is not an option
in a civilized society, why not coax gays into traditional values rather than rail incoherently
against them?

There's a less elaborate argument for gay marriage: it's good for gays. It provides role   14
models for young gay people who, after the exhilaration of coming out, can easily lapse into
short-term relationships and insecurity with no tangible goal in sight. My own guess is that
most gays would embrace such a goal with as much (if not more) commitment as straights.

Even in our society as it is, many lesbian relationships are virtual textbook cases of monogamous commitment. Legal gay marriage could also help bridge the gulf often found between gays and their parents. It could bring the essence of gay life—a gay couple—into the heart of the traditional straight family in a way the family can most understand and the gay offspring can most easily acknowledge. It could do as much to heal the gay-straight rift as any amount of gay rights legislation.

15   If these arguments sound socially conservative, that's no accident. It's one of the richest ironies of our society's blind spot toward gays that essentially conservative social goals should have the appearance of being so radical. But gay marriage is not a radical step. It avoids the mess of domestic partnership; it is humane; it is conservative in the best sense of the word. It's also practical. Given the fact that we already allow legal gay relationships, what possible social goal is advanced by framing the law to encourage those relationships to be unfaithful, undeveloped, and insecure?

Against Gay Marriage
What Heterosexuality Means

Dennis O'Brien

Writer Dennis O'Brien published this article in Commonweal *in November 1991.*

1   My firmest conviction on this debate is that it will end with no conviction. To reach some common view would require an agreement on the meaning of *marriage*—no easy subject; an agreement on whether homosexuality has a meaning—or is it just a natural fact; finally, we would have to find a tone of "sexual wisdom" for the discussion—we are usually too passionate about our passions for wise dispassion.

2   The very day that *Commonweal* asked me to comment on the subject, I happened to read a personality squib in the local paper about the movie actors Kurt Russell and Goldie Hawn. It seems that they are "together" after previous unhappy marriages. They now have a four-year-old son and they would consider marriage if their current arrangement proved difficult to the youngster. Since Hollywood is usually the avant-garde of the culture, it may be that marriage of any kind is a charming anachronism. I assume that the reluctance to enter marriage is that it destroys the honesty and commitment of "true love." Genuine commitment does not need the sanctions of judge or priest. In fact, it shows a weakening of ardor to rest fidelity on formality.

3   I have no doubt that there are deep and abiding homosexual commitments. What would formal marriage add? Legal marriages do help in divorce proceedings because there is a known system for dissolution and disposition of claims. If legal rights are an issue, they can, of course, be settled by (non-marriage) civil contracts. Should Kurt and Goldie break up this side of marriage, there are "palimony" settlements and similar suits have been brought for homosexual partnerships.

4   If the sole meaning of "marriage" is legal, then marriage of any sex may become a matter of "indifference." Perhaps truly loving couples should be as "indifferent" to marriage as

our Hollywood pair. That there have been homosexual palimony cases would suggest that the law already brings homosexual partners into some sort of "coupled" network of legal restriction. It seems a short step from palimony to matrimony.

If there is an *issue* regarding homosexual marriage, it must rest on some deeper political or "religious" concerns. I do not mean what the newspapers think of as "political": who has the clout to carry the day. I am interested in the basic values of the American *polis.* What does our society express about itself and the human condition through its sanctioned institutions?

One might believe that the American *polis* avoids deep value issues; America is a debating society of opposing philosophies and life styles. Arguments are settled, if necessary or at all, by clout not cultural commitment. On the other hand, it is doubtful that any *polis* can exist at all without a cultural sense, however suppressed. American democracy rests on a powerful set of assumptions about human nature and society which legitimate the character of its institutions. Would homosexual marriage harmonize with our underlying values? I am not certain I can answer that question, but it is worth pointing out that "nonnormal" marriages have previously received constitutional scrutiny. The most famous are "the Mormon cases" which ruled on the legitimacy of polygamy (as a religiously protected right). The Supreme Court struck down polygamous marriage in part on *democratic* grounds. "Polygamy leads to the patriarchal principle . . . which, when applied to large communities, fetters the people in stationary despotism, while that principle cannot long exist in connection with monogamy" *Reynolds* v. *United States* 98 US 145 (1879).

I am not overwhelmed by the sociology of the Court's opinion, but the justices were correct in attempting to connect marriage customs with the deeper values of the society. If homosexual marriage were to be seriously advanced, similar large concepts should be brought into play.

Are there potential problems for the *polis* if homosexual marriage becomes a legally sanctioned institution? There are some obvious social concerns. Heterosexual arrangements remain the mainstay for creating the next generation—which is not an incidental issue for any continuing social body. Surrounding heterosexual arrangements with political blessing and legal structures could be judged to have special social utility on that ground alone. Giving heterosexual marriage a positive place in the legal structure does not, however, imply that homosexual relations need suffer from negative legal stricture. What consenting adults do, and so forth—but the state is not obliged to bless every bedroom. (The Athenian *polis,* while it practiced a form of sanctioned homosexuality, did not amalgamate that practice to marriage.)

A *religious* position on homosexual marriage would go beyond the merely legal and the larger political values. (I believe that homosexuality should not be discussed as a straightforward *moral* issue; *moral* issues generally deal with specific acts but the concern here is a life choice. The church has thought traditionally that a religiously celibate life choice was more exalted than marriage. For all that, marriage did not thus become "immoral.")

Is the *meaning of marriage* (as religious sacrament) consonant with the *meaning of homosexuality*? The latter meaning may be even less recoverable than the former. To the extent that superficial accounts of homosexuality treat it as a direct expression of a biologically determined appetite, they displace it from the web of cultural development that would assay the worth of homosexual life patterns. If all there is to homosexuality (or heterosexuality) is natural determinism, we could remove it from the human spiritual agenda.

11   I would like to believe that sex is a human artifact for all that it has a biological base. (Human eating habits are not just feeding behavior. The prevalence of fantasy in sex certainly suggests heavy human seasoning of an essential appetite.) Assuming that sex has a human meaning, it seems plausible that homosexual life patterns differ from heterosexual if for no other reason than that male bodies and female bodies are different. If we were only accidentally related to our bodies (angels in disguise, ghosts in a machine), then how these mechanisms got sexual kicks might not *fundamentally* invade our sense of person and human value. *Playboy* and Puritanism both assume the triviality of bodies; they are for playful/sinful distraction only. Catholics seem more stuck with incarnation—and somewhere along that line would be a Catholic answer to the question posed.

12   I am no fan at all of the "natural law" arguments about procreative sexuality as presented in *Humanae vitae.* These arguments assume that one can read the moral law off the book of nature. Social Darwinists argued that because humans are naturally aggressive, war was morally desirable. (The same mistake occurs when someone argues from a natural urge for hetero/homosexuality to the moral obligation to carry forward the urge.) But for all that nature gives no dogmas, nature presents an ur-text for human meaning. Heterosexual marriage is a deep story developed from the ur-text of genital biology.

13   What difference could there possibly be in homosexual relations? Well, perhaps homosexual relations are better sex. After all, one knows one's own sex's response better than the heterosexual response. "It takes one to know one!" (As Oscar Wilde said about masturbation: "cleaner, more efficient, and you meet a better class of people.") The sexiness of homosexuality may or may not be the case, but I believe that reflection on hetero/homosexual embodiments would reveal quite different erotic story lines. It seems eminently plausible that bedding with an other (strange?) sex is as different as travel abroad can be from staying at home.

14   One could conclude that the homosexual story line was valuable—perhaps more valuable than the heterosexual. But not all things are possible in either variation. There are distinct spiritual problems with homosexual "marriage" in the Jewish and Christian traditions. Franz Rosenzweig states a deep truth when he attempts to explicate Jewish "faith": "the belief of the Jew is not the content of a testimony, but rather the product of reproduction. The Jew, engendered a Jew, attests his belief by continuing to procreate the Jewish people."

15   Underneath all the heated argument about artificial contraception, abortion, population control, family planning and the lot, the traditional Jewish *mitzvah* for procreation expresses human solidarity with a Creator God. The Christian claim for an embodied God moves in the same spiritual territory. (I do not imply that family size scales one up in blessedness.)

16   Kierkegaard regarded marriage as spirit's proper synthesis of recollection and hope. Without getting into deep theological water, it is certainly the case that heterosexual marriage normally carries with it the meaning of recollection and hope. Normative heterosexual marriage recollects parents in the act of parenting and literally embodies hope in the bringing forth of children. Homosexuals may, of course, recall parents and be hopeful for the future but they do not, of course, embody a family history. In so far as these Judaic faiths

are not finally enacted in the realm of attitudes, they seem destined to give a special place to embodiment. Procreative "marriage" seems to me to be a special and irreplaceable central symbol of the tradition.

Gay Rights, Gay Marriages

John Leo

Syndicated columnist John Leo published this argument in U.S. News and World Report *in May 1993, at the time that the prohibition of same-sex marriage was being tested by the courts in Hawaii.*

The next big gay controversy is here, touched off by the state supreme court of Hawaii. The court opened the door to legal gay marriage. It ruled that Hawaii's ban on same-sex marriages "is presumed to be unconstitutional" unless the state can show, in a lower-court trial, that the prohibition is "justified by compelling state interests." 1

The issue has been bubbling toward the surface for years, mostly in the churches, partly in campaigns around the country for city "domestic partners" legislation that offers gays some spousal benefits of married couples. 2

During the week of the gay march on Washington, gay marriage was the centerpiece of a long article in the *New Republic* by its editor, Andrew Sullivan, a gay, conservative Catholic. He called it "the critical measure necessary for full gay equality." 3

There's a traditionalist argument in favor: Society ought to sanction almost any arrangement that promotes personal commitment and social stability. But the most common argument, like most advanced by interest groups these days, is a charge of bias, inequality and "privileging." If gays are the social equals of straights, why can't they marry too? 4

This is a potent argument. Egalitarian arguments seem strong: privileging seems unfair. But all societies privilege certain activities and practices and discourage others. Because of family disintegration, we are finally trying to privilege two-parent families and discourage one-parent families. 5

We privilege parents over nonparents in some ways because we know that parenting is difficult and expensive and essential to society. Marriage is privileged for the same reason. Society has a crucial stake in protecting the connection between sex, procreation and a commitment to raise children. If it didn't, why would the state be involved with marriage at all? All couplings, gay or straight, would be merely private matters, settled by contract or handshake, not licenses. 6

TRUE PARTNERS

Are gays entitled to many benefits that married couples get? I think so. Committed couples should have the same health-plan coverage as straights, for instance. When a lover dies, a gay or lesbian shouldn't lose an apartment, or the right to control the funeral. 7

8   But this can come about through domestic-partner legislation or registered bonding ceremonies. The insistence on calling these arrangements marriages is quite another matter. It's an attempt to overhaul tradition, language and common sense for perhaps one tenth of one percent of the population interested in appropriating heterosexual practice and ceremony.

9   Many gays, like Andrew Sullivan, favor marriage because they honor it, but another motive is at work, too. Some gay activists are frankly interested in diluting or breaking down heterosexual norms and downgrading the nuclear family to one lifestyle choice among many.

10   But marriage isn't just about lifestyle or personal fulfillment. It's also about children and the continuation of the human project. Popping loose the connection between marriage and procreation (or at least the possibility of procreation) seems like an extraordinary step, profoundly altering a conception of marriage that goes back thousands of years.

11   We don't even know what the immediate effects would be. Would it effectively convert the emerging policy of tolerance for gays into one of de facto approval? For instance, at some public schools, 8- and 9-year-olds are currently being taught about gay sex. Parents are protesting, but if the state says gay and straight marriages are equal, apart from "age appropriateness," what grounds for protest would be left?

12   Polls show that large majorities of Americans approve of some spousal rights for gays but reject the idea of gay marriage. That seems to point to a compromise based on domestic-partner laws. But large majorities do not always count for much in the age of litigation.

13   It's worth noting that the apparent victory for gay marriage in Hawaii turned on the word "sex" in the state's equal-protection law forbidding discrimination "because of race, religion, sex, or ancestry." (The state law doesn't protect sexual orientation.)

14   This seems to mean that prohibitions against sex discrimination, which most states have, can be contorted into justifications for gay marriage. Julian Eule, a constitutional-law expert at the University of California at Los Angeles, said the court's reasoning "converts all homosexuality issues into gender issues." Quite a trick.

15   The court itself found that a right to same-sex marriage "is not so rooted in the traditions and collective conscience of Hawaii's people that failure to recognize it would violate the fundamental principles of liberty and justice. . . ." But it managed to conjure up the right anyway by stretching the meaning of sex discrimination.

16   This is yet another example of our judicial problem. We vote for one thing; relentless litigation and imaginative judges turn it into something wildly different. In this case, it may amount to a fundamental reordering of society, all done without any input from the people.

Gay Marriage, an Oxymoron

Lisa Schiffren

This article appeared in the New York Times *on March 23, 1996. Lisa Schiffren is a freelance journalist who was a speechwriter for Vice President Dan Quayle.*

As study after study and victim after victim testify to the social devastation of the sexual revolution, easy divorce and out-of-wedlock motherhood, marriage is fashionable again. And parenthood has transformed many baby boomers into advocates of bourgeois norms.

Indeed, we have come so far that the surprise issue of the political season is whether homosexual "marriage" should be legalized. The Hawaii courts will likely rule that gay marriage is legal, and other states will be required to accept those marriages as valid.

Considering what a momentous change this would be—a radical redefinition of society's most fundamental institution—there has been almost no real debate. This is because the premise is unimaginable to many, and the forces of political correctness have descended on the discussion, raising the cost of opposition. But one may feel the same affection for one's homosexual friends and relatives as for any other, and be genuinely pleased for the happiness they derive from relationships, while opposing gay marriage for principled reasons.

"Same-sex marriage" is inherently incompatible with our culture's understanding of the institution. Marriage is essentially a lifelong compact between a man and woman committed to sexual exclusivity and the creation and nurture of offspring. For most Americans, the marital union—as distinguished from other sexual relationships and legal and economic partnerships—is imbued with an aspect of holiness. Though many of us are uncomfortable using religious language to discuss social and political issues, Judeo-Christian morality informs our view of family life.

Though it is not polite to mention it, what the Judeo-Christian tradition has to say about homosexual unions could not be clearer. In a diverse, open society such as ours, tolerance of homosexuality is a necessity. But for many, its practice depends on a trick of cognitive dissonance that allows people to believe in the Judeo-Christian moral order while accepting, often with genuine regard, the different lives of homosexual acquaintances. That is why, though homosexuals may believe that they are merely seeking a small expansion of the definition of marriage, the majority of Americans perceive this change as a radical deconstruction of the institution.

Some make the conservative argument that making marriage a civil right will bring stability, an end to promiscuity and a sense of fairness to gay men and women. But they miss the point. Society cares about stability in heterosexual unions because it is critical for raising healthy children and transmitting the values that are the basis of our culture.

Whether homosexual relationships endure is of little concern to society. That is also true of most childless marriages, harsh as it is to say. Society has wisely chosen not to differentiate between marriages, because it would require meddling into the motives and desires of everyone who applies for a license.

In traditional marriage, the tie that really binds for life is shared responsibility for the children. (A small fraction of gay couples may choose to raise children together, but such children are offspring of one partner and an outside contributor.) What will keep gay marriages together when individuals tire of each other?

Similarly, the argument that legal marriage will check promiscuity by gay males raises the question of how a "piece of paper" will do what the threat of AIDS has not. Lesbians seem to have little problem with monogamy, or the rest of what constitutes "domestication," despite the absence of official status.

10   Finally, there is the so-called fairness argument. The Government gives tax benefits, inheritance rights and employee benefits only to the married. Again, these financial benefits exist to help couples raise children. Tax reform is an effective way to remove distinctions among earners.

11   If the American people are interested in a radical experiment with same-sex marriages, then subjecting it to the political process is the right route. For a court in Hawaii to assume that it has the power to radically redefine marriage is a stunning abuse of power. To present homosexual marriage as a fait accompli, without national debate, is a serious political error. A society struggling to recover from 30 years of weakened norms and broken families is not likely to respond gently to having an institution central to most people's lives altered.

For Better or Worse?
The Case for Gay (and Straight) Marriage

Jonathan Rauch

This article first appeared in the New Republic, *May 6, 1996.*

1   Whatever else marriage may or may not be, it is certainly falling apart. Half of today's marriages end in divorce, and, far more costly, many never begin—leaving mothers poor, children fatherless and neighborhoods chaotic. With timing worthy of Neville Chamberlain, homosexuals have chosen this moment to press for the right to marry. What's more, Hawaii's courts are moving toward letting them do so. I'll believe in gay marriage in America when I see it, but if Hawaii legalizes it, even temporarily, the uproar over this final insult to a besieged institution will be deafening.

2   Whether gay marriage makes sense—and whether straight marriage makes sense—depends on what marriage is actually for. Current secular thinking on this question is shockingly sketchy. Gay activists say: marriage is for love, and we love each other, therefore we should be able to marry. Traditionalists say marriage is for children, and homosexuals do not (or should not) have children, therefore you should not be able to marry. That, unfortunately, pretty well covers the spectrum. I say "unfortunately" because both views are wrong. They misunderstand and impoverish the social meaning of marriage.

3   So what is marriage for? Modern marriage is, of course, based upon traditions that religion helped to codify and enforce. But religious doctrine has no special standing in the world of secular law and policy (the "Christian nation" crowd notwithstanding). If we want to know what and whom marriage is for in modern America, we need a sensible secular doctrine.

4   At one point, marriage in secular society was largely a matter of business: cementing family ties, providing social status for men and economic support for women, conferring dowries, and so on. Marriages were typically arranged, and "love" in the modern sense was no prerequisite. In Japan, remnants of this system remain, and it works surprisingly well. Couples stay together because they view their marriage as a partnership: an investment in

social stability for themselves and their children. Because Japanese couples don't expect as much emotional fulfillment as we do, they are less inclined to break up. They also take a somewhat more relaxed attitude toward adultery. What's a little extracurricular love provided that each partner is fulfilling his or her many other marital duties?

In the West, of course, love is a defining element. The notion of lifelong love is charming, if ambitious, and certainly love is a desirable element of marriage. In society's eyes, however, it cannot be the defining element. You may or may not love your husband, but the two of you are just as married either way. You may love your mistress, but that certainly doesn't make her your spouse. Love helps make sense of marriage emotionally, but it is not terribly important in making sense of marriage from the point of view of social policy.   5

If love does not define the purpose of secular marriage, what does? Neither the law nor secular thinking provides a clear answer. Today marriage is almost entirely a voluntary arrangement whose contents are up to the people making the deal. There are few if any behaviors that automatically end a marriage. If a man beats his wife, which is about the worst thing he can do to her, he may be convicted of assault, but his marriage is not automatically dissolved. Couples can be adulterous ("open") yet remain married. They can be celibate, too; consummation is not required. All in all, it is an impressive and also rather astonishing victory for modern individualism that so important an institution should be so bereft of formal social instruction as to what should go on inside of it.   6

Secular society tells us only a few things about marriage. First, marriage depends on the consent of the parties. Second, the parties are not children. Third, the number of parties is two. Fourth, one is a man and the other a woman. Within those rules a marriage is whatever anyone says it is.   7

Perhaps it is enough simply to say that marriage is as it is and should not be tampered with. This sounds like a crudely reactionary position. In fact, however, of all the arguments against reforming marriage, it is probably the most powerful.   8

Call it a Hayekian argument, after the great libertarian economist F. A. Hayek, who developed this line of thinking in his book *The Fatal Conceit.* In a market system, the prices generated by impersonal forces may not make sense from any one person's point of view, but they encode far more information than even the cleverest person could ever gather. In a similar fashion, human societies evolve rich and complicated webs of nonlegal rules in the form of customs, traditions and institutions. Like prices, they may seem irrational or arbitrary. But the very fact that they are the customs that have evolved implies that they embody a practical logic that may not be apparent to even a sophisticated analyst. And the web of custom cannot be torn apart and reordered at will because once its internal logic is violated it falls apart. Intellectuals, such as Marxists or feminists, who seek to deconstruct and rationally rebuild social traditions, will produce not better order but chaos.   9

So the Hayekian view argues strongly against gay marriage. It says that the current rules may not be best and may even be unfair. But they are all we have, and, once you say that marriage need not be male-female, soon marriage will stop being anything at all. You can't mess with the formula without causing unforeseen consequences, possibly including the implosion of the institution of marriage itself.   10

However, there are problems with the Hayekian position. It is untenable in its extreme form and unhelpful in its milder version. In its extreme form, it implies that no social reforms   11 should ever be undertaken. Indeed, no laws should be passed, because they interfere with the natural evolution of social mores. How could Hayekians abolish slavery? They would probably note that slavery violates fundamental moral principles. But in so doing they would establish a moral platform from which to judge social rules, and thus acknowledge that abstracting social debate from moral concerns is not possible.

12   If the ban on gay marriage were only mildly unfair, and if the costs of changing it were certain to be enormous, then the ban could stand on Hayekian grounds. But, if there is any social policy today that has a fair claim to be scaldingly inhumane, it is the ban on gay marriage. As conservatives tirelessly and rightly point out, marriage is society's most fundamental institution. To bar any class of people from marrying as they choose is an extraordinary deprivation. When not so long ago it was illegal in parts of America for blacks to marry whites, no one could claim that this was a trivial disenfranchisement. Granted, gay marriage raises issues that interracial marriage does not; but no one can argue that the deprivation is a minor one.

13   To outweigh such a serious claim it is not enough to say that gay marriage might lead to bad things. Bad things happened as a result of legalizing contraception, but that did not make it the wrong thing to do. Besides, it seems doubtful that extending marriage to, say, another 3 or 5 percent of the population would have anything like the effects that no-fault divorce has had, to say nothing of contraception. By now, the "traditional" understanding of marriage has been sullied in all kinds of ways. It is hard to think of a bigger affront to tradition, for instance, than allowing married women to own property independently of their husbands or allowing them to charge their husbands with rape. Surely it is unfair to say that marriage may be reformed for the sake of anyone and everyone except homosexuals, who must respect the dictates of tradition.

14   Faced with these problems, the milder version of the Hayekian argument says not that social traditions shouldn't be tampered with at all, but that they shouldn't be tampered with lightly. Fine. In this case, no one is talking about casual messing around; both sides have marshaled their arguments with deadly seriousness. Hayekians surely have to recognize that appeals to blind tradition and to the risks inherent in social change do not, a priori, settle anything in this instance. They merely warn against frivolous change.

15   So we turn to what has become the standard view of marriage's purpose. Its proponents would probably like to call it a child-centered view, but it is actually an anti-gay view, as will become clear. Whatever you call it, it is the view of marriage that is heard most often, and in the context of the debate over gay marriage it is heard almost exclusively. In its most straightforward form it goes as follows (I quote from James Q. Wilson's fine book *The Moral Sense*):

> A family is not an association of independent people; it is a human commitment designed to make possible the rearing of moral and healthy children. Governments care—or ought to care—about families for this reason, and scarcely for any other.

16   Wilson speaks about "family" rather than "marriage" as such, but one may, I think, read him as speaking of marriage without doing any injustice to his meaning. The resulting proposition—government ought to care about marriage almost entirely because of children—

seems reasonable. But there are problems. The first, obviously, is that gay couples may have children, whether through adoption, prior marriage or (for lesbians) artificial insemination. Leaving aside the thorny issue of gay adoption, the point is that if the mere presence of children is the test, then homosexual relationships can certainly pass it.

You might note, correctly, that heterosexual marriages are more likely to produce children than homosexual ones. When granting marriage licenses to heterosexuals, however, we do not ask how likely the couple is to have children. We assume that they are entitled to get married whether or not they end up with children. Understanding this, conservatives often make an interesting move. In seeking to justify the state's interest in marriage, they shift from the actual presence of children to the anatomical possibility of making them. Hadley Arkes, a political science professor and prominent opponent of homosexual marriage, makes the case this way:

> The traditional understanding of marriage is grounded in the "natural teleology of the body"—in the inescapable fact that only a man and a woman, and only two people, not three, can generate a child. Once marriage is detached from that natural teleology of the body, what ground of principle would thereafter confine marriage to two people rather than some larger grouping? That is, on what ground of principle would the law reject the claim of a gay couple that their love is not confined to a coupling of two, but that they are woven into a larger ensemble with yet another person or two?

What he seems to be saying is that, where the possibility of natural children is nil, the meaning of marriage is nil. If marriage is allowed between members of the same sex, then the concept of marriage has been emptied of content except to ask whether the parties love each other. Then anything goes, including polygamy. This reasoning presumably is what those opposed to gay marriage have in mind when they claim that, once gay marriage is legal, marriage to pets will follow close behind.

But Arkes and his sympathizers make two mistakes. To see them, break down the claim into two components: (1) Two-person marriage derives its special status from the anatomical possibility that the partners can create natural children; and (2) Apart from (1), two-person marriage has no purpose sufficiently strong to justify its special status. That is, absent justification (1), anything goes.

The first proposition is wholly at odds with the way society actually views marriage. Leave aside the insistence that natural, as opposed to adopted, children define the importance of marriage. The deeper problem, apparent right away, is the issue of sterile heterosexual couples. Here the "anatomical possibility" crowd has a problem, for a homosexual union is, anatomically speaking, nothing but one variety of sterile union and no different even in principle: a woman without a uterus has no more potential for giving birth than a man without a vagina.

It may sound like carping to stress the case of barren heterosexual marriage: the vast majority of newlywed heterosexual couples, after all, can have children and probably will. But the point here is fundamental. There are far more sterile heterosexual unions in America than homosexual ones. The "anatomical possibility" crowd cannot have it both ways. If the possibility of children is what gives meaning to marriage, then a post-menopausal woman who applies for a marriage license should be turned away at the courthouse door. What's more, she should be hooted at and condemned for stretching the meaning of marriage beyond its natural basis and so reducing the institution to frivolity. People at the Family Research Council or Concerned Women for America should point at her and say, "If she can marry, why not polygamy?"

22   Obviously, the "anatomical" conservatives do not say this, because they are sane. They instead flail around, saying that sterile men and women were at least born with the right-shaped parts for making children, and so on. Their position is really a nonposition. It says that the "natural children" rationale defines marriage when homosexuals are involved but not when heterosexuals are involved. When the parties to union are sterile heterosexuals, the justification for marriage must be something else. But what?

23   Now arises the oddest part of the "anatomical" argument. Look at proposition (2) above. It says that, absent the anatomical justification for marriage, anything goes. In other words, it dismisses the idea that there might be other good reasons for society to sanctify marriage above other kinds of relationships. Why would anybody make this move? I'll hazard a guess: to exclude homosexuals. Any rationale that justifies sterile heterosexual marriages can also apply to homosexual ones. For instance, marriage makes women more financially secure. Very nice, say the conservatives. But that rationale could be applied to lesbians, so it's definitely out.

24   The end result of this stratagem is perverse to the point of being funny. The attempt to ground marriage in children (or the anatomical possibility thereof) falls flat. But, having lost that reason for marriage, the antigay people can offer no other. In their fixation on excluding homosexuals, they leave themselves no consistent justification for the privileged status of *heterosexual* marriage. They thus tear away any coherent foundation that secular marriage might have, which is precisely the opposite of what they claim they want to do. If they have to undercut marriage to save it from homosexuals, so be it!

25   For the record, I would be the last to deny that children are one central reason for the privileged status of marriage. When men and women get together, children are a likely outcome; and, as we are learning in ever more unpleasant ways, when children grow up without two parents, trouble ensues. Children are not a trivial reason for marriage; they just cannot be the only reason.

26   What are the others? It seems to me that the two strongest candidates are these: domesticating men and providing reliable caregivers. Both purposes are critical to the functioning of a humane and stable society, and both are much better served by marriage—that is, by one-to-one lifelong commitment—than by any other institution.

27   Civilizing young males is one of any society's biggest problems. Wherever unattached males gather in packs, you see no end of trouble: wildings in Central Park, gangs in Los Angeles, soccer hooligans in Britain, skinheads in Germany, fraternity hazings in universities, grope-lines in the military and, in a different but ultimately no less tragic way, the bathhouses and wanton sex of gay San Francisco or New York in the 1970s.

28   For taming men, marriage is unmatched. "Of all the institutions through which men may pass—schools, factories, the military—marriage has the largest effect," Wilson writes in

The Moral Sense. (A token of the casualness of current thinking about marriage is that the man who wrote those words could, later in the very same book, say that government should care about fostering families for "scarcely any other" reason than children.) If marriage—that is, the binding of men into couples—did nothing else, its power to settle men, to keep them at home and out of trouble, would be ample justification for its special status.

Of course, women and older men don't generally travel in marauding or orgiastic packs.   29 But in their case the second rationale comes into play. A second enormous problem for society is what to do when someone is beset by some sort of burdensome contingency. It could be cancer, a broken back, unemployment or depression; it could be exhaustion from work or stress under pressure. If marriage has any meaning at all, it is that, when you collapse from a stroke, there will be at least one other person whose "job" is to drop everything and come to your aid; or that when you come home after being fired by the postal service there will be someone to persuade you not to kill the supervisor.

Obviously, both rationales—the need to settle males and the need to have people   30 looked after—apply to sterile people as well as fertile ones, and apply to childless couples as well as to ones with children. The first explains why everybody feels relieved when the town delinquent gets married, and the second explains why everybody feels happy when an aging widow takes a second husband. From a social point of view, it seems to me, both rationales are far more compelling as justifications of marriage's special status than, say, love. And both of them apply to homosexuals as well as to heterosexuals.

Take the matter of settling men. It is probably true that women and children, more   31 than just the fact of marriage, help civilize men. But that hardly means that this settling effect of marriage on homosexual men is negligible. To the contrary, being tied to a committed relationship plainly helps stabilize gay men. Even without marriage, coupled gay men have steady sex partners and relationships that they value and therefore tend to be less wanton. Add marriage, and you bring a further array of stabilizing influences. One of the main benefits of publicly recognized marriage is that it binds couples together not only in their own eyes but also in the eyes of society at large. Around the partners is woven a web of expectations that they will spend nights together, go to parties together, take out mortgages together, buy furniture at Ikea together, and so on—all of which helps tie them together and keep them off the streets and at home. Surely that is a very good thing, especially as compared to the closet-gay culture of furtive sex with innumerable partners in parks and bathhouses.

The other benefit of marriage—caretaking—clearly applies to homosexuals. One of the   32 first things many people worry about when coming to terms with their homosexuality is: Who will take care of me when I'm ailing or old? Society needs to care about this, too, as the AIDS crisis has made horribly clear. If that crisis has shown anything, it is that homosexuals can and will take care of each other, sometimes with breathtaking devotion—and that no institution can begin to match the care of a devoted partner. Legally speaking, marriage creates kin. Surely society's interest in kin-creation is strongest of all for people who are unlikely to be supported by children in old age and who may well be rejected by their own parents in youth.

Gay marriage, then, is far from being a mere exercise in political point-making or   33 rights-mongering. On the contrary, it serves two of the three social purposes that make marriage so indispensable and irreplaceable for heterosexuals. Two out of three may not be the whole ball of wax, but it is more than enough to give society a compelling interest in marrying off homosexuals.

34   There is no substitute. Marriage is the *only* institution that adequately serves these purposes. The power of marriage is not just legal but social. It seals its promise with the smiles and tears of family, friends and neighbors. It shrewdly exploits ceremony (big, public weddings) and money (expensive gifts, dowries) to deter casual commitment and to make bailing out embarrassing. Stag parties and bridal showers signal that what is beginning is not just a legal arrangement but a whole new stage of life. "Domestic partner" laws do none of these things.

35   I'll go further: far from being a substitute for the real thing, marriage-lite may undermine it. Marriage is a deal between a couple and society, not just between two people: society recognizes the sanctity and autonomy of the pair-bond, and in exchange each spouse commits to being the other's nurse, social worker and policeman of first resort. Each marriage is its own little society within society. Any step that weakens the deal by granting the legal benefits of marriage without also requiring the public commitment is begging for trouble.

36   So gay marriage makes sense for several of the same reasons that straight marriage makes sense. That would seem a natural place to stop. But the logic of the argument compels one to go a twist further. If it is good for society to have people attached, then it is not enough just to make marriage available. Marriage should also be *expected.* This, too, is just as true for homosexuals as for heterosexuals. So, if homosexuals are justified in expecting access to marriage, society is equally justified in expecting them to use it. I'm not saying that out-of-wedlock sex should be scandalous or that people should be coerced into marrying. The mechanisms of expectation are more subtle. When grandma cluck-clucks over a still-unmarried young man, or when mom says she wishes her little girl would settle down, she is expressing a strong and well-justified preference: one that is quietly echoed in a thousand ways throughout society and that produces subtle but important pressure to form and sustain unions. This is a good and necessary thing, and it will be as necessary for homosexuals as heterosexuals. If gay marriage is recognized, single gay people over a certain age should not be surprised when they are disapproved of or pitied. That is a vital part of what makes marriage work. It's stigma as social policy.

37   If marriage is to work it cannot be merely a "lifestyle option." It must be privileged. That is, it must be understood to be better, on average, than other ways of living. Not mandatory, not good where everything else is bad, but better: a general norm, rather than a personal taste. The biggest worry about gay marriage, I think, is that homosexuals might get it but then mostly not use it. Gay neglect of marriage wouldn't greatly erode the bonding power of heterosexual marriage (remember, homosexuals are only a tiny fraction of the population)—but it would certainly not help. And heterosexual society would rightly feel betrayed if, after legalization, homosexuals treated marriage as a minority taste rather than as a core institution of life. It is not enough, I think, for gay people to say we want the right to marry. If we do not use it, shame on us.

1. Discussions of same-sex marriage often zero in on a definition of marriage. How do these articles define marriage, and how do they use that definition in their overall arguments? What do these writers say is at stake in how marriage is defined?

2. Analyze and evaluate disagreements among these writers about the social value and legitimacy of same-sex marriage by applying the first set of guide questions from page 465. How do you account for the differing points of view?

3. Choose one of the arguments for closer analysis, applying the second set of guide questions on pages 465–66.

4. Which argument do you think makes the most thought-provoking case for its position? What audience is that argument trying to reach?

OPTIONAL WRITING ASSIGNMENT   Imagine that you have to deliver a speech on the subject of same-sex marriage to a strongly resistant audience. (For example, imagine speaking in favor of same-sex marriage to an older, conservative audience; conversely, imagine speaking against same-sex marriage at a meeting of PFLAG [Parents and Friends of Lesbians and Gays].) Using the strategies of delayed thesis or Rogerian argument (see pages 165–66), develop a speech that attempts to lower the level of hostility to your ideas, reduce threat, highlight common ground, and promote a slight movement toward your position.

EGG DONORS AND REPRODUCTIVE TECHNOLOGY

Eggs No Longer Cheaper by the Dozen

Thomas A. Shannon

Thomas A. Shannon, a professor of religion and social ethics at Worchester Polytechnic Institute in Massachusetts, originally published this article in the May 1, 1999, issue of America.

1   An advertisement that appeared recently in the newspapers of several Ivy League colleges seeking a smart, tall, healthy and athletic egg donor for $50,000 reveals much about America and the fertility business. Clearly we have now passed into a model of fertility services that implements the motto "If you can afford it, you can get it." Also the ante for egg "donors" has been raised considerably, from about $1,000 to $5,000 and now to $50,000. Surely, for a month of somewhat risky injections of drugs and aspiration of the eggs we have gone beyond reasonable compensation to clear bribery. And with the cost of attending one of the Ivys (or almost any college) approaching the $50,000 per year mark, this may indeed prove to be an offer some cannot refuse.

2   Yet several problems remain. The ad is predicated on what I call the genetic fallacy: If your genes are good, so is everything else. Unfortunately this is not true. Good genes may take one a long way, but they are no guarantee of a healthy life. Neither are good genes (should we even be able to define such a reality) a guarantee of being a decent, kind or even successful person. We know that there are a lot of jerks around, and their quantity and longevity suggest that even they have their share of good genes. There are simply no guarantees in life, and even the most sophisticated genetic planning and screening cannot change that.

3   Second, given the parental expenditures and expectations in obtaining the prized egg, what will happen if the child does not come up to snuff? Even assuming that the father's SAT score was over 1400, that he is over 5 feet 10 inches and athletic, the child may still turn out to be short, not interested in academics and a klutz. The genetic fallacy raises its ugly head again, for the child may disappoint the inflated expectations of the parents. What if the child does not want to attend an Ivy? Or what if—the fertility gods forbid—the child is not accepted (though one of my students suggested that the child might be considered a legacy because of the egg's origin)? The ad seems to suggest high expectations for the child (and all parents want what is best for their child), but the margin for error seems quite narrow here.

4   An ad such as this also raises, even if unintentionally, the strong scent of eugenics, the attempt to breed in or out certain qualities. In the past this has led to genocide, racism and regressive immigration policies. In the future it may lead, thanks to both prenatal diagnosis and ads such as this, to accepting children only if they possess traits we desire or try to program into them. Children might no longer be loved for who they are but only if they meet their parents' expectations. Childhood is already difficult enough; but if one is a constant disappointment to parents because the characteristics they so carefully selected and purchased are absent, how much more difficult will growing up be! Furthermore, the classism and racism of this ad are fairly obvious and blatant. Why intensify these tendencies of our society with ads such as this one?

5   This ad makes clear that the market has indeed taken control of reproduction and that body parts are now commodities to be exchanged for what the market will bear. Perhaps the time is ripe for a national discussion of the cost, methods and access to reproductive services and clinics. Shouldn't we reevaluate a notion of reproductive freedom that equates freedom with the capacity to purchase whatever reproductive services I can afford? In this matter of choice, we need to remember that we have to think as carefully about what we choose as we do about guaranteeing our right to choose.

Egg Heads

Kathryn Jean Lopez

This article appeared in the September 1, 1998, issue of National Review.

Filling the waiting room to capacity and spilling over into a nearby conference room, a group of young women listen closely and follow the instructions: Complete the forms and return them, with the clipboard, to the receptionist. It's all just as in any medical office. Then they move downstairs, where the doctor briefs them. "Everything will be pretty much normal," she explains. "Women complain of skin irritation in the local area of injection and bloating. You also might be a little emotional. But, basically, it's really bad PMS." 1

This is not just another medical office. On a steamy night in July, these girls in their twenties are attending an orientation session for potential egg donors at a New Jersey fertility clinic specializing in in-vitro fertilization. Within the walls of IVF New Jersey and at least two hundred other clinics throughout the United States, young women answer the call to give "the gift of life" to infertile couples. Egg donation is a quickly expanding industry, changing the way we look at the family, young women's bodies, and human life itself. 2

It is not a pleasant way to make money. Unlike sperm donation, which is over in less than an hour, egg donation takes the donor some 56 hours and includes a battery of tests, ultrasound, self-administered injections, and retrieval. Once a donor is accepted into a program, she is given hormones to stimulate the ovaries, changing the number of eggs matured from the usual one per month up to as many as fifty. A doctor then surgically removes the eggs from the donor's ovary and fertilizes them with the designated sperm. 3

Although most programs require potential donors to undergo a series of medical tests and counseling, there is little indication that most of the young women know what they are getting themselves into. They risk bleeding, infection, and scarring. When too many eggs are matured in one cycle, it can damage the ovaries and leave the donor with weeks of abdominal pain. (At worst, complications may leave her dead.) Longer term, the possibility of early menopause raises the prospect of future regret. There is also evidence of a connection between the fertility drugs used in the process and ovarian cancer. 4

But it's good money—and getting better. New York's Brooklyn IVF raised its "donor compensation" from $2,500 to $5,000 per cycle earlier this year in order to keep pace with St. Barnabas Medical Center in nearby Livingston, New Jersey. It's a bidding war. "It's obvious why we had to do it," says Susan Lobel, Brooklyn IVF's assistant director. Most New York–area IVF programs have followed suit. 5

Some infertile couples and independent brokers are offering even more for "reproductive material." The International Fertility Center in Indianapolis, Indiana, for instance, places ads in the *Daily Princetonian* offering Princeton girls as much as $35,000 per cycle. The National Fertility Registry, which, like many egg brokerages, features an online catalogue for couples to browse in, advertises $35,000 to $50,000 for Ivy League eggs. While donors are normally paid a flat fee per cycle, there have been reports of higher payments to donors who produce more eggs. 6

7   College girls are the perfect donors. Younger eggs are likelier to be healthy, and the girls themselves frequently need money—college girls have long been susceptible to classified ads offering to pay them for acting as guinea pigs in medical research. One 1998 graduate of the University of Colorado set up her own Web site to market her eggs. She had watched a television show on egg donation and figured it "seemed like a good thing to do"—especially since she had spent her money during the past year to help secure a country-music record deal. "Egg donation would help me with my school and music expenses while helping an infertile couple with a family." Classified ads scattered throughout cyberspace feature similar offers.

8   The market for "reproductive material" has been developing for a long time. It was twenty years ago this summer that the first test-tube baby, Louise Brown, was born. By 1995, when the latest tally was taken by the Centers for Disease Control, 15 percent of mothers in this country had made use of some form of assisted-reproduction technology in conceiving their children. (More recently, women past menopause have begun to make use of this technology.) In 1991 the American Society for Reproductive Medicine was aware of 63 IVF programs offering egg donation. That number had jumped to 189 by 1995 (the latest year for which numbers are available).

9   Defenders argue that it's only right that women are "compensated" for the inconvenience of egg donation. Brooklyn IVF's Dr. Lobel argues, "If it is unethical to accept payment for loving your neighbor, then we'll have to stop paying babysitters." As long as donors know the risks, says Mark McGee of the University of Pennsylvania's Center for Bioethics, this transaction is only "a slightly macabre version of adoption."

10   Not everyone is enthusiastic about the "progress." Egg donation "represents another rather large step into turning procreation into manufacturing," says the University of Chicago's Leon Kass. "It's the dehumanization of procreation." And as in manufacturing, there is quality control. "People don't want to say the word any more, but there is a strong eugenics issue inherent in the notion that you can have the best eggs your money can buy," observes sociology professor Barbara Katz Rothman of the City University of New York.

11   The demand side of the market comes mostly from career-minded babyboomers, the frontierswomen of feminism, who thought they could "have it all." Indeed they *can* have it all—with a little help from some younger eggs. (Ironically, feminists are also among its strongest critics; *The Nation*'s Katha Pollitt has pointed out that in egg donation and surrogacy, once you remove the "delusion that they are making babies for other women," all you have left is "reproductive prostitution.")

12   Unfortunately, the future looks bright for the egg market. Earlier this year, a woman in Atlanta gave birth to twins after she was implanted with frozen donor eggs. The same technology has also been successful in Italy. This is just what the egg market needed, since it avoids the necessity of coordinating donors' cycles with recipients' cycles. Soon, not only will infertile couples be able to choose from a wider variety of donor offerings, but in some cases donors won't even be needed. Young women will be able to freeze their own eggs and have them thawed and fertilized once they are ready for the intrusion of children in their lives.

13   There are human ovaries sitting in a freezer in Fairfax, Virginia. The Genetics and IVF Institute offers to cut out and remove young women's ovaries and cryopreserve the egg-

containing tissue for future implantation. Although the technology was originally designed to give the hope of fertility to young women undergoing treatment for cancer, it is now starting to attract the healthy. "Women can wait to have children until they are well established in their careers and getting a little bored, sometime in their forties or fifties," explains Professor Rothman. "Basically, motherhood is being reduced to a good leisure-time activity."

Early this summer, headlines were made in Britain, where the payment of egg donors   14
is forbidden, when an infertile couple traveled to a California clinic where the woman could be inseminated with an experimental hybrid egg. The egg was a combination of the recipient's and a donor's eggs. The clinic in question gets its eggs from a Beverly Hills brokerage, the Center for Surrogate Parenting and Egg Donation, run by Karen Synesiou and Bill Handel, a radio shock-jock in Los Angeles. Miss Synesiou recently told the London *Sunday Times* that she is "interested in redefining the family. That's why I came to work here."

The redefinition is already well under way. Consider the case of Jaycee Buzzanca. After   15
John and Luanne Buzzanca had tried for years to have a child, an embryo was created for them, using sperm and an egg from anonymous donors, and implanted in a surrogate mother. In March 1995, one month before the baby was born, John filed for divorce. Luanne wanted child support from John, but he refused—after all, he's not the father. Luanne argued that John *is* Jaycee's father legally. At this point the surrogate mother, who had agreed to carry a baby for a stable two-parent household, decided to sue for custody.

Jaycee was dubbed "Nobody's Child" by the media when a California judge ruled that   16
John was not the legal father nor Luanne the legal mother (neither one was genetically related to Jaycee, and Luanne had not even borne her). Enter Erin Davidson, the egg donor, who claims the egg was used without her permission. Not to be left out, the sperm donor jumped into the ring, saying that his sperm was used without his permission, a claim he later dropped. In March of this year, an appeals court gave Luanne custody and decided that John is the legal father, making him responsible for child support. By contracting for a medical procedure resulting in the birth of a child, the court ruled, a couple incurs "the legal status of parenthood." (John lost an appeal in May.) For Jaycee's first three years on earth, these people have been wrangling over who her parents are.

In another case, William Kane left his girlfriend, Deborah Hect, 15 vials of sperm be-   17
fore he killed himself in a Las Vegas hotel in 1991. His two adult children (represented by their mother, his ex-wife) contested Miss Hect's claim of ownership. A settlement agreement on Kane's will was eventually reached, giving his children 80 per cent of his estate and Miss Hect 20 per cent. Hence she was allowed three vials of his sperm. When she did not succeed in conceiving on the first two tries, she filed a petition for the other 12 vials. She won, and the judge who ruled in her favor wrote, "Neither this court nor the decedent's adult children possess reason or right to prevent Hect from implementing decedent's pre-eminent interest in realizing his 'fundamental right' to procreate with the woman of his choice." One day, donors may not even have to have lived. Researchers are experimenting with using aborted female fetuses as a source of donor eggs.

And the market continues to zip along. For overseas couples looking for donor eggs,   18
Bill Handel has the scenario worked out. The couple would mail him frozen sperm of their choice (presumably from the recipient husband); his clinic would use it to fertilize donor

eggs, chosen from its catalogue of offerings, and reply back within a month with a frozen embryo ready for implantation. (Although the sperm does not yet arrive by mail, Handel has sent out embryos to at least one hundred international customers). As for the young women at the New Jersey clinic, they are visibly upset by one aspect of the egg-donation process: they can't have sexual intercourse for several weeks after the retrieval. For making babies, of course, it's already obsolete.

Egg Donor, or Seller?

Katrien Naessens

Katrien Naessens, a Belgian citizen and a biology major at Harvard University, wrote this article in response to the egg donor ad that sparked a flurry of journalistic commentary—the ad offering $50,000 for eggs of a college woman who met certain specifications. This article was originally published April 9, 1999, in the Christian Science Monitor.

1   At first I am amused by the item. My friend Cara has just shown me an advertisement in our Ivy League college newspaper. It offers $50,000 for an egg donor who is athletic, taller than 5 feet, 10 inches, and has SAT scores higher than 1400.

2   "That could be me," I joke, offhand. We are amused because we think that someone who wants a baby so desperately would not impose such restrictions on the donor. We think the couple must be vain to want only an aesthetically pleasing baby. Though this type of thing is nothing new, usually compensation runs $3,000 to $6,000.

3   "$50,000, isn't that a flagrant financial bribe?" Cara asks.

4   More friends join us, and we contemplate the article for a while. One friend notes that perhaps the prospective parents are also tall and Ivy League graduates, and they simply wanted a baby that resembled them. I prefer to believe this, as I want confidence in humanity. I want everyone to have clear, uncorrupt motives.

5   "You should do it, Kat," Cara says.

6   This flicks a switch inside me. I remain quiet, but I inwardly imagine myself with $50,000 in my bank account and the effect that would have on my life. I am going to be a doctor someday, and my dream is to work in developing countries where I can really help people. The only obstacle to my dream is money; I can't afford four years of medical school. And $50,000 is halfway through medical school—halfway to what I want most in the world. I want to save lives, and all I have to do is help start one.

7   How can I refuse?

8   I contact the agency and they send me the information I need to apply to be an egg donor. They say their client has "shown interest in me."

9   My inner turmoil begins, there is so much more to consider than I had anticipated. It seems simple. After all, as a biology student I know very well I'm only donating a few cells. No different from donating blood, or an organ, or selling my hair as they used to do 100

years ago! And what a noble gesture, helping a family conceive a child when they can't do so themselves.

I know I want children when I am older, and I understand the frustration it must cause to find out you cannot have your own. Helping a family by donating an egg that I know I won't need myself would surely be a generous gift. 10

But here lies the conflict. Donating an egg for this couple would not be a "gift" and is certainly not generous on my part. If I were going to be noble enough to help a childless couple to conceive, truly a charitable gesture, shouldn't I be doing it for free? 11

I question my motives. Why must I be lured by the money? I realized that I would be selling part of my body, just to get to medical school. Selling my body? Isn't that prostitution? The comparison troubles me. 12

I write to the agency that I have decided against donation. I tell myself the procedure is too invasive, and I don't want to risk taking the drugs prescribed to do it. 13

The truth is, I'm not worried about the medical procedure, nor am I against egg donation. It's not unethical. But personally, I wouldn't donate a kidney for $50,000, I wouldn't sell my DNA to a bioengineering firm, and neither can I do this. 14

I sometimes still wish $50,000 would fall into my lap and secure my future. But I'm glad I didn't give my eggs. I won't have to live with the idea that somewhere out there is a child that is half of me. 15

What a strange thing, to generate a life somewhere across the States with no effort, no involvement. Would the child ever have forgiven me for selling him, for $50,000, if he found out? 16

From Bastardy to Cloning: Adaptations of Legal Thought for Unorthodox Reproduction

Bruce Wilder

Bruce Wilder is a physician and official counsel to the Pittsburgh law firm of Wilder, Mahood & Crenney, P.C. This article appeared in the Spring 1999 issue of Human Rights: Journal of the Section of Individual Rights and Responsibilities.

From its beginnings, Anglo-American law has shown a trend toward preserving the rights of children who happen to have been born under circumstances other than the social and religious ideal. The "ideal," of course, is that children are born as a result of sexual intercourse between a man and a woman married to each other. Indeed, the institution of marriage itself is centered around procreation, and the Church openly frowned upon the idea of sexual intercourse if procreation were not the object—i.e., if sexual intercourse were engaged in solely for sexual gratification. While the diagnosis and treatment of infertility have comprised the main driving force behind the development of assisted reproduction technologies, parallel advances in molecular genetics have combined with it to present new possibilities of eliminating "defects" in the genome, and the possibility of "enhancing" the genome, of children being conceived by assisted reproduction technology. 1

THE GENESIS OF REPRODUCTIVE LAW

2   Barrenness has been a powerful subject of legend and mythology for centuries. It usually connotes infertility in the female, and it should not come as any surprise that the woman was the one who was identified as being barren if no child was born to a couple. The woman either gave birth or she did not. If a man were infertile, in most cases there was no way to prove it. A reading of Genesis suggests that the idea of surrogate motherhood has existed a long time. In one instance Abraham's wife, Sarai, realizing her barrenness, asked her husband to impregnate her handmaid, Hagar, so that he might have progeny. After Hagar became pregnant, both she and Sarai appear to have had second thoughts. Through Sarai's jealousy, Hagar and the child were sent into the desert, where the angel of Jehovah encountered them at a spring, and said to Hagar:

> Thou shalt call his name Ishmael, because Jehovah hath heard thy affliction. And he shall be as a wild ass among men; his hand shall be against every man, and every man against him, and he shall dwell over against all his brethren.[1]

3   The name Ishmael may be synonymous with social outcast,[2] at least in the Judeo-Christian world. Interestingly, however, in Islam—where polygamy is accepted—Ishmael is considered a prophet. The spring mentioned above is traditionally identified with a Meccan well near the Kaaba, which Muslims believe was built by Ishmael and Abraham. Muslims recognize Arabs as Ishmael's descendants, as distinguished from the Israelites, the descendants of Isaac, who was the half-brother of Ishmael.[3]

4   The story of Jacob and Leah and Rachel, and their handmaids Bilhah and Zilpah, is a little less like a surrogate mother arrangement because of the fact that at least Leah was not infertile. Here, Jacob, with the blessing of God and of their father, Laban, seems to have had a bigamous relationship with Rachel and Leah, as well as—at the requests of, and with the blessings of, Rachel and Leah, respectively—extramarital relationships with their handmaids, which resulted in the birth of several children. It does not appear that Jacob's children suffered any adverse consequences.[4]

5   In Deuteronomy, bastards were dealt with more severely. As if it were not enough to punish the adulterer or rapist with death by stoning, "A bastard shall not enter into the assembly of Jehovah; even to the tenth generation shall none of his enter into the assembly of Jehovah."[5]

6   For centuries, in England, an out-of-wedlock child was regarded as a non-person not entitled to support from the father or an inheritance from either parent.[6]

7   The concept of adoption goes back at least to the Code of Hammurabi, and its purpose appears to have been to continue the pattern of male inheritance in the society.[7] The law dealing with modern adoption is a relatively recent phenomenon. And it has only been relatively recently that the law has, for the most part, treated adopted children—at least those adopted as minors—in the same way as biological children born within a marriage.[8] While adoption is not a form of reproduction, we can look to the development of law in that area, and the important policy considerations that its development reflects, to guide us in advancing and improving law in the area of unorthodox reproduction.

NEW IDEAS FOR A NEW DAY

Courts and legislatures have struggled with the new reproduction technologies because   8
the increasingly numerous biological permutations of procreation simply do not fit well with
our traditional concepts and constructs. Physicists will tell you that Newton's classical theories of motion, energy, and mass work as well today as they did in his time, except when
we are dealing with velocities that approach the speed of light or with particles of sub-
nuclear size. They will further tell you that it was the recognition of the fact that Newton-
ian classical mechanics did not work under either of those circumstances that gave rise to
the development of the theories of relativity and of quantum mechanics in the early part of
this century. Similarly, the myriad kinds of reproduction technology that have developed in
the last few decades, and particularly in the last decade, along with the emerging possibilities for the future, demonstrate the need to rethink the fundamentals of how we determine
the legal relationships between children, their biological progenitors, and the people who
will be their parents and legatees.

With few exceptions, our jurisprudence has had difficulty freeing itself from the idea   9
that the biological father is presumed to be the legal father of a child, and that the woman
who bears a child will be the legal mother, because "for millennia, giving birth was synonymous with providing the genetic makeup of the child that was born."[9]

My thesis, on the other hand, is that there are certain legally significant acts by adults   10
that occur either before or after the birth of a child that establish a parent-child relationship. I contend that our focus should be on determining what acts are "legally significant"
in that regard, and what acts are not, with some measure of predictability. For reasons
of simplicity and practicality, I suggest that this kind of approach is to be favored over the
traditional paradigm of presumptions based on biological relatedness, with its exceptions,
exceptions to exceptions, and so on. However, such a new approach must not lead to results that vary significantly with established law in the more traditional fact patterns.

The law's initial attempts to rely on what I shall call the "biological paradigm" have   11
often been harsh, in that, as we have shown above and will show by further example, they
often visited gratuitous penalties on the child, who obviously had no control over his or her
genesis. Gradually, but too slowly, the law has evolved to correct some of these injustices,
but it has taken centuries and, in our own time of rapid change in the methods of unorthodox reproduction, a fair amount of tortuous litigation in an environment of a hands-
off approach by legislatures.

The National Conference of Commissioners on Uniform State Laws has addressed some   12
of these problems. Their Uniform Status of Children of Assisted Conception Act (USCACA),[10]
published in 1988, was a bold attempt to provide some consistency and uniformity of state
law in the area of assisted reproduction, but only two states, Virginia and North Dakota,
have adopted it in any significant form.[11] The Uniform Parentage Act (UPA),[12] which has
been much more widely adopted by the states, is currently undergoing revision, and in its
new form, will modify and incorporate the provisions of the USCACA.

California has not adopted USCACA. But what if it had? In the case of *In re Marriage*   13
of Buzzanca,[13] a couple procured a human embryo, to which neither of them had any

biological connection, and arranged for it to be implanted into a surrogate for the purpose of providing themselves with a child. After a pregnancy resulted, and less than one month before the birth of the child, the husband filed for divorce and disclaimed any legal relationship with the soon-to-be-born child. The trial court ruled in his favor and even went so far as to declare that the child had no legal parents, not John Buzzanca, not Luanne Buzzanca, and not the surrogate, because they were "genetic stranger[s]" to the child. Fortunately, on appeal, common sense prevailed, and both John and Luanne Buzzanca were found to be the legal parents of the child. The *ratio decidendi* of the ruling was based upon the fact that both John and Luanne had caused the birth of the child by arranging for implantation of the embryo into the surrogate for the purpose of having a child of their own. The court looked to well-established law of donor insemination and likened John's actions to those of a husband who consents to artificial insemination of his wife, and, by analogy, also reasoned that Luanne was also a parent. "In each instance [of John and Luanne], a child is procreated because a medical procedure was initiated and consented to by the intended parents."[14] It is fair to say that the court at least implied that their actions in arranging for the embryo to be implanted into the surrogate, and their contract with the surrogate, were sufficient for them to be deemed to have intended to be legally bound as parents of the child that would result. Under USCACA, neither the sperm donor nor the egg donor would have been the child's parents, and the "intended parents," John and Luanne, not the surrogate, would have been the child's parents at the time of birth, assuming a valid surrogacy agreement.[15]

14   This "intent to parent" doctrine, for which the *Buzzanca* court had looked to an earlier California case, *Johnson v. Calvert,*[16] has not yet carried the day, however. The biological paradigm is still alive, if not well. For example, an Ohio trial court, in a declaratory judgment action by a couple who created an embryo from their own egg and sperm and had it implanted into a surrogate, rejected the "intent" doctrine of *Johnson* and relied on the fact that both the husband and wife were the genetic parents. It was very easy for the court to do that without causing any of the problems that occurred in *Buzzanca* because both the husband and wife wished to be the parents of the child, and the surrogate, who was the sister of the wife, had no intention of asserting parental rights. The case only came about because the Akron City Hospital, where the child was to be born, indicated that it would not list the husband and wife as parents on the birth certificate and informed them that the surrogate would be listed as the child's mother, and that the child would be designated as "illegitimate."[17] The *Belsito* court could have easily reached the same result without rejecting the ruling of the California Supreme Court by declaring that the Belsitos were deemed to be the legal parents because they created an embryo, arranged for it to be implanted into the surrogate, and established their intent to be legally bound as parents of the child by virtue of the contract with the surrogate, all legally significant acts.

15   Looking at a more mundane situation that does not present any difficulty using the biological paradigm, we could ask, How would a legally significant acts doctrine play out in a case where a married woman has an extramarital affair that results in the birth of a child, and the husband learns about it within the applicable statutory period, and disclaims any legal relationship to the child? The legally significant act of the wife's paramour was having had sexual intercourse with her, and the DNA test would simply be evidence that such an

act occurred, and that it was that act that resulted in the birth of the child. Here again the biological paradigm and the legally significant acts approach reach the same result, as they should. That is, the husband could disclaim the parent-child relationship, and the paramour would be liable for child support.

Another hypothetical may be helpful here. For medical reasons, it may be advantageous to insert nuclear DNA from one oocyte into another oocyte, from which its original nuclear DNA has been removed. The resulting oocyte would contain nuclear DNA from one person and cytoplasmic or mitochondrial DNA from another person. Under the biological paradigm, who is the mother of the resulting child? Under the legally significant acts analysis, the mother would be the adult female person whose acts and/or consent caused or permitted the oocyte to be synthesized, if you will, and to be fertilized and implanted, with the intent to be legally bound as the child's parent.   16

FURTHER COMPLICATED ISSUES

Ordinarily, we think of parents as a male and a female, usually married to each other. Obviously, there can be parents of opposite sex who are unmarried. There may be legal parents of the same gender, where adoption under those circumstances is permitted, or there may be parents, one of whom is transgendered, i.e., holding himself or herself out, legally recognized or not, as of a gender different from his or her genetic or birth gender, whether or not that person has had sexual reassignment surgery. Decisions in some cases of same-sex couples have seemed to disfavor such arrangements for child rearing, ostensibly because of concern over the effect of such adult lifestyles on the child's development. Moreover, our law has, at least implicitly, limited the number of legal parents to two. Such a limitation is, admittedly, somewhat arbitrary, but for the most part is in keeping with a wide range of lifestyles in our society. As at least one court has pointed out, "society and the law recognize only one natural mother and father."[18]   17

Consider the case of *Karin T. v. Michael T.,*[19] where a lesbian, not biologically related to the child of her partner, but who had obtained a marriage license, participated in a marriage ceremony as a man, and participated in the artificial insemination of the child's mother, later sought to be absolved of any support or other parental obligations to the child. The court did not look to the presence or absence of any biological relationship to the child and instead used the doctrine of equitable estoppel, which falls more readily within a legally significant acts analysis than into any biological paradigm. In other situations, where a custody dispute arises between a lesbian couple who have raised a child who is biologically related to one of the women, the nonbiological partner has usually been denied any parental rights, often to the detriment of the child, and even to the consternation of the court itself. This again demonstrates the flaw in a biological paradigm analysis.[20]   18

If we consider the problem of establishing parent-child relationships in human cloning, the scent of biological paradigm has the potential to take us further off the trail of fairness and sanity in the law than ever.   19

Although no one has successfully cloned a human being using somatic cell DNA transfer, it certainly could occur within our lifetimes. It is probably possible today to separate human embryonic cells at, say, the eight-cell human stage, grow each of them into another   20 eight-cell embryo, again separate them, and on and on. The resulting embryos with identi-cal genomes could then be frozen for thawing and gestation at a later date, while one of their number could be implanted and brought to term. After that person has grown to adulthood, his or her clones-to-be might then be thawed, implanted, and brought to term years later.

21   If, and when, we as a society decide to permit the cloning of human beings, it is all-important to define the role of the state in the regulation of cloning. First, that state role should be limited to making sure that cloning is done with reasonable safety and without undue risk of birth defects and other severe medical complications. The state should not be in the business of determining who may or may not clone or be cloned, or what traits may or may not be passed on.

22   The issue of genetic enhancement has been raised, not only in the context of possible cloning, but in the discussion of already extant reproduction technologies. There may be noth-ing wrong with eugenics when it is practiced by individuals, and when the techniques used do not involve significant risk of medical complications. However, the legal or illegal sale of gametes or embryos, with the potential for being sold at a premium based upon a particular genome, remains deeply problematic as an ethical matter. When the state decides to regulate eugenics, things can go terribly wrong, as we have already learned, even in our own country.

23   Elegant arguments for and against cloning of human beings have been advanced.[21] Per-haps we place too much emphasis on problems of personal identity. Anyone who has raised a child through the teen years will readily understand how powerful and pervasive is the innate drive for each human being to establish his or her unique identity and persona. In any event, our law must develop to ensure that the status of children born through cloning is protected. That means that they come into this world with the same rights and privileges (such as legal parents, heirship, and unique legal identity) as do other children, i.e., that, among other things, they must not be required to be organ donors or to bear the name, persona, or identity of the person from whom they are cloned.

24   In formulating new law[s] to protect the rights of children born as a result of unortho-dox [forms of] reproduction such as cloning, our focus should be [on trying] to define what legally significant acts by individuals who bring about [the birth of these children] establish parental rights and responsibilities, inheritance rights, and a unique legal identity for the individual, and [on ensuring] that all [children] are born with these legal attributes.[22]

ENDNOTES

1. Genesis 16.
2. *Merriam Webster's Collegiate Dictionary* (10th ed.).
3. *The Columbia Encyclopedia* (5th ed., 1993).
4. Genesis 30.
5. Deuteronomy 23:2.
6. W. Blackstone, *Commentaries* 459; *Davis v. Houston, 2.* Yeats 280 (1878), cited in J. Wilder, *Pa. Family Law Prac. and Proc.* Section 27-1 (4th ed.).
7. J. McNamara, *The Adoption Advisor* 2 (1975), cited in J. Wilder, *Pa. Family Law Prac. and Proc.* Section 32-1 (4th ed.).
8. *In re Estate of Tafel,* 449 Pa. 442, 296 A.2d 797 (1972).
9. *Belsito v. Clark,* 644 N.E.2d 760, 763 (1994).

10. 9B U.L.A. (West 1998 Pocket Part).
11. Id.
12. U.L.A. (West 1998).
13. *In re Marriage of Buzzanca,* 72 Cal. Rptr. 2d 280, 24 Fam. L. Rep. 2019 (1998).
14. Id., 24 Fam. L. Rep. at 2022.
15. See note 10 supra, "Alternative A."
16. *Johnson v. Calvert,* 19 Cal. Rptr. 2d 494, 851 P.2d 776 (1993).
17. See note 9 supra, at 764. The *Belsito* trial court rejected the "intent to parent" rationale, noting difficulties of application and proof, public policy, and "failure to recognize and emphasize the genetic provider's right to consent to procreation and to surrender potential parental rights."
18. See note 9 supra, at 763, citing *Michael H. v. Gerald D.,* 491 U.S. 110, 109 S. Ct. 2333, 105 L. Ed. 2d 91 (1989).
19. *Karin T. v. Michael T.,* 127 Misc. 2d 14, 484 N.Y.S.2d 780 (1985).
20. *Nancy S. v. Michele G.,* 279 Cal. Rptr. 212, 228 Cal. App. 3d 831 (1st Dist.) (1991).
21. J. A. Robertson, Human Cloning and the Challenge of Regulation, *New Eng. J. Med.* 339(2): 119–21 (1998); G. J. Annas, Why We Should Ban Human Cloning, *New Eng. J. Med.* 339(2): 122–25 (1998).
22. [This paragraph has been edited for clarity. EDS.]

Superior People

This article originally appeared on the editorial page of Commonweal, March 26, 1999.

Advertising is the lingua franca of the modern age. Everyone has something to sell or something they want to buy, and advertising is what brings sellers and buyers together. Guaranteeing the quality of the merchandise is a routine advertising technique. Take the venerable Charleston, South Carolina, wholesalers Austin, Laurens, & Appleby. They had a boatload of highly valuable merchandise ready for a competitive consumer market. Assuaging prospective customers' concerns about any hidden defects in their inventory was important. "To be sold on board the ship *Bance Island,* on Tuesday the 6th of May next, at Ashley Ferry; a choice cargo of about 150 fine healthy NEGROES, just arrived from the Windward & Rice Coast," reads the firm's eighteenth-century ad. "The utmost care has already been taken, and shall be continued, to keep them free from the least danger of being infected with the SMALL POX, no boat having been on board, and all other communication with people from Charles-Town prevented." [1]

Selling human flesh is an ancient practice, and one that seems to find a new manifestation in every age. It's not impossible to imagine an Austin, Laurens & Appleby–like advertisement appearing somewhere on the Web, or perhaps in a student newspaper at a prestigious university. [2]

The *New York Times* recently reported that the following ad—illustrated with drawings of a baby carriage and a stork delivery—has been appearing in select college newspapers across the country: "EGG DONOR NEEDED / LARGE FINANCIAL INCENTIVE / [3]

INTELLIGENT, ATHLETIC EGG DONOR NEEDED / FOR LOVING FAMILY / YOU MUST BE AT LEAST 5'10" / HAVE A 1400+ SAT SCORE / POSSESS NO MAJOR FAMILY MEDICAL ISSUES / $50,OOO / FREE MEDICAL SCREENING / ALL EXPENSES PAID."

4   What, no blonde hair, blue eyes, and pure Aryan bloodline required? If this pitch for a eugenically "superior" donor is any indication, American culture seems to have made as little progress over the last 250 years in securing the intrinsic dignity of human life as it has in elevating the quality of advertising copy. For when it comes to the commercialization of human reproduction and the marketing of human eggs, we are fast returning to a world where persons carry a price tag, and where the cash value of some persons (or at least of their genetic "endowment") is far greater than that of others. Still, it is hard to believe that campus newspapers, otherwise notoriously sensitive about economic and social injustice, as well as the exploitation of women and minorities, would see fit to run such ads. Egg donation, after all, entails both present and possible future medical risk, not to mention that donors are selling their own genetic progeny to the highest bidder. Are nineteen-year-olds able to make truly informed decisions about such things? Is consent voluntary or subtly coerced when such large sums of money are involved?

5   The response to the ad has been robust—after all, $50,000 will pay almost two years' tuition at an Ivy League school. Of course, there is an aspect of absurdity in the idea of screening a genetic reproductive partner on the basis of SAT scores and height. One can imagine a whole new SAT coaching industry springing up to help dolts with a meager 1350 SAT qualify for egg donation. Athletic coaches will be swamped with requests from the egg-bearing but uncoordinated. Or think about the potential for graft and corruption in the business of certifying that candidates have "no major medical issues." And won't a few vertically challenged prospective donors, stunted at a mere 5'9", devise clever ways to add an extra inch? Already it appears that students at less prestigious state colleges and universities are demanding equal opportunity in the egg race. Will today's egg procurers, following in the entrepreneurial footsteps of Austin, Laurens & Appleby, let boatloads of such "fine, healthy" specimens go to waste?

6   A year ago on this page ("Eggs for Sale," March 27, 1998), we noted the moral dangers and the threat to human dignity signaled by the escalation of fees for donor eggs. At that time, Saint Barnabas Medical Center in New Jersey had made headlines by upping its fee to $5,000. That looks like chump change now. There is little surprising in the most recent tenfold increase in what people are willing to pay to gain a genetic advantage—some of it real, some of it illusory—for their children. The logic of the marketplace is inexorable. If left unregulated by the medical profession or by the state, the business of reproductive technology will become little more than a tool of the wealthy and an increasing rebuke to those who forswear such opportunities for eugenic "improvement." In the widespread practice of aborting Down's syndrome and other "defective" fetuses, American society is already establishing a dangerous pattern for its genetic future. These private "choices" implicitly fuel resentment against those who "unnecessarily" bring handicapped children into the world, not to mention against the handicapped themselves and their "cost" to society. And as the $50,000 egg ad exemplifies, it is but a small step in logic from aborting for physical or mental handicaps to selecting or engineering for intelligence, height, athletic ability, or other "desirable" qualities. Bryan Appleyard writes in his important new book *Brave New*

Worlds: Staying Human in the Genetic Future (Viking), the "key problem with privatized eugenics [is that] it amounts to a judgment on the existing human population." Appleyard warns that the more control technology gives us over procreation and genetics—and it will give us increasing control over attributes such as sex, intelligence, and physical size—the easier it becomes to "generate new classes of human inferiority."

Advocates for untrammeled "reproductive freedom" argue that genetic information   7
and the spread of private eugenic practices will not threaten the dignity of those who may be regarded as mentally or physically "inferior." That judgment seems naive at best, if not disingenuous. We are just beginning to feel the subtly corrosive effects that eugenic abortion and genetic screening have on our ideas about the value of children and human life, the meaning of sex and procreation, and the nature of the family. Yet already our children need only open their college newspapers to see how the new classes of human superiority and inferiority are taking shape.

Reproductive Medicine and Ethics

Richard Taylor

Richard Taylor is an author, well-known philosopher, and professor emeritus at the University of Rochester. This article first appeared in the Spring 1999 issue of Free Inquiry.

Several far-reaching social changes in the past few decades have undermined the clus-   1
ter of norms known as "family values." These changes include the rise of feminism, the availability of contraceptives to unmarried people, the liberalization of divorce laws, the widespread acceptance of homosexuality, and, above all, the establishment of a constitutional right to abortion, which had hitherto been treated as a crime.

Now, however, the threat to those norms, which conservative religionists still cling to   2
with tenacity, comes from recent developments in reproductive medicine and, especially, from in vitro fertilization, the fertilization of human eggs in a dish. This has created possibilities of parenthood never before contemplated and given rise to situations that are impossible to reconcile with traditional ethics. What these developments appear to prove, in fact, is the validity of what Joseph Fletcher called "situation ethics."

Traditional ethics, which is as old as Western culture, presupposes that there are cer-   3
tain basic rules of morality that should govern all conduct. These are thought of as absolutes, such that departure from them amounts to compromising morality itself. Strict adherence to those rules is, accordingly, the measure of one's rectitude. It is this way of thinking that underlies the so-called family values.

The situationist, on the other hand, maintains that our actions should be governed, not   4
by fixed rules, of whatever supposed origin, but by their likely outcome, given the situations in which we are called upon to act. And, it is further maintained, there will always be situations in which established moral rules should be discarded.

5   Reproductive medicine now creates, with increasing frequency, situations so far beyond normal experience that even the most basic of such rules, those governing marriage and parenthood, lose their validity. The concept of parenthood, especially, has become hopelessly ambiguous.

6   The larger consequence of this is that traditional Judeo-Christian ethics, widely supposed to be mandated by God, is thrown into question too. If that ethical system can no longer govern the most basic of human relationships, those of marriage and parenthood, then how can it be adequate for far more complex relationships, such as those involved in war, human rights, the treatment of criminals, and so on?

7   What we are here calling traditional ethics rests on four assumptions that are seldom questioned. These are (1) that there is a real distinction between moral right and wrong; (2) that the moral rightness of our actions is what ultimately counts, such that no consideration of practical consequences can override it; (3) that the distinction between moral right and wrong results from moral principles or rules; and (4) that the basic concepts embodied in such principles are clear and unambiguous.

8   None of these assumptions survives the situations that modern reproductive techniques supply. Consider the following story, recently in the news. A California couple, John and Luanne Buzzanca, strongly desiring children, finally faced the fact that they were both infertile. They then resorted to in vitro fertilization, using anonymous donors for both eggs and sperm, plus a surrogate mother, who was paid to carry and bear the child and who then, as contractually arranged, happily turned the baby over to Mrs. Buzzanca. The husband, meanwhile, who had agreed to this arrangement and signed the contract to this effect, filed for divorce. When called upon for support payments for the child, he declined, noting, quite correctly, that he was not the child's father and therefore had no such obligation. The matter ended up in court and the judge agreed. In fact he had no choice, for statutory law expressly exempted any man from having to support another man's children. But then the judge went farther, declaring that Mrs. Buzzanca was not the child's mother either, since this baby had been born to another woman and had, in fact, no genetic tie whatever to Mrs. Buzzanca. Thus, by the application of seemingly obvious and clear rules and concepts, this child, though never orphaned, had no parents at all.

9   Or, for another recent example, consider the Iowa woman who was strongly desirous of children but was prevented by the anatomical fact that she had no uterus, although ovulation was normal. Her mother, on the other hand, had no such shortcoming, although she was postmenopausal. Mother and daughter arrived at a plan to fertilize the daughter's eggs in vitro, using her husband's sperm, and then let the mother carry and give birth to the resulting child. And that is exactly what happened. This, of course, gave rise to media accounts of the woman who bore her own grandchild, and it does, indeed, raise the question of the meaning of motherhood. What name, for example, should appear on the records of the obstetric ward as the mother? Or on the birth certificate? Both mother and daughter, it should be noted, are Roman Catholics, and of course the Church, following traditional ethics, declared this whole procedure to be inconsistent with its teaching. It seemed to the two women, however, to be a natural expression of their love and the solution to a problem. They were, then, situationists, even though they did not know it and would doubtless deny it if asked.

10   What a departure all this is from the time, not long ago, when people simply got married and, in the normal course of things, had children. If there were no children then the

wife was deemed "barren." The birth mother was the mother, and her husband was the father. If she had a child by another man she was an adulteress. The child of an unmarried woman was illegitimate and its mother drenched in shame.

The simplicity and certainty expressed in that cluster of concepts is still viewed with yearning by advocates of family values, but it can never be restored. Even if the vast social changes that have undermined it had not occurred, still the developments of modern medicine render it untenable. 11

The birth of triplets was once quite rare, and quintuplets attracted international attention. Now, thanks to modern reproductive medicine, we read of septuplets and even octuplets. The possibility of motherhood absolutely ceased at menopause. Now it is estimated that there are at least 100 post-menopausal late-life mothers, one of whom gave birth at age 63. 12

The purpose of in vitro fertilization is, of course, to make motherhood possible to women for whom it would otherwise be hopeless. When, however, it was realized, some time ago, that the infertility could be on the part of the husband, then the solution, involving the minimum of technology, was found in the anonymous donation of sperm. Physicians who thus assist childless couples—and even, now, unmarried women and lesbian couples—readily find healthy donors with good genetic backgrounds among medical students and other associates. The use of in vitro fertilization to overcome female infertility is simply the reverse of this, but it is much less simple, because the woman thus helped carries and bears the resulting child, and egg donation is far more complex than sperm donation. It is also much less common for the donor of eggs to remain anonymous. In fact, a common practice is for that donor, and her background, to be made known to the prospective mother and even to meet with her and enter into a formal contract. Such disclosure of identity rarely occurs in the case of semen donors. 13

Surrogate motherhood, which of course does not by itself require special medical technology, has nevertheless had a profound effect on traditional notions. A surrogate mother not only carries and bears a child but is normally the source of the egg. She thus fulfills completely the concept of being the child's mother, even though another woman is standing by to claim that role, as contractually arranged, her husband having contributed the sperm. The practice has been attacked as adultery, even though there is no carnal contact between the surrogate mother and the sperm donor. It has also been attacked as the selling of children, even though it is a man's own child that is supposedly "sold" to him. For such reasons as this, surrogate motherhood is generally banned by law. There is, on the other hand, no such prohibition of surrogate fatherhood, that is, sperm donation. 14

It is, however, the fertilization of human eggs in a dish that has had the profoundest effects upon ethics. It originated in England in 1978, and the world was rocked with astonishment at the first such normal and healthy "test tube baby." The technique did not become common in the United States until ten years later, and not until several years after that was it made available to women in their early forties. Now it is no longer rare for women in their fifties to bear children, using anonymous donors of eggs. 15

In 1994 there were over 40,000 cases of in vitro fertilization in the United States resulting in nearly 10,000 births. Today it is estimated that over 40,000 children owe their existence to this procedure. The probability of success by this method, it has been found, is greatly increased by the use of egg donors, as opposed to using the mother's own eggs; indeed, the success rate is more than doubled, to the point that nearly half of such 16 procedures result in pregnancy. This is significant in view of the high cost and the very considerable discomfort and pain involved in the production of human eggs, by hormonal stimulation and surgical removal of the eggs.

17   In vitro fertilization has also given rise to a whole new set of problems concerning the status and use of human embryos. The procedure often results in far more embryos than are needed to achieve pregnancy, and the question arises, What to do with them? They can be kept frozen indefinitely and then used to achieve pregnancy for other women and thus have considerable market value. But these embryos, even though they may be composed of only four, eight, or perhaps 140 cells, are in a very clear sense human beings—not fully developed human beings, to be sure, but human nonetheless. And yet to prohibit their sale on this ground would be totally irrational. What is the alternative? To flush them down the sink?

18   The clash with traditional ethics becomes even more apparent in light of the fact that the undifferentiated tissue of human embryos holds great promise for the alleviation and perhaps the cure of degenerative diseases, especially Parkinson's disease and Huntington's disease. Law prohibits government funding of research involving embryos, but the effect of this is that such research is privately funded, and secret. No law prohibits radical use of aborted fetuses, illustrating once more the absurdity that can result when we try to impose traditional norms on new situations. In Australia it is forbidden to do research using the tissue of any embryo that could become a human being, so scientists there send the embryos to Singapore, where the placental cells are removed, and the embryos, now no longer capable of becoming human beings, are returned to Australia for research.

19   Doubtless other high-tech reproductive methods await us, to stir ever greater controversy. What has been done so far has contributed greatly to human happiness, rendering parenthood possible to many for whom it would otherwise be hopeless, and giving rise to research of enormous promise.

20   Each advance is going to generate controversy, clashing with norms that apply fairly well to common situations but not to uncommon ones that emerge from modern medicine. We have to choose between allegiance to these established norms, which is the choice of conservative religionists, and human well-being, the choice of the situationist.

FOR CLASS DISCUSSION

1. New reproductive technology, including the use of egg donors, raises controversial issues on many fronts.
   a. What ethical issues emerge?
   b. What legal issues emerge?
   c. What medical issues emerge?
   d. What issues emerge concerning public policy, health-care costs, and insurance costs?

2. Discussion of reproductive technology often turns to the landmark *Buzzanca* case in Orange County, California. Summarize in your own words the details of the *Buzzanca* case. What was the original trial court decision? What was the argument of the appellate court in overturning the trial court's decision?

3. Imagine a case in which an infertile couple enters into contract with a surrogate mother to bear a child using another couple's frozen zygote. Imagine further that the original couple divorces (as in the *Buzzanca* case) but that all three women in the case decide they want custody of the baby. What criteria would you use to decide whether the genetic mother, the gestational mother, or the woman whose "intent" led to the surrogate pregnancy should have custody of the child?

4. Choose one of the arguments for closer analysis, applying the second set of guide questions on pages 465–66.

OPTIONAL WRITING ASSIGNMENT   You and your friends have read the following classified ad in your student newspaper (Note: This is a real ad, taken from a university newspaper in 1999):

EGG DONORS NEEDED.   Give the gift of life. Loving couple eagerly seeking egg donor. If you are college educated, caucasian, height/weight proportionate, with fair hair and eye color, age 21–30, with healthy lifestyle and family history, please help a couple who very much want a child. Besides our sincere gratitude, you will be compensated $2000; medical expenses will be covered. All inquiries are confidential. Please call [name removed] at [telephone number].

One of your friends is thinking of answering this ad and becoming an egg donor. Drawing on the reasons discussed in the articles, develop the strongest case you can think of either to persuade your friend to make the call and help this couple or to dissuade her from taking this step.

ENVIRONMENTALISM VERSUS CULTURALISM

The Makah Manifesto

Keith A. Johnson

In the mid-1990s, the Makah Nation, a Native American tribe on Washington's Olympic Peninsula, informed the United States government that it intended to resume its ancient cultural practice of whaling—a right guaranteed to the tribe in an 1855 treaty. The announcement touched off a worldwide debate on issues of international whaling. The Sea Shepherd Society, a powerful antiwhaling organization, led the antiwhaling resistance against the Makah. The following argument, originally published in the Seattle Times *on August 23, 1998, was written by Keith A. Johnson, president of the Makah Whaling Commission and a member of the Makah Tribal Council.*

1   I am a Makah Indian and president of the Makah Whaling Commission, comprised of representatives from 23 traditional whaling families of our tribe. For the past three years, we have been reading the attacks made on us by animal-rights organizations, aimed at stopping our whale hunt. These attacks contain distortions, exaggerations and outright falsehoods. Reading these things has sickened and angered me and I feel I must respond.

WHAT WE PLAN TO DO

2   We plan to conduct a whale hunt this year, sometime in October or November. While we are legally authorized to take up to five whales per year, our management plan limits the number of landed whales over a five-year period to 20, or an average of four per year. But I want to point out that our whaling commission will issue a permit only if there is an unmet need in the community, so it is possible that as little as one whale per year will be taken.

WHY DOES THE TRIBE WANT TO DO THIS?

3   Whaling has been part of our tradition for more than 2,000 years. Although we had to stop in the 1920s because of the scarcity of gray whales, their abundance now makes it possible to resume our ancient practice of whale hunting. Many of our tribal members feel that our health problems result from the loss of our traditional seafood and sea-mammal diet. We would like to restore the meat of the whale to that diet. We also believe that the problems that are troubling our young people stem from lack of discipline and pride and we hope that the restoration of whaling will help to restore that. But we also want to fulfill the legacy of our forefathers and restore a part of our culture that was taken from us.

HOW DID WE GET A LEGAL RIGHT TO HUNT?

4   Before entering into negotiations with the Makah for cessions of our extensive lands on the Olympic Peninsula in 1855, the United States government was fully aware that our people lived primarily on whale, seal and fish. They knew that we hunted several species of whales and had a substantial commerce in whale oil that had brought us prosperity. When U.S. Territorial Gov. Isaac Stevens arrived at Neah Bay in December 1855 to enter into negotiations with our leaders, he was met with strong declarations from them that in exchange for ceding our lands to the U.S., they demanded guarantees of their rights on the ocean and specifically, of the right to take whale. The treaty minutes show Gov. Stevens saying to the Makahs:

"The Great Father know what whalers you are—how you go far to sea to take whale."

He went on to promise U.S. assistance in promoting our whaling commerce. He then   5
presented a treaty containing the specific guarantee of the U.S., securing the right of the
Makahs to continue whaling. The treaty, accepted by us, is the only treaty ever made by
the U.S. that contained such a guarantee. The treaty was ratified by Congress in 1855 and
has since been upheld by all the courts, including the U.S. Supreme Court.

To us, it is as powerful and meaningful a document as the U.S. Constitution is to you,   6
because it is what our forefathers bequeathed to us. In fact, one of our whalers has said that
when he is in the canoe whaling, he will be reaching back in time and holding hands with
his great-grandfathers, who wanted us to be able to whale.

WILL THE MAKAHS SELL ANY OF THE WHALE MEAT?

Absolutely not! Yet, animal-rights groups such as The Sea Shepherd Conservation   7
Society continue to insist that we secretly plan to sell whale meat to Japan. That claim has
been repeated endlessly by other animal-rights groups. It is utterly false.

Although our treaty guaranteed a commercial right, we have agreed to limit ourselves   8
to noncommercial whaling. We have no plans to sell whale meat in the future.

Though it may be difficult for some people to accept, we are acting out of purely cul-   9
tural motives. In fact, it is costing our tribe an enormous amount of money to carry on the
whale-hunting program. It is, if you please, part of our religion, because for us, culture
means religion.

IS THERE ANY CONSERVATION ISSUE?

Absolutely not. The Eastern Pacific or California gray whale has been studied by sci-   10
entists around the world and it is established that the gray-whale population is currently at
an all-time high of around 22,000. The population continues to increase at 2.5 percent per
year, despite an annual harvest which has gone as high as 165 by Russian aborigines called
Chukotki.

The gray whale was removed from the endangered-species list in 1994 and the popu-   11
lation is now considered to be at its maximum level.

In fact, some biologists have raised the question of whether the number of gray whales   12
may be nearing the carrying capacity of their range, that is, the number that can be supported by the food resources. No reputable biologist or whale scientist has suggested that
our taking five whales a year will present any conservation threat whatsoever to the gray-
whale stock.

The fact that no one can legitimately argue that this is a conservation threat is one of   13
the main reasons why two of America's leading conservation organizations have refused to
join in the attack on our whaling: The Sierra Club and Greenpeace. There are animal-rights
activists within those organizations who are trying to get them to come out against our
whaling, but they have steadfastly refused because they do not see this as a conservation
issue.

THE WISHES OF THE TRIBE

14   Our attackers continue to claim that we are disregarding the views of the majority of our members. They repeatedly publicize in the media and elsewhere the views of two women who are members of the tribe and are outspoken opponents of whaling. While we respect the right of all of our members to hold and to express their views on any subject, I must respectfully point out that these two women do not speak for anywhere near the majority of the tribe and there are other elders who strongly support whaling.

15   In the last opinion poll we held on this issue, 85 percent of those voting favored whaling. There is a faction within our tribe that is opposed to whaling, but they are a distinct minority.

16   I can say proudly that the Makah Tribal Council and the Makah Whaling Commission represents the strongly held views of the majority of our members.

17   We were the premier whalers on the American continent and were able to enjoy a prosperous life because of our whaling trade. Our forefathers bequeathed our right to whale to us in our treaty and we feel that a treaty right which cannot be exercised is no right. I can tell you that our tribe is not prepared to abandon our treaty right.

HOW WE PLAN TO CONDUCT THE HUNT

18   We will hunt the whale from one or two sea-going canoes, each carved from a single cedar log by Indian carvers. Each canoe will be manned by a crew of eight whalers and will include a harpooner and rifleman. Both these men will be stationed in the bow. The harpooner will use a stainless steel harpoon mounted on a wooden shaft. It will be connected to the canoe by a rope with floats attached. The harpooner will throw the harpoon at the whale. Immediately afterwards, or simultaneously, the rifleman will fire a special high-powered rifle using a .50-caliber round.

19   We are using this specially designed rifle and this ammunition on the specific recommendations of Dr. Allen Ingling, a veterinarian and specialist in arms and the humane killing of animals. This weapon has been tested by Ingling, who has worked with the National Marine Mammal Laboratory of the National Marine Fisheries Service. Ingling has instructed us on the target area to be hit so as to bring about almost instantaneous loss of consciousness and death of the whale.

20   The use of the special rifle has been attacked by many animal-rights groups as brutal and [un]traditional. I believe these attacks are dishonest. In the 19th century, we didn't use such a weapon; we used harpoons and spears. The whale often died after a prolonged and agonizing time from internal bleeding. That was not humane.

21   I don't hear any of these animal-rights groups attacking us for conducting the hunt with a canoe. The lives of at least eight people will be at risk on the dangerous waters of the Pacific in October and November to hunt the whale. That is our traditional method. If we wanted to abandon all cultural tradition, we would simply use a deck-mounted cannon firing a harpoon into the whale. No, our canoe has been carved by traditional carvers and will be paddled by eight whalers who have sanctified themselves by rituals that are ancient and holy to us. The hunt is being conducted in a manner that is both traditional and modern.

THE DIRE PREDICTION

The Sea Shepherd organization has been making sweeping claims that if we hunt a whale, whales will begin attacking humans throughout the waters of the state and devastate the whale-watching industry. This is complete nonsense.   22

First of all, most of the whaling watching is focused on orcas, not gray whales, and takes place in Puget Sound and the eastern area of the Strait of Juan de Fuca. As for gray whales, whale watching on this species is primarily concentrated in Westport, far from any area where we will be hunting whales.   23

The idea that whales will somehow begin to act aggressively against human boats or change their migratory path to avoid boats is false. The whales passing through the waters of Washington state have come here after being hunted and attacked in the Bering Sea by the Russian indigenous people called Chukotki. The Chukotki have been hunting the gray whale for more than 40 years and there is no evidence that gray whales have attacked other boats. Nor is there any evidence that whales communicate with each other and spread the message that humans are the enemy, to be attacked or avoided.   24

This is a fantasy promoted by animal-rights activists.   25

WHAT IS OUR CULTURAL NEED?

It is hard for us to explain to outsiders our "cultural" attitudes about whaling. Some of us find it repugnant to even have to explain this to anyone else. But let me tell you about my own case.   26

I have a bachelor's degree in education from Central Washington University, Ellensburg. I was the first Makah teacher in the Neah Bay School System from 1972 through 1976. I received my principal's credentials from Western Washington University, Bellingham, in 1975 and served as vice principal of the Neah Bay Schools in 1976 and between 1990 and 1997.   27

Have I lost my culture? No. I come from a whaling family. My great-grandfather, Andrew Johnson, was a whaler. He landed his last whale in 1907. My grandfather, Sam Johnson, was present when the whale landed and told me he played on the whale's tail. I lived with my grandfather for 16 years and heard his stories about whaling and the stories of family whaling told by my father, Percy, and my uncle, Clifford.   28

When I was a teenager, I was initiated into Makah whaling rituals by my uncle. While I cannot divulge these sacred rituals, they involve isolation, bathing in icy waters and other forms of ritual cleansing that are still practiced today. I have been undergoing rituals to prepare me for the whaling this year. Other families are using their own rituals. I am proud to carry on my family legacy and my father is overjoyed because he is going to see this in his lifetime.   29

I can tell you that all of the Makah whalers are deeply stirred by the prospect of whaling. We are undergoing a process of mental and physical toughening now. We are committed to this because it is our connection to our tribal culture and because it is a treaty right—not because we see the prospect of money.   30

We are willing to risk our lives for no money at all. The only reward we will receive will be the spiritual satisfaction of hunting and dispatching the whale and bringing it back to our people to be distributed as food.   31

32   Recently, the Progressive Animal Welfare Society (PAWS) distributed a brochure in which they implied we have lost our cultural need for whaling because we have adapted to modern life. They cite our ". . . lighted tennis courts . . . Federal Express . . . and other amenities . . ."

33   Well, excuse me! I want to tell PAWS that the two tennis courts on our high-school grounds have no lights. How about the fact that Federal Express makes deliveries to our reservation? Does that mean that we have lost our culture?

34   These attacks on our culture and our status are foolish. No one can seriously question who we are; we are a small Native-American tribe whose members were the whalers of the American continent. We retain our whaling traditions today. It resonates through all of our people from the youngest to the oldest, and we don't take kindly to other people trying to tell us what our culture is or should be.

THE DOMINO EFFECT

35   Animal-rights groups have been scaring each other and pumping up the claim that if we whale, it will mean the collapse of all restrictions against commercial whaling and whaling will be resumed everywhere. This is nonsense. If there are other indigenous people who have a legitimate whaling culture and whaling tradition, then they should be allowed to whale just as we do. The rest is all hype.

36   The leader of the pack attacking us is The Sea Shepherd Conservation Society. They have been responsible for a steady stream of propaganda aimed at inflaming the public against us, some of which has been repeated by other anti-whaling groups, who have assumed it was factual.

37   Who is Sea Shepherd? They are a California-based organization that has for years operated on the fringe of mainstream conservation groups. They have built a flourishing organization supported by contributions from around the world. They portray themselves as the swashbucklers of the ocean because they have sunk whaling ships. This action has earned them the label of a terrorist organization and they have been barred from attending the deliberations of the International Whaling Commission even as observers since 1987.

38   They applied for readmission in 1995 and the IWC sanction again denied them admission.

39   They threatened to sink our boats if we whaled without IWC sanction, smug in the assumption that we would never get approval from the IWC. They have since churned out reams of material attacking us.

40   We can't hope to keep up with this barrage by Sea Shepherd and others. These groups are well-financed. Sea Shepherd operates two ocean-going vessels, a submarine, an airplane, a helicopter and other waterborne craft. It seems to me that Sea Shepherd is actually in the commerical whaling business and we're their best ticket now.

THE ETHICAL ISSUE

41   The arguments and claims by Sea Shepherd and the other anti-whaling groups are designed to inflame the public against us and to attack the honesty of our motives. They mask the real aim of these groups: To prevent the killing of a single whale.

Some people honestly believe that it is wrong to kill one of these animals. Maybe their minds are made up, but I want to say to them that we Makahs know the whales, probably better than most people. We are out on the waters of the ocean constantly and we have lived with and among whales for more than 2,000 years. We are not cruel people. But we have an understanding of the relationship between people and the mammals of the sea and land.   42

We are a part of each other's life. We are all part of the natural world and predation is also part of life on this planet. So orca whales attack and eat whales and whales calves as well as seals and fish. Those who regard the orcas simply as cute may prefer to ignore this side of their nature. But there is a reason they are called "killer whales." In fact, they were originally called "whale killers."   43

I want to deal with the claims of those who would romanticize the whale and ascribe almost human characteristics to it. To attribute to gray whales near-human intelligence is romantic nonsense—as any professional whale biologist can tell you. The photographs of gray whales surfacing to be petted by people are all taken in the calving lagoons of Baja, Calif., and Mexico. This behavior is not exhibited by gray whales anywhere else, particularly by migrating whales passing through our waters.   44

The whales we will hunt are migrating whales and we will not hunt any mother whale with a calf.   45

Whales have captured the public's fascination. The world has had a similar fascination with our cultures, but whenever we had something you wanted or did something you didn't like, you tried to impose your values on us.   46

Too often white society has demonstrated this kind of cultural arrogance. To us the implication that our culture is inferior if we believe in whaling is demeaning and racist. The Makah people have been hurt by these attacks, but nevertheless, we are committed to continuing in what we feel is the right path.   47

We Makah hope that the general public will try to understand and respect our culture and ignore the attacks of extremists.   48

Where Is the Whales' Manifesto?
Sea Shepherd's Response
to the Makah Manifesto

Paul Watson

Paul Watson is the founder and president of the Sea Shepherd Conservation Society. This argument appeared on the Sea Shepherd Web site with the following URL: www.seashepherd.org/wh/us/mkmanif.html. We accessed the site on November 18, 1999.

Makah Whaling Commission President Keith Johnson's "Makah Manifesto" appeared in the *Seattle Times* on August 23. It was short on facts but long on arrogance, venom, and   1 righteous indignation largely directed at the Sea Shepherd Conservation Society for having brought unwanted public attention to the Makah's whale hunting scheme.

2   It is ironic and sad, yet appropriate, that I find myself leading the fight to *oppose plans by the Makah Tribal Council* to slaughter four Eastern Pacific gray whales in the waters of Washington state.

3   A few weeks ago in Seattle, a sympathizer for the Makah's whaling initiative, demanding to know why I cared so much about four whales, yelled at me "Where were you when they were shooting Indians at Wounded Knee!?"

4   "I was there," I answered.

5   I received my life's mission to protect the great whales while serving as a medic for the American Indian Movement (AIM) at Wounded Knee, South Dakota, in 1973. I was holding the other end of the stretcher when a U.S. Marshall's bullet struck down medic Rocky Madrid as we were running through a hail of lead. I assisted Leonard Crow Dog in removing the bullet. I was made a warrior brother to the Oglala Lakota Nation and was given the name Gray Wolf Clearwater. In the sweat lodge ceremony, I had a vision, a dream wherein an arrow struck a buffalo. The arrow had a long string attached to it. The buffalo asked for my help and I broke the string and chased the hunter away.

6   Wallace Black Elk interpreted my dream. "Your mission is to help the buffalo of the sea—the whales," he said. "It will not be easy."

7   Two years later, in a high-speed zodiac, Bob Hunter and I became the first people to place our bodies between a whale and a harpoon. We were confronting the Russian whaling fleet sixty miles off the coast of Northern California in the first Greenpeace whale campaign. Never did I dream that more than twenty years later I would be returning home to defend the whales once again in American waters, this time from Americans.

THE REAL STAKES

8   Native Americans have been on board Sea Shepherd's ships on many campaigns, including our 1991 boarding and seizure of the replica *Santa Maria* in Puerto Rico, pre-empting the 500th anniversary celebration of the Columbus voyage. We secured a formal apology from the Spanish government for the conquest and exploitation of native Americans.

9   This is not an issue of race or culture. It's an issue of global whale conservation. In the Makah Manifesto, whaling commissioner Johnson attempts to assure the *Seattle Times'* readers that it is no such thing. It's just four whales. Commissioner Johnson avers that the Sierra Club, despite the urgings of "animal-rights activists . . . who are trying to get them to come out against our whaling," has "refused to join the attack" because it doesn't "see this as a conservation issue."

10   In fact, the Makah approached the Sierra Club in a bid to secure their support for the hunt. The Club appointed a 12-person task force to look into the issue. The task force did so, concluded that the hunt was environmentally unsound, and voted 11–1 to condemn it. The dissenting vote came from the chair, an Alaskan Eskimo. Citing her cultural heritage of whaling, she overruled the vote and dissolved the task force. As a result, the Sierra Club has opted to take no position on the hunt. Sea Shepherd is not investing this time and expense, committing our entire fleet, to oppose a tribal whale hunt of four or five whales. We

know our opposition is headquartered in *Tokyo* and *Oslo.* Last year, at the Monaco meeting of the International Whaling Commission, Tadaio Nakamura, representing the Japanese delegation, asked "What is the difference between cultural necessity for the Makah and cultural necessity for the Japanese?"

If cultural necessity becomes a reason for whaling, the slaughter will be unrelenting.   11
The Makah will be killing the grays for the benefit of the Japanese. Whether or not the meat is sold to Japan directly, the Japanese whaling industry will profit enormously because the Makah will be turning the key to overturning the global moratorium on whaling. Commissioner Johnson can say that it isn't so, but it is indeed the case that if the Makah succeed in changing the basis for aboriginal whaling to a cultural need, as opposed to a subsistence need, the Japanese, Icelanders, Norwegians, and many others will claim the same right.

The United States has been a great whale conservation nation for three decades. We   12
are preparing to throw that away in order that a few Makah whalers may "traditionally" blast a whale from the water with .50-caliber assault rifles. Meanwhile, in Tokyo, the recruitment of the United States into the ranks of the whale-killing nations will be noted in the boardrooms of the Japanese whaling industry with a quiet satisfaction.

If the Makah kill those whales this October, the harpoon cannons of the North Atlantic,   13
North Pacific, and Antarctica will be pouring the blood of thousands of whales into the sea.

PERCEPTION VS. REALITY

While we may debate that point (as, either way, it constitutes a conclusion based on   14
an event which has not yet occurred), Commissioner Johnson's manifesto was replete with more than a few outright lies, two of the largest ones coming in the same sentence: "[Sea Shepherd] threatened to sink our boats if we whaled without [International Whaling Commission] sanction, smug in the assumption that we would never get approval from the IWC." Contrary to much popular opinion, feverish rumor, and inaccurate reporting (energetically disseminated by the Makah), we have never threatened to sink the Makah's boats, and the Makah never got approval from the IWC for their whale hunt. That second widespread misperception is the result of an energetic *"spin" effort by the U.S. delegation* following the 1997 IWC meeting. This has misled many people, but has not changed the fact that the Makah did not get specific permission to hunt whales from the international body that is the ultimate permitting authority on whale hunting. Nor does it alter the fact that the clause requiring a recognized subsistence need in order to receive an aboriginal exemption to the ban was included in the IWC resolution addressing the issue for the express purpose of clarifying the point that the Makah have no such authorization and are therefore barred from a hunt as a matter of international law.

Whaling commissioner Johnson says "We have no plans to sell whale meat in the   15
future. Though it may be difficult for some people to accept, we are acting out of purely cultural motives."

There's a reason why the *Seattle Times'* readers should find this difficult to accept: 16
Because the Makah have previously affirmed that the hunt has a financial motivation, and that they have every intention of selling whale meat in the future. On May 25, 1995, three weeks after the Makah Tribal Council first cited its need to kill whales for purposes of

spiritual and cultural revival, *Seattle Times* columnist Don Hannula related a conversation with Makah fisheries manager Dave Sones in which Sones said "the tribe hopes in the future to do some commercial whaling. There are markets overseas for the meat and oil." Hannula further reported that Sones told him "the value of a Gray whale is estimated at a half-million dollars." Statements like these—which abruptly ceased shortly after the Makah retained the services of the public relations firm of Miller & Associates to handle the whaling issue—make a dramatic contrast to Mr. Johnson's latter-day claims of cultural purity.

17   There is another statement the Makah Tribal Council would like everyone to forget: In 1991, in pressing the National Marine Fisheries Service for the removal of the Gray whale from the Endangered Species List, the Makah's lobby group asserted that this move was "aimed not at allowing the hunting of Gray whales but so that research money can be shifted to other species in need of monitoring, such as salmon or marine birds."

18   "It is costing our tribe an enormous amount of money to carry on the whale hunting program," says commissioner Johnson. They're not alone. Clallam County officials are seeking $150,000 in Federal funds to underwrite estimated policing costs of the hunt. They have already received $10,000 from the Justice Department. Over $200,000 in federal funding has gone to support the Makah's whale hunt lobbying efforts, including the cost of food and travel to France, New Zealand, Oman, and Alaska by tribal members. The whale hunt has already paid off handsomely for the Makah Tribal Council, at taxpayers' expense. In the face of this jackpot, commissioner Johnson has the gall to say "Sea Shepherd is actually in the commercial whaling business and we're their best ticket."

19   And while U.S. taxpayers, the vast majority of whom overwhelmingly abhor the killing of whales, are forced to pick up the tab for the Makah's whale hunt, whaling commissioner Johnson proudly asserts that the majority of the tribe backs the plans of the Makah Tribal Council and Makah Whaling Commission. He doesn't say how these groups go about securing their backing. Seven Makah tribal elders have gone on record in opposition to the whaling scheme. They have been called "traitors" by the MTC and have been subjected to threats, intimidation, and firings. "It's grandmothers fighting this fight against them," tribal elder Dottie Chamblin says of the MTC. "The tribal council issued a memo that nobody was to talk to the newspaper. . . . They wanted to banish those of us who oppose whaling from the reservation. This fear of banishment really stopped a lot of people from helping us."

THE RACE THING

20   Makah tribal officials are very good at calling us liars and propagandists, and have been doing so steadily for the last three years. They are equally proficient at playing the race card. A sympathetic national media (including this newspaper and the Sunday *New York Times Magazine*) has been saturated with the reverse racism inherent in the "noble native" take on the hunt. They have effectively created an atmosphere in which concern for the welfare of whales is now perceived as a de facto attack on native rights and the cultural heritage of an oppressed minority.

21   Where is this stepped-up campaign based on heavy-handed accusations of racism, political incorrectness and invocations of white guilt really coming from? The recent history

of a situation Sea Shepherd has been involved in for some time north of the border offers
a telling parallel.

In 1985, the environmental movement had the barbaric Canadian seal hunt on the
ropes and heading for extinction due to successful combined campaigns of direct action,
media work, public education, letter writing, boycotts, and a European ban on the import
of baby seal pelts. That year, the Canadian Department of External Affairs got an idea about
how to blunt or divert international censure of the hunt. In contemplating "the manipulation of public attitudes," they determined that "defusing the basis for individual action/
commitment" should have been the government's goal when international outrage over the
hunt first began to build, but now it was necessary "to take dramatic counter-action that
will dissipate the initial commitment. Such action could be based on contradictory emotional themes of interest to the same target publics, e.g., preservation of traditional indigenous cultures." ("Defence of the Fur Trade," CDEA discussion paper, May 1985.)   22

It worked. The government p.r. machine cranked up, and the "traditional" Canadian
seal hunt managed to survive the collapse of the much larger commercial hunt. Though reduced from 80 to 90% of what it had been before, the hunt was kept alive, and so was able
to roar back to life ten years later as a government-subsidized commercial enterprise, larger
than it had ever been.   23

The Canadian Department of External Affairs' confuse-&-conquer strategy was not new,
but it is seldom recognized by the people who are duped by it. The Makah Tribal Council's
p.r. consultants are clearly advising them that this is the strongest card they can play, but
no amount of cultural agit-prop can obscure the reality of what the Makah are planning to
do. The near-desperation inherent in commissioner Johnson's attempted defense of the indefensible is evident in this extraordinary paragraph near the end of the Makah Manifesto:
"The photographs of gray whales surfacing to be petted by people are all taken in the calving lagoons of Baja, California, and Mexico. This behavior is not exhibited by gray whales
anywhere else, particularly by migrating whales passing through our waters."   24

Setting aside the fact that Mr. Johnson, a former school teacher, evidently does not
know that Baja, California, is part of Mexico, one must wonder exactly what point he is trying to make, and what he thinks "migrating" means. Does he not know that the whales
being petted in Baja are the very same whales the Makah intend to blast into oblivion off
the Olympic Peninsula? Does he believe they become different whales when they move
from one place to the other? Does he think the failure of the whales to engage in the same
behavior off the coast of Washington as they do off the coast of Mexico is a prerequisite for
their execution? It is statements like these that cast doubt upon Mr. Johnson's assertions
that "we Makahs know the whales, probably better than most people . . . we have an understanding of the relationship between people, the mammals of the sea and land."   25

This, of course, is another way of saying "we know better than you"; that the Makah
are culturally superior and above the national and international laws that prevent other
American citizens from sailing forth with heavy weaponry to put a few slugs into passing
cetaceans out of nostalgia for the cultural traditions of our hearty whaling ancestors.   26

When the Makah hunted whales, they did not hunt out of a cultural or traditional
impulse, they hunted in order to survive. This, and the arduous and dangerous nature of
the hunt, was the entire grounding for the hunt's cultural context. Without that purpose,   27

the hunt has no meaning. The need for the Makah to hunt whales has passed into history. What they contemplate now, as minutely described by Mr. Johnson, is an unreal, half-hearted, techno/traditional hybrid, further bastardized with military .50-caliber rifles and power boats (which commissioner Johnson neglected to mention), which are being used in order to eliminate insofar as possible the physical perils of what was once a nearly equal combat arising from a basic necessity.

28   From this primal equation arose the body of cultural traditions around the hunt. Without that equation, the hunt is an act of make-believe, an empty gesture toward a vanished past with only one component that will have a real, immediate meaning: The violent death of a living creature that has every right to be left alone.

Makah Whaling: We Must Either Move Forward or Be Left in Dustbin of History
Stephen D. Bennett

This argument appeared as a letter to the editor in the Seattle Times *on May 24, 1999.*

Editor, The Times:

1   I watched the TV coverage of the Makah whale hunt. (Actually, it looked more like the Keystone cops hunting whales.) What a sad sight. We were led to understand that this whale hunt is as much a "spiritual" experience as it is a connection with the past. I don't see much traditional or spiritual about being towed out to sea by an aluminum power boat with a .50-caliber gun to blow the whale's brains out after one of these brave "warriors" manages to wound it.

2   Then, after the kill, I understand the whale will be sold to Japan. What on earth does this have to do with traditions, or spirituality? Why can't these people move into the 20th century like civilized folk?

3   Maybe we should let everyone return to their traditional past so they could re-connect with their roots.

4   Perhaps in Central America the Aztec descendants could reinstate human sacrifice for spiritual purposes. Maybe some of the other cultures could try cannibalism to re-establish their connections with their past.

5   Maybe I should re-connect with my ancestral past and burn my neighbors at the stake because they are rumored to be witches. What is the difference? These are all nothing more than acts of savagery.

6   We must either move forward or be left in the dustbin of history. If we want to have our traditions remembered, we should write them in history books, teach our children about them, even re-enact them, but not in real life (or death).

7   Just because our ancestors did it doesn't make it right for us to do it, too.

Flouting the Convention

William Aron, William Burke, and Milton Freeman

This article appeared in the May 1999 issue of Atlantic Monthly.

THE ONGOING CAMPAIGN TO BAN ALL COMMERCIAL WHALING IS DRIVEN BY POLITICS RATHER THAN SCIENCE, AND IS SETTING A TERRIBLE PRECEDENT

This month the International Whaling Commission will hold its fifty-first annual meeting, in Grenada. Once again pro- and anti-whaling forces will barrage the commission and each other with press releases, angry denunciations, and publicity stunts. Once again politics will drown out science and will push the commission into a state of posturing irrelevancy. And once again the result will be a disservice to the people who whale, to the commission itself, and, most troubling, to international environmental law and sound resource management. Indeed, the continuing dysfunction of the IWC—one of the most prominent conservation groups in the world—should worry everybody who has concerns about preserving our natural heritage.   1

In 1946 a fifteen-year effort by whaling nations to exert multilateral control over the whaling industry finally produced the International Convention for the Regulation of Whaling, the fundamental purpose of which was "to provide for the proper conservation of whale stocks and thus make possible the orderly development of the whaling industry." The convention established the fourteen-nation IWC, which was empowered to regulate the industry but was granted no authority to amend the convention itself. In adopting, revising, or terminating regulations the IWC is required always to follow the convention's intent—namely, as explicitly stated in Article V, "to provide for the conservation, development, and optimum utilization of the whale resources," taking into consideration "the interests of the consumers of whale products and the whaling industry." Simply put, no possible interpretation of the convention allows for putting an end to whaling when credible scientific opinion supports the sustainable use of abundant whale resources.   2

The IWC started off badly. For nearly thirty years after its inception it tolerated whaling at unsustainable levels. Many of the largest species declined so precipitously that in 1972 the United States began calling for a ten-year moratorium on all commercial whaling. The proposal was intended to shock the IWC into getting its house in order—that is, putting into effect a management system that would both maintain the whaling industry and allow whale populations to recover. When the moratorium was voted down in 1972 and 1973, activists threatened to boycott goods from whaling nations; targets included Russian vodka, Japanese cameras and TV sets, and Norwegian and Icelandic fish products. The whaling industry was forced to compromise.   3

In 1974 the IWC endorsed the New Management Procedure—an Australian plan, with strong backing from the United States, that essentially banned whaling of all overexploited stocks but permitted commercial catches of abundant stocks at levels that would not threaten their existence. The plan satisfied the IWC Scientific Committee, most of whose   4 members had objected both to the excessive size of the earlier whale quotas and to the idea of a moratorium on commercial whaling, which they also viewed as excessive. The NMP took effect in the 1975–1976 whaling season. Since then not one whale population has been jeopardized by a commercial whaling operation.

5   Such success was not enough for the anti-whaling forces, however, who seized on the fact that the NMP called for scientific data, such as abundance estimates, growth rates, and identification of regional stocks, that were difficult to obtain with precision. Most of the Scientific Committee believed that the gaps in data were not important enough to stop controlled whaling. But the United States and other anti-whaling countries, urged on by the emerging animal-rights movement, tipped the scales in their own favor by recruiting additional nonwhaling nations to the commission—increasing its membership from the original fourteen to forty. (Any nation can accept the 1946 convention and become an equal voting member of the IWC.) Citing the alleged data-collection problems, the newly inflated IWC passed a moratorium on all commercial whaling in 1982. The vote for this moratorium marked a significant change: instead of trying to force the IWC to comply with the convention and support only sustainable whaling, the anti-whaling majority was trying to force the commission to flout it.

6   In a small compromise that has turned out to be an empty gesture, anti-whaling nations asked the Scientific Committee to undertake a comprehensive assessment of whale stocks by 1990—at which time the IWC was to reconsider the fate of the moratorium. The committee was also asked to develop an up-to-date replacement for the NMP. The result was the Revised Management Procedure, completed in 1993, which permitted whaling only if impartial systematic surveys had determined that an individual stock was not in danger. When the commission resisted even this modest plan for sustainable whaling, the chairman of the Scientific Committee quit.

7   In 1994 the RMP—a risk-averse successor to a management scheme that had already proved successful by terminating the harvest of all whales in jeopardy—was accepted in principle by the commission. In practice, however, the IWC has yet to allow a return to commercial whaling; instead it has deliberately dragged out negotiations over monitoring and enforcing the RMP. By focusing on increasingly arcane questions of logistics, costs, and methodology, each needing lengthy debate, the anti-whaling majority has successfully pushed the target for the whaling nations ever further into the future—a procedure that has been likened to moving the goal posts.

8   The cause of this charade is obvious: a majority of the IWC wants to halt all commercial whaling, no matter what the convention says. Indeed, Australia, Great Britain, New Zealand, and the United States—and, more recently, Austria and Italy—have explicitly stated that they will not approve commercial whaling under any conditions. In 1991 the Australian commissioner stated flatly that there was no longer any need to hunt "such large and beautiful animals" for food. Conceding that no scientific reason exists to ban all whaling, the U.S. commissioner announced in 1991 that he would defend the U.S. position on ethical grounds.

9   Such an approach, based on moral judgments rather than science, plainly violates both the convention and the international rule of law. And because anti-whaling activists will

accept nothing less than a total ban, they leave no room for good-faith negotiation and compromise. The whaling industry will not cooperate in its own elimination, nor will the governments of whaling nations permit their citizens to be victimized. As a result, scientists, whalers, and activists are locked in a never-ending battle. The bitter standoff violates international law, fosters tensions between otherwise friendly nations, and undermines environmental legislation. Worst of all, the cynical actions of the IWC's anti-whaling majority constitute a clear warning to all nations engaged in negotiating multilateral environmental agreements: Beware, for the United States and its allies may suddenly adopt new interpretations of long-standing principles, and use them against you. Even if you accept treaties, these countries may (for purely domestic reasons) apply sanctions against you for actions fully in compliance with those treaties.

Despite guidelines accompanying the International Convention for the Regulation of   10
Whaling that refer to only twelve whale species (right, pigmy right, bowhead, humpback, blue, fin, Bryde's, minke, sei, sperm, and Arctic and Antarctic bottlenose), many IWC members act as if the convention covered all whales—and even all cetaceans, the order of eighty-three species of aquatic mammals that also includes dolphins and porpoises. Few scientists deny that several species of whale—including the blue, the right, the bowhead, and the humpback—have been severely overhunted by commercial whalers and are now properly regarded as endangered. But almost all scientists admit that most other species are in no danger of extinction. Minke and pilot whales, for example, have populations of more than a million, and sperm whales have a population of about a million. Gray whales (probably more abundant now than ever) and some regional stocks of sei, Bryde's, and fin whales (less abundant than in earlier times, but not dramatically so) are in no sense endangered by controlled hunts.

Unsurprisingly, researchers continue to argue that endangered species should gener-   11
ally not be hunted. However, the IWC allows native peoples in Alaska and Siberia to hunt limited numbers of bowhead along with gray whales to meet their needs. Neither species has been adversely affected by such hunting. Estimates of the bowhead population in the late 1970s ranged from 500 to 2,000 animals; the current bowhead population is believed to exceed 8,000. The rise in the estimate is due in part to population growth but mostly to better survey techniques. It is estimated that the gray-whale population has increased from about 7,000 animals in the 1930s to more than 26,000 today, despite authorized subsistence catches of 140 or more a year. The difference is thought to reflect population growth.

Just because it is possible to harvest whales without placing their populations in jeopardy does not mean that the practice is acceptable. Whale protectionists often claim that whales are extremely intelligent—as smart as, if not smarter than, humankind—and that the killing of such highly sentient creatures is wrong. But whales have been studied intensively for decades, and there is still no strong evidence that they are uniquely intelligent. Many species throughout the animal kingdom demonstrate behaviors and abilities just as complex as those demonstrated by whales.

Another major objection to whaling is that it is an inhumane practice carried out un-   12
necessarily. Let us be clear: "humane killing" is an oxymoron. The best we can hope for in killing animals is that death be as quick and as nearly painless as possible. Experience has

shown that in the whaling industry this is largely achieved—just as it is in the food industries that kill millions of cattle, sheep, pigs, and chickens every day.

13   Some whaling-ban advocates feel that whaling has no place in the contemporary world.
They point to the fact that many industrialized countries, despite having engaged in commercial whaling twenty or thirty years ago, are now fervent opponents of whaling. If this
is the case, the advocates ask, why should Norway and Japan and a few other countries continue whaling? The trouble is that this argument assumes that there are no fundamental
cultural differences between whaling and nonwhaling societies: the former are simply considered to be stuck at an earlier stage of development, in need of being goosed up the ladder of progress.

14   Anthropologists believe otherwise. The societies that have abandoned whaling hunted
whales principally for oil. Until the late 1960s whale oil was used for many purposes—in
submarine guidance systems, for example, leading the Pentagon to object to listing sperm
whales as an endangered species. Indeed, the IWC was established in part to ensure the
profitability of the whale-oil business, which it did by setting quotas measured in units of
oil. When substitutes for whale oil became available in the 1970s, nations that whaled primarily for oil stopped hunting whales.

15   Things were different in other nations, especially Norway and Japan, where whaling is
an ancient occupation worthy of the respect and support that Americans award to, say, the
running of a farm. Norwegians view whaling as part of the hard, honorable life of a fisher-
man—a reliable slow-season activity that helps fishing communities to make it through the
year. The Japanese who come from a long line of whalers have deeply held moral beliefs
about maintaining their family tradition. To be prevented from honoring their ancestors in
this manner is a source of shame. After the 1982 moratorium some Norwegian fishers went
bankrupt. The same thing happened in Iceland. Given the abundance of the whale stocks,
these nations ask, why can't such people be free to practice their traditional livelihood? Anthropologists have long observed the primary role played by traditional foods in the social
structure and moral norms of a community—a role that is captured in the widely repeated
aphorism "you are what you eat." Asking people to give up their customary diet is in many
ways like asking them to give up part of their identity.

16   The Japanese are particularly angered by the IWC's ongoing failure to fulfill its legal
obligations to whaling-treaty members. They point to the extensive research—much of it
done by non-Japanese scientists and endorsed by the IWC Scientific Committee and the international scientific community—suggesting that an interim reinstatement of coastal
minke whaling (until the implementation of the RMP) would not be harmful. When such
research is ignored or trivialized by the IWC itself, it is easy for the Japanese to conclude
that the United States and its anti-whaling allies are irrational, dishonorable, and racially
prejudiced. To Japan and other countries, a Western antagonism to whaling and to the use
of whale products smacks of cultural imperialism.

17   To counter the pleas of countries like Norway and Japan, the anti-whaling members of
the IWC assert that worldwide public opinion now opposes commercial whaling. But the
convention's acceptance of whaling is not an isolated anachronism. In recent years United
Nations conferences have twice had an opportunity to oppose whaling, and have twice

declined to take it. In 1982, soon after the IWC adopted the whaling moratorium, 119 states signed the UN Convention on the Law of the Sea, an agreement that permits whaling on the high seas. Individual nations may forbid their nationals to take whales, and coastal states may prohibit all takes within their national waters, but unless states jointly agree otherwise, whaling can go on. In 1992 the UN Conference on Environment and Development reaffirmed the provisions of the Convention on the Law of the Sea, explicitly rejecting efforts by anti-whaling forces to exclude whales from the list of resources open to sustainable use and development. Both actions show that there is no international consensus against whaling.

Despite this lack of a consensus, in 1994 the New Zealand commissioner stated that his country would "work to maintain the moratorium on commercial whaling because it reflects the current reality of world opinion"—an assertion subsequently repeated by the British and U.S. commissioners. The evidence does not support this claim. Public-opinion polls have for years indicated that people in putatively anti-whaling countries do not know that many whale species are not near extinction—and that when they learn this fact, they are willing to support whaling. In April of last year, to cite a recent example, Responsive Management, an American polling firm specializing in environmental issues, released a survey of attitudes toward whaling in Australia, France, the United Kingdom, and the United States. At the outset of the survey 92 percent of those polled admitted that they knew little or nothing about minke whales, the species now of most interest to whaling countries. When informed that the minke is not endangered, that its harvest is traditional in some places, and that an IWC-managed hunt would ensure that there would be no adverse effect on whale numbers, 71 percent of U.S. respondents said they would endorse regulated whaling for minkes. A majority of respondents from each of the other three nations also favored minke whaling under these conditions, though the majority was not as large. [18]

These results are not surprising. Most people in the West know that they personally benefit from the slaughter of large numbers of food animals every year, and that in general it is perfectly lawful to take non-endangered animals in regulated hunts. Responsive Management found that only six percent of the Australian and U.S. respondents opposed whaling on the grounds of animal rights. [19]

Perhaps sensing that informed public support for a total whaling ban would be weak, whaling-ban advocates frequently resort to campaigns that can most kindly be referred to as "artful." Despite a decades-old scientific consensus that most whale species do not face extinction, Greenpeace and other anti-whaling groups continue to decry a supposed illicit trade in whale products, implying that a large global market for such products exists. This has not been the case for decades, and is not likely to be so again. Nor are there large numbers of potential whaling interests anywhere in the world waiting to resume uncontrolled whaling once the moratorium is lifted, as whaling-ban advocates also claim. What is at work here is politics—and the opportunity for anti-whaling organizations to raise substantial revenues through emotionally powerful but deceptive campaigns. [20]

The whaling industry has done much to deserve activists' ire, and public-awareness campaigns about its behavior are laudable. But they are also simplistic and misleading—often [21] deliberately so, to attract funding and support. The slogan "Save the whale," for example, was far more effective in awakening public concern than the scientifically correct "Save the particular whale stocks threatened by overhunting" would have been. Unfortunately, the slogan was hijacked by a small group of animal-protection activists, who mustered public support for a whaling ban by creating the false impression that all whale stocks were in danger. Politicians found it easy to follow this lead.

22   With the arrival of cheaper substitute oils in the early 1970s, the whaling industry in most countries approached collapse. As the small, unprofitable whaling industries in Australia, Brazil, France, Germany, Great Britain, the Netherlands, Peru, Spain, and the United States closed down, no significant constituencies in those countries remained to counter the claims of activist groups, and a whaling ban became a political freebie. By militating against whaling, these countries could project an environment-friendly image abroad without antagonizing business or labor interests at home.

23   In the United States senators and representatives from both parties have eagerly advertised their anti-whaling credentials. In June of 1996 the House Resources Committee, not otherwise known for its commitment to environmental activism, unanimously resolved to ask the IWC to block whaling by the Makah Indian tribe of Washington state. The chief proponent of the resolution was Jack Metcalf, a Washington Republican who, *The Seattle Times* tartly noted, was regarded as having "one of the least-green voting records in Congress." And last May the Senate, fresh from its refusal even to consider a treaty on global warming, unanimously resolved to "remain firmly opposed to commercial whaling."

24   In the ongoing campaign to ban whale hunting altogether, the ends do not justify the means. By spurning all attempts at compromise, today's anti-whaling crusaders have the potential to disrupt the large-scale environmental legislation of tomorrow.

25   To address such issues as global warming, the overuse of freshwater supplies, acid rain, overfishing in the oceans, the introduction of species to new environments, and other international environmental problems, the nations of the world will have to negotiate with one another—and for negotiations to be successful, *all* sides will have to compromise. Necessarily, the sacrifices will be harder for poor countries than for rich ones—note the reluctance of Third World nations to sign a greenhouse-gas agreement. But the sacrifices must be agreed upon and implemented in good faith. For Western nations to provide clear evidence in a highly visible forum that they are willing to flout past agreements, as they have with whaling, dims the prospect for reaching new ones in the future.

26   Because of the intransigence of anti-whaling nations, the IWC is rapidly becoming irrelevant. Some nations that want to whale but view the commission as a science-free forum for ecoposturing—Japan and Norway in particular—have taken advantage of the convention's provisions for opting out of IWC decisions. Other whaling nations, such as Canada and Iceland, have simply exited the IWC. Today almost all whaling is conducted by nonmembers in accordance with general international law or by IWC members ignoring the commission's (nonbinding) decisions. Fortunately, the latter nations, mainly Norway and Japan, have chosen to limit their catches to sustainable levels. But the example of an international environmental agency politicizing itself into irrelevance is alarming.

The means for protecting whale populations, allowing a resumption of controlled whaling, and rescuing the IWC from itself already exist: a plan known as the Revised Management Scheme. First proposed in 1992 by Australia, and supported by five other nations, including the United States, the Revised Management Scheme incorporates the Revised Management Procedure and adds an observer program and other safeguards to ensure that whaling operations do not endanger whale populations.   27

Under such a plan a return to large-scale commercial whaling is highly unlikely. The reasons are economic, biological, and social: Inexpensive substitutes have eliminated the market for whale oil, and the market for whale meat is very limited. The slow growth of whale populations means that large-scale whaling is unlikely even to be possible for the foreseeable future. And whales today are protected by the most important safeguard of all: an ecological awareness, which is now firmly implanted in the minds of the public and politicians alike, that nowhere existed during the ruinous heyday of industrial whaling.   28

Pointing to the recently revealed cheating of the Soviet Antarctic whaling fleet, whaling-ban advocates claim that the ban can't be lifted because whaling nations can't be trusted. But the cheating took place before any observer program existed. Together with other enforcement methods, observer programs have proved effective in regulating the take of dolphins in the eastern tropical Pacific Ocean and of fish in the United States' exclusive economic zone of the North Pacific. An international observer program independent of the IWC was implemented last year by four North Atlantic whaling nations. But attempts to put together an observer program within the IWC are moving extremely slowly, because anti-whaling nations see that putting it in place will remove a barrier to whaling.   29

As a first step toward rescuing the International Whaling Commission, the Revised Management Scheme should be completed and fully implemented without further delay. Ending the charade at the IWC would induce more whaling countries to follow its dictates— and would for the first time bring most or all of the whaling industry under a science-based scheme of international regulation. It would also suggest that nations in diverse economic and cultural circumstances can cooperate and compromise for the mutual environmental good—something that will be in ever greater demand.   30

Letter on "Killing Whales"

Paul Watson

Paul Watson is the president of the Sea Shepherd Conservation Society. This letter, a direct response to "Flouting the Convention," appeared in the October 1999 issue of Atlantic Monthly.

William Aron, William Burke, and Milton Freeman ("Flouting the Convention," May *Atlantic*) assert that the creation of an on-board observer program is a safeguard that will   1 assure sufficient regulation for the return of commercial whaling. They downplay the devastating cheating of the Soviet whaling fleet, which killed the most-endangered species of whales indiscriminately in vast numbers for more than twenty years, reporting only about one tenth of their kills, with the assertion that "the cheating took place before any observer program existed."

2   Wrong. The biologist Vassili Papastavrou reported on the scandal in the April 23, 1994, issue of *Science:* "The deception continued even in the presence of IWC observers. Although the observer scheme was international, observers were simply swapped between the Soviets and the Japanese." In 1994 a Norwegian whaler violated his quota—taking one for the road—with an observer on board.

3   The authors declare that "observer programs have proved effective in regulating the take of dolphins in the eastern tropical Pacific Ocean." Wrong again. The Inter-American Tropical Tuna Commission is among those "observer programs"; its laxity is legend, and its record of enforcement is invisible. The efforts of activists, consumer outrage, and the 1990 U.S. ban on the import of tuna caught in purse-seine nets at the dolphins' expense are what saved the dolphins of the eastern tropical Pacific from certain extinction.

4   The authors deny claims of "a supposed illicit trade in whale products, implying that a large global market for such products exists. This has not been the case for decades."

5   In fact, no one has ever implied "a global market." The market is Japan and the nations of Southeast Asia. With whale in the Tokyo markets reaching $300 for a kilo of meat and blubber, no further implications are necessary. The number of busts of whale-smuggling operations has been rising for the past ten years, and the introduction in 1995 of DNA-sampling techniques that have positively identified the meat of endangered fin whales, sperm whales, and humpback whales sold under the cover of Japan's "research" minke-whale kill likewise speaks for itself.

6   The authors aver that the ideal of "quick and . . . nearly painless" death has been "largely achieved" in the whaling industry, "just as it is in the food industries that kill millions of cattle, sheep, pigs, and chickens every day." The comparison of cows in a slaughterhouse (necessitating a comparison of wild with domestic animals, which are bred in a controlled stock of known numbers) to a wildlife hunt that targets the largest members of the species—that is, pregnant females—should require no comment. The speed and painlessness of its death would come as news to a whale that is shocked into semi-consciousness at the end of a pair of low-voltage electric lances for upwards of thirty minutes and then drowned while being dragged upside down to a factory-processing ship.

7   The authors cite ancient tradition and traditional diet and its importance in "the social structure and moral norms of a community." In Japan whale meat as popular dietary tradition had its last flowering from 1946 to 1960, when Douglas MacArthur ordered an intensive whaling program to alleviate the postwar food shortage. Today Japan's aging political elite, struggling to keep an irrelevant industry alive, has been trying every marketing ploy it can think of to maintain some kind of popular taste for the postwar staple (home delivery, personal snack packs, school lunch programs), but the younger generation is generally repulsed by the thought of killing whales. Thus whale meat remains an expense-account menu item for the highest-ranking members of the *keiretsu.*

Reply to Paul Watson

William Aron, William Burke, and Milton Freeman

The authors of "Flouting the Convention" reply to Paul Watson in the letters section of the October 1999 issue of Atlantic Monthly.

The article to which Paul Watson refers was published not in *Science,* a world-respected peer-reviewed professional publication, but in *New Scientist,* a popular magazine. Its author was identified as a zoologist, but his role in a major animal-rights organization was not mentioned. The article provided a lurid account of plotting by the Russians and disparaged the IWC Scientific Committee for meeting "in camera" as representatives of the governments appointing them rather than as disinterested scientists. The author failed to note that the cheating was reported by a senior adviser to the President of Russia at an international scientific meeting in Galveston, Texas, the year before his article appeared. He didn't reveal that he had attended Scientific Committee meetings (representing a nongovernmental organization) and that most members, like those of the IWC itself, are from anti-whaling nations, including the United States, Australia, and the United Kingdom. Scientists from these and other anti-whaling nations played key roles in developing the Revised Management Procedure that, if implemented, would permit controlled sustainable whaling that would allow whale populations to continue to grow. [1]

The IWC observer program is credited by the IWC Secretary with leading to a dramatic improvement in official records of whale catches. Although Russia apparently cheated after observers were required, the extent of the cheating is still being investigated. That it was serious before 1972, when the observer scheme was introduced, is undisputed. [2]

That observer programs can work when the political will exists is proved by the fact that the United States has placed its citizens on every foreign fishing vessel operating within the U.S. zone in the North Pacific since the 1970s. Japanese, Koreans, Poles, and Russians who want to fish in our zone have had to accept observers and pay the costs. This is true for the U.S. vessels that have replaced the foreign fleets. Mr. Watson's depiction of the role of observers in the eastern tropical Pacific has little relation to fact. The dolphin-mortality-limit program administered by the Inter-American Tropical Tuna Commission, in which observers play a key role, has been extremely successful, owing in major part to the work of the commission and its professional staff. Because of the effectiveness of national and international observer programs, we believe that an international IWC observer program can work and avoid the problems of the past. [3]

Mr. Watson's arguments about whales as a source of food and economic wealth are confusing, contradictory, and distorted. Whale meat as a "popular dietary tradition" probably peaked in Japan in the postwar period, a time of real shortages of food, especially of meat. As alternatives became available and IWC quotas more restrictive, whales became less important to the Japanese diet. Even so, whale meat remained one of the least-expensive sources of animal protein available to the Japanese until the whaling moratorium. Mr. Watson's assertion that whale meat may cost as much as $300 per kilo must be treated with [4] caution. Such a price could apply only to a very special cut of whale meat (called *onomi*), found near the tail fin and representing a minute proportion of the whale's mass.

5   As for Mr. Watson's claim that whale smuggling has been rising for the past ten years, this is wishful thinking. Independent checks of whale meat in Japanese markets, stores, and restaurants by TRAFFIC (the wildlife-monitoring unit of the IUCN—The World Conservation Union) in the past have indicated that all meat from whales either legally taken by the Japanese or legally imported before an import ban was enforced by Japan can be accounted for.

FOR CLASS DISCUSSION

1. The Makah whaling issue raises numerous questions concerning culturalism and environmentalism. How are culture and history part of the most important arguments in favor of the Makah's being allowed to resume limited whaling? How do some of the writers challenge these cultural arguments?

2. What environmental arguments oppose the Makah's claims?

3. Like many heated issues, the controversy over whaling involves definitions that have high stakes. For instance, according to these writers, what is the difference between commercial whaling and cultural whaling? Which articles emphasize definitional lines of argument? Where do the writers of these articles agree and disagree on facts, values, definitions, and analogies/ precedents?

4. In your own words, summarize the argument of William Aron, William Burke, and Milton Freeman in "Flouting the Conventions."

5. Choose one of the arguments for closer analysis, applying the second set of guide questions on pages 465–66.

OPTIONAL WRITING ASSIGNMENT   In every state and region there are issues that pit the cultural practices and economic interests of some group of people against environmental concerns such as protecting endangered species, preventing pollution, or preserving natural resources or natural beauty. For example, are environmental groups in your area opposing farmers or loggers, or suburban homeowners? Are wilderness advocates pitted against recreational vehicle owners, motor bikers, or power boaters? Are builders of mass transit or freeways or commercial buildings pitted against neighborhoods or open space for parks? Is your state or region wrestling with any of these problems: deforestation, excessive mining, overbuilding, overfishing, overuse of pesticides and fertilizers, erosion of topsoil, expansion of tourism, controversies over dams, or increasing restrictions on the use of state parks? Identify such an issue in your state or community. After acquainting yourself with the various views on this issue, write an op-ed piece of about 500 words that takes a stand in favor of the environmental position or in favor of allowing the cultural practices or economic interests of some group to prevail.

CORPORATE RESPONSIBILITY AND WORLD MARKETS

The Neoliberal World Order:
The View from the Highlands of Guatemala

John D. Abell

John D. Abell is a professor of economics at Randolph-Macon Woman's College. This article originally appeared in the NACLA Report on the Americas *in August 1999 (NACLA stands for "North American Congress on Latin America").*

From the perspective of poor rural Guatemalans, the current global crisis has little to do with interest rates or budget deficits. It has everything to do with the fact that policies aimed at the developing world are far removed from the needs and realities of the majority of the world's peoples.

It had been a productive morning so far. The family I was helping had picked close to 200 pounds of red, ripe coffee beans and we were relaxing around a cooking fire where the women had prepared a feast of beans, tortillas and avocado. Life seemed peaceful for the moment. Bellies were full. Beautiful Lake Atitlan, the jewel of Guatemala, was glistening in the distance. The only serious issue that remained this day was the matter of getting a couple of 100-pound sacks of coffee two miles down the side of the Toliman volcano to the coffee-processing plant where they would be weighed and scrutinized for leaves and stems prior to the payout.

Our discussion at lunch ranged from coffee prices to politics, focusing especially on the recent Peace Accords. Yes, everyone agreed, life had improved since the cessation of hostilities in December 1996, if only because the Guatemalan military was no longer dragging their sons off the streets and soccer fields to fight in the counterinsurgency war against the Guatemalan National Revolutionary Unity (URNG). Also, sleep came a lot easier knowing that the chances of a visit in the middle of the night from a paramilitary death squad were significantly reduced if not entirely eliminated.

Had any of the benefits of the Accords on the economy or judicial reform trickled down their way? Beyond a basic recognition that the Accords had left land-holding patterns untouched, they were not aware of many details. Their lives had remained essentially unchanged, they told me, living from day to day, eagerly awaiting the coffee harvest in hopes that it would be profitable enough this year to allow them to keep their kids in school and to pay their medical bills.

I asked if they were aware of the global economic crisis that had engulfed Asia, Russia and Brazil, and if they were concerned that Guatemala might be next. Don Ramon, the patriarch of the family, patiently explained to me that during his entire lifetime, and that of his father—indeed, he said, for nearly 500 years—Guatemala had been going through an essentially permanent economic crisis. How, he asked, could a country possibly have a healthy economy when most of its people go to bed hungry each night, and when they do not have land or any control over their lives? How could the latest problems from Asia or wherever make their lives any worse?

6   I was thinking about this lesson in real-world economics the next day when I stumbled on an issue of *Newsweek* devoted to the global financial crisis.[1] One of the broad themes running through all the stories was that while calm was returning to financial markets, economic recovery in the developing world was slow in coming. Indeed, there is abundant evidence that poverty and suffering is widespread. In the arctic regions of Russia, for example, people whose life savings vaporized in the early days of the ruble crisis faced starvation during one of the worst winters on record. In Jakarta, fathers who were once gainfully employed have now joined their families in the garbage dumps scrounging for their next meal. For many people, life—which was never very easy—has become precarious and desperate.

7   Many are beginning to blame the global financial system itself for such outcomes.[2] With countries like Malaysia setting a "dangerous" example by establishing restrictions on the movement of foreign capital, there is genuine fear in the establishment that some serious backsliding may be in the offing among those countries that had so eagerly embraced the neoliberal agenda. This may help to explain why Klaus Schwab, president of the World Economic Forum, selected "Responsible Globality" as the theme of this year's conference in Davos, Switzerland. Globalization is not going away anytime soon, says Schwab. The key, therefore, for lifting people out of poverty, is an improved infrastructure—"procedural, legal and institutional mechanisms"—to help harness the global revolution. "The new dividing line between richness and poverty," he suggests, "is not between the haves and have-nots, but between the knows and don't knows. The best way to help the poor is to enable them to take advantage of a global knowledge-economy."[3]

8   Don Ramon's eyes would probably glaze over if I told him that there was a fellow by the name of Klaus Schwab who was of the opinion that it did not matter that he was a have-not, and that he could improve his life if he would just take advantage of the "global knowledge-economy." If Don Ramon could speak with Mr. Schwab, he would surely tell him that his knowledge of the coffee business is just fine, and that what he needs is not a fancy Internet hookup or a Web page, but rather a higher price for his coffee and more land on which to grow it.

9   Each of the 100-pound sacks (referred to as a quintal) that Don Ramon's sons carried down the mountain that day only brought the family approximately $14. They only have half an acre of coffee and, because of the age of the trees, will be lucky to harvest a total of 2,500 pounds this year. If they can avoid the thieves who prey on small producers—lying in wait to take a family's harvest at gun point—they will earn an extra $360, a nice supplement to Don Ramon's weekly income of $17, but still not yet within striking distance of Guatemala's average annual income of $1,500.

10   Another way to think about the Ramon family's precarious position in the global economic order is to suppose that with a bit of luck some of their coffee ended up in the inventory of an upscale U.S. coffee shop. For every $4 cup of cafe latte sold, Don Ramon would receive about $0.02—less than 1%. Coffee processors and exporters, transportation

companies, advertising agencies, roasters, retailers and other intermediaries would take the remaining 99%.

In spite of all that, Don Ramon is one of the lucky ones. Most people have no hope of owning their own land. In Guatemala, just 2% of the population owns 80% of the land. Not coincidentally, three-quarters of Guatemalans live in poverty, with nearly 60% of the population unable to meet minimal nutritional needs. Eighty-five percent of children under age five experience malnourishment to some degree, and stunted growth affects up to 95% of non-Spanish speaking children in some regions of the country.[4]   11

Don Ramon is luckier still because of his steady $17 per week job as a bee keeper. For many highlands residents, however, not only is land an impossible dream, but work itself has become scarce. Many highlands families survived for generations as residential employees of the giant coffee plantations, a throwback to the days of the colonial encomienda, or royal land commissions, where the indigenous were expelled from their own lands and, through a variety of forced-labor laws, made to work on the estates. The Constitution ostensibly protects modern plantation workers by obligating owners to provide workers with housing, clean water, a minimum wage (currently $2.80 per day), schooling and health care—not a bad deal, on paper. In reality, many of those services are not provided, including payment of the minimum wage. More often than not, a daily wage of only $2.10–$2.60 is paid. Guatemala's own Ministry of Labor estimates that there is only 15% compliance with payment of the minimum wage in rural areas.[5] Since workers are generally poorly educated, not aware of their legal rights, and with no local authority to whom they can turn, owners can operate with impunity. Nevertheless, there is some limited degree of security for the families in this arrangement, no matter how inequitable.   12

A trend begun on the coastal sugar plantations in the 1980s, which is gaining more and more acceptance on the coffee estates of the highlands, is to use seasonal or sometimes daily contract laborers instead of permanent employees. For the owners, efficiencies—i.e., cost-savings from not having to provide year-round wages and benefits far outweigh the uncertainties associated with having to hire and supervise temporary workers. There is also a secondary financial benefit that comes from releasing hundreds of families into the labor market. Their presence in the contract labor force helps to put further downward pressure on an already distressed labor market, allowing the owner to pay wages far below the legal minimum. For the families, on the other hand, who have been kicked out of the only homes they have ever known for generation upon generation, life takes a turn for the worse. They have little choice but to join the ranks of the seasonal work force. Their wages, which were never totally adequate in the first place, get cut in half or more since seasonal work is just that—seasonal. Plus, without land, there is no means to grow one's own food. Housing, medical care and schooling become additional complicated financial matters.   13

With at most six months of work at the subminimum wages of approximately $2.30 a day, feeding and caring for a typical highlands family of six is nearly impossible. All hopes will be pinned on a bountiful coffee harvest. The months of January and February are the peak months and entire families will head up the mountainsides at daybreak to pick coffee for the owner. They are paid by the pound, and with all hands working feverishly they may pick 300 pounds a day. At a pay scale averaging $0.023 per pound, the family may bring home approximately $6.90 every day during this peak period. It is imperative that these   14 two months go well for the families because nearly 70% of their annual income is earned at this time. The yields are so much lower in the month before and the month after that only 25–30 pounds per day, or $0.62 per day, can be counted on.

15   With some luck, the father and possibly an older son may get hired for an extra couple of months for weeding, pruning or planting on one of the plantations. Additional work could conceivably be found on one of the coastal sugar plantations, though the harvest season tends to overlap with that of coffee. At any rate, the family's income for the season will be in the vicinity of about $715, an amount that will cover only about a third of the required minimal daily caloric intake of a basic corn and beans diet.[6] In addition, housing, medical care, school and clothing will take as much as a third out of this already strained family budget. Income-earning opportunities during the rainy season for families like the Ramons are limited. The occasional odd job—shining shoes, selling prepared foods in the market, or for the desperate, begging or prostitution—brings only a modicum of financial relief. It is not hard to see where the high statistics on malnutrition come from when so many families face similar circumstances. It is also easy to see why a plot of one's own land is so critical for survival.

16   To my knowledge, former U.S. Treasury Secretary Robert Rubin, the architect of U.S. neoliberal economic policies during the 1990s, and his former deputy and now successor, Lawrence Summers, never invited Don Ramon or any of the rest of the world's poor campesinos to any of their free-market strategy sessions. Nor have I seen any accounts of their visits to the countryside to share a meal and a discussion with the Don Ramons of the world for whom the benefits of trickle-down economics are slow to arrive.

17   Indeed, the current global crisis has little to do with the fact that Secretary Rubin has not gotten interest rates or exchange rates right, or that the various countries' budget deficits are too high, or some other statistical imbalance. It has a lot to do with the fact that policies aimed at the developing world are far removed from the needs and realities of the majority of the world's peoples. Such policies, implemented by the rich and powerful, assume a textbook world in which producers and consumers operate at arm's length, negotiating until a price and quantity are determined that clear the market and benefit both parties to the transaction. Overlooked are the more realistic scenarios whereby Don Ramon and other small producers receive take-it-or-leave-it prices from agribusiness concerns that control the world's markets.

18   A survey done by the Association for the Development of San Lucas Toliman, a highlands community in the heart of the coffee-growing region, indicated that small coffee producers need to receive a price of $28.50 per 100 pounds in order to cover their production costs and to put an adequate diet on the table. But the reality is that market prices have not been that high in years.[7] You can be sure that if there is a glut of coffee on world markets—and if the powerful coffee merchants have their way, there will always be a glut—prices will fall for Don Ramon and his family. On the other hand, cafe latte prices will hold firmly, or possibly rise a bit at the fashionable coffee houses.

19   U.S. Treasury policies, which draw upon free-trade concepts first espoused by the British economist David Ricardo over 200 years ago, are supposed to work like this: Guatemala should produce those products in which it has a comparative advantage, such as coffee, sugar and bananas. The United States, its largest trading partner, should do like-

wise, focusing on goods like sport utility vehicles (SUVs), computers and information services. Then, by trading freely with one another, their respective national incomes will be higher than if each country attempted to be self-sufficient in the production of all goods.

So how much coffee would a landowner in Guatemala have to produce to be able to afford to purchase the latest $50,000 SUV? At an average wholesale price for top-end, gourmet coffee of $100 per 100-pound sacks, the landowner would need to produce 250,000 pounds of coffee beans.[8] This would entail the use of approximately 50 acres of land.[9] The landowner would have to employ approximately 21 workers during a four-month harvest season and pay them approximately $0.23 per hour.[10] This would add up to a collective wage bill of about $5,700, or 11% percent of the cost of the SUV. If the plantation in this example happened to be among the country's largest, it might be in the vicinity of 600 acres, enabling the owner to buy a fleet of nearly 12 SUVs per year.[11]

On the other hand, suppose that one of the boss's workers also wanted to purchase a vehicle. If he were somehow able to save every single cent of his paycheck it would take him 18 years to accumulate enough money to buy a $5,000 used car. To buy an SUV he would have to share the purchase with each of his 21 co-workers and they would each have to save the entirety of their paychecks for nine years.

Such free-trade policies will be deemed successful as long as they can continue to generate 20% returns year in, year out, in the U.S. financial markets. But how long can this continue? The investment guru Peter Lynch emphasizes in his television commercials for Fidelity Investments that there is nothing magical about successful stock-market investing. Good portfolio performance results from doing one's homework, from carefully scrutinizing those companies that have strong profit potential. What is not mentioned, however, is how those profits come about, and especially how critical the connection is to the developing world.

Profits, of course, arise when sales revenues exceed the costs of production. Don Ramon might be amazed to realize just how vital he is to the amassing of global corporate profits—he figures critically in both variables in the profit equation (revenues and costs). To the coffee merchants, his family's 2,500 pounds of coffee sold at $14 represents just another cost of doing business. The more small growers like him there are around the world, the more coffee is produced. And with more coffee comes lower production costs for the coffee multinationals. The lower coffee prices are, however, the less food Dona Ramon can afford to buy for her family's meals. But that is not the concern of the coffee companies.

The Ramon family is also critical to the revenue side of the equation. Here is how that connection works. The United States produces many more goods than it is capable of consuming domestically. In certain industries such as agriculture, this imbalance is quite significant. For example, wheat production exceeds domestic consumption by as much as 50% in a given year, corn by 25%. In order for corporations to provide investors with healthy annual returns, not only do they need to hold the line on costs, but they also need to find overseas outlets for their surpluses. To follow our example, this entails finding markets for as much as 50,000,000 metric tons of wheat and corn per year.[12] Exports, therefore, represent an increasingly large share of gross domestic product (GDP), having grown from less than 6% to nearly 15% of GDP in the past ten years. Also, developing countries have become increasingly more important as destinations for U.S. surpluses during this period, increasing their share of U.S. exports from 35% to 45%.[13] In countries like Guatemala, the well-to-do have been consuming imports from the United States for years. It is people like Don Ramon and his highlands neighbors who are being called upon more and more these days to do their share.

25   We have created a system that generates enormous profits for a select few who sell products like soft drinks, snacks and cigarettes to the masses around the world. The glitch occurs when the masses can no longer afford to buy these things. When this happens, the system begins to grind to a halt. In other words, the system is sustainable only as long as the masses are actually able to participate in it—that is, when they are paid a living wage. And the system has limited sustainability when the people who actually have enough disposable income to buy these consumer goods number less than 10% in most countries of the developing world.

26   For the moment, thanks to aggressive advertising—as well as high sugar and nicotine content—Don Ramon and the remaining 90% in Guatemala who are among the have-nots are obediently consuming soft drinks, snacks and cigarettes like there is no tomorrow, much to the detriment of their health and well-being. It is not an uncommon sight to see a family that cannot afford to send its kids to school or buy them shoes spending their hard-earned quetzales on Coca-Cola, Chiclets, Doritos or Marlboro cigarettes. However, it seems unlikely that the means exist for the Ramons and their neighbors to increase their purchases of these products year after year so that the companies that peddle these products can continue to expand. Amazingly though, stock market investors continue to place their bets that somehow the multinationals will continue to reach more people throughout the world with their advertising, or convince those already in their grasp to dig deeper into their pockets to buy even more.

27   Herein lies a core capitalist contradiction. With the goal of increasing global profits, corporations are searching all over the world for new customers like Don Ramon, promising them unlimited happiness if they would just buy their products. The corporations' hope, on the other hand, is that someone else will pay these customers a high enough wage so that they can afford the products. So far, no one appears willing to do so.

28   Like the global corporations, Guatemala's oligarchy also faces a contradiction. In its effort to maintain power, prestige and wealth, it refuses to treat the indigenous and campesino poor of its country humanely—to share the richness of the land. Without land, the poor are forced to work as seasonal laborers or to assemble clothes in the maquiladoras for wages that cannot put food on the table, much less buy consumer goods or luxury items. Guatemala's producers thus have no choice but to become ever more dependent on export sales. What they find, though, is that the oligarchy in nearly every other developing country is doing the same thing, from Brazil to Indonesia to Russia. Prices around the world fall as a result of the collective attempt to run trade surpluses. The people who have to tighten their belts as a result are not the landowners—they do not want to give up their SUVs and their country clubs—but rather the Don Ramons of the world.

NOTES

1. *Newsweek International,* February 1, 1999.
2. See, for example, the four-part *New York Times* series "Global Contagion," February 15–18, 1999.

3. *Newsweek International,* February 1, 1999, p. 56.

4. *Bread for the World: Hunger 1990* (Washington, D.C.: Bread for the World Institute on Hunger and Development, 1990).

5. Tom Barry, *Inside Guatemala* (Albuquerque: Inter-Hemispheric Education Resource Center, 1992), p. 97.

6. At current market prices for corn ($0.11 per pound) and beans ($0.54 per pound), it would take $5.20 per day to provide a family of six with the minimal daily required calories (2,900—men, 2,340–women, 1,485–children) based on figures from the National Academy of Sciences. An annual income of $715 per year covers about 38% of the cost of the basic diet.

7. In an effort to address poverty in the area, the Association pays small coffee growers who meet exacting quality standards the above-market price of $28.50 per 100-pound sack. For more on this effort and other sustainable projects of the community, see John Abell, "Peace in Guatemala? The Story of San Lucas Toliman," in J. Brauer and W. G. Gissy, eds., *Economics of Conflict Resolution and Peace* (Brookfield: Ashgate Publishing Co., 1997), pp. 150–178.

8. This assumes a ratio of five-to-one raw bean to wholesale (what is known as green coffee).

9. This assumes a yield of approximately 5,000 pounds per acre.

10. This assumes each worker can pick on average 100 pounds per day. The actual day-to-day yield will depend, of course, on the stage in the harvest.

11. Barry, *Inside Guatemala,* p. 104. The exact average is 582.

12. Agricultural data from: U.S. Department of Agriculture, USDA Economic Research Service, an online data service.

13. Guatemala has gone from essentially being self-sufficient in the production of corn, importing only a negligible amount in the 1960s, to importing 25% of its domestic needs in the 1990s from the United States and other countries. Cheap U.S. wheat has swamped the domestic wheat industry such that nearly 100% of all wheat consumed domestically is imported.

Kaske versus Nike

Lawsuit Filed in the State of California against the Nike Corporation for Unfair Business Practices

What follows is the main text of a legal brief filed in the state of California against the Nike Corporation on April 20, 1998. Following the conventions of legal briefs, supporting documents are called "exhibits" and would have been attached to the original brief filed in court. We obtained this document from the antisweatshop site, "Corporate Watch: The Watchdog on the Web," accessed on October 6, 1999, at http://www.corpwatch.org/trac/nike/lawsuit.html.

INTRODUCTION

1. This private attorney general action against defendant NIKE INC. ("NIKE") charges that NIKE, in order to maintain and/or increase its sales, made misrepresentations by the use of false statements and/or material omissions of fact, including but not limited to the following:

(a) claims that workers who make NIKE products are protected from and not subjected to corporal punishment and/or sexual abuse;

(b) claims that NIKE products are made in accordance with applicable governmental laws and regulations governing wages and hours;

(c) claims that NIKE products are made in accordance with applicable laws and regulations governing health and safety conditions;

(d) claims that NIKE pays average line-workers double-the-minimum wage in Southeast Asia;

(e) claims that workers who produce NIKE products receive free meals and health care;

(f) claims that the GoodWorks International (Andrew Young) report proves that NIKE is doing a good job and "operating morally"; and

(g) claims that NIKE guarantees a "living wage" for all workers who make NIKE products.

[. . .]

NIKE'S UBIQUITOUS AND SUCCESSFUL PROMOTIONAL SCHEME

2   10. In order to promote, advertise and market its athletic shoes and apparel, NIKE expended almost $1 billion in the fiscal year ending May 31, 1997. NIKE had annual revenues of $9.2 billion. (*See* "NIKE INC. 1997 ANNUAL REPORT," attached as Exhibit A.)

3   11. According to sports-marketing specialists, by the 1990's, seven times as many athletes were parties to working agreements with NIKE as with any other company. Over half of the NCAA championship basketball teams of the past 10 years had worn NIKE products, and more than 60 big-time colleges were "NIKE schools"—this, in most cases, because their coaches were NIKE coaches. In total, NIKE has promotional arrangements with over 200 colleges and universities, including the University of California at Berkeley. For example, the University of North Carolina reportedly receives $7 million from NIKE. Well over 200 of the 324 NBA players wore NIKE shoes—over 80 of them by contract. And, 275 pro football players wore NIKE shoes, as did 290 Major League Baseball players. (*See* Donald Katz, *Just Do It: The Nike Spirit in the Corporate World*, Adams Media Corp., Holbrook, MA.,1994, p. 25 [hereinafter, *"Just Do It"*].)

4   12. Recently, NIKE paid the Brazilian National Soccer Team an astonishing $100-plus million to become a "NIKE team."

5   13. NIKE was so masterful at connecting its business aspirations to customers and high-profiled athletes and teams that NIKE's revenues by fiscal 1993 were as large as those garnered from NBA, NFL and Major League Baseball TV deals, tickets and retail paraphernalia sales combined. (*See* Katz, *Just Do It, supra,* at p. 25.)

14. The success of the pervasive NIKE advertising and promotional campaign has been phenomenal. One *Time Magazine* story about the baby-boom generation quoted a social historian saying that the ethos of the largest American generation could be summed up in three words: "Just Do It." Scott Bedbury, an Advertising Director for NIKE, said, with respect to the slogan, "Just Do It," "This thing has become much more than an ad slogan. It's an idea. It's like a frame of mind." (*See* Katz, *Just Do It,* pp. 145–46.)   6

NIKE'S SWEATSHOP STIGMA

15. NIKE's carefully cultured image has come under attack in the past few years. Various human rights groups have provided documentary evidence that: 7

   ■ Thousands of mostly young, female workers in Southeast Asian (Indonesia, Vietnam, China) factories that produce NIKE products were being exposed to reproductive toxins and suspected carcinogens. (*See, e.g.,* Exhibit B: NIKE document entitled, "Ernst & Young Environmental and Labor Practice Audit of Tae Kwang Vina Industrial Ltd. Co. Vietnam," January 13, 1997; this NIKE document was released by the Transnational Resource Action Center.)

   ■ These workers were not earning a "living wage" even though they work unimaginable hours—oftentimes 12 to 14 hours per day. (*See* Exhibit C: "Working Conditions in the Sports Shoe Industry in China," published by Hong Kong Christian Industrial Committee, Asia Monitor Resource Center Ltd., October 1997; *see also,* Exhibit D: NIKE letter to Prema Mattai-Davis, Executive Director, YWCA of America, from Dusty Kidd, dated September 28, 1997.)

   ■ NIKE workers in Southeast Asia have suffered corporal punishment and corporal abuse. (*See* Exhibit E: Nguyen, "Report Provided by Thuyen Nguyen of Vietnam Labor Watch on March 29, 1997, After He Returned from 16-day Fact-Finding Tour of Vietnam Factories in Vietnam.")

   ■ NIKE young female workers have suffered sexual harassment.

   ■ NIKE workers in Southeast Asia have been forced to work overtime in violation of applicable laws regulating wages and overtime.

   Each of these allegations is more fully described below. NIKE disclosed none of these facts to California consumers either in the promotion of its shoes or at the point of purchase, or in any other manner. As more fully described below, in response to the public exposure of NIKE's labor policies and practices in Southeast Asia, NIKE has misrepresented to the California consuming public that in some instances the allegations herein alleged were untrue, or, if true, NIKE was not responsible for such acts.

16. The media have continued to expose NIKE's actual practices. *See, e.g.,* CBS News, *Financial Times, The New York Times, The San Francisco Chronicle, Greensboro*   8

North Carolina News and Record, Buffalo News and *The Oregonian,* all of whom have run stories and articles which expose NIKE's actual practices. (*See* Exhibits F to L.)

9   17. Recently, Reggie White, the Green Bay Packer all-pro defensive end, an ordained minister and a "NIKE athlete," has called on NIKE to start manufacturing athletic shoes in the United States instead of in Southeast Asia. (*See* Exhibit M.) Michael Jordan, who is synonymous with NIKE, is planning to view working conditions in the Asian factories that produce NIKE products, said that:

> I'm hearing a lot of different sides to this issue so . . . the best thing I can do is go to Asia and see it for myself. If there are issues . . . if it's an issue of slavery or sweat-shops, [NIKE executives] have to revise its situation.

(*See* Exhibit N: Marantz, "A Model of Understatement," *The Sporting News,* December 22, 1997.)

NIKE IS LEGALLY RESPONSIBLE FOR EVERY
WORKER WHO PRODUCES NIKE PRODUCTS

10   18. The vast majority of NIKE's products are manufactured by subcontractors in China, Vietnam and Indonesia. The vast majority of the 300,000 workers who actually make NIKE products are women under the age of 24.

11   19. NIKE is legally and ethically responsible for the workers who make NIKE products. Beginning in or after March 1993, NIKE, pursuant to its contracts with each of its subcontractors, has assumed legal responsibility to:

(a) require compliance with applicable governmental regulations regarding minimum wage;

(b) require compliance with applicable governmental regulations regarding overtime;

(c) require compliance with applicable health and safety regulations;

(d) require compliance with environmental regulations; and

(e) ensure that workers will not be put at risk of physical harm. (*See* Exhibit O: NIKE Memorandum of Understanding with its Subcontractors.)

12   20. NIKE has represented to the public that NIKE has assumed full responsibility for these workers. In a NIKE document entitled "Please, Consider This . . . ," NIKE states:

> NIKE takes *full responsibility* for working conditions wherever its products are produced.

[Emphasis added.] (*See* Exhibit P.)

21. In a letter dated January 15, 1996, Lilian Bours, PR Manager Nike Europe, repre-   13
sented that the NIKE Memorandum of Understanding is "legally binding." (*See* Exhibit Q.)

22. In a letter dated June 18, 1996, to University Presidents and Athletic Directors,   14
including universities which have contracts with NIKE to wear its equipment and
to display the "NIKE Swoosh," and copied to NIKE CEO Philip H. Knight, Steve
Miller, Director NIKE Sports Marketing, represented and certified that NIKE is in
compliance with applicable government regulations regarding minimum wage and
overtime, as well as occupational health and safety, and environmental regulations,
and that NIKE enforces these standards through daily observation by NIKE staff
members. Mr. Miller stated:

> First and foremost, wherever NIKE operates around the globe, it is guided by prin-
> ciples set forth in a code of conduct that *binds* its production subcontractors to a signed
> Memorandum of Understanding. This Memorandum strictly prohibits child labor, and
> *certifies compliance with applicable government regulations regarding minimum wage
> and overtime as well as occupational health and safety, environmental regulations,*
> workers insurance and equal opportunity provisions.

> Nike enforces its standards through daily observation by staff members who are
> responsible for mandatory adherence to the Memorandum.

[Emphasis added.] (*See* Exhibit R.)

THE CODE OF CONDUCT AND MEMORANDUM OF UNDERSTANDING ARE USED BY NIKE AS MARKETING TOOLS TO ATTRACT CONSUMERS

23. In 1992, NIKE established its own Code of Conduct, which NIKE claims applies   15
to itself and to all of its business partners. (*See* Exhibit JJ.)

24. NIKE's Code of Conduct and Memorandum of Understanding were intended,   16
among other things, to entice consumers who do not want to purchase products
made in sweatshop and/or under unsafe and/or inhumane conditions. For example, in a candid acknowledgment of the linkage of sales to good company practices
and in an overt appeal to customers to consider the Code of Conduct when shopping, NIKE's Director of Communication, Lee Weinstein, wrote in a letter to the
editor published in the *San Francisco Examiner* on December 14, 1997:

> Consumers are savvy and want to know they support companies with good prod-
> ucts and *practices* . . . During the shopping season, *we encourage shoppers to remem-
> ber that NIKE is the industry's leader in improving factory conditions.* Consider that
> Nike established the sporting goods industry's first code of conduct to ensure our work-
> ers know and can exercise their rights.

[Emphasis added.] (*See* Exhibit S.)

NIKE'S CLAIM THAT ITS CONTRACTS PREVENT CORPORAL PUNISHMENT AND SEXUAL ABUSE AT FACTORIES WHICH PRODUCE NIKE PRODUCTS IS DECEITFUL

17   25. In March 1993, NIKE signed an agreement representing that it would "only do business with partners whose workers are . . . not put at risk of physical harm." Athletic Footwear Association's Statement of Guidelines on Practices of Business Partners, signed by NIKE in March 1993. (*See* Exhibit T; *see also,* Exhibit O: NIKE's Memorandum of Understanding.) In a document entitled "The Nike Code of Conduct: What it is, How it Works," NIKE represented that the "key provisions of the Code include: . . . zero tolerance of corporal punishment or abuse, or of harassment of any kind." (*See* Exhibit U.) In a NIKE document which was distributed to the media entitled "NIKE Production Primer," dated March 1996 (*see* Exhibit V), NIKE represented that " . . . NIKE expatriates ensure safe working conditions and prevent illegal working conditions."

18   26. Notwithstanding NIKE's representations and its legal and ethical duties to ensure that workers are not subjected to corporal punishment, reports of corporal abuse at factories which make NIKE products abound:

- On March 8, 1997 (International Women's Day), a supervisor forced 56 female workers to run twice around the 1.2-mile factory perimeter as punishment for failing to wear regulation company work shoes. Twelve of the women suffered shock symptoms, fainted, and were hospitalized. (*See* Exhibit E: Nguyen, "Report Provided by Thuyen Nguyen of Vietnam Labor Watch on 29 March 1997 After He Returned from 16-day Fact-Finding Tour of Vietnam Factories in Vietnam.")

- Forty-five Vietnamese workers were forced by their supervisors to kneel down with their hands up in the air for 25 minutes. (*See* Exhibit F: CBS News Report, "48 Hours," Transcript, October 17, 1996.)

- On November 26, 1996, 100 workers at the Pouchen factory in Dong Nai, Vietnam, were forced to stand in the sun for an hour for spilling a tray of fruit on an altar which three supervisors were using. (*See* Exhibit W: VN Fact Sheet, "Hear Laps Story.")

- In Indonesia, an American inspector from NIKE reprimanded a supervisor because an incorrect color was being used on the outsoles. The supervisor, in turn, lined up six workers and smacked each of them with an outsole. (*See* Exhibit X: Jeff Atkinson and Tim Connor, "Sweating for Nike," Community Aid Abroad, Melbourne, Australia, November 1996.)

- In certain Vietnamese factories, workers cannot go to the bathroom more than once per eight-hour shift and they cannot drink water more than twice per shift. (*See* Exhibit E.)

- Fifteen Vietnamese women were hit over the head by their supervisor for poor sewing. (*See* Exhibit F: CBS News Report, "48 Hours.")

27. In Vietnam, at the Tae Kwang Vina plant, a supervisor fled the country after he   19
    was accused of sexually molesting several Vietnamese workers. However, in a
    speech to NIKE shareholders on September 16, 1996, NIKE CEO Philip H. Knight
    sought to minimize the incident by saying that the supervisor was just trying to
    wake the female workers and must have touched them in the wrong place. Sig-
    nificantly, the Vietnamese government took a different view: it instigated extradi-
    tion procedures against the supervisor. (*See* Ex. S, F, and W.)

WAGE AND HOUR VIOLATIONS
AT FACTORIES IN CHINA AND VIETNAM

28. Pursuant to its Memorandum of Understanding, NIKE is under a legal duty to en-   20
    sure that its products are manufactured in accordance with applicable govern-
    mental laws regulating wages and overtime. And, NIKE has represented that its
    products are manufactured in compliance with applicable laws and regulations reg-
    ulating wages and overtime. (*See, e.g.,* Exhibits O, P, Q, R and S.) The represen-
    tations are intentionally and/or recklessly misleading and deceptive and/or were
    negligently made because they omit material facts: documented violations of the
    prohibitions of China's and Vietnam's labor laws against forced overtime and
    against excessive overtime at plants which produce NIKE products.

29. The Wellco Factory in Dongguan, Chang'an, China, employs 8,000 workers who   21
    make NIKE products. The ratio of women to men is seven to one and they are very
    young, between 18 and 25 years old. (*See* Exhibit C: "Working Conditions in
    Sports Shoe Factories in China.")

30. The Asia Monitor Resource Center Ltd. and the Hong Kong Christian Industrial   22
    Committee documented the following wage and hour violations at the Wellco plant:

    ■ Workers work eleven hours per day in violation of both Chinese law and
      NIKE's Code of Conduct. In addition to this, workers must work overtime. The
      overtime of 2.4 hours (on top of the 11-hour work day) violates China's Labor
      Law.

    ■ Workers who refuse overtime are subject to termination. This violates both
      China's Labor Law and NIKE's Code of Conduct which states that coerced
      labor is not acceptable.

    ■ Workers receive only two to four days off every month. This violates both
      China's Labor Law and NIKE's Code of Conduct which states that workers are
      entitled to at least one day of rest every week.

    ■ In violation of Chinese Labor Law, pregnant workers are treated with disre-
      spect and have been, on occasion, unjustly terminated. (*See* Exhibit C.)

31. In the same October 1997 report, the Asia Monitor Resource Center Ltd. and the   23
    Hong Kong Christian Industrial Committee documented the following wage and
    hour violations at the Yue Yuen Plant in Dongguan, China. Yue Yuen is a huge factory

employing between 50,000 and 60,000 workers. About 80 percent of the workers are women between the ages of 18 and 22 years old. The documented violations at Yue Yuen include:

- In violation of Chinese law, workers must work 10 to 12 hours per day, six or seven days per week, not including overtime. This means a normal work week of 60–84 hours which exceeds the limit set by Chinese law.

- Eighty percent of the workers who were interviewed said that on top of the normal 10 to 12 hour workday, they worked an additional two hours of overtime.

- In the survey, half of the workers were paid by piece rate and stated that they did not receive any extra pay for overtime work. This violates China's Labor Law, Article 44, which requires that overtime pay should be at least 1.5 times the regular wage. (*See* Exhibit C.)

24   32. In Vietnam, the facts give the lie to NIKE's representations that overtime is not compulsory. In late 1996, Ernst & Young, at NIKE's request, conducted an audit of the Tae Kwang Vina factory in Bien Hoa City, Vietnam. The audit report was delivered to NIKE in January 1997 but *was kept secret* until November 1997 when it was leaked to the press. Ernst & Young examined the payroll register of 50 workers at Tae Kwang Vina. Ernst & Young found as follows:

> We noted 48 cases where workers were *required* to work above the maximum working hours.

[Emphasis added.] (*See* Exhibit B: the Ernst & Young Audit of Tae Kwang Vina, at p. 3.)

25   33. Thus, in 96% of the cases (48/50), Ernst & Young found that workers producing NIKE products were *required* to work overtime.

26   34. In addition to the Ernst & Young audit, Vietnam Labor Watch has documented instances in which workers were forced to work overtime to produce NIKE products. According to Vietnam Labor Watch, most workers who produce NIKE products are forced to work 500 hours or more per year of overtime. This is in clear violation of Article 69 of the Labor Law of Vietnam which restricts overtime to 200 hours per year. (*See* Exhibit E.)

27   35. In an eye-witness visit to the factories which produce NIKE products, Thuyen Nguyen was able to observe the women employees' sense of desperation, physical exhaustion and pressure to work overtime to meet high production quotas. On March 29, 1997, Thuyen Nguyen reported that:

> Many of the things I learned during my two-week visit I had already known from earlier reports. But meeting these workers face-to-face made me realize just how bad the conditions are. I cannot describe to you these women's sense of desperation. Many of them told me they had lost weight since coming to work at the Nike factories. They complained of being tired all the time. Most of the women I spoke to work 10 to twelve hour days, six or seven days a week. . . . Forced and excessive overtime to meet high

quotas is the norm. . . . If workers refuse, they are punished or receive a warning. After three warnings, they're fired.

(*See* Exhibit E.)

36. In sum, NIKE's representation that its products are manufactured in compliance with applicable laws governing wages and hours is deceitful.   28

NIKE'S CLAIM THAT ITS CONTRACTS PREVENT HEALTH AND SAFETY VIOLATIONS AT FACTORIES THAT MAKE NIKE PRODUCTS IS DECEITFUL

37. By its Memorandum of Understanding, NIKE is legally and ethically responsible to ensure that its subcontractors comply with applicable governmental health and safety, and environmental, standards. (*See* Exhibit O.) In a 1996 document entitled "Please Consider This . . . ," NIKE stated that: 29

> NIKE takes *full responsibility for working conditions* wherever its products are produced . . .

[Emphasis added.] (*See* Exhibit P.) In its letter of January 15, 1996, to University Presidents and Athletic Directors, NIKE represented that the Memorandum of Understanding certifies NIKE's compliance with "applicable government regulations regarding occupational health & safety [and] environmental regulations." (*See* Exhibit R.) At the NIKE Annual Shareholder Meeting on September 22, 1997, NIKE CEO Philip H. Knight represented that the air quality in NIKE's Vietnam shoe factory was better than it is in Los Angeles:

> You go into the new shoe factory in . . . Vietnam today. There are no surgeon masks, and you'll find air quality better than it is in Los Angeles.

(*See* Exhibit Y.)

38. Notwithstanding NIKE's Memorandum of Understanding and NIKE's representations, thousands of young (18–24 years old) female workers are exposed to reproductive toxins, and other harmful chemicals, in the solvents and glue which are used in the production of NIKE shoes. These reproductive toxins include, but are not limited to, toluene. In addition to being a reproductive toxin, toluene has the following acute and long-term health consequences: 30

Solvent	Acute Health Consequence	Chronic Health Consequence
Toluene	vertigo; headaches; narcotic coma	irritation of the mucous membrane; euphoria; headaches; vertigo; nausea; lost appetite; alcohol intolerance; autoimmune illness

Workers who produce NIKE products have been and are also exposed to acetone which has the following acute and chronic health consequences:

Solvent	Acute Health Consequences	Chronic Health Consequence
Acetone	unrest; nausea; vomiting; progressive collapse; coma; kidney and liver damage	headache; drowsiness; throat irritation; coughing; vertigo

31   39. NIKE's own documents confirm that workers who produce NIKE products have been exposed to highly toxic and dangerous chemicals. In the previously described audit of the Tae Kwang Vina plant in Bien Hoa City, Vietnam, Ernst & Young found the following:

- The problem of harmful fumes (caused by toluene) needs more attention.

- Dust in the mixing shops exceeds the standard by ten times.

- More than half of the employees in mixing, roller, P.U., stockfit, lamination, TPR (sections using chemicals) do not wear protective equipment (mask and gloves) even in highly hazardous places where the concentration of chemical dust and fumes exceeds the standard.

- In the stockfit section where employees can smell toluene fumes, only thin cotton mask and gloves are available. (*See* Exhibit B, at p. 7.)

32   40. On December 9, 1996, Ernst & Young found that the toluene and acetone levels dramatically exceeded the permissible levels:

- *Toluene:* the level at the Assembly I-sole fit, Assembly Ultra Violet, Sole sinking, Attaching room of Stockfit section; Sole fit Ultra Violet, Attaching room of Assembly line and Mixing section exceeded the standard from six to 177 times.

- *Acetone:* the level at Assembly I-sole fit, Assembly Ultra Violet, Attaching room of Stockfit section; Sole fit of Ultra Violet of Assembly line exceeded the standard from six to 18 times. (*See* Exhibit B, at p. 8.)

33   41. In addition, Ernst & Young found that dust in the mixing room exceeded the standard by 11 times. (*See* Exhibit B, at p. 8.) Ernst & Young also found that employees working in sections with noise at more than 85dB(A) had no earplugs and still worked more than eight hours per day. (*See* Exhibit B, at p. 8.)

34   42. Notwithstanding the well-known and well-documented adverse health effects of each of the above-listed chemicals and the amount of those chemicals used in the manufacturing of its products, NIKE officials amazingly say that they have little information about the long-term health effects of exposure to solvents. Dusty Kidd, Director of NIKE's Labor Practices department, downplayed the danger, saying

most workers' exposure is limited because they do not stay more than two or three years in the factories. NIKE's Kidd said the goal is to meet United States OSHA standards, but that NIKE does not know how many factories meet these standards. According to Kidd, "It's a work in progress." (*See* Exhibit L: Jeff Manning, "Poverty Legions Flock to Nike," *The Oregonian,* November 1997.)

NIKE'S CLAIM THAT IT PAYS DOUBLE THE MINIMUM WAGE IS DECEITFUL

43. In a document entitled "Nike Responds to Sweatshop Allegations," NIKE represents that the "average line-workers' wage in Asian subcontracted facilities is double the government-mandated minimum." (*See* Exhibit Z.)   35

44. The Ernst & Young audit directly contradicts this claim. According to Ernst & Young, the minimum wage for workers is $40 per month. According to Ernst & Young, workers at the Tae Kwang Vina factory in Vietnam received an average wage of $45 per month. (*See* Exhibit B, at p. 2, p. 3, and p. 3, p. 12.)   36

45. Another recent study of wages of workers who produce goods for NIKE in Vietnam shows that NIKE's claim of paying double-the-minimum wage is not true. Mr. Vo Minh Quang, Director of the Dong Nai Labor Bureau, and Mr. Nguyen Dinh Thang, President of the Dong Nai Confederation of Labor, reported that: 37

> Most workers here in Dong Nai received at most $40 (U.S.) Per month or 440,000 VND (Vietnam Dong). According to [Vietnam minimum wage laws], this pay is not even legal.

(*See* Exhibit AA: "The Truth Behind Nike's Recent Public Statement, excerpted from a newspaper entitled *Thanh Nien* and translated by Vietnam Labor Watch.)

46. In March 1997, Vietnam Labor Watch interviewed 35 workers of four factories which produce NIKE products. Vietnam Labor Watch examined the pay stubs of some of the workers. The pay stubs, attached as Exhibit BB, show as follows: 38

Exhibit No.	Basic Pay without Overtime per Month	Net Pay, Including Overtime, after Deductions for Meals/Health	Hours of Overtime per Month
1 & 2	Not legible		
3	387,000 (VND)	521,600	40
4	387,000/418,000	458,000	36
5	517,000	593,000	31
6	517,000	575,000	53
7	517,000	551,200	29
8	517,000	595,700	21

These pay stubs show that, even with overtime hours that often exceed Vietnam's legal limits, workers do not earn twice the minimum wage of 444,444 VND.

39   47. Indonesia provides another example that disproves NIKE's representation that it pays double-the-minimum wage. To attract companies such as NIKE, the Indonesian government set the national minimum wage below what was deemed necessary to support the workers' minimum "physical needs." Significantly, as NIKE has conceded, throughout much of the 1990's, NIKE subcontractors received government exemptions from paying even the minimum wage. (*See* Exhibit CC: Jeff Manning, "Life in Global Arena Grows in Complexity // NIKE Criticized for Production in Asian Lands," *Minneapolis Star Tribune,* November 29, 1997.)

40   48. In sum, NIKE's representation of double-the-minimum wage is both false and based on misleading statistical data.

NIKE'S CLAIM THAT IT PROVIDES FREE LUNCHES IS DECEITFUL

41   49. In its document "Nike Responds to Sweatshop Allegations," NIKE represents that:

In addition, compensation extends beyond wages to include . . . free meals . . .

(*See* Exhibit Z.) The identical representation was made by NIKE CEO Philip H. Knight in a letter dated June 21, 1996, to the *New York Times* asserting that NIKE "provides free meals, housing and health care." (*See* Exhibit DD.)

42   50. As documented by Vietnam Labor Watch in their analysis of workers' pay stubs, workers who produce NIKE products were forced to pay 9¢ U.S. for their lunches. (*See* Exhibit BB.) To put this in context, workers at the Tae Kwang Vina plant earn approximately 16.8¢ U.S. per hour ($45 per month for 267 hours). In addition, the pay stubs show that the workers paid for their own health care. (*See* Exhibit BB.)

NIKE'S RELIANCE ON THE GOODWORKS INTERNATIONAL REPORT IS DECEITFUL

43   51. On February 22, 1997, hundreds of persons filled San Francisco's Union Square on the opening day of Niketown, a multi-floor NIKE superstore, to urge prospective customers to stay away, citing widespread labor abuses by contractors who make NIKE products.

44   52. Two days later, NIKE CEO Philip H. Knight announced that NIKE was commissioning an independent investigation of its Asian operations. NIKE contracted with Andrew Young, former U.S. Ambassador to the United Nations, to conduct the investigation. To conduct this investigation, Andrew Young founded a firm called "GoodWorks International" (hereinafter, "GoodWorks").

53. GoodWorks released its report in June 1997. (*See* Exhibit EE.) On the same day   45
that GoodWorks issued its report, NIKE took out full-page advertisements in major
U.S. newspapers (*New York Times, Washington Post, U.S.A. Today, San Francisco
Chronicle,* etc.) (*See* Exhibit FF.)

54. In addition, NIKE has repeatedly used the GoodWorks Report in various public   46
statements. For example, at the September 22, 1997, Annual Shareholders' Meeting, NIKE CEO Philip H. Knight, stated:

> So I think we continue to make good progress, and I think that any independent
> party will find as Andrew Young that we are *operating morally.*

[Emphasis added.] (*See* Exhibit Y.)

55. NIKE's representations that the GoodWorks Report supports claims that NIKE is   47
"doing a good job" and "operating morally" are misleading because NIKE inten-
tionally omitted the following facts:

(a) The GoodWorks Report did not address, directly or indirectly, wage, hour and
overtime violations at factories which produced NIKE products. Mr. Young has
stated, "I was not asked by NIKE to address compensation and 'cost of living
issues' which some . . . had hoped would be a part of this report." (*See* Exhibit
EE, p. 3.)

(b) The GoodWorks Report did not address the life-threatening health and safety
issues documented in the Ernst & Young audit of the Tae Kwang Vina factory.
(*See* Exhibit B.) Even though the Ernst & Young audit was completed three
months before Andrew Young visited Vietnam, Andrew Young did not address
a single violation which was documented in the Ernst & Young audit. In fact,
Andrew Young did not even visit the Tae Kwang Vina plant. Either NIKE with-
held the Ernst & Young Tae Kwang Vina audit from Andrew Young, or Andrew
Young and/or his staff negligently or recklessly ignored the Ernst & Young report. In any event, NIKE knew, or should have known, that the GoodWorks
Report was deficient in its failure to address the potentially life-threatening
health and safety violations at the Tae Kwang Vina plant (as documented by
Ernst & Young).

(c) As NIKE knew, or should have known, the GoodWorks Report listed consultants who were never consulted. For example, the GoodWorks Report lists
Anita Chan, a renowned researcher of the Australian National University, as a
person whom GoodWorks contacted. Mr. Young states as follows:

> Early in the process, I wrote and called a number of the important interna-
> tional and U.S. N.G.O.'s [non-governmental organizations]—both to inform them
> of our assignment and to solicit their input and advice.

(*See* Exhibit EE, p. 7; Appendix, p. 16.)

48   56. In a letter submitted to the *Washington Post,* Anita Chan categorically denies that she was either phoned or contacted by Andrew Young or anyone else from Good-Works. She goes on to list various health, safety and wage violations in China which she would have brought to Mr. Young's attention had she been phoned or contacted. (*See* Exhibit GG.)

49   57. NIKE also knew, or should have known, that the alleged photograph of Andrew Young with the caption, "Andrew Young meeting with plant management and union representatives in Vietnam," was misleading. This photograph, along with others purporting to show Andrew Young with "union representatives," came as something of a shock to the Vietnamese Confederation of Labor, which represents workers at the NIKE factory. They do not know these individuals. Mr. Vada Manager, a NIKE spokesperson, has admitted that these individuals receive salaries from the company, not from the union or the government. (*See* Exhibit HH: Stephen Glass, "The Young & the Feckless," *New Republic,* September 15, 1997.)

50   58. In sum, NIKE's representations that the GoodWorks Report is proof that NIKE is "doing a good job" and that NIKE is "operating morally" are misleading.

NIKE'S CLAIM THAT IT GUARANTEES A "LIVING WAGE FOR ALL WORKERS" IS MISLEADING

51   59. On October 27, 1997, NIKE issued a release datelined Washington, D.C., and entitled, "Nike Addresses Concerns Regarding Women's Issues and Highlights Leadership in Worker Initiatives." (*See* Exhibit II.) The release quotes Kathryn Reith, NIKE Manager of Women's Sports Issues, who represented that NIKE guarantees a living wage for all workers. Ms. Reith stated that:

> NIKE is fulfilling our responsibility as a global corporate citizen each and every day by guaranteeing *a living wage for all workers* . . . and creating opportunities for women's financial independence.

[Emphasis added.]

52   60. This statement is false. On September 28, 1997, a month before the Kathryn Reith statement quoted above, Dusty Kidd, Director of NIKE's Labor Practices department, wrote:

> I am fully cognizant of the call on the part of some for a "living wage." That is generally defined as sufficient income to support the needs of a family of four. We simply cannot ask our contractors to raise wages to that level—whatever that may be—while driving us all out of business, and destroying jobs, in the process.

This letter was written to Prema Mattai-Davis, Ph.D., Chief Executive Officer, YWCA of America. Dusty Kidd copied Doug Stamm, NIKE's Director of Public Affairs, on the letter. (*See* Exhibit D.)

[. . .]

[The remainder of the brief outlines the legal codes Nike is alleged to have violated. ED.]

Job Opportunity or Exploitation?

David Lamb

This news analysis by journalist David Lamb appeared in the Los Angeles Times *on April 18, 1999.*

Asia: To Vietnam's impoverished, a $65-a-month position at a Nike factory is a prize. Though the company has cracked down on labor abuses in the last few years, critics say the moral questions go beyond that.   1

BIEN HOA, Vietnam—Nguyen Thi Dong has never heard of Tiger Woods or Michael Jordan and has never worn a pair of sneakers. But she knows this for sure: Her assembly-line job at the Nike plant here rescued her from poverty. It is a job she wants to keep for "10 years anyway, maybe forever."   2

Dong, who is 27 and has a seventh-grade education, lives with her parents in a small house that has electricity and a TV. When the prices of rice and chicken are low, she can save a few dollars from her $42 monthly paycheck. Her sister also works for Nike. Her best friend hopes to hire on soon.   3

The factory to which she bicycles six days a week is clean, modern, well-ventilated. When told that U.S. human rights groups had—until recent company reforms—accused Nike of running sweatshops staffed by underpaid, overworked, mistreated laborers, she replied: "That's strange. Why?"   4

In many ways, Dong is a symbol of the clash between the agrarian and industrialized worlds. She is the cheap labor that factories migrate in search of, and in her small world, the line between opportunity and exploitation is a thin one. Jobs are scarce in Southeast Asia and getting scarcer because of the continent's economic crisis, and for millions of unskilled Vietnamese, a job at Nike would seem a prize not much shy of hitting the lottery.   5

Nike's five Taiwanese and South Korean subcontractors in Vietnam pay an average monthly wage of about $65, more than twice what a teacher earns and considerably above the salary of a young doctor at a state-run hospital. With a payroll of 43,000, Nike is Vietnam's largest private employer, and its footwear and apparel account for 7% of the nation's exports. The turnover at the Tae Kwang Vina plant here in Bien Hoa, 18 miles northeast of Ho Chi Minh City (the former Saigon), is less than 1% a year.   6

"If they didn't have jobs here, most of the women you see would be planting rice or working part-time city jobs," said Than Thi Hoa, 31, who makes $175 a month supervising 1,300 workers and is part of Vietnam's emerging middle class. She and her husband, an army officer, both have motor scooters. Their home has running water, a refrigerator, a stereo and a TV. Their daughter goes to an upscale school. They save about 10% of their income.   7

Make no mistake, though. Nine hours a day on an assembly line—stitching, trimming, gluing, painting, cutting, boxing, meeting quotas in silence—is no walk in the park. And the five subcontracted plants in Vietnam that produce Nike product can hardly claim an unblemished record in labor relations or working conditions.   8

9   At various times in 1995 and 1996, workers at one plant were forced to run around the perimeter of three warehouses for punishment. A dozen fainted in the 100-degree heat. At another plant, a Taiwanese forewoman lined up 125 assembly-line workers and slapped them with the sole of a sneaker. A Korean forewoman at a third facility made workers lick the factory floor for misdemeanors, and employees at yet another factory were led in chants of "Loyalty to the boss!"

10   In 1997, Nike's image was further tarnished when Dara O'Rourke, an environmental researcher at UC Berkeley, made public a report that accounting firm Ernst & Young had prepared for Nike's internal use. Among its findings: Laborers at the Tae Kwang Vina plant were working 65 hours a week in 1996, and air quality in the factory was so bad that 77% of them had respiratory problems.

11   "The truth is, Nike's factories were never any worse—and in some ways were better—than other companies' factories here," said Brian Quinn, Vietnam representative for Harvard University's Institute for International Development. He has tracked Nike's operations in Vietnam for the last four years.

12   Scores of foreign-run factories, producing everything from trucks to detergent, have popped up in Vietnam since Hanoi started moving toward a free-market economy in 1989. Here, for example, in the industrial zone where Nike is situated on the site of an old U.S. military base, there are 80 factories that produce, among other things, textiles, cigarettes, electronics, semiconductors and champagne. Among the widely known companies that have set up shop here are Nestlé and Sanyo.

13   "But Nike got targeted early," Quinn said, "and its first reaction was to close the doors to independent monitors, journalists, inspectors. When that happens, people say, 'Let's go see what's wrong there.' It was a serious failure to communicate."

14   Nike apparently also failed to understand Vietnam itself. Although it is one of the region's poorest countries—per-capita income is about $1 a day—Vietnam has tough labor unions. Strikes are legal, the Communist government is active in its defense of workers' rights, and Vietnam's historical sense of having been taken advantage of by foreigners often makes the country suspicious, inflexible and difficult to deal with.

15   Last May, Philip H. Knight, Nike's founder and chief executive, bowed to international pressure. He defended Nike's record of creating jobs and improving factory conditions in Asia but, in announcing sweeping reforms, admitted, "The Nike product has become synonymous with slave wages, forced overtime and arbitrary abuse."

16   As part of those reforms—which include a new openness—a journalist and his interpreter were recently given unrestricted access to Nike's factories. They found that the quality of the free daily cafeteria lunches provoked some upturned noses. But otherwise, there were no substantive complaints about wages, working conditions or the conduct of foreign supervisors.

17   "It's a good job, better than what most of my friends have," said Vo Tien Sy, 23, who earns $47 a month, 10% over the minimum wage that foreign companies must pay in Dong Nai province. "My only complaint is that they cut overtime to 200 hours a year. I'd like more overtime."

18   In addition to reducing overtime, Nike in the last year has raised the minimum age for employment at its footwear plants to 18 (although children can work at 14 in Vietnam with their parents' permission). New ventilation systems have been put in place, lead-based

paints have been eliminated, solvent-based adhesives are being replaced with water-based ones to reduce hazardous chemicals, and independent monitors have for the first time been given access to Nike plants.

A spokesman for the Vietnam Labor Union Federation said that for the first time in memory, his office received not a single complaint last year about working conditions at Nike plants. Even O'Rourke, the Berkeley researcher and long-time Nike critic, has praised the company's initiatives. He said in March that the number of workers at the Tae Kwang Vina factory reporting nose and throat complaints fell to 18% of the labor force in 1998 from 86% in 1997. Although he said problems remain, he gives Nike high marks for making progress.   19

"Things are changing, and for the better," said another frequent critic, Medea Benjamin, director of Global Exchange, a San Francisco–based human rights organization focusing on labor issues.   20

She added: "There's been significant progress in health and safety issues, and letting in independent monitors is a major step forward. But we still criticize Nike and others for not being the best-paid places around to work, for not lifting workers out of poverty."   21

Economists reply that multinational factories have a responsibility to pay competitive wages but not to change the living standards of a nation. If Nike suddenly doubled or tripled wages, they say, its assembly lines would be full of doctors, teachers and bureaucrats. The repercussions would be devastating to Vietnam's economy.   22

"The bottom line is that I'm competing with 80 other companies in this industrial zone for the same work force," said Tae Kwang Vina's president, C. T. Park, standing among stacked cartons bearing shipping labels to Tokyo; Singapore; Karachi, Pakistan; Ashdod, Israel; Laakdal, Belgium; Memphis, Tenn.; and Wilsonville, Ore.   23

"If we don't offer competitive wages and a good work environment and benefits—we've built a kindergarten, we run night classes for workers who want to continue their education—our workers are going to walk across the street to other jobs," Park said. "If that happens, I'm out of business, because machines don't make our footwear. People do."   24

Global Exchange and a Kinder, Gentler Nike

Stephanie Salter

This news story appeared in the San Francisco Examiner *on March 21, 1999.*

For years, whenever Global Exchange had anything to say about Nike Inc., you could count on it being bad.   1

An international workers advocacy organization based in San Francisco, Global Exchange regularly goes after toy and apparel manufacturers who practice exploitative and abusive business in countries that are too poor to resist. Because Nike is a colossus of the industry—whose success is as much about image peddling as product—Global Exchange has made it the target of especially harsh and relentless criticism.   2

The group's investigators have been 86ed from Nike factories, thrown off Nike properties and generally dissed up and down by defensive Nike execs.   3

4   But a few days ago, an astounding thing occurred.

5   Global Exchange's co-director, Medea Benjamin, publicly praised Nike for taking a couple of "profoundly important" steps toward improving conditions for garment workers around the world.

6   Tossing down the gauntlet to other shoe and clothing manufacturers, Nike promised that, if other companies follow suit, it will disclose the names and locations of all its factories that produce gear for colleges and universities. It also has agreed to allow some of its most severe critics to examine conditions in Nike factories in Vietnam.

7   "This is very exciting and a big breakthrough," said Benjamin. "We've been in direct dialogue about this with Nike for the last six months. We really feel like they're getting it. This is like the kinder, gentler Nike coming out."

8   Most of the kinder-gentler is no doubt a result of the public relations drubbing Nike has taken since reports of its abusive off-shore practices first began to surface. When CEO Phil Knight's outraged denials were met by even more and better-documented charges, the company retreated into the old everybody's-doing-it defense.

9   The critics kept yelling. At the same time Nike stock began to show signs of an oversaturated athletic shoe market, social justice–minded college students began haranguing their university administrations to boycott "sweatshop" produced shoes and equipment—even the freebies.

10   Most schools have denied such demands, but several influential universities have not. Pledging that their official clothing and gear will come only from companies that disclose the names and addresses of their factories are, so far, the University of Wisconsin, Georgetown, Duke, Brown, Cornell and Harvard.

11   According to Benjamin, there is another big factor in Nike's turnaround. Her name is Maria Eitel.

12   Hired last year as the company's vice president for corporate and social responsibility, Eitel appears determined to prove wrong all the people who predicted she would be "more like a lap dog than a watchdog." Where other Nike execs argued with Benjamin in the nation's newspapers or via letter and fax, Eitel was the first to say: Let's sit down and talk, face to face.

13   "I think she personally has made a big difference," said Benjamin. A former TV reporter, White House spokesperson (Bush administration) and Microsoft executive, Eitel returned the compliment.

14   "Medea's done a fabulous job in raising awareness around the world," she said.

15   Eitel is a long way from proclaiming that Nike was arrogant, insensitive and negligently out-of-it when it came to conditions in its factories. But she does admit the company "made some mistakes" and adopted "a definite posture" that only made matters worse.

16   The primary reason Nike has come around to working with its critics, she said, had little to do with the bottom line and much to do with employee morale.

17   "Believe it or not, there is a real family feeling here. There are a lot of people within Nike who are really socially conscious. Anything that has an impact on our employee base is important," said Eitel.

18   Working for a company that was getting skewered on newspaper front pages had a decidedly negative impact. And employees said so.

19   Eitel maintains that "Nike gets held to a higher standard than other companies."

She said it plans to live up to that standard. 20

"It's not like, if you run a really good factory and provide a positive work experience, 21
you can't make money," she said. "I believe you can make more."

That is something Global Exchange and the other garment industry critics have been 22
saying for years. So now, Nike is listening. Are Reebok, Adidas, New Balance, Converse and
the rest of the athletic apparel industry?

"Everyone in the business knows that Nike's willingness to do this blows away all the 23
justification about how companies 'can't compete' if they disclose (locations) of their factories," said Benjamin.

And everyone should also know that, until they follow Nike's lead, they can count on 24
one thing: Global Exchange and the rest of the workers' rights warriors will never, never
go away.

Sweatshop Reform: How to Solve the Standoff

Aaron Bernstein

This article originally appeared in Business Week, *May 3, 1999, in the Social
Issues section. Aaron Bernstein is a staff writer for* Business Week.

Sweatshops are the hot topic on college campuses these days. In recent months, stu- 1
dents have been demanding assurances that clothing with their universities' logos be made
under humane conditions. Some 50 universities have responded by agreeing to join the Fair
Labor Assn. (FLA), a sweatshop-monitoring group founded last fall by a Presidential task
force of apparel makers and human rights organizations.

But the students want more. On Apr. 15, United Students Against Sweatshops (USAS), 2
representing students at some 100 colleges, demanded that universities quit the FLA and
create a more rigorous monitoring plan. They want companies to publicly disclose the location of their foreign factories so human rights and labor groups can independently verify
any monitoring. And they want employers to pay a so-called living wage that meets workers' basic needs in different countries. The FLA would do neither, though it's still debating
the wage issue. "Universities must hold themselves to higher standards by rejecting the
FLA's weak code," says University of Michigan sophomore Peter Romer-Friedman.

The students make valid points. Even some apparel executives privately concede that 3
some disclosure may be needed to keep companies honest. A living wage is probably a
workable idea, too. In fact, companies such as Nike use a version of it to help set wages in
some countries.

But no monitoring effort will work unless it's embraced by a critical mass of the U.S. 4
apparel industry. So far, just four companies have joined the FLA: Nike, Reebok, Liz
Claiborne, and Phillips–Van Heusen. Other companies on the Presidential task force bowed
out because they found the FLA's goals too onerous. Since last fall, the surviving four and
the White House have been unable to recruit other apparel makers or major retailers. Nor
are companies crying to join a second effort—featuring a living-wage standard—launched

last year by Avon Products, Toys 'R' Us, and the Council on Economic Priorities (CEP), a New York public-interest group. Instead, most manufacturers and even some retailers, including Wal-Mart Stores Inc., are devising a less stringent code through the American Apparel Manufacturers Assn.

5   By undermining the FLA, students are inadvertently fostering the weakest approach. Instead, they should try to get the apparel industry to join the FLA, not leave it. Students should also pursue retailers, who control pricing power in the industry. "It's important that we have higher labor standards, but everyone has to adopt them, including retailers, or those of us who stick our necks out will be out of business," says Phillips–Van Heusen CEO Bruce J. Klatsky.

6   The debate over sweatshop codes of conduct shows just how tricky it is to put a floor under global labor standards, even in a single industry. The apparel business involves hundreds of thousands of factories in widely disparate economies. Exposés have alerted U.S. consumers to abuses, yet consumers' desire for bargain goods means companies still face fierce competitive pressures. And it's unclear what the economic toll would be if anti-sweatshop efforts lift prices.

7   **Job Loss.**   One possible result: Consumers might buy less clothing, potentially reducing employment. A living wage, the most costly demand, poses the greatest risk. "The worry is that a living wage might cause some workers to lose their jobs," says Dani Rodrik, an economist at Harvard University. Still, slowly raising labor standards around the globe would benefit most workers now toiling in sweatshops. Given the uncertainties, the best approach is to set up a common monitoring system, such as the FLA's, that tackles the most egregious abuses first. Then the bar could gradually be lifted to include ideas like living wage.

8   Each of the three anti-sweatshop efforts takes a somewhat different path to higher labor standards. All have a code of conduct for issues such as health and safety, child labor, and overtime. The CEP's is the most stringent—it calls for a living wage. Companies on the FLA task force refused to follow suit, which was one reason U.S. unions quit the group last fall. Ultimately, the FLA agreed that companies must match the local industry prevailing wage. The group also agreed to discuss the living-wage idea again later, and the White House commissioned the Labor Dept. to do a preliminary study. Meanwhile, the AAMA, whose members include Sara Lee, Jockey International, and VF, chose the weakest standard. It calls for companies to pay the legal minimum wage, which in some countries is so low as to be meaningless.

9   The monitoring systems diverge even more. The CEP and the AAMA both take a factory-based approach. Each group is setting up an association to accredit monitors, most likely auditing firms. Companies, either manufacturers or retailers, can then submit their factories or their suppliers for audit. Each factory that passes is certified to be in compliance with the group's labor code—so they can tell the public they're "sweatshop-free."

10   The FLA system, by contrast, focuses on an entire company. Garment makers or retailers must set up internal monitoring systems to ensure that their factories or those of suppliers are in compliance with the FLA's labor standards. Outside monitors will randomly audit 30% of a company's factories in the first three years and 10% in subsequent years. The FLA will certify those that pass as in compliance with the code.

11   Each approach has strengths and weaknesses. Company-based monitoring requires U.S. executives to police their own factories or those of suppliers. This is probably the best way to achieve real change because it forces companies to take a direct hand in solving the

problem. And under the FLA plan, monitoring results will be disclosed to the public every year, giving companies an incentive for true reform. Still, random spot checks by outside monitors could leave many abuses undiscovered.

Factory-based monitoring better suits commodity manufacturers and retailers, which use hundreds or even thousands of suppliers and change many of them each year. Demanding that entire supply chains be certified "sweat-free" would rope many more factories into the system. But neither the CEP nor the AAMA has set timetables for requiring companies to certify any portion of their vast web of contractors. And outside groups would not see monitors' findings, as with the FLA's plan. "The FLA has the only plan that provides public accountability by companies," says Michael Posner, head of the Lawyers Committee for Human Rights and a member of the FLA task force.   12

Whatever oversight system is used, the underlying economic issue is whether tough standards such as a living wage do more harm than good. The same applies to labor rules in trade pacts. Malaysian Prime Minister Mahathir Mohamad and other leaders of low-wage countries have long argued that such standards would price them out of global markets. Low-wage countries would lose investment and jobs, they say, hurting the local economy and the workers the standards are intended to help.   13

The issue is particularly acute in apparel, a cutthroat business where relentless competition has driven production to ever cheaper sources of labor. In the past decade, U.S. apparel imports have soared to 61% of the $101 billion wholesale apparel market, up from 47% in 1987. Most of the rise has come from U.S. manufacturers exporting partly finished clothing to Mexico and the Caribbean for the most labor-intensive sewing, and then importing it back to the U.S. for sale. At the same time, production has moved from middle-wage countries such as Taiwan to low-wage ones such as Costa Rica.   14

Low Rise.   Certainly, U.S. consumers pay less for clothes today as a result. The U.S. Consumer Price Index for apparel has risen at half the pace of the overall CPI since 1982, the lowest rise in any major item except energy.   15

But there's also evidence that U.S. retailers and apparel makers share in the bounty. In most advanced economies, wages track productivity over the long term. But U.S. apparel imports have shifted to countries where workers have little bargaining power or are often squelched by authoritarian governments—precisely the countries most likely to breed sweatshops.   16

One indication is the huge discrepancies between productivity and wages. In Mexico, for example, apparel workers are 70% as productive as their U.S. counterparts, yet they earn just 10% as much per hour, according to surveys by Kurt Salmon Associates Inc., an Atlanta-based apparel consultant. "The people really making the money are U.S. retailers," says Raoul Verret, vice-chairman of Werner International Inc., a New York apparel-management consultant.   17

Harvard's Rodrik has found similar results. A new study of wages and productivity in 138 countries shows that "at least part of the cost of higher labor standards would come out of profits, though a low-wage country's competitiveness could suffer, too," says Rodrik.   18

Of course, no one can define a living wage down to the penny. But the idea can be used to check for gross labor abuses. One way is to use a method similar to the way the U.S. defines poverty, which is to assemble a market basket of food needed for a basic daily   19 diet. Nike used such an approach to respond to the economic collapse in Indonesia, where the company raised wages for its 80,000 footwear workers by more than 30% in the past year. "We don't see the wage issue as off the table" in the FLA discussions about codes of conduct, says Maria Eitel, Nike's vice-president for corporate responsibility.

20   At this point, private-sector codes of conduct hold the most potential for curbing sweatshops. Labor standards in trade pacts such as NAFTA are weak and aren't well enforced. And tougher rules adopted by the International Labor Organization years ago have been largely ignored.

21   Nor is the market likely to solve the problem on its own. Eventually, companies may be able to charge higher prices for sweatshop-free clothes, just as they do for environmentally friendly products. But today, "it's naive to think the public will pay more because someone says their product is made with the right labor conditions," says Reebok International Ltd. CEO Paul Fireman. "It's up to the manufacturers to take responsibility."

22   Retailers, too, could play a huge role in setting new rules for global suppliers. As part of an AAMA pilot program, Wal-Mart has asked a contractor to undergo a factory audit—one of the first among big U.S. retail chains. Real progress toward curbing labor abuses will be made only if many more companies agree to a set of minimum standards. That should be the students' first goal.

What's a Living Wage?

Here's one way the Council on Economic Priorities suggests defining a wage that meets basic needs in different countries:

1. Establish the local cost of a basic food basket needed to provide 2,100 calories per day per person.
2. Determine the share of local household income spent on food. Divide into 1 to get total budget multiplier.
3. Multiply that by food spending to get the total per person budget for living expenses.
4. Multiply by half the average number of household members in the area. (Use a higher share if there are many single-parent households.)
5. Add at least 10% for discretionary income.

EXAMPLE   Assume the basic food basket costs $15 a week, there are 5.6 people per household, and families spend 40% of their income on food. A living wage would be $15 × (1 ÷ .4) × 2.8 (half of 5.6 people) + 10% = $115.50 a week.

Data: Council on Economic Priorities Accreditation Agency.

FOR CLASS DISCUSSION

1. Visit your campus bookstore and look at the labels of T-shirts and sweatshirts bearing your college or university logo. Who manufactures these garments? Where were they assembled? Try to ascertain whether your college or university has been involved in any discussions of sweatshop issues.

2. Suppose you wanted your college or university to take a stand on sweatshops. Based on the readings in this unit, what course of action would you recommend? What further research would you need to do?

3. The World Trade Organization (WTO) is an international organization that mediates trade disputes among its member organizations. Because its mission is to reduce restrictions on free trade, it typically rules against countries whose trade practice treats foreign countries unequally. Based on the readings in this unit and on any further research you might be assigned to do, what are the arguments for and against free trade?

4. When the World Trade Association held a conference in Seattle in early December 1999, thousands of protesters disrupted its proceedings. Defenders of the WTO, who support free trade, praise multinational corporations for creating jobs in Third World countries and bringing technological advances to all nations. To what extent would the writers of the readings in this unit share the WTO's views about the benefits of multinational corporations? Imagine a panel discussion that included the writers of the readings in this section but also included Don Ramon from John D. Abell's "The Neoliberal World Order: The View from the Highlands of Guatemala"; one of Nike's Vietnamese factory workers quoted in David Lamb's "Job Opportunity or Exploitation?"; college activists against sweatshops; defense and plaintiff lawyers in *Kaske v. Nike*; CEOs of multinational corporations; and some of the leftist protesters who opposed the WTO meetings in Seattle.
   a. What points of view would emerge from this panel discussion?
   b. What position on free trade would you want the president of the United States to have?

OPTIONAL WRITING ASSIGNMENT   Imagine that the editorial staff of your college or university newspaper is doing a series of articles on sweatshops following disclosure that your campus bookstore buys its college-logo apparel from a manufacturer that uses overseas assembly plants. Write an op-ed piece for your campus newspaper persuading some campus constituency to accept your views on this issue.

credits

Page 5. Wilfred Owen, "Dulce et Decorum Est."

Page 16. "Illinois Court Won't Hear Case of Mom Who Refuses Surgery" and "Homeless Hit the Streets to Protest Proposed Ban." Reprinted with the permission of the Associated Press.

Page 19. Gordon F. Adams, "Petition to Waive the University Math Requirement." Reprinted with the permission of the author.

Page 28. George F. Will, "Lies, Damned Lies, and . . ." from *Newsweek* (March 29, 1999). Copyright © 1999 by the Washington Post Writers Group. Reprinted with permission.

Page 40. Ellen Goodman, "A New Campaign for Pay Equity" from the *Boston Globe* (1985). Copyright © 1985 by the Boston Globe Company. Reprinted with permission of the Washington Post Writers Group.

Page 129. David Langley, "'Half-Criminals' or Urban Athletes? A Plea for Fair Treatment of Skateboarders." Reprinted with the permission of the author.

Page 149. Eric Sorensen, excerpt from "The Tradition vs. Full-Blown PR Problem: Now Come Reactions to a Very Public Death" from the *Seattle Times* (May 18, 1999). Copyright © 1999 by the Seattle Times Company. Reprinted with the permission of the *Seattle Times*.

Page 163. Marybeth Hamilton, from "First Place: A Healing School for Homeless Children." Reprinted with the permission of the author.

Page 166. Ellen Goodman, "Minneapolis Pornography Ordinance" from the *Boston Globe* (1985). Copyright © 1985 by the Boston Globe Company. Reprinted with the permission of the Washington Post Writers Group.

Page 175. George F. Will, "The Perils of Brushing" from *Newsweek* (May 10, 1999). Copyright © 1999 by the Washington Post Writers Group. Reprinted with permission.

Page 218. John Leo, "The Stereotypes No Phantom in New 'Star Wars' Movie" from the *Seattle Times* (July 6, 1999). Copyright © 1999 by John Leo. Reprinted with the permission of the author.

Page 220. Kathy Sullivan, "Oncore, Obscenity, and the Liquor Control Board." Reprinted with the permission of the author.

Page 223. Vicki Schultz, "Sex Is the Least of It: Let's Focus Harassment Law on Work, Not Sex" from the *Nation* (May 25, 1998). Copyright © by the Nation Company, L. P. Reprinted with the permission of the *Nation*.

Page 247. Daeha Ko, "The Monster That Is High School" from the *University of Washington Daily* (May 9, 1999). Copyright © 1999 by the *University of Washington Daily*. Reprinted with the permission of the publisher.

Page 250. Judith Kleinfeld, "The Morella Bill, My Daughter Rachel, and the Advancement of Women in Science" from *Academic Questions* (Winter 1998–1999). Copyright © 1998 by the National Association of Scholars. Reprinted with the permission of Transaction Publishers. All rights reserved.

index

Checklist for Peer Reviewers

Understanding the Writer's Intentions

- What is the issue being addressed in this essay?
- What is the writer's major thesis/claim?
- Where does the writer present this thesis/claim? (See pp. 85–86, 165–68.)
- Who disagrees with this claim and why?
- Who is the primary audience for this argument? How resistant is this audience to the writer's claim? Does the writer regard this audience as supportive, undecided, or resistant? (See pp. 153–56.)
- Does the writer show awareness of the obstacles preventing the audience from accepting the writer's claim?
- If proposing an action, does the writer address a specific, appropriate group of decision makers? Is the writer aware of the constraints operating on these decision makers?

Reconstructing the Writer's Argument

- Can you summarize the writer's argument in your own words? Can you summarize it in one sentence as a claim with *because* clauses? (See pp. 83–86.) If you have trouble summarizing the argument, where is the source of difficulty?
- Can you make an outline, flowchart, or tree diagram of the writer's argument? If not, where do you have trouble perceiving the argument's structure?

Identifying the Argument's Claim Type

- Is the writer's main claim one of the claim types discussed in Part Three (category or definition, cause, resemblance, evaluation, proposal)?
- If so, does the writer use argumentative strategies appropriate to that claim type (for instance, using examples to support a categorical claim; using criteria-match arguing for definitional or evaluative claims; describing causal links for cause/consequence claims; arguing from category, consequence, or resemblance to support a proposal claim)?
- How well does the argument anticipate and respond to possible objections associated with each claim type?